The Fulbright Difference, 1948-1992

Studies on Cultural Diplomacy and the Fulbright Experience

The Fulbright Experience, 1946-1986,
edited by Arthur Power Dudden and Russell R. Dynes

The Fulbright Difference, 1948-1992,
edited by Richard T. Arndt and David Lee Rubin

Studies on Cultural Diplomacy and the
Fulbright Experience

The Fulbright Difference,
1948-1992

Edited by
Richard T. Arndt and David Lee Rubin

Foreword by
Stanley N. Katz

Afterword by
Robin W. Winks

Transaction Publishers
New Brunswick (U.S.A.) and London (U.K.)

Copyright © 1993 by Transaction Publishers, New Brunswick, New Jersey 08903

Library of congress Catalog Number: 92-28068
ISBN: 1-56000-085-6
Printed in the United States of America

Library of Congress Cataloging-in-Publication Data

The Fulbright difference, 1948-1992/edited by Richard T. Arndt and David Lee Rubin; foreword by Stanley N. Katz; afterword by Robin W. Winks.
    p.   cm.   —(Fulbright Association series)
    Includes bibliographical references and index.
    ISBN 1-56000-085-6
    1. Fulbright Association—History. 2. Educational exchanges—United States—History. 3. Scholarships—United States—History. I.   Arndt, Richard T., 1928- . II. Rubin, David Lee. III. Series.
LB2375.F86   1993   92-28068
307.19'62'0973—20   CIP

For
Fulbrighters Everywhere

There are nearly two hundred thousand alumni of the
Fulbright Program planted all over the globe—seedlings,
striplings and tall trees.

This book is dedicated to them, and to the man from Arkansas
who made their unsuspected dreams spring to life.

TABLE OF CONTENTS

ACKNOWLEDGMENTS

Full responsibility or blame for this book, every comma and phrase of it, falls to the editors. Yet it is rare that one volume, even a collective work like this one, should have incurred so many debts. To repay them all requires a chronology of its creation: at every step of the way indispensable contributions moved it forward.

It began where others left off. Arthur Power Dudden and Russell R. Dynes, in their pioneering *The Fulbright Experience, 1946-86: Encounters and Transformations* (New Brunswick: Transaction, 1987), brought to light forty-five episodes of change. In that volume the opening contribution focused on "questioning" the Fulbright experience; Robin Winks then set about stitching a larger quilt from the "Tissue of Clichés" that his thematic analysis of those memoirs revealed. The present volume was designed to explore the insights of the first book and especially to dwell in the space defined by those two contributions. Our title designates this continuity: it is the title of that groundbreaking book's last chapter, taken in turn from Dr. Cardozo's closing essay.

In December 1989 a panel on the Fulbright contribution at the Chicago meetings of the American Historical Association brought Professor Winks and the principal editor together with Stanley N. Katz of the American Council of Learned Societies and Deborah Dash Moore of Vassar College, under the aegis of Cassandra Pyle, director of the Council on International Exchange of Scholars. That session did more to focus this book's agenda than could have been understood at the time.

The principal editor, at that time, was in the midst of four active yet contemplative years with the Woodrow Wilson Department of Government and Foreign Affairs of the University of Virginia, where a combination of stimulating student seminars and penetrating collegial interchange was filling in some of the gaps left by earlier graduate work in French literature and too many years in government service. During those years a theoretical framework for the analysis of cultural diplomacy began to take shape, built on the vital foundation laid by Frank Ninkovich in *The Diplomacy of Ideas* (Cambridge, 1980) and pressed forward by the theoretical orientation of departmental friends and by colleagues in other fields too numerous to list, at Virginia and elsewhere. To Mr. Jefferson's University, profound thanks are due.

By the Spring of 1990, one Charlottesville friend had developed into a colleague: David Lee Rubin of the University's French Department was a critical element in thinking about the nature of the book, about the process of eliciting proposals then drafts, and about working critically with the drafts in such a way as to maximize quality and minimize annoyance; he was as well a godsent source of information on modern publishing. His acceptance of the role of co-editor was a turning point.

By then we had defined a simple question: if in fact the Fulbright experience changed lives, how did it achieve that end and what were the results? From the beginning we agreed to press beyond easy answers—the new job found, the spouse discovered, the expertise acquired, the friendship formed. The authors who survived this first round and provided drafts were then peppered with editorial questions, a process documented to some extent by Gerald and Margaret Dietemann in their lively essay. Some drafts shuttled between author and editor as many as six times, pressed ever onward by new questions. A few gave up in annoyance, others dug in their heels and declared a moratorium. But the greatest number expressed gratitude for having been read critically, taken seriously, and pushed to greater self-awareness. To the forty authors and co-authors who stayed until the end, our gratitude for patience well beyond the call.

Early we called for contributions from across the U.S. and abroad. The Fulbright Association's newsletter carried the call in several numbers in 1989. Direct communication with Fulbright Commissions went out all over the world, with special stress on the older programs. Many responded and special thanks are owed to the Commissions and their directors in Belgium, Finland, India, Portugal, Spain, Sweden, and the UK.

The Fulbright Association in Washington, it goes without saying, played an indispensable role. Its Publications Committee, chaired by Professor Winks and including David Lee Rubin, Joseph Tulchin of the Woodrow Wilson Center for Scholars, Sheldon Meyer of Oxford University Press and board-member Robert Wright, offered interest, support and advice. The Association's board expressed continuing support over the two-year period. One remarkable boardmember was able to encourage the Hurford Foundation to make a generous contribution which advanced discussions with our publisher. The Association's Legal Committee, chaired by Loren Hershey, and its general counsel Jeffrey Yablon and his colleague Rosanne Sullivan, of Shaw, Pittman, Potts and Trowbridge, watched contractual questions, as did the Association's President Michael DeLucia. Jane L. Anderson, the Association's director, could always be counted on; and Debbie Laredo provided vital fax, copying, and mailbox services. Of the hundreds of conversations with Fulbright alumni from all over the world, we believe it can be said that no voice was wholly lost.

In the final stages Lisa Tulchin, of the Library of Congress staff, and Robert Amyot, of George Washington University, provided sturdy support, imaginative advice, and sharp eyes in formatting the manuscript for publication. And the remarkable team at Transaction gave continual stimulation, wise advice, counsel and friendship.

To all those in the chain of actions leading to this volume, responsibility for which we repeat resides only with the editors and the individual contributors, our gratitude and thanks. If this book lives up to the faith their help implied, may it be their bounty.

Dr. Katz, while maintaining his service to history at Princeton, presides over the American Council of Learned Societies. ACLS, as Ninkovich has chronicled, was a designer of the original Fulbright structure. Today it shelters the Council for the International Exchange of Scholars (CIES), the heart of the post-doctoral program. In these remarks, Dr. Katz participates in this accidental symposium by relating his gradual, persistent and committed journey to the Program's interior.

FOREWORD

Stanley N. Katz

It is May 13, 1992 as I write, here in Mexico City. Last night, we celebrated the fiftieth anniversary of the Benjamin Franklin Library. This morning I sit at the desk of the Assistant Cultural Attaché in this well-staffed USIS post.

The Franklin Library was the first of the USIS libraries, and it is still one of the largest. I came here to deliver the anniversary lecture. Last night I talked to an audience of a hundred or more on American Pluralism, Democracy and Higher Education. Remarkably well-informed discussion of the problems of American higher education followed, at the reception after my talk. This is not entirely surprising, in view of the fact that many in the audience had been in the U.S. as "Fulbrights" (the real Fulbright Program, as I shall explain, has barely begun here) or as International Visitor Grantees, for short-term visits. The Library, it is obvious, is rich in information resources and it has vigorous programs of intellectual outreach; it has developed a constituency of informed Mexicans—and one can imagine their opposite numbers, the Americans scattered all over the U.S. who have held Fulbrights here. Nearly everyone I spoke with last night went out of the way to remark that the time spent in the U.S. had transformed his or her life—as it has all of ours.

Recent developments in cultural relations between Mexico and the U.S. point to a new emphasis in the overall USIA program—the establishment of

Fulbright commissions in countries whose "Fulbright" activities were previously run by and through the USIS post. The establishment of new commissions in Eastern Europe is mentioned nowadays as the most dramatic example of the return to a Commission-oriented policy at USIA, after years of neglect. But for me the new North American Commissions in Mexico and Canada are even more important than the same developments in Eastern Europe.

Setting aside the reasons why it has taken forty-odd years to get here, these commissions are epoch-making: led by distinguished academic figures, both together symbolize a truly new era in North American foreign relations, one in which the three countries of the region are at last according each other full respect. It is fitting that the fulfillment of that respect should take the form of a Fulbright agreement, a Fulbright commitment, and a Fulbright Commission. In Mexico the new body is called the U.S.-Mexico Commission for Education and Cultural Exchange. Like the Commission in Spain, on which it is partly modeled, the Commission here is complemented by a separate and largely private-sector body with its own board, the Fund for Culture. It will raise non-governmental funds for cultural exchange activities.

For those of us who have remained active in Fulbright activities, developments like these in Mexico are heartening signs of the Program's vitality and its potential. Binationalism is showing signs of resurgence, after its hiatus. Private funding and substantial host-government funding are helping expand the Program, though such sources—and their understandable demands for participation in decision-making—complicate program planning. Still, there is a trend to mutualism, not only in keeping with the Senator's original goals but also particularly important in the new multilateral world in which we are beginning to live. The emergence of mutuality in North America is therefore a symptom and a symbol of the global post-Cold War era.

As I said, Fulbright changed our lives. I went to the UK, to King's College, London, in 1959-60. When I returned to the U.S. in August of 1960, I was calmly and clearly determined to pay back to the Program, in service, some portion of the incalculable riches it had given me. But at first, other than a lifelong friendship with the UK Commission Executive Director William L. Gaines and his Associate Director, my son's godfather Derek V. Lawford, there was little to link me to the Program, and this was so for a good many years.

Then I began serving regularly on the American History Committee of the Council for International Exchange of Scholars. In 1981 I became Chairman of CIES. It was a time when it seemed to me that the American political process might kill the Program altogether, after years of barely visible erosion.

In the CIES chair, I found myself paying back, a lot faster than I might have expected or wanted. Later, CIES was transferred from the American Council on Education to the American Council of Learned Societies, of which I had just become President. The two of us, the Program and I, were becoming inseparable. Again I found myself spending much of my time with Fulbright, and so it has continued, with American Specialist selections for USIA and other activities, like the Committee I currently chair for USIA's Division for the Study of the U.S., reviewing the agency's American Studies work.

Over more than three decades, I have learned a great deal about the Program and USIA—occasionally more than I wanted to know. And I have come to a conclusion that will surprise few readers of this important volume: the continued health and success of the Fulbright Program require commitment, close attention, patience and occasional sacrifice on the part of those, academics and otherwise, who believe that a government role in cultural exchange is vital to international intellectual life. Senator Fulbright and his colleagues in those early years understood the need for constructive engagement between the private intellectual community and the government, through exchange programs. Despite recurrent difficulties, the process has succeeded well beyond anything the good Senator might have imagined at the end of World War II.

Here in Mexico developments are enormously encouraging, though I think I might be writing the same thing if I were in Brasilia or Rawalpindi. But it is not a free lunch, it never was: the price of success in the Fulbright Program is eternal hard work—vigilance is assumed. America must lead the world in sustaining its support of the Program and in maintaining its quality. And those who will, who must pay that price are the beneficiaries of the Program, people like me who, understanding its needs, care deeply enough about it to fight for it. We may count ourselves blessed in that there are growing numbers of such people and growing awareness on their part of their responsibilities, as the enormous energy which has gone into this book so dramatically reminds us.

INTRODUCTION

Richard T. Arndt

The Fulbright difference is not worn on a sleeve . . . .
—Michael Cardozo

There have doubtless been Fulbright grantees, returned from their experience abroad, who do not report a life-change. The fact is, I have never met one.

Working with the forty authors and co-authors in this volume has led to a few observations. One conclusion: most people do not instinctively see their Fulbright experience, any more than they see their daily lives, as part of history. Only a few of them think in conceptual terms, even in retrospect, about the process of cross-culture exposure and immersion, as few fish—in Barbara Clarke Mossberg's metaphor—think about water. And with few exceptions (most of them foreign), people, even the highly self-aware Fulbright family, seem either naturally inclined or socially and culturally trained to reticence; they do not like to delve too deeply into themselves, at least in public. Few tend to reflect very deeply, at least without stimulation, either on the miracle of the Fulbright Program's very existence or on the unique self-defining quality of the Fulbright experience.

"A modest program with immodest aims," says the Senator. The statement's modesty reflects the man. No other nation in the world's history ever set out to carry on exchanges with virtually every other country in the world, in a framework of binational agreement about the purpose of such exchanges. No formal government-sponsored exchange program ever succeeded in persuading dozens of participating nations to share in its costs. No program has continued for nearly half a century and amassed an alumni body of nearly 200,000, in every nation of the world.

If this volume helps generate greater awareness of the Fulbright achievement, whether among its participants or in those outside the experience, it will have carried out its first objective. As of this writing, a world network of these former participants is only beginning to take shape. Fulbright associations are growing in dozens of countries and communications among

1

them are on the rise. But it took many years for this process even to begin, and its growth has been slow. Members of this network in process are becoming aware of its potential, and some are beginning to speculate about the uses of the special internationally qualified people who share the Fulbright experience or who manifest its values. This book serves as an example of what might be—it could not have happened without the support of that growing network.

Still, as I write in the Spring of 1992, it seems to me that few alumni think of the half-century since World War II as a unique era in U.S. and in world history precisely because of the Fulbright Program. Yet the idea of a Fulbright Moment, as Darshan Singh Maini boldly names it, is more than an immodest assertion, this volume suggests. Few have thought that their role in it might have any significance: Fulbright fish swim in its enabling water with little awareness of what water is or how they would survive without it.

Dr. Maini points out that, viewed in the context of historical communications between nations, we have lived for almost half a century through a systematic American effort to exchange students and scholars with every country of the world, in purposeful, implemental, and programmed ways. In that half-century, the changes across the globe have been staggering. To impute the difference to the Fulbright Program would go too far; but it is not unreasonable to argue as Dr. Maini does that the last half-century has been at least as deeply marked by the spirit of the Fulbright idea as by any other single implemental concept that comes to mind.

It is also true, though none of these authors tackles the question directly, that the Fulbright experience differs, in the minds of its participants, from any other educational exchange. Authors here speak of the honor of selection into a tiny group of the excellent, others dwell on the remarkable access which Fulbright machinery provided for them abroad and in the U.S., some note that the Fulbright experience extends well beyond the year of the actual foreign study into a continuing process, others write soberly of the lofty goals of the Senator and building the foundations of world peace, others express amazement that a government-sponsored program imposed little if any political interference, some speak of the unspoken commitment to "repay" that they implicitly accepted along with their grants, of expanding the Fulbright impact more broadly, of seeking ways to knit together the family of alumni and to turn these talents and energies to appropriate uses in the service of humankind. There is more to the Fulbright Moment than the elapsing of fifty years.

This volume then aims first to continue laying the groundwork for understanding the meaning of this half century, this Fulbright era, and the difference it has made. At the same time it attempts to sharpen some of the questions such insights raise. These are issues for the historians of tomorrow —whether they study the history of society, politics, culture, intellect or diplomacy.

These historical issues should also concern Fulbright alumni today. Those who found benefits in the experience, however inchoate, may come to understand through this volume that they are part of an ongoing and continuing, if ever fragile, national and global process. To augment this awareness is our second purpose.

The volume has a third purpose in public policy. The issues raised here should attract the attention of today's administrators of the Fulbright Program and those policy-makers in the public and private sectors of every nation who need to understand how Fulbright has already changed our world and how it must be nurtured if it is to continue making a vital difference on the human planet we share.

*   *   *

For historians, the genesis of this book needs to be clear: beginning from the first volume in 1987 and the implicit commitment to a second, even if two steps do not make a series, the intent was to continue building the history of the Program. After a panel at the 1989 meetings of the American Historical Association, the idea took shape during the Spring of 1990 in discussion with co-editor Rubin at the University of Virginia; a call for proposals began to circulate. Several numbers of the American alumni association's quarterly newsletter, each mailing reaching at least 8000 people around the world, made the announcement. Direct communication with overseas Fulbright Commissions, especially those whose origins extended back before 1960, invited proposals. Reserving the right to refuse any proposal and to question all drafts, we focused on two major goals: getting below the anecdotal surface and making the collection as international as possible. A third goal would prove harder than we thought: we wanted to reach the earliest grantees, aware as we were of the passing of time.

Word of mouth worked as well. The idea was discussed at various conferences, seminars, and local chapter and association meetings in the U.S. and around the world. An unrealistic deadline was pushed back more than once because the proposals, then the draft essays, especially those coming from abroad, were torturously slow to appear. Some were in fact rejected at the proposal stage, usually on the grounds that the author showed little understanding of the need to go beyond narrative to questions of structural change. Foreign essayists had to be reassured about their English and in some cases helped to carry out their full meaning in a language not their own, though only two contributions were actually translated.

Fulbright Commissions around the world reacted in different ways to the invitation. Some provided inestimable help, picked the perfect essayist, and helped keep the project on track by managing international communications. Others—because of an excess of work, an absence of willing writers, other priorities, or inability to help in the indispensable communications process— were less forthcoming. A note on the growth of technology: at the outset the fax was a relatively unknown instrument, but by the end of the process we were corresponding with authors in Belgium, Finland, Portugal, Spain, Sweden, and the UK by this revolutionary tool.

After months of anguished expectancy, we were discouraged: there were not enough essays of quality to merit continuing. By the Spring of 1991, we were in a slump. There were too few essays, fewer prospects and some outright negative reactions: concerns about excessive tooting of the Fulbright horn, about giving the Program an elitist image, or about the book's taking vital human energies from other pursuits. At this point, we began a more insistent personal solicitation of our network of Fulbright friends. A second wave of essays resulted, some of a quality as to require rethinking the earlier work. By now, describing our goals, we were paraphrasing Tocqueville, asking authors to document changes in their "habits of heart and mind," as well as in those they touched. This brought a burst of contributions and mandated the final closing of the editorial door in March of 1992.

*   *   *

In constant consultation with committee and association colleagues, we then faced the problem of organization: there were thirty-seven essays, of which twelve from abroad, of a depth and density sufficient to justify publication. The temptation was to cluster them according to countries—for reasons difficult to understand, there were two or more essays from or concerning India and Pakistan, France, Italy, Scandinavia, the Iberian peninsula, Iran, Africa, what were once called "the Bloc countries," and the UK. Another possibility was classification by type of experience—university teaching, graduate or post-doctoral research, secondary teaching, BA generalists, "professionals" and others. The democratic idea of random selection, listing authors alphabetically, had some merits. Another idea was to work from major themes like self-discovery, professional enrichment, crossing cultural lines, the discovery of America, its proper study, "anti-Americanism" and "Americanization," or the meaning of freedom and its most successful political construct Democracy.

In the end the decision went to chronology. The reasons for this decision will be made clear by the introductions to each decade. All introductory and abridging material is the work of the principal editor.

There is little doubt that the Fulbright Program has evolved over the years, and in its random way this book documents some of those changes. As these essays fell together, implicit and explicit trends in the Program emerged. Administrators and policy-makers will find that the material thus presented provides a view of the sweep of half a century. For them, a careful reading may suggest what the future may hold. More generally, Fulbright fish will find, I believe, that they are seeing things about water they had not noticed before.

The hope is that the internationally experienced general reader for whom this volume is intended will have far more acute perceptions than ours of the separate strands of these essays' collective meaning. Irving Louis Horowitz calls the book a "symposium," but with apologies to Ann Tyler and Barbara Mossberg an "accidental" symposium might be more accurate. For, while the editors and others have managed some small control over the contents, the whole—like the Fulbright Program itself—is a complex carpet whose figures can better be seen by the outside viewer than by any of the weavers.

As Professor Winks pointed out in 1987, the astonishing variety of the Fulbright experience, as displayed in the earlier volume, trivializes most generalizations about its nature. Those who lament this variety, who claim it represents administrative or policy chaos and argue for channeling the Fulbright Program towards "doing a few things and doing them well," should note the passionate endorsement by these writers of its real genius: infinite variety, flexibility, and the capacity to generate transforming experience.

Indeed I suspect and hope all readers will pursue their own strands in this weave. After forty-three reflective years as a self-conscious Fulbrighter, many of them as a toiler in the Program's administrative or support vineyards, I have my own list. But I prefer to leave readers as free as the Fulbright Program does to follow their own paths, to browse among these deeply personal evocations of change and growth, to fill in their own gaps of memory, remembering that every essay by its very presence in this volume attributes these life-changes specifically to the Fulbright process.

On the other hand it would be coy not to underline some of the obvious themes which have emerged almost by magic, without collusion on the part of the authors, from this accidental symposium (with the exception of the editors and the authors of the Foreword and the Afterword, no author has seen another's work). There are a number of common themes, even if it is increasingly clear with time that no two Fulbright experiences are ever even remotely similar. Still, when Fulbrighters put their minds to it, it would appear they go through very similar soul-searching on very similar subjects.

For one thing, Fulbright seems to be virtually synonymous with self-discovery and, by extension, with self-realization. Every Fulbrighter plunges deeply into another language, even Americans in English-speaking countries, and to some degree each becomes aware that language structures thought. In some the experience helps in a negative sense, weeding out lesser aspirations like Per-Erik Lönnfors' athletic ambitions. The discovery of self, as reported by our authors, seems to go hand in hand with the notion of service: again and again authors speak of their newfound or reinforced commitment to helping humankind, usually because they have learned that individual actions can make a difference. A corollary of the service orientation of these authors is their desire to share the Fulbright experience with others, to make it available more widely, and to multiply its potential. This orientation to service, most often focused on international assistance, can begin with very personal involvement at home in local community affairs, as Frank Jossi reports after harrowing experiences in Peshawar on the margins of the Afghan War, or as Dr. Tavares da Silva reports from Lisbon.

Part of the discovery of self has to do with personal identity, and with this goes the discovery of country and culture, whether it be the nation of birth, an adoptive nation or even some country or culture of the mind. A persistent sub-theme of identity is ethnicity—a surprising number of authors deal with Jewish identity, including for example, the amazing story of a foreign Fulbrighter who uncovered during a U.S. stay a little-suspected family history of cultural survival after forced conversion from Judaism five hundred years before!

National identity and ethnicity bring us squarely into the political arena. The political historian will find rich fare in these pages. Faced with alternative political and social systems and styles, both Americans and foreigners range from rejection to avid acceptance, though most dwell in the ambivalent terrain between. To understand the riches of another socio-political system seems to have been a sometime goal of many of the authors; but with the discovery of riches there soon comes the awareness that for every advantage there is a price to pay. South Asia, in these pages, seems to pose both the greatest shock and the highest temptation, ranging from the astonished discovery that arranged marriages *can* work to the advantages of sacred cows—innocence abroad goes through many stages on its way to wisdom.

Confronting alternative political systems, Fulbrighters, especially naturally self-critical Americans, turn their own governmental systems over in their minds. But they come face-to-face, sooner or later, with the question of the U.S. impact on others—for want of a better word, call it imperialism, be it deliberate or accidental, be it by military, economic or cultural means. At the same time, they discover that the anti-Americanism which shocks so many

Americans abroad is the price of this perception of powerful U.S. forces, most often cultural and technological in nature and as such rarely recognized by Americans until they live abroad. Tiziano Bonazzi develops this point in his sensitive analysis of the footdragging by the Italian university system in accepting historians of the U.S. He reminds us how seriously the world takes the threatening process loosely called "Americanization" and how casually unaware Americans can be of their impact on others. The cultural dilemmas of colonialism, and of its parent structure imperialism, run through these pages. The wounds of the post-colonial era have not yet healed, and the persistence of even an unintended version of colonialism by economic, cultural, and technological means is a hard discovery for egalitarian Americans to handle. Both American and foreign authors in this volume touch on these themes again and again—Americanization is implicit on almost every page of this book, and its naturally-generated antibody, known generically as anti-Americanism, never lies far beneath the surface.

This dilemma remains in the long run a burden for those who learn that they are seen to dominate, because it is so often concealed from the dominator. Dipping back forty years into the far-seeing essays Leslie Fiedler wrote while a Fulbright lecturer in Italy in 1952-54, we might conclude with him that anti-Americanism is less an affront to Americans than agonizing self-criticism by foreign hosts. But these pages show that it affects sensitive Americans today as well.

Few of these writers are unaware of the tensions between intellect and politics. Many touch generously on the meaning of "the Embassy," of the U.S. Information Agency in Washington and its USIS posts in the field. Cultural and educational exchange, even handled by Fulbright Commissions abroad—specifically designed to provide distance between foreign policy and academic exchanges—reflects the politics of U.S. international relations. USIA, the administering agency for the Program, was not founded until 1953, five years after Fulbright. An outgrowth of the Office of War Information, it inherited the wartime Voice of America and its mission of "telling America's story abroad." In its dedication to an American Truth, USIA is designed to serve American foreign policy. The word "information" in its name has served Americans since World War I as a gentle euphemism for what other nations call "propaganda."

Yet the U.S. style of propaganda differs markedly from that of other nations. There is first a proclaimed American public distaste for lying in any form. More important, prominent within USIA there is a basic component designed to promote honest exchange of academics committed to the search for truth: the Fulbright Program. Fulbright has always been the heart of USIA's educational and cultural dimension. USIA's way of doing propaganda is kept as honest as circumstances permit by Fulbright and other cultural-educational elements, e.g. books. Fulbright's relationship to foreign *policy* should never be overlooked, even if its authorizing legislation refers most often to foreign *relations*. Within USIA, Fulbright is—or should be—the difference.

Take for example American Studies. As early as the forties, it was deemed useful by USIA and therefore by the Fulbright program to help develop university-level teaching and research about the U.S. in foreign universities. A third of the authors in this book were involved, at one end or the other, in American Studies, broadly defined as university-level study of the U.S. in any field (not as the promotion of the multidisciplinary field known in many American universities as "American Studies").

As the years have passed, younger scholars like Richard Horwitz have begun to focus on the contradictions implicit in politically motivated acts of scholarship—or are they scholar-motivated acts of politics? Yet the value of the growing international movement as a means for serious academic study of the U.S. is rarely questioned. For one thing Americans have begun to understand how much can be learned by viewing the U.S. as others do through comparative approaches to human experience. For another, the movement has begun to produce an important body of scholarship of its own. Horwitz, Bonazzi, Mossberg, and many others less explicitly, examine critically the idea that teaching others about the U.S. is a useful tool, certainly in foreign relations and probably in foreign policy as well, over time. Ultimately they admire the fruits of the movement to foster study of the U.S. abroad. Like Churchill, they might be said to believe that Americans do this sort of thing worst of all—"except for all the others."

The elusive question of how to teach foreign students objectively about a nation whose overwhelming power affects the intimate daily life of virtually every denizen of our tiny planet is not resolved in these pages. Rather the dilemma of power and intellect, of an educational exchange program insulated from but largely financed by the U.S. government for purposes of foreign relations, remains just that, a dilemma. These pages can do little more than help define it.

To this index of themes, we could add others. One is skills acquisition and technology transfer in fields as apparently dissimilar as art education, law, library science, design, sociology, journalism, city planning, engineering, business, social work, history, economics, women's studies, education, nursing, and university administration—an oddly selective list, excluding for example most of the sciences and reflecting in that a characteristic of the Fulbright Program. Another: the experience has fostered re-examination of questions like the role of women and the emergence abroad of "American" ways of looking at that issue. It has sparked reexamination of the idea of academic merit as a moral value and political screening device, of the nature of freedom, of the nature of journalism, of economic justice, of the impact of bottomless poverty, of war, of hunger, of history itself.

The largest concept these authors treat, even if the word is seldom mentioned (less so by the Americans), is Democracy. From the beginnings of the Program in Burma until today, one can see in these pages the fine but hidden hand of the democratic ideal in the Fulbright structure, even though that structure was skillfully designed—like the U.S. Constitution—so that no individual, party or foreign policy *diktat* could direct it along any specific path. Clearly it has ever worked its wondrous, overarching though often accidental purpose of *displaying*—not preaching—the U.S. style of democracy. The foreign authors write openly of democracy; but most of the U.S. authors, like their missionary forbears, believe that in their overseas assignments their very lives would demonstrate the U.S way of democracy with sufficiently compelling force. Paraphrasing Archibald MacLeish, these authors might be said to suggest that a Fulbrighter should not Mean but Be.

If the Fulbright Program has meant anything in its five decades, it has meant the fulfillment of individuals, in a context of freedom, through study and learning: and it has meant the implicit commitment of many of these participants to share this richness with others, towards the end of helping build democracies of trust wherever they can. This is perhaps the deepest structural value built into the Fulbright Program. In this assumption resides the politics of the Program.

We have heard much in the last decade about the need for the U.S. to project its democratic values. If this book, random accident that it may be, tells any story at all, it is that since 1948 the Fulbright Program has been doing precisely that.

*   *   *

Earlier I urged readers to follow their own itineraries as they dipped into these essays. Yet it seems irresponsible to leave a book so fraught with public policy implications without some kind of explicit conclusion. The BFS White Paper in 1990, launching a "continuing conversation" on Fulbright issues, indeed virtually demands that this volume join that dialog. As the Fulbright Program approaches its fiftieth anniversary, it is a time for forthright statement.

Conclusions normally end a volume. In this case they will precede. They are my own, flowing from the immediate role I have played for at least four years, pressing questions on the past, along the illustrated itinerary of this book.   More generally, in articulating below five loosely-grouped sets of conclusions, my longer-range association with the Program and its alumni comes into play; these conclusions represent not only ongoing discussion with forty-odd authors over these years, but also those with hundreds of Fulbright alumni all around the world and with past and present colleagues of Fulbright associations over many years.   Obviously, I take sole responsibility for these interpretations.

First, on the nature and character of the Fulbright Program, this collection reaffirms the indispensability of binationalism in Fulbright program design and execution—Fulbright is a two-way process.   A decision to do Fulbright exchanges virtually demands a binational Fulbright commitment, hence a Fulbright Commission; but a commitment to binationalism has consequences.   These pages demonstrate the two-way nature of the individual Fulbright experience.   They pages also tell us that Fulbright is process: once launched, the experience triggers an ongoing way of looking at the world which, these writers testify, continues to grow throughout a lifetime.

There are calls here for excellence and independence in program participants.   The idea has always been to choose the best people in the U.S. and abroad, then trust them to find their own way in their work and then in their careers—reaching for the kind of integrity often linked with the word "academic."   The university and its peer review systems, with all the flaws, are still the only mechanism structured to evaluate and judge certain kinds of human excellence; if Fulbright wants the best, it needs the universities at its core.

There are other hints here as well that better coordinative interchange and planning with other government and private programs would help.   USIA's long-forgotten mandate to coordinate all U.S. government exchanges abroad could, in its university dimension at least, be taken up by BFS as a way to extend the impact and sharpen the relevance of the Program.   Another conclusion can be drawn only in its absence from these pages: no writer suggests here that the U.S. government responsibility can be handed off to the private sector.   Fulbright can coordinate private sector activities, can be guided by gaps they have left, and occasionally can be supplemented by private contributions.   But Fulbright was designed to be and must remain a U.S. government responsibility.

Three concepts then—binationalism, the integrity of university values, and wisdom in the exercise of U.S. government responsibility—lie at the base of the Program's honesty, its variety, its adaptability, its sensitivity to place and time, its power of growth and adaptation, and ultimately its contribution to foreign relations.

Second, the administration of the Program concerns many of these writers. Budgets are bottom lines, by definition reductions and abstractions; merely to watch their rise and fall is to abandon vigilance. Once allocated, Congressional funds can be spent for many things—all are good, but some are better than others. Concerned citizens can influence the Program's direction if they are informed. All these writers hint at the need.

These essays seem to me as well to suggest rebuilding and reinvigorating the Program, focusing first on the traditional academic core so as to achieve a sound binational mix of pre-doctoral students (including the lost dimension of "unfocused BA generalists") and post-doctoral researcher-instructors, in a university-to-university context. Such well-intended variations as "professional" exchanges, costly U.S. orientation and "enrichment" programs, secondary teacher seminars, university affiliations—these have tended in the last decade to wag the core. Not that any of these should be dropped; they can be redesigned, assigned new priority and placed in an appropriate university framework. Innovative variation can only work when the core is unassailably strong.

Refocusing the university role hangs on another implicit administrative conclusion, emerging from Fulbright history. In 1968 the BFS began the progressive loss of the academic character its founders intended, through the inappropriate intervention of politics. If Fulbright is to be a high-quality university-oriented program, it is obvious that the political process must help the universities earn back control of the BFS.

Third, there are repeated suggestions here that the academic and scholarly world should begin serious and systematic research into "the Fulbright Moment." We need more collections like this one as sources for scholars, as well as policy-makers; building on that basis, intellectual and cultural historians can begin to study the Fulbright factor in the developments of this last half-century. Only in that we can we begin to follow out and understand more fully some of the suggestions this volume provides.

Fourth, program conclusions abound in these writings. For example, I believe it is clear that the Fulbright Program, a well-designed machine even if it needs minor repairs and a bit of careful oiling, is in fundamentally sound shape. But it suffers seriously from two kinds of under-use: first, the failure by many nations, especially our own, to exploit the resources it generates, both American and foreign—for example, no Fulbright alumni sit on the BFS; this is the more tragic in that there is in today's world an obvious and acute need for the very Difference these pages delineate.

Equally serious under-use is revealed by the Program's enormous surplus capacity. The Senator, like other close observers, has spoken for years of the Program's potential for absorbing doubled, quadrupled, even octupled funding in little time, with little administrative overhead and less waste; as ever a program multiplied by seven or eight would still cost less than one Stealth bomber. The Program needs new initiatives less than a rededication to the structure the founders built, to the spirit they created, and to the rough proportions reflected by the size of country-programs in the early years. Grant stipends must rise, coming closer to true expenses and salaries foregone—why should families have to borrow to accept a Fulbright assignment? The need for a major expansion of Fulbright funding is not like the familiar bureaucratic whine about insufficient resources; what is called for here is a major *qualitative* change, one that can only be brought about by doubling and redoubling the program.

We hear much nowadays about the new needs of a changed and changing world. But has the change been so great? Have the fundamental values of humankind changed? Is learning different from what it was? Flexibility is the Fulbright genius, this book argues. There are few tasks the Fulbright Program could not find some way to tackle, if it set out to do so. The machinery is in place, and the costs are comparatively small. It is time to use Fulbright as it was used in the early years, with imagination, with integrity and with enough scope to meet worldwide needs.

Fifth, I think I speak for the forty-odd people who have contributed time and energy over a three-year period to the making of this book when I say that not one of them dissociates the Fulbright experience from the idea of peace; none of them can imagine a world in which the Fulbright flagship will not be out there churning the waters ahead, leading us towards new ways of living together on our little planet. All believe Fulbright must go steadily forward, seeking ever to change the minds of people everywhere, to build the structure of civil societies and democracies of trust throughout our world, and to set humankind not to seeking but literally to waging the only kind of peace that matters, the peace based on understanding.

$$*   *   *$$

It is time now to listen to our authors, as from the forties to the nineties they try to recollect and discern what Fulbright meant to them and in their lives.

PART I

THE FORTIES: CREATING THE MYTH

The first Fulbright Agreement was signed with China in November 1947. A hasty agreement with the British colonial government of Burma followed, just before Burmese independence in January 1948. By the end of the forties, Australia, Belgium and Luxembourg, Egypt, France, Greece, Iran, Italy, the Netherlands, New Zealand, Norway, the Philippines, Turkey and the UK all had agreements and functioning Fulbright Commissions—only seven in Europe. Fresh from the War, the Allies fell into place first—the surplus war materiel was there, for one thing. But the "developing" countries were there from the first.

World War II had everything to do with the Fulbright Program: its horrors pushed the young Senator from Arkansas to find ways of avoiding another such conflagration; its leftovers provided the early funding; five or more years of interrupted European-American intellectual commerce meant that masses of U.S. university professors of the highest calibre were eager to return to nourishing foreign intellect and libraries; and thanks to the ASTP language-area-study programs of the U.S. military during the War and to the GI Bill afterwards, a new generation of ordinary Americans, unlike earlier American elites who rounded off their education with a Grand Tour, had the motivation, the preparation, and the means to study abroad.

There were precedents for the idea of academic exchange in U.S. foreign relations: the Boxer Indemnities, Belgian Relief in the twenties, Finnish World War I debt repayments, and the programs begun in 1938 when the Department of State reluctantly agreed to accept a benign role as coordinator of overseas educational and cultural relations. These provided relevant background and experienced staff for the Fulbright initiative.

More important, at least in the Senator's mind, were private exchanges like his beloved Rhodes Scholarships, shaping a vision of vastly expanded government-sponsored exchanges. An important U.S. export of education had been undertaken in the early nineteenth century by the missionary movement; this evolved into its lay form in the philanthropic era; literal and spiritual

13

descendants of the missionaries provided leadership and staff for those early programs.

The fundamental idea of the Fulbright Act: while avoiding damage to fragile rebuilding economies, to channel funds from the sale of surplus military equipment into scholarships, literally swords into plowshares of the mind. The first legislation provided no dollars for bringing foreigners to the U.S. When the Smith-Mundt Act of 1948 began to take effect in 1950, the Fulbright Program became a two-way flow.

There was no shortage of funding: on the Fulbright-chartered S. S. Washington carrying graduate students to France in October 1949, two contributors (who discovered their shipmate-hood in the process leading to this volume) report there were over 250 pre-doctoral students going to France—no more than five make the trip today. Stipends were generous. Robert Clifford reports allocations in Burma of $200,000 per year, a great deal of money in 1948 Burma.

Three contributors mark these early years. In Rangoon, energetic Embassy officers seized the Fulbright opportunity in 1948, despite political counter-indications, and patched together a program moment wherein much of what followed in Fulbright history can be found; it included the performance of the beautiful man history remembers as the Ugly American. In France, an ASTP- and GI-Bill-trained Francophone sociologist began the long itinerary from his Brooklyn neighborhood through the various ethnic fractions of Europe's Nation States; and in Dijon an unfocused BA generalist set out to discover America.

The times were heady. The War was won, there was a UN, economies were on the mend, there seemed to be no end of available money, the U.S. had the answers, and tomorrow *had* to be better. Rumblings in Eastern Europe were no more than that, and China was still "ours." Yet the grantees of 1949, before they returned home, lived through the Berlin Airlift, the closing of China, and the crossing of the 38th parallel by North Korean troops. In Korea, Burma, and Vietnam, disaster was already in process.

The author served in the China-Burma-India theater during World War II, then as Economic Officer at the Embassy in Rangoon in 1948-49. Later he would serve in seven other developing countries as a foreign service officer and as a United Nations economic advisor. Helen Hunerwadel was with the first group of Fulbright grantees to Burma. Following the death of her soon-to-be famous husband, she stayed on with Point Four programs and continued her work in two-year tours in Iran and Surinam. In Burma, building on the previous work of missionaries, American and Burmese Fulbright grantees were in place in the Fall of 1948. Despite the precarious political conditions into which the Americans went, they compiled a remarkable record. Mr. Clifford's description of the very earliest Fulbright effort in the developing world reveals the choices which had to be made, in a program of university exchanges, where no real university was yet in operation and where national and international politics held sway. One line of thought would lead to the Fulbright Program as it later took shape, the other to the programs of technical assistance which over the years have been fostered by a very separate AID and its predecessors. In Burma in 1948, Fulbright was still in one piece, ready to define itself better but unmistakably an opportunity to be seized by imaginative Americans, for the needs they saw.

1

BURMA BEGINNINGS: FULBRIGHT AND POINT FOUR

Robert L. Clifford, with Helen B. Hunerwadel

Even today arguments take place over whether the first Fulbright Program began in China or Burma. The answer is simple: the first agreement was signed in China on November 9, 1947, but the first participants began work in Burma.

The program in Burma, with American grantees in place in the Fall of 1948, played out against a backdrop of uncertainty and confusion, flowing from the granting of independence to a country not yet recovered from World War II and the Japanese occupation.

Postwar Burma is a story of inexperienced leadership obsessed with grasping not only political but complete economic control of the nation. Only the second of more than a hundred of Europe's colonies to gain eventual independence, Burma had few examples to follow. Despite their inability to maintain law and order, its leaders embraced immediately a vague concept called "socialism" as the mechanism for instituting tight and pervasive control of all economic and natural resources. The first Fulbright grantees implicitly and explicitly endeavored to suggest possible alternative routes to economic and social development.

Few readers know much about Burma. I may thus be excused for providing a few background details. The country has some of the richest natural resources of any area of the world. The middle Irawaddy River basin has high-grade petroleum located relatively close to the surface; the hills of the Shan States are rich in lead, tungsten and other ores, and the Tenasserim Peninsula has tin. Tropical forests with teak and other hardwoods cover more than half the country, and its fertile soil and fine climate made the country a major exporter of rice.

In the days of the Burmese kings, these resources were undeveloped and unavailable to world markets. Understandably Burma caught the attention of 19th-century European colonial expeditions. By 1886 the British had annexed all of Burma to the Government of India. They established law and order, set up a civil administration designed to further economic and social development, and created Government College, the beginning of education. Ports, railways and river shipping promoted trade with Britain and India as well as investment. American and British missionaries brought education and health services, particularly for the hill peoples, less developed and therefore more open to "Christian" teaching—they constituted a third of the population.

The British Empire was the principal trading area for Burma's raw materials. Seventy per cent of its exports went to India and Britain; in 1936-37, 74% of its imports originated from within the Empire. A skilled work force was recruited from outside Burma, largely in India, although by the early 1900's key professional engineers and technicians in the petroleum and mining industries came from the U.S. Before World War II, Burma produced 5% of the world's rice, with nearly 40% of its total production exported. Over 70% of its teak entered the world market and Burma produced about 7% of the world's lead, tin, tungsten and zinc.

Its thriving and relatively serene atmosphere was shattered by the War. In January 1942 the Japanese invaded southern Burma and drove the British and Chinese forces north. By the onset of the May monsoon, the invaders had occupied all but the northern mountains. By 1944-45, the Allies had recaptured Burma. At the War's end, the modern sector of the economy lay devastated.

The political structure was likewise shattered. Growing disorder spread throughout the country. Remnants of the Japanese-trained Burma National Army, amnestied in early 1945 by Mountbatten, swarmed over the countryside. The Attlee government declined to dispatch the two infantry divisions which could have restored order and in 1947 the British opted for Burmese independence. Many of the Chins, Kachins and Karens, ethnic groups which had supported the Allies, were reluctant to trade the protection which British rule had provided for the traditionally despotic Burmese rulers but the Union Jack was lowered on January 4, 1948. Two weeks before, on December 22, 1947, an educational exchange "Fulbright" agreement was signed with the British government.

The new Burmese government took the form of a parliament composed largely of plains Burmans under Prime Minister U Nu. A new constitution established the state's right to nationalize any sector of the economy it chose. Members of the cabinet had studied the socialist economics of their day, Laskian interpretations of thirties Fabianism, at Rangoon University and in London. They believed that government control of the economy, including natural resources, would lead to a better life for the people. Lacking practical experience of any kind, they believed that Burma's wealth had been "drained away" and "exploited" by the British. They were convinced that unprecedented prosperity awaited the country if only the Union government could take over the development of all resources. U Nu and his government set about expanding economic controls. Beyond the railroads, ports and airfields, it quickly took over the Irawaddy Flotilla steamer lines and imposed bureaucratic regulations in other areas.

The cabinet eyed the British and Indian companies hungrily; the long-time expatriate owners soon slowed reinvestment in new facilities and productivity dropped. The government was naive in its expectation: they thought foreign capital would be enough to run these enterprises for the benefit of the people. It slowly dawned on them, as it would on the hundred other newly independent colonies, that human resources at all levels, bringing the necessary managerial and technical know-how to run these complex operations, were more vital. By 1949 they realized that both capital and manpower for large-scale economic enterprises were in disastrously short supply and appeals went out to Britain and the U.S.

It was too late: disaster had already struck. A few months after independence, civil war broke out between the plains Burmans (70% of the population) and the hill tribes. It engulfed the country and chaos ensued: banditry increased, as law enforcement agencies proved incapable of maintaining order. Political discontents—the People's Volunteer Organization, Red Flag and White Flag Communists, mutinous army and police units—declared their opposition and took control of several areas in the south. By early 1949 Karen units in the army and some Kachins rebelled against Rangoon.

In these troubled years, it was difficult for Washington to recognize the state of near-anarchy into which Burma had slipped. Life was tolerable for the small embassy staff in Rangoon, in its own residential compound; the missionaries had their compounds as well, although in 1949 bandits or "dacoits" had destroyed several. Travel in the north was still possible, but getting out of Rangoon was tough—the Rangoon-Mandalay railroad was frequently cut and two local airlines struggled to maintain service to about a dozen towns, but the airports were periodically taken over by insurgents. Arriving passengers never knew what they would find on the ground—insurgents, cows on the runway, no gasoline, whatever.

In Rangoon, the Embassy decided to try to implement the potential of the Fulbright Act of 1946 for Burma. No more unsettled place in the world could have been found for that first experiment in educational exchange, yet it was done. Congress had provided funds to allow Americans to study and work in other lands and to help citizens of other countries to study in the U.S. Original funding came from the sale of surplus U.S. military equipment in Burma and was budgeted at $200,000 per year in Burmese Rupees.

In Burma, Fulbright was unique in four respects: it was the first country program to be implemented, it included medical and agricultural education and assistance from the start and thus was a prototype for the Point Four technical assistance projects yet to come, it was not administered by USIS, and it was soon engulfed in civil war.

Veteran Burma-hand J. Russell (Rusty) Andrus, Second Secretary of the Embassy, was asked to guide the program. He had extensive knowledge of the local scene: as a Baptist missionary in the thirties, he had been Professor of Economics at the Baptists' Judson College, later part of the Rangoon University. He spoke several local dialects and had former students scattered all over Burma. He was a more logical choice to shape a Fulbright program in Burma than the very limited USIS staff. No one worried at the time about his natural bias towards the hill people and his tendency to give them equal footing with the plains Burmans.

I arrived in Rangoon in July 1948 as Economic Officer and was immediately appointed to the U.S. Educational Foundation in Burma (USEFIB) as Treasurer. The board, appointed by the Ambassador, had eight members: three other Embassy officers, including the USIS Public Affairs Officer, and four Burmans, including U Htin Aung, Rector of Rangoon University; U Cho, Director of Public Instruction; and Sao Saimong, Educational Officer for the Southern Shan States.

Our initial program called for six Americans to come to Burma and several Burmese to study in the U.S. Confusion in Washington—we had moved very fast—stalled implementation for a few months. But things began in late 1948. The first three grants were aimed at Rangoon University, famed "Burma Surgeon" Gordon Seagrave's "Hospital in the Hills," and Sao Saimong, who had been known to Rusty Andrus before the War. Whatever success we had was owed largely to the character of the initial recipients and their remarkable wives.

Dr. Gordon Seagrave and his wife had started their famous hospital in the 1920s; he was a fourth-generation Baptist missionary. After the War, this hospital and its nurses' training school were incorporated as the American Medical Center in Burma, with a 200-bed hospital, four-year nursing training for frontier girls, and teams providing out-patient care to nearby villages in both the Northern Shan and the Southeastern Kachin states. The first grant provided training for two of his hill nurses in Jersey City, New Jersey. Seagrave was gratified, after a life-time of service, that his government had extended this token of support. So the first foreign Fulbrights to go to the U.S. were in nursing.

The second was a teacher of economics. Dr. Ernest L. Inwood, of the Department of Economics of the University of Nevada at Reno, was Visiting Professor of Economics at Rangoon University. Delayed by red tape, he arrived after half of the academic year had elapsed. He, his wife Alice and three children lived in a furnished faculty house. Rusty Andrus briefed him about the economy and personally introduced him around the unsettled campus. Burma's two colleges—Judson and Government Colleges—had by then been merged by government decree into a single university, controlled by the government. In 1948 amalgamation was in process. Six Americans from the old Judson faculty had returned and a handful of British-educated Burmese joined them as faculty in the new university, offering a BA and a BS to less than a thousand students.

Inwood's lively curiosity about the country, its culture and its people, helped him teach a full load in undergraduate economics but the unrest discouraged him from leaving the capital city. One day he phoned in great excitement to report that a battery of artillery had taken up positions across the road from his house. I told him to take a photo, "Otherwise people back in Reno will never believe you." One night the battery officers knocked on his door and asked if they could spread out their maps on his dining room table under decent light so they could plot firing data against Karen troops in nearby Insein.

In many such ways it was a comic opera war, but thousands of people were being killed, in the south for example, and hundreds of villages were being burned. In Rangoon the atmosphere was tense—the sound of firing in Insein could be heard day and night. Inwood retained his cheerful outlook, and his family seemed to enjoy this unique setting. The academic year ended in March 1949 and they returned to Reno in April, completing only five of their nine months.

The third Fulbright project was agricultural education and home economics. Oscar and Helen Hunerwadel arrived in early February 1949. He had been a pioneering agricultural extension agency in Tennessee between 1920 and 1940. Helen was a teacher and a practicing home economist. They had retired to Florida, but the Fulbright opportunity induced them to set out for Rangoon, via BOAC's flying boat, to serve as Agricultural Advisor to the Southern Shan States in the mountains—Sao Saimong's territory, about 275 miles northeast of Rangoon.

Arriving at Heho airstrip, they were met by Sao Saimong, who drove them 25 miles up the mountain to Taunggyi, a rambling town of about 15,000 located on a fertile plateau. Sao and his wife Mi Kim Khiang helped them get settled in the government bungalow which had been reserved for them; but the civil war worsened, planes stopped flying, and the Hunerwadels were stranded with only their hand luggage—no household necessities, books, magazines, mail, no communications with USEFIB or the Embassy, not even the promised transportation. The Americans in Rangoon referred to them as "those poor Hunerwadels," or "the Fulbright guinea-pigs."

Though frustrated and even scared, they soldiered on. Local officials seemed delighted for help in running the new agricultural training school and advice on modern practices. The Hunerwadels used the time to barge about on foot, learning about the people, being friendly, establishing trust.

The Shans did not readily accept outsiders and preferred minimal contact with the central government. They lived in a semi-autonomous state in their fertile, damp valley, hedged in by mountains running north and south. Descendants of Chinese settlers from the sixteenth century, they liked their isolation.

Many had been skeptical, if not downright suspicious, about the Hunerwadel assignment. But Otto's approach was wise. The level of agriculture in the Shan states, while backward compared with his middle Tennessee farm, was not much below that found in some of the mountainous areas of East Tennessee where he had spent his youth. He was able to make immediate and practical suggestions to Shan officials and farmers. He never hesitated to dirty his hands or clothes as he demonstrated his techniques. He jeeped to wherever help was needed. It took several months for the Hunerwadels to adjust to a new country, language and customs. But their enthusiasm and the practical value of their suggestions inspired confidence and their influence spread.

Otto's primary assignment was to help run the new Agricultural Teachers' Training School. Forty young men from all over the southern Shan states took both academic and practical courses. In his endeavor to add scientific modern farming methods to the curriculum, Otto began preparing lessons in agriculture. These were translated into Burmese and distributed to the students. Helen helped with this and taught English in the school.

His demonstrations soon attracted widespread attention. At the 47-acre experimental farm, he showed students and farmers better ways to prepare soil and plant seeds, use fertilizers, pesticides, fungicides, weed-killers and sprays, and improved methods of planting, cultivating, irrigating and crop storage. Within months, greater quantities and better quality crops were being produced at the experimental farm.

Meanwhile he advised appropriate government officials. He was careful to pay due respect to the Sawbwas (local chiefs) of the various states. He showed a blacksmith how to make simple farm and garden tools, such as a light-weight, long-handled goose-neck hoe to replace the heavy short-handled grubbing hoe, and metal points for wooden ploughs to turn the soil more efficiently. He demonstrated rope-making and splicing, fence-building. He advised a miller on improving the texture of his flour, suggested changes in the curing methods used by tobacco farmers. He introduced better and more prolific varieties of wheat to meet a growing demand for bread—a taste developed during the Japanese occupation when rice was in short supply. They also loved sweets—cakes and cookies—and welcomed Helen's demonstrations.

Otto was especially proud of his broom factory. He introduced a tough broom corn, raised from Tennessee seed, then cured the resulting broom straw, used local bamboo for handles, and rigged a crude but efficient machine to bind the straw to the handle. These were a great improvement on the traditional short-handled brooms that required crouching. Otto taught his students how to make these brooms and to construct the simple binding machine. When students left school, each was given a handful of broom-corn seed and a blueprint for the machine.

The Hunerwadels made frequent visits to rural villages through the Shan states to demonstrate modern farming techniques. In each village, they answered questions about specific farming problems, then distributed seeds. Helen gave food-canning and juice-bottling demonstrations. She showed how to make vinegar from wasting fruit, how to make cotton mattresses, how to churn and make butter, how to make yeast bread. They made a 1000-mile tour of the mountainous northern Shan states, stopping in 24 villages. American seeds, furnished by the new International Cooperation Agency (ICA, a predecessor of Point Four and AID), were distributed at each stop. At both Kutkai and Lashio for example, 200 villagers attended four-hour workshops on better farming practice and canning-bottling.

Much of the local fruits and vegetables were going to waste for lack of transportation. Canning made food available year-round and reduced expensive imports. Briefly in Rangoon, Helen appealed to the Shan Government and obtained the royal sum of $560 to buy equipment for teaching canning. Then she made a quick trip to the U.S. to purchase the equipment. Realizing that sea transport would be too slow, she went on a begging spree. She collected $800 worth of home canning, kitchen and farm equipment, including 300 tin cans and a can sealer, as well as some farm and garden seed—including the precious broom-corn. She found a surveyor's level for laying out terraces, a corn sheller, a scythe and snath, a knapsack sprayer, a cyclone seed-sower. A large fibre-board suitcase packed with several varieties of small budded Florida citrus trees, packed in damp graybeard moss, traveled back on the BOAC plane with her. During the five-day trip, the pilots were helpful: "We will look after your little trees. We'll keep them in the cockpit and sprinkle them occasionally, so don't worry." She used the Shan money and some of her own to ship the equipment to Burma by air freight, helped in the packing by her son. A wood-burning American kitchen range donated and shipped ahead by Sears, Roebuck had already arrived in Taunggyi.

Meanwhile a new building had been built near the school, complete with cabinets, counters and tables designed by Otto. The new equipment and the Sears stove were set up there and became Helen's famous "Canning Kitchen." Thousands, including top officials, came from all over to see it. The first canning class opened in July 1950. When the last class was completed in March 1952, 160 people from all over Burma—local women, businessmen, community leaders—had been taught home canning. The businessmen saw the potential for a canning industry in the Shan states. Other students organized a small-scale cannery, the Producer's Canning Cooperative Society, fostering a new industry for Burma. The country's largest newspaper *The Nation*, reporting the Hunerwadels' departure on home leave in February 1951, referred to Helen as "the Mother of the Canning Industry in Burma." A decade later the army set up a large cannery in Kalew. As the then-Secretary of USEFIB wrote to Helen in 1962, "The canning industry you promoted in Taunggyi has been taken up by the present government and is making great progress. You can therefore have the satisfaction of having done some permanent good to Burma through your Fulbright assignment." A difference indeed!

Meanwhile the civil war was spreading through southern Burma. Karen and Kachin insurgents effectively cut off Rangoon from the up-country for several months in 1949. Only travel by air was feasible. In August 1949 the war spilled into the Shan states. The First Kachin Brigade moved from the Burma plains into the Shan states, occupying Taunggyi. The Embassy, concerned about the safety of the Americans there, sent me with another officer by plane to Lashio and then by jeep 244 miles south. En route we encountered the First Brigade moving north. Karens and Kachins had supported the Allies during the War so they were friendly to Americans, particularly to those like myself who had served in Burma.

Government officials were terrified. Sao Saimong fled, after advising the Hunerwadels not to venture outside. Helen, trying to reassure his abandoned wife, said to her, "God will bring us through." Her answer: "We Buddhists have no God."

Finally a five-vehicle caravan took two dozen Americans and Britishers on a fast-moving twelve-hour drive to the airport at Lashio, going through nineteen roadblocks and crossing battle-lines twice on the way.

The three-month stay in Rangoon proved helpful to the Hunerwadels, who were good at turning adversity to advantage. It gave them time to edit their agricultural lessons, get them accurately translated, and turn out a textbook entitled "Practical Agriculture for the Shan States." While Helen worked on the book, Otto spent much his time filling in as a teacher of botany at the Teachers Training School until a Fulbright could be recruited to take over. The time in Rangoon provided opportunities to meet and explain their work to central government officials, including the President. These men later helped further their projects and get needed supplies into Taunggyi.

Looking back, I see that Otto Hunerwadel and Helen were engaged in both an educational exchange program—there were Burmese students in the U.S. about whom I have no information—and also in pioneering a technical assistance program, on the model of the old U.S. extension service. His and like projects became models for future foreign aid programs. In 1950 Truman launched the Point Four Technical Assistance program, now AID. Otto's contract was picked up by Point Four in 1951, while Helen was awarded her own Fulbright grant. Otto then focused on agricultural extension work and Helen continued her canning classes.

In July 1952 Otto Hunerwadel contracted malaria in Taunggyi while Helen was on leave in the U.S. The treatment produced something worse: a severe phlebitis. He was moved to a hospital in Rangoon where he died of thrombophlebitis that same month. Was he perhaps the first Fulbrighter? He was certainly the first to die in his place of original assignment.

Burma never recovered from the collapse of law and order and the stifling of economic life in its first years of independence. It never regained its pre-War export trade. The most important economic sector in the country became the black market.

Obviously the Fulbright Program continued, despite problems. Two Oregonian pre-doctoral students—Charles Brandt of Portland and Samuel Dashiell of Dallas—arrived in 1949, Dashiell to study land-utilization and Brandt to investigate village cultures. They settled in Shan villages before the Government restricted up-country travel. Three professors arrived to teach at Rangoon University, though one departed early. In 1949 the Embassy decided it had to restrict the inflow of Americans.

A major crisis in U.S.-Burma relations came in August 1950 when Dr. Seagrave was arrested in Namkhan and accused of "treason" because he had given medical supplies to the Kachin Brigades when they occupied his hospital grounds a year earlier. He was lodged in the central prison in Rangoon and eventually brought to trial. Defended by the four best trial lawyers in Burma, who volunteered their services, he was acquitted after two trials. He was allowed to return to Namkhan only in December 1951, after the editor of *The Nation* launched a campaign on his behalf. He died there in 1965 and is buried on the grounds of the hospital he and Marion and so many others worked valiantly to build.

*   *   *

What did it all mean? Forty years ago most underdeveloped countries in the world depended, like Burma, on agriculture. They needed modern inputs of both technology and materials to increase production of food and commercial crops as well as to improve the quality of rural life. But few bilateral or multilateral development assistance programs in the Third World have given any priority to agriculture and rural development.

As American missionaries had learned years earlier, the success of an assistance program in situations like Burma's in the forties depends largely upon the personal relationships between teacher and students. The Hunerwadels and the Seagraves exemplified the patient, humane and caring attention that encouraged the exchange of practical ideas. Americans can take pride in the work accomplished by this early and short-lived Fulbright Program. The U.S. was the first country in the world to establish agricultural extension services to individual farmers. In the U.S. such services were based on agricultural colleges and research centers. The Hunerwadels transferred this practice overseas.

The work of these early Fulbright pioneers has not been unrecognized. Gordon Seagrave's medical work was immortalized by his three well-known books. Otto Hunerwadel instead became the prototype for the hero of Lederer and Burdick's *The Ugly American* (1958). Contrary to the misconceptions of those who have read only the title, the "ugly" hero was the helpful American serving in the bush and performing neighborly deeds traditional in American society. The local residents called him "ugly" to distinguish their beloved teacher from the more self-important, self-serving and better-dressed Americans. Lederer and Burdick have prominent journalist U Maung Swe say this: "In this section of the Shan States, everyone is pro-American because of the Hunerwadels. They came to Burma to help us, not to improve their own standard of living."

Forty-odd years later, the Fulbright Program has compiled an illustrious record throughout the world. Its role, style and function have been defined by policy and practice over time in a fairly recognizable way. Our modest efforts in 1948 must look very strange from the viewpoint of Fulbright history. In 1948 we were offered an opportunity. In a country gripped by rebellion and insurgency, we were trying to do what we could. We were looking for a way of bringing American experience to a country which needed it. Was it premature? Perhaps so, but we tried anyway.

Today, events in Burma indicate continual and persistent deterioration. And yet the down-to-earth grass-roots undertakings of the early Fulbright grantees won enormous goodwill and made a lasting impact by a simple method: we brought straightforward American approaches to problem-solving into a country where hostility and confusion reigned. We were able to do something because we had magnificent human beings who dedicated their lives to their work there. Were we naive? Perhaps. Were we right to try? Perhaps not, but then history is made of such glorious mistakes.

The author, Emeritus Professor of Sociology at the University of Massachusetts in Boston, took the ship that launched the Fulbright program in France in 1949. Before that, accidents of war and the GI Bill had already taken him into research on ethnicities within a national unity. His own origins in the neighborhoods of Brooklyn in the thirties fueled a personal commitment to a lifetime of concentration on this subject. Fulbright took him to France, then to its Alsatian region, and from there he went on to study the Flemish and the Walloons, the Catalans and the Spaniards, and the other complex cases of sub-cultures within national entities throughout Europe. As this book moves towards the press, ethnic conflict rages in Yugoslavia, in once-Soviet Georgia, as it does in Ireland, and throughout the Third World, while in Washington delegations of Palestinians and Israelis warily eye each other across the conference table. Professor Robbins reminds us that he has worked as a social scientist and not as a statesman, raising the question of whether Fulbright-generated research and wisdom could be more fully utilized in the service of the nation.

2

OTHER CULTURES AND SINGULAR PLURALISMS

Richard Robbins

> *So it is in traveling, a man must carry knowledge with him if he would bring back knowledge.*
> —*Samuel Johnson*

In the thirties, the Depression years, New York City still had large numbers of foreign-born and second-generation, as it does today, though with a different set of countries of origin. Growing up in Brooklyn, native-born of Russian Jewish stock, I saw the ethnic mosaic as a reality—in the streets, in the stores, in the subways where two women on one side spoke Italian and the man opposite read his daily *Vorwärts* in Yiddish. True, bigotry was endemic, on all sides—we were called "Christ-killers" and our high school New Utrecht was called Jew Utrecht. No doubt we struck back with our own epithets, but there remained a kind of live-and-let-live tolerance. We had, after all, the immense solidarity of the ethnic neighborhood, with all its institutions. Without minimizing the depth of the racism and the ethnic conflict, and remembering that no firmament of civil rights law, no landmark court decision yet existed to protect greater equality of opportunity, we nonetheless came together in the neighborhoods and the schools, across ethnic, religious and color lines.   The great suburbanization of the metropolis, which would drastically diminish diversity by segregating inner and outer city by race and class, was two decades away.

That kind of city socialization can lead, by the time of adolescence, to a powerful desire to know more about and even to visit the old Europe from which our folk had come. We were primarily absorbed in the American goals: pursuing upward mobility, resisting discrimination, working out our sense of cultural identity in a country strongly bent on assimilation.   Nonetheless we could imagine a return journey to our "roots," so we studied as much European geography, history and foreign language as possible.

What we could *not* imagine, we young ethnics of the thirties, was the enormous impact of World War II—its global scale, its transformation of the socio-economic life of the nation, and above all its personal consequence—military service. Suddenly "the system" reached into our familiar urban world and sent us, by virtue of war, to the far corners of the earth. In my case there were four years in the far Pacific—Saipan, Guam, Iwo Jima et al.

On the positive side, two obvious unanticipated consequences of the War: the GI Bill provided federal support for hundreds of thousands of veterans to pursue higher education and got me a BA at Brooklyn College.   And the Fulbright Act, funded initially from war surplus sales, enabled American scholars to study and teach abroad. For me, it was France: a year in 1949 and two others (1962, 1965).

A third and less well-known factor had developed during the War.   The Army had established language-training centers in major universities across the country, under the Specialized Training Program (ASTP). So a lowly private ended up in 1942 at Georgetown's School of Foreign Service. We had been selected to become French language interpreters in the coming invasion. Month after month we soldier-students immersed ourselves in French language, politics, history, economics.

Had I already been a sociologist at that time, a student of Max Weber's theory of bureaucracy, I could have predicted the outcome: oversize Georgetown diplomas in hand, we were embarked for the Pacific! But the damage was done: ASTP training later helped me complete my BA in less than a year. Then the GI Bill took over and carried me through the MA at Washington State University and part of a PhD in sociology and anthropology at the University of Illinois. Still, it took the Fulbright Program to bring my diplomas to life.

Our band of over 200 bound for France in 1949, by ship of course—the S.S. Washington, was one of the very first. That spring, applying for the program, I was halfway through my doctorate. The GI Bill was exhausted and a teaching assistantship had taken its place. I had decided to specialize in immigration; an earlier concentration on American immigration, immigration policy and the assimilation process now had to be brought into conjuncture with an international, comparative framework (Taft and Robbins 1955). The American dimension was now inseparable from the larger format of international migrations and the vast displacement of refugee populations in Europe and Asia. Witness the first break in the restrictive and racist American "national origins" formula in 1948, when thousands of displaced persons from Europe were admitted under special quotas, and the repeal of Asian exclusion in 1965 (Robbins 1966).

The Fulbright selection process that year was incredibly quick. I resigned my assistantship—though classes had already begun, I married, I packed and we set sail. Just before departure, we learned that married couples would receive an extra $20 per month!

I look back now, forty-odd years later, to that experience in France. As we know, Senator Fulbright and the Congress made it possible for scholars to extend their research interests abroad, advancing their own work and more generally furthering the cause of international understanding. Yet there was something more for us ethnics of European background. Here was our opportunity to return to the Europe that had nourished our grandparents and sent them on their way to those neighborhoods of our childhood, whether in New York, Boston or Chicago. We would return not as tourists but as scholars whose American education had fulfilled our forbears' expectations —"My son, my daughter, the professor."

Over these years I have been able to live almost literally what Joseph Addison described as his fondest dream: "Could I transport myself with a wish from one country to another, I should choose to pass my winter in Spain, my spring in Italy, my summer in England, my autumn in France." Autumn in France in 1949 and the many subsequent autumns elsewhere brought childhood dreams and ideas to life.

Paris in 1949 had not freed itself altogether from the grim burdens of war. Life remained austere: the economic miracle still lay ahead. Coffee and sugar were rationed for part of that year. The old buildings of the University and its institutes seemed grayer than in the pre-war pictures. But Paris is Paris, nearly always exhilarating. Nothing could dampen the enthusiasm of a young American academic charged with studying sociology at the Sorbonne and carrying out a modest research project on post-war migratory patterns and refugee movements.

The academic side was conventional. We could see that after gigantic upheavals French higher education had returned to what it was—*plus ça change* . . . . It was still a centralized, formal system, characterized by highly abstract lectures intoned by great names to students in rows of seats under high-vaulted ceilings in mammoth lecture halls. Attending the lectures was not critical—you could buy transcripts at the bookstores—except to observe the eminent author in real life. American social scientists could imagine their pre-eminent role-model Emile Durkheim arriving at the Sorbonne in 1902 in just such a setting, "called" to Paris from Bordeaux, as all distinguished scholars inevitably were, to be a *chargé de cours*. It had taken the encrusted bureaucracy ten years, and then only by ministerial decree, to change the title of his chair from "Education" to "Science of Education and Sociology."

At the heart of the system were the rigorous examination stages from the *lycée* on up. In theory this produced a sterling meritocracy. In practice there was a tradeoff: it severely restricted the prospect of upward mobility through higher education for young people of merit from working-class backgrounds. Foreigners of course took no degrees and we escaped this torturous obstacle race, but we received all the perks of French students, including the cheap barely-edible blood-sausage-and-wine meals at the state-funded dining halls. Even then there were a few signs, portents more exactly, that the hierarchical and inegalitarian system would have someday to be leavened. But May '68 was still almost twenty years away.

Even then, generalizations about French universities, as about any university life, had to be tempered by recognition of the great diversity among individual professors. In my case the old school was represented exactly by Georges Gurtvitch, who delivered—in a remarkable but difficult Russian-German-French accent—lectures of daunting abstraction and complexity each of whose many sociological *paliers* contained sections, sub-sections and sub-sub-sections!

At the other extreme, in Raymond Aron's lucidly French expositions on such theorists as Comte, Marx and Weber, we could take an actual esthetic pleasure; we knew too that the next day, in his other familiar European role as intellectual-journalist, we could read his front-page editorial in *Le Figaro* on, say, developments in Soviet totalitarianism.

Claude Lévi-Strauss, at the Collège de France, addressed a distinctive group, not only conventional students like us but administrators and missionaries from France *outre-mer*—the colonial empire was not yet in collapse. His remarkable books on structuralism and on mythology were yet to come; what we heard was a stimulating amalgam of general anthropological perspective and field experience perhaps best exemplified by his *Tristes Tropiques*. Georges Friedmann taught industrial sociology; he represented the emergent new face of European sociology, wherein traditional European grand theory would be extended and modified by an infusion, mainly from the U.S., of empirical research. Friedmann had in his sights both theorists and the workers at the Renault plant.

My own research began with the adaptation of Polish immigrants in Roubaix, in the north of France. I studied as well France's participation in the newly-formed International Refugee Organization. My ultimate goal remained the comparative understanding of the different forms of cultural or social pluralism—ethnic, religious, linguistic and so on—within and across the borders of France and other European nation-states. But I learned more, or at least something different, outside the Sorbonne and beyond my research in Roubaix.

University life consisted of late afternoons and evenings on the streets and in the cafés, among French, non-French, European and African friends and acquaintances. That informal education contributed to my eventual preoccupation with ethno-nationalism and other forms of ethnic pluralism. Having devoted my life to this question, the present breakup of the Eastern European nation-states holds few surprises.

In that setting forty years ago I learned, in sum, that my love for France, persisting to this day, ran parallel to my recognition that for France, as for all nation-states, the scholar's generalizations are conditioned by realism; they invariably contain their own contradictions and shades of grey.

For example, I came to a different understanding of the social role of the Catholic Church in France and elsewhere. Given my family tradition of democratic socialism and my adult sociological study of the revolutionary role of the Church as part of a junta with army and landed aristocracy in countries like Spain with earlier feudal class structures, I had a straightforward view of the Church in terms of class structure. Lenin's "opiate of the people" made no sense at all, but neither did I believe the Church really followed its own encyclicals on labor and social justice. Paris taught me that the Church was an extraordinary institution, timeless in faith but whose structure incorporated *both* resistance to change and acceptance of change, both rigidity and resilience. I knew the Church of Franco's Spain; the Catholicism of the worker-priest movement; the Catholic spirit of community exemplified by Emmanuel Mounier's *personnalisme*; the relationship of the Catholic ethos to social justice as seen in the work of Simone Weil—all that, I read about and experienced in Paris. Later at the Jesuit-run Boston College I taught the course on American Catholic social structure and carried out research with John Donovan on social change in the urban parish. That deeper, more complex vision of the Church I had found in Europe got through to my students. Later, through my association with Gordon Zahn, Catholic pacifism became as accessible to me as the official Catholic doctrine of the "just war" (Mounier 1962, Zahn 1962 and 1967, Robbins 1965).

In France as a Fulbright at the beginning of the fifties, I learned to look for manifest proclamations and latent realities in my special field of racial and ethnic realities. French anti-semitism had subsided without disappearing; it would rise again, as it had before, from Dreyfus to Pétain. On my first day at the Sorbonne I saw, scrawled on a wall, *Au four encore les juifs!* I came to see that the great and profound French tradition, since the Revolution, of asylum for the exile and protection for the foreigner would be periodically undermined by a fierce chauvinism and xenophobia. The manifest France of *liberté, égalité, fraternité* would prevail in the end, but not before the latent France would surface in the form of one nativist movement or another. Today's version, the "national front" of Jean-Marie Le Pen, is sustained by stagnating economic conditions and an abiding French fear of ethnic heterogeneity. The Arabs, North Africans, Africans, whoever, "are taking our jobs, and they are not really French," one says. To be sure, quantitative restrictions on immigrants in the light of changing economic and social conditions are sometimes required, but neo-fascist "fronts" are not concerned with that problem, they seek only to stamp out some "internal enemy."

I learned that in some ways French colonialism, harsh as it was, was less racist than the British kind, given its premise of integrating Asian and African elites into an advanced French *civilisation*: "They are more French than we French are." Students from Indochina, Senegal and other possessions told me the obverse: brutal economic exploitation, meaningless parliamentary representation, massacre of indigenous people in Madagascar-Malagasy. That year I was delegate and interpreter at a Friends Service Conference on youth and international cooperation at Lake Garda in Italy; many delegates came from former colonies. The representative of France gave an expressive speech on the greatness of France and what its civilization had brought to non-Western peoples, not only industrial technology but the ideas of Voltaire, Rousseau, St. Simon et al. The representative from Pondichéry, a tiny French enclave in India, gave the response: "I know well this French *civilisation*. I have a

Lycée education. At the Lycée I learned all about *liberté, égalité, fraternité.* And these are the principles we are using to drive you French the hell out of Pondichéry!"

Finally it was borne in upon me that the reputation of France as a race-free haven for Americans of color, a generalization I had first heard in Harlem years before, while broadly true and well-deserved, did not always apply. Two cheers for that happy French indifference, far better than either prejudice or patronization, displayed towards strolling interracial couples. But in more mundane matters of jobs and housing, the writer James Baldwin, a close friend, and other blacks in France, both American and from the colonies, spoke of serious problems.

Yet on balance the Paris of cosmopolitanism, mutual tolerance, individualism and the freedom to be oneself was real. That Paris, that France, has generally prevailed, though interrupted periodically by racism and nativism. For my part, I found that realism reinforces attachment. When I knew the more complex and difficult France, I grew more attached, more determined to take up my central sociological theme: how national unity incorporates ethnic diversity, how a culture is knit together from sub-cultures in a broader setting. Paris was not France, there were the provinces; nor was France Western Europe—there were countries like Belgium and Spain as well, engaged in their own forms of federalism and pluralism.

The second time round as a Fulbright, I was visiting professor of sociology and American studies at the University of Strasbourg. Strasbourg stood for a nation—France, but also for a region—Alsace. This time we went *en famille*, with two children promptly enrolled in nursery school, a little Montessori sub-culture in itself, run by the synagogue with instruction in French and Hebrew. At the University I taught courses on American capitalism and ethnic relations in English, sociology in French. But my chief interest still lay outside Academe, in sub-cultures within cultures.

Alsace presented a challenging first case, especially rural and village Alsace (as children we were wrongly taught to say Alsace-Lorraine, but that term refers only to the period of German control immediately after the Franco-Prussian war). Occupying the northeast corner of France between the Rhine and the Vosges mountains, Alsace has been strong in agriculture and industry. Alsatians remember two German occupations—the oppressive control, street signs made over, the German language installed, French forbidden in the schools and men pressed into serving the German military. The architecture and the dialect are more Germanic than French. Yet there is today no possibility of an ethno-national association with Germany. France the nation commands basic political identity: you are first and last *citoyen de*

France, then Alsatian. In contrast to what I found in East Europe, ethno-nationalist separatism is irrelevant. Conflicts with Paris center on decentralization, equitable distribution of resources, national-regional control of education. Problems are regional; but they are not *ethno-nationally* regional. Thus Alsace lies at the easy end of the spectrum of national pluralism, in contrast to harder nuts like Belgium and Yugoslavia.

What is Alsatian-ness? Strasbourg was not the place to frame an answer. Like Brussels a center for the new Europe, it is transnational in a sense, with an extensive Europe-oriented civil service. So I set out with colleagues to find my village: Weiterswiller, on the slopes of the Vosges 50 km from Strasbourg. Rapid socio-economic change has not obliterated its Alsatian sub-culture, though farming has virtually disappeared and most inhabitants work in nearby towns or commute to Strasbourg. Its core, as is often true in Europe, is linguistic: to be Alsatian is to speak the dialect. It is distinctive in its religious pluralisms: 75% Catholic, 25% Protestant, and between the two churches an abandoned synagogue—the Nazi deportations and now the characteristic migration of youth to the cities has virtually ended a once-vibrant rural Jewish community in Alsace. One Jewish family survives sporadic anti-semitic incidents; it no longer practices the old middleman trade (Raphael and Weyl 1977).

For nearly a quarter-century, I have lived in Weiterswiller in periodic time-spans of months, broken by residence in Strasbourg. I see now what eluded me at first: a pattern not terribly European in shape and perhaps closer to the American model of assimilation. The Alsatian sub-culture is receding and Weiterswiller is becoming, like thousands of other villages across France, a microcosm of the nation in general. But not quite. Regionalism recedes in France but does not vanish. The dialect holds on more tenaciously than expected. Folk culture declines but is not lost altogether, and the younger generation—as in Brittany—is interested in cultural revival. Folk literature must be carried orally because the dialect is not a written language: the regional newspaper appears in French and German. Most of all there persists, in psycho-social terms, that intangible *esprit*, a sense of wanting to be Alsatian in temper, not readily defined. The Alsatians at least have avoided an ethno-national political stance; there is no aspiration to make the region a nation-state. This is no small accomplishment in a Europe of fierce revived nationalisms. The French regional formula works well enough (Ardagh 1980).

But the French case cannot be generalized too widely. Since the Revolution and Napoleon, who says France says centralization. Under DeGaulle and afterward, regionalization and decentralization have been important. But the nation-state remains the main theme, regional sub-cultures the variations.   In the seventies I moved to harder cases: more complex and troubling ethno-national cross-border situations in Belgium and Spain, then Bulgaria, Hungary, Rumania, Czechoslovakia and the former USSR.   In Belgium I found my ethno-national area along the linguistic boundary running east and west, in a village area due east of Brussels. Dutch-speaking Flemish north of the line and French-speaking Walloons to the south have come to terms politically: one Belgian state encompasses two regional-linguistic communities, entitled constitutionally to equal participation in a genuinely bilingual educational system. In Spain I chose a section of Barcelona, capital of Catalonia.   There, with Franco's death in 1975, a new constitution established a national-federal Spain. The three most clear-cut "autonomous communities" (Catalonia, the Basque Republic and Galicia) are defined in ethno-national and ethno-linguistic terms and their integrity affirmed. In both countries the case is made for a viable policy of ethno-national pluralism. It is nonetheless assumed that there will be continuous conflict.

These and other ethno-national homelands are shown on the map opposite (Connor 1977). It should be emended of course to show German unification (1990), the breakaway of Slovenia and Croatia from Yugoslavia followed by civil war (1991), the end of the USSR (1991) and its replacement by a yet-undefined Commonwealth of Independent States.

For Europe in general, ethno-national pluralism—the system whereby modern nation-states remain sovereign while providing territorial, political and cultural entities within them with representation and access—constitutes the only sensible solution. Two conditions are essential: significant economic stability, and a process for arriving at the basic agreement within a democratic political framework. The most elaborate forms of confederation, common-wealth or union cannot survive massive unemployment and steeply dwindling supplies of consumer essentials. Perhaps a third condition: no faking. There are too many shams in history, where the central state cedes folk-dancing and ethnic museums but no power or representation to the constituent nationalities. Calling nationalities "republics" does not make them so.

What are the alternatives? Forced assimilation? It deprives the ethnos of its cultural integrity. Secession? It can lead to destructive fragmentation and balkanization, usually with violence.   Perhaps voluntaristic and gradual assimilation, but that is a different story, a story for the far longer range. Today the central issue remains, as it has for 200 years, the crisis of nationalism (Kohn 1967). Like it or not, the nation-state continues as *the* central organizing force in our lives. I doubt the new integration, Europe '92 and after, will prove me wrong.

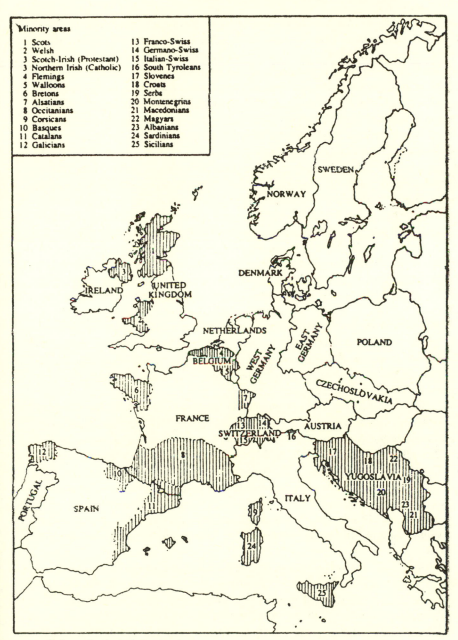

Minority areas

1 Scots	13 Franco-Swiss
2 Welsh	14 Germano-Swiss
3 Scotch-Irish (Protestant)	15 Italian-Swiss
3 Northern Irish (Catholic)	16 South Tyroleans
4 Flemings	17 Slovenes
5 Walloons	18 Croats
6 Bretons	19 Serbs
7 Alsatians	20 Montenegrins
8 Occitanians	21 Macedonians
9 Corsicans	22 Magyars
10 Basques	23 Albanians
11 Catalans	24 Sardinians
12 Galicians	25 Sicilians

Selected ethnic homelands.

For we have inherited the double legacy of the French Revolution. Good Nationalism produces a nation-state which is the protector of the rights and the focus of the obligations of *all* citizens, however they may differ. Bad Nationalism produces a nation-state which tramples the principle of common citizenship, dividing those who belong from those who do not. Worse still, Bad Nationalism is by definition expansionist, invoking the same principles to conquer "inferior" peoples around them.

I sometimes wonder what the Senator thinks of all this. The enormous resurgence of powerful, traditional nationalisms in Europe and the Third World might be deeply disturbing to him. His life's work has meant an effort to demonstrate that national sovereignties and interests can adapt successfully to international cooperation, containing war and advancing peace. His perspective, optimistic but grounded ever in realism, was shared by many of the best students of modern nationalism in the years following World War II. On the other hand, it is possible that the Senator, who struggled all his career with the compromises imposed on him by the sub-cultures of his own native state, was looking for something that could only happen over time. Reflect on the vision of this man and how his region and his own German-American ethnicity shaped it: raised in the far northwest corner of a tiny Southern state, he had grandparents who lived through the humiliations of the Civil War. His university years were spent in Arkansas, but four years of Rhodes-sponsored European residence took him far from home. Since the early forties he has ceaselessly worked towards ways for the weak and the strong to live together in some kind of peaceful balance.

I wonder then if he is so surprised by the fragmentation of the emerging Europe. He might say it was expected all along, that the nationalisms of Europe have been so long and so violently suppressed over the last two centuries that it is natural for them to burst forth, even as our own nationalisms split tragically only four score and seven years after the beginnings. He might say, as the sponsor of the UN Resolution in 1943, that broader U.S. support of the UN over the last half-century might have put us far ahead on the road to Good Nationalisms. But he might also say that there are some things which we cannot circumvent, things we must live through, things that only time can change.

Unlike the Senator, I could not change our world. I have contented myself with trying to understand it, to articulate it and perhaps to touch a few students. My forty years of study have turned up a basic home truth: the acceptance of ethnic diversity within national unity is an index of Good Nationalism. In France, where the regional sub-cultures live in fairly steady balance with the center, the xenophobic "fronts" are eventually constrained by the tradition of openness and the protection of inalienable rights.

Fulbright and ASTP helped me find the right country. And it is to the model of *regional* France, as of Flanders-in-Belgium and Catalonia- in-Spain, and in my case, New England-in-U.S., where I have completed the long journey from Brooklyn, that I remain attached. Reflecting on France and my Fulbrights, I need to devolve Addison's dream from nations to regions: some year I would choose to pass my winter in Provence, my spring in Bretagne, my summer in Aquitaine, my autumn in Alsace. Then home to Massachusetts.

REFERENCES

John Ardagh, *France Today* (Rev. ed.), London: Penguin, 1990.

Walker Connor, "Ethnonationalism in the First World," in Milton J. Eisman (ed.), *Ethnic Conflict in the Western World*, Ithaca, NY: Cornell, 1977 (by permission).

Hans Kohn, "Nationalism," *Encyclopedia of the Social Sciences*, New York: Macmillan, 1967.

Emmanuel Mounier, *Be Not Afraid: A Denunciation of Despair* (tr. Cynthia Rowland), New York: Sheed & Ward, 1962.

F. Raphael and R. Weyl, *Juifs en Alsace*, Toulouse: Privat, 1977.

R. Robbins, "American Jews and Catholics," *Sociological Analysis*, Spring 1965.

_____, "Sociology and Congressional Law Making: Immigration," in A. Shostak (ed.) *Sociology in Action*, Homewood, Illinois: Dorsey, 1966.

D. Taft and R. Robbins, *International Migrations*, New York: Ronald, 1955.

G. Zahn, *German Catholics and Hitler's Wars*, New York: Sheed & Ward, 1962.

_____, *War, Conscience and Dissent*, New York: Hawthorn, 1967.

Forty-year-old memories, when the floodgates open, turn torrential. In this essay, the writer attempts with only partial success to channel this flood into three thematic channels: the demystification of Romantic American views of Europe, the discovery of war and politics, and the functioning of a university system in a country long dominated by a small, highly intellectualized elite. A fourth theme, the elusive question of French perceptions of the U.S. and American views of France, is never far from the surface.

3

TILTING AT MYTHS

Richard T. Arndt

In the lonely hills above Dijon's famous *Côte*, the plateau-edge where grapes for the world's finest wines grow, the motorbike faded beneath me and coasted to a halt. It was a hazy afternoon in the early Spring of 1950 and I was exploring the Burgundian hills around Dijon, to which a spin of the brand-new French Fulbright Commission's roulette-wheel had assigned me. I had set out in search of the manor where the poet and liberal statesman Lamartine had lived his last years; I had lost my way and was meandering through newly-planted wheatfields.

Americans are born somewhere near engines. I knew what most of us learn by owning our first cars, but the manual in my saddle-bag, in mechanic's French, was not immediately clear. Someone at my side said, "It's the sparkplug." The old peasant in wooden shoes and wide-brimmed straw hat, stooped by the weight of his years if not the centuries, might have stepped from Millet's *Angélus* or Markham's "Man with a Hoe." He repeated, "It's the sparkplug. With these two-phase one-cylinder engines it's always the sparkplug" (what I actually heard was, "It's the candle, with these two-time motors it's always the candle").

He took an English key (wrench) from my tool-kit, removed the single plug, scraped the carbon out of its gap with an antique pocket knife, put things back together, and suggested I lean on the mushroom (step on the accelerator).

The motor hummed. He was gone before I could construct a sentence of thanks.

The moment has remained. Only later did I begin to understand how it marked a change in my world. My visions and expectations of France, of Europe, had been shaped by pervasive and dominant Romantic images and myths, some of my own creation, some from my education and some generated by the subtle machine that grinds out the endless enchantments of Francophilia. Forty-odd years later, I begin to realize how unprepared I was for this old man and his mechanical sophistication.

A Princeton French major in the forties knew the language of Racine better than that of *Le Monde*, better even than that of Chaucer or Spenser. In the forties, at least in my small sector of the college, we were lovingly but relentlessly urged to an esthetic vision which held that living one's life as a work of art was the highest goal, that art alone mattered and was its own object.

The esthetic imperative did not contradict the university's mission of preparing a service-oriented national elite—"Princeton in the nation's service" was the motto, first articulated by the same Woodrow Wilson whose ultimate disciple was just beginning to emerge in the person of a young Senator from Arkansas.   Estheticism-as-service, largely a matter of style, tinted my itinerary, from the lower middle class on the Jersey side of New York through Princeton on nothing a year, with too little scholarship help and too heavy a work schedule. Estheticism beckoned to us from the university's impeccable Gothic cloisters and towers—in Jersey fieldstone, not ivory. It led me into the French Department and shaped my view of France, a nation which long used style and grace to keep peace between its administrative elite and those it ruled, while shining as a beacon of world intellect and culture. Princeton allowed my education to be a-political. My teachers, generous men—they were all men, just as all but three of my secondary teachers were women— professed the Central Jersey Brahmin style.

The way French literature was presented all but ignored politics, except for the Enlightenment, where politics became "ideas." Even in the writings of Montaigne, Stendhal, Balzac, Zola, Malraux and Sartre (a 1948 visitor to Princeton), little challenged the estheticist view.   More than that of most countries, literary life in France focused then in a tiny group living in three *arrondissements* of Paris. My senior thesis—I blanch at the thought of rereading it—dwelt on the novels of André Gide, a refined, classical, cautiously daring yet lofty contemporary writer and critic whose flirtation with Communism went completely past me. True, hardier stuff like Zola on the peasantry and the working class impressed me, but at a safe distance; I saw films like Marcel Carné's *Le Jour se lève* and Jean Renoir's setting of Zola's *La Bête humaine*, in which a handsome young Jean Gabin incarnates a Stakhanovite worker-hero married to his magnificent locomotive. But nothing at Princeton prepared me for this old man in the hills of Burgundy.

I was in fact painfully young, perhaps the youngest of that first French Fulbright litter. I was vaguely aware of the government sponsorship, the sources of Fulbright funding in converted war materiel; I was certainly unaware of any attendant political contradictions. To me, it meant a year in the country I had studied and even worshipped for much of my adolescent life. I had proposed to examine the French impact of the American novels of the twenties and thirties, a subject for a lifetime. In a pamphlet sent with my passport, Eleanor Roosevelt reminded us that we were all Ambassadors of America. Practical Ambassador that I was, I took a year's supply of toilet-tissue.

A farewell reception at the French Consulate on October 18 and then the close quarters aboard the reconverted troop-ship S.S. Washington introduced me to the 270 or so new BA/BS's and advanced graduate students bound for France (5 or 6 make the trip nowadays). The voyage was a perpetual bridge game in intimidating company over the cheapest drink on the menu, twenty-five cent Cognac. I listened a lot, and we practiced our French. Arriving via Le Havre at the Gare St. Lazare late in the evening of October 26, we were swept into a whirl of orientation activities by the newly-minted Commission. I overlooked my twenty-first birthday.

Wandering through Paris in the daze of my young years, I remember little—orientation was, generally is, a garble. Details and people come back but little substance or structure—a briefing by the *New Yorker* legend Janet Flanner, remarks by America's arbiter of diplomatic grace Ambassador David Bruce, a visit to the St. Etienne-du-Mont beloved of Robert Delaunay, to Sacré-Coeur, the usual things. I gaped and stared—this was the France I had read about. Looking back, I see now that my curiosity was gorging on the magic of history, of time and its incrustations, on that deep-layered historical dimension in life that still does not come readily to hand in our young republic. On this corner, Coligny was assassinated, here the Rite of Spring was first performed, there Marie-Antoinette waited for the end, up there Quasimodo—or was it Charles Laughton?—swung between the towers. And the theatre: the legendary Louis Jouvet doing *Ondine* by the living Giraudoux, the brash, brilliant Jean-Louis Barrault doing the living Gide's translation of *Hamlet*, and the Comédie Française, doing Corneille and Molière the old-fashioned way. The shabby, war-weary City of Light glowed with meaning, from inside.

Dijon, a city of 100,000 then four hours by train to the southeast, was another matter: my only literary memory was what Henry Miller, in one of the *Tropics*, had recounted of his nightmarish months as a *pion* in Dijon's Lycée Carnot, whose halls years later would be graced by my older son. But for me Dijon was still France. And in my France, everything—even dirt—was beautiful. An odorous and filthy wall with flaking stucco and years of shredded posters was a work of art—it was a *French* wall.

My encounter with the peasant-mechanic marked the outset of the careful peeling away of myth which had to be done before getting anywhere near French realities, near the honest stone under the flaking surfaces. Romantic visions are lovely, sweet and dangerous—no one wants to leave them. It takes faith to strip them away, the faith that whatever lies beneath may be more important and as beautiful, or perhaps not beautiful at all—with apologies to estheticism, does it matter? I began then to knock heads with myth, to find the path that led out of the ivory-tower's maze, to learn the pain of demystification. The old man reminded me of the plural roots which reach deep beneath an elite society. His presence hinted at the rich growth that could spring up in France and that would ultimately create another nation. I cannot say that France taught me, as David Woo puts it, ". . . to prefer real hell to any imaginary paradise." But it did its best, and I began to learn.

Politics and its extension, war, forced their way into my life in France. It was too early for World War II to have passed entirely into mythology, and too early for Cold War slogans. Four years after victory, war was all around me, sometimes overlooked but never far, and always hard to read. It had exhausted France, more than the proud French liked to admit. The physical damage had only begun to be repaired; cities like Caen would never be the same. Long-deferred maintenance, over-exploitation of natural resources, a depleted economy and human terror had taken a toll: France—even Paris—was shabby, threadbare and frightened.

Dijon had scarcely been nudged. True, there were yellow *Abri* (shelter) signs stenciled every fifty yards. And the Mayor, a colorful, portly priest, was said to owe his limp to a wound incurred in the Resistance (he would achieve the barroom equivalent of Count Nesselrode's culinary fame—his name stuck to a cocktail made of two local products and since called a Kir). There had been some resistance fighting around Dijon, there was an unfortunate accidental slaughter at Comblanchien, the rail yards had been bombed by the Allies; but the damage was slight. A common opinion held that the Germans, while nasty, had behaved "correctly." Much of Dijon, Catholic Dijon at least—and the Catholicism of Dijon, heavily influenced by St. Bernard of Clairvaux and by nearby Cîteaux and Cistercian thought, was puritan and fundamental—had come to terms with Pétain's Vichy. Coins in ersatz metal were still in circulation all over France, bearing the Vichy motto *Travail, Famille, Patrie* in place of *Liberté, Egalité, Fraternité*. And by 1949 the younger generation had already begun to entertain thoughts about the moral compromises of their elders.

Mark Clark's Fifth Army had liberated Dijon, pausing long enough so that my friend the Director of the student hostel, a former monastery which American troops had taken over from the Germans and where I lived, said ruefully one day, without a trace of anti-American animus, what many of Dijon's people echoed: "We had *two* Occupations, theirs and yours." No ingratitude, merely a statement of fact: armies are armies, war is war, no one including the victim behaves very well. Goodhearted U.S. airmen from the base at Chaumont to the northeast came for weekends to the strait-laced city, equipped with imported beer and floozies, and left their mess behind. Auxerre, to the northwest, home to student-colleagues, had never recovered from its selection as a rest area for the survivors of the Arnhem-Nijmegen disaster depicted in Cornelius Ryan's *A Bridge Too Far*. The War and its memories marked the beginning of my political education. In the U.S. politics was a game, akin to today's Super Bowl rites. In Europe politics killed.

What took years to see, under the facade of French dignity and pride, was the pain and humiliation of what had happened—the corrosive doubts about pre-War decadence, the abject collapse known as the Debacle, the moral ambiguity of the Vichy period, the elegant compromises of the world's most polished administrative system, the disturbing sub-stratum of anti-semitism, the rhetorical snares of anti-Communist theory, the emergence of a vicious indigenous French *milice* going the Nazis one better, the behavior of the paradoxically civilized Germans—dramatized by Vercors' *Le Silence de la mer* or by *Hiroshima mon amour*, and the discovery that even good-hearted American GIs were warriors.

The poverty, the hunger, the deprivation, the shame, the deaths were carefully camouflaged. Only pride stood tall. It took the turn of the seasons for me to realize that most of my co-students owned only one wool garment or a single shirt, that they and the women of their families spent hours patching and darning and mending. William Maxwell's sensitive *The Chateau* catches this stoic, heroic and touchingly vain French effort in the forties to keep up appearances at all costs—above all, it seemed to me, with us Americans, casually unaware of the troubling cultural threat we posed. The people I knew needed to live up to the very myths I was just beginning, with affection, to strip away.

The dollar was at an embarrassing high and provincial Fulbrights were overpaid. That first year, with a Fulbright Commission in faraway Paris still inexperienced at non-Parisian costs and allowances, all of us earned considerably more than the University's Rector. None flaunted it. Some skimped and stretched their nine months into twelve. My motorbike—and a periodic binge of *pâtisserie*—were my only vices. Living at the student hostel, with two or three meals, cost me less than a dollar a day.

The American colony consisted of two GI Bill "students," two English-teaching *assistentes* living over the Post Office, and half a dozen Fulbrighters. One read Valéry while tending with his delightful wife to two infant sons, shocking their French neighbors by feeding the infants *eggs*! Another did economics, stayed through a doctorate, and later became massively successful at handling money, less so at politics. Another, a Hispanic-American, disappeared sadly from view. One young man tried with painful sincerity to understand and ward off the advances of one of his teachers. Another was a paratrooper-poet, writing the lines that would win him a Hopwood Prize at Michigan before he retreated to his beloved farm in Iowa.

At the hostel, I saw the clasped hands of the Marshall Plan for the first time when the director gave me a can of powdered milk. The Burgundian farmlands were producing their bounty, milk was no longer in short supply, he had a few cans left over, and he was pleased to give me back something of my country's largesse, gone slightly stale. My friend M. Ballot opened another insight into the Marshall Plan difference. He owned a fine hardware store, full of surprises, in central Dijon. One day, in search of a hacksaw blade, I followed him to a store-room where he showed me case after case of Marshall Plan goods, given to France for its economic recovery and sold by the government through commercial outlets like his. He found the blades and gave me one, refusing payment. He kissed the box as he put it back on the shelf. "Sans l'Amérique, sans l'Amérique . . . ," he said, his eyes misty behind thick glasses. Was it La Rochefoucauld who warned us that gratitude was the hardest virtue to practice, that we resent our saviors? Not M. Ballot. He and I parted that day with an especially firm handshake. I stopped by regularly for chats.

The War and America meant something else to Charly Rouxel, a 15-year-old who had learned English from the GI's. He was hooked on a lifetime love-affair with the U.S. His tiny but magnificent mother ran the Cours Pigier, a commercial school. Charly's well-meant suggestions for my first translation exercise at the University had disastrous results. He and his cronies, including various priests and maternal friends, set out to "fix me up real good"—the issue was housing. It took a while to learn there was none to be had in Dijon that year and I ended up to my ultimate relief in the hostel. Charly showed up in New York six years later, drove across America with a friend and a guitar in a $50 used car, and was last heard of making a grand success of selling second-hand machine-tools out of Cincinnati.

After the mysteries of war and politics came those of the French university, my single greatest challenge. Nothing, even Oxonian Princeton (founded 1746, probably before Dijon), prepared me for this. The University, actually the Faculty of Letters or "la Fac," was dingy behind its sooty facade. Our classes in French literature took place for the most part in one badly heated room: long wooden trestle desks and chairs defied belief. In 1990, visiting my younger son at the Fac, I peered into those rooms: nothing has changed, only the steam-cleaned facade gleaming in the sunlight.

Deciphering the University had its sorrows and its glories. Take my admission. There was no way to identify myself without my diploma, the original, no copies accepted. Airmailed by my mother and still dog-eared from the trip, it made my reputation. The Fac's administrative office was staffed by a single long-suffering, impatient and perpetually irritated woman who told me with considerable effort that it would of course have to be translated into French by an official translator. Now, Princeton indulged then, and still does I hope, in touching kinds of antiquarian drollery: I asked her where I could get my diploma translated from *Latin*? The game changed: *Comme c'est merveilleux*, of course no translation would be required. I became a favorite of the grumpy lady, who thereafter never missed a chance to smile, shake hands and greet warmly the American whose university used Latin.

There were no classes in French literature to speak of except on Thursday. A new graduate, I was addicted to attending classes and, having already understood that my French was too superficial to allow me to get very far under the surface of my project, I managed to find a few other things worth doing other days of the week, mainly in the English Department—I was the American who went to class. Thursday was the big day: most of my fellow students were earning some kind of meager living as primary teachers or dormitory supervisors in *lycées*. Thursday afternoon was a school holiday and the Fac was geared to their needs.

There were no lecture courses or surveys, only *le programme*, the curriculum. It consisted of a list of a dozen books, some of them no longer than thirty pages, none of them written after 1923, and with them a single thematic subject. Take it or leave it, that was it. If you did not feel like studying Joachim Du Bellay, you could come back next year. On the other hand, if you knew Othello inside out it did not much matter whether you had read Hamlet or Lear, that was only *culture générale*. Subjects like psychology, anthropology, sociology were nowhere to be found (in fairness we had neither anthro nor sociology at Princeton until my last year)—a tentative course in psychology was taught in the philosophy department. The whole approach, the very contrary of the American survey-course, was intensive, based on close reading and detailed analysis of a few texts. True, we spent inordinate time worrying about twists and turns in the "psychology" of the characters in literary works—unfettered by any systematic study of psychology the French found room for lots of talk about it. As a Columbia teacher later remarked, "You Americans read Freud, but we have Racine."

La discussion, literary and political, was the national sport. Any subject would do: a movie had to be followed by a two-hour dissection at a café—I discovered that films, more than "entertainment," were works of craft, of the human mind, and ultimately of art. With friends, there was a lot of talk, about almost any subject. Perhaps memory has slipped but I do not recall entering the university library—I bought my books with generous Fulbright allowances. Everyone shook hands, with a short, sharp single chop, no matter how many times per day we met. And everyone used *tu*—followed by verb forms Princeton never taught.

The handshakes had little to do with friendship, only camaraderie and fellow-suffering. The structure pitted every student against the others. What bound us was our shared terror at the power of the *Profs*, who seemed to delight in exquisite forms of classroom torture. No recitations to speak of, no exams, no discussion, no assigned reading, no questions in class. Lectures were casually delivered on the assumption one was lucky to be able to hear them. Everything was geared to June exams and nothing happened until then.

Nothing that is except for Thursday at 1 PM, the one compulsory element in the weekly curriculum: *explication de texte*. The Prof-torturer was an aging but still-handsome survivor of the nineteenth century who had written volumes on sentiment and sensibility in the eighteenth century and who admired long-dead writers of purple critical prose. He was missing a thumb, reportedly shot off in a boudoir; he delighted in counting off five key points on the four remaining digits. Thursday was his moment. He strode commandingly into the hall. We leapt to our feet. He waved us negligently to our seats and laid out the paragraph or page that was to be covered next week—meanwhile his eyes darted around the room until he found next week's victim. Then the day's designee took his place beside the Master and launched into his agony.

At Columbia my teacher Jean Hytier, trying to define *explication*, once mused that, of all the things that marked the French, it was the most typical: "One is tempted to go so far as to define the Frenchman as a little guy who does *explications de texte*." In Dijon it was a set of rites for which all were prepared and it went through its several stages at a stately pace: one "situated" the text in its larger context, then read it (a good reading was said to obviate the need for explication, but no one achieved that in Dijon), then analyzed it—always in some miraculous way dividing it into three parts. The general student performance was fairly unimpressive, but then that was the idea: it was a curtain-raiser for the main event.

The Master began his critique. He too had his rituals: a few words of faint praise: "What you have done is intelligent (or: not stupid, perceptive, clear, whatever); you did this well (that less well, this other fairly well, this was completely overlooked, whatever); in sum, that was good (very good, not so good)." Once he said, memorably, "That was good, very good. In fact, not bad." But after a minute or two of such remarks, he would invariably come to the same verbal pivot: "But . . . what you *should have said* . . . ." Then, in the grand style, with dignity, élan, careful staging and some degree of sparkle, there emerged The Truth. His performance, designed to impress and indeed to a certain extent impressive, had several purposes: to remind us how inferior the preceding speaker had been, to prove that there was only One Truth and that he was Its keeper, and to discourage the weak from pretending to the priesthood of literature. There might be the vague suggestion, but only for the chosen, that if you worked at it and above all observed him closely, you too might some day achieve something almost as good.

The most impressive student performance of the year focused on the grisly scene in Stendhal's *Le Rouge et le noir* in which Mathilde de la Môle makes a kind of passionate love to the severed head of her guillotined lover Julien Sorel. The student's performance caught the Master short; he had to admit it was a superior job. But he swung into his routine anyway, building his oration to an exquisite climax: the student had missed the only point of any importance, the scene was in poor taste!

There were three kinds of Prof: aging survivors, young comers and second-team Parisians who arrived by train on Thursday morning and stayed until Friday afternoon. One Parisian in particular had his origins in Burgundy, attested by a strong local accent. He had the laudable audacity to introduce that year the Fac's first course in Comparative Literature. I had early incurred his annoyance by doing the unspeakable thing: raising my hand, not to ask a question—bad enough—but to correct a *lapsus* he had made, convulsing my colleagues, adding to my reputation and making an inadvertent statement about the U.S. We delighted in catching him in the act: reading his lectures aloud from books which one of us had invariably read. By then I had drifted into sitting among the "graduate students," those who had their *licences* (BA/MA) and were preparing the state-controled *agrégation*, approximately equivalent in those days to American PhD orals but run as a savage national competition. In Dijon the academic student imagination reached little higher than the *agreg*.

It took years before I understood that provincial university and its problems—perhaps the problems of all the 17 or so underfunded French universities of the time.   Surely in the forties no more than 8-10% of the eligible age-group went beyond the lycée at all.   No one in 1949 told me about the skimming off of the best, who went to the famous *grandes écoles*, the Super Schools which siphoned off all the top lycée students.   Another slice was accounted for by those who could afford to move to Paris.   The provincial universities got the rest of the 10%.   The Profs then had to teach them, to screen out most, and to prepare the exceptional few for the preposterously scant number of careers in secondary or, exceptionally, university teaching. Unlike the dazzling student element which peopled the Super Schools, the students at the Fac had no support funds and this affected their performance; the University had even less, as the Fac's single spavined mimeograph machine reminded us.

Few made it.   Of all my student colleagues and one older friend, an earlier product of the system, I have tracked four Dijon friends who stayed in the provinces to complete the *agrégation*:   one used her towering gifts as a teacher of Latin and Greek at the best Parisian lycées; the other three—one in history, one in English and one in Greek and Latin studies—taught at provincial lycées, persisted through the exhausting state doctorate process, and ended up at the Fac, one as Dean.   Meanwhile those shunted off to the Super Schools graduated into the fraternal governmental bodies known as *les Grands Corps* then to the famous ENA.   Even now they run France, as Jane Kramer remarked, "with a pencil."

If I have dwelt on the sorrows, there were also glories.   I lived among these Profs and a few aspirants who mattered.   With all their minor vanities and their major skills (like Latin and Greek, French of course, and unnerving articulateness), these men and women embodied the life of literature, of scholarship, of humanism, of ideas in a way that has all but disappeared in the U.S. and increasingly is fading in Europe.   That was really all they lived, all they had time to live given their crushing workloads—except for the Profs at the tip of the pyramid they were overwhelmed by work, and they were paid very little.   They scraped for every franc they could to buy the heavily-discounted books which lined the walls of their studies, but buy them they did. They favored a dynamic bookseller whose condescension towards them mirrored society's attitude—as he confided to me one day, they were to him "a bunch of petty provincial *agrégés*."

The ruthless pyramidal selection system, the conveyor-belt to elite status, produced a special kind of disobedient dependency in those who did not go all the way. As an under-class, the Profs, the intellectuals of Dijon, seemed to matter little in the French scheme of things; they were a harmless, non-ruling, powerless part of the elite. True, they ruled in the satrapies of their classrooms, and perhaps that power corrupted as much as other kinds. They taught because that was the role the world had assigned them. Few of them had any real alternatives and, once in the system with its long-range perks, it was folly to leave. Some of them were brilliant, most of them were good, and all of them—though it was not always easy to see—cared not only for ideas but for the students to whom they tried to transmit them. They lived a provincial French version of the life of the mind, they lived it with genuine style and in it found a peculiar kind of richness. With few rewards for being so, they were scholars. And like the chiseled cameo signatures of France, developed for a banking system obsessed by forgery, they were complicated and gnarled and curled and spiky and even flamboyant, yet strong, and sometimes very beautiful.

France taught me about the connections between politics and education, or elite-formation as my political scientist friends say. Politically Dijon's intellectuals sounded further left than I—it would take years to see the curious coincidence by which those who entered the *grandes écoles* and staffed the Establishment were farther right. Over the years I have come to understand that particular Left's fascination for a vague ideal of a populist, utopian, post-Revolutionary, St. Simonian kind of socialism, one which Mitterrand would be quick to abandon when he discovered the difference between socialism as opposition and as power. The Profs' approach to politics, as I think I see it now, was through ideas—the system allowed them, in their powerlessness, a simple choice: vote to support the status quo, or protest. Protest amounted to little more than formalized griping; certainly they had no experience of the processes of day-to-day consensus-building and power-sharing that we are alleged to practice in America. Voting, except possibly at the local level, did not seem to make a lot of difference to them—and it permitted a convenient form of protest; I guessed at their pain in having politics reduced to just another subject for *la discussion*. Was there as well a sense of relief?

In party terms, the teacher unions—though few of my friends—leaned to the PCF. The Cold War was not yet a commonplace. These intellectuals in the provinces were not terrified by French communism, nor much indeed by the Soviet variety; they believed Stalin was mortal. The idea of the USSR attracted them, I suspect, for its capacity to focus a protest statement about

France at little visible cost. Still, it was 1950, the year of the Berlin blockade and the airlift; North Korean troops would cross the 38th parallel in June; and Dijon had acquired a forlorn little group of Czech student-émigrés from the Prague coup of 1948, as it had acquired Germans from the Saar, some even wearing the leftover green lodens of the Wehrmacht. Rightly or wrongly, Dijon's skeptical intellectuals were fond of the Soviets, if only for literary and historical reasons. As I see it now, they were persuaded the Soviet Union would evolve sooner or later into something more civilized; they feared that anti-Soviet rhetoric and policies would stiffen Soviet resolve and delay rather than advance its demise; they believed that the more dialogue the better—surely it would soon dawn on the Soviet citizenry that they were being had. They had trouble believing in the USSR as a military threat, at least to France. In short, they thought that the emerging U.S. approach was probably wrong, possibly counter-productive, and embarrassingly pointless.

In the midst of all this, I was a naive bystander. Politics aside, I saw this odd but glorious priesthood of ideas as an attractive path to the country of the mind. But another Fulbright discovery got in the way, politics of another kind. In Dijon I discovered the rich, foliate and interwoven fabric of anti-American-ism, of the unintended U.S. role in the political thought of Europe. Whatever missionary genes had ended up in me (the French called it "puritanism," a marvelously flexible term which explained whatever in the Americans did not fit into their own experience) fairly bristled whenever the U.S. was attacked. Anti-Americanism triggered my politicization.

It has taken years to begin to see what I was up against, the complex fabric, the rich weave of sometimes contradictory thought patterns and myths which can only be attacked in the separate strands of the fabric, the intersecting threads of self-love and self-hatred which color it. Only recently have I come to understand how little it mattered. There were as many versions of anti-Americanism as there are hues in the rainbow of European political opinion, and ultimately it was not aimed at us so much as at themselves.

That year the left variety was the obvious kind: it was easy to blame it all on the PCF and its foreign sponsors. Many friends took a playful left position, because its vocabulary was more current, because fascism was the all-too-present and familiar alternative, because the prominence of Marx in the curriculum had provided a beguiling theoretical construct, and because Establishment France was rough on the Left.

Raised in 1930s America to a broad faith in something called the New Deal, then schooled in an art-for-art tradition, I had grown up seeing politics as a spectator sport and an impediment to serious concerns. The more curious then that my first political statement, two passionate basketball games against the CGT-dominated railroad workers' team, took place in Dijon. My second as well, at a showing of a Soviet film at the PCF center. The film had been banned in France, or at least not circulated. A grad-student friend and I watched this turkey, a film about the Soviet Luther Burbank, named Michurin as I recall; it had everything, including fat capitalist cigar-smokers in vests trying to lure this hero of the people to the U.S. with offers of fame and riches. Afterwards the organizers sought unanimous support of a two-pronged Resolution to the effect that the film should be allowed to circulate in France and that it was a truly magnificent work of art. For my gutsy colleague the second was one prong too many. She jumped to her feet to vote in the negative. I joined her, an act of considerable courage for me (it had been hammered into me that I was a "guest" and should avoid politics—fine by me). We were subjected to a chorus of hisses and catcalls of "turnip" (*navets*, stinkers). I had stood up to be counted, albeit on an esthetic question, and tasted the pride and pain that go with such acts.

A more subtle and ultimately effective left anti-Americanism than the clumsy PCF version emerged during a lecture by a British Council visitor, a towering art historian of the Baroque period. During his dazzling performance, he jabbed repeatedly at the U.S. for buying up European art, demonstrating, he hinted, the obvious fact of American immaturity and its impoverished culture. But there was more: the lecturer, blindingly well informed, was systematic. A pattern soon took shape around his killer metaphor: the American "looting" of art treasures was merely an economic variant of the Nazi effort; both sprang, he implied, from equivalent moral depravity. The speaker: Sir Anthony Blunt.

*   *   *

We read our lives, late or soon, in the book of our actions—Fulbright always seems to mean self-discovery and acceptance. I began to recognize, that year in Dijon, that hidden behind a high-energy ability to cover both sides of the street lay a set of preferences: I was better at learning languages than at thinking philosophically in them; I preferred engaging with people to analyzing them, exploring the countryside to probing an archive, playing basketball with the Dijon "Dukes" to browsing in second-hand bookstores, playing a dilapidated piano to writing papers, getting something done to getting something read, studying the general inter-connectedness of things to uncovering the bedrock beneath any one of them.

Two choices in the balance: the Generalist vs. the Specialist, and the life of Action vs that of Contemplation. Ultimately, my decision to leave the American university world and take up cross-cultural activism in the framework of our nation's diplomatic function was hammered out during my Fulbright year. Even in my second and third university incarnations, at Princeton and Virginia as at Columbia, the need for action outweighed the consolations of philosophy. I prefer to think it has been contemplated action and that my generalist stance respects the specific depths of the problems I gloss; but it has been generalism and action nonetheless. It is a Fulbright choice and it began to come clear in Dijon.

Jefferson had his own experience with the French; he warned us about the dangers of foreign study. For better or for worse, I have never recovered from Dijon. It set out an agenda sufficient to fill a restless lifetime. It showed me that myths and lies are not the same and that, while facts will unmask some lies, myths fall away less easily. It revealed the first of the mythic windmills at which I have been known to charge.

With time I learned that, if lies are easier to unmask than myths, successful liars surround us—American politics is full of them; good liars practice a high skill and the best of them get away with it. I learned too that humankind lives by myths; that many myths, perhaps most, are better left in place; that new myths—some grown from lies—flash into being every day, to be sorted out by time; and that the indispensable myths, like Rilke's unicorn, need loving care.

Dijon fueled an irrational commitment to a life of service. It polished to a high degree the language with which I can communicate, even today, with at least half the educated world outside the U.S. Its historical dimensions fed the need to see life as a process only to be understood over time. It revealed the irreducible and unavoidable realities beneath the games of politics; it warned me that avoiding politics is a form of participation—with or without us, politics happens. Dijon taught me war: I learned in France that, with apologies to Clausewitz, war gets to extend politics by other means only after the ultimate catastrophe of political failure. I began to understand there that elites do not necessarily imply elitism. I learned too that criticism can be an expression of responsibility, that love without it cannot deepen. Dijon rationalized and fed my love for another country, so different from mine; in doing so it internationalized me beyond repair.

Surely I shall never pay my full debt to the Senator and his dream, nor to the idea of the great American republic which nurtured both. Nor shall I ever be able to repay what France has so generously given. May these words then serve to honor the memory of an old man who once cleaned my single spark-plug.

PART II

THE FIFTIES:
GROWING AND FLOWERING

The groundswell of Fulbright agreements begun in the forties crested in the fifties. In Europe, Austria, Denmark, Finland and Sweden were in place by the Fall of 1952, as were Ceylon-Sri Lanka, India, Iraq, Korea, Pakistan, South Africa and Thailand in the developing world. In two defeated Axis powers, Japan first then Germany, massive "re-education" efforts by the Allied occupants accommodated Fulbright Agreements in August 1951 and July 1952 respectively. Other European countries—Iceland, Spain and the culturally-European Israel came in by late 1958. Mainland China closed, then Taiwan opened in 1957. Meanwhile Latin America burst onto the scene; agreements were signed between March 1955 and November 1957 with Argentina, Brazil, Chile, Colombia, Ecuador, Paraguay and Peru (Uruguay would follow in July 1960). The first alumni of the program had returned to their universities; they triggered proliferating overseas exchange programs, e.g., the classic junior-year-abroad programs. Seeds were sprouting all over the world.

As the number of participating countries grew, and as military surpluses declined, Fulbright funding became a more serious matter for Congress, which in the early days could pretend the Program cost nothing. Even with the Senator in the powerful position of Chairman of the Senate Foreign Relations Committee, individual country programs were already noticeably smaller, with the exception of Japan and Germany; in India, another priority nation, Public Law 480 turned wheat sales into exceptionally generous support for Fulbright.

The decade began with the Korean War. By now the Cold War was in full bay. Politico-military episodes in Iran and Guatemala were alleged to have U.S. backing, and by the end of the decade Cuba would set off on its long journey. In Southeast Asia there was turmoil—the French in Vietnam already had their hands overfull.

Dwight D. Eisenhower moved from the presidency of Columbia University to the White House. There was no evidence that partisan political concerns would affect the Program, seen by both sides—both Smith and Mundt of Smith-Mundt were Republicans—as an important national asset, and by some as an important weapon of the Cold War.

53

A new player came on the scene in 1953, the U.S. Information Agency (USIA). Before, cultural diplomacy and informational affairs had been handled out of the Department of State, in two separate offices occasionally united under one director. After 1953, a powerful new agency of government had as its mission to "tell America's story," dispersing the kind of "information" which our enemies, and some friends, called propaganda. The Cultural Attachés overseas, in the early days borrowed for the most part from the university world and thus enjoying a certain kind of academic independence, came more closely under USIA control; foreign service professionals specialized in cultural work gradually took over the cultural jobs. Senator Fulbright, fearing propaganda more than foreign policy, had managed to keep his program in the State Department, away from USIA; but in the field, the Cultural Attachés were hired, fired, transferred and "managed" by USIA. Meanwhile the Fulbright Commissions were attracting an unusual breed of internationalist American as their administrators, men like Alan Pifer, later head of Carnegie, in London, Richard Downar, later with ACLS, in Cairo and Rome, historian Carl Anton in Bonn, and anthropologists George and Elaine Harris in China, among others.

At the end of the fifties, tentative "Fulbright" arrangements were made with many of the countries in the Soviet orbit. Because of the impossible controled bureaucracies of these countries, these programs were instituted under complex reciprocal "cultural agreements," the only way of operation that could be devised. A special American screening body (IREX) was devised to handle these exchanges. A minor precedent had been established: the idea of a Fulbright country program without a formal binational commission. It would grow.

Of the eleven contributors to this section, two came to the U.S. in the second year of the program in 1950: Belgium's equivalent of the Librarian of Congress and one of France's most vital social scientists. The Class of 1951 is represented by a French business major, who wedded an American Fulbrighter to Paris two years later in what may be the first Fulbright-Fulbright marriage. In 1952 a young American critic went to Rome, never—in one sense—to return. A young woman from Florence arrived in Cambridge in 1954 for what turned into a ten-year stay. In 1956 a young couple in social work and folk art began a lifelong love-affair with India and South Asia; a Columbia apprentice sociologist was learning flawless Swedish and less sociology at Uppsala, and a young future-journalist from the less tender side of Chicago was exploring Vienna and the repercussions of Budapest 1956. By the end of the decade, another ASTP grad and Italianist by courtesy of the GI Bill was already an important observer of Italian politics when he returned to

Italy as a senior Fulbright. And a young historian from Bologna was off to Rochester, to trace patterns of American thought along lines laid out by Perry Miller and F.O. Matthiessen.

These authors, with the exception of the senior Norman Kogan, went as young, impressionable people from the best universities who set off to find their truth in another land. The U.S. was discovering Europe and the rest of the world, and the world was beginning to deal seriously with the U.S., or at least its universities. A complete history of the fifties would be peppered with the names of various greats who were eager to spend a year in the capitals of Europe, though none of these legends could be lured into contributing to this volume.

The period 1949-65 surely represents the apogee of the Fulbright Program and the cradle of its myths. Our eleven contributors do not tell it all, but the claw tells us much about the lion. There runs through these contributions from the fifties a memory of simpler times, of a government which saw no contradiction in making sizable investments in overseas education for the young yet scrupulously refrained from interfering with them. In Congress the Program was in the care of the Senator from Arkansas. There was ample funding. There was perhaps, as Professor Bonazzi suggests, a certain kind of comfort in the rhetoric of the Cold War, of which it could at least be said that, like World War II, it reduced overwhelmingly complex political questions to Manichean simplicity. For Fulbright, it was a good time.

Henri Mendras, Alain Touraine and Michel Crozier, key figures in modern French social science, began reshaping the discipline in the early fifties. Mendras and Crozier at the University of Chicago and Touraine at Harvard rediscovered the great French figure Emile Durkheim, who had been set aside by French thought but nurtured in the U.S., as well as a variety of American figures who had created urban sociology in the years when academic communications between France and the U.S. were scant. Back in France Mendras, as he relates, was "assigned" to work on the French peasantry. By the time his magisterial study was published in the late sixties, France's peasants had all but disappeared. Broadening his approach to the general question of social change, he brought out his remarkable Seconde Révolution française *(published in English as* Social Change in Modern France 1945-85: Towards a Cultural Anthropology of the Fifth Republic, *Cambridge, 1991). The only writer in this volume who was technically not a Fulbright grantee, his witty retelling of the Chicago days captures the heady excitement of the Old Continent's discovery of what had been going on in the U.S. during the 1930s and during the War.*

4

ON BEING FRENCH IN CHICAGO, 1950-51

Henri Mendras

In this volume, I confess to being an interloper. My year at the University of Chicago in 1950-51 was funded by the French government. But my colleague Michel Crozier was there that year as a Fulbright grantee and we did not draw fine distinctions. Alain Touraine, the third of those early apprentice sociologists who would draw on their American experience to reshape French sociology, would only go to Harvard via Fulbright a year later.

In 1950, for an aspiring sociologist, going to Chicago was like a Muslim going to Mecca. One hoped to return with the title of Hajji, anointed by the reigning high priests of sociology who dwelt there. The Chicago School, which in the twenties had literally invented urban ecology by analyzing

56

Chicago's ethnic minorities (Park, Burgess, McKenzie, *The City*, 1925), was very much alive. There were survivors around the campus—I had the rare privilege of lunching once with Ernest Burgess. But there were also the "young Turks," those who would soon reorient sociological research and give birth to what we now call ethno-methodology. People like Lloyd Warner were in full scholarly flower.

Eric de Dampierre and I took a Cunard Line ship from Le Havre to Quebec. It was populated by elderly Scottish ladies—nowadays do I dare call them old maids?—returning to their homes in Canada after visiting the land of their ancestors. From wharf-side in Quebec, a train took us to the suburban outskirts of Chicago where we experienced our first culture shock: there were no sky-scrapers out there, only modest houses made of wood.

There is little doubt in my mind that it is better to enter America by such a side-door than through the triumphal arch of New York. Old friends and classmates like Touraine and François Bourricaud went straight to Harvard and dove immediately into an "intellectual" milieu which fascinated them by its richness but struck them as singularly disconnected from American social problems. In 1977 Touraine commented on the Harvard he encountered:

> A highly refined intellectual world, but in my eyes lacking courage: it did not dare look society in the face but was content to cover it over with the false splendor of reassuring theories. The triumph of functionalism in those days cannot be understood without acknowledging that self-satisfaction, that uncritical approach to American society which flowed from the country's formidable power, its integrative strength, and its vigorous fight against social deviance, in those early days of the Cold War.

In the years of my youth, we young citizens of France had flung ourselves into sociology as a way of understanding the extraordinary disarray of our society and its deep and manifold problems. We did sociology with a keen sense that there were urgent problems to be solved and that the responsibility was ours. Today the younger generation finds it difficult to understand the state of our nation in those times. And of course Americans cannot possibly imagine the shock which America represented for those of us who came directly from post-War France.

In Paris, we were a handful of apprentice sociologists, ten or twenty at most. The masters under whom we studied, for all of whom sociology was no more than a marginal preoccupation, consisted of half a dozen men: a Professor of Canonic Law, a Professor of Labor History, a Professor of Philosophy and the like. A single survivor of Durkheim's school seemed to us very old and insignificant. The striking consequence: we were firmly convinced we were following in no one's footsteps, there was no inheritance, no tradition; we had to and were going to reinvent social science for the uses of our times.

In Chicago I found precisely what I was so passionately seeking: a chance to "take a look," to plunge my hands up to the elbows into the crankcase of a society. Oddly enough my first memory points the other way: Louis Wirth, saying to me: "Aha! Here is a Frenchman bringing us theory and ideas." A considerable surprise to me since I had come with the opposite intention, to learn the techniques of the sociologist's craft. Wirth was deep into the work which would lead to his monumental *On Cities and Social Life* (1964), in which he built on Max Weber and the Chicago School to arrive at a new understanding of the urban way of life. His question caught me by surprise because ideas and theories seemed to me to take fairly low priority. A few months of seminaring brought me to see what he meant, and that in retrospect was not the least of the lessons I learned in Chicago.

I was amazed at the importance of Durkheim in the Department's teaching. In Paris, the masters were blithely burying him. I had only read, as I recall, his *Rules of Sociological Method*; to me it had seemed an outmoded book, passing off the obvious as revolutionary discoveries. Only later, much later, when I began teaching in France, did I sit down to read Durkheim carefully; then it was clear to my new eyes not only why my French masters had not spoken of his work but why my American masters considered me a total Durkheimian. This philosopher of society, a potboiler in Paris, was seen in Chicago as the founder of all rigorous and empirical social science.

My second visit was to David Riesman, who gave me a thorough grilling. One of his questions surprised me: "Have you read Tocqueville?" It was totally unexpected because no one in France, at least at the Sorbonne, considered the great liberal aristocrat who gave us *Democracy in America* to be a sociologist. I was in fact able to answer his question affirmatively but only because I had studied political theory, what we called the history of political ideas, at Sciences Po'—a mile away from the Sorbonne but centuries away in time.

It took a while to see that my idea of the sociologist's profession was far too narrow. In American sociology there was an important concern for social thought. It cropped up everywhere, especially in the group around John U. Nef of the Committee on Social Thought and of course with men like Edward Shils.

Other discoveries will seem more familiar to any foreigner who has discovered the art of studying in the U.S. I reveled in the joys of direct access to faculty and to books in the marvelous libraries. The business of wandering through the stacks, leafing through a dozen or more volumes before finding the one that might be useful, was an extraordinary experience—and of course a completely novel one. After all I had come from a country which allowed you to order no more than one or two books at a time from the dogged guardians of the libraries, only to learn that neither book provided what was needed.

The teaching methods implicit in the idea of small seminars had its novelties as well, even after the seminars of the Ecole Pratique des Hautes Etudes, that towering graduate research establishment in Paris, just beginning to grow strong then; it was built around the "human sciences"—which for us meant the social sciences plus history. In Chicago, the professor said little and it was the students who related progress in the work they had undertaken. My sharpest memory was the seminar run by Everett C. Hughes, where people who have since become famous came to talk about subjects which seemed more like folklore than science. I remember one speaker who told us about the life of professional musicians. Lloyd Warner's seminar had another feature: it took place in a kind of living room or lounge where we all spread out on deep sofas and discussed the early returns from Yankee City, the first results of a monumental piece of social analysis based on a small American town—the first volumes were then in the press. It all seemed a bit frivolous, to a Parisian student who had acquired the habit of sitting reverently on the hard wooden benches of the Sorbonne.

Despite these exotic elements, or perhaps because of them, I learned my craft as I wanted to and as it was impossible to do, in those hard years, at the Paris end. I constructed questionnaires and samples, and I rang doorbells in the neighborhoods around the University to get the questionnaires filled out. In fact George Gallup had trained a few pollsters in Paris and they were doing the first public-opinion surveys in France, but we had no idea how to build a questionnaire, how to handle different kinds of interviews, or how to analyze the results. I recall my stupefaction on reading one of Rogers' early works in which he explained that it was crucial to let the interviewee follow out the thread of associational ideas and above all not to orient the interviewee in one direction or another. It was almost the opposite of what I had observed in Paris.

In Chicago I learned all the little tricks you need to overcome your own and the interviewee's natural anxieties when you ring each bell, the games you play so as to be accepted when the door opens. As I think back on it, it was incredibly easy, especially for a foreigner. I used to imagine what it would be like in Paris: the hefty French ladies in curlers who would open the door a crack, with the security chain firmly in place, then slam it in my face. Later, in my research in rural France, where access is always much easier than in urban petty bourgeois neighborhoods, I often thought with envy about those two or three streets in Chicago where I could get into one house out of five.

In one regard I was fortunate. I had left France madly in love and this saved me the endless time young people spend in the various rites of courtship and dating, as it was quaintly called in the U.S. It also gave me a regular chance to think about my American experiences, as I turned them into transatlantic letters. On the other hand, this little detail deprived me of the chance to learn English as well as I should have. To this day my spoken English suffers from a bad limp.

Driven by the need to learn my trade even better, I tried to get involved with a large-scale research program. To my considerable surprise, there was nothing in the Department of Sociology. This turned out to be a piece of great good luck: a young assistant professor of politics agreed to take me along with two other PhD candidates for a research project near the Arizona border deep in the heart of Utah. Edward Banfield was off to study rural sociology in Mormon country, with his wife and two children. With no ceremony whatsoever, he set me down in a town of about one hundred inhabitants and gave me a single order: "You're on your own!" As a method of apprentice-ship, it was in truth totally unexpected—yet it is in the end precisely what I have done ever since when I send my students out to study French villages. I learned then that, in the final analysis, methods of inquiry in true scholarly research matter much less than educating the sociologist's eye, by putting a set of precisely defined research problems into the student's head.

My months in Utah were tough, for one thing because the Mormons were serious folk who didn't kid around and who, I must confess these many years later, struck me as a bit simple-minded. At Sunday services, each of them stood up and recited without a trace of embarrassment the naive banalities which the Lord inspired in them. The experience took me straight back to my own village in the Aveyron where an elaborate and age-old ritual had the peasants performing chants in Latin, a language of which they understood not a single word, yet singing with total conviction and totally out of tune.

Of course, I had a car. More important, I had a horse! It was an unthinkable luxury for a young lad fresh from the miseries of post-War France, just beginning to struggle back to her feet after the travails of the Occupation. Imagine my glorious cowboy fantasies, as I rode out daily through that breathtaking landscape. On the Fourth of July there was my first rodeo.

My little town was dirt poor. There were no chairs in the household that took me in, and one of the children of the town's bishop ate his dinner standing up when my friend Jean-René Tréanton stopped by on his way from

Yale to Berkeley. One day, after rounding up a herd of colts on a hillside, I was surprised to see people bargaining with the butcher to rent space in his freezer. They had slaughtered a calf, which they were sharing among two or three families, and they needed a place to store it. Not a surprising matter today in Europe, but in 1951 it was another matter, even in the U.S.

I was looking at the underside of America, at the real life of those cowboys and Indians we French knew from the Westerns. I watched them live their daily lives in rough and difficult ways, with totally unexpected religious and moral imperatives. The little sociology of religion I had studied in France helped me understand the universe in which those Mormons were living, and my deep exposure to the experience of that sect which had grown into a powerful church has stood me in good stead throughout my career.

Fieldwork was a way of learning how material conditions and situations affect and limit the researcher; dealing with these limitations taught me as much as the interviews I was conducting in flawless Rogerian non-directive style. That same year Laurence Wylie was going through the process of choosing his famous village in the Vaucluse: his final decision hinged on housing for himself and his family.

After two weeks, stifled by life in my tiny town, I went back to research HQ and told Banfield I knew everything there was to know about the town, hence that there was no need for me to go back there. At great length, we discussed the observations I had made in my notebooks and the interviews I had transcribed. With infinite patience and kindness he showed me that I had made some small progress in learning about my town but that there was a lot more to be done. In short, he bucked up my morale and sent me back to work. I must say that the Banfield family, his wife Laura and the two children, did as much for my morale as his recommendations. I owe them a great deal, when it comes to my understanding of America.

We all took part in the life of their town, St. George, Utah. I recall a presentation I was invited to make at a Rotary luncheon, and an open house with a couple who had retired to a hilltop overlooking the town. Getting into close contact with total strangers who showed off their kitchen machinery with charming openness and innocence amazed me. I came from a sector of French society in which the doors of a home opened only to relatives, and indeed only to those who were acceptable. And even with such carefully-screened guests, we would never have dreamed of letting them go beyond the two public rooms, the salon and the dining room. Life was a daily surprise and constant learning.

That is how I learned my craft, and that double experience—the University and fieldwork—has shaped my life ever since. More, it was there that I found my vocation as a rural sociologist. Returning from Paris with my

Mormon monograph under my arm, I soon found interest in publishing it, diptych fashion, together with a study of my native village Rouergat. Everyone drew the same immediate conclusion from the book: Mendras is our rural sociologist. That is how research policy, such as it was, functioned in those days in Paris: Georges Friedmann parceled out the sub-fields of sociology in great dollops: workers to Touraine, bureaucrats to Crozier, *bidonvilles*—tent cities or Hoovervilles at the margins of the big cities—to Dofny, literature to Roland Barthes, films to Edgar Morin, schools to Viviane Isambert, women to Madeleine Guilbert (an accident which got her the Order of Lenin medal), cities to Tréanton, labor to Jean-Daniel Reynaud . . . and Mendras gets the peasants.

In truth, we were a small group. Moreover the different sectors of society were *terrae incognitae* into which our masters launched us as though we were exploring the darkest corners of Africa. They would set us up with some sort of job with the CNRS (France's National Research Center), or some kind of research money from government agencies. With this modest support, we embarked on the discovery of our special terrains, with no tools other than our bare hands.

Not everyone could spend a year in the U.S. But the influence of the American way of doing sociology spread quickly, so quickly indeed that it created its own violent counter-reformation. One section of our generation went to war against American "Quantiphrenia," under the inspiration of Georges Gurtvich. Obviously the quarrel was foolish and petty, but it helped us assimilate what we had learned abroad, then reshape it to fit French intellectual traditions and the peculiar characteristics of our social structure. In my own case, I tried to use statistics wisely, even deftly: what I learned with Banfield fed back easily into the geographic and ethnographic traditions I had learned from my teachers in France. Still, I think it took us all a while to get used to France again; as a result we all remained a bit marginal with regard to the Parisian intellectual world. This forced us to be original, and it contributed in turn to the unusual success we encountered relatively soon and with relative ease. This happened for the very reason that our discipline was new and that it met a clear need of our society at that special moment.

As for me, I began by studying the attitudes of farmers towards modernization, using the tools I had learned to handle—in essence, the questionnaire and an approach which drew out the uniqueness of each individual. That led me to see that peasant society, then still very much alive in France, could not be understood by the systematic interrogation of individuals but that we had instead to try to understand them in the role they played inside their own local social structures. In other words, their openness towards progress did not result from individual experience but was dictated by the structure of their village. It was the village itself which had to be studied first.

That led to my particular way of studying locales, developed with Marcel Jollivet over twenty assiduous years. It was viewed by most of my colleagues as old-fashioned, hence out of date. It was of course excusable for anyone studying the peasantry, but seriously retrograde in terms of real research. My friends missed the meaning of my work with Lloyd Warner on Yankee City and with Everett C. Hughes, who had taught me the meaning of the significant case. It is ironic that Hughes was totally unknown in France until the mid-seventies when he was discovered by sociologists from the critical tradition; under the banner of ethno-methodology, his way of going about things has now been glorified by an entire sector of French sociology. Thus in the seventies, the idea of putting problems back into their local context came into style for questions well outside the rural domain: cities, religion, business, and so forth. Passing into history, one feels older. Recently several younger colleagues have undertaken a study of the "rebuilding of French sociology (1945-60)." It is a bizarre experience, becoming a historical object.

Where do things stand today? The new generation of French sociologists is numerous beyond my ability to count; there are professors of sociology in all French universities—there are now 70 of them. And there are research centers in universities, in the government bureaucracy, and in private business. Forty years ago we were no more than a handful, today there are several thousand of us. It is hard to believe that the spread has taken place so rapidly. Surely none of this would have happened without the help and support of our transatlantic colleagues.

It is therefore all the sadder for me to report my concern that our American brothers and sisters may be lagging behind. Viewed from Paris, American sociology today looks a bit routine, lacking in imagination. One wonders why. Sociology's relationship to its surrounding society is naturally different in a country the size of the U.S., where the walls shielding the universities from political power are still strong. Many French sociologists today do not hesitate to pass themselves off as *intellectuels*, playing the specific role which French society has always assigned to intellect. From Voltaire to Gide and Sartre, writers in France have always been expected to be moral pontiffs, to consider themselves the conscience of their contemporaries and their era, licensed to pronounce on Good and Evil. Today France's writers have shunned the pontifical role, and it has fallen into the hands of the social and human scientists, principally the historians and the sociologists. Certain of them have become virtual media stars; others, less garrulous, seem not to be able to resist the occasional temptation to issue a pronouncement on some problem that falls roughly within their competence—the media is always delighted to find time for them. There is little doubt that our sociologists visit the Prime Minister in the Hôtel Matignon or the President in the Elysée Palace more often than their Harvard or Yale colleagues visit the White House. Does this make them better sociologists? Perhaps not, but it focuses their attention, sharply and persistently, on the overall shape of society and . . . it makes for interesting careers!

Meanwhile, in the American universities, our colleagues are specializing more and more. Already burdened by the American tendency to think of the U.S. as the center of the world, they are creating a sociology focused on their own society, which looks a bit parochial viewed from Europe; they specialize more and more narrowly on fewer subjects, and these almost by definition seem to be ever more particular and partial topics to which we must affix the adjective "American." Europeans, on the other hand, are forced into a comparative mode, in space and time: the diversity of social structures and historical traditions inside and around France makes this unavoidable. French sociologists depend less upon their discipline in narrow terms, for one reason because they can understand nothing if they are not keenly aware of history. A second factor may explain more: they profit from the fact that ethnologists and anthropologists are turning back towards the city and seeking new European fields to till, with their comparativist mindset and different theoretical tools. Two obvious elements of inspiration for this approach: the anthropology of Claude Lévi-Strauss and the work of the historians Marc Bloch, Georges Duby and Fernand Braudel.

Paris today is where social and human science is happening. It may be consoling, but I would think troubling as well, to report that it all started in Chicago.

Libraries, it is said, are the heart of universities. And surely the university, since the beginning, has been the heart of the Fulbright Program. In 1950 Herman Liebaers landed in Hoboken, New Jersey, a tough-minded francophone Fleming who had survived the War and now was dedicating his life to the service of the Book. Forty years later he tells a tale of the growth of European libraries, as stimulated by contact with American models, American-designed international networks and associations, the rapid developments in information science, and some exceptional human beings. His essay, deeply personal and generous to those who helped accomplish this transatlantic transfer of library methodology, should serve as a starting-point for historians interested in the infrastructure of intellectual relations between the two continents since the War. But it also reveals his lifelong dedication to the Fulbright process in Belgium, a latecomer to a country which nurtured contacts with the U.S. as far back as World War I and perhaps farther, to the voyage of the Mayflower, long the symbol of the Belgian Fulbright Commission.

5

THREE CENTURIES AFTER THE MAYFLOWER

Herman Liebaers

The year of this writing, I celebrated the fortieth anniversary of my return from my first visit to the U.S. in 1950-51. As a young librarian at the Royal Library of Belgium, Fulbright sent me to spend three months visiting a hundred libraries around the country. My affiliation with the Library of Congress (LC) led to a contract to evaluate the Belgian collections, as the first librarian from Belgium to visit after the war. I then stayed three months more as a Special Fellow of the Belgian-American Educational Foundation (BAEF). Later my second tour would cover art museums and graduate art departments.

How many times have I been back since 1950? I am tempted to say either slightly less or slightly more than a hundred. I tried to go systematically through my old diaries but got sidetracked into counting my visits to the

USSR—about fifty. Not long after, filling out a form for the Japan Foundation, I learned that I had visited Japan a dozen times. None of these numbers is accurate, but the proportions are about right: I go through life thinking I know a little about Japan and twice as much about the U.S. as about the Soviet Union.

After the pseudo-statistics, what conclusions? In Japan I hardly ever knew after a long discussion on which points there was agreement. If there is the slightest chance of understanding, it disappears as soon as figures are quoted. In Tokyo as well as in Washington, figures are essential. Not so in Moscow. The problem in the USSR pre-Perestroika was that, even with old friends, it was difficult to draw the dividing line between plain-talk and double-talk. How far is one following the party line? In the U.S. I no longer feel like an alien, though I am still a keener observer in New York than in Brussels. In the U.S. nothing is completely different or exactly the same as in Europe.

The intellectual and professional impact of my American experience, which the Fulbright grant triggered, fills many pages of my book *Mostly in the Line of Duty* (1980). I shall not repeat myself here, only revise and sharpen earlier thoughts.

From that first visit, two reflective memories. The first relates to the evaluation period at LC, a unique professional experience which I have recommended to all I have sent since to the U.S. or elsewhere. Instead of listening to careful descriptions of operations in one division after another, then conscientiously transcribing my notes at night, I worked in each relevant division. It proved a shortcut to understanding how a large and complex institution like LC operates. LC always remained my point of reference when later later I had to make important decisions.

My second memory relates to my second tour. I had run the Brussels Art Seminar, a summer school financed by BAEF and the Belgian Government. Fifteen American Fellows and fifteen Europeans attended two-month courses on Flemish art of the fifteenth century. From 1949 until 1955, six times, it turned into an exercise in social and national psychology. The American students were present from the very beginning, had prepared their subjects well, were excited at seeing original art works in their authentic environment. But the Europeans, more particularly the Italians, arrived two or three days late, had not prepared their subjects in advance, and were more interested in meeting American colleagues than in looking at art, which of course they could do at home. The miracle was the sudden interaction, the immediate and deep influence of one group on the other. As soon as the Italians arrived, everything became louder and livelier and the seminar got its real start.

Lifelong friendships resulted from these encounters in the presence of the Flemish primitives in Bruges, Ghent, Brussels or Paris. In Europe young American scholars needed only a small incentive to feel at ease—art and its history became the binding force and motivation.

Unique benefits flowed from this experience—the last time as exciting as the first. The Americans helped me understand the difference between Northern and Southern Europe, between the Cisalpine Flemings & Co. and the Transalpine Italians & Co. The differences between these two major European civilizations bear constantly and will continue to bear for many years on the difficult path towards federation set in motion by the Treaty of Rome thirty-four years ago and heading rapidly towards a new Europe.

I tend to aggregate the Fulbright Commission and the BAEF. Why? During World War I, the U.S. decided to set up Commissions for Relief (in Belgium the CRB) in all countries occupied by German forces. Belgium was then the only country to turn the surplus funds into educational exchange programs, an important forebear of Senator Fulbright's idea. Thus the Belgian-American Educational Foundation or BAEF in 1920. Later it was natural for BAEF to assist the Fulbright Commission in Brussels to launch a program similar to its own. When I left the U.S. in 1950, the Secretary of the BAEF was also Acting Director of the Fulbright Commission.

The BAEF was only part of the Belgo-American use of surplus money. The Fondation Universitaire and the Fonds National de la Recherche Scientifique, related initiatives, shaped higher education and research in the years following the first war. As Woodrow Wilson wrote, "Nothing that the American people have had the privilege of doing during the war has more deeply enlisted their interest and sympathy than the relief of the sufferings of the stricken population of Belgium."

Gradually the Fulbright Commission began to develop a life and a character of its own. Before my return in 1951, Gene Horsfall, an American Fulbright alumnus, had already taken over as executive director, followed shortly by George Wickes (1952-54). Wickes brought previous familiarity with Belgium since he had been Assistant Secretary of the BAEF in 1947-50 and special representative of the CRB to the Brussels Art Seminar in 1949. For many years he has been Professor of English literature, first at Duke, then at the Claremont Colleges, and finally at the University of Oregon (American mobility is still one of the main differences with Belgium—if in the U.S. one stays at the same university, something is wrong; if in Belgium one does *not* stay at the same university, something is wrong).

Wickes was succeeded by the late Dorothy Moore (1918-90), who was for many years—from 1954 to 1978—the incarnation in Belgium of the Fulbright idea of educational cooperation with the U.S. After her marriage to André Deflandre, Dorothy took Belgium as her second homeland. She helped establish a realm of deep understanding between Belgians and Americans directly and indirectly involved with Fulbright activities.

Year after year, I worked with the Commission. During orientation, I introduced American Fulbrighters to the use of our libraries, a task less simple than it sounds. I regularly got the discussion started by saying that Belgian library collections were richer than their catalogues suggested. It ended by my whispering that Belgian librarians are better than their libraries. No need to be a librarian in Belgium to know that the average quality of an American library is higher than that of Belgian counterparts. All Fulbright grantees, and before them BAEF fellows, have borne witness to this fact.

There were of course tiny clouds in my blue American skies. After the first visit, I was so full of the discovery of an overwhelming library world that I hardly took any notice of the damage being done to the American image by the campaign of Senator Joseph McCarthy against so-called un-American activities. Not so during my second extended visit in 1954 when, night after night, I witnessed the immoral TV shows staged by the famous Senator and his associates. I felt sorry for those he led in a direction which we in Europe had known since the thirties and from which the American forces finally freed us. In my mind the contrast between the two Senators, McCarthy and Fulbright, was a beacon of hope, and I retain my faith in healthy American self-criticism. Both Europe's qualities and deficiencies had crossed the Atlantic with the same speed and had developed in their own way on the fertile American soil.

A late sequel to the McCarthy damage touched me directly. I had been working closely with an American civil servant attached to UNESCO, Julian Behrstock, before, during and after the International Book Year of 1972. I did not then know that he had been one of eight American staff-members of UNESCO accused of un-American activities. Then-Secretary General, Luther Evans, who as Librarian of Congress had stood up to McCarthy, had to let seven of his American compatriots at UNESCO go, but he was able to save Julian.   When the Freedom of Information Act was passed, Julian was bewildered by what he found in his secret file; he wrote the disturbing story in his book *The Eighth Case*. The passing of such an Act in itself shows the brighter side of public life in the U.S. Julian is now working on *McCarthyism at the United Nations: A Memoir of Dissent*.

These sad paragraphs do not diminish my unlimited confidence in the democratic values of American life.   Though most librarians and other professionals I meet are proud of their country and its achievements, they never expected blind admiration from me. On the contrary, my interlocutors wanted me to feel like a distinguished representative of old European wisdom. Yet I shall never forget a conversation with a printer at the Lake Side Press in Chicago. As I looked at his new press, I was introduced as a visitor from Europe. "Oh," he said quietly, "Europe is hell and America is paradise." He came from one of the Baltic republics, he said, and went on: "My father was killed by the Germans and my mother by the Russians." Then he drove up the speed of his press and the noise ended our conversation. This happened not long after the war; a European in America had no reason to be proud of what his continent had done.

Most of the people I met were not like the pressman in Chicago. Nearly all my conversations were from librarian to librarian, scholar to scholar, man to man, saying what they and I wanted to say, not necessarily to hear, a simple and direct link with a shared community. Later I blamed myself for not having listened carefully enough to the silence of those who were exluded from the community of free men during the McCarthy hysteria.

The old continent's prejudices die hard. In 1957 the Fulbright Commission and the Embassy's Cultural Affairs Office organized a meeting of American-experienced European librarians, most of them Fulbright alumni. Librarians from twelve European countries gathered for a three-day seminar to exchange impressions and ideas. The keynote address by Harvard Librarian Douglas Bryant concerned "American Librarianship at Mid-Century." My summary was the European answer. Both papers were later published in the *Library Journal*. The main difference between the two continents: a mosaic of activities in Europe and a major difference between Northern and Southern Europe, reflected accurately in the different languages, as opposed to a systematic, quietly formulated approach in the U.S., the result of a consensus and not of monolithic thinking.

Over the years at the Royal Library, we established six national studies centers of which at least three have an American slant:

1) The National Center for the History of the Sciences (1958). As a Fulbright, I had met the Belgian scholar George Sarton at Harvard, the founder of a new scientific discipline. I invited him to return to his native land to help set up the Center and he did.

2) The National Center for Scientific and Technical Documentation (1964). We had sent the late August Cockx (1928-91) to the Linda Hall Library in Kansas City to learn how the sciences could be included in library operations. Under his direction the Center developed rapidly, with typical Belgian pragmatism—no theoretical considerations, no formalistic statements. Soon the first computer to appear in a European national library was operational.

3) The Center for American Studies (1965). Director Francine Lercangée spent a year at the Berkeley Law Library before joining us. She had accompanied her husband, a Fulbrighter at the Law School. Later an ACLS grant enabled the Center to acquire the basic research materials so sorely lacking in Belgian libraries. From the beginning, the Brussels Center linked to the Kennedy Institute in Berlin, larger and politically more important but oddly located from the viewpoint of what was then Europe. The present executive director of the Fulbright Commission in Brussels, Margaret Nicholson, came to Belgium on a Fulbright grant and served as Francine Lercangée's American assistant at the Center, where she wrote her *Catalogue of Pre-1900 Imprints Relating to America in the Royal Library* (1983). Over the years these two "American" ladies of the Royal Library developed a kind of Belgo-American support community.

Fulbright meant more than binational links, there were multinational activities. UNESCO, once an American dream, was another of my institutional homes. The poet and Librarian of Congress Archibald MacLeish, an early architect of the Fulbright Program, was one of the dreamers. He wrote of UNESCO: "Since wars begin in the minds of men, it is in the minds of men that the defenses of peace must be constructed." Senator Fulbright chaired the American delegation to the founding sessions of UNESCO and hopes were bright that this specialized UN agency would make a major contribution to world peace. Education, science and culture, the three mandates of UNESCO, require peace if they are to develop harmoniously, bringing together the great intellectuals of the world. Generous in its early contributions, the U.S. began to be defeated systematically under Secretary General M'Bow by an automatic majority of developing and communist country votes. Under the Reagan administration, which had shown little interest in the fields covered by UNESCO, withdrawal became inevitable. After M'Bow and under Federico Mayor, UNESCO began rebuilding its position in the world of education, science and culture, but the U.S. is still reluctant to rejoin.

A European today can also anticipate growth in these fields within the multilateral framework of the European Community. Yet, like UNESCO, EEC is a multilateral organization based on governments. People like me, deeply influenced by the U.S., do not trust governments when it comes to the life of the mind. There is little doubt that the responsible citizen contributes less to public life in Europe than in the U.S. and the difference is government interference, with the result that personal dedication is replaced by power.

Looking at the growth of the library world from Brussels, one is reminded that almost a century ago in 1895 the Institut International de Bibliographie was founded here. It would soon change the face of European librarianship, its ways of storing and retrieving knowledge and information, even to the point of rejecting traditional vocabularies, e.g. calling librarians "documentalists." A sterile war between the old-fashioned librarians and modern documentalists has done a lot of harm to library development in Europe. In the U.S. "general librarians" and "special librarians" have avoided damaging quarrels.

As President of the International Federation of Library Associations (IFLA), I promoted cooperation with the Fédération Internationale de Documentation (FID) and its leader Helmut Arntz. Theoretically FID stands closer to the U.S. because of similarities between the Dewey Decimal Classification and the Universal Decimal Classification; but practically my familiarity with American procedures made it easier to agree to cooperate. Both secretariats moved under the same roof in the Hague; and an international conference at the Rockefeller Foundation's Villa Serbelloni helped fuse the two professional organizations. This happened many years ago, and the two still live under the same roof. There I learned that good American expression, to "proceed with all due speed."

Then there was the Washington-based Council on Library Resources (CLR). In 1973 I became a staff-member and later the only non-American board member and Director. Here modern American librarianship was at work, challenged by problems which had not yet surfaced in Europe: networking, management, the economics of librarianship, research in library science, etc. Pressed by CLR President Jim Haas to set up a European equivalent, it took me six years and considerable goodwill in different parts of Europe to produce a weaker comparable institution, the European Foundation for Library Cooperation (EFLC)/Groupe de Lausanne. The French name, chosen because we received seed-money from the Canton de Vaud, reminds us that language is still a paradigm of all things European.

Europe does not yet understand foundations. EFLC had a slow but good start. Though its First European Conference on Automation and Networking (Brussels, May 1990) succeeded professionally as well as financially, it remains a weak brother to CLR. The explanation: the difference between the European and the American foundation worlds. Early aware of this difference, I admired the freedom of action of the American foundations. Now the European Cultural Foundation in Amsterdam is helping Europe move to a sounder situation. Two trends favor this change: first, the too-much-government attitude is growing everywhere as public opinion in Europe shifts towards American-type skepticism. Second, the European Foundation Center (EFC) in Brussels, modeled on the Foundation Center in New York, raises high hopes—it was set up on the very day the Berlin Wall was torn down, November 9, 1990.

Coming from a small European country, I find it redundant to say that American contacts broadened my intellectual horizons. I saw my American colleagues as more forward-looking than I. At a young age, at least from a European viewpoint, I became a national librarian—and inherited an obsolete institution called the Royal Library. All my transatlantic experience and connections were needed to put this library back on the world map. What were the American ingredients? One was professional mobility. Another: broader horizons and a sense of the future, stirring a bolder approach to the challenges of time.

Another: the centrality of libraries to civilization. A few hours before the failed coup of August 1991 in Moscow, Vyacheslav V. Ivanov, Director of the Library of Foreign Literature, and James R. Billington, Librarian of Congress, had an informal discussion on the intellectual responsibility of libraries. This high-level performance found both speakers switching from Russian into French or English. Those present caught phrases like: "the electric erosion of wisdom through unmanaged information," or "the librarian is the indispensable navigator in the flood of information," or "the libraries are the strongest bridge between democracy and culture." It took America to remind Europe of all this.

Something about individuals and institutions in the U.S. struck me as well during my first visit: the number of memorial names I found everywhere, on buildings, in parks, halls, museums, universities, hospitals and like institutions. One conclusion was that individuals were more important than institutions. Another was that responsible citizens who became public figures were important actors in shaping the social image of the U.S. A thread of individuals runs through my American experience.

The starting point would be the 1958 Vienna meeting of European national librarians, where the American observers were Quincy Mumford, Librarian of Congress, and Brad Rogers, Director of the National Library of Medicine. Rogers pioneered in developing the Index Medicus into Medline, which still keeps the U.S. ahead of Europe in computerized medical information. Mumford was my second LC chief, after Luther Evans. Evans, who soon left for UNESCO, came to Brussels in 1955 to open the IFLA conference. He blamed librarians, in his rough Texan way, for spending too much on buildings. A couple of years later I was involved in my own expensive building project! Quincy Mumford then attended my luxurious new building's opening ceremony in February 1969.

My next LC chief was Daniel Boorstin, whose Pulitzer Prize-winning *The Americans* had impressed me. It explained a major reason for America's rapid development, the willingness to accept new technologies in daily life. His example of the sewing machine, which Parisian tailors had destroyed out of fear, sticks with me. There were other LC greats, for example Deputies like Verner Clapp, Rudy Rogers, John Lorenz and Bill Welsh, all of whom brought new ideas to my attention. At home I was blamed for being too American! These LC figures worked in a great institution which I knew and admired. Though a young foreigner at the time, I shared the general disappointment that Clapp, the most brilliant and imaginative librarian I ever met, was not appointed Librarian. The episode revealed the typical American response to such a mistake: the Ford Foundation, through a generous grant, set up CLR and Clapp became its President. For over thirty years, CLR has influenced library and information sciences in the U.S. Some of this influence flowed out to the international level.

After LC, IFLA allowed me to meet outstanding librarians. The late Foster Mohrhardt, former Director of the National Library of Agriculture and former president of the ALA, helped me most when I presided over the IFLA and he was vice-president. A major problem: dealing with the difficult Soviet membership. Foster, who hid intellectual depth behind his kidding, introduced me as well to Japanese librarianship and to the Library Center of the Kanazawa Institute of Technology. In Japan we traveled with the president of the University of Hawaii, a Nisei who spoke eloquently about his mission of developing the Pacific American as opposed to the Atlantic American. Foster told him I thought I had already shed my European parochialism by visiting America's East Coast!

Bob Vosper is America's best ambassador at large for librarianship. With his gentle voice and elegant style, he too spoke at the dedication of the new Royal Library. Like Foster a former president of ALA and vice-president of IFLA, he and I have roamed about the world.

Rudy Rogers was Deputy at LC when we went to Manila in 1967 as UNESCO experts for the First Conference of Librarians from Southeast Asia. Shortly afterwards he became Librarian at Stanford, then Yale, where I was often his guest before, during and after his chairmanship of IFLA's Program Development Committee. He was wonderful at presenting broad and complex subjects in a clear, magisterial way. In 1984, at the New Information Technologies and Libraries Conference in Luxembourg, his keynote address on Western information theory hit a high point in the first systematically organized attempt to transfer information technology from America to Europe.

Jim Haas, CLR's third president, had been vice-president of Columbia University. Thanks to him, IFLA became the strongest international library organization. He urged librarians in Europe to unite to relieve CLR of part of its international obligations.   As Jim's respondent, I became expert in translating American values, professional and others, into European terms.

In 1975, a major transition: I went from Book to Crown. At the peak of my career, I left my profession. Unexpectedly I was invited by the King to become his main advisor. I told His Majesty that there was no Royal Palace in my intellectual horizon and accepted gracefully—one does not refuse the King's invitation. For eight years I served the Crown, as I had served the book for thirty years before.

Belgium, a constitutional monarchy like the UK, became independent in 1830 and it superimposed on its liberal constitututuion a rigid French institutional system centralized to the limit. The overcentralization in this northern nation's capital is rather more typical of southern Europe: the North is reformed and the South Roman Catholic. Christian churches in the North operate from bottom up and in the South from top down. The dividing line, for four hundred years, started in Brussels and moved east where it hit until recently the border between Western and Eastern Europe. At the western edge of the East-West line, Belgium has gradually realized that all political wisdom did not come from the South. The process of moving from a centralized state to a federal one, begun twenty years ago and to be completed in another decade, is unique in Europe. It took place smoothly and gently because it was handled democratically.

The division of duties among the King's advisors left me no political responsibilities, so I was responsible for the King's and the Queen's public life in and outside the country. The U.S. had become so important to my way of life that I soon found an opportunity to suggest a private visit to the U.S. The King had already made a state visit to the U.S. many years before, a technical impediment. Twice I accompanied the King and Queen to the U.S., first to Yale. Three reasons. First, the Master of Berkeley College, Robert Triffin, was a Belgian economist who had become an American and served as monetary advisor to President Kennedy. The King and Queen stayed at the College, an excellent way of getting a feel for American university life. Second, Yale was a living museum of contemporary architecture (Gordon Bunshaft's Beinecke Library for rare books had been repeated in Brussels as a bank, losing the refinement of the original). Third, the BAEF had historical links to Yale—for example, its current president Emile Boulpaep teaches at the Medical School.

When the King and the Queen were dinner guests of Yale President Kingman Brewster and watched him join in a performance of the Whiffen-poofs, Yale's legendary singing group, they saw a basic difference between professors in the U.S. and on the continent. That evening provided a better explanation than all those I had tried over the years. In 1977 the King gave a formal dinner in Brussels in honor of three Belgian Nobel Prize winners— Albert Claude, Christian de Duve, and Ilya Prigogine. I reminded him that all three had done research at American universities.

The second visit took place on the occasion of the Belgium Today program, sponsored by the National Endowment for the Humanities, BAEF and the Belgian Embassy, in celebration of the sesquicentennial of Belgian independence. It was then that the King got acquainted with the Smithsonian Institution. He was a guest of President Carter; luncheon at the White House remains in the memory because it occurred on the sad day of the failure of the hostage rescue operation in Iran.

As my term came to an end, the King appointed me Royal Commissioner for the restructuring of the national research institutions. We took the Smithsonian as a model, and in my report I mentioned its principle of unity in diversity, exactly what a country like Belgium needed. My report had been gathering dust for years, forgotten in a drawer with others, when in 1990 it was turned into law. In it I barely recognize the Smithsonian.

To return to my network of monumental people whom the Fulbright process brought into my life, I have saved Clark Stillman for last. He and Frances came to Belgium in 1932 as BAEF fellows. A brilliant linguist from Ann Arbor, he was soon fluent in French and Dutch and taught American literature at both state universities, Ghent and Liège, until the War ended their eight-year stay. Afterwards he returned as Public Affairs Officer at the Embassy. The Stillmans' keen literary interest meant they befriended all the best Dutch and French writers. Soon after their return to Belgium, all were invited to a fairly wild party, attended as well by a shy young librarian —though Clark remembers our first meeting at a Royal Library exhibit.

Clark's translations were as good as translations can be. Revised by Frances, herself the author of a general prosody of Belgian, French and Dutch-language poets, they brought to the Anglophone world the work of Emile Verhaeren, Maurice Maeterlinck (Belgium's only Nobel in literature), Guido Gezelle and Karel van de Woestijne. A frequent house-guest was the major Flemish novelist Marnix Gijsen. Clark left diplomacy to become the secretary then president of the BAEF. He greeted me, on arrival as a Fulbright in October 1950, at the pier in Hoboken, New Jersey. I was introduced to the New World by an unusual American. Together we ponder questions like this one. As my Europe and America grew closer, why have the two continents moved culturally apart today? Why have the U.S. and Europe drifted so far away from each other in a relatively short time? In my view, world events of the last two years shed light on the answer. The decolonization of the Soviet empire, a generation and a half after the French and British decolonizations, suggests that the much-earlier decolonization of North American may explain the relative swiftness with which it was to discover its own identity. My dialogue with Clark has no ending.

If the impact of the U.S. on my professional and intellectual life has any substance and value, I owe it to him almost as much as to Senator Fulbright: the Senator sent me off from Brussels and Clark met me in Hoboken. After these two men, a series of librarians over the years became close friends. With hindsight I am tempted to conclude that friendship follows profession, just as profession precedes politics, in Europe as in the U.S. It amounts to an attitude in life by which a foreigner has a hundred times more chance of becoming a friend than a foe.

Clark was never a librarian but through books he became my best friend. He is an extremely selective collector, opening his books with care and closing them just as cautiously. From Clark I learned that most Americans leave their office doors open. Now, forty years after my Fulbright year, three hundred odd years after the Mayflower and in the twilight of my life, I have no office. But the door will always remain open.

There have been many marriages of Fulbright to Fulbright, across national lines. While it is not certain that the Dietemann marriage in February 1953 was the first, it was certainly among the earliest, beating the editor's by more than a month. The following essay resulted from an extended correspondance, one which will give the reader some insight into the to-and-fro process which went into many of these essays. Gerard Dietemann went to Syracuse from France, later married Peg, and worked with American multinational businesses in the U.S. for his entire career. Peg (Margaret) Dietemann went to France to study literature and returned to various university jobs in teaching and administration, resulting in a second Fulbright grant years later, to advise on university development in Morocco.

6

MARRIAGE, FULBRIGHT STYLE

Gerard and Margaret Dietemann

In June 1991 we were asked by the principal editor of this volume, who had noticed in our membership renewal that Gerard was among the earliest if not the first foreign Fulbrighter to marry an American Fulbrighter, to try to tell our story. The facts were simple: Gerard went to Syracuse University in 1951-52 from the Ecole des Hautes Etudes Commerciales (HEC) in Paris. Margaret, or Peg, then studied Comparative Literature at the Sorbonne in Paris in 1952-54, after undergraduate studies in English at Syracuse. We were married in Strasbourg in February 1953. As the editor noted, "The marital (and, I blush to say, the sexual) history of the Fulbright Program remains to be written." We have opted for the former.

To stimulate discussion, the editor threw us a raft of questions, some probing, some relevant and some less so, some off the mark. The following transcribes parts of a lively written interview which resulted.

PD: You are calling for analyses of "deep structural changes" in people as a result of the Fulbright Program. To me it seems logical that our marriage, like most marriages, created enormous changes in our "habits of heart and mind," with apologies to Tocqueville.

GD: You throw us a curve in asking us to describe our experience so as to fit into the "fairly thick intellectual context of the rest of the contributions." Difficult enough. But you ask the unanswerable: "If the U.S. invested in you both and then took a hands-off approach to you, was it money wasted or well-spent (in *national* not personal terms)?" For the moment I will not address the "hands-off"question, as I can imagine no approach short of Gestapo tactics which could have made much difference in how we have behaved over the forty years since our scholarships.

PD: We thrashed your question up one side and down the other. Was the money spent on us as usefully spent as most government appropriations? What did it produce? It helped educate two individuals who worked steadily and conscientiously, paid their taxes, educated four children, refrained from most of the seven deadly sins, and stayed out of jail. It did not create two individuals who produced great art, literature, philosophy or science. But, public moneys have rarely produced any of the above, so it is probably not grossly immodest to say that the money was reasonably well-spent.

You also asked us several questions about what we learned because of the Fulbright Program that we would not otherwise have known. We shall try to answer those questions as honestly as possible, although even there we hit a few imponderables, not to mention honest answers likely to outrage a few readers. Nevertheless, we shall try.

A little background information is in order. At the end of my Fulbright studies in France we returned to the U.S. and my French husband spent his entire professional life working for American corporations. He thus became part of the so-called "brain-drain" which brought many bright, educated young people to the U.S. during the 1950s. If he had not come here, I would have remained in France. Fulbright-Fulbright marriages are of necessity ones in which one partner becomes an expatriate. Two facts influenced our decision. Housing was almost unfindable in Paris in 1953, and the French government was reluctant to accept American credentials for teaching positions. We both immodestly believe that our decision to come here was America's gain and France's loss—though our natural humility would never have permitted this assertion if you had not pushed us to the wall. At any rate, while finishing his MBA and CPA, Gerard took his first job working for a small corporation willing to hire a foreigner. Then, armed with appropriate American creden-tials, he served in a variety of financial positions for a variety of American multinational corporations. In spite of their confidence that anyone they needed to deal with overseas would speak English, they were often happy to have someone who was fluent in both French and German. They were not always so happy to have an employee who did not believe that everything which needed to be said in a report could be written on a single page. Nor were they pleased to hear from him about the difficulties they were likely to encounter because of cultural differences in the countries where they had manufacturing or licensing operations. And he was never a part of an "old boy network." Nor did he ever learn how to use the metaphors of contact sports to describe business activities.

What did the Syracuse MBA program teach you that HEC had not?

GD: It taught me cost accounting (now usually called management accounting). In France during the very early fifties, business education was highly theoretical and still very much tied to France's closed, protectionist economy. No practical applications of accounting were taught, in part because national conditions, lack of world competitive pressures on Franch industry, and the French franc's continuing devaluation created a business ambiance in which most cost-accounting applications seemed irrelevant. (My exposure to the principles and applications of management accounting remains one of the most important experiences of my professional life. At present, in retirement, I am at work on an article about managerial accounting designed for use in Eastern Europe, which, like France in 1950, is converting to a free economy and in need of a tool for examining its progress and increasing its efficiency.)

I also had my first look at the role of advertising and at the uses of the methods of Operations Research.

On the down side, I was subjected to several courses in psychology which I found painfully simplistic and naive. The texts were childish, the examples laughable, and I found it hard to believe that educated people could entertain the mechanistic concepts of human behavior which underlay the courses or subscribe to the foolish meliorism which they expounded.

What were the intellectual differences in the mindset or worldview and in the focus of the French and American schools?

GD: HEC and Syracuse University were, and are, so different that comparison is almost impossible. The former is a small, highly selective school, entered by competitive examination (*concours*).   Less than one applicant in ten is accepted, and most students do not even attempt the entry examination because of the difficulty of the national tests. It was at the time the only *grande école* of its type in France.

Syracuse was a large, somewhat regional private university which drew most of its students from nearby public and private high schools and tended to accept any which fell into the middle range of preparation. I do not know if it has since raised its entrance requirements.

While I did not perceive much difference in the intellectual depth or teaching expertise of the teachers in the two institutions, there was a great difference in the intellectual baggage and the mindset of the students. French students at HEC in 1950 were caught up in the intellectual ferment of the times. The influence of Jean-Paul Sartre and of many other equally competent although less fashionable philosophers on receptive young minds was enormous—whether or not we accepted their theses. I still cherish some of the books I brought with me to America. Among them is a best seller of the day, *Les Grands Appels de l'homme contemporain*. This transcript of a series of lectures which young French students attended in record numbers treats such subjects as scientific humanism, Nietzschean man, Marxist man, human liberty according to Sartre, the humanism of Gide, Valéry, Alain Duhamel, Christian man. The early fifties were heady times for French students.

Most of my fellow students at Syracuse were so wrapped up in the part-time jobs which financed their cars and Saturday night dates that they had little time or energy to examine their world. Through no fault of theirs, American students at that time had never been exposed to such an intellectual diet. Worse yet, as the days of frantic McCarthyism approached, all philosophical discourse was suspect, especially when it involved multisyllabic words. I quickly learned to avoid such discourse with my fellow students. Again, I do not know whether or not that has changed. I hope so. And I suspect that if I had been sent to a metropolitan university I would have found myself in a less parochial environment.

At any rate, I left an intellectually active, multilingual metropolitan environment in France to find myself in a monolingual provincial setting. Whether the Fulbright administration should consider my case in placing students I do not know.

As a brain-drainee, how did you handle the transfer from France to the U.S.?

GD: I never worked in France for a French company. Therefore I have no means of comparison.

How do you explain the permeability to foreign talent of the U.S. work force, as contrasted with the (to some, unbelievable) closed-shop approach of the French?

GD: It was certainly easier for me to find work in the U.S. than it would have been for my American wife to be hired as a teacher in France. But let's not exaggerate the difference. The U.S. was in the midst of a huge post-war expansion; France was just starting her recovery. That certainly made part of the difference. But I soon realized that in the U.S. a foreign accent labeled its speaker as "dumb." I deliberately chose accounting as the branch of business least language-based, accepted the poor pay and lack of prestige associated with junior accountancy, and completed an American MBA and CPA so that I could compete on reasonably level turf with people who did not sound "foreign."

My French credentials made as little impression on my American employers as Peg's American degree made on the French Ministry of Education. As to the French "closed-shop," I agree that in our case it did a disservice to French children. On the other hand, it does illustrate the importance the French attach to education that they screen their teachers so rigorously.

Has it not begun to dawn on France that such protectionism is harmful in the long run?

GD: That is a leading question. Even if it could be shown that American schools do a superior job of educating children, I would not address it.

How did your Fulbright experience feed into the business world and your success there?

GD: I have already mentioned the importance of managerial accounting which I learned during that Fulbright year. It created my career and my continuing professional preoccupation. As to my success in American business, I held upper-middle management positions with Corning Glass, Colgate-Palmolive and the Carrier corporation. I suspect that my language skills were the second most useful ones I had, and those I owe to my incredible foresight in choosing to be born in Alsace, and to the French educational system's steely insistence that I learn English. While my American colleagues could negotiate with and learn from the English-speaking top management of European firms, with my fluency in French and German I could talk to almost everyone. My employers knew it, and therefore to some extent my handicapping foreign accent became an asset. I was a useful negotiator.

What was comp-lit like at Syracuse as opposed to France in 1953?

PD: I can't say as I never studied Comparative Literature at Syracuse; I was an English major with a large number of electives in French and Chemistry.

What did you discover in a French University that was good? Bad?

PD: As I look back, I realize that the classroom aspects of my stay in France left very little mark on me, although conscientious student that I was I attended lectures and small group meetings more faithfully than the French students with whom I studied. You learn what you want to learn, and what I wanted to learn was to speak fluent and graceful French and to put together a home in Paris where Gerard would not be ashamed to bring his friends. Stated that boldly, it sounds awful now—the very thing the whole international women's movement has tried to put an end to. But I was very much a child of my time. I wanted to please, to charm, not to instruct. Intellectually I was both worse and better prepared than the French students in my classes. Worse, because the sort of close textual analysis which they all knew how to do was new to me. It was not until years later when I studied for a doctorate at Cornell that I learned the tricks of that trade. Better, because in Comparative Literature my command of French was better than my classmates' command of English. And because after years in American public schools which required very little homework, I had had time to read much more widely, albeit randomly, than they had. It is a little noted advantage of the watered-down curriculum of American public schools that it offers a real bookworm plenty of time to use the local public library. Many do as I did.

What was your reaction to the omnipresent and persistent and subtle (mainly cultural but also political) anti-Americanism of the French?

PD: I would like to answer the political part of the question first, not because it is the more important, but because it is more dramatic. During my Fulbright years in Paris, Julius and Ethel Rosenberg were convicted of treason and executed by electrocution. They left two sons who were small children at the time. Prior to the executions, French Communists papered the city with posters of President Eisenhower, his face alight with his hallmark grin. On closer examination you could see that each tooth was an electric chair. On the day of the electrocutions, each poster became a sort of shrine with bunches of flowers in milk bottles and vases lined up beneath the grinning face.

Gerard and I lived in a small apartment on the Ile Saint Louis across from an active Communist Party cell. Before the executions we joked about joining the party because the cell had a swimming pool and we had neither bath nor shower. (Better Red than . . . dirty?) Both of us were totally apolitical. The Rosenberg affair gave the French Left a political field day by providing them with "evidence" of the cruelty and vindictiveness of the capitalist system, and the bloody-mindedness of American society.

I wanted to believe that the poster and shrines were no more than another piece of the political game-playing I had learned to ignore or ridicule. Somehow I could not. For the first time I could find no defense for what my government was doing. I had no reasonable answer to the accusations leveled at my country and by extension at me. I learned that while most anti-Americanism was mean and self-serving, it had occasional justification. It was a humbling experience for a small town patriot.

Now, to the cultural part of your question. I confess that the almost universal assumption of my French colleagues that I was an air-head and a spoiled brat amused me. Looking back after forty years I find that they were more or less correct, but not because of my nationality. Twenty-two year-olds simply do not have the repertory of experience which gives much wisdom or true altruism. My apologies are hereby extended to younger readers who will not believe the truth of this assertion, for many years to come.

I was living a storybook romance which glorified all things French. Therefore, I explained away what would otherwise have upset me. But I was not so happy playing grown-up citizen of the world that I failed to notice that the famous *esprit critique* on which the French so prided themselves was often rationalized chauvinism. Americans had not suffered the Nazi occupation; they were, therefore, overgrown children. Americans had lots of material possessions; therefore, they were crass materialists. Americans had not been educated in French schools; therefore they were uneducated. Et cetera, ad nauseam.

I was also struck by the fact that the vast amount of unstructured time which I had in high school was what French students had at the university. My undergraduate years at Syracuse were highly structured. That has changed now, I believe, but when I was an undergraduate, attendance was taken in every class and there were frequent examinations, papers and projects. *In loco parentis* was still the order of the day; I signed in and out of my dormitory, returned evenings prior to set closing hours, and accepted rigid visiting regulations. In France, I found that except for comprehensive examinations given at the end of the academic year there were no requirements at all. And I noted that many of the French, newly released from the rigid confinement of the lycée, were like visiting fireman at a convention. I was not surprised that so many failed. The system seemed to me to be designed to encourage failure. I began to suspect that the universal assumption in France that so many failed because the requirements were so demanding and because the level of instruction so high was just another rationalization.

On the other hand, it was clear that French education gave students a belief in their own worth, in their own intelligence, in their own "rightness" which I did not have. They were all, as far as I could see, convinced of their own superiority. Somehow, American schools had never been able to instill this delightful feeling in me. I assumed that what I knew was a tiny portion of what was to be known, and that much of what I knew was probably wrong, and almost certain to be superseded by new concepts not yet known. I have since wondered if this feeling, which I have found to be shared by many Americans, was not a product of the frontier mentality compounded by a national inferiority complex. I know this sounds bizarre, that it flies in the face of what are generally perceived as typical American qualities of self-assurance, of "can-do," of Yankee bravado. Yet the fact remains that I discovered my own weakness, and strength, to be founded in this willingness to suspend judgment—a willingness lacking in the teachers in my classes and the students I talked with at bull sessions in France.

So what did I learn? To speak clear and correct French. To appreciate French culture and my own. More importantly, to love and admire people even when they confuse vanity with knowledge. To see more clearly the ways in which my compatriots and I also confuse vanity and knowledge. To question, even more deeply than I had done before, how I knew what I knew and how sure I could be that it was correct.

What was your return like: did people accept or reject your French (Europe)-taught insights?

PD: I returned to America with a three-month-old son born in Paris and a second boy already *in utero*. It was at least three years later that I had time to think of anything except keeping them alive and healthy. When I emerged from my coma, I found pretty much what I expected. Some people envied me my experience and assumed that I now possessed knowledge of great value—although they were not sure what it might be, or if it could be imparted to non-initiates. Others let me know indirectly that I had compromised the promising career for which I was destined. (It was never entirely clear to me whether it was the babies or Gerard or the French who had done the compromising.) Nobody rejected the academic insights I had gained; but, then, I never played the silly role of Eurosnob and intimated that because they had not had the advantages of a "European Education" they had had no education at all.

What was it like having another Fulbright thirty years later (1981) and how did the two experiences compare? What was your precise assignment in Rabat?

PD: I spent six weeks during the Spring of 1981 in Morocco. The Rector of Mohamed V in Rabat had requested an American college administrator capable of lecturing and teaching in French about the form and function of the American University. At the time that I applied for the short-term Fulbright granted to honor his request, I was Assistant Vice President for Academic Affairs at Iona College in New Rochelle, New York. I had previously served as Assistant Dean and Acting Dean at LeMoyne College in Syracuse, New York. In my application for the lectureship I explained that I did not hold a degree in Post-secondary Administration, and that what I knew about college administration had come from on-the-job training in two medium-sized private institutions. I volunteered to translate Iona's Faculty Handbook to use as a text, and to describe the day-to-day activities of an academic administrator as I had experienced them. And that is exactly what I did. I spoke first to a large gathering of deans and department chairmen, then traveled from school to school and college to college in Rabat, Casablanca, Fez and Marakesh to speak informally and answer questions.

Many of the questions concerned what Moroccans found as the incredible diversity of American schools, and the even more incredible ways by which they are funded. I sometimes sensed that my auditors found it difficult to believe such facts as that some private universities receive more federal funding than state universities, that each of the fifty states has a separate educational system with separate regulations, that program enrollment is based on student demand rather than national need. The most common question was not a question at all, but a request to help them to get computers. When I made it clear that I had no access to free computers, and that I was not sure that computing facilities for administrative record keeping should be their first priority, many visibly lost interest in my lectureship.

As to my advice to them, I was confident that it was correct and appropriate to Morocco because I did not advise anything specifically American. I did my best to stick to simple common sense. What did I advise? 1) That to the extent possible student scholarship money be predicated on some sort of service to the school. The notion of Work-Study funds has always seemed to me to be a good one, and in Morocco it would give students a stake in their own educations which they do not seem to have. 2) That card catalogs and reference works be moved out of locked and inaccessible back rooms and placed in easily accessible parts of the library. 3) That all examinations contain questions which cannot be answered from lecture notes alone, and that reading lists be distributed at the start of each course. (What I saw was massive rote memorization of class notes as the most common form of study.) 4) That the most able and experienced teachers be assigned some large introductory sections. (There, as in the U.S., most beginning students never see a top-rate teacher because the more capable professors are the less they teach. I suspect that this piece of advice was as little heeded in Morocco as it would be here.) 5) That chairmanship be rotated throughout the senior members of each department so that each person can share the headaches and learn first-hand what can and cannot be done. (This too is seldom done in the U.S., although it would cut back-biting and chronic discontent significantly.) 6) That all students be required to present for admission at least a minimum high school preparation in basic mathematics, Arabic, science and history. (Most students choose high school course sequences which lead into only one *Faculté* and, when their true interests mature during their university years, find themselves trapped. Not only are there few bridges between *Facultés*, but even these possibilities of program change are blocked by their lack of basic preparation.)

As to my basic "assignment" in Rabat, it was not until I had finished my stay there that I learned that the national ministries were considering institution of specifically "American" post-secondary structures. I would not have recommended that if I had known. American post-secondary education has many wonderful aspects, but it is wasteful. An emerging nation has better things to do with its time and money than use them to copy such a complex and expensive way of educating its young people.

That is the answer to the question about whether either of us was ever told by our U.S. sponsors what to do or say or how to behave. I agree whole-heartedly that America's hands-off approach was both the only sensible one and one which honors the integrity of the U.S.

What kinds of social and political attitudes traceable to the Fulbright experience have you tried to instill in your children?

PD: Our children are quite simply the result of the Fulbright Program. Without it, we would never have met and married. They have always been aware of that. In their early years Senator Fulbright ranked with Santa Claus and the Easter Bunny. That said, one of the great lessons of parenthood is the discovery that one's children are not one's clones or puppets. Each of our four children has reacted to the internationalism of his or her background in a different way.

Yet commonalities do exist. Each believes mastery of more than one language is the single most important tool for living in today's world. Our son Christopher may have been the only undergraduate engineering student in his class at Princeton to use his meager pool of electives to take courses in French and German. Margaret majored in Geography at the University of Michigan;

she is now married to an English geographer. Her four young daughters are imbued with the concept of "spaceship earth." Our son Stephen, born in Paris near the end of my Fulbright experience, is an artist and architect. He is entirely at home in the world of art which is by its very nature international. Our youngest child Chantal is a graduate student in mathematics. She has roamed Europe alone with a backpack and train pass. Her apartment is a sort of free hotel for hordes of European friends who come to visit and to enjoy the splendid international cuisine which she seems to produce effortlessly.

They all share the certainty that no cultural or national group has a monopoly on either vice or virtue. In fact, as far as we can determine, nobody appears "foreign" to them. We assume that this is what is meant by the term "citizen of the world," and that the creation of such citizens is one of the primary differences sought by the Fulbright program.

Leslie Fiedler's first Fulbright took him to Italy for two years in 1952 as a medievalist. Despite his lack of formal training in American literature, he was soon pressed into service to help satisfy the very early demand for university-level teaching in that subject. Beginning in Rome, he expanded his teaching to include the universities of Bologna and Ca' Foscari in Venice: his students from those early days were destined to hold the first chairs in American Literature in the Italian university system. By the time he returned to the U.S. two years later, he was well on the way towards becoming one of the leading U.S. critics of American literature, indeed something of an enfant terrible in the best sense of the term. His entire career since then has concentrated on the U.S., in recent years at the University of Buffalo. Much of the meaning of Leslie Fiedler's Fulbright stay in Italy has long been in print. With his permission and that of the University Press of America, we have added a post-script to his lyrical evocation of the meaning of the Italian venture in his life, selecting four passages from essays written and first published in the years 1952-54, then gathered in An End to Innocence: Essays on Culture and Politics *(Beacon: Boston, 1955).*

7

FULBRIGHT I: ITALY 1952

Leslie Fiedler

My first Fulbright Fellowship took me to Italy at what seems in retrospect to have been exactly the right time for me and my host country. It was, to be sure, a marriage made not in heaven but by faceless bureaucrats playing the role of fate, which is to say, like all the best things in my life, it was unplanned, unforeseen, just happened to happen. Yet in a sense the timing seemed right. When I arrived in 1952, I was exactly thirty-five, *nel mezzo del cammin* as I kept saying over and over to myself like a charm. Nonetheless, though my head was full of such tags from Dante (I had as a freshman in college begun to translate the *Commedia* with all the blithe *chutzpah* possible only at seventeen), I had never wanted, intended to go to Italy.

I had of course dreamed during my first twenty years, trapped in Newark, New Jersey, of escaping to Europe sometime, somehow. But it was to a mythological Paris I had dreamed of escaping, a Paris which, when I got there in reality, I found not really sympathetic. Not like Rome, at any rate, with which I fell desperately, almost idealistically in love at first sight. Indeed, for the first year I lived there (I was eventually to stay for two years—almost dying, begetting my fifth child, a true *Romana di Roma*, but that is a story for another day), I could do nothing but walk and listen and touch and smell. It was not only Rome's swarming daylight streets I felt obliged to explore but, especially perhaps, its silent dusky depths—excavated more in time than space, like the Mithraic temple beneath the Basilica of San Clemente or the bone-encrusted crypt of the church of the Capuchins.

I was eternally surprised as I penetrated the Baroque twists and turns of the city I wooed, as I caressed its crumbling travertine surfaces; yet at the same time I found it all disconcertingly familiar, myself oddly at home—not just with the improbable place in which I found myself, but with that very self. It was as if I were discovering for the first time my true face in the face I saw reflected in the basins of Rome's fountains: especially perhaps in the Tortoise Fountain which I came upon at a gateway to the old Ghetto, where there had lived for so long those who were flesh of my flesh and bone of my bone though they had spoken in an alien tongue—not Hebrew, nor Yiddish, much less my own American, but in the language of Dante, his *lingua materna*.

It was however in my own *lingua materna* that I talked when finally I ceased walking long enough to talk—as after all I was being paid to do: addressing students from the University of Rome at the Center for American Studies in the Palazzo Antici Mattei. It was, I believe, the first time a course in American Literature had been given in Italy under official university auspices—thanks in large part, I also believe, to the good offices of the then-Professor of English at that University. If I do not here mention his name, it is not out of lack of gratitude but because—despite my initial New World skepticism—I came to believe that he was indeed, as all those around me warned, a *jettatore*. After all, my watch stopped after our first face-to-face encounter and could never be fixed. [Editor's note: the Italian word "jettatore" means a "caster of spells." The celebrated author of *The Romantic Agony*, a postwar returnee to Rome after years of exile at the University of Manchester, was referred to by all Italians who knew him not by his name, but as *l'Innominabile*, "the Unnamable One," because he was alleged to possess mysterious and even diabolical powers which, even when he did not wish it, interfered with the functioning of mechanical objects.]

Despite all of which, his decision turned out to be in this case a fortunate one; my lectures were given at the very moment at which—as neither he nor I suspected—the study of our literature was about to become a part of the curriculum in the Italian system of higher education. Indeed, where there were in 1952 none, there are today in that system well over fifteen Chairs of American Literature; some of them are held by those who once listened to me talk about our authors living and dead, along with Agostino Lombardo and Bianca Maria Tedeschini-Lalli, both then in the employ of the Fulbright Commission, who guided and advised me so warmly and so well.

It was from them I first learned that, until the end of World War II and the arrival of American Fulbright grantees, those who had sought to introduce our writers to Italian readers had been extra-academics like Cesare Pavese and Elio Vittorini, for whom writing about our country and our culture had been a political gesture, a protest against the Fascist insularity which had sought by fiat to keep Italy's artists within the walls of a narrowly defined "Mediterranean Culture." Consequently, even as I was teaching students (eventually at the University of Bologna and at Ca' Foscari in Venice as well as Rome) and lecturing to more diverse audiences from Ascoli Piceno to Caltanisetta, I was also learning from Pavese and Vittorini.

Not only was I reading and coming to relish their fictions, but I was rereading, reassessing our own in their translations, through their eyes. I actually once met Vittorini and talked to him—or rather tried to, almost talked to him, since he confessed as we began to begin, "Sono sordo muto in Inglese," (I am a deaf-mute in English)—and I, shy about speaking Italian in any case, became doubly shy. Pavese was, alas, dead before I arrived in Italy; but observations from his published essays on writers from Dreiser to O. Henry kept ringing in my head—as did certain cadenced phrases from his extraordinary translation of *Moby Dick*. Moreover one of my dearest memories of Italy is of a night when, full of grappa and arm-in-arm with Gabriele Baldini, I made a tearful pilgrimage through the streets of Torino, pausing at places where Pavese had done that translation and where he had taken his own life.

Those now long-gone years were, moreover, as crucial to my own subsequent career as to the future development of American studies in Italy. In the years since, I have found it hard to convince anyone that I had never before taught a course in American Literature. Indeed, I had never even *taken* one, either as an undergraduate at New York University or as a PhD candidate at the University of Wisconsin. In fact, during my graduate years I had acquired a contempt for anyone who specialized in that area, concentrating instead in the more "scholarly" areas, requiring mastery of other languages, that is, the Middle Ages and Renaissance. But in Rome I found I was expected as an American to talk only about American literature—no questions asked and no protests possible.

At first I was dismayed, offended by what seemed to me to be the arrogance and condescension implicit in the assumption that, considering whence I came, I should and could do nothing else. My attitude changed, however, as I became aware of the real desire in my students not merely to know but to identify with all that was unique in our books and in the society which had produced them, of their half-conscious awareness of what I had myself not suspected until that moment, the convergence of their culture and ours—the coming Americanization of world culture, high and low.

I do not mean to suggest that I was entirely unprepared to deal with our literature and even to define its uniqueness, though to be sure the latter was easier to do at a distance, in the midst of another culture. I had after all not only read Hawthorne, Melville and Mark Twain deeply and passionately despite my resolve to keep my relationship to them strictly amateur. I had also written and published in 1948 an essay called "Come back to the Raft, Ag'in, Huck Honey." In this little piece, more a lyrical meditation really than critical analysis, I suggested that at the heart of our literature, classic and modern, there was a uniquely American myth of love, a dream of inter-ethnic male bonding outside of civilization, which is to say a world dominated by women.

Though this was initially greeted with scorn rather than assent, I was moved in my new-found home away from home to begin fleshing it out, incorporating into my own *lingua materna*, without at first quite realizing it, a *linguaggio* which made it available not just to the Italians to whom I lectured, but eventually—as it turned out—to the whole non-American reading world. For this reason, the four books which finally came out of this effort and which constitute the bulk of my critical work (*Love and Death in the American Novel*, *Waiting for the End*, *The Return of the Vanishing American*, *What Was Literature?*) have been translated in whole or in part not just into French, German, Italian and Spanish but into Chinese, Korean, Japanese and Thai.

Nowhere however have they been as fully and lovingly translated as they have in Italy. Needless to say, it is a special pleasure to read myself in what has been called the "language of Earthly Paradise," though I think of it rather as that of a second homeland—not paradisal, of course, but paradise enough for me. It is moreover an even greater pleasure to learn that my compatriots in the spirit continue to think of me as one of them. Succeeding generations of younger Italian scholars—most notably perhaps Guido Fink and Franco La Polla, who have grown up reading me and influenced by my work—have extended some of my insights in ways I could not have foreseen and which therefore have especially delighted me. One of them in fact was moved to remark not so very long ago that I "have never been loved much" in my own country, implying that in his I was, which is of course true.

In any case, whatever I have given to Italy, Italy has given me much more. And for this thanks are due to Senator Fulbright, who made our improbable mating possible—as I had the opportunity to say to him at long last in the course of a celebratory meeting at which he was given an honorary degree by the University of Siena in October 1989.

It was a fitting climax to my then-latest visit to a land which I have never left in spirit and to which I dream always of returning in the flesh.

On Discovering America (1952)

For shipboard reading enroute to Italy, I took along with me *The Marble Faun*. It was a toss-up between that and *Innocents Abroad*. There seemed to be no use in trying to kid myself—no American just goes to Italy; he makes willy-nilly a literary journey, and his only choice is between melodrama and comedy. Hawthorne or Mark Twain? You pays your money and you takes your choice—if it is a choice; for after all each writer confesses, according to his own conventions, the same meanings of the voyage: a Pilgrimage to the shrines of the idea of man (or more accurately, I suppose, to the visible forms of a culture in which that idea is entombed) and a Descent into Hell . . . . The Descent into Hell is for us the real pleasure of the venture, while the Pilgrimage threatens always to become a bore . . . .

I am never able to doubt that the portrait of America I find reflected here is a portrait of my own America. Unfair, I may find it, even occasionally dishonest, but it never seems to me the limning of something else. I have, indeed, felt here as I have never felt before that there is only *one* America. To be sure, an occasional home-grown speaker, visiting under the auspices of the U.S. Information Service, and reviving the familiar banalities about the infinite variety of our land and the misrepresentation of writers like Faulkner, will arouse in me a suspicion that the monolithic America the Italians dream is a hoax. But, at this distance and inside another view, I see clearly my own ironies and dissents as a necessary part of an overall pattern; and this does not upset me. I have come across occasional detached Americans who seem eager to attest, by loudly certifying their own dissociation from that picture. "Yes," they declare, "it is true of those others, but we, on the other hand . . . "; and they devote themselves to exposing unfortunate American influences in current Italian movies and novels. These are the last true Innocents Abroad, the last claimants to what seemed once our unquestioned birthright. For whoever admits his complicity in the existent America, down to the crassest Philistine, avows a sense of guilt . . . .

The point of view of the subtle Fascist-apologist Emilio Cecchi, author of an "almost legendary travel book" *America Amara* (Bitter America, 1938), is met head-on by Cesare Pavese, the brilliant novelist and translator of *Moby Dick*. His collected essays have just appeared posthumously, not only the studies of American literature, but a fascinating series developing a new theory of the relation of myth and literature. In his earliest pieces, written between 1930 and 1934, he boldly spurns the comforting official theory of the American artist as the enemy of his own culture, the foe of the upstart "puritan" system of values, which the Fascist press was always discovering in the act of "threatening our 2000-year-old culture" . . . . Pavese sets himself the task of showing how certain works which, read as satire or polemics, create an anti-America, read as poetry, reveal an essential, positive America, America's consciousness of itself; a complex and ironic affirmation, which must also be taken into account along with the strikes, the lynchings, the "materialism," and the "emancipated women" that are its occasions . . . . This search for an anti-rhetorical rhetoric and the honesty which prompted it were essential to America, and not the "babel of clamorous efficiency," "the cruel, neon-lighted optimism," which, after all, were precisely what the Fascists would have liked for Italy—"granted always a civilized veneer of Roman hypocrisy." In the mirror of America, the young Italian intellectuals recognized themselves, their deepest longings, which the official culture wanted to persuade them were spiritual vices. "America was not another country . . . but only the giant theater where with greater candor was played out the drama of us all" . . . .

As early as 1947, Pavese was able to head a new essay, "The days are gone in which we discovered America!"; and the intellectuals, who just after the war were generally Communists and are now more and more merely disillusioned, have been explaining to themselves and everyone else for nearly five years now that they really translated American literature in order to find out what they themselves were not; that American books are no longer as good as they were in the 1930's; that America, having lost Fascism as an ideal opponent, has lost its vitality; that the American GI has been Europeanized to the point of dissipating his "exotic and tragic straightforwardness" etc., etc. Meanwhile, the more conservative writers who once "defended the West" against America have now discovered us as allies in a new "defense of the West." The very youngest generation is discovering new utopias, a few in Moscow, even more in the vanished Social Republic of Mussolini—but without real conviction or enthusiasm. It is, alas, a time for common sense . . . .

(From "Italian Pilgrimage: The Discovery of America," first published in *Kenyon Review*.)

On Anti-Americanism (1954)

I have been haunted, ever since my return to the U.S. from Italy, by the image of a typical discussion at the end of which, as inevitably as in a recurring dream, I find myself heated, shouting a little, defending America with a passionate self-righteousness I should like to disown. But it is a true recollection and I cannot disavow it. What *was* I doing, playing the earnest advocate, the patriot at bay—I who, by temperament and on principle, have always been a critic and dissenter, and who had hoped in Europe to open a dialogue based on fairness and moderation? . . . Several friends had told me . . . of how they too had found themselves for the first time forced into the role of apologists and ambassadors extraordinary. But I [took what they said] as a figure of speech, a hyperbole to express their exasperation with European intellectuals.

I was prepared to meet with frankness the Europeans who trotted out the conventional criticisms of our culture; to grant that some of us, many of us, indeed, are smug, boorish, conformist, contemptuous of what we do not understand, virtually cultureless. I was resolved not even to assert in protest what I have long known—that the average European has as little living connection with his country's traditional culture as any Midwestern farmer; for I knew that in Europe at least no one is proud of such ignorance, that the European is likely to be in regard to culture a pretentious hypocrite rather than a surly Pharisee. And this difference I was ready to admit was a European advantage.

I suppose I had not quite realized that the European intellectual would not, as we ourselves do, hate our failings in us, but rather hate us for these failings, taking our faults for our essence. And surely I assumed that no European would forget that he had, indeed, learned our faults from us . . . .

I had even hoped that my own small heterodoxies might serve as evidence that not all Americans think alike out of ignorance or choice or abject surrender. But I soon realized that any unorthodox comment I might make would be taken solely as testimony against my country, though I might personally be credited with a courage to which I had no claim . . . . Such evidence of virtue on my part would be greeted with overt praise, and not a little concealed contempt . . . . It is only too easy to become the "Good American" of the anti-American Europeans; all one has to do is to talk before them precisely as one has always talked among friends at home, critically, skeptically, bitterly.

But the "Good" in "Good American" has exactly the tone and weight of the same adjective applied to the "Good Jew" of the anti-Semite. One is good in so far as he is different—i.e., not really a Jew or an American, not really the unmodifiable legendary figure of contempt. The anti-Americanism of many European intellectuals has reached a stage where it is almost immune to facts.

Some Americans (especially the young, whose own America is as mythic as that of their European friends) submit to the role imposed on them, flattered by the social success it brings and by the sense of belongingness that costs only a willingness to bear witness on demand. But most American intellectuals will not abide so ignoble an exploitation; and they fall into the counter-strategy of patriotic defense. It takes only a little while to bring to the surface of one's mind the virtues of his society, which he has, behind all criticism, always taken for granted: its hostility to hypocrisy, its eternal discontent.

He finds quickly that most Europeans are not only ignorant of these virtues but choose to remain so. A sufficiently platitudinous comment on our simplicity and animal vigor, or on the nastiness of McCarthy, is perfectly acceptable. But a favorable remark on the structure of our courts, or an unfavorable one on such legendary figures as Alger Hiss or the Rosenbergs, brings forth the supercilious smile . . . . It is at this point that the shouting properly begins.

One soon learns that it is unwise to be polite about the most hackneyed and apparently harmless observation. Grant without qualification that American soldiers are ignorant . . . and your interlocutor will follow up by observing in a conspiratorial tone, "It's easy for us (*us!*) to understand how such barbarians can be persuaded to use germ warfare against Korean peasants!" Or admit the abuses of the Congressional investigating committees, and you will be expected to grant that the U.S. has resigned from Western civilization. One must refuse the gambit, protest loudly from the start. . . .

"The Soviet Union has nothing in common with us," [he tells you], "but America, now! When we criticize America, we are criticizing ourselves. Culturally you represent the most advanced stage of what we are all fast becoming."

Now one knows that this is, in a sense, true. American serious literature among the intellectuals, American mass culture among the people, moves inexorably into Europe. The Americanization of cultural life on all levels is a complement to, perhaps a cause of, anti-Americanism.

"Why do you make your forecast so sadly?" you ask your European friends. "Under our system you will survive. You will be harrassed by movies, television, the comic books; but you will be permitted to fight back and you may win in the end. Under the Soviet system of mass culture, you would have to choose among conformism, silence, or death!"

"Would the death of an intellectual be so terrible an event?" Your interlocutor gives you his most cynical and pityingly European smile.

Here is the giveaway, the clue to why anti-Americanism has become a psychological necessity to many Europeans. The self-distrust of the intellectuals, their loss of faith in their function and in the value of their survival, blends in with the Marxist dogma that one's own bourgeoisie (if you are a bourgeois yourself!) is the worst enemy. Conditioned by this principled self-hatred, the European intellectual finds it hard to forgive America for being willing and able to let him live; and even harder to forgive himself for knowing that he could be, in our "McCarthy-ridden" land, if not happy at least unhappy in his customary way. Both these resentments he takes out on a mythicized image of all he hates, which he calls America . . . . In the end, anti-Americanism of this type permits the European to indulge simultaneously in self-hatred and self-righteousness. So handy a psychological device is not readily surrendered.

Yet unless it is surrendered, unless the European intellectual learns to see the menace as well as the promise of his future not in a legendary America but in his actual self, self-pity will answer self-righteousness on both sides of the Atlantic—and we will delay yet longer in taking up that dialogue between the European and American intellectual upon which the solution of our problems, cultural and political, in part depends. Perhaps for now a real basis for disagreement is all we can hope to find; but certainly it is better for us to shout at each other in the same world rather than to smile condescendingly from our several nightmares. (From "The 'Good American,'" first published in *Encounter*.)

On a Seder in Rome (1954)

On the long ride home [after a disastrous effort to celebrate the Passover at Rome's Synagogue], my wife and I argued bitterly, chiefly because I, for some reason I can no longer recall, refused to admit how miserable the whole evening had been. Finally I was yelling so loud that the two other passengers were watching me, delighted to be so entertained. Despite it all, the children had fallen asleep, and had to be awakened for the hike home; but they were surprisingly cheerful.

We had almost arrived, when someone hailed us. It was an American girl we knew and her Italian husband, both Jewish, both very young, and determinedly liberal.

"A big day," I said, thinking wearily of the holiday.

"The strike, you mean," he answered. "We really tied them up tight! This should be a lesson for De Gasperi and the Vatican, too." He seemed as enthusiastic about it as if he had arranged it all himself.

What was the use of arguing? "We're just coming from a Seder," I said to change the subject. "A Seder! I'll bet." He laughed, hoping it was a joke.

"No—no—I'm serious. And tomorrow we're having another—a *real* one at home, so the kids will really understand it."

At that his wife could no longer bear it. "How can you do it?" she cried in horror, turning from me to my wife in search of an ally. "Do you mean to say that in this day and age you tell your children"—she could hardly manage to say it—"you teach them that we're the *Chosen People?*" (From "Roman Holiday," first published in *Commentary*.)

On America and Europe (1952)

. . . Ever since Columbus it has been normal to discover America by mistake. Even in the days when it was still fashionable to talk about "expatriation," the American writer was discovering the Michigan woods in the Pyrenees, or coming upon St. Paul in Antibes. How much more so now, when the departing intellectual does not take flight under cover of a barrage of manifestoes, but is sent abroad on a Fulbright grant or is sustained by the GI Bill. The new American abroad finds a Europe racked by self-pity and nostalgia (except where sustained by the manufactured enthusiasms of Stalinism), and as alienated from its own traditions as Sauk City; he finds a Europe reading in its ruins *Moby Dick*, a Europe haunted by the idea of America.

The American writer soon learns that for the European intellectual, as for him, there are two Americas. The first is the America of ECA [the Marshall Plan] and NATO, a political lesser evil, hated with a kind of helpless fury by those who cannot afford to reject its aid. The second is the America invented by European Romanticism—the last humanistic religion of the West, a faith become strangely confused with a political fact. . . . Overwhelmed by a conviction of human impotence, [the European intellectual] regards with horrified admiration a people who, because they are too naïve to understand theory, achieve what he can demonstrate to be theoretically impossible.

Of all the peoples of this world, we [Americans] hunger most deeply for tragedy; and perhaps in America alone the emergence of a tragic literature is still possible . . . . Only where there is a real and advancing prosperity, a constant effort to push beyond all accidental, curable ills, all easy cynicism and premature despair toward the irreducible residuum of human weakness, sloth, self-love, and fear; only where the sense of the inevitability of man's failure does not cancel out the realization of the splendor of his vision, nor the splendor of his vision conceal the reality and beauty of his failure, can tragedy be touched. It is toward this tragic margin that the American artist is impelled by the neglect and love of his public. If he can resist the vulgar temptation to turn a quick profit by making yet one more best-selling parody of hope, and the snobbish temptation to burnish the chic versions of elegant despair, the American writer will find that he has, after all, a real function.

Indeed, he is needed in a naked and terrible way, perhaps unprecedented in the history of Western culture—not as an entertainer, or a sustainer of a "tradition," or a recruit to a distinguished guild, but as the recorder of the encounter of the dream of innocence and the fact of guilt, in the only part of the world where the reality of that conflict can still be recognized. If it is a use he is after and not a reward, there is no better place for the artist than America. (From "Looking Backward: America From Europe," first published in *Partisan Review*.)

In Professor Martellone's student years, the Italian undergraduate curriculum terminated with a doctorate. Italian Fulbrighters still go to the U.S. at a post-doctoral level then discover the need to fill in pre-doctoral gaps. At Harvard she was a research fellow intent on doing American history, as focused in the experience of Italian immigrants; she discovered that a year at Harvard was not enough. Her major and important research on the Italian-Americans of Boston's North End was concluded during a ten-year teaching career at Smith College. She is alone in this volume in writing of the Fulbright "contract," meaning her responsibility to give what she could to the U.S. and to Italy. She returned to the University of Florence in the full knowledge that she would virtually have to begin all over again, a new career in a university world which had no real place for a historian of the U.S. and which gave little or no value to what she had already accomplished. A Second Generation U.S. historian, like Tiziano Bonazzi, she sheds different light on the same phase of Italian intellectual history he describes. Both were pioneers in forcing their university system to open a niche for serious teaching and research in American history.

8

AMERICAN ENCOUNTERS, BRIEF AND OTHERWISE

Anna Maria Martellone

Growing up in Italy, for my generation, meant that our vision of the U.S. was partial, to say the least.

Unlike Italians from further south, I had only a few relatives who had become Americans, notably two uncles each of whom faithfully sent me ten dollars a month after my father's death. Twenty dollars a month was not a lot of money, but in the postwar poverty of Italy it was an unambiguous sign of American affluence and generosity, akin to what Italians had experienced in contact with American "liberators" at the end of World War II.

Intellectual sources were similarly restricted. Like most Italians at that time I knew more about America's literature than its history. American literature became known in the thirties through the work of critics and writers like Emilio Cecchi (*Scrittori inglesi e americani*, 1935) and Cesare Pavese, whose translation of *Moby Dick* appeared in 1932. Growing up in the forties and studying at the University of Florence in the early fifties, I knew the impact Cecchi, Pavese and Elio Vittorini's mythical anthology *Americana* had made on the reading public—I say mythical because its first printing, under the Fascists, quickly disappeared. Pavese's collected essays (1951) and the 1954 translation of F.O. Matthiessen's splendid *American Renaissance* were milestones. Intellectuals like Vittorini and Pavese influenced my generation and awakened an interest in American literature and an attraction for the U.S., nurtured of course by American films.

American history had no counterpart pioneers. USIS in Florence had a good library, which we used as often as not to study our own books in comfort—in those premises I read my own copies of Marx and Engels for the Modern European History exams. We browsed there on the fiction described by Pavese and Vittorini, not on history or sociology. Instruction in history at the University was strictly ethnocentric; chronologically speaking it gave more attention to the Middle Ages and the Renaissance than to what had happened since. As a student of modern history, my only exposure to U.S. history was a course on the origins of the War, exceptional in its focus on contemporary issues and therefore packed with students.

Architect friends launched my life-long curiosity about U.S. architecture. Beyond them, I found only one real source of information, however superficial: the many American "buyers" from stores like Neiman-Marcus and Gimbel's whom I met during part-time work in a big American buying office. They seemed genial, easy-going and optimistic, always ready to take an interest in the young people working around the office, especially those who helped them find what they wanted. Training as an assistant buyer was not without its temptations: it brought me into contact with a host of Americans, men and women of all ages. Most told me to "look them up" when I finished the University, promising to find me a "wonderful job" in the U.S.—if you were intelligent and hard-working, they said, you could really strike it lucky there.

No promise of wonderful jobs could take me away from my basic purpose—university teaching, or journalism, or publishing. Fulbright was a means of doing historical research in a good American university, while seeing the country that had nurtured so many masterpieces and projected itself in so many alluring movies. Yet my basic information was scanty. Even my thesis advisor Delio Cantimori declared himself unable to supply me with ideas or projects.   It was he who advised me to talk with Gaetano Salvemini. Salvemini had resumed his chair at the University after the years of anti-Fascist exile at Harvard. A seminar with that great and generous man the year before had opened the door. Two or three hours of discussion produced a simple idea: that the history of the countless Italians who had emigrated to the U.S., neglected by our elite-oriented historians, needed doing. The project: to study an Italian community in America during the years of the great mass migrations from Southern Europe. I designed a project focused on Boston's North End and the Fulbright Commission accepted the idea.

I departed in a state of ambivalence. I was elated by the prospect of leaving home, of being on my own for the first time, of seeing America. But there were disquieting things, some in the realm of feelings and impressions. In Pavese's novel *The Moon and the Bonfires*, the protagonist returns to his native Piedmont hills after working in the U.S. and says, "It is like the moon, there is nothing there at all." Could the U.S. turn out to be a step into an empty desert, an opening to a better future but a meaningless present, without family or friends, and without the comfort of my Tuscan cypresses or the Brunelleschi cupola?

There were more concrete fears. To get an American visa in 1954, one had to swear abstinence from three plagues: prostitution, infectious diseases, and Communism. The land of freedom made free entrance difficult, in an arbitrary and discriminatory way. The exclusion of anyone even faintly "tainted" with Communism brought to the fore the harsh reality young Europeans found hard to accept: a world divided into two blocs. We saw less clearly than we do today that the Cold War and Senator McCarthy, cutting into our image of America, had turned the yearnings for an American land of freedom during our Fascist years into a new kind of ambivalence.   A year before, the Rosenbergs had been electrocuted despite protests from every nation in the world including the Vatican. They at least may have been guilty of sharing nuclear information with the Soviets, but the case of Robert Oppenheimer on the other hand represented a clearer challenge to freedom of conscience and scientific integrity. Was I going to a land of luck or one of suspicion and fear? Divided of mind and perhaps a little frightened, I left the Rome airport on a steamy late afternoon of summer.

Above New York the sky was full of giant soft and foamy clouds, whiter than I had ever seen and certainly unlike anything in my familiar Italian skies. The woman next to me turned to her husband: "Herbert, we're home." I was not home, and I wept a little. But all my relatives were at the airport and reassurance returned. In a few days they drove me to Bard College.

It was called "orientation"—scores of foreign students "getting oriented" and a handful of highly disoriented and very lazy Americans making up credits in summer. God forbid we should model ourselves after their casual behavior, their incredible clothes and their bottomless apathy!

My suite-mates agreed. There was a beautiful Indian, a sturdy and well-mannered Chilean and a supercilious Englishwoman a bit older than the others. We talked but it was more listening for me: my English was inadequate. I could read and compose passable letters in the clichés of the commercial world. But conversation had been limited to my buyers and our tight little horizons—customs duties on ceramics, gloves and raffia articles. Classroom English was less a challenge than talking with my teachers at dinner.

"Orientation," for Americans, means throwing together dozens of people from all over the globe, in some lovely and secluded place, then talking at them. I took refuge in making friends with other foreigners. Europeans predominated and, sticking together, we constituted a foretaste of Europe 92. This led naturally to the familiar sport of griping about the U.S. We ranged from the food to the stifling political atmosphere. Their faces are gone but I remember them all: Brian the flashy Irishman, Alois the accomplished Austrian, Eberhard the intense German, Claude the witty French girl, Rob the elegant young Netherlander, and five or six less memorable Scandinavians from the distant marches of Europe. From this bizarre human stew two Americans somehow emerged: Donald and Mira, my first ordinary Americans—unlike my buyers they were real people with whom some part of me could identify.

Donald, a second-generation Italian-American, knew a little Italian. His father had emigrated from Campania to Massachusetts and started a small truck-gardening business, in sharp contrast to my Pugliese uncles, skilled artisans who worked for wages in New York. Donald was not like my cousins, who went to work as clerks immediately after high school and who valued money and material improvement. The cousins were jittery, always in a hurry, and delighted to consider themselves 100% Americans. Donald instead was calm, patient and lazy; he played the guitar, sang Spanish and Portuguese songs, and traveled when he could. Identifying with the lands south of the U.S., he loved Mexico. I visited his Massachusetts home in the country and met his nice, gentle parents. They worked hard in their extended gardens; they had achieved financial comfort but they worried about their son. Donald did not worry; he wanted to take a group of us to Mexico but his "analyst" (my first encounter with the concept) advised against it—when we finally went we would get no farther than Georgia. Concluding that he was crazy, I bought a few paperback on analytical theory—I was already persuaded that Americans spent too much time on their psyches; I still have those books, or rather their replacements.

Mira was another kind of American, a special breed known as a New Yorker. She belonged to the American Civil Liberties Union and Americans for Democratic Action, about which I knew nothing. A Stevenson Democrat in 1952, she was "liberal" but too far left for American comfort in those times. She talked too fast, with a peculiar accent I would only later identify. Later I would understand that Mira had leapt right out of the Thirties, from the New Deal to the Eisenhower years; she had landed in a state of total disaffection. She lived by a magazine she called "PR," the *Partisan Review*. One afternoon, between bursts of energetic labors over *The Federalist*, I tried PR but gave up when I found I needed the dictionary more often than for Mr. Madison and his friends.

Orientation dragged on. Field trips took us to West Point, to Hyde Park, and to IBM in Poughkeepsie. During the question-period at IBM, one of us asked a question he was convinced would be devastating: whether IBM used truth serum to screen prospective employees. The speaker, obviously convinced that all foreigners asked stupid and irrelevant questions, looked irritated.

A week with a family on the other hand was priceless, a contact with the outside world. The T's, a young couple of German-Dutch origin with two small children, lived in Rhinebeck, N.Y. My photos of them remain but the T's are gone from my world. Truly good people, they were patient with me; we shared an interest in Italian cooking. A big church party was my first encounter with one of the strains of American religiosity, the mixture of religion and socialization. At their home I leafed through the Bible for the first time in my life—like many Italian Catholics I took religion for granted and worried little about God's word. Mr. T owned an auto repair shop. The family lived in a little house with small windows and too many curtains; like my uncles' houses in Queens and Brooklyn, it was too cluttered to be handsome. What I had seen as an Italian-American trait turned out to be a lower-middle-class phenomenon.

By now I could converse about many things, including politics. While I avoided explaining the Byzantium of Italian politics, I wanted to learn about the American kind. The T's were Republican, conservative, optimistic, naïve and uninformed in some ways, but democratic and advanced in others. He was an elected town official, so one night we went to a town meeting about trees. One group wanted to cut some down, the others were incensed at the thought. There was talk of raising money for a new fire-engine. To me it was pure fascination: the participants were informed, interested, tolerant, amazingly free of ideological bias, down-to-earth, practical—in sum, civilized. Years later, reading Henry Baxter Adams on the democracy of nineteenthcentury New England towns, Rhinebeck came rushing back. In that short week, I did so many "American things": I shopped at the A&P, went on a blind date, began to feel a sense of relief, of release from my past, of starting anew in a world where life was easier, where everyone was friendly and optimistic.

It was exhilarating to be free from oppressive memories. This sense of generalized freedom had little to do with the American social and political scene at the moment and everything to do with my own growth in a new and freer ambiance. Feeling much more free and happy than I had been at home, I was beginning to understand that freedom to grow and pressures to conform were two sides of the single coin of American society.

Yet I could not conform in every area. Why had Americans allowed McCarthy to go so far before rejecting him? At Bard the Europeans had their own experience of political participation—why did American students not protest? Mira and Donald were different, Mira in her activist Democratic militancy and Donald in his general dissociation from the majority. We Europeans, more politically-minded, were naïve enough to want to register our own dissent from American conservatism. On a field trip, we decided to march into a neighboring town singing the Internationale. No one noticed—doubtless they had never heard the socialist hymn. All told it was a silly gesture and perhaps even a dangerous one. Above all, it was pointless: none of us had anything to do with Communism or our respective national CPs, even if we did come from countries with strong and honorable socialist traditions where CPs were not outlawed. Surely it occurred to no one to worry that some successor to Senator McCarthy might use the episode to prove the subversive effect of the Fulbright Program through the systematic import of Communist students!

After Bard, I looked forward to Cambridge and Harvard, yet with anxiety. To enter the hallowed gates of Harvard—actually the Radcliffe Graduate School—was bad enough, but finding lodging in Cambridge was a real source of worry. A more serious fear: I was shifting my historical focus from "modern" Europe, specifically Italy 1500-1700, to patterns of immigration among Boston's Italian-Americans. Deeper still, there was a new politico-historical commitment in my work, breaking away from the traditional Italian history of elites to the study of the underprivileged classes.

In reflection, I was embarrassingly naïve. Take for example American academic practices. I had no idea what a "Dean" was. So, at the suggestion of one of my buyers, I had written a peremptory "Dear Dean" letter to the

Dean of Radcliffe asking that she find me housing. Receiving no answer, I presented myself at the Dean's office. With Donald and the others, I was on my way south and, while they waited outside, I burst in with two heavy suitcases and demanded to know where I was to live so that I could drop off my luggage. My irritation at not receiving an answer to my letter must have showed. Only weeks later did I realize I was addressing Dean Cronkhite herself! May the reader permit me a moment of apology to that great figure of patience and aplomb, wherever her spirit now may dwell. Her response was astonishing, I now see: she picked up the telephone and calmly placed a call to Rockport. In a minute it was settled: on return I was to be well housed. I did not know then that I was also heading towards one of the great encounters of my life: Catharine Wilson Pierce.

Our meeting was memorable. Cambridge, after Georgia and the Blue Ridge, was touched by the pink, blue and green light of late afternoon as I walked towards 987 Memorial Drive. I felt an unexpected sense of longing, a hint that I would miss this place for the rest of my days. I rang the doorbell at the solid Neo-Gothic brick house. Catharine stood at the head of the stairs, a tall grey-haired and slender woman, her eyes shining and a bright, warm smile lighting her face. In a pleasant, elegant but subdued living room, three windows looked out on the Charles. There, over sherry and almonds, we had the first of a thousand long evening conversations. Memorial Drive, number 987, became my Cambridge home that year and my second home for many years thereafter.

The idea was for Catharine, an art historian and one of Radcliffe's first PhDs, to practice her Italian. But her Italian could not keep up with her searching curiosity. We soon lapsed into English and stayed there, discussing Florence, my studies past and present, courses and teachers at Harvard, my reactions to people and ideas, my friends, my projects, my dreams. Her curiosity, her capacity to listen, her eagerness to learn, to exchange thoughts—all this left her Italian language needs far behind.

Niece of the great historian Frederic Bancroft, she was born in 1890; she had traveled everywhere, had a special love for Italy and Japan, and maintained a supportive relationship with a number of foreign scholars, among them the great University of Chicago historian Akira Iriye, in Cambridge that year as a Fulbright from Japan. Her enormous curiosity for all human beings and cultures gave her a rational and tolerant appreciation of diversity. She was brought up, as a true "proper Bostonian," to be sober in manners, terse of speech, acute in listening.

Today's ethnic-conscious world would not understand her towering open-mindedness and receptivity, would brand her a WASP and dismiss her.

To me, she brought only credit to that vanishing breed. She died last year, after a century of life. I owe her the substance of whatever intellectual and emotional understanding of Cambridge and Boston I gathered that year and have kept since then. I owe to her the bonds of deep affection for America I have kept intact over the years. In her house I first recognized the golden vein of luck which had guided me since the foamy clouds of New York.

Harvard has its own magic. The Yard, one of the most harmonious places I had ever seen, and the Square, less rundown than today, seemed to me the hub of a newly-glimpsed universe. As a Visiting Research Fellow, I was not bound to take courses, but I audited many and read everything I could. Oscar Handlin, the reason for choosing Harvard, was on sabbatical that year so I taught myself immigration history in Widener Library. Paul Buck and Howard Mumford Jones graciously admitted me to their seminars, though neither believed I could keep up with the pace of the readings. There *was* a lot to read every week, and adherence to a syllabus and a schedule was a new experience—even if Cantimori's seminars in Florence were no joke. The pace here was quicker, the readings were foreign to me, and the material flowed well beyond the boundaries of the "history" I knew. There was a lot of sociology and psychology, and much talk about inner-directedness, peers, pressure-groups and the like. Only Marcus Lee Hansen's work provided genuine enjoyment. To experience American history as seen by a full-blooded liberal, I tried the younger Arthur Schlesinger. But the crowds were daunting and the speed of his lectures outstripped my capacities. Instead I read him on Jackson, a welcome diversion from the sociology I was getting everywhere else.

To assuage my nostalgia for European history, I turned to Myron Gilmore's "Ren and Ref." An adoptive Florentine himself, he was one of the great teachers, a friend of Cantimori's, a man of gentlemanly countenance and manners. His kindness extended to reading my Italian dissertation on a sixteenth-century Florentine political writer and offering to publish part of it in the *Journal of the History of Ideas*, provided I could turn it into English. I never did—I was interested in too many things.

Graduate students had stalls in Widener and the historians soon got to know each other. Measured by Widener time, we were hard-working—most of us were there all day. Student life in Florence was easier, until June exams, and there was time for diversions: film clubs, political debates and demonstrations, concerts and operas, and endless discussions. Faculty relations were impossibly difficult, but if you caught an ear and someone thought you worth while, relations could go well beyond narrow academic concerns—into politics, novels, movies, anything. The Harvard faculty, more accessible, tended to stick to the subject; it was hard to get to "talk" about mutual interests, as though we were citizens of the same city. I wondered what they *cared* about. But Catharine was there for that.

Thanksgiving found me a bit claustrophobic and sad. Soon after Christmas I took off by bus for Chicago, St. Louis, and New Orleans. Encounters and impressions flood back from those three weeks: I suffered loneliness and discomfort in a variety of YWCAs, bounced from elation to gloom and back. After muggy Louisiana, the snow of New England was a relief. I had paid my debt to the spirit of adventure, to the open road—in my fashion. After my version of the American Grand Tour, I came back to my second home.

At Widener my historian friends tended to be Europeanists. We talked of *Les Annales* and Marc Bloch and social history. I was beginning to *enjoy* reading English and increasingly I found the language congenial to my way of thinking, quicker than Italian and more to the point. It astonishes me today to recall how much I packed into those few Cambridge months: Faulkner, Andrew Marvell, Henry James, Byron, Lionel Trilling, Alfred Kazin, Norman Mailer, Allen Tate, René Wellek, Emile Durkheim, Erich Auerbach, Tawney, Max Weber, Thorstein Veblen, even William Buckley, Jr. Of the new novels, I have kept only a few—mainly May Sarton's *Faithful Are the Wounds*, evoking F.O. Matthiessen, whose suicide still haunted Cambridge. By now I had acquired a lifelong tendency to think in English. And I had established friendships with two or three people who remained my intellectual and emotional referents for a long time.

The winter seemed endless. What next? My restlessness reflected frustration at not getting to American "realities"—segregation, gangsters, political corruption, prejudice, and racism. Living a charmed life in the ultimate academic grove, I feared life was beating somewhere else. A visit to Greenwich Village in New York, with its painters and writers, left me wondering whether I would not have learned more about America uptown at Columbia. Back in Cambridge, I tried going "across the river" to Boston and the Public Library, in the belief that it would give me a better feel for the "real" city. I mapped different ethnicities, class differences, architectural styles, walking Boston's several districts: the financial section, the Italian North End, Boylston Street, Downtown Beacon Hill, Back Bay, the West End. I tried to read Boston like a beloved old manuscript. Was it that the closed garden of Cambridge was just another secluded "academical village," or was the somnolence I saw the climate of the fifties? In New York, many different forms of dissent took shape, but in Boston?

Getting deeper into the study of immigrants, acculturation, assimilation and alienation, I still found it hard to understand the underlying tensions as my

American friends saw them. In Italy I had learned about class and political alignments, but I had no experience with the tensions of religion and race. Two or three of my closer friends, indeed the ones I found most intellectually stimulating, more widely read, livelier, easier to talk to, were Jewish. Another was an Italian-American and Catholic and the other a Mexican-American (also a Catholic I suppose, though I smelled an agnostic). The rest were WASPs of mixed northern European origin from various Protestant denominations.

Without my Jewish friends, I would have paid no attention to these distinctions, but each of them carried a chip on the shoulder. The brightest of them labored under a burden, or privilege—her family had changed its name two generations back. For her, it was difficult for Jews to get into good schools because of quotas, in the schools they were rejected by the good fraternities and clubs, and so on. The universe was divided into Jews and Gentiles, for her; she could never marry a non-Jew. My other Jewish friends, less vocal, considered Jewishness a source of pride yet a handicap.   The Italian-American knew about quotas too; he wondered how he had gotten a Harvard scholarship. Italians were southern Europeans and Catholics, hence inferior in American eyes. The Mexican, an exceptional historian and now famous, also felt discrimination—even if I could feel nothing but jealousy of his talent—and disliked looking "Mexican."

In my country one assumed everyone was Catholic, but no one cared. Mussolini himself had never persuaded Italians that there were good races and bad. What then was bothering my American colleagues? I was taken aback when my hyper-sensitive Jewish friend referred to our Mexican colleague as a "greaser." Had the assimilation I read about in Widener actually taken place? We had not yet learned to talk about "ethnicity," we still studied "immigrants"; America after all was the land of consensus, the famous "melting pot." I have lived and worked with these questions for nearly forty years.

By April my quandary was clearer: what next? Perhaps an extension— but I was turned down. A "wonderful job" at the buying office? A Harvard PhD program, with light teaching?   But an American PhD, even from Harvard, meant nothing in the Italian university world. I wanted and needed more time in the U.S., but I knew my life was in Italy.

Once again my golden luck came through: an offer to teach Italian at Smith College, generated by Salvemini. The rest is history: ten years at Smith earned me tenure, an Associate Professorship, the bi-annual direction of Smith's year-abroad program in Italy, and a Green Card.

Ten years of Smith and Green Card notwithstanding, I was still a Fulbright Visitor in spirit. I had a commitment to acquire skills in America, to give Americans what gifts of intelligence and talent I could, then to return to Italy enriched by my experience and ready to share it with my compatriots. I stayed longer, to finish what I had set out to do and perhaps, just a little bit, to prove to myself I could make it in the U.S.

In my years there, I lived in the certainty that America, for me at least, was the Land of Good Encounters. Given time I knew I would have the opportunity to make the encounter, then to try my American luck against Italian odds. It happened: a final encounter took me back to my beginnings. On "Mass" Avenue behind Widener, the tide turned. I ran into an Italian visitor, a then-young Professor of History who knew my work and who told me it was time to stop learning, time I went back home, perhaps to teach America to young Italians. Shortly afterwards I did.

I was glad to go back to Italy, though starting a professional life anew was not easy. But I was pleased because in returning I was fulfilling my commitment as a Fulbright visitor. Besides, if I may be allowed to say so, the whole story made beautiful sense. It was like having drawn a perfect circle, starting from that distant point, a Fulbright grant to a postwar Italian. Many years later, I am still aware of that unique chance to grow, to mature as a person while yet keeping faith with my beginnings and my aspirations. I always knew, even in the midst of doubts and uncertainties, that I must not waste that priceless opportunity. I have never ceased being grateful for it.

Arthur Robins is Emeritus Professor of Psychiatry at the University of Missouri in Columbia. In 1956-57 he and his wife Betty were Fulbrighters in India. As others have noted, it is a bewitching land. The Robins family was beguiled and transformed. In subsequent years, they would become South Asian experts of stature, with two more Fulbright grants to India and Malaysia, two other research grants to India, and two UN consultancies, including major assignments in then-East Pakistan and Iran. This essay stresses the contrast between the UN and the Fulbright experiences to shed light on an elusive question: why is a Fulbright experience different from just any overseas experience? Beginning with the effects of the long-term and deep-immersion process which in their times were the hallmark of the Fulbright Program, they relate the effects on their family and on their surrounding community in a midwestern American university town. The Robinses exemplify the repeat-Fulbrights, a class often criticized for parasitism, bilking the taxpayer and other vices. While reminding us of the painful financial aspects of accepting a Fulbright award, they quietly demonstrate in this essay why certain people are called back to service in the Program: for the simple reason that they are good at what they do.

9

ON STEPPING INTO RIVERS: FULBRIGHT AND UN EXPERIENCES

Arthur J. and Betty D. Robins

No one, observed Heraclitus, steps into the same river twice; the river and the person are always changing. In this essay, we explore differences in the rivers and environments into which we stepped, features of the programs, and changes in us, during three Fulbright experiences and two UN consultancies. The contrast between these two kinds of overseas experience is instructive.

The Fulbrights: the University of Delhi School of Social Work, India (1956-57), the Shri Nataraj Damodar Thackersey University, Tata Institute of Social Sciences, University of Bombay (1981-82), and the National Institute of Public Administration, Malaysia (1988-89). The UN consultancies: Advisor to Government of East Pakistan, Dacca (1961-62) and Advisor to the Government of Iran, Teheran (1968-69). There were also a three-month National Science Foundation grant in 1979 and a 60-day University Grants Commission Fellowship in 1989, both for research in India.

At the high level of mission statements, one expects lofty and glittering generalities. Public Law 87-256, which authorizes the Fulbright Program, defines its purpose: "to enable the government of the U.S. to increase mutual understanding between the people of the U.S. and the people of other countries." "Mutual understanding," never defined, refers to "a state of cooperative or mutually tolerant relations between people," according to my dictionary. Mutual understanding, an instrumental goal, suggests higher goals. Senator Fulbright, on the program's 40th anniversary (1988), described these as ". . . joint ventures for mutually constructive and beneficial purposes, such as trade, medical research, and development of cheaper energy sources. To formulate and negotiate agreements of this kind requires well-educated people leading or advising our government. To this purpose the Fulbright Program is dedicated" (Fulbright 1988).

The Senator obviously contemplated some contribution to the nation from the Fulbright experience. He hoped that 40 years of aiming at "mutual understanding" might contribute to action on significant problems of mutual concern. Yet the Fulbright Program has little or no control over whether this understanding it generates serves our government or the nation. In our case, the senior author's first Fulbright appointment led to a UN assignment, in which capacity he served as an international, not a national, civil servant. UN offices track Fulbright appointments better than our government does: I am unaware of any U.S. government mechanism to involve former Fulbrighters in the planning or implementation of joint international ventures. Without the help of our government, Senator Fulbright's vision remains a pious hope.

In contrast with the Fulbright aim of mutual understanding, the UN aims at technology transfer and problem-solving consultation. The consultant provides technical help to the client in order to increase the latter's effectiveness or efficiency. The UN consultant helps consultees generalize learning to future problem situations. Mutual understanding *may* develop, as the consultant works with his consultee, assuming that the consultant can cope successfully with the special demands of international consultation; but it is not the goal, it is a by-product. Those demands derive from the fact that international consultation to newly developing countries, in contrast with traditional consultation, involves clients who may not have solicited consultation, who may not desire it, who may not have defined the problem for consultation, who may not have the basic competence to use consultation, and who, having incurred no cost for the service, may have little stake in using it.

In contrast, the Fulbrighter typically is chosen binationally and places his substantive competence as a scholar at the service of his students and colleagues. His mission is not to help his colleagues become more proficient in their roles nor to help solve problems, though that may happen as well—technology transfer of a sort does occur among colleagues. The expected outcome of the Fulbright experience is mutual understanding between the Fulbrighter and his students and colleagues in the host country; hopefully it is a positive understanding. In a climate of mutual respect, one can develop an appreciation of new social institutions. One may learn that some things that seem to be "wrong" cannot be fixed, at least by the mere import of American culture. And the Fulbrighter may have to disabuse colleagues of any tendencies, particularly those who have studied in America, to apply slavishly their American experience.

The premium that a UN consultation places on achieving specific goals puts an odd kind of pressure on the consultant that is not felt in a Fulbright academic assignment. The importance of getting the job done may tempt consultants to assume *mutatis mutandis* the infamous White Man's Burden. "Driven by the need to produce results, to achieve concrete objectives, the consultant may take over administrative functions, thereby fostering dependency and stifling the initiative of his client . . . . The consultant's assumption of an operational role [is] a usurpation of indigenous responsibility, no matter how willing the abdicating client has been to transfer his burden to the consultant." (Robins 1964)

In sum, our experience of UN consultation underlines the desirability of preserving the academic nature of the Fulbright program. True, the two can intertwine: my most recent Fulbright (Malaysia 1988-89) had consultative characteristics. Although it was one of our most satisfying foreign experiences, in hindsight it is also clear that initial planning might have clarified the difference between the Fulbright and consultant roles. A formidable contract-like copy of "Terms of Reference" arrived shortly before our departure for Malaysia. It referred to impossible timetables for specific products, e.g. a few weeks to produce a reliable and valid instrument to assess the effectiveness of training in "Islamic values." I assumed at the time, correctly as it turned out, that the rigid phrasing was more rhetoric than reality—had I thought otherwise, I would have declined the appointment.

In the Malaysia case, my willingness to satisfy the multiple teaching assignments that were thrust upon me after my arrival may have compensated for the lack of closure on other items (I am still working on some of these). The announcement had mentioned working only with the National Institute's Bureau for Institutional Research.   But when the heads of various centers which compose the Institute reviewed my background in social work, management, psychology and psychiatry, almost all of them requested my services.   I was flattered and gratified by their eagerness to use me for a variety of tasks and to learn everything that I could teach, so I did my best. Their attitude contrasted sharply with my American experience, where students often seem to be the only consumers who are happy to be short-changed.

There is a financial difference as well: UN salaries are considerably higher than Fulbright awards, and the perks are more extravagant. The UN, even on the verge of bankruptcy, requires first-class travel. On the Fulbright side, there is a parsimonious quality: I was on leave without pay during our first visit to India (1956-57), having served only three years at my university when the award was received.   Since the grant did not include dependent travel, we sought a bank loan. Unable to meet me during the day, time being critical, the banker suggested I come to his home after hours to discuss the loan.   After judging our major asset, our home, to be unsuitable collateral ("People still remember foreclosures during the great depression, so we steer clear of second mortgages"), he elicited information about other assets, mostly household appliances, until the $4,000 loan was technically covered. This, mind you, was not a transaction with a pawnbroker but with a prudent banker, albeit of an era now past. Without him, we could not have accepted the Fulbright.

There is a bright side to low pay and no perks. At the Delhi School of Social Work in 1956, chatting with the school's director and his wife, Madhov and Phyllis Gore, we watched American consultants board the USAID van to take them to one of New Delhi's Golden Ghettos, where many foreigners lived. We lived within walking distance of the University. Phyllis said, "I am glad you don't have transport and a housing allowance. You would be living in Sundarnagar and we would never have gotten to know each other."

Remuneration is a tricky question. I remember meeting Senator Fulbright at the 1987 conference of the Fulbright Association. I saw him walking across the lobby of the conference building and impulsively rushed to him. We shook hands and he held on, in his warm and gentle manner. I thanked him for my two Fulbrights and a pending third and acknowledged the impact upon my life. He did not release my hand, so I continued, thanking him for the wonderful outcomes for my wife, including her publications on Indian art. Still he held my hand. So I discussed the impact on our daughter, who is in international marketing (seven years in China, five in France), and on to our son. I was about to get to the impact on our dogs when we were interrupted. The next day Senator Fulbright, a panel moderator, begged the audience's indulgence while he got something off his chest. His inspiration for the Fulbright program, he said, had been his Rhodes Scholarship: he had conceived it as a program for graduate students, not faculty with their "whole damn families." He noted that, while the appropriations for the Fulbright program had significantly increased in recent years, the number of Fulbright awards had decreased. "So what's happening? Are you putting it all into dependency allowances, family travel, children's education, etc.? Well, that's all I have to say." I slithered down in my seat because I feared that he might point at me and add, "There's the fellow who got me to thinking about this." (The Senator reaffirmed his views in an interview reported in a recent Fulbright Association newsletter.)

In our family, we are grateful that the Senator's early conception was not allowed to remain that way. Someone at the 1987 meeting noted that, in the nineteenth century and right up until 1939, many professors had private wealth and made the Grand Tour at their own expense. Today most of us do not have such resources and we need, yea require the Fulbright Program for intellectual renewal. Our first Fulbright to India, as I told the Senator, was a milestone in our lives. We had been encouraged to go, despite the lack of sabbatical support, by colleagues who held Fulbrights in India: Noel Gist in sociology (1951-52) and Howard Hirt in geography (1953-54).

In Delhi in 1956, the director of USEFI was Isabelle Thoburn, whose missionary forebears had extensive connections with India. Her missionary tradition probably determined the selection of our first lodging arrangements, a shabby room in the same Connaught Circus hotel where Ghandi's assassin had stayed while planning the murder. In contrast to our room, the hotel restaurant was staffed with magnificently appareled waiters, one posted behind each diner. Disembodied white gloved hands unobtrusively refilled glasses. Our uneasy daughter asked us to tell the silent servant behind her chair to go away.

Despite such experiences in elegant living, we assure the Senator that acceptance of a Fulbright award still involves enough financial sacrifice to satisfy the severest puritan. Each of our three Fulbright years in fact left us in debt. True, money does not motivate one to seek a Fulbright; but neither should a Fulbright family's willingness to undertake personal debt be a test of motivation. Both faculty and graduate students contribute to the achievement of the Program's objectives. Families indeed are an advantage, if only in their multiple points of effective contact with the host culture. A reasonably happy Fulbright family may even help challenge the common notion that Americans have devalued the institution.

A Fulbright means discovery. The heady thrills of exploring a new society on our first Fulbright have not been matched since. We have attempted many times to analyze India's fascination. We enjoyed the novelties—the weekly tea dances at Gaylords, the obligatory staff of house servants, the invitations to official functions (in those early days Fulbrights were honored guests at many state receptions—we met Nehru and President Radhakrishnan). At the same time, we were appalled by the poverty of the bustees, the life of the sidewalk dwellers, the inescapable street beggars showing every kind of disability. We did not dismiss India's social ills as consistent with cultural values or acceptable in the cultural context, any more than thoughtful Indians indulged in such rationalizations. One can *understand*, for example, why female infants do not get the same medical care given to male infants, but that does not mean condoning the practice.

What made us want to return to India so many times? First, enduring warm relationships with kind, thoughtful, unpretentious human beings. As a prime example, the Gores. She has a master's degree in social work, he a doctoral degree in sociology, both from Columbia. His remarkable abilities have been recognized by many honors. Through their eyes, we saw not only India but America. On home visits as a student social worker in New York, she had been surprised by the fact that welfare recipients had telephones, radios, and refrigerators. They were shocked that American families turned over care of their dead to commercial firms, since the Indian family saw this as an important family function. Both the Gores and we saw this as one of the evolutionary changes in the American family, not as callousness nor as an embarrassing deficiency of American character. The traditional Indian extended family has also changed. It is not always the ideal arrangement it initially seemed to be to those of us to whom family cohesiveness under one roof was appealing only so long as we did not have to experience it.

There probably are Americans who, enamored of a new culture, take a zero-sum approach, that is, their attraction to the host country must be balanced by demeaning the American way of life. And the insecure may believe that deprecating American society will ingratiate themselves with their hosts. We never encountered a Fulbrighter of that type, so we look to our daughter for an example. She told us of a visiting American professor of journalism in China who seized every occasion to show his solidarity with communism by castigating America. An African-American, he was not totally without a basis for his opinions. But Lisa's mastery of Mandarin allowed her access to what his Chinese acquaintances, all of whom would have undergone any sacrifice to come to America, thought of his gratuitous America-bashing. I am reminded of Joe Louis' explanation to a reporter of why he was supporting the war effort despite the treatment of "your people": "There's lots wrong with America, but nothing that Hitler can fix." The Chinese knew that China had no solutions for the professor's complaints.

The second reason for focusing on India: the high value placed upon my professional contribution. I was not a threat to anyone's career ambitions, nor a competitor for scarce resources or other rewards. I was outside the indigenous pecking order and was thus judged on my own merit (true also of subsequent tours in India and in Malaysia).

Third, the visual and performing arts of India were a major attraction. In 1956, Betty began developing a deep and professional interest in those aspects of Indian culture. Because much of Indian art has religious significance, her studies helped her to develop a substantial knowledge of Hinduism. All of this was applied to significant activities back home.

Fourth, the whole *gestalt* of Indian culture—the vividness, the cuisine, the contrasts—helped overcome the negatives. Even street-dwellers had a certain dignity as they conducted their lives in open view of passersby. The grace of the women as they carried heavy loads on their heads made one momentarily forget the burdens they bore. Again, we could appreciate the ability to tolerate adversity without seeing adversity as acceptable.

Finally, we shamelessly confess, as educators who appreciate respect, that it is good every so often to receive the red carpet treatment. On our first Fulbright, Betty went to a furniture rental shop. Asked about her husband, she impulsively referred to me as *Dr.* Robins, hoping to elicit preferred treatment—intact items and prompt delivery. "PhD or MD?", asked the proprietor. Embarrassed to be caught putting on airs, she murmured, "PhD." "Then your husband is an important person," was his sincere response.

Four years after India, I was eligible for sabbatical leave. When a UN appointment to East Pakistan materialized, I declined a Fulbright research award. Reasons: the vagaries of doing research without language proficiency, and the UN remuneration—our family was larger and we had only recently paid off the debt from our previous Fulbright. Seven years later, I again declined a Fulbright to Iran in favor of a UN position. Yet despite their advantages neither of our UN assignments brought the satisfaction that our Fulbright experience had. Was that the cause or the result of our enjoying the societies of East Pakistan or Iran somewhat less? A mix, most likely.

In 1979, in India for several months, I was invited to go to Bangladesh to lecture in Dacca at the same institution where I had earlier served as a consultant. As my taxi drew near the destination, I could hear the noise of a large crowd. A horde of students had gathered in front of the building where I was to speak; they were responding with cheers and chants to the cues of a leader. The welcome seemed a bit extravagant. Alas the cheers were not for me: I found the faculty staying prudently inside the building and learned that the students were protesting police brutality at a sister university. My lecture was never delivered. Dacca University students, eighteen years before, had been on strike during our entire year in then-East Pakistan. *Plus ça change!*

The pervasive discontent in East Pakistan and Iran inevitably affected us. Our friends and colleagues in India, in contrast to those in East Pakistan and Iran, exuded optimism about India's future. Many in India exemplified a selfless Gandhian kind of spirit. East Pakistan and Iran had little of that. Faculty colleagues predicted that the widespread popular dissatisfaction would one day come to a head. In both countries it did, within a decade of our departure.

The College of Social Welfare and Research Centre in Dacca, off the campus of Dacca University, kept open during the strikes. Social welfare students, vulnerable to physical abuse by the strikers, had to be circumspect. Processions of students marched from time to time in protest of government policies. Serious work was difficult. The Peace Corps, arriving in East Pakistan shortly after us, was soon accused of tinkering with the Basic Democracy Scheme and expelled (the Scheme was a government program designed to maximize popular grassroots participation). The village-level "Basic Democrats" elected representatives to the next higher level and so on up to Parliament. The catch: the *government* selected the village-level members. Such blatant authoritarianism made my assignment unattractive.

Much the same context obtained in Iran. The government had demonstrated little interest in social welfare, not even mentioned in the five-year plan. The morale of the mostly inexperienced social work school's faculty was low. Hyperbole and puffery characterized the Shah's White Revolution, the name coined for his progressive efforts. An American sociologist's banned book (Jacobs 1966) documented the dysfunctionality for economic development of Iranian social institutions. SAVAK, the secret police, and its informers were thought to be everywhere.

I recall a soirée organized by the Embassy Cultural Attaché on the subject of social welfare. My counterpart, the director of the Teheran College of Social Work, was asked during the discussion why she did not use her influence to talk with Prime Minister Hoveyda about improved welfare planning. Jokingly, she said, "One doesn't talk to him, one listens." The next morning she was visited by SAVAK agents who spent three hours seeking an explanation of her "grievances" against the government. She suspected that an Iranian professor, who had seemed to sleep through most of the session, had reported her remark. Her remarkable autobiography reached me just as this volume went to press (Farman Farmaian 1992).

We are Jewish. While both East Pakistan and Iran had predominantly Muslim populations, the fact had no visible effect on our experience in either country. Islam is Malaysia's state religion but this fact diminished in no way our professional and personal satisfaction with that assignment. The UN in fact had not permitted us to visit *Israel* en route to East Pakistan. In Dacca, we found a Jew heading the Chamber of Commerce.

The UN was wrong on another count: citing the Muslim attitude towards dogs, it had admonished us to leave our pet at home. We later learned that a dog was in fact a status symbol in the upper middle class. Profiting from our observations in Dacca, we ignored the pre-Iran UN briefing and brought our dog to Iran, picking him up at Customs after we had been there for three weeks. On seeing the large dog, our cook locked herself in the kitchen. Gradually, she was intrigued by the new experience. Much of his time was spent in the kitchen, where his appreciation of her cooking further endeared him. Her tears at our departure were not for us but for the dog. She begged us to leave him with her—a new dimension in mutual understanding. One unpleasant incident occurred in Isfahan—a crowd teased the dog by throwing burning cigarettes at him. But that hardly warranted leaving him in America for a year. In fact, we probably should have left him in Teheran.

Briefings on foreign cultures are always approximate: they may help to avoid gross gaucheries, but they also tend to perpetuate stereotypes. Many predictions of the dire consequences of violating cultural norms, we have come to believe, can be nullified by being one's natural self in the context of mutual respect, of mutual acceptance of difference in values and beliefs, so long as the differences do not offend universal human values. Moreover, people from both the host culture and the visitor's culture can and do learn to change. A homely (as they say in India) example will illustrate our meaning. Lunch at the institution's cafeteria in Iran invariably consisted of an immense pile of rice on an oversized plate, together with a small bowl of meat in a sauce. Custom called for the diner to empty the bowl on the rice and consume the mixture. To the accompaniment of much giggling by onlookers, I would put a small portion of my rice into the bowl and decline the rest. By year's end, most of my colleagues and many of the students were emulating my reverse procedure. "It never occurred to us before"—the rice became the figure; the meat sauce, the ground. The traditional perception, perhaps deriving from the relative costs of the items, was abandoned in favor of a tastier dish and greater alertness during afternoon classes. Can significant behavior of the people of the host country be brought to useful change if one gives up the "walking-on-eggs" approach that briefings inspire?

Good briefings of course do have their uses. The UN briefing on East Pakistan warned that the lack of entertaining activities meant family members would get to know each other very well. Our nine-year-old daughter posed a disquieting question: "What happens if we find out that we don't like each other?" Insight, she intuitively realized, does not—despite its central role in psychoanalytically-induced behavior change—necessarily bring about positive outcomes; getting to know other's societies does not necessarily lead to love or even respect for them.

Some host-country customs on the other hand were so engaging that we found ourselves, without thinking, continuing them in America. We still fall into the gracious Hindu gesture of palms pressed together, used as a greeting or politely to decline an invitation. Some overseas behaviors on the other hand soon disappeared from our repertoire because they might be misconstrued as affectations, just as Indians were not impressed by imitative behaviors they saw as "going native." Wearing a sari was disapproved when the western woman did not modify her stride to suit the grace of the garment. There may be a tendency to gush over aspects of the host culture, particularly when one is warmly welcomed. For example, some previous Fulbrighters to Malaysia had reported lyrically on Islam because they met so many nice Malays. Indeed, we found many Malays to be considerate and hospitable. But while Islam is important to them we could no more ascribe their attractive characteristics to religion than we could trace the charm of our Chinese and Indian Malaysian friends to their Buddhism or Hinduism.

Fulbright experiences do not mean contacts only with foreigners. At the Delhi School of Social Work in 1956, we had only three years of academic life behind us. A doctorate, for a social worker, was relatively rare at the time. It added weight to my resumé, as well as research competence. I felt secure about my ability to teach in India, since I was to teach the same courses I taught at home. Then I learned that Helen Wright, Dean Emeritus, University of Chicago, was to be Chief of the USAID social work education project at the School! A self-styled curmudgeon, the formidable Dean Wright had given me a traumatic interrogation five years earlier, when I sought admission to her doctoral program. Admission was offered, but I chose what appeared to be a user-friendly program at the University of Minnesota.

At meetings of the Delhi faculty, the Indians frequently referred questions on educational issues to me. Loathe to overshadow Dr. Wright, I deferred to her. But the Indian faculty, consistent with their male-dominated society, persisted, "We are asking for *your* opinion." Still, we got along well—Dean Wright claimed not to remember the admissions interview—and were able, as old India hands (having arrived a month or so before her), to help with some of her everyday living problems. Having to hold my own with Dean Wright, along with what I learned from her, made the year a professionally maturing experience.

Fulbright rhetoric often overlooks the positive outcome of such meetings with other Americans abroad. Recently I asked someone who had been a visiting professor of finance in China whether he had met our daughter working in finance there at the time. He told me that he had gone to China to meet Chinese, not Americans. Given her intensive contacts with Chinese officials and her fluency in Mandarin, I think he missed an opportunity. Insulating oneself in an American expatriate community is one thing, selectively meeting knowledgeable fellow Americans along with people of the host country is another.

Home from our first Fulbright, we sought to meet Indian students. Our university had an AID contract to develop agriculture in Eastern India, and several Indian civil servants were there for advanced studies. We had brought back a variety of Indian musical instruments and had marvelous musicales at our home, soon known as India House. We helped introduce Indians to the American community. We arranged for performances and interviews on a local television show, sometimes with amusing consequences. On camera, the host urged her Indian guests to taste what she was advertising—genuine Boone County Ham!

In 1958 I became university coordinator for a program conceived by Burvill Glenn, of SUNY Buffalo, who had been a Fulbrighter in Pakistan. His plan brought eight Asian professors to the U.S. for an academic year, rotating among eight participating universities. Fitting those lectures into existing courses proved a problem. At my suggestion, we dropped out of the program and instead brought one visiting professor for the entire year to one department. Subsequently a National Defense Education Act grant funded our Center for South Asian Studies. Over the last 30 years, the Center has helped finance the addition in several departments of faculty who teach India-related content.

Since those early days, the Indian community in Columbia, Missouri, has grown. We no longer chase every Indian we spot on the streets. Some are close colleagues. There is still a need for people in our town to understand India, but there are now institutionalized ways of educating them. Columbia now has a Cultural Association of India.

Through her activities in the arts, Betty contributed significantly in Columbia and beyond to an understanding of India. Under various sponsorships, e.g. the art league, the University's art department and the museum where she was the South Asian curator, she organized informative exhibits. One emphasized the similarities between everyday Indian and American arts and crafts, such as quilts, samplers, toys, kitchen utensils. Common elements of function and design demonstrated the closeness between the two cultures. She organized Indian arts and classical dance programs, using her wide contacts in India to learn what artists were visiting the U.S., then bringing them to Columbia. She co-authored a book with a friend who had been stimulated by our experience to seek a Fulbright to India (Bussabarger and Robins 1968) and recently was consultant to the Denver Art Museum on a project involving their South Asian collection.

By the time of our second Fulbright (1981-82), fourteen years had elapsed. I had held two UN consultantships and a variety of academic experiences transcending disciplinary boundaries, with additional professorships in management, psychology and psychiatry. There was a new confidence to assume any teaching assignment that was reasonably related to my experience. For my first Fulbright, I had shipped duplicate sets of notes separately so that a single catastrophe would not leave me bereft. My confidence was put to actual test on my second Fulbright—the suitcase containing my teaching materials was lost. When the materials caught up with me a month later, I decided that the notes I made after the loss were better than the original set. By 1981, I no longer worried about losing notes. One wonders how much improvement in teaching might occur if lecture notes were periodically destroyed.

The second India Fulbright forced me to develop new courses and seminars: the women's university to which I was primarily assigned had neither a program in familiar social work nor psychiatry. My diverse background fed into seminars and short staff courses for human services organizations. The focus on continuing education was more challenging than teaching resident students. I was also more flexible in meeting host institution teaching needs that had not been specified earlier. This proved more the case on my third Fulbright in Malaysia when I was asked, after arrival, to offer training in new subjects. Preparing for those tasks challenged me to integrate my knowledge of the four disciplines in which I have held professorships and apply it to a new educational mission. Again, a large continuing education component provided the stimulation of students who brought work experience to the classroom.

Today, we are 35 years away from our first Fulbright, 20 years from our second and 2 years from our third. The first had the most impact: it determined in large measure our future personal and professional interests, and it stimulated our shared interests in the social institutions of India—political, religious, economic, artistic, and familial. Ideas provoked by the first visit have found expression in our research, teaching and publications. From that first Fulbright we gained more than we gave, although it is always difficult to quantify the utility value of such exchange. Subsequent Fulbrights enabled us to give at least as much as we received, even if measured only by the quantity of my teaching duties. The applicants handbook for 1992-93 warns applicants "not to stress how a Fulbright grant will benefit only you and your career. Remember that the program is intended to foster mutual understanding between cultures and nations." The injunction is partially belied by the request, both in the application and evaluation forms, for information on expected and achieved professional and personal outcomes.

Regardless of who benefited more, all our Fulbrights generated mutual understanding. Over the years, we have watched developments in India. We have sometimes, together with our Indian friends, been distressed by what we see. Yet we have always understood India's basic dilemma: it must build a nation which commands the loyalty of diverse groups in a highly pluralistic society at the same time that it pursues social development involving the conflictful distribution of resources among those groups. If "Unity in Diversity" is the slogan of nation-building, "Unity in Adversity" is the slogan of development. India's achievement stands in contrast with the crumbling of the USSR and Yugoslavia under the weight of both diversity and adversity.

A rural Missouri lady once introduced her companion to us: "We're good friends, we done fell out already." Like hers, our relationship with India has been tested by occasional disagreement. It has survived. Perhaps that statement encapsulates a vital Fulbright outcome. Our teaching abroad has helped us achieve an understanding that allows both our hosts and us to express what we like and do not like about our respective societies and why. Understanding can never remove the potential for conflict. But it can and should be expected to identify the bones of contention and to facilitate resolutions that work, at all levels of human organization.

Mutual understanding, we said earlier, is not an end in itself. Senator Fulbright would have it lead to joint ventures and contribute to a truly new world order. The mature individual, someone has said, seeks neither independence from nor dependence on his fellows but, rather, interdependence. So it should be with nations—the Fulbright experience can further awareness and acceptance of interdependency. But there must be a systematic effort on the part of governments, both ours and theirs, to use the experience of Fulbrighters from America as well as those who come here. The Fulbright Association is only one potential means to that end.

Heraclitus' observations on the river and the person did not touch on the interaction between the two. The rivers, in our case the environments, induced salutary changes in us; and in turn we exerted a modest and perhaps favorable influence upon our environments. It is now time for mutual understanding generated over forty years to serve the higher goals envisioned by the Senator, whatever he thinks about families.

REFERENCES

Robert Bussabarger and Betty Dashew Robins, *The Everyday Art of India*, New York: Dover, 1968.

Sattareh Farman Farmaian, *Daughter of Persia*, New York: Crown, 1992.

Fulbright, J. William, Speech on the 40th anniversary of the Fulbright Program, in *Directory of Visiting Fulbright Scholars and Occasional Lecturers* (1987-88), Washington, D.C.: Council for International Exchange of Scholars.

Norman Jacobs, *The Sociology of Development: Iran as an Asian Case Study*, New York: Praeger, 1966.

Arthur J. Robins, "The Foreign Consultant's Role in Newly Developed Countries," in *Studies in Asia*, R. K. Sakai, ed. Lincoln: University of Nebraska Press, 1964.

The author, a brand-new "unfocused BA generalist" when she went to Vienna in 1956, already had a strong bent to contemporary history. She practiced it in Vienna in notably non-academic ways. Budapest '56 contributed to her discoveries and led her to journalism, a sixteen-year career with the Chicago Daily News and membership in the select group of American syndicated columnists—her work appears three times per week in 120 newspapers in the U.S. and Latin America. Five books include: The Young Russians *(1975), the autobiographical* Buying the Night Flight *(1983), and the recent* Guerilla Prince, *a biography of Fidel Castro (1991). In this reflection on the "big pictures" of a new and reshaping world, she makes a compelling case for major augmentation of the Fulbright potential at a time when, in the world's history, it becomes more obvious than before that it is a national and international imperative.*

10

FROM VIENNA, WITH LOVE
AND UNDERSTANDING

Georgie Anne Geyer

The Vienna I came to that remarkable autumn of 1956 was the antithesis of the entire American experience. Its legendary beauty was still there, but now it was mired in the sorrows of a wrongful war lost and of a desperate poverty not known since long before the golden days of the Hapsburg Empire.

Where America in the heady aftermath of World War II was pure positivism, Vienna was subsumed melancholy. While America was exuberantly rebuilding Europe and Japan, Vienna was searching for its lost soul. Austria looked a lot like "us"—the same European roots and culture—but in truth she was very different; that is why living for a year in her heart was so revealing.

Only the year before, the Four Power Occupation of Austria ended and the peace treaty was signed. The Americans, the Russians, the French and the

British went home, finally and completely, from World War II. But the occupation of Vienna had been wholly unlike other occupations after the War: the city's utter charm, even after the most terrible of wars, made veritable friends of the four powers there. Because of the special historical mellow *gemütlichkeit* of the Austrians, because of their special charm and warmth, even the occupation by the Great Powers was friendly. Still, in their leaving, the mellowed occupiers left Vienna again alone there in central Europe, with her delirious waltzes, her legendary palaces and her baroque fears.

I settled into Vienna in September of 1956 and quickly decided with youthful sobriety that, were I to die tomorrow, I would now have "lived" (that was big with us children of the fifties, "living," and it was always in quotes). With great good fortune, I found a room in an apartment on the Westbahnstrasse with two lovely Austrian girls from the beautiful southern province of Kärnten, Ingrid and Erika. The better friends and comrades we became, however, the more jealous and unsettled became the strange little old man who owned the apartment.

He was always snooping around, his bulging voyeur's eyes popping out suddenly from behind treacherous doors. The happy and comradely little eyrie on the Westbahnstrasse was not to last. At the old fellow's urging, I gave a big Thanksgiving dinner in the flat, to which I invited all twenty-three of my new friends from twelve nations. Not having cooked in his odd kitchen before, I misjudged the time the chicken would take to cook. While we waited, and waited, and waited, my group got high on Austrian Gumpolds-kirchner wine, my favorite, in twelve languages. And the next day Georgie Anne was out on the Westbahnstrasse.

It is at this point that I need to unburden myself of a guilt I have carried for thirty-six years. I must speak what was formerly unspeakable and let life move on ahead, at last on a clear track. I did not go to class in Vienna.

There: I have finally said it. But having said it, I must hasten to add that the fault was not really mine. I tried to go to classes at the University; indeed, I tried hard. But my Fulbright had been sought for the study of German and Austrian history from the 1930s to the 1950s—and no one had warned me they taught no such history at the University! Vienna was still too traumatized by the war even to begin to think about examining the cancerous warts of its recent history. Besides, "contemporary history" was classified disdainfully as a form of "journalism," prophetic in my case. So silence reigned.

I am pleased however to report that, being a practical girl from the South Side of Chicago, I quickly regrouped. I decided that the university cafe was a splendid place from which to study the Austrian historical character. I avidly took German lessons and within two months spoke fairly fluent German. My epiphany came when the Herr Professor who was head of the Fulbright Program in Vienna, noting the fact that I attended every possible meeting with Austrian students and might have been said to oversocialize, urged me on with a pleased smile: "Just keep doing what you're doing—you help to make up for all the Fulbrighters who do nothing but study!" Thus was crime early rewarded. Still, it was part of the Fulbright accident—I often wonder what would have become of me had I set out to study Bismarck. In fact, the absence of formal university courses forced me, willy-nilly, to learn the skills of synthesis, analysis, extrapolation, interviewing, note-taking and memory— in short, the tools of journalism.

Then, just as I was settling into a wonderfully mellow relationship with Vienna, the world just east changed dramatically. In October, that same fall, Hungary erupted into a totally unexpected revolution. ·For a 21-year-old American, romantic and idealistic as well as intellectually seeking, with the American's positivist view that things were surely and necessarily moving and evolving towards an ever-better world, the Hungarian revolution was devastating. The scoundrels of history had won, the noble rebels were smitten; force and artifice again reigned in the world.

Working at the border with international student brigades helped relieve my terrible feeling of powerlessness. But it was all over soon. Only days after Hungarians went out into the streets of Budapest to fight the Russian tanks, we in Vienna could hear Radio Budapest going off the air, saying to the West: "Help us, help us, we are going off the air . . . Help us . . . ."

That experience marked a critical change towards realism for the idealistic American in me. It was the first time, but certainly not the last, that I would see to my distress and disorientation that human progress was far from inevitable. Yet it also began to teach me an invaluable lesson: you cannot always *will* life, but you can *shape and form* it.

Leaving Vienna in the fall of 1957 and returning home to begin a career in writing and journalism (how, I knew not!), I realized I had been practicing those arts, at least by Austrian standards, all year long. And at a deeper level, I had intuitively absorbed much of the tragic sense of Vienna.

A terrible case of hepatitis kept me in bed the next year and came close to killing me; strangely and symbolically, in confirming the reality of my own mortality, it gave me time to brood about the relativeness of societies and cultures (and of human lives?) that I had absorbed abroad with joy and with pain. I began to understand how those other less optimistic cultures than ours had had to learn throughout history that everything does not always "work out in the end." Nor—and this is even harder—do all people want the same thing.

From Vienna I brought with me into the next phase of my life a number of invaluable tools, none more important than language. I had loved learning German—I had worked on it with a tutor almost every day, while sipping the Slivovitz which his mother kindly proferred. I realized that a language is like a creature: it grows inside you until one day it begins speaking to other people in sounds and tongues you never knew before.

I had also learned the primary importance of distance in understanding, or trying to understand, another culture. Many Americans think that liking, or loving, or knowing another culture means somehow immersing yourself in that culture and giving yourself up, to the extent of actually pretending to give up your own identity in order to embrace another. Losing yourself! Becoming one of them! Identifying with their ways!

Nothing could be more wrong, no approach more false and counter-productive. In order really to engage in the strange and sensitive exchange that takes place in beginning to know another culture, one must first be firmly rooted in one's own. One must, as far as it is humanly possible, know oneself. It is disrespectful to assume that another people's historic experience is something you can enter at will. Indeed it is willfully and arrogantly disrespectful to your own culture because it assumes that your culture is so puny and pitiful that it has no hold on you at all.

Later, when I covered the Arab world as one of the first women foreign correspondents there, I would see that I was rather good at it because I presented myself honestly and forthrightly (and, not incidentally, with the self-respect that comes with this) as what I was: a Western, Christian woman foreign correspondent who knew who she was but cared who they were and who could respect them because she respected herself. More years later, when I was the only journalist investigating the "new worlds" of Central Asia in the defining winter of 1992, I discovered the fifteenth-century Uzbek poet Ali Shir Nava'i had asked the same key questions about mankind: "How can I expect people to find me if I do not know myself?"

These sensitivities, plus a close-to-obsessive concern with knowing people's histories—another mark of respect I might add—stood me in good stead when I became a foreign correspondent for the Chicago Daily News and then a syndicated columnist. Young journalists and students invariably asked me how I "controled" my interviews, those with leaders like Castro, Khaddafi and Khomeini; the answer (totally unsatisfactory to them I realize) was History, another Fulbright discovery.

Let me give an example. In 1978 in Paris I interviewed that great "friend of humanity and of children" the Ayatollah Khomeini. It was December, only a few weeks before he went back to Iran to overthrow the Shah and institute one of the most bloody, atavistic and regressive "revolutions" of all times. When I was ushered into a little French summer house where Khomeini was temporarily staying, I knew a little Iranian or Persian history; I knew in particular that Persian Shiites were permitted to "dissimulate" when their faith is under attack.   This is an historic tenet, forced upon the Shiites by the constant conquests of Mongols and others; it not only allowed them to lie to save themselves and their faith from those ceaseless marauders, but it meant "dissimulation" was a virtual habit.   So, when I sat for a rare hour with the Ayatollah, before those dark, sinister eyes, I *knew* that he was carrying out that strange cultural prerogative.   When he told me that "his" Iran would be a democracy and that women would be free to be doctors and professors, I knew very well that he was dissimulating before the hated foreigner.   When, in those same weeks, the Afghan-American Zalmay Khalilzad, professor at Columbia University, went to see Khomeini, his attendants did not know that Khalilzad understood Persian.   He overheard them saying to the Imam: "Tell the American professor the Ayatollah wants democracy and rights for women— that is what the Americans like to hear."

It was less easy to act on such knowledge than to have it, I might add. I never quite understand what to write when you are trying to quote a person honestly yet tell the reader the person is lying. What I did that time was to quote Khomeini and then tell the reader that the Persian Shiites dissimulate, a notably unsuccessful way to deal with cultural complexities. I never have hit upon a particularly graceful way of dealing with the problem.

Another Fulbright dimension was the discovery of fun. To be honest with myself, I have to admit that my reasons for going into this strange business of foreign journalism, trying to understand another culture, then putting my findings into evocative journalistic writing that can inform or move others and finally perhaps even reaching some catharsis of my own—these reasons were not all disinterested or community-serving. Basically, I can now admit, I did it because it was fun—so much fun, indeed, that it should have been illegal or immoral, by my youthful value system. Fulbright was in fact for many of us a kind of moral relief. It made discovery respectable, even noble. It showed us that this kind of joyous "fun" of discovering, learning, and enjoying is what life is—or ought to be—all about.

The joy of sitting at a breakfast table in some strange hotel in some new country, watching people I never knew before and seeing how they acted! The breathtaking gasp of seeing a lost city in some desert, "new" to me because I had never seen it before! The romance of gleaming moonlight in the Galapagos, with sea lions innocent in their paradise, swimming with me in their lack of mistrust of humans! The exciting fear of sitting on a darkly-forested mountainside in Guatemala with Marxist guerillas as they told their story, all the time surrounded by 3000 government troops! The good-humored irritation of my fiancé, hating my love for hotels above homes and muttering, "The three most beautiful words in the world to you are not 'I love you' but 'Room service, please'"! The way I finally came to think of my strange and difficult life as a kind of continuous play in a perpetual off-season resort!

Those are just a few of the personal things, over many years, that came out of the life that began for me in Vienna that vintage year of 1956—my career in journalism, my work as a foreign correspondent, my books on other countries, and my love affair with the world.

Beyond the personal, when I look at the bigger screen, when I move beyond those memories and look at the whole immense Fulbright Program that crosses and crisscrosses the globe, I see still larger pictures whose shadows reflect other ideas in my life.

Think of it this way: until 1989 the Fulbright years were the years of the Cold War. The Program was certainly not begun as any antidote to Soviet expansionism, nor was it explicitly intended to serve that purpose—though even the Senator would say so if he thought it would help fund the program. But the fact was that it came to be in truth and in reality a major weapon in that "war." Yet it was generally assumed that Fulbright was a soft weapon, like "psy-war" or the "information war." True, its main intent was nothing less than informing and transforming Mankind. But this transformation was not to be political—in the immediate sense of the word—nor certainly military; it was and is assumed that the Fulbright Program is a kind of harmless, pleasant adjunct to the "real" issues, those of politics and security.

I would like to argue here that such a supposition could not be more wrong. The Fulbright Program was not on the periphery of the gigantic struggle for democratic and free-willed change in the world since 1945, it was the very center of that change. It was a vast and unique commitment, in history, to the peaceful and non-restrictive exchange of invididuals among and within many societies—an invitation to explore, to see, to know "the other," and then for the Fulbrighters to do what they would (or would not) with their knowledge. And it became terribly appropriate to its time because, in truth, the struggle of this era of Man's history has been primarily cultural.

Why cultural? In previous centuries man grappled with man through war, the imposition of religion and economic competition. Only in this century, since 1917 when Communism and Democracy first faced each other in a contest for hegemony, did each side set out to make the other believe in its particular "faith." On both sides, the fight took place in the schools, in the intellectual communities, and inside the highly-distilled belief-systems of the elite communities. This change was mammoth in its proportions and in its implications.

Look at what the Cold War has seemed to mean to nearly everyone. We have tended to look at the struggle that has dominated the thinking and the behavior of the world since 1945, and in fact since 1917, as an imperial and military contest for power and hegemony, for sovereignty over land and space, and for a primitive idea of victory over men's bodies. But the truth of this long and onerous period has in fact been instead a far more complicated fight to see which system—Utopian Marxist collectivism or liberal capitalistic democracy—could first and best and most completely *transform Man*.

Let me not dwell too much on early history. The cultural struggle obviously began with the Bolshevik Revolution, ushering in an era of class struggle and collectivism in every human activity. Some of this reached the U.S.: there were pseudo-collectivist ideas in parts of the New Deal, for instance. Enormous amounts and levels of influence flowed outwards from Russia all over the world; many Europeans and Americans sympathized with the developments in Russia, believing they had seen a future which worked. At the same time, despite towering barriers erected by the Soviets, the counter-influences of democratic thought, of individualism, of notions of free enterprise flowed eastwards. In the time of Krushchev, young Russians began to travel first to Eastern Europe, then to Western Europe, and finally to the U.S. By 1958 a formal "Fulbright" program was in place with the USSR and Yakovlev was at Columbia. All this meant that ideologies were being copmpared and criticized.

What exactly was going back and forth between the democratic West and the Marxist East in those decades since World War II? Think of it this way: in essence, the East under Communism—and Mother Russia in particular—was construed around the counter-idea of collective responsibility, of collective redemption and of aberrations on both sides, these constructions were the major ones.

Once the two sides began to make war, not in white heat but in the freezing cold, these quintessential realities in each culture began literally to infiltrate each other. Marxian, "leftist," or collectivist ideas began to affect U.S. universities, unions, churches, bureaucracies and corporations. Statist ideas transformed American institutions in many ways, not all of them of course for the worse, as the two systems vied for suzerainty in the world. It was a time when America's youth and its intellectuals visited Cuba, Russia's Third World surrogate in the Americas, and when carefully selected Soviets were permitted to visit the West. It was a war of ideas, penetrating and very real.

It was at heart a struggle for a kind of modernizing redemption. From Angola to Cuba to Vietnam, the Soviets worked diligently at and dreamed fantasmagorically of transforming random Man into a disciplined automaton, formally called "socialist new man." At the same time, in its regions of influence in the world, from Egypt to South Korea to Brazil, the U.S. vied in trying in parallel fashion to form "democratic and free enterprise man."

It was a thoroughly new kind of fight, in many ways a grand contest. But it was tremendously disorienting for many parts of the world. What we can now see is that this cultural contest, not for men's bodies but for their souls, confused, confounded, corrupted and even destroyed many traditional cultures (in the industrialized world the effects were more complex).

The traditional cultures could simply not absorb or adapt to the pounding blitzkrieg of these carriers of change. One need only look at Iran under the Shah, at Cambodia under the Khmer Rouge, at Peru under the threat of the Sendero Luminoso, and at all of Eastern Europe today in the wake of communism to see how the assaults on traditional beliefs and structures have driven many whole peoples into trauma or even into madness. Indeed we now have case study after case study of how the best-meaning attempts at "modernization" have created a world of dangerous disorientation and even national insanity among men torn too precipitously from their past. Thus, while there is indeed a new level of international organization and of cooperation between Americans and former Soviets in the Third World, there is another dangerous level of ideas and activities underneath, ideas that may doom even the best intentions.

In the industrialized world and in the former superpowers, there is another kind of disorientation. The cultural conflict—which was going on all along in parallel with the military struggle—has in great part led to the confusion over where we are today. The military part was easy; the cultural part is utterly bedeviling. It has led to the disorientation and despair that one finds in Eastern Europe and the Soviet countries today, as understandable as it is dangerous. For with the fall of communism, with this unprecedented and implosive collapse of a totalist ideology from inside without being conquered in war and with its military might intact, we are seeing something terribly, frighteningly new.

How does a vast nation, formerly held together by a rigid and unforgiving ideology, find itself again in a world in which it must finally accept the ultimate humiliation of embracing the actual ideology and system of the enemy? How does it impart ethical principles of free enterprise business and systems of democratic being and patterns of a work ethic that are totally foreign to its historic memory and experience? How do we deal with this new factor in foreign affairs of cultural collapse?

Cultures collapse when the underlying beliefs and tenets that kept them together no longer hold. They collapse when their economic systems are not built on an understanding of human nature. In the Soviet Union, for instance, no one saw the reality of the human need to earn profits and to develop individual initiatives. We find ourselves today in a particularly dangerous place in human history with regard to multi-ethnic societies like the Soviet Union, Yugoslavia, and our own. The fact is that once ethnic, racial and special interest groups begin to return to their parent groups, the idealistic and basically artificial glue that held these societies together is no longer strong enough to stand against the atavistic old ties of blood, history and ancient mythic hatred.

In the Soviet Union and elsewhere, this cultural collapse came about for specific reasons. In their ideologized contest—and it had all the passion of a religious crusade—both big powers literally invaded each other's culture and soul. It is after all a reciprocal process: in long conflicts like this one, you become something of your enemy; each side takes on some of the colors and beliefs of the other. For the developing countries, what we were doing amounted to more than a cultural hurricane, it was basically an attempt at secular evangelization, one democratic and the other Marxist. Third World societies hungered for modernization but lacked the tools to do it, a recipe for disaster. Within the superpowers, the illusions and the corruptions were more subtle.

American ideas of democracy and free enterprise filtered in slowly but finally struck East Europeans and Russians with cyclone force. In the collapsed Soviet Union today, Russians say over and over that they could no longer sustain their faith in the Marxist mystique or in real collectivism once they had seen the prosperity of Europe and the U.S. Mikhail Gorbachev himself began his long itinerary when he secretly visited France in the late seventies and saw that Russia was not keeping up. Meanwhile the international American radios—Radio Liberty, Radio Free Europe and the Voice of America—patiently, systematically, ubiquitously and relentlessly beamed news of the world directly into the USSR, a cultural ripping asunder of the web of falsehood that unfortunate society's leadership had woven to protect itself from outside realities.

America of course, at least we hope so, is a long way from cultural collapse; yet even among ourselves we have serious questions. There are the obvious ones, like the state of our cities and our schools. There are more amorphous questions, like the decadence that accompanies drug-use, out-ofwedlock children, and the terrible criminality that infects our cities. And on deeper levels, there are questions about our role in the world. What is the U.S. to be in the "new world order"? How do we deal with the illusions that our monumental cultural victory implies—can we now go home and enjoy life? How do we find a new consensus when the old one, based on a common enemy and the idea of a consuming if cold war, has lost its cohesive quality?

It was a war of ideas, and in that war the West with all its less-than-perfections surely won. It won because its system is more in line with human nature, with that natural morality which rejects ideas like killing one's parents for state ideological reasons. It won because its economies were immeasurably more functional than the East's. And it won, I have no doubt in saying, because programs like Fulbright, cultural and educational programs, allowed people from all nations to go somewhere else and take a deep, long look for themselves.

We who care about human exchange, ideological dialog, and intellectual and scientific give-and-take; we who do more than care, who see exchange as the locus of the real fight, the only path towards a manageable peace—we face new and important questions in our world. They are questions which I believe point to the real genius of the Fulbright Program and the experience it generates because I believe, and I see in this world since 1945, that the sensible and commonsensical type of human and intellectual interchange fostered by cultural exchanges like Fulbright has shown us the way things should have gone.

I would argue indeed that, in the light of what we can clearly see now about this historically unprecedented exchange of people and ideas over the last half-century, the Fulbright Program, almost alone . . . did . . . things . . . right!

While USAID on our side and the Comintern on the other, and many other programs and policies on both sides, were throwing indigestible change at these peoples of the world, Fulbright was systematically and patiently giving the individual human beings, whether Gabonese or French or Indian or American, the simple chance to go to another country and learn and accept things (or learn and not accept them). No demands were made, except of course a certain level of professional study and of personal behavior.

Fulbright thus put the choice of where a person, a people or a country should or would go partly in the hands of some of its most promising people. Its impact brought about the gradual transformation of peoples through organic reorientation; its own people could choose whether to accept or deny or accept in part what they found elsewhere. The Fulbright process completely by-passed the traumas that accompany change imposed from the outside, especially when imposed without consideration for the capacities of a given culture to absorb or to deny. Without perhaps really planning it and certainly without knowing the nature of the struggle that lay ahead, Fulbright created no Irans or Cambodias.

One last example. The most horrendous movement at the world's doorstep today is the Sendero Luminoso, or Shining Path, of Peru. It is the murderous new Khmer Rouge, and if it comes to power, Peru will be as much a bloodbath as Cambodia in 1975. Sendero, one of those movements that aims at starting "anew," at "Year Zero," and destroying every alternative to its power, began at the University of Ayacucho, high in the Peruvian Andes, in the mid-sixties. Its leaders were not Indians but *mestizos* or mixed bloods, most of them in the Philosophy Department.

They were relatively unimportant until 1968 when the Peruvian military, then led by Leftist reformist officers, took over the country, determined to transform everything. The problem was that Ayacucho had been "the" center in Peru for foreign aid--everything from USAID, the German aid programs, church programs, etc. But in response to the military takeover, every group literally withdrew in protest overnight. Ayacucho had been awakened by the foreigners; and then they left it, suddenly, half-awake. This was of course the most dangerous eventuality, and from that moment on Sendero Luminoso grew—out of the trauma of people uprooted from their traditional past and then left alone in a traumatized situation. One has to wonder what would have happened in Ayacucho had the programs been of the Fulbright variety?

And so, many of us have come to the "radical" idea that the world would be far ahead if a nation's attention to the needs of other nations had been paid via the Fulbright approach. Indeed I am far from alone in believing today that, except for some American aid programs which are essential (e.g. drug-fighting, or some kind of stabilizing economic assistance), the world and we ourselves would be far better off if all of our aid had gone into Fulbright programs or to Fulbright-style programs. Through the Fulbright process, the world could have looked around, seen what it wanted and did not want, and then gone home to develop in accordance with its own local cultural necessities and imperatives.

As I look back, I see many things, most of them beginning with my Fulbright year. I see how Vienna warned me and prepared me for a time we did not know was coming and how it prophesied the tragic clouds that would darken my own positivist land—the disaster of Vietnam, the cultural breakdown of our families and cities, the things we had always thought "could not happen here." I see too that it warned me about a renegade heresy of cultural exchange, the notorious "multiculturalism" in the U.S., posing new problems for us as the U.S. has broken away from its historic idea of the melting pot into a nation of indigestible ethnic groups. Perhaps the next step should be Fulbright exchanges between blacks and whites, Jews and Muslims, Hispanics and Anglos, right here inside the U.S.

What a changed world! Hungary, which seemed then so tragic and hopeless, today leads Eastern Europe towards freedom and free enterprise. Development soars in the Pacific Rim countries of Asia; and other cultures race ahead of us, showing us clearly now that it is not race or creed or national origin that determine development but culture! And knowing that—knowing it empirically for the first time in modern history—is a boon to mankind; it proves the falsehood of racism, of ethnic and religious hatred, and instead it invites us to join in the search for growth and development by adopting the cultural qualities such growth demands. In the same light, I see another pressing new need: for scores and hundreds of Fulbright relationships between the former Soviet Union and the West.

And as I think of these contemporary imperatives, now and then my eyes mist over and I see an idealistic but realistic young American walking into the grey Vienna of 1956 and beginning to understand.

Thousands of Fulbrighters from the earlier years have already left us. Their stories remain to be told. One such case is that of Lois Roth (1931-86), about whom we are fortunate to have unusual documentation, a trove of letters and papers remaining after her death. This essay analyzes the meaning of her Fulbright experience through its revealing aftermath, a career-change to educational and cultural diplomacy—first, in a decade with the American Scandinavian Foundation, then in two decades with USIA. Focusing on the first year of her first assignment as Assistant Cultural Attaché in Tehran, this memoir does more than merely tell her story; it shows the kind of work which must be done before historians can begin to put together the mosaic, the thousands of individual experiences which some day may define what the Fulbright Era meant in this century.

11

FROM FULBRIGHT TO CULTURAL DIPLOMACY: A MEMOIR OF LOIS ROTH

Richard T. Arndt

Lois Roth spent a Fulbright year in Sweden in the mid-fifties, at Uppsala University, in sociology. It transformed her life. I knew her well, as a colleague in Tehran and as my wife from 1973 until her death in January 1986.

Before her Swedish experience, as she told it, she had drifted. Born to comfortable New York parents, she imbibed at New York's Fieldston School the special set of humanist internationalist values of the school's sponsor, the Ethical Culture Society. She tried Elmira College but after two years returned to New York, to major in sociology at Barnard College. After a desultory experiment with marriage, she returned in the mid-fifties to graduate studies at Columbia's famous Department of Sociology, stocked with the most important names in American social science, while working in Columbia's undergraduate student activities office. Columbia, under the leadership in the thirties of Nicholas Murray Butler and with major figures like James T. Shotwell, G. Rexford Tugwell and Philip Mosely on the faculty, had stood since the twenties as a major force in shaping the liberal internationalist Ecumene, in Frank Ninkovich's word.   The great university on Morningside Heights intensified her internationalization.

A beloved Swedish-American second mother and an inspiring Columbia teacher raised her awareness of the social experiments that Sweden had already launched.   She set herself to learning the language and applied for a Fulbright grant.   In the fall of 1956 she set off for Uppsala.

We have little documentary access to the events of the year in Uppsala. Lois Roth's story instead must be read in the actions of the decades that followed.   Returning from Uppsala with a facility in Swedish which would amaze Swedes to the end of her life, she found work with the American Scandinavian Foundation in New York.   It was a perfect fit—before she left, she would be special assistant to three successive Presidents.   She plunged into a new career in an ideal place to develop her gifts and her Fulbright-focused need for a life of international service.   She had discovered an activist way of involving herself in international understanding, in carrying out her need to share what she had learned.

At ASF, she did everything: wrote book reviews for the quarterly publication, translated (including the first of the Martin Beck detective stories for Pantheon Press), typed, made and served coffee, lectured around the U.S., escorted college summer groups to Scandinavia, showed prominent Scandinavian visitors around New York, organized exhibits, helped run a fellowship program, answered research questions, nurtured board-members and chairmen, engineered ASF dinners and social events, and gave wise counsel to her bosses.   Her fondest memory: escorting Halldór Laxness, Icelandic Nobel Prize-winning novelist, to a performance of "West Side Story" and watching him discover America, through his tears, via Leonard Bernstein's poignant re-telling of the Romeo and Juliet legend.

In the late fifties and early sixties, she helped expand the ASF portfolio to include Finland, convincing the Ford Foundation to sponsor forty prominent Finns, over a five-year period, for visits to the U.S. of up to six months.   She did little else during that period, serving as program designer and escort for most of them.   In the early sixties, she arrived in Finland for a visit on the same day as Vice-President Lyndon B. Johnson. She delighted in showing the front page of the Helsinki newspaper, with her picture "above the fold," twice the size of Johnson's on the lower half of the page.

By the end of the fifties, she had already begun to worry about staying with ASF too long.   In the fall of 1961, enthused by the Kennedy campaign and by the appointment of Edward R. Murrow as Director of USIA, she filed an application for lateral entry into USIA.   Her file languished: women were not a high-priority recruitment issue for USIA then—the rules of the day, mired in the past, still stipulated that only single women would be accepted; on the day of her marriage, a woman officer was required to resign. In 1961 there was expansive recruiting, but of men only (I was accepted at precisely the same time). In the two groups which shared training sessions in the summer of 1962, about forty people in all, there was one woman—a political appointee who herself would be the principal instrument for raising USIA's understanding of the importance of women.

By the fall of 1966 change had begun and single women were in demand. The Near East division of USIA, looking for someone to send to Tehran, reactivated her file; she reported to Washington for training in January 1967, arriving in Tehran on March 16 to serve as Assistant Cultural Attaché. I was the Cultural Attaché she assisted.

Among other discoveries, she found herself from the first day on the other side of the Fulbright desk, an administrator of the Program and all that went with it in those years of vigor. Her energy was already legendary and it explains why the records of her first year in Tehran are copious: a dutiful daughter had left home. She began writing regular letters to her parents, with carbon copies to a small group of friends. In this prehistoric venture in desk-top publishing, she set out to make her life in Tehran as accessible and as vivid as she could, writing at least once a week for the next five years. Some of the remarkably lively letters run to ten pages or more.

This memoir focuses on that first year in Tehran. The new experiences of an apprentice cultural diplomat, the excitement of daily discovery, her obvious enchantment at the change in landscape, her new angle of vision regarding the Fulbright Program, and her attempt to describe all this meaningfully to her parents and friends are writ throughout these letters. In her five years and four months in Tehran, she would hold three jobs, first as Assistant then as Deputy Cultural Attaché and finally as Director of the mammoth Iran America Society (IAS), which taught English to 5000 Iranians daily, ran Tehran University's only Student Center, had five separate building complexes in Tehran, Isfahan, and Shiraz, with numerous restaurants, three theatres, art galleries, a small library and an impressive range of activities, all funded except for four USIS salaries by income from English teaching.

Her career would take her to the top of USIA's educational and cultural affairs division. Cultural and educational diplomacy to her was a total mission; she took to it as though she had been doing it all her life—in fact, since Uppsala she had. A USIA VIP visiting in 1969 asked her, as he asked all younger officers, how she saw her future with the agency. Her answer was unique in his experience: she saw her work "in terms of growth"—so long as it provided a learning context, she asked no more.

Fulbright was central in her mind. From the moment of her return to New York, but more visibly in Tehran, hardly a day passed without her making some kind of contribution to the direct and indirect goals of the Fulbright process. In the fall of 1968 she would spend two months as Acting Executive Director of the Fulbright Commission during a change of directors.

She was straightforward about her intent: to repay her debt. She was one of the legion of first-generation Fulbrighters who returned to the U.S. with a sacred flame, developed institutional ties, and helped turn their institutions in the directions that their Fulbright experiences had shown them. Now she was part of the program itself.

In Tehran, Fulbright and its products were all around her. As she notes, the Program in Iran in 1967-68 was already sizable for a country of 26 million. When in 1967 the Six Day War brought a group of refugee Fulbrighters from neighboring countries to Iran, the American side of the program more than doubled—"Thank goodness we have an efficient, free-standing and more or less well-staffed Fulbright Commission," she wrote (6/67).

The Iranian side of the program was less impressive. Before she went to Tehran, a short-sighted political decision had been reached in Washington, flowing from Congressional concerns about too many Iranian students in the U.S. (there were 20,000 then as compared to 50,000 now) and their tendency to overstay—many extended back to the Mossadeq years of the early fifties and were, in effect, unacknowledged refugees. During her time in Tehran, this decision would be cautiously reversed and a thin trickle of Iranian pre-doctoral students connected with Fulbright projects would begin to flow to the U.S.

The opening of her first letter home sets the tone for what follows: (3/21/67) "Eid-e-shoma mobarak! Happy New Year—in Iran today is the day! After a first evening or two of homesickness, I am well. Tehran is unbelievable. It is the beginning of Spring with forsythia, japonica quince and flowers everywhere. The mountains rise to 14,000 feet right outside my window. The entire country is shut down for a few days since the Persian New Year combines our Christmas, New Year, Easter and Spring all rolled into one. Everyone seems to work on an around-the-clock basis that combines work and social life. The Cultural Attaché (Cultural Affairs Officer, or CAO) is a Fulbright alumnus—he and his wife have only been here six months; they have been fabulous to me . . . . I do not yet know the eight Iranian staff in the Cultural Section and it will take time. The office is well located in the central northern part of the city—a big seven-story building with our own print shop, photographer and so forth. The Library is on the ground floor . . . . I saw a small house the first day I was here, my predecessor's . . . , within walking distance of the Fulbright Commission, the office, the university and the CAO's house."

Ten days later: (3/31/67) "In the lobby of the Sina Hotel, waiting for the Georgia State College Brass Ensemble, delayed by many hours in their flight from Afghanistan . . . . The hotel manager here studied architecture at the University of Colorado and is very solicitous—he brings me tea . . . . By the way, if you think that today's waiting is a waste of the taxpayers' money, I remind you that it is Friday, our day off."

A week later: (4/6/67) "The Georgia Brass: one concert, one reception, one party for them every day. Visiting Fulbright Professor Harold Deutsch, Chairman of History at the University of Minnesota, here for five days. I am in the office, it is Friday and we are closed. Spent the morning at the TV station with the Brass Ensemble. The CAO picks me up for a concert at 4 PM. I've heard three already, including one at the Shah's Youth Palace last night . . . what a propaganda place that is!!"

She was off and running. The early letters capture her excitement and as well a commitment that "combines work and social life." Fulbrighters, especially unfocused graduate students like her, are often involved in a total learning situation; every encounter represents growth, because language-learning is central to the agenda. The values she had discovered in herself during her Uppsala year included the joy of work well done, even work around the clock; at ASF she had already discovered the pride of total commitment. The adult educator she was knew that life and work flow together happily where continual learning is involved. She also knew that in a strange airport where no one speaks English a friendly face is a special human gift—"I also went to the airport three times (the airport is impossible so we meet and bid farewell to everyone)."

The USIS office made its demands, but most work was done outside. Within the first month she had agreed to take a semi-weekly student discussion group at the Tehran University Student Center ("Imagine, [the Iran-America Society] runs a student center, the only one, for the University of Tehran, right across the street from the University!"). In 1968 she agreed to handle a tiny individual class in English for the francophone Dean of the Faculty of Law and three hand-picked potential U.S. graduate students, in support of a pending Fulbright project in legal education and research. Colleagues recall her as tireless—a letter reporting on the visit of the Los Angeles Symphony tells of heroics: no sleep for fifty hours, then four hours of sleep before dragging out of bed to greet a group of returning exchange grantees at the airport.

Yet she insisted on retreating regularly from frantic activism, stepping back to see what was happening. She turned the monthly Cultural Section report to Washington, despite evidence it was not leaving USIS Tehran, into a way of taking stock. And she welcomed visits like this one: (7/22/67) "A consultant to the new Assistant Secretary of State for Educational and Cultural Affairs Charles Frankel is out here with family for a month, helping us think about what we are doing, here and in the whole Northern Tier: Jay and Myriam Hurewitz, a Columbia Middle East specialist and political scientist, a very interesting and thought-provoking guy."

Her perceptions of Iran's politics sharpened quickly and she learned her lessons well. When 1978 came, she would be surprised only by the timing of the Shah's collapse and the improbable alliance of forces which produced it, not by the collapse itself. Her Jewish background sharpened her insights into the politics of the Middle East; she was surprised and impressed when she got beyond the simpler views of her New York days; she saw, for example, the wisdom of cooperation between Iran and Israel: (4/28/67) "Last night I thought I might get home but got an invitation for dinner with Abram Sachar, President of Brandeis, a dear man here looking into ties between Brandeis and Tehran University, in a Muslim country which quietly gets along with Israel." Israeli friends worked in an agricultural development project in nearby Ghazvin and another was attached to Israel's discreet embassy, around the corner from her office. More exciting, a glimpsed chance for cooperation between the U.S. and the USSR during the Six Day War in 1967. All this was part of her early apprehension of the complexity of contemporary political process on the international level, a process into which educational exchanges fed.

The Six Day War was a dramatic interlude: (6/5/67) "Right now, the world seems to be going totally crazy. They are monitoring the AP wire service reports upstairs and it is all very confusing. No one knows whether the Arabs or the Israelis fired the first shots. Meanwhile we hear rumors: Haifa in flames, Jerusalem pounded, Cairo bombed, with varying reports as to damage and number of planes down. Meanwhile the Tehran papers say everyone loves the Shah in Germany, but the Paris Tribune, confiscated here this week, said there were riots among Iranian students in Berlin." And: (6/11/67) "It is a beautiful and warm Sunday afternoon. I am on standby for duty at the airport, the embassy or wherever—we are expecting evacuees from Jordan this afternoon and everything is being kept hush-hush, to keep some hothead from taking potshots at the planes. We are expecting about a thousand today. The contingent from Baghdad arrived yesterday and the day before in two car-caravans, and they are pretty well settled in hotels throughout the city . . . . I've said I would take four people right away, and if they can supply the beds I will increase it to eight. The icebox is full . . . . Drove to Isfahan on June 6. It was eerie to be driving across that desolate landscape, cut off from news, knowing that a war was going on nearby. Iran is all business as usual: they hate Nasser here, and things are stable enough so that, even with the Shah away, there is little chance of trouble from the Left or the Right . . . . Pretty cute of the U.S. and the USSR to get together on this one. Maybe that is a good sign for the long run."

A strong developmental cast to her thinking flows primarily from the educator's stance but also from the Iranian imperatives of the sixties. She may have picked up some of this in Sweden, but surely she could not miss it in an Iran obsessed with its own growth. Rather than take refuge in high principles about the Fulbright Program's purpose of mutual understanding, or about its focus on academic exchange not training (in USIA rhetoric, "development" was AID's business), she sought to channel the energy in Iran's concerns.

She helped gear the entire USIS and Fulbright program to a simple goal—meeting Iran's perceived needs—from that would grow the flowers of mutual understanding. She believed totally in binationalism: one does not do exchanges *to* people but *with* them, with their full consent and their contribution in program design. The Fulbright Program, from the administrator's viewpoint, was an investment in people and a human process; she looked for sectors of importance in Iran, then for Iranians and Americans who could make a difference.

Library Science, for example, was a project which became a life interest: (6/11/67) "Last night a reception given by the Iran Library Association, fourteen members, many of them Fulbright returnees, lured together by the USIS Librarian; they have all been trained by Fulbright lecturers in Library Science (another Fulbright project). It was held at the new Faculty of Education at the University, the most exciting university group in town, headed by Fulbrighter Dean Manouchehr Afzal (also a Fulbright project). Their library actually has open stacks, almost unheard-of here. It was encouraging to see, to remind me that we *can* do something useful here." Then, nine months later: (3/27/68) "Yesterday a cocktail business meeting at my house with our American Fulbright professor of library science and the CAO, to talk about an Iranian idea to start a major documentation center here, with computer links to the U.S. and Europe."

Most of the Fulbright Commission's projects focused on the vital and central Tehran University. (1/19/67) "Our Fulbright musicologist from Illinois, Alexander Ringer, is back with us. Two other unusual men on the way: an engineering curriculum specialist and a specialist in international legal research and education. All are working on curriculum reform at the University—a subtle assignment. The legal opening in particular could reach far out into this society, in ways that are unpredictable, if we can structure a project and get Fulbright to fund it." (2/2/68) "Our engineering visitor is as different as he is interesting.   Chairman of Mechanical Engineering at Brown, a Polish refugee, still very European and elegant, the remarkable Joseph Kestin is out here for eight full weeks to consult and advise on curriculum reform at the Faculty of Engineering, very French- and German-oriented—he is the perfect man to bridge the gap between the U.S. and—not Iran but Europe! I am learning in depth about the problems of Tehran University." (3/27-68) "As is the way with my life, I had a very small working dinner: the American-educated, newly returned Chancellor of the major technical university here, our expert in engineering curriculum, and the CAO—we got right down to technical manpower training problems. Dr. Kestin was to leave two days later and we needed feedback to help shape program decisions. The talk was so interesting that dinner only broke up well after midnight, when we had to go once more to the airport."

Another Fulbright project: Social Work Education. She learned quickly to look forward to the annual fall visit of Henry Ollendorff, founder of the Cleveland program for youth leaders and social workers. And she worked closely with the remarkable Sattareh Farman-Farmaian, directress of Tehran's School of Social Work: (5/6/67) "On Monday I was out to the airport again, this time to meet the Dean of the School of Social Work at UCLA: program for him at the new and exciting but terribly problem-ridden Tehran School of Social Work—we place Fulbright lecturers there every year. At the end of the day, I went to the Fulbright House to learn how to fulfill my role as Assistant Treasurer of the binational US-Iran Commission, part of my job—I have been bonded up to $25,000."

The Fulbright Commission, in her first two years, was a major focus of her life: (5/13/67) "Wednesday ended with a delightful evening at Fulbright House, a lecture on different approaches to foreign policy, buffet dinner in their garden . . . . Escorting a USIA VIP to nearby Lake Karaj for relaxation, on the way back we stopped at the Agricultural College and had tea with the Fulbright-returnee Dean of the School of Forestry: water, trees, plants, flowers, a real oasis in the desert."

Development for her, like education, was a process. Educational and cultural exchanges, necessarily a two-way street, had an important time dimension: because societies are in constant change, an idea which is foolish one year may make sense later; on the other hand an investment may produce something different and even better than planned. Above all she knew that few educational investments pay off in less than a dozen years. She often referred to her work as planting trees, not marigolds.

Her years at ASF, worrying about where the funding would come from, gave her a business-oriented approach to Fulbright investments. She quickly learned to appreciate the project-approach of the Commission, focusing various resources on a single field and trying to build a small and lasting dimension into the country, one that might withstand the reactive pressures that traditional societies invariably devise to retard new ways of doing things. The alternative to project focus, what she called a "scatter-gun approach," was unthinkable.

Sociology had taught her to look under the surface: Sweden and Finland had been her first intimate case-studies in depth, Iran was her next. She knew where the pulse of a society could be touched and she used that knowledge; she stressed the use of Fulbright as an "infrastructural" investment, working with those elements, scarcely visible below the surface of a society, upon which over time more visible structures might be built. Beyond the Commission's projects in library development, social work education, public administration and local government, and education as a discipline, she was dogged in exploring and opening other fields: legal education and research; university administration, university curriculum development and manpower planning; engineering education; Iranian Studies for Americans and American Studies for Iran; university-level humanities, specifically music and art.

Sweden had shaped her social awareness. She saw politics as the central factor in human life. Iran, for all its apparent progress and promise, had buried various important questions deep below the surface; hiding these critical questions was for her a form of political dishonesty which could not be maintained in the long run. She believed Americans had a responsibility to provide gentle and diplomatic but persistent reminders about the nature of political process in a functioning democracy; she often argued that the study of politics, for example, did not necessarily lead to chaos or treason, as Iranian leadership tended to fear. The quasi-official ban on the teaching of political science and government was an ostrich tactic: for her, sound government depended on knowing what was going on, hence the social sciences in a university framework and their research capacities should be turned to that end. In the same context, she maintained highly discreet relations with certain opposition figures, in one case serving as mail-box for a correspondence between an important writer and her American writer-mentor.

The Six Day refugee scholars had included a number of social science researchers, an uncomfortable presence for Iran's establishment, which resisted by stonewalling requests for research permits. The need for some kind of concerted action by the academic community, supported by the Embassy, was clear. (11/67) "Profesor Charles Adams of McGill University is trying to arrange for a Tehran 'research arm' of his university. Meanwhile the CAO is in New York and elsewhere trying to convince various Iran scholars that the formation of an American Institute of Iranian Studies with Fulbright assistance is a high priority, if only to help coordinate this kind of activity. If it does not begin soon and start handling some of these projects, it will be a shame."

(4/14/67) "Next, Saul K. Padover traveling under Fulbright auspices. A great deal of thinking and planning has gone into Padover's visit . . . how to use him most effectively for 'program purposes' here in Iran, where political science makes people nervous? I am learning more and more what a hotbed of intrigue and politics this country is, not unusual in this world of ours. I am doing my best to keep out of it." (4/21/67) "A three-day colloquium planned for Saul jointly with the Iran America Society (IAS) and the Fulbright Commission, focusing on the American constitutional experience—not a subject much talked about in this allegedly constitutional monarchy." (4/28/67) "Saul Padover, one of the really great human beings and scholars I have ever known. Colloquium on Innovation in a Dynamic Society. What a guy! The first lecture and dinner were held at the Fulbright House. The second and lunch at the CAO's house. And the third with dinner at the IAS. Things like this are not usually done in Iran and we were not sure it would work—but it did! About forty or fifty high-level academicians and government people showed up for each lecture. I think we really made a dent, if only through the force of Saul's great humanism. Needless to say, constitutionalism is a sensitive subject."

Her belief in the American democratic experience, especially in constitutionalism, shines through her admiration for Padover; with this went her faith in the American Supreme Court hence in American legal systems, common law and due process, as close to a deep religious conviction as anything in her life. Yet she believed that the U.S. experience could never be a model for Iran or any other nation. Careful study of the U.S. experience could do no more than help define the options which faced nations at similar critical points of conflict. Long before U.S. rhetoric boasted of projecting American democratic values, she was doing it—quietly and effectively.

"Democracy requires democrats, and democrats can only be educated over time," she would say when Americans complained about the failures of Iranian politics. Comparing a French-educated university Chancellor with a Professor of Medicine who had done his undergraduate work in the U.S., she coined what we used to call Roth's Law: the understanding of democracy in Iran is directly proportional to the years spent in the U.S. prior to age 20. Of a French-trained elite member, she once said, in a kind but sad tone, "Poor man, he never had the benefits of a democratic education." At the micro-level, she hated the pervasive nepotism of the Iranian system and believed that merit systems and peer review were processes which had to be implanted, by hard bargaining if necessary: (11/14/67) "We got a free grant for the World Youth Forum, the old Herald Tribune Forum, and were informed that the Ministry of Education was the proper channel. Yesterday they called to say they had *one* candidate. I went down to see them with our trusty Iranian advisor and told them, like Dr. Johnson, 'It just won't do.' We would rather lose the grant than budge on the point of our having a choice; it may not exactly amount to a merit system, but we are trying to combat the easy nepotism which is standard here." She won her point with the Ministry.

She was no cultural imperialist; she understood that some things, e.g., national literacy and the preservation of the cultural heritage on which a nation's identity rests, are better handled on a multilateral basis than by a single nation, especially one which is already far too important in that country's self-image. She reports dining with people, including "a nice guy and his wife—he works for UNESCO on the literacy campaign here, on which we pin high hopes—better *they* do it than the U.S."

She followed one project, in local government, through her five years in Tehran. (Labor Day, 1967) "Last Saturday I gave a formal lunch for ten: five shy young Iranian District Governors we are sending on the International Visitor Program on a sixty-day visit to the U.S., plus five Embassy-AID-USIS types. This is the beginning of an important project in local (and self-) government, designed to show young administrators how much people can do for themselves with proper motivation, attitudes and backing." Then, the return: (11/14/67) "After the Los Angeles Philharmonic madness and the CAO's departure for the U.S. with five francophone Tehran University Deans, dragged myself out of bed to meet the young District Governors, back from the U.S. You remember how timid and unassuming they were when they left? Well, they are great, all jabbering away in English. The Deputy Chief of Mission will do a luncheon next week. Marvelous boys (boyish, even in their late twenties), full of idealism and with an apparently deep understanding of what they saw in the U.S. All are said to be in line for early promotion." She kept in touch with those first five "boys" until she left Iran in 1972. I know no one who knows where they are today.

First for her came the human factor: what made Saul Padover great in her eyes was his humanism more than his scholarship, his humanity more than his ideology; and her local government "boys" were first of all wonderful people. She knew that the first adjective that came to the Iranian mind about a person they admired was "sincere." In a context laced with cynicism, her kind of sincerity worked in the long run.

She had a special faith in the American role, in the capacity of sensitive Americans to help others see themselves more clearly, through our national pluralist instincts. A visual person, she had also learned how to see beauty in places which a society like Iran's overlooked. She knew why an exhibit of Iranian naive painting might contribute to Iran's search for its own identity, at the same time reminding them that Americans cared for something important in Iran—as she wrote of Fulbright musicologist Alex Ringer, "He ties Persian music into the history of Western music and helps us make an important point: that the U.S. cares about more in Iran than its oil." America's peculiar attributes, summed up in the very idea of pluralism, meant it had the ability and therefore the responsibility to serve as a touchstone for others, to help them spin the threads that could be woven into a sense of national identity. (10/3/67) "Major event: a stunning big exhibit of 'Coffee House Paintings' at the IAS, truly marvelous stuff. This is my predecessor Barbara Spring's parting gift to a country she loves: a marvelous way to show, through American eyes, the colossal beauty in Iran that resides in seemingly ordinary things—like these naive paintings, done by itinerant artists, which decorate the humble coffee shops along the Iranian roads."

Perhaps at the center lay tolerance, seeing difference in other societies as a rich possibility rather than a threat. She avoided comparing things to the way they are in the U.S. and pitting nations or cultures against each other. In a moment of discouragement she compares Iran unfavorably with her beloved Scandinavia: (7/20/67) "With my Persian Fulbright friends and their three-year-old boy, [to the Caspian]. After return, latent reaction, a bad mood, maybe just plain homesickness. I guess, when all is said and done, I don't really have the temperament for Iranian culture. You have to wade through ten pounds of garbage before you get down to essentials—if you ever do. There is a small elite of rich, Western-educated sophisticates that you can talk to, but it is so small and smug. I've been homesick for Scandinavia, the freshness, the honesty, the healthiness of it." But it passes quickly: in a letter two days later she has bounced back.

She was in fact remarkably aware of and resistant to cultural relativism. Her balance-wheel, fine-tuned in Scandinavia, ran true; she knew how to understand without necessarily agreeing or approving; she also knew that picking quarrels or scoring debating points was no way to help people learn, let alone influence or persuade them. Tolerance may have come to her from Fieldston, understanding a society in its own terms from sociology. To these, she added patience, energy and a fundamental wisdom about people based on her concern for them. These were her Fulbright-reinforced virtues.

Seeing things from the educator's bias, she was calmly aware of the conflicts built into her role as a USIS officer, employed by a PR- oriented agency. Her university mindset from Columbia and Old World Uppsala remained. Indeed, it would only be reinforced: she believed that the best way to tell America's story was to involve good people in deep, meaningful, helpful, useful and critical *learning* experiences of the other country, to focus on process, and to let the exchangee's own desires and needs determine the fundamental purposes of the visit. Exchanges done in this spirit meant understanding would happen by itself in the longer term. She was biased towards universities: universities were the site of the most effective and focused learning of this kind. She believed that, in times of peace, propaganda is pointless and, more specifically, she knew that the Fulbright Program would be destroyed if it were ever perceived, either by its administrators or its products, as propaganda. She would always believe that the best propaganda, at least in a climate of peace, flows from its absence.

The Iranian Revolution of 1978 and its aftermath, six years after her departure—she was then in Paris and surrounded by elements of the Iranian diaspora—were difficult for her. The fall of the Shah came sooner than she expected; she was saddened, not surprised. She never entirely shook off a tendency to a personal sense of failure. From the start she found ways of expressing her compassion, friendship and support: hundreds of Iranians came through our homes in Rome, Paris and Washington. To all she gave warmth, concern and love. To a special few, digging into her trove of beloved Persian treasures, she would give back one of the beautiful objects Iran had given her.

If ever there was a life deeply and totally pledged to the Fulbright ideal, it was the last three decades in the rich life of Lois Roth. And all that began at Uppsala. She knew the Senator well, but she was never able to tell him so. That is why I have tried.

Professor Bonazzi, by his own taxonomy a Second Generation Italian historian of the U.S., teaches at the University of Bologna. In this essay he writes a virtual biography of the postwar Italian intellectual class. Rather than content himself with describing some of the problems encountered by young historians trying to change the fundamental structure of the Italian university and the mindset left by twenty-odd years of Fascist re-education, he gives us a deeply personal statement of the reasons for European resistance to the study of the U.S. and for the unintended ironic counter-productiveness of Cold War rhetoric, affecting even the carefully-insulated Fulbright Program. He gives as well an insight into the broader definition of "Americanization" which helps explain much European ambivalence towards the U.S.

12

THE BEGINNINGS OF
AMERICAN HISTORY IN ITALY

Tiziano Bonazzi

It is September 1991 as I write this, and I feel like a man deprived of his past. Less than a month ago, the abortive coup in Moscow closed the era of the Cold War, the giant confrontation between superpowers that has marked half a century of world history—and my life.

My memories begin with war—the World War II bombings vaguely remembered, the images of a half-destroyed, poverty-stricken and slowly recovering Italy, the moral split between Fascism and anti-Fascism, and the glories of the Resistance, legends I absorbed from my family.

In those years, the late forties and early fifties, everyone I knew shared the values of democracy and anti-Fascism that underlay republican Italy. But what those values were, what they meant was a matter of violent debate. I was caught up as a teenager in the cross-fire of Communist and anti-Communist, pro- and anti-American ideologies. They were days of ideological integrity, of political love and hate. Families, my own included, divided over these issues.

149

The world stabilized into two wary but non-warring camps. The Cuban missile crisis in 1962 gave us a last shudder, but when that crisis was over domestic problems like the Italian economic boom and changing life-styles came to the fore. The East-West confrontation became a given more than a threat, a general frame of reference for everything that happened more than an issue. In the Parliament, Christian Democrats and Communists waved bloody shirts at each other. But they knew the rules: one side was in charge of governing, with no serious possibility of defeat, the other was a legitimate and permanent opposition.

Then came 1968 and the student revolt. The movements were strongly anti-American but not pro-Soviet. Fiercely ideological, the various revolutionary groupings mixed libertarian sentiments with Leninist ideas. They failed, the more radical elements and the die-hards ending up in the tragic cul-de-sac of terrorism and the Red Brigades. The early eighties saw the final and utter defeat of these young revolutionaries. But Italian society by now had been transformed by libertarian ideals, women's and gay lib, the "greens," and a revolution in life-styles—all this grew from the turmoil of the previous decade. Many of us, a middle-aged generation by now, felt uneasy in the newly mobile and disorderly society that sprang from the ashes of a failed revolution. Our society had dispensed with both hard-core ideologies and stable values.

Thank God, the Big Two were still there. Their continuing combat was a monument to stability in a world of change, a reasonable framework within which to reenact the old games of love and hate—or was it a titillating mixture of the two? Today what shall I make of my Cold War and New Left memories?

At least the Americanist and the U.S. historian in me is—or should be—happy. More than once I have argued that the Cold War and its ideologies hampered the growth of U.S. history in Italy (1986). Catholics and Marxists, the two main divisions of the Italian intelligentsia, held in the fifties and sixties a Eurocentric vision of history. They saw the world position of the U.S. as the result of historical and political mechanisms that could best be understood from a European viewpoint. America's European origins made any separate inquiry into American history irrelevant: it was assumed that no real qualitative change had occurred on the other side of the Atlantic. American power was no more than a continuation of European history. The refusal to come to terms with American history enabled both Catholics and Marxists to harden their stereotypes of the U.S., myths that proved useful in their internal debates and fed into their respective ideologies. In the social sciences, after much hesitation, Italians absorbed ideas and methods from the U.S., but not American history.

We cannot, however, maintain that Italian culture was "unable" to open itself to American history. Cultures are complex and historically-rooted structures. They do not change according to abstract and rationalistic patterns. Deep American influence on post-war Italy and the accompanying process of "Americanization" have only recently been approached by scholars (D'Attore 1991, Paggi 1989, Vezzosi 1983). The meaning of Americanization is still unclear: it points to something real but not yet fully defined. True, in the fifties sociology was reshaped along American lines, in the sixties political science and organization studies responded to transatlantic influences, education had earlier been marked by the work of John Dewey, and American influence is clear in psychology. But none of this implies unbridled fascination with the U.S. nor a process of passive acculturation. Besides, the same thing was happening everywhere in the world in this last half century, in the social sciences a process of internationalization more than Americanization. It was a process in which the U.S. played a leading role but was by no means the only actor.

This brings us closer to what I believe was the general import of Americanization for Italy and for the rest of the world. It meant a grafting of American elements onto foreign cultures through an often ambivalent process in which three factors interacted: enthusiastic acceptance, "anti-American" responses, and misunderstanding about the real meaning of what was actually flowing from beyond the Atlantic. The end result, in Italy and elsewhere, has been "creolization," to use Umberto Eco's word (1984), the mixing of opposites to create new elements in the culture which contribute to change.

We know (Ventone 1991) that in the immediate post-war period anti-American reactions were strong not only among Communists and Socialists but also among Catholics, both Church and laity. Catholics and the Christian Democratic party, strong supporters of the alliance with the U.S. as a means of stopping Communism, still feared the Protestant and pluralist nation whose individualistic values and mass civilization endangered the communitarian traditions of the Italian people, the family, and the hierarchy of values steeped in Catholic ethics and theology.

Most political Catholics thus resisted the introduction of American lifestyles well into the sixties, when they had to find subtler and more modern ways to defend their approach to life and society because their previous positions were marred by obvious contradictions. They soon accepted the idea that economic reconstruction and prosperity in post-war Italy could only be based on a free-market economy. This idea was bouyed up by the political competition for popular consensus with the Communist Party; that competition in turn made it necessary to show that Western-style democracy meant a better

life. The economic development that actually followed in Italy brought about
the very social and cultural consequences that Catholics feared. Italian society
ended up modernized and Americanized, and many of the new society's
features displeased the same Catholics who had called for them.

Americanization did not mean that Italy became an ersatz U.S. No
American would ever recognize Cincinnati in Bologna or Bari. An American
knows that a good part of what Italians call "American" pop music is actually
British, and he would probably pay little attention to the distinctly Italian pop
music that in this country vies for popularity with "American" rock. The
Americanization of Italy reflects less the importation of U.S. goods—there are
few American cars on the Italian peninsula—than the acceptance of a pragmatic
and flexible set of values, a primacy of individual over group choices, an
erosion of ideologies, and a strong social mobility whose roots and structures
more than its actual contents can be traced to the U.S. Americanization has
not been a passive phenomenon marred by "anti-American" resistance but a
creative intermarriage, or better, by analogy with racial intermixtures, a
métissage. It has less to do with the real America than with the birth of an
international societal system organized around mass consumption and the new
communications, a system whose roots are mostly in the U.S. but whose
branches extend everywhere.

This does not mean that the U.S. played no active political role in the
process. The Americanization of Italy, as I watched it, cannot be understood
apart from U.S. economic and military policy, nor outside the context of an
alliance in which Italy plays the lesser role. America's dominant power and
Italian creative adaptation have concerted to bring the "American empire,"
such as it is, to this corner of the world. What matters is that the unique
American notion of "empire" left room for a two-way relationship with Europe
and for the creolization I have already noted.

In cultural relations, the U.S. as part of its Cold War effort developed
policy guidelines and instruments devoted to diffusing the American "dream."
American propaganda operations were guided by a single notion: the
superiority of American-style democracy and its no-nonsense, practical
approach to life. To us, it seemed a peculiar ideology, whose main premise
was that free and direct intercourse with American culture could not fail to
convince honest, rational aliens to accept and spread its main tenets.

This was the ideology of the Fulbright Program, at least as viewed from
the Italian peninsula. I am convinced that, apart from obvious political
considerations in picking the "right" grantees, this was the main rationale
behind the creation of the various Fulbright Commissions in Europe and
elsewhere. And I also believe that this has been the reason for the Fulbright

impact and success in countries like Italy. Italians reacted freely, in highly personal and often creatively negative ways, to their exposure to American life and culture. Returning, they took an active and sometimes crucial part iin the *métissage* of Italian culture and in its internationalization.

A quick glance at the Commission's alumni lists supports my point. There are leading figures like art historian Lionello Venturi, semiologist Umberto Eco, sociologists Franco Ferraroti, Luciano Cavalli, Alberto Izzo, Alberto Martinelli, Guido Martinotti, jurists like Giovanni Bognetti, Mauro Capelletti, Sabino Cassese, Gino Giugni, Antonio La Pergola, Federico Mancini, Guglielmo Negri, Stefano Rodota, political scientists Giovani Sartori, Gianfranco Pasquino, Pier Paulo Giglioli, Stefano Passigli, economists Siro Lombardini and Giorgio Basevi, demographer Massimo Livi Racci, historians Giorgio Spini, Alberto Aquarone, Carlo Cipolla, Carlo Ginzburg, Giuseppe Mammarella, historian-columnist Mauro Calamandrei, to name only a few—readers outside Italy will not recognize all of these names but it is enough to say that everyone is there.

And all this without mentioning American literature and its specialists, from Agostino Lombardo to Claudio Gorlier, Sergio Perosa, Biancamaria Tedeschini-Lalli, and Cristina Giorcelli. They bring me to American Studies and its position in post-war Italian culture.

By "American Studies" I do not mean what is meant in the U.S., an autonomous interdisciplinary field. That approach never took root in Italy because the higher education system, lacking the concept of colleges, has less flexibility than American universities. Italian students, after the baccalaureate at age 19, enroll directly in a Facoltà. These are organized along professional lines (Medicine, Engineering, Literature, Architecture, Dentistry, Political Science, etc.). Four to six years of study lead to the *Laurea*, long honored in Italy with the title of Doctor. Curricula rarely extend outside the boundaries of the Facoltà. This means that students of American history today study no literature, film, art and architecture, or popular culture. "Area Studies" or courses in "civilization" do not work in a system designed to produce excellence in a single disciplinary field.

American Studies, in the American style, was significant in the U.S. itself in the forties and fifties as an instrument of cultural analysis, and American cultural diplomacy made use of it in other countries with success. Though it could not work in Italy, this did not hinder the spread of American cultural influence along more Italian lines, further proof of the bi-directional nature of processes of this kind and perhaps of the flexibility of the Fulbright approach.

In post-war Italy, my Italy, America's literature blossomed first, following the path laid out by anti-Fascist writers and intellectuals like Cesare Pavese,

Elio Vittorini and Giaime Pintor who discovered in the thirties the "democratic newness" of American writers and used them in their fight against official Fascist culture (Lombardo 1981). In the fifties American literature as an academic discipline was recognized in many universities. Meanwhile the translation of American novels proliferated and many of them became best-sellers (Gorlier 1981). My generation grew up reading classic writers like Melville, Poe and Mark Twain and contemporaries like Hemingway, Steinbeck, Faulkner, Fitzgerald, Dos Passos, Edgar Lee Masters, and William Saroyan, all in Italian. In 1954 an important translation appeared: Matthiessen's *American Renaissance*.

The teaching of American literature and the translation of its writers are two sides of the same coin. Literary scholars rapidly refined their critical tools and broke away from the fascination with the myth of the "new democratic nation, savage and free" that served so well in the thirties and forties. Guido Piovene, in his important and popular *De America* (1954), pointed out that it was necessary and possible to understand America in its own terms and to explain the "otherness" of American civilization vis à vis Europe by making use of the tools of science instead of the metaphors of myth. Still, myth was the only available approach to America for the general reading public and for the man on the street awash in American movies.

It is all too easy to say that America as myth prevailed over America as fact, that literature did not help understand America objectively, the efforts of critics and intellectuals notwithstanding. Cultures after all are strongly centered on themselves and, while change may in fact be spurred by actual contacts with outside realities, the mechanisms are infra-cultural in nature. Both scholars and the general public reacted creatively, according to their cultural needs and their instruments, to what they encountered—a few books in translation stripped of context, or a sophisticated and integrated view of American literature as part of American civilization. At both levels, literature made a difference, becoming an integral part of the cultural horizons of the people concerned and contributing to the dynamics of Italian cultural change. The crucial differences between the scholar's understanding of America and that of the man on the street cannot be separated as one separates myth from science. Both contributed, in different but related ways, to the complex process of Americanization. What matters more is the ready acceptance and even enthusiasm in Italy for American literature, which answered a deeply felt need for change at various levels of Italian culture.

Historical study of the U.S. in Italy has an altogether different itinerary. Historiography—the critical awareness of how history is done and hows its biases operate—is deeply ingrained in Italian skepticism. In the post-war period, history still dominated the social sciences because of the historicist teaching of the idealist philosopher Benedetto Croce, the single most important influence on Italian intellect in this half-century. For Croce, as well as for both Catholic and Marxist historians, history meant Europe. Croce's Liberty, the Catholics' Church, and the Marxists' Capitalist and Socialist Revolutions were all distinctly European, spreading from there to other continents and cultures. If now the dominant position of the U.S. in international affairs made it mandatory to know that country better than before, it was contemporary America, not its history, that demanded attention. In the final analysis, the glaring differences between Europe and America could be explained as a consequence of the lead taken by modern America in the main processes of the contemporary world—capitalism, democracy, secularization. The roots led back to Europe.

The rapid development of the social sciences during the fifties and the concurrent American influence (Sani 1983) gradually reduced the influence of historicism and of history in Italy. Paradoxically, it also made U.S. history less appealing to historians. Present-minded and anti-historicist, the American social sciences stressed a problem-solving, analytical and quantitative approach to short- and middle-range phenomena, an approach that ran counter to historical research, reinforcing the idea of the U.S. as a nation with no past. There were contradictions in the Italian perception of the social sciences, as well as in the disciplines' view of themselves, but such clashing insights fed the vision of the U.S. as a land of change and flux, a land of the future. Under these conditions, no treatment of America had to deal with the American past. It needed to relate instead to a model—positive or negative, to be followed or fought—for the future of mankind.

Interest in U.S. history was superficial. Neither the ideological debate nor the scientific-scholarly-intellectual debate had much use for it. We have to search carefully among the members of a minor sector of Italian intellect, the so-called *laici* or intellectuals of the laity, to find genuine interest in U.S. history during the fifties and sixties. Heirs to the secular tradition of classical European liberalism and somewhat less to reformist socialism, young lay intellectuals were seized with the difficulties of implementing and defending the republican Constitution of 1948 against Communist ideology, catholic populism, and the more general resistance to modernization. These lay intellectuals began by seeing constitutionalism, pluralism, the separation of church and state, and the protection of individual rights as essential ingredients of modern democracy and they soon turned to American political and constitutional history, and to the American Revolution as well, for examples that might help explain the mechanisms of liberal democratic politics and political institutions. These were my masters.

U.S. history then came on the scene not as the result of outside pressures, such as the minor and hotly contested influence of U.S. propaganda's historical materials. It happened instead when an active component of Italian culture needed comparative evidence to support its views. Untrained as Americanists and woefully short of resources—Italian libraries held almost no books on the U.S. and its history—the lay intellectuals were able to pinpoint those features of American history that interested them and to write about them. Aldo Garosci's analysis of the political theory of the Federalist Papers (1954) and Alberto Aquarone's comparative study of the Philadelphia Convention and the French National Assembly of 1789-91 were among the fruits of this early season, along with the translation of the Federalist Papers (1955) and the publication of two volumes of basic documents on the birth of the U.S. (Aquarone et al. 1961).

To Nicola Matteucci, now a leading figure in political theory, we owe the effective weaving together of European and American intellectual and constitutional history under the concept of Western Constitutionalism. Strongly influenced by legal scholars like Edwin Corwin and by legal historians like Charles McIlwain, whom he translated, Matteucci made Constitutionalism the central feature of the distinctly Western attempt, born in the Middle Ages and culminating in the U.S. Constitution and in the principle of judicial review, to limit political power by legal means (Matteucci 1965, 1976). Through his work based in my native Bologna, American history found a way to become an integral part of scholarship within the Italian cultural tradition. Matteucci and the *laici,* who began their work on the U.S. in the fifties and sixties, reveal as well the difficulty our historiography had in coping with the "otherness" of any non-European culture.

Outside the *laici*, there was little work done on American history, with the solitary exception of the Florentine Giorgio Spini. Spini was well-known as a scholar of modern European history and the Reformation. His deep interest in American history led him to support studies in this field well into the eighties. A Protestant and a Socialist, Spini's convictions led him to see U.S. history as a fertile ground for inquiry on topics like religious freedom and personal liberty; meanwhile his keen understanding of American radical currents made him one of the first Italians to understand the American New Left. We owe him one of the most important early Italian works on American history, his *Autobiografía della giovane America* (1969), an investigation of the contribution of colonial historiography to shaping political and religious values and an American national identity.

The fifties and early sixties also saw the first spate of Italian translations of U.S. historians. Largely under the influence of the intellectuals I have noted, often backed by vigorous financial support from USIS, publishers like Comunità, Il Mulino, Opere Nuove and Neri Pozza translated U.S. historians. In Bologna Il Mulino made available classic authors like Francis Parkman, Frederick Jackson Turner, Beard, J. Franklin Jameson and McIlwain, as well as contemporary historians like Samuel Eliot Morison, C. Vann Woodward, Perry Miller, Louis Hartz, Walt Rostow, Richard Hofstadter, Arthur Schlesinger, Jr. and others.

These First Generation Italian Americanists, in their effort to fit U.S. history into a broad and sophisticated political culture, proved invaluable for Italy. But they were unable to tear down the wall of indifference that surrounded the discipline. And the political ties that linked many of them to the U.S. and to the American presence in Italy made their work suspect in some circles. Italy of the early sixties was not ready to give official recognition to U.S. history.

Things changed a few years later. The decline of idealism in Italy, the impact of Vatican II on Catholic thought, and the Third World's struggle for independence all left their mark on Socialist and Communist ideology. This in turn eroded the Eurocentric base of the historians. They sought to look anew at the nature of the U.S., whether as imperialist power or as leader of a "Free World" that was fast becoming the First World in common parlance. Moreover Vietnam, the New Left and the women's movement had demonstrated the manifold faces of America—an imperialist and racist power, yet also the cradle of a new type of radicalism.

While the U.S. was attracting increasing attention, the Italian universities were exploding in the sixties. An almost five-fold growth, with disastrous results for the universities, nonetheless led to the creation of additional academic positions in new disciplinary areas. U.S. history became an official academic discipline. The "fathers," men like Spini and Matteucci, were able to recruit younger scholars—Anna Maria Martellone in Florence and myself in Bologna. Meanwhile Raimondo Luraghi in Genoa had completed his move from military history to the U.S. by publishing his huge history of the American Civil War (1966). And Gian Giacomo Migone and Massimo Teodori had begun teaching in Turin and Lecce.

Thus the Second Generation of Italian historians of the U.S., my own, came into being. It was different from the first in that its members were able to make U.S. history their profession and in that we came from varying cultural and political backgrounds; our existence reflected emergent Italian needs and social changes.

To take my own example, I was dragged almost unwittingly into American history by the broad historical mechanisms then at work. My undergraduate studies in Law at the University of Bologna brought me into contact with Felice Battaglia, Professor of Legal Philosophy, or Jurisprudence as it is called in the U.S. A leading idealist, he was a broad-minded and lively intellectual who was interested in a new field, Sociology of Law. He assigned me, as the subject of my senior thesis, the legal thought of Roscoe Pound, whose *Interpretation of Legal Theory* had just been translated by Il Mulino (1962).

My tutor was Matteucci, Battaglia's assistant, already deep in his study of the American contribution to constitutionalism. He encouraged me to apply for a scholarship to the Johns Hopkins University Center in Bologna, a branch of Hopkins' School of Advanced International Studies founded in 1955 with considerable U.S. funding support. The Center's students came both from the U.S. and from all over Europe; thirty-six years later its influence in Italy and Europe has been sizable.

In those days it still had an American Studies dimension, backed by USIS. I joined the program and it was in the Center's rich library collection, under the tutelage of the delightful Southern gentleman Clement Eaton, that I formally engaged battle with American history. A year later, with Fulbright (and later Harkness) help, I left for the University of Rochester, where I had been accepted as a researcher on early Massachusetts and Puritan political thought. Il Mulino had just given us Perry Miller's two volumes on the New England mind (1962), of major importance in my development.

Such circumstances allowed future professional Americanists to enlarge the scope of their research: we were free to work in new ways and from perspectives that were novel in Italy. I was alone then in using intellectual history to seek the cultural roots of liberalism and the creation of political order, in focusing on the American Revolution and the history of political ideas and institutions (Bonazzi 1970, 1977). Yet these themes flowed directly from the concerns of my masters. In Genoa Raimondo Luraghi, via the Civil War, studied the American South as an example of the fate of an agrarian society, of its values and mores, in the age of Capitalism (1966, 1978). In Florence Anna Maria Martellone, after a Fulbright to Harvard and a decade in the U.S., picked up a neglected field: Italian communities in America. Italian historians had studied emigration from the Italian side, looking at the push factors leading to mass departures at the turn of the century. Martellone's study of Boston's Little Italy (1973) broke new ground in observing their experience on American soil.

Among these Second Generation Americanists, Gian Giacomo Migone and Massimo Teodori followed a less academic path. They reflected the Italian Marxist and non-Marxist radical interest in the U.S. The late sixties and early seventies saw the publication of anthologies and studies on U.S. student and black movements, as well as translations of New Left and black authors, responding certainly to great public interest in these questions. Teodori, close to American libertarian ideas, did original work on the American New Left, with the sub-textual intention of bringing these ideas into Italian political life (1970), later practicing his ideas as an elected member of the Italian Parliament for the tiny Radical Party. Migone, a neo-Marxist intellectual active in the student movement, spearheaded the interest of the Italian New Left in the U.S. His interest in international relations and the U.S. impact on Italy led him to study the financial support given to Mussolini by American banks in the twenties.

A diverse group, the Second Generation came from different backgrounds, knew each other only slightly, and shared little at first other than their passion for American history, a willingness to devote their lives to it, and personal acquaintance with the U.S.—all spent time there in the sixties for study and research, all with Fulbright assistance at least in the beginnng.

With the advent of the more numerous Third Generation, I shall quicken my story, sparing the reader the enumeration of the dozens of fine young scholars who have come into being in the seventies and eighties. Early in the seventies, Spini had seen the need for concerted action by historians to help develop the field; he formed the crucial Committee for North American History. Meanwhile the dormant American Studies Association, formed earlier by the literary scholars, sprang back to life; the historians joined but also kept their own organization.

The seventies were a period of deep social and cultural turmoil: revolutionary groups to the left of the PCI proliferated, "red" and "black" terrorism flourished, and the Italian secret services maneuvred. Yet the economy was growing, civil society was changing at a disturbing pace, and the universities were beginning to recover from the earlier explosion.

Student movements gave us most of the Third Generation Americanists. Italian neo-Marxist radicals had leapt from American libertarian ideas to a hard-core ideology of their own, and young historians among them were fascinated by social history, whose methods allowed them to do historical analysis of working-class culture and spontaneous class consciousness. In search of a "usable proletarian past" free of PCI dogma, they discovered the social history of the American workers' movement; they found a model close to their ideals of political action and mass democracy in the old American

IWW, the Industrial Workers of the World. Visits to Italy by the late Herbert Gutman, leading American historian of work—also a Fulbright-initiated contact—helped many younger scholars develop research approaches to these problems.

Now young people could begin their careers as Americanists and get thorough training in the U.S. Yet the impulse to write American history came, as it had for the lay intellectuals, from inside Italian culture, from the hunger for a history that was relevant to the Italian political debate—cultures come to terms with outside reality through active mechanisms of their own, not through passive assimilation.

By the beginning of the eighties, Italy could count five full professors of American History, a dozen associate professors and a small group of tenured "researchers," a minor but integral part of the historians' profession. The criteria of professionalism are all there: different schools of thought, varied research interests, a persistent if limited stream of publications, a PhD program, and an English-language journal *Storia Nordamericana*, born in 1983. Meanwhile, as ideological furors cooled, there was a further mark of professionalism: not so much a retreat into pure scholarship as an awareness, even among the more militant historians, of the complex and ambiguous links between politics, values and research.

In 1984 at Bellagio, another outpost of the American intellectual "empire" funded by the Rockefeller Foundation, Stanley Kutler and Stanley Katz led a conference on U.S. history. I noted then that Italy had not yet made an innovative contribution to the discipline at the international level, but that originality in a strictly scholarly sense is not what we should be seeking. The transfer and interpretation of cultural patterns is also important. Studying the history of remote nations or periods involves the historian in a relation that is above all scholarly or ethical; the Americanist, however, cannot escape the immediate political relevance of his subject. The U.S. erupted into Italian culture in a dramatically political manner and now looms large at all levels. This has not failed to leave its mark on historiography. Italy's alliance with the U.S. is an unavoidable fact; besides, the two countries share a common civilization. We in Italy are used to using history as a basis for thinking about political issues. It would be a mistake if Italian Americanist historians failed to provide the nation with the knowledge needed for its vital debates.

Things are never easy, progress is never linear. A few years later I noted a sense of fatigue among Americanists. The field was not growing. History was a zero-growth discipline, allocated few new positions by the central university authorities. Worse, fellow historians were denying openings to Americanists. Just as in the case of Latin American, Middle Eastern, Far

Eastern and even Russian history, professionalization meant living at the margin. We had to learn the tough rules of academic politics, now that ideological debate and its visibility were disappearing (Bonazzi 1989).

And now the Cold War, my Cold War, is over. My sense of the U.S. and its history was forged on its anvil. I come from another era. Is the same true for the Fulbright Program and its achievements? My discipline developed in the context of an ideologically loaded concept, Americanization. Yet I still believe, as I did in 1984, that setting higher standards for U.S. historians, making history ever more professional, does not rule out a constant search for a "usable past," nor a quest for the inner dynamics of the American nation and its society, nor even a way to understand the complex, so-often misunderstood mechanisms of its impact abroad.

The end of the Cold War forces us to reconsider the terms of the problem. I shall not try to prophesy the future of U.S. history studies in Italy, but certainly the past forty years teach us lessons. They tell us that history is a peculiar and elusive discipline, deeply tied in with national culture and experience; it is not a ware that can be marketed easily. An example: to give American democracy and the U.S. a purportedly non-ideological foundation, American historians in the U.S. often tended to identify democracy and history. Americans tended to and still see their version of democracy less as a local way of handling the issues of governance than as a univeral solution. After 1945, the U.S.—whether in candor or disingenuity is of no concern here—offered its democracy and therefore its history as models for democracy-hungry Europeans. In the forties Europeans, not only Italians, accepted American democracy and the U.S., though with reservations; but in almost every country they depreciated American history. Setting aside parochialism, divergent interests, power relations and the like, it is clear that both sides had a grip on some portion of the truth. Lifestyles can be borrowed, adapted or accepted, so can ideologies. But no one freely accepts another nation's history as a model for his own past or future.

American history encountered thirty or more years of stone-walling and resistance in Italy, often in the name of foolish and counter-productive party interests and ideological vagaries. The deeply rooted cultural resistance was less impolite, manifesting itself in silence as absolute lack of interest. Yet whenever they could serve usefully, one heard the Americanists' voices. Successful professionalization of the discipline drew on various uncontrollable factors: massive educational growth, political relevance, cultural attractions.

U.S. history was not "exported" to Italy, its rooting here—and the metaphor of trees and roots runs throughout this essay—has been a far more delicate process than any outsider can imagine. American Studies in Italy started from scratch, amidst immense material, psychological and political obstances; they have succeeded in Italy as a part of the internationalization of Italian culture.

I wonder sometimes whether Fulbright officials in the U.S., or in Italy for that matter, are satisfied with these forty years of effort. Those who must address the question in terms of foreign policy considerations have an especially difficult job. American history has fed Italian partisanship through these decades, but the partisanship sprang from the dynamics of Italy; it has allowed for genuine discussion and research. But the major contribution: a scholarly discipline has been planted and nurtured. It can only continue to grow. Italy will have greater access to truths about the U.S. than it did before.

The Fulbright Program, through its open-ended politics, contributed to all this. As a tool of cultural diplomacy, it put Italian grantees directly in touch with American society and provided access to its deeper levels of meaning. It gave them the possibility of reacting freely, negatively if necessary, to their perceptions of a diverse and complex society. International Italian politics then conspired to limit the outreach of the Program yet destroyed neither its pluralism nor the basic confidence in cultural intercourse and dialog that constituted its ideology. The Program has helped create the possibility for the American past to become relevant to the self-analysis of another culture.

Now we turn, all of us, to our post-Cold War future. The process will not be different from that of the past: cultural cross-fertilization. But if we do not respect the past, the task will require even more of our creative energy.

REFERENCES

Alberto Aquarone, *Due costituenti settecentesche*, Pisa: Nistri Lischi, 1955.

Aquarone, Negri, Scelba eds., *Le formazione degli Stati Uniti d'America. Documenti*, 2 vols. Pisa: Nistri Lischi, 1961.

Tiziano Bonazzi, *Il sacro esperimento: Teologia e politica nell'America puritana*, Bologna: Il Mulino, 1970.

_____, "Trends in Italian Historical Research into North American History," *Storia Nordamericana*, I,2, 1984, 5-21 (full bibliographies in both).

_____, "American History: The View from Italy," *Reviews in American History*, XIV, 4, Dec. 1986, 532-41.

_____, "L'America settentrionale," in Luigi De Rosa ed., *La storiografia italiana degli ultimi vent'anni*, 3 vols., Bari: La Terza, 1989, III, 339-62.

_____, ed., *La Rivoluzione americana*, Bologna: Il Mulino, 1977.

D'Addio, Negri eds., *Il Federalista*, Pisa: Nistri Lischi, 1955.

Pier Paolo D'Attorre, "Sogno americano e mito sovietico nell'Italia contemporanea," in Attorre ed., *Nemici per la pelle*, Milano: Franco Angeli, 1991, 15-53.

Umberto Eco, "Il modello americano," in Eco, Ceserani, Placido eds., *La riscoperta dell'America*, Bari: La Terza, 1984, 23.

Aldo Garosci, *Il pensiero politico degli autori del Federalist*, Milano: Comunità, 1954.

Claudio Gorlier, "La situazione del romanzo americano in Italia," *Quarderni dell'Istituto di Studi nordamericani di Bologna*, 3, 1981, 41-54.

Agostino Lombardo, "L'America e la cultura letteraria italiana," ibid, 3, 1981, 7-39.

Raimondo Luraghi, *Storia della Guerra Civile americana*, Torino: Einaudi, 1966.

_____, *The Rise and Fall of the Plantation South*, New York: New Viewpoints, 1978.

Anna Maria Martellone, *Una 'Little Italy' nell'Atene d'America*, Napoli: Guida, 1973.

Nicola Matteucci, *Charles McIlwain e la storiografia sulla Rivoluzione americana*, Bologna: Il Mulino, 1965.

_____, *Organizzazione del potere e libertà*, Torino: UTET, 1976.

Gian Giacomo Migone, *Gli Stati Uniti e il fascismo*, Milano: Feltrinelli, 1980.

Luigi Paggi ed., *Americanismo e riformismo*, Torino: Einaudi, 1989.

Giacomo Sani, "La riscoperta delle scienze sociali in Italia," in Vezzosi, op.cit.

Giorgio Spini, *Autobiografia della giovane America. La storiografia americana dai Padri Pellegrini all'independenza*, Torino: Einaudi, 1969.

_____, "New Trends of the American Left," in *Storia Nordamericana*, 3, 1, 1986.

Massimo Teodori, ed., *La Nuova Sinistra Americana*, Milano: Feltrinelli, 1970.

_____, *La fione del mito americano*, Milano: Feltrinelli, 1974.

Angelo Ventone, "L'avventura americana della classe dirigente cattolica," in Attorre ed., *Nemici*.

Elisabetta Vezzosi ed., *Le relazioni Italia-USA dal 1943 al 1953*, Firenze, 1983.

Elisabetta Vezzosi and Laura Manetti, "A Bibliography of Italian Studies on North American History 1945-83,"*Storia Nordamericana*, 1,2, 1984, 22-182.

Other significant authors:
  Elena Aga-Rossi
  Piero Bairati
  Luca Codignola
  Ennio Di Nolfo
  Antonia Donno
  Ferdinando Fasce
  Valeria Lerda Gennaro
  Federico Romero
  Massimo Rubboli
  Carlo Mario Santoro
  Malcolm Sylvers
  Arnaldo Testi
  Loretta Valtz-Mannucci
  Maurizio Vaudagna

Norman Kogan, Emeritus Professor of Political Science at the University of Connecticut, was born in the pre-Fulbright generation. A product of World War II, marked by a fortuitous encounter with a great Italian émigré figure, he was well launched in his field of contemporary Italian political history before the Program was created. Participating later as a senior researcher, he has watched Fulbright exchanges between Italy and the U.S. and taken part in aspects of its administration since the beginning. In this provocative overview, at once a highly personal and yet abstract and theoretical statement about the American connection to Italian intellect, he establishes a context in which the contributions of the other three writers on Italy in this volume can be more fully understood. The four essays taken together provide a unique view of the evolution of democratic liberal thought in Italy during this half-century and of the modest contribution of American ideas to this self-discovery.

13

ITALIAN INTELLECT AND FOREIGN INFLUENCES

Norman Kogan

From time to time I have marveled at my good fortune in having made my academic and professional career in the decades after the Second World War. It was a period of expanding opportunities and broadening horizons for those lucky enough to have grown up and lived in the advanced industrialized countries of the world.

In my more pessimistic moments, I speculate as to whether this period is coming to an end. Perhaps it is. But no great historical insight is required to recognize the post-war difference: the contrast between the restrictions placed on American scholars in the Great Depression of the thirties and the relatively open possibilities of the succeeding decades.

One such possibility was travel abroad for study and research. After 1945 everything conspired to create a climate for educational exchange. And the rewards—increased knowledge and burgeoning professional employment—were attractive. Fulbright filled out a big part of that picture.

I learned Italian because of the War, in the Army's ASTP, then practiced it in an unusual assignment to an Italian "co-belligerent" army battalion. (After Italy's separate surrender in September 1943, all prisoners of war were then called upon by the new Badoglio government to collaborate with their captors; those who did were called by this name.) My assignment lasted for the rest of the war.

After the war, another stroke of educational fortune: the GI Bill made graduate education a viable possibility. I decided to specialize in Italian Studies. Because of my interest in politics, economics, and contemporary history, I found myself concentrating on Italian political parties and on Italy's foreign relations. It was not long before foundation research awards, including Fulbright, opened the gates to recurrent residence in Italy and proximity to the archives, files, and human documents which are the stuff of the contemporary political historian.

Living in post-war Italy was expensive, except for Americans, who profited from a booming economy and a strong dollar. It was difficult for the Italians, even with the post-war economic miracle, but they forged steadily ahead. For me, life was busy and productive. I had access to the essential ingredients and adequate funding was relatively easy. The active political players posed a harder challenge. Knowing people who can help is an asset anywhere, and for a contemporary political historian it is crucial. In Italy, however, it is indispensable: *la racommandazione* opens doors, doors that otherwise remain tightly shut.

In my case, the magic name—and the most important figure in my life—was Gaetano Salvemini. It was my special privilege to have been associated with him as a graduate student: a letter written to him at Harvard from my departmental base in Chicago launched a long friendship and endowed me with a trunkload of unassorted papers which kept me busy for years. Salvemini, certainly the most distinguished anti-Fascist émigré scholar in the U.S., was a goldmine of knowledge. But he also knew and commanded the respect of the leading anti-Fascists who inherited Italy in the post-war period. This combination of learning and connections, coming from one of the most generous humans I have ever been privileged to know, allowed me to do the kind of research that even the best libraries cannot support. Interviewing the active political and economic elites gave me an understanding both of the substance and the process of Italian political life, literally as it unrolled before our eyes.

The indispensable human element in scholarship on Italy in fact extends to all fields. For whatever reason—the inadequacy of library collections, the understaffing of universities and museums, the then small and self-protective intellectual elite—the goodwill and encouragement of authoritative people is vital even to those working on classical Rome, the Renaissance, or any other aspect of Italian history and culture. More American researchers have worked in the humanities, the social sciences and the fine arts in Italy than in the sciences; but even in the natural and applied sciences, access to the laboratories and research institutes requires previous personal relationships.

That is part of the Fulbright role. The Program in Italy has been, at least for the first three decades, a major and continuous granting agency in all these areas. The Program has always been, except for the first year, a two-way business, with more Italians traveling west than Americans east. As of 1990, according to two papers (1978, 1987) by the remarkable Cipriana Scelba, long-time director of the Commission in Rome, about 4700 Americans had worked in Italy and 5500 Italians had gone to the U.S. The quality has been high: people like Italian Nobel physicist Carlo Rubbia, American Nobel economists Franco Modigliani and James Buchanan, American Nobel physicist Emilio Segre (the Italian-born and educated Modigliani and Segre, like Enrico Fermi, lived and worked in the U.S. beginning in the late thirties). Other Italian Fulbrighters have become cabinet ministers, judges of the Constitutional (Supreme) Court, foreign service officers, members of parliament, industrial-ists, university presidents, deans and scholars, prominent journalists and the like. My impression: the vast majority of them returned to Italy with positive attitudes towards the U.S., with new ideas about how to do things, and with some of the old intellectual categories in disrepair. They then became, through the effective network of the Fulbright Commission, willing helpers to Americans working in Italy. This was my network as well.

The intellectual component of politics in Italy matters a great deal, unlike the politics of certain other nations. I recall one conversation which revealed a deep change in political thinking. In 1973, I was engaged in research under Fulbright auspices on the new regional governments that had been established in 1970, a fairly revolutionary idea which has been long in taking root. I interviewed the president of one of the southern regions, a Christian Democrat, a man who in the U.S. would have been equivalent, more or less, to the governor of a state. We soon discovered a common wartime experience: while my co-belligerent battalion of Italians worked in an army post in Pennsylvania, he had served as a co-belligerent on the West Coast. This touched off a long reminiscence about his experiences in the U.S. as a prisoner of war, then as a co-belligerent. He concluded, "Without that wartime co-belligerent experience, I would be a Communist politician today." The history of the impact of the American prison camps and co-belligerent units on their European residents remains to be written, but I do not think it unfair to suggest that it was an unusual but important precursor of the Fulbright Program in Italy and Germany. Direct contact with Americans has a way of making a difference.

The state of co-belligerency was left deliberately ambiguous. In 1943, the government of King Victor Emmanuel III and his prime minister Marshal Pietro Badoglio wanted to reverse alliances and become a member of the UN alliance. The British and the Americans, especially Churchill, would not hear of this. The British wanted to impose a punitive peace treaty on Italy, which could not be done to an ally. And the Allies needed all the help they could get. The idea of co-belligerency was the way out: neither ally nor enemy nor neutral. Badoglio called on Italian prisoners to work with the Allies. The individual prisoner could either volunteer or remain in a prison camp. Members of the dreaded Fascist Militia were excluded.

This ambiguous status was not easy to handle. The men were organized into units, companies and battalions; they were led by the very officers who had earlier lost the respect of their troops. Americans attached to these units quickly became the ultimate source of authority. Still, life was easier for the co-belligerents than for the prisoners of war: they had gradually expanded extra privileges and the food was better. On Sundays visitors were permitted. Towards the end of the war, soldiers were allowed to leave the camps with American escorts to visit the surrounding towns. Naturally the townspeople were suspicious and even hostile; they did not understand co-belligerency and resented enemy prisoners wandering around the streets.

After ASTP, this was my second pre-Fulbright experience. I learned a great deal through contact with these men; I was introduced, for example, to that enduring misfortune of Italian life: their deep and extensive regional clannishness and the special hostility of North and South. My battalion came from all over Italy; but the men naturally grouped into region-based cliques or friendship circles, the same groupings that characterized the Italian-Americans already resident in the U.S. In the summer of 1945 I was escort to six young men on a weekend trip to a Philadelphia social club, where a relative was an officer in the club. There I learned that membership was restricted to those whose families came from north of the Po valley. My six charges were Piedmontese, it turned out. At first I tended to attribute such attitudes to the less well-off and less educated Italians, but I was wrong: in 1973, at a dinner in Turin, a prominent academic intellectual harangued me on Cavour's great mistake—going south of the Arno, south of Florence.

Now the significant fact is that my regional president saw his political alternative as Communism. It reflects the important role of Marxism and of the Communists (PCI) in the Italian system. In 1991 the Communists changed the party name to Democratic Party of the Left. But since 1947, when the Socialists split into two parties—the Italian Socialist Party (PSI) and what became the Social Democratic Party (PSDI), the PCI has been the second party of Italy. Only the Christian Democrats (DC) have exceeded the PCI in numbers. This is the more strange in that in cultural and intellectual terms it can be argued that the Communists have been the leaders.

Religion at least in part lies somewhere near the base of that anomaly. Italian high culture has been a lay affair for seven or eight hundred years, as epitomized by Dante in the *Commedia* and *De Monarchia* and his Ghibelline preference for the Holy Roman Empire over the political pretensions of the Papacy. In later centuries lay forces and clerical forces won and lost political battles. But the intellectual battles went mainly to the lay elements, except in the Spanish-dominated seventeenth century. Galileo could be forced to recant; but Galileo's ideas prevailed over time.

The Italian state was created in the middle of the nineteenth century by lay forces, basing their legitimacy on intellectual concepts like nationalism and positivism. The first half of our century was dominated by the ideas of the lay philosopher and historian Benedetto Croce, operating within a variant of Germanic philosophical idealism (though I have long suspected that the influence of philosophical idealism in Italy was as much the product of German political and economic leadership in Europe after 1871 as of German philosophy).

Through the centuries the tensions between Church and State in Italy, between lay and clerical ideas, between different religions, never reached the extremes they did elsewhere in Europe. Nothing in Italian history compares to the religious wars in France or Germany, in terms either of destruction or bloodshed. Salvemini used to insist on the point that Italy never had this kind of war and credited the good sense of the Italian people in avoiding extremism in fact, if not always in language.

Gaetano Salvemini was a central figure, perhaps *the* central figure, in this period—a symbol for Italian intellectuals, a remarkable, true, and great Italian. The Fascist regime denounced him as anti-Italian, but he on the contrary considered the most profoundly anti-Italian idea to be Fascism itself. He was among the first to have the courage to oppose the dictatorship openly. In 1924 he and his friend Ernesto Rossi founded the journal *Non Mollare* (Don't Give In). In 1925 a royal decree took away his Chair at the University of Florence and deprived him of property and citizenship. With the police hot on his heels, he escaped across the Alps into exile. After a decade of academic and political action in France and England, he arrived at Harvard to take up the Lauro De Bosis Lectureship in Italian Studies founded by the actress Ruth

Draper, fiancée of the young anti-Fascist martyr. From his Cambridge platform, Salvemini waged a struggle against Fascism through his teaching, his writings, and his public lectures. It was there that I was fortunate enough to know him.

An inspiring and even charismatic man, he was very much an individualist. He fought his enemies but also his friends, even those who shared his anti-Fascist commitment. The Mazzini Society is a prime example. He helped found this refugee organization early in the war, then split from it. The Society had decided it had only one choice: to work with the Anglo-American governments in the struggle against the Axis powers. Salvemini, pointing to Churchill's "One man and one man alone" speech, believed that Churchill intended to maintain Fascism in Italy but without Mussolini; he thought Roosevelt had not only bowed to British leadership in the Mediterranean but was ready to work with reactionary monarchical elements in Italy. Salvemini was perhaps as hostile to the Savoy monarchy as he was to Mussolini and Fascism.

He was the more hostile to Fascism in that, as a young man, he had begun like Mussolini as a Marxist socialist. In 1909 he split with the Socialists because the party was neglecting the southern peasantry. Abandoning Marxism, he became an independent radical. In 1948 I remember showing him a State Department document from 1943 listing exiled Italians who might collaborate with Allied forces during the occupation of Italy: it described him as "an old Socialist." His reaction: "Yes, I am an old Socialist, but my socialism comes from the Sermon on the Mount and the golden rule." At a memorial service after his death in 1957, Ignazio Silone put it this way: "Marxism woke him up when he was young, but it did not blind him or stifle his mind."

Salvemini was a humanitarian, not a Christian socialist. His early education had been sponsored by an uncle who was a priest, and he attended a seminary in secondary school. But he became strongly anticlerical, and his hostility to the Vatican augmented when it agreed to collaborate with the Fascist regime. His mistrust carried over to the American Catholic hierarchy.

In 1948 his chair in Florence was restored and he retired from Harvard, but he delayed his departure so as to vote in the 1948 election, not because he wanted to vote for Truman but because there was a Church-opposed referendum item on the Massachusetts ballot to legalize birth control (the item lost). In the same election Henry Wallace had split with the Democratic Party to run for the presidency as a Progressive. Salvemini"s reaction: "He is in favor of peace; that's fine. But he never says, 'Peace on what terms? Peace on whose terms?'" He was already suspicious of the Soviet-sponsored international peace movement.

He had tried and failed to mobilize Italian-Americans into political activity in the anti-Fascist cause. The episode revealed his tendency to rhetorical oversimplification: "Ninety-eight per cent of these Italo-Americans know nothing about politics and don't want to know," he said to me once. Later his cynicism about Italian politicians before, during, and after Fascism colored his thinking. He told me: "There are only three honest politicians in Italy," referring less to financial integrity than to intellectual and moral honesty. None of the three was a Socialist. He was cynical perhaps, or more exactly a skeptical realist; but his skepticism about past and present never diminished his hope or the quality of his fight for a better future. He was an old man when he returned to Italy; still he lived in the present and the future rather than the past. In the early fifties I wrote to announce the birth of a son. He wrote back congratulating us on having the "courage to bring a child into this world of the atomic bomb."

In Florence, the system did not permit him to teach modern or contemporary history: he had to teach ancient and medieval history, on which he had written his doctoral thesis. Disappointed but not dismayed, he noted that there were at least twenty-six theories on the fall of the Roman Empire; discussing them, he would find ample opportunity to deal with recent and current events.

His success was never political. He was an intellectual and a moral example to a generation of young intellectuals in Italy, most of whom never knew him. I did, and his presence in my life was the third element in the pre-Fulbright sector of my itinerary.

As my regional president knew (he was also a university professor of history), the history of Italian political thought since the war is entwined with Marxism. After 1945, Marxist ideology moved front and center. Despite the modifications of the brilliant Antonio Gramsci, a standard version of Communist thought prevailed; I doubt that Gramsci's ideas had much to do with the PCI's post-war strategies. His major idea, the war of position, was certainly followed by the PCI. But this strategy of penetrating society and culture sooner or later to obtain hegemony over a nation's values, norms, and behavior was not unusual in the communist movement. No Communist party out of power has an alternative to this strategy. Even movements that never heard of Gramsci followed the same general lines, seeking contacts and alliances with potential friendly forces—so long as the Soviet Union was not impeding them, as happened more than once in the twenties and thirties. By the fifties the PCI had achieved virtual independence from Soviet orders, at least in its domestic strategies. But it still believed that its moral and ideological ties to the USSR were a source of strength. Only in the late sixties and seventies did most Communists abandon this belief.

For most Italian Communists and Marxist Socialists, their Marxism was simplistic and even innocent: a few slogans, myths of proletarian goodness, class solidarity. "Land to the peasants," "workers unite," the legend of the October Revolution, Lenin, and the like. Beyond this, there was little solid knowledge. In 1957 a Communist senator told me, "There are no more than 25,000 knowledgable and believing Marxist-Leninists in all of Italy" (the population of Italy at the time was over 50 million and the PCI had two million card-carrying members). Granted, the senator, a university professor, set high standards.

Behind the intellectual attraction of Marxism lay the prestige of the Soviet victory over the Nazis. As philosophical idealism had been linked to German power, now Marxism was connected to the emergence of the Soviet Union as the dominant power in Europe.

A major difference between the late nineteenth century and the post-war era: the leading political, scientific and intellectual power was no longer centered in Europe. Now Europeanized countries outside the Continent, especially the U.S., cast their influence around the world, including old Europe itself. It was clear that the U.S. was able to block Soviet domination of Western Europe primarily through science, politics and economics. Culturally and intellectually it was not so simple. Wherever Marxist movements had deep roots, American cultural influence was embattled. Examples: France, Italy, and West Germany until 1959, when the German Social Democrats at Bad Godesburg cast off their Marxist heritage.

Marxist categorizations distorted American liberal democratic and pragmatic ways of looking at life for Italian intellectuals. Meanwhile the integralist wing of the Christian Democrats was equally suspicious of U.S. behavior. The profit system repelled them, as it did the Marxists; it was un-Christian and evil. In 1965 I clipped a newspaper account of a statement by Pope Paul VI to the effect that liberalism was a greater enemy to Catholicism than Marxism.

So far I have been using the word "culture" in its meaning of "high culture," the intellectual and aesthetic constructs of people who have advanced education and capabilities for theoretical reasoning. At the level of "mass culture" on the other hand, American influence predominated. Materialistic mass consumption, so despised by Marxist and integralist intellectuals, was exactly what was wanted by the masses, who had always been poor and who had suffered much under Fascist rule and war. The thirst for goods and services was identified with the U.S. Mass entertainment felt the influence of

Hollywood. At advanced levels American leadership in science and technology had extraordinary impact.

And in a different field American social sciences made remarkable inroads, considering the large numbers of Italian social scientists already committed to a Marxist perspective. In the late 1970s I lectured on U.S. foreign policy at an Italian university; afterwards the chair of political science commented that I had approached international relations within the framework of power politics whereas, he said, "I look at international relations as part of the class struggle."

The inroads of American social science require some explanation. First, Italian social scientists open to American perspectives and techniques were found in the non-Marxist, non-integralist and lay groups. The others abstained, did not apply for grants to the U.S., did not associate with Americans working in Italy. Second, Italian Marxists in large part were never as dogmatic, extremist or rigid in their thinking as were their counterparts in other countries; they were ready to learn what was worth knowing from wherever it came. In the late seventies, the orthodox PCI figure Armando Cossutta was accusing his more flexible comrades of substituting "sociologism" for Marxism—it was an attack on the ideas of Max Weber as transmitted through American sociological thought. Third, American private foundations contributed to the dissemination of social science knowledge, as did the translation programs of the USIS and of course the patient annual exchanges of the Fulbright Program. None of what was learned was swallowed whole, something to which Italians are not prone; but more and more of it stuck to the ribs as time moved on.

Italian skepticism is a national trait, as is realism. The writer Mario Soldati once said that few Italians do things for abstract reasons. Intellectuals may speak or write in theoretical terms but their actions stay close to their interests. When Communism appeared to be the wave of the future, it was in the interests of many to stay close to the crest. Even non-Communists and anti-Communists had to explain themselves in the framework established by Marxism so that Marxists set the tone of the debate, and the liberals and Catholics were kept on the defensive. In the sixties, when left-wing Catholic intellectuals were incorporating the class struggle into their social doctrine, PCI Secretary General Palmiro Togliatti was already saying that the class struggle in classic Marxist thought no longer made sense (Gozzini 1964). By the late seventies, Giorgio Napolitano of the *miglioristi*, the social democratic wing of the PCI, was calling his party a former Marxist movement.

It is significant that the decline of Marxist thought in Italy preceded the collapse of Communism in the Soviet Union and Eastern Europe. It even preceded the decline of PCI strength among Italian voters. In 1973 Enrico Berlinguer, then head of the PCI, proposed an "historic compromise" between Marxism and Catholicism. After a decade of dialog between Marxist and Catholic intellectuals, a dialog that emerged from Vatican II, the compromise undermined fundamental Marxist doctrine, even if Communist strategic efforts to incorporate Catholics as allies or even as members of the PCI dated back to World War II.

Communist electoral strength peaked in 1976. By 1978 and 1979 a decline had begun and it has continued ever since. In 1976 over 34% of the voters chose the PCI; by 1991 the vote was down to 22%, according to figures derived from parliamentary, regional, and local elections. For over two decades, at least since the Soviet invasion of Czechoslovakia in 1968, PCI leadership has tried to distance itself from the international communist movement and from the Soviet Union in particular. Success was only partial, but among intellectuals the decline in prestige and influence of Marxist dialectics led to a revival of democratic liberal ideas, not only in politics but in economics, well before Glasnost. The social-democratization of both PCI and PSI has meant the acceptance of parliamentary or presidential forms of democratic government, going back to the 1970s. By the late seventies, both parties had endorsed selective privatization of parts of the public sector economy and an effort to manage an incomes policy. In parallel were attempts to modernize and secularize the Christian Democratic Party, whose integralist sectors still resist liberal outlooks. Polls today indicate that a substantial majority of the Italian population considers profit-making to be a moral act: in the "hot autumn" of 1969 workers struck and rioted to destroy the profit system, today they strike for profit-sharing.

Neither the intellectuals who consider themselves part of the ruling class nor the general public give high marks to the Italian state, to political parties, or to public administration. Yet when Aldo Moro was kidnapped and murdered by the Red Brigades in 1978, a moment of great danger for the state and its political system, the people rallied to the state. So did most intellectuals, though some ducked the issue and a few sided with the terrorists. Reform is complex: still, most concrete proposals involve varying the machinery of parliamentary democracy. Not even the neo-Fascists dare propose change to a non-liberal democratic form of government. The present system works badly, but the intellectuals want to improve not wreck it. In the words of two of them, "Italian society has by now so profoundly absorbed democratic values and principles that it can no longer be content with any kind of democracy, but demands for itself a democracy that functions . . ." (Fusaro and Ravaglia 1987).

The process of interaction with America during all this has been subtle, gradual and indirect. It is difficult to estimate with any precision the degree of influence exercised by the U.S. or by American intellectuals in this transformation to "profoundly absorbed democratic values." Obviously the most important features are internal. The society, and the intellectuals who articulate and mold the society's values, have responded to the tremendous changes of the last forty-five years. A traditional rural society has been transformed into a modern urban society, even if there are severe cultural lags. These changes can be measured in economic and demographic statistics: Italy now has the fifth largest economy in the world and is crowding France for fourth place; population growth is down to zero, and in the central and northern regions the death rate exceeds the birth rate by a small margin.

Difficult as it is to measure, even for someone who has watched the waves and ripples for fifty years, there is little doubt in my mind that the major external influence on Italian political thought has been American. The Italian constitution of 1948 incorporates a number of American doctrines like judicial review and a bill of rights. Italy has participated in the Americanization of life-styles that mark all modern and semi-modern societies, most markedly in the fields of material accumulation, mass communications, and mass culture. It is subtler in the areas of high culture and advanced ideas but there is little doubt the American impact has been substantial. And in that picture American libraries, translations, and scholarly exchanges have played a patient and persistent part over time.

Still it may be permitted to remind the reader that Italians are intelligent, too intelligent to carry ideas to ultimately absurd conclusions and too experienced to swallow any concept whole. It may also be useful to remember that America has not gotten away scot-free: Italy is a contagious friend. But the question of what contact with Italy may have done to America in return is a subject for another day. I know only what it has done to me.

REFERENCES

Mario Gozzini, ed. *Il dialogo alla prova*, Florence: Vallecchi, 1964.
Carlo Fusaro and Gianni Ravaglia, *La scommessa delle riforme*, Rome: Edizione della Voce, 1987.

PART III

THE SIXTIES: WEATHERING CRISIS

In the sixties, the proud program would stumble. In 1967 and 1968, a highly personalized feud between Representative John J. Rooney of Brooklyn and Columbia University philosopher Charles Frankel, then director of the State Department's educational and cultural affairs, would all but destroy it: in two years, budgets were cut by half. Even the Senator was powerless in the face of Rooney's animus. Fulbright discovered its precarious mortality. The first five years of the decade, an optimistic buildup by the Kennedy team, were followed by near-collapse.

This was the more distressing in that, with President Kennedy, it had been decided that the program, which had always been funded by the U.S. though adminstered binationally, should seek foreign government cost-sharing. By now, the American commission directors overseas were a rarity, at least in Europe; a new class was coming into being: foreign executive directors, mythical figures of the likes of Ulrich Littman, Cipriana Scelba, Ramón Bela, Daniel Krauskopf and Dorothy Deflandre, were in place. Thanks in part to them, the idealist binational rhetoric of the plea for joint-financing was warmly received in the early sixties and foreign funding began to flow. But the Rooney cuts were seen as a betrayal: in France, when its contribution not only failed to increase American funding but appeared to have been used to justify a sharp drop in American appropriations, the rose lost its bloom.

In the dying moments of the Johnson administration, a precedent was shattered: to the Board of Foreign Scholarships, which in its first twenty years of existence had only three or four members outside the university world, Johnson appointed three outgoing White House staffers. The Republicans took note and the BFS in its second two decades would have two dozen non-academic representatives—it has never regained the academic character its designers intended. At about the same time the great American foundations, which had since the post-missionary era played important roles overseas and had worked implicitly hand in hand with Fulbright, began to cut back their international efforts.

The growth of new commissions and agreements overseas slowed markedly, and various agreements became inactive. A flurry of new agreements were signed early in the sixties, carrying over the momentum of the fifties (in chronological order, Portugal, Nepal, Ethiopia, Cyprus, Ghana, Malaysia, Afghanistan, Tunisia, Liberia and Yugoslavia), but after the Yugoslav agreement of November 1964, eighteen years would pass before the next Fulbright agreement was signed. In the first two decades of Fulbright history, forty or more commissions were founded; in the second twenty-year period, one.

The reasons for the slackened pace are difficult to pin down. Certainly some agreements had been signed prematurely, in countries like Burma—where the Program was not fully understood or where political upheaval would soon wipe it away. Certainly the climate in the House of Representatives was stormy. A more complex factor: once a commission exists, it attracts to itself a variety of natural clearing-house functions, e.g., counseling students who want to study in the U.S. This in turn means salaries and raises administrative costs. As a percentage of program, auditors pointed out that in some commissions it took 30% of the total budget to administer the program, without realizing that in many cases the "administrative" expenditures were as important as the grant-program. U.S. expenses were high as well: though the screening and placement agencies, the Institute of International Education (IIE) and the Council for the International Exchange of Scholars (CIES), drew on voluntary support from the universities, the costs of a functioning peer-review process were high.

Some observers advance another hypothesis: USIS posts wanted more control over the independent binationally-administered Fulbright commissions, heavily protected in the U.S. by the Board of Foreign Scholarships, the two independent academic screening and placement bodies, the Senate Foreign Relations Committee, and the strictures of the university world and the peer review process. There was understandable impatience in the fast-moving USIA at the slow pace of commission decisions. And the idea that a Fulbright country program could operate without a commission, as practiced in Eastern Europe, may have seemed an attractive alternative.

Six contributors represent the sixties, only one American, a three-time Fulbright teacher of art, literature and humanities in Berlin, Istanbul and Tehran. The others came to the U.S.—a Finn who worked out his approach to the ethics of journalism at Syracuse; a Swede who outstripped his country's capacity for research on the Soviet economy; a Portuguese teacher of English literature who discovered the American feminist movement and would put it to good use after the demise of Salazar; a remarkable Indian who, with the help of a great American teacher, built a bridge between his country and the suburbs of Seattle; and the thought-provoking Darshan Singh Maini, who went to Cambridge to study Henry James and found more there than expected.

The crisis years in the second half of the sixties were a watershed for more reasons than Congressman Rooney. Charles Frankel, justifying his resignation from the direction of State's cultural programs, pointed to the brooding growth of Vietnam in the American consciousness.   The universities and the government, after years of a tense but creative partnership, had drawn apart over the issue.   Something had changed in the climate for the Fulbright Program.   Its consequences would take a while to develop and reveal themselves.

Presently head of the Finnish News Agency in Helsinki, the author found three treasures at Syracuse University's Journalism School during his Fulbright year: a capacity for work beyond his earlier imaginings, the partner and love of his life, and a passion for press freedom. A fourth factor was his discovery that basketball was only a game. Discreetly neglecting the others, this essay focuses on how the American version of press freedom, as a culmination of the wisdom of civilization, has been challenged around the world but has steadily lifted all boats on its tide, a tide not so much of truth as of that open flow of truth and error, lies and myth, without which the filtering process required to find enduring truth can never take place. In defending the press' right even to print lies, he traces the itinerary abroad of a burning American passion. Does it burn so brightly, he wonders, in today's America?

14

A BRIEF ESSAY ON TRUTH

Per-Erik Lönnfors

Dr. Bird mumbled in his moustache. Research methods . . . term paper . . . brief essay on truth . . . 10-15 pages . . . footnotes . . . outline . . . bibliography. He left the classroom.

Someone interpreted. In one week we were to hand in a term paper with the title "A Brief Essay on Truth." This in addition to three other writing courses with weekly assignments.

It was 1960. My first class in Research Methods at Syracuse University's School of Journalism set the pace for two semesters as a graduate student there by grace of Fulbright. With a degree from Helsinki in Business Administration behind me and with journalism in mind, I had come to the U.S. to fill a few holes in my education, liberal and otherwise.

Dr. Bird wanted something different. Graduate school was no place for seeking truth at a leisurely pace with like-minded students. My American colleagues, paying fortunes for their education by Finnish standards, were applying a basic economic principle: gather a maximum of credits in a minimum of time. Not to do the same would have left me completely alone, out of rhythm with the entire graduate school, waltzing to a rock beat.

Truth had to be found in six days and crammed into twelve pages—with footnotes. Thanking my fortune at having studied English as my third and optional foreign language after Finnish and Swedish, I set out to combine Europe's academic standards with American productivity.

"Beauty is truth, truth beauty," volunteered my roommate, a physicist. A nice equation, brief enough, but no footnotes. In a week, with the help of Socrates, Bertrand Russell, Wittgenstein and my battered Remington, I had Truth neatly wrapped up. In the Court of Truths, mine got an A from Judge Bird. At home, an A meant almost Nobel-laureate standards.

At Syracuse, I turned into a human workshop, producing papers at a speed no one at the Helsinki School of Economics could have imagined. In two semesters, 3 major term-papers, 17 papers for Dr. Bird, and 26 other written assignments, in addition to attending classes, passing exams and taking the comprehensives in Mass Communications. Syracuse did not give me a liberal education, it taught me how to work.

*   *   *

Women? Graduates were of course separated from undergraduates, and grad school appeared to be sexless. One either lived in voluntary celibacy or sublimated sex to Research Methods.

I experienced the power of American women. One day a woman asked a professor to open a window because it was too warm. He interrupted his lecture to do as he was asked. Was it because of a profound understanding of the employer-employee relationship? Or was it the position women had acquired during the pioneer years when they were in scarce supply? In Europe the situation was unthinkable.

My Keatsian roommmate suggested a date with Linda, another cultural shock. She chose a movie we had to reach by cab, she picked the restaurant and ordered our meals. I paid the bills, two weeks' household budget. No Fulbright allowance for dates. All for a goodnight kiss.

My roommate knew a very different girl, in New York. He spoke the truth. She was the opposite, in every respect, including her Greek origins. We have been married for thirty years now and have three children and two grandchildren.

Beauty is truth.

*   *   *

Just once, when I almost gave up under the stress, Dr. Bird had to teach me me another key American value: give up and you regret it your whole life.

He refused to allow me to drop a single course. Back to my Remington and onwards, until the MA was done.

Often since I have run into this business of never giving up. I understand what the American philosopher Vince Lombardi meant when he said that winning is not the best thing, it is the *only* thing, as well as what another philosopher—was it Yogi Berra?—meant when he said it is never over until it's over. I learned to understand the great depth of American character which lay beneath Nixon's need to assert he was "no quitter."

One thing I quit was serious basketball. Playing with a top-division team in Finland, I had assumed I would return from the U.S. a star. But the demands of the J-School left time for little play. With a roommate we did one-on-one, starting out for fun and ending up learning something when the game soon got serious—another American trait? "Crush the enemy," said George Patton, a hero of my roommate. I outplayed him. As always with Americans we were good friends afterwards. I wonder, deep in his soul, if he ever forgave me? I had applied Bird theory and even Patton theory, with no oriental concern for saving the opponent's face. The Experiment in International Living's motto: "You learn to live together by living together."

I talked my roommates into sharing the cost of the *New York Times*, a great investment. It compared with Syracuse's *Herald-Journal* as a New York girl compares to one from Syracuse. Henry Ward Beecher said, "Newspapers are the schoolmasters of the common people. That endless book, the newspaper, is our national glory." The *Times* was my second American university.

That year happened to be exciting for American political life. Hospitable fellow-students let me watch the Nixon-Kennedy TV debates and live through an unforgettable election night, till four AM. A tanned JFK, in person, strained his hoarse voice for one more brief speech during a whistlestop campaign that included Syracuse. I was euphoric about the American system of democracy and its free press.

Tiberius, Voltaire, Milton had said it earlier, but my prophets were Jefferson: "Were it left to me to decide whether we should have a government without newspapers, or newspapers without a government, I should not hesitate to prefer the latter." And Lincoln: "Let the people know the facts and the country will be safe." And most important, as the years have passed, Walter Lippman: "The theory of the free press is that the truth will emerge from free reporting and free discussion, not that it will be presented perfectly and instantly in any one account."

England, Sweden and France had of course given constitutional guarantees of free speech earlier. For me the U.S. Constitution said it best: "Congress shall make no law . . . abridging the freedom of speech, or of the press."

A full century before I returned from America, Felix Heikel—then editor of my newspaper *Hufvudstadsbladet*—had journeyed to the U.S. Afterwards he quoted an American voter: "I did not vote for Grant because he is a genius. Greeley has a better head, but Grant is an honest and capable man, and people need such men to govern them." Heikel's comment in 1873: "Lucky people!"

In 1961 I left the U.S. with a lot of basketball unplayed but full of idealistic and ultimately naive admiration for American democracy. I have no memory of the slightest self-doubt on the subject.

These three treasures then I acquired during my Fulbright year: a foreign wife, the capability to produce masses of text of passable quality, and a monumental belief in the blessings of press freedom. They have accompanied me ever since, through six years of newspaper and magazine journalism, seven of diplomacy in Stockholm and Washington, nine of newspaper management and eight of news agency journalism and management. Of these three, my wife is a blissfully private matter. My working capacity is nothing to brag about, having deteriorated with time (and perhaps wisdom?). That leaves my belief in the freedom of the press as an agent of truth. Let me try to trace what has happened to it since Senator Fulbright took me off the basketball court and set me on my present track.

*   *   *

At Syracuse I never believed that the sheer production of words would bring us closer to the truth. Unless of course truth lies in work itself. This is a plausible argument, in philosophy at least, but hard to prove.

"News," said Ben Bradlee, "is the first draft of history." Who are the drafters? Much of it is written by the news agencies. The truth about the world, in a single day, is expressed in about 33 million words--the number turned out daily by the four major international news agencies, according to a UNESCO survey in the mid-eighties. At the time, the Associated Press accounted for 17, UPI 11, Agence France Presse 3.4, and Reuters 1.5. For purposes of comparison, six of the biggest national news agencies *together* produced only about a million words daily. Today a few international news bureaus provide the world with its daily truth. In terms of *foreign* news, just two—AP and Reuters—dominate absolutely. With some 1200 correspondents all over the world, these two provide most of what we know about what happens daily outside our national boundaries. The *Encyclopaedia Britannica* Annual collects the world's history. A few years ago, this version of truth amounted to a million words, culled from the news agencies' 33. In 1771 the first edition of the entire *Britannica* contained 3 million words; my 1966 edition has 36 million—has world truth in 200 years increased only twelvefold? In any case, whatever the drafters write is pretty much compulsory reading for a journalist like me.

In 1887 the Finnish News Agency was founded. Its task: to provide newspapers with the "most important" news of each day. But what news is important? The *Britannica* has one answer. For most of us that question is answered by the news media, generally persuaded that they correctly interpret the needs of their consumers—who better, they ask?

Of the news agencies' 33 million daily words, many are repeats. Assuming only 10 million words of original daily news—a generous estimate which eases calculations, the Finnish News Agency receives about 300,000 words of international news every day. Of that, the agency sends on about 13,000 words (about 0.13% of the world's production) to its newspaper and broadcasting customers. Of these 13,000, the average newspaper uses a couple of thousand, and broadcasters less—no more than 0.013% of the world's truth.

So much for the whole truth. As for its being nothing but the truth, we can only hope. The most important? All "that is fit to print"? More hope needed. Polonius: What do you read, my lord? Hamlet: Words, words, words.

*   *   *

Of all the radical ideas born in the sixties, few consumed more words than mass communications. Not many years after Syracuse, I tangled with another Finn—an American graduate in Mass-Com—in a Great Debate. Kaarle Nordenstreng, with a background like mine and a sincerity I have no reason to question, arrived at opposite conclusions from mine. Each had his own truth. He became an advocate for UNESCO's Mass Media Declaration and its New World Information and Communication Order. As for me, a die-hard practitioner albeit in the same field, I ended up on the other side of the fence, first as a member of the Finnish National UNESCO Committee, then as Board Member and later Chairman of the International Press Institute (IPI).

In a decade of debate, the UNESCO paper-mill at Place de Fontenoy in Paris, with the assistance of researchers all over the world, produced a mountain of documents on mass communications. On November 22, 1978, this mountain gave birth to a mouse with a big name: the Declaration on Fundamental Principles Concerning the Contribution of the Mass Media to Strengthening Peace and International Understanding, to the Promotion of Human Rights and to Countering Racism, Apartheid and Incitement to War. Perhaps UNESCO financed some useful mass communications research, but much of the result today has no more worth than my old term-papers at Syracuse—and probably less value as academic training.

Throughout the debate, the U.S. stood up for the same ideals of free speech I had imbibed at Syracuse, to the point of withdrawing from UNESCO—at least in part because of the mass communications argument. Fighting for press freedom, among others, were the World Press Freedom Committee. In 1981 WPFC and Tufts University's Fletcher School of Law and Diplomacy organized a conference in Talloires, in France near the Swiss border: the Voices of Freedom Conference of Independent News Media. Sixty-three delegates came together from 21 countries. Today the Declaration of Talloires is often called the "Magna Carta of the Free Press." To my sorrow I did not participate.

In the end the great UNESCO debate left no imprint on the world history of mass communications. The participants might have remembered Hamlet's step-father: "My words fly up, my thoughts remain below./ Words without thought never to heaven go." The dusty papers produced by UNESCO are now sharing a similar fate: "Imperious Caesar, dead and turned to clay,/ Might stop a hole to keep the wind away."

The strong winds of historic change building up in the late eighties, especially in Eastern Europe, were a more permanent matter—or so it seems today. They too had their Hamlets, but some of their words were trickier than others. "Objective reality," for example, is a Marxist-Leninist idea, hopefully today drifting towards the dustbin of history along with kindred doctrines. Nordenstreng illustrates its meaning through his definition of international news value (Nordenstreng, Ahmavaara and Peltola, *Informational Mass Communication*, Tammi: Helsinki, 1973): "The importance of a news item is determined in the first place by the extent to which the event described affects the lives of the audience either directly or indirectly, *regardless of whether or not the audience is itself aware of this effect*" (my italics). Admire his easy solution to the dilemma of which news is important: Big Brother Knows Best, or spoon-feeding.

Could Keats have written: "Beauty is Objective Reality, Objective Reality Beauty"? Poor Keats died too young to know Lenin's aphorism, "The author is the engineer of the soul." The best he could do was declare poets the "unacknowledged legislators of the world."

That is how my Fulbright principles withstood the assault of the Mass Media Declaration.

*   *   *

The UNESCO debate surely made little difference to the world press and the exercise of its freedom, though I sometimes wonder where things would have stood without Talloires. But another declaration turned out to be much more important, perhaps unintentionally: the Final Act of the Conference on Security and Cooperation in Europe (CSCE), often called the Helsinki Third Basket.

As a drop in the ocean of history, I was involved. I helped Finland's visiting Ralph Enckell, when I was Press Attache in Washington, to convince the State Department it should support the Conference. The chain leading to that role led straight back to Syracuse. Returning to my newspaper in Helsinki, I had found a pile of reprints of an article of mine—a retread of a Syracuse paper—on Public Relations, my Syracuse major. They had forgotten to show me the article, picture and all, published by the Public Relations Society. The article led to several job offers. I took one, editing a promotional magazine in English on Finland. This led in turn to an offer from Ambassador Enckell, then in Stockholm, to do a book on my country for Swedish consumption. This led in turn to Enckell's inviting me to join him there, then in moving me to Washington—to no regret of my wife.

Enckell was disappointed in then-Secretary of State William Rogers: "A typical American lawyer and no diplomat. He doesn't understand that process may matter as much as product or results. He asks, 'What's in it for us?'" The U.S. was suspicious of Finland's motives in promoting the Conference. Someone had apparently convinced them we were running errands for the USSR.

The CSCE convened in Helsinki in 1975. Its Final Act was signed by the heads of state of all the European powers including the USSR and its satellites, the U.S. and Canada. What the U.S. and the West would find "in it for us" was Basket Three, concerned with human rights. At the time few made the connection: the Soviet Union and other signatories had pledged themselves to foster the "freer flow and wider dissemination of information of all kinds, to encourage cooperation in the field of information and the exchange of information with other countries, and to improve conditions under which journalists from one participating state exercise their profession in another participating state."

Obviously nothing of the kind was immediately carried out in Eastern Europe. But the Final Act carried their signatures. It served as a point of reference for dissidents and fighters for press freedom. The Helsinki process played an incalculable role in the wave of freedom that washed over East and Central Europe in the late eighties. Information crossing national borders quickly began to expose the gross inequities and injustice inflicted on people of the same cultural and historical background. Brecht's words about some who walk in the shadow and others who live in the light, referring originally to class differences, took on a new meaning in Europe.

Many factors caused the revolutionary events that led to the historical changes in Eastern and Central Europe in 1989 and in the Soviet Union in 1991: the collapse of the Communist economic and political system, the absurdity of the nuclear arms race and its cost, distress over miserable living standards and malfunctioning societies, the total lack of confidence in the leadership—and dictatorship—of the Communist parties. Through all these runs the thread of freedom of speech and expression. The liberalization of East Europe, whatever comes next, is one of history's great victories for the free word. In the tradition of Tiberius, Voltaire and Milton, Jefferson, Lincoln and Lippman. At least that is how it looked to a Syracusan Fulbrighter.

*   *   *

My accent in English is still foreign—I started too late and came too late to the U.S. But the year at Syracuse gave me a touch of American identity I have never lost. In fact, I have nurtured it. My two oldest children began school in Washington, then returned later as exchange students. My wife has twice chaired the American Women's Club in Helsinki. We have had many embassy friends over the years. Son Paul surprised his California host family by making the basketball team at Cupertino High. Helena did the same in Ephrata, Washington, broke the school record for free-throws, and was offered a scholarship at Seattle University.

In Stockholm another Syracusan, Don Henry, lured me into joining a third-division team in the YMCA league. An American of Phillipine origin joined us and we started applying the Patton doctrine. We ended up in the finals playing Acropolis, a team of Greek immigrants. We hustled enough so that half their team fouled out—we won by a point. On the way to the locker-room, a Greek player spit in our Phillipine friend's face, shouting, "You f-ing immigrant." What immigrants hate most is other immigrants.

You learn to live together by living together.

*   *   *

What comes next in our world? Freedom of speech was always guaranteed in the constitutions of the "socialist" states, as it is in Article 35 of the Constitution of the PRC: "Citizens of the People's Republic of China enjoy freedom of speech, of the press, of assembly, of association, of procession and of demonstration." So what happened in Tienanmen Square?

Try Article 51 of the same Constitution: "The exercise by the citizens of the PRC of their freedoms and rights may not infringe upon the interests of the state, of society and of the collective, or upon the lawful freedoms and rights of other citizens." The same free principles applied in Eastern Europe. Freedom of speech and of the press, but subordinated to the interests of the State and the collective. Defining those interests was left to the Party.

Beginning in 1985, Glasnost began to change this. I asked my colleague at TASS, whom as Manager of the Finnish News Agency I knew well, what Glasnost meant for TASS. "Now we are telling the truth," he answered. As it later emerged, TASS had taken the first step on the ladder leading to the levels of truth common to the West—by admitting having lied before. It was a start.

The party organ *Pravda*, which name itself means Truth, never repented. After all, it had always represented truth, the ultimate truth, the objective truth. In the thirties, when the paper misspelled a name, the owner had to change his name. The conformity theory of truth.

New openness and truthfulness in the Soviet papers almost immediately boosted their circulation enormously. But economic reforms lagged behind and left the country with another set of lies, as fatal as the media's. Statistics were made to lie for the same reason that Johann Jacoby had given Friedrich Wilhelm: "It is the misfortune of kings that they do not want to hear the truth."

Prices too were lies. A subway ride, 5 kopeks in 1935, cost 5 kopeks in 1968. A three-room flat still cost 15-20 rubles a month, a kilo of bread 25-40 kopeks. But a four-person Lada car cost 7500 rubles and a color TV cost 700. Prices before January 1992 had no relationship to cost of production or demand. But price is the language of products. Low, it says: "Produce less of me." High, it says, "Produce more." People in Moscow screamed for more housing, but prices screamed louder: "Fewer flats." When prices lie, distribution does not work. With no price mechanism, government has to have huge inventories of goods. The high investment in the Soviet economy happened because only high stockpiles can increase consumption, but only very slowly.

Even the Soviet economy needed free speech.

*   *   *

The press in Eastern Europe was controlled in three ways by the Party which, as we already know, had a monopoly on defining the State's interest. In the Central Committee of the Party, Agitprop (Lenin defined the press as the "agitator, propagator and organizer of the proletarian revolution") controled the finances, the administration, and the contents of the press. The Party not only appointed the editors, it provided newsprint and presses. It also put in

Party *politrucs* to oversee what was published. When the Party was over-thrown, it left the media as empty as Party headquarters. No owners, no operating capital, no one to tell them what to write.

At the Moscow University School of Journalism, I kept Dr. Bird and Research Methods in mind when I asked what sources they taught their students to use. Our hosts did not understand the question. I explained "news sources." "Oh," they said, "they of course use official documents." The journalist as parakeet.

No owners or administration, no capital or revenues, no norms of journalistic ethics. The press in Eastern Europe faces three different vacuums. Three holes to plug with half-understood concepts like private ownership, market economics and a free-press ideology. Not as easy as it sounds.

The "socialist" countries live a different reality from ours in the West. The role of the press in consequence is also different. Economically they suffer shortages while the West lives with abundance. Russian Jews entering Israel do not cry when they cross the border, they cry when they see the supermarkets and realize the misery in which they have spent their lives. If there are no goods, why advertise? For empty shelves? If the shelves had any goods at all, they would disappear before the ad had time to appear.

For the press, there is a fight going on for values long since established in the West. This means the approach is more ideological, more nationalistic, than in the cooler-headed and factual western media. Politically, they are experiencing the birth of democracy, where the West has been shaping democratic process for decades, scores of years, centuries. For the press, this again means a fight over values and norms. How can they be pluralist in our sense of the word? Their situation resembles that of the West a century or so ago.

For these shattering problems, Syracuse provided no answers. In the reality of Eastern Europe, journalism textbooks can offer only empty phrases. More words, more Hamlet. Free speech, as a value, is absolute. It cannot be subject to compromise. But it will surely develop along different paths in different historical, social, economic and political contexts.

*   *   *

Something links Fulbright and basketball—my main Fulbright contacts over the years have been in the gym. When I got back to Helsinki, Fulbright Director Bill Copeland, a fine historian of China, was arranging Saturday afternoon pickup games for Fulbrighters, embassy personnel and a few Finns. Bill too was a Bird-Patton-Berra theorist.

I played on the Finnish team one day, the American the next, a minor identity crisis. I was often put on the defensive by Europeans criticizing

American values; but then the Americans went after European values through me as well. Thank God for the common ground of free speech—on that we could always agree. So I wandered in my mid-Atlantic space. Saturday's expert on fadeaway jump-shots delivered Monday's lecture on *Moby Dick* as Puritan literature and Reagan's rise to the presidency.

Tensions rose when the Finns began regularly winning the Saturday games. An embassy friend brought in the Marines, literally. Youth and muscle reclaimed the day for the Yanks. But politics stepped in. The Marines never passed off, it was every Marine for himself. The one Finn on the American team was the one with access to the free gym. No more Saturday basketball for the Fulbrights. A parable lurks in that story. Knowing you can't win them all, I began to wonder about the American value of win-win.

*   *   *

Free speech won a major battle in Europe in 1989. But it lost one in the Gulf War of 1991. The war was quickly over. The war for freedom of speech is never over. As Chairman of the IPI, I opened the proceedings at our General Assembly in Kyoto in May 1991. I said, "January was a black month for press freedom. It was as black as the oil, killing innocent birds in the Persian Gulf. It was as black as the berets of the commandos hitting civilians in the Latvian capital of Riga. In January, the free world was gasping for air, like a sea bird smeared with oil."

In January 1991 word power was world power. But it was in the wrong hands: word power was exercised by the military censors, not by a free world press. In the Gulf as in all wars, truth was the first casualty. "These reports are subject to allied military reporting restrictions." Soon after the beginning, international journalists were expelled from Baghdad. Then began the CNN show. Some called it the best TV journalism they had ever seen. In the U.S. not everyone agreed.

Modern manipulation of the press, learned first in the Falklands then polished in Grenada and Panama, was put to efficient use in the Gulf. The press, taken by surprise, was completely controled.

It contradicted everything I had learned at Syracuse. The U.S. commitment to free speech began to blur in my mind. What had Felix Heikel said in 1873—something about electing honest and capable men? Watergate and Irangate raised doubts, I repressed them. But the Gulf? I shall watch and wait for the American free press system to stage a comeback from the censorship of that episode.

*   *   *

Are there other dangers looming? Free speech can work as an agent of truth, but it is constantly under pressure. New factors emerge every day. Take the element of speed in reporting.

News through history has traveled at different speeds, according to the technology of the time. The news from Marathon reached Athens by foot. Then came horse couriers, carriages, pigeons, smoke signals, trains, cars, telegraphic cable, radio waves, lasers and satellites. The news of Napoleon's abdication took 44 days to reach Finland in the winter of 1813, but Gorbachev's resignation took place on live TV in real time: does this foster truth?

We Finns say truth travels slowly but lies have long legs. Mark Twain said a lie can travel halfway around the globe while truth is putting on its shoes. *Die Zeit*, on the Gulf War:

> Truth may be the first casualty of war, but ultra-fast television is degraded into a means of propaganda. Given censorship, the impatient television gobbles up all time for considering, for checking and weighing information—time that democracy urgently requires. The triumph of the news could spell the demise of democracy, which would be replaced by the rule of speed. High-speed journalism uses military methods, draws near the military, and risks losing its independence and credibility.

Another factor: the limited angle of vision of the screen. Like the oft-repeated pictures of precision-bombs hitting their targets, TV shows again and again the baskets scored; it leaves out the team-work, the failures, the mid-field maneuvring, the preparation, the essential contexts, the victims.

Pace Baudelaire, the best translations may also be the truest, as it is paradoxically with truly beautiful women. But the fastest news is seldom the most truthful.

As Aesop's hare suggested, too much sleep damages the memory capacity. Radio and television news has no memory. It disappears into air as soon as it is spoken, even when it is repeated. But the newspaper is its own memory. *Verba volant, scripta lettera manet*—the written word stays where the spoken words fly away.

For the world's society, a 33-million-word first draft is cut to a few thousand, delivered in sound-bytes of a few seconds, wrenched from historical and social context. We are falling victim to Alzheimer's disease, soon we will know only what is happening in real time. No history, no future. What a responsibilty for the dailies and the periodicals! Erwin Canham said long ago that people cannot and need not absorb meanings at the speed of light: "The day of the printed word is far from ended. Swift as is the delivery of the radio bulletin, graphic as is television's eyewitness picture, the task of adding meaning and clarity remains urgent."

Is the successor of Syracuse's J-School, the Samuel Newhouse Mass Communication Center, still teaching journalists to do research and to write?

*   *   *

If speed makes for problems, what about winning? Today I wonder if my roommate emerged from the Syracuse gym better educated than I. Winning brings a simple but deceptive emotion. Losing is a more profound learning experience, you learn about yourself. Americans worship winners, as they worship youth. It is fine for the younger years. But over time I have drifted away from Patton-Nixon theory. I see sports as a lesson in losing, not winning. Perhaps baseball is a more profound game than football—every team has to lose fifty or more games in a season, and for every hit a good batter is permitted eight or more misses. Losing in sports prepares us even for the ultimate loss—the semantics of sports (a "deadly" forehand, or "sudden death" overtime) remind us what it is all about. Like the films of Lucchino Visconti and Ingmar Bergman and others, reflecting their own struggles with death.

The winner can fool himself, the loser faces reality. The moment of truth comes when a matador and a bull look each other in the eye. Life is a game of tennis with an unbeatable opponent. You prolong the game by playing well, but the last ball will always pass you. Game, set and match—face the truth.

*   *   *

I understand it when I see a lie in newspapers or anywhere. I am less happy when they say I am being told the truth. Because if I see and read only one truth, I know this cannot be right—if only because truth, in theory, requires an opposite in order to exist. Light defines shadow.

I do not believe anyone claiming to tell the "truth." When a source claims the whole truth, the journalist gets suspicious. The news agency journalist, competing against speed, uses a simple operational definition of truth: truth happens when two independent sources give the same information. That is why I am happy to find a lie—then I know that the truth has been tested. This kind of happiness hits me often.

In Stockholm in 1968 I was asked to correct Wilfred Fleisher, the Washington Post correspondent; he had reported Soviet officers in uniform in the Finnish border town of Lappeenranta, implying that the USSR was putting military pressure on Finland. At lunch I asked him if he had been to Finland. No. Would he accept an invitation to visit? No, it would embarrass his son who was working in the American embassy in Helsinki. I told him his son was already embarrassed because he knew there were no Soviet officers in Lappeenranta. The Post never printed a correction. Even Homer naps.

During Irangate, the IPI had its board meeting in Israel. We met Peres and Shamir on different occasions, the same day. Both explicitly denied involvement in Irangate. A few days later Israel admitted its role. The IPI board had been told lies. It is bad enough reading lies in newspapers but that is nothing compared to being told a lie to one's face.

The world press is full of lies, lies that influence world history. The student death that triggered the Velvet Revolution in Czechoslovakia in 1989? There was no dead student. The famous battle in the Gulf of Tonkin? No battle. Reagan was no Signal Corps photographer in World War II, and the JFK I admired in 1960 turns out to have been a womanizer.

None of this destroys my belief in a free press. Its strength lies not in that it is always and ever right but instead in the many texts, voices and pictures, often contradicting each other, which give the consumer the means to form his or her own opinion. The basis for protecting publishers of false information is that otherwise the truth would too often be suppressed. In science, as Niels Bohr said, the opposite of one profound truth may be another profound truth.

The lie is the prerequisite for truth. No lies, no truth. Suppress lies, you suppress truth because you do not know what the truth is. A lie is a truth that has not yet been rehabilitated. The lie of hypocrisy, says La Rochefoucauld, is the homage vice pays to virtue. The main requirement for a journalist is suspicion. Hamlet wrote to Ophelia:

> Doubt thou the stars are fire;
>   Doubt that the earth doth move,
> Doubt truth to be a liar;
>   But never doubt I love.

We arrive at beauty and love by searching for truth. Or we arrive at truth through love and beauty. Over the years I have learned more and more to prefer the latter. My roommate and John Keats were both right: beauty is indeed truth, truth beauty: "That is all ye know on earth, and all ye need to know."

Gunnar-Adler Karlsson, by his own description, has been seen in his native Sweden as an "American"-influenced maverick, a victim of the process of "Americanization" described by others in this volume. He spends most of his time today in his Institute for Social Philosophy, on the enchanted Mediterranean island of Capri. A political economist who has long focused on the Soviet economy, he tells of outstripping his country's capacity to develop high-level research in his field and turning to the Fulbright Program for a year at both Harvard and Berkeley. He relates the unusual case, in an advanced industrialized society, of a high-level research Fulbright who seems to have outgrown the academic teaching and research structures of his own country, not as a brain drained to the U.S. but as a brain his homeland has not found a way to use. His essay speaks as well to a remarkable formative pre-Fulbright U.S. experience, and to the natural progression from this program to the American post-graduate world.

15

FULBRIGHT KICKS

Gunnar Adler-Karlsson

My father had not the slightest idea of it, but I later came to understand that in my home province he was the representative of American capitalist imperialism. He was the local wholesaler of bananas in Biekinge, in southern Sweden. In 1933 when I was born, that region still lived in another version of García Marques' *One Hundred Years of Solitude*. As a child I never heard the name of United Fruit. I doubt my father knew he worked for it.

We lived close by the port of Karlshamn, the "harbor of Charles." It was dominated by a big margarine factory. We often visited the foreign ships. I was fascinated by their brown and yellow sailors, carrying bananas from Guatemala, coconuts from Africa, soybeans from China. Before I started school my fantasies roamed over the whole world.

At sixteen, I got a chance to come into contact with the American part of it when I applied for a scholarship. To the surprise of my parents and more so of my teachers, I was chosen as the only Swede that year to go to Camp Rising Sun in Rhinebeck, New York. It had been founded before World War II by an idealistic American, George E. Jonas.

It was a private, small-scale Fulbright Program. "Freddy," as we called Mr. Jonas, was one of the most lovable father-figures I have ever met. His idea was to bring together promising youngsters at the impressionable age of 15-16 years in an international community. Some 25 American boys and 20 foreigners from as many nations spent the summer together in something like a Scout camp. The program however was much less practical. Our time was filled with discussions, with common creative projects in music, theatre and a camp newspaper, or with a bit of native Indian mysticism around a weekly campfire, uniting us all in a big global brotherhood. Freddie carefully observed every single boy, in my case trying to soften a bit of the stiff Prussian self-discipline in which I had been raised. Camp Rising Sun left an international imprint on me and a feeling for American generosity that nothing—even Vietnam—has been able to delete.

That scholarship might pass for an early indicator of ability. An early sign of idealism may be found in my first article. It was written in 1954 during my military service, for the so-called cadet newspaper. In it I called for giving one per cent of our gross national product as aid to poor and underdeveloped nations. That is, it had the same content as, for instance, an editorial in the International Herald Tribune of June 6, 1991. Thirty-five years later the western world is giving only a third of one per cent of GNP to foreign aid.

After our unpleasant version of military service, I went to the University of Stockholm to study the law. There I met Marianne. The law professors made less of an impression. They were all busier with profitable legal practices than with teaching or with the search for a balance between Right and Might.

One stimulating professor of economics, Ingvar Svennilson, took me in charge. After my law degree, he arranged for support for five hard years of further study in economics. He led me to focus on the communist pricing system and its effect on Soviet foreign trade, the subject of my thesis in 1962. Until recently that book has proved frighteningly up-to-date: absurd marxist pricing principles have been damaging the Soviet economy for three or more decades. They lie at the bottom of an economic conundrum: as I write in late 1991 neither Gorbachev nor Yeltsin has dared cut through it all with a serious market deregulation, lest political repercussions become too explosive.

Why did I apply for a Fulbright? Of Sweden's 9 million inhabitants, only a few are expert in each field and specialty. The few Swedish Sovietologists at the end of the Fifties were either involved in secret work or some semi-secret variant. One sat in the Foreign Office, one was in military intelligence, and a few knowledgable people formed a brain trust in the export community. None was teaching. Most were unwilling to share insights with a young and unknown scholar. We were in the middle of the Cold War. My subject was more sensitive than I had imagined. In England, West Germany and the UN Economic Commission for Europe, I got in touch with other experts. Most were similarly "secret" or tied into practical work, thus unhelpful. In the U.S. two academic institutions beckoned: Harvard's Russian Research Center and Berkeley's Slavic Center. Professor Svennilson suggested the Fulbright route to a half-year's study at each. Having married Marianne—a classical archaeologist—in Athens in December 1960, we set out for Harvard the following Summer.

All this happened thirty years ago. How to channel the flood of memories? How to separate out exactly what the Fulbright experience meant in the now fuller cauldron of my mind? More generally, what can such a cultural project as Fulbright be expected to do for and to anyone, at any time, in any place?

Common genes dispose us to common behavior but common homes and education less so: " . . . the effect of being reared in the same home is negligible for many psychological traits," writes Thomas Bouchard, who specializes in the question of Nature vs. Nurture. To a Sovietologist, the inability of cultures to affect personalities in a lasting and systematic way gives hope. It helps understand why a ruthless totalitarian indoctrination has failed to wipe out the spirit of Russian freedom, even in an extremely repressed population. But the same principle should sound a note of caution for something like the Fulbright Program. Nothing systematic should be expected.

What culture *can* do seems more stochastic, influential but in a random way. During a long train ride, for example, one may chance to meet an interesting person so stimulating that it changes one's behavior in a lasting manner, provoking us to exert innate abilities more than before, perhaps even giving a new direction to one's life and work. In the strongest case, it can be something like a religious conversion. What culture can do, at its best, is to give us a kick. I see the Fulbright Program as a systematic attempt to provide such kicks, perhaps in both senses of the word.

Which of the kicks of 1961-62 seem important today? The first was academic excellence. At Harvard, over which another Rising Sun boy now presides, I found hard-working, disciplined, continuously-publishing no-nonsense scholars everywhere I looked. People came to their offices early in the morning, remained there, had intensive lunch discussions and more intensive weekly seminars; the library services were prompt and perfect.   Totally different from what I had seen back home, it provided a model to imitate.

In my field, I had the privilege of meeting some of its most eminent scholars. Abram Bergson, the grand old man of American Sovietology, took care of me. Alexander Gershenkron, Marshall Goldman, Franklyn Holzman, Charles Kindleberger at MIT, and Marshall Shulman, to mention a few of the best, helped in many ways. They taught me how to study. To Marianne's horror, I still often get to my typewriter at 5 AM.

Abram Bergson and his wife once took us to Thoreau's Walden. Bergson was the first scholar to have cut through the muddle of Soviet statistics, making it possible to estimate the size of the economy in relation to that of the U.S. He had laid out an immense puzzle of details. It had cost millions, mainly from the RAND Corporation, then rumored to be "the CIA of the Air Force." Over lunch at Walden, I asked why RAND had devoted so much to him and his project. The essence of his answer: to know where to drop atomic bombs. His research was involved and engaged in the Cold War. Obviously scholars in the USSR were being similarly enlisted. I wondered to what extent that was true of other American and western scholars.

Marianne and I were much impressed at the time by the Theatre of the Absurd, notably Beckett's *Godot* and Ionesco's *Rhinoceros*, illustrating the behavior of a sometimes irrational humanity. Bergson, on the "rational" side of Sovietology, was unsurpassed; but we were shocked by his lack of interest in the absurdists' "humanistic" insight into the behavior that surely lay behind the Cold War.

The question fed into my sense of the Fulbright experience: was the goal really to understand, or was it to win? One of the most enthralling lecture series I heard at Harvard was Merle Fainsod's analyses of the Soviet communist party.   You left each lecture quivering with hatred for that monstrous power apparatus. So far as I could judge, Fainsod said nothing that was not so. But where was the classical *sine ira et studio*, the ideal that one should study without wrath or bias?

As a "neutral" with a deep and even unscientifically emotional interest in the Cold War, my main concern was peace. I was terrified that a third world war might explode upon us, atomic bombs and all. "Mutual understanding," the key concept of the Fulbright Program, was something I took very seriously: if the U.S. and the USSR did not develop a deep mutual understanding of each other's systems, the risks of ultimate conflagration were much higher. But these are nice words that idealistic youngsters can easily believe. During my stay at Harvard, listening for example to the spellbinding Merle

Fainsod, I began to wonder if I, as well as Sweden's neutral policy, were not a bit naive.

A good number of the scholars I met seemed more interesting in "winning" over the Soviet, atheistic, communist system than in understanding it. In the autumn of 1961, the Cold War was intense. Only a few years before the Soviets had invaded Hungary. The Berlin Wall had just gone up. Shortly after I got to Harvard, a man I had met—Dag Hammarskjold, the Swedish UN Secretary General—died in a plane crash in Africa. He had been heavily denounced by the Soviets for UN involvement in the Belgian Congo crisis and rumors circulated that they had brought down his plane. Feelings were running high.

American scholars, and even more the many refugees I knew, wanted to win more than to understand. "What would have happened had we tried only to 'understand' Hitler without fighting him? Why should we try to 'understand' the equally horrifying Stalinist system?" Such questions are not easy to answer. Put differently, what should a nation do in a conflict between two sides if only one side is prepared to understand and the other maintains a ruthless indoctrinating system which turns its adherents into senseless janissaries or mankurts? In such a case, is it not a duty to give students a similarly intense hatred for the opponent?

Fainsod had a deep understanding of the facts. But when you are fighting a totalitarian system, he maintained, mutual understanding is not an option: the opponent will not permit it. The best you can attain, in those circumstances, is one-sided understanding. But then? Is the understanding of what is true and just not a value in itself? Indeed is it not a weapon, a power of its own?

Marshall Shulman, author of one of the best books at that time on Stalin's foreign policy and a former diplomat in Moscow, took me to lunch à trois with the editor in charge of all Soviet material for *Time*. In the course of our conversation, this man—whose name I have gratefully forgotten—flatly told us: "We at *Time* are not out to tell the truth. We are out to fight Communism." He was, to me, a paid mercenary.

In the West we cherish the truth. In the academic world it is or should be the primary value. But this man was telling me that truth was subordinate to the struggle. He mirrored the attitude of the renowned communist ideologist Gyorgy Lukacs: asked about the moral value of lying, Lukacs proclaimed, "communist ethics makes it the highest duty to accept the necessity of doing evil." I certainly did not want communism to win. But if in the struggle against communism we in the West give up our highest democratic values and adopt the immorality of communism, what is left to fight for? That meeting with the *Time* man, a minor kick, sharpened my watchfulness against those journalists, professors and politicians who, in the heat of the struggle, forget about principle.

Looking back, we say now that the U.S. has "won" the struggle against Soviet communism. On *why* it did, scholars are never likely to agree. My own conviction, after thirty years of Cold War studies, is that the U.S. "won" largely because it invariably promoted, as with the Fulbright Program, the western values of open societies and mutual understanding, at least to the extent possible. In the long run, these values are more efficient weapons than secret and devious actions by CIA or the Star Warriors. Given patience, sheer truth can make the walls of both Jericho and Berlin come tumbling down. Somewhere in *Philoctetes*, Sophocles has Neoptolemus say: "I would rather fail acting nobly than win by acting basely." That summarizes the most useful kick of my Fulbright year, at least from an ethical point of view.

Another: if it had not been for Fulbright, I would never have become a collaborator of Gunnar Myrdal. Myrdal often said he was more American than Swedish. It was he, I believe, who coined the concept of the American Creed. He was immensely proud that, when Kennedy was shot, his desk held a copy of Myrdal's *Challenge to America*. Myrdal became the teacher of my academic life—for better or for worse.

He had published his *American Dilemma* in 1944. In 1945 he was Minister of Trade for Sweden. In 1946 he was named head of the UN Economic Commission for Europe (ECE). He was, beyond compare, the most successful Swedish social scientist and our champion at getting honorary doctorates all over the world.

In his best-selling *Der Neid*, German writer Helmut Schoeck claims that jealousy is the central human characteristic. No Swede has been exposed to as much jealousy as Gunnar Myrdal (am I wrong in thinking that the only American Senator with a global fan-club of bright, grateful and influential admirers of all ages may have had a similar experience?). The Swedish economists admired Myrdal's sociology but said he was no economist, the sociologists vice versa. The *American Dilemma* was never reviewed in Sweden, not even once. He spoke of that the last time I saw him, a few weeks before the end. After his *Asian Drama* (1968), proposals for the Nobel Prize started dropping in from all over the world, so many that they could not be ignored. But to devalue the prize, his economist colleagues decided to have him share it with his worst ideological enemy, Friedrich Hayek (the same Senator I mentioned earlier has been nominated eighteen times without success for the Nobel Prize). Even after death the jealousy continued: on the day he died a leading Swedish economist, via the media, said contemptuously that Myrdal had been nothing but a "super-journalist."

We met by a fortuitous accident. Derek Bok, already president of Harvard and himself a Fulbright alumnus, had married Myrdal's daughter Sissela. Myrdal came to Cambridge for a visit in late 1961. We had met earlier in Sweden and now he invited us to dinner at the Boks' home. At 63, he was already a bitter man. His ego, which from the beginning had not been small, was badly wounded. He had developed an enormous need for relating the great deeds he had done. They were fascinating the first time.

It was into this context that I came. He suggested I write the first serious study on a rather secret side of the Cold War, the U.S.-led attempts to break the back of the Soviet economy under the guise of a "strategic" embargo policy. He was very persuasive. He told me about archival materials and mentioned a top-secret source to which I would have access.

His persuasion succeeded, but only because of a contingent fact. In Cambridge, Marianne and I lived in a small room at 1709 Cambridge Street. Our charming host-family had also rented a room to a boy from Thailand, Suchati Chuthasmit. We became friends. He was working on a thesis at the Fletcher School. By chance I read through his manuscript and it was precisely on the theme that Myrdal was suggesting. Knowing I had a good, independent starting-point, I agreed to join Myrdal when I returned to Sweden in 1962.

So Derek Bok's marriage, Myrdal's visit, Chuthasmit's thesis and my Fulbright grant combined to give me another kick, one that kept me busy researching and writing *Western Economic Warfare 1947-67*, published seven years later. Today Chuthasmit is one of Thailand's leading diplomats, at the moment Ambassador to Indonesia and a major force behind the initiative to create an ASEAN Free Trade Area by the year 2000.

Could Myrdal have united Europe in peace with the help of the ECE, given a chance? Later, when we discussed economic warfare more deeply, I came to understand that that was precisely what he had wanted me to prove. This had been his vision in 1946, but then came the Marshall Plan, out of which grew the OEEC-OECD framework and the economic embargo policy. The organization in Paris that was to distribute Marshall aid took any real power away from Myrdal's ECE. It destroyed his potential instrument, his hope to unify all Europe from the Atlantic to the Urals in an intricate pattern of economic interdependency. With hindsight it is easy to say this was a naive vision, given Stalin's reckless will to power. But in 1946 such visions might have been nurtured.

However he may now be judged, Myrdal was a great man. His importance for the U.S. has recently been described in Walter A. Jackson's *Gunnar Myrdal and America's Conscience* (1990). As for me, that dinner in December 1961 gave me the most important kick of my entire professional life, with repercussions that led to my own Institute on the "Pearl of the Mediterranean," the island of Capri where I now live. I shall come to that story.

Our move from Cambridge to Berkeley took the long road. The sea voyage from Göteborg to New York had not been perfect—Marianne caught the flu just before departure and spent most of her time in bed. Entering New York Harbor, we watched, close together then as now, while the classical skyline emerged out of the morning mists. It was impressive, it gave us hope for a new life, but it had been a dull trip. We decided on some compensatory travel.

At the end of the year we spent a fine Christmas week with Marianne's parents in Vero Beach, Florida. We were duly shocked by the obvious racism: our part of the beach was closed to blacks. A life-guard explained to us that they were not permitted because the water would be polluted if a "nigger" went into it.

From Florida we flew to Mérida in the Mexican Yucatan. There I saw the only free market I ever found in all my life. It was an open area in which about 5000 Indians tried to sell simple shoes to another 5000 Indians selling bananas. Remembering my childhood and the economic basis of my early education, I see why this market has always remained with me. In the Spring of 1991 I used it in a series of lectures in Moscow and Poland, where far too many people believe even today in the saving power of something they call "the free market." In reality, markets are rarely free; they are regulated by law or manipulated by cartels. In Mérida I glimpsed Adam Smith's original 1776 conception of this potent idea.

From Mérida to Mexico City, we alternately hitch-hiked and took local fifth-class buses, seeing a form of life we never saw in Sweden. Staying in Uxmal, for example, we walked among the fabulous Mayan statues and I climbed the pyramid of the Temple of the Magician. Nature was wild and we were lonely. The few people we saw around were carrying guns. We asked why. "There are lots of pumas around," was the answer. Swedes grow up in security "from the cradle to the grave." We were as lucky as we were naive.

In Mexico City, we spent memorable days with an old Rising Sun alumnus, Alessandro Benbassatt, who had already won national fame as a hero of the speedways and occasionally the bullring (unfortunately later on he drove fast one time too many and died). Around New Year's Eve he took us to La Gitanería Blanca. During a gorgeous and entertaining evening, I had the usual business to do in the gentleman's room where I was stunned to find a man with a Kleenex whose job it was to wipe my penis dry. I came to realize that class differences may take unexpected forms. A few days later, despite strong warnings from our hotel porter, we found our way to the Gitanería Negra, where Marianne and I were probably the only white tourists in a crowd of some thousand Indians, watching a simple but warm performance of music and dancing.

My naiveté found other expression in a train ride from Guadalajara to the U.S. border a few days later, when a casually prepared tamale gave me one of the worst nights of my life. In Nogales at the U.S. passport control, a guard saw me half dead and said, "I know exactly what it is. Leave your passports with me and go to the hotel over there. I'll send the doctor." We realized what progress means, not to mention helpfulness.

In Berkely my ingenuous Swedish quality was exposed to another serious strain, a methodological temptation, somewhere between scholasticism and philosophical reality. It started from a simple point: why do we pay so little for vital water and so much for useless diamonds? An old formulation, it is still arguably the deepest problem in economics, one which explains why the Soviet pricing system is not so dull a subject as it seems. Marx and Adam Smith had the same answer: because it takes so little work to get a glass of water and so much labor to find a diamond. This so-called labor theory of value explained, for them, the market price of commodities. Prices should be proportional to the amount of labor going into their production. This basic idea of Marx was developed by the Soviet planners in theory and in practice.

Then should not capitalists get something for the capital they put into the production process? No way, said the marxists. But the planners soon learned that if you have no rate of interest on capital, there is no way of allocating available investment capital. So the Soviet economists, and lots of western ones as well, started tinkering with mathematical methods of "imputed interest rates," to find out where best to invest scarce capital.

Gregory Grossman, who coined the concept of the "command economy," was my principal host at Berkeley. He introduced me to the literature of the field and suggested I go more deeply into it. One discussion took place during a trip with the Grossmans to the redwoods. In the deep shadows of the mighty sequoias, where we grilled our food, he tried to persuade me to go into the mathematics of this problem. For someone with basic training in the law, someone who had read for instance a hundred highly different cases of family disputes, the big statistical aggregates of human beings in economics, shuffled around as mathematical symbols, seemed utterly unrealistic. I retain today, with no regrets, the opinion I gave him then in that ancient grove: that such logical methods verge on scholasticism. As a nice liberal, Grossman let me keep my legal and philosophical ideas. In his mind he probably scratched me off his list of serious economists.

Behind all the fuss about prices lies another question: the value of human beings. According to the labor theory of value, anyone who works is a valuable member of society. The equality of human beings finds support in this theory. But if you accept its successor theory, born in 1871, you lose this support. Diamonds have a high value, the successors argued, because the demand for diamonds is higher than their supply. Clean water, says the modern version, will only get a value when it has become so rare that its supply will be scarcer than that of Coca-Cola. If a man works with something for which volatile demand is falling, the price of the product will fall and he himself will lose his economic value on the market, join the unemployed, and became a valueless burden on society.

The labor theory of value was an attempt to find a fixed economic value for human beings as well as goods—before God or work we are all equal. The inconstancy of values, flowing from modern theories of supply and demand, can thus be understood as an economic variation of the nihilism which flourished around 1870, the time of Turgenev's *Fathers and Sons* and Dostoyevsky's Ivan Karamazov, who argued that "if God does not exist, everything is permitted" and therefore that no fixed values exist.

These speculations still have importance. If humankind, to take an example for the 1990s, is seen to be in surplus supply, with a population explosion adding a new U.S. every three years, should we then treat human beings like coffee beans in Brazil, drowning them in the South Atlantic or burning them in huge bonfires as disposable goods?

Despite Grossman's gentle prodding in the direction of scholastic economics, I have never regretted my decision to keep to my more philosophical approach and to try at least to pose the important questions. Grossman forced me to think through that choice and helped me greatly. A resistible kick but a kick nonetheless.

In Berkeley I also discovered Purgatory. How? We enjoyed an intense student life, more than we could say for our months in the pristine Harvard Yard. In 1962 the build-up to 1968 had already begun. One day Nixon gave an open-air speech and the lively students, already blaming him and "the system" for the sins he would later commit, made for good entertainment. Similar if less spectacular events made me think hard about one of the deeper differences between communism and capitalism, that is between utopianism and realism. I love Utopias—who doesn't want to peer into Heaven? But contrary to the marxists I have always tried to remember that we live our real lives in something more like Purgatory. Movements towards a perfect social Heaven are extremely arduous. At Berkeley I found out that many a simple-minded intellectual thinks it is as easy to change reality as it is to shuffle words on paper. I have never been able to join any movement demanding Paradise Now. I am sure we are fated to stay a little longer in our Purgatory—and we had better accept it. One more Berkeley lesson that has stuck for life, another kick.

Despite his sins, I still admire Nixon's Machiavellian handling of foreign policy, especially China. In the best of all worlds, we have to accept the fact that crooks often become kings, or kings crooks. But few political systems are constitutionally balanced enough to kick out the Crook-Kings when they go too far. The U.S., for all its vices, is one of these partially-balanced systems.

Not that I am short of doubts about the American system. In California we formed two lasting impressions of politics and poverty. Sundays Marianne and I took long walks in the hills behind the "upside" of Berkeley. Once we stumbled on a hotel, if I remember correctly the Claremont. Inside, it was a madhouse. Lots of fancy-dressed people running about, an enormous crowd in an enormous hall, much noise, a man shouting from a podium, another lifting his hands high. The noise rose to thunder. Everyone clapped and cheered and hugged each other. It was a political convention!

Another doubt arose from our walks. We had little money and we frequented a number of cheap restaurants, mainly Chinese and Mexican, on the outskirts of San Francisco. While enjoying the enchiladas and Szechuan beef, we were depressed by the visible and outrageous poverty. Nothing like it in Sweden. Germany just after the War, that was as close as I could come. Today I understand more. A country with a liberal immigration policy, which permits poor immigrants to fend for themselves on the labor market, may do a lot of good for its poor neighbors. It may in fact help them more than a nation like Sweden, which gives more in foreign aid but refuses to take poor immigrants into an unregulated labor market. Sweden keeps poverty outside its borders. The U.S. generously permits it to come in and get to work.

In 1962 I did not see that far. So our doubts about the U.S. system, the fruit of our Fulbright-Berkeley experience, entered into my first booklet, *Functional Socialism* (1967), a defense of the Swedish "middle way," built on a then-new analysis of the concept of ownership. While not happy with certain brutal social-darwinistic aspects of the U.S. system, my book was even more a hefty critique of the Soviet system and of the student nonsense that was to appear a year later. The Swedish Social Democratic Party, to which I did not belong but in which I had good friends, needed a theory of the sort. My book was translated into several languages and circulated from Japan to Argentina. It was used in several U.S. university programs in Scandinavian Studies. In 1989 before reunification, I was told it was studied in East Germany.

Our success at compensatory traveling induced us to return to Sweden via Asia that year. The Fulbright Commission permitted a minor variation by which we flew to Honolulu and Japan, then from Japan via a Swedish freighter to Europe. Looking back today I see that American generosity not only helped us develop our chosen fields of study and gave us a first-hand impression of the U.S. but it also permitted us to glimpse the world through a stay in Hawaii, interesting weeks in Japan, then a delightful crossing of the Indian Ocean with numerous Asian ports of call. In Aden, tense then with hatred of the English whom we resembled, we used our last cash for an oriental carpet which, ironically, has always reminded us more of our Fulbright year than of Aden.

Back in Sweden, I joined Myrdal's new institute and devoted five years to the study of the economic side of the Cold War. In Europe that subject was pretty much under wraps. But I had access to secret materials and knew what I was writing about. RAND some ten years later published a study of the same subject and, so to speak, justified my results by quoting them extensively. Myrdal, when the book was in press, told me that if I took the manuscript to the Soviet Embassy I would first get a $100,000 spying fee from the KGB, then five years in jail when Sweden's CIA found out!

Sweden in fact played a very minor role in the book, but my study revealed a few secrets about the most established Swedish power-groups. A minor scandal in the media ensued, with various results—fortunately in the West you do not have to go to Siberia. The worst punishment they could think of was to exile me to Denmark, where I spent fifteen years at the University. In 1976 Marianne got a scholarship and we went to Capri to study Italian. Three years later we found a little house and opened the Institute for Social Philosophy, at which all Fulbrighters are welcome. Our closest neighbor is Gelsomina, the Jasmine, the island's best restaurant. We invite groups and individuals, mainly from the Nordic countries, often those who have read one of my fifteen books. Once in a while we arrange English- or German-language seminars about global issues. In 1992 we shall ask if "the unity of knowledge" can contribute to "the unity of the world." We like our problems *big*.

In our humble way we are trying thus to promote the deepest Fulbright ideal, as I see it, that of preventing war through mutual understanding. I like to think that our present activity is one small ripple of the wave originating from the stone the Senator threw into human history.

Let me report on such a ripple in the Moscow of 1991. I was there in April just at the time when Yeltsin had demanded that Gorbachev step down. Economic chaos was obvious as was the ominous slide towards political anarchy. The smell of a military coup was in the air. Knowing that the KGB would honor my six lectures by attending, I decided to deliver a message to the leaders through the myth of Cain and Abel.

The failures of mutual understanding after all go back to these first brothers of our world. Their story has become the Ur-archetype of human history, by which tens of thousands of early "family kingdoms" have been reduced, mainly through warfare, to the present 166 members of the UN. Remember the story: both made a sacrifice to God. God preferred Abel's smoke. Cain was named Number Two. He did not like it, no one does. So he killed his brother.

In Moscow in every lecture I used the story. I spoke of other symbolic fratricides: Romulus and Remus, Oedipus' sons Eteocles and Polynices, and even the first Russian epos *The Song of Ivan's Army* (c. 1150) in which the brothers Igor and Oleg were at each other's throats. Then came the Fulbright message: "Imagine that Cain had not killed Abel. Imagine that the two brothers had developed mutual understanding, enough to join forces against common enemies. Then the Babylonian captivity might not have occurred. The Jewish disapora and all the persecutions and pograms might never have come to pass. For 3000 years Israel might have been a strong and united nation with fixed borders in the Middle East, if only Cain and Abel had been wise enough to cooperate. Today, my friends, the names of Cain and Abel are Yeltsin and Gorbachev!"

The audiences and—who knows?—perhaps the two gentlemen got my point. Shortly afterwards they joined forces. When the drunken adrenolino-maniacs or power lunatics tried a few months later to expel Gorbachev, Yeltsin saved him, even if only months later they parted political company.

Stones thrown into human history can do such things. So too with well-placed kicks.

Dr. Tavares da Silva, one of Portugal's leading fighters for women's rights, tells of a Fulbright experience at a small U.S. college in the early sixties. Intending to study American literature, she encountered two unexpected forces: the New Frontier, and the to-her cautious beginnings of the American feminist movement. Back in Portugal, the Salazar regime was still strong. But a seed had been planted, and it grew in fertile soil. She would never be the same, and when the liberalization of Portugal began after the death of Salazar she was ready to step into a major role, first in Portugal then in the new Europe, as a leading player in the politics of equality for women.

16

LEARNING EQUALITY AND DEMOCRACY

Maria Regina Tavares da Silva

My Fulbright experience happened in 1962-63. Those who lived them—in both the U.S. and Portugal—know they were interesting years; the circumstances of that period shaped and determined the nature of my learning. A new graduate of the University of Lisbon in 1960, in English and German Literature, I was just starting to try my wings with various professional experiences. The year in America was both an end and a beginning to my life.

As a European, I had traveled a great deal: Spain of course, France, Italy, Switzerland, Austria, Germany, Belgium, Holland were already part of my living world. But there was a desire deep down for something else, for the unknown, for a new world—or was it The New World?—another continent, another culture. I had no need for further academic degrees, I longed instead for new visions of the world, new adventures, a way of going beyond the horizon my eyes could see.

Immediately after the University, I applied for a Fulbright and was selected. I was to spend 1961-62 at the University of Arkansas in Fayetteville, home of Senator Fulbright though I did not know it at the time. For reasons of an unclear X-ray, my visa was delayed then postponed. My first dream was frustrated. I was furious with the unfairness of the American bureaucracy. I did not know there was a mysterious design behind all this.

Life went on. While beginning a teaching career, I was already drifting into deeper involvement with social issues in Portugal, something which had begun during my university years. I worked on various problems related to the condition of women, mainly in basic education and community development in diverse faraway impoverished areas of the country.

Then a second opportunity knocked, another invitation to an American year. Links had been established between a Portuguese women's organization and its partners doing similar things in the U.S. Through these channels came the possibility of admission to tiny Grailville College in Cincinnati. I jumped at it and the Fulbright Commission agreed. I carefully collected my X-rays.

It was a small college with most of the usual departments—Agriculture, Home Economics, Community Development, American Literature, Fine Arts, Theology and Religious Education—but it had a single basic concern in all areas: to locate, articulate and develop issues affecting the role of women in society. My areas of study were American Literature, continuing my university studies towards a career in the teaching of literature, and Community Development, drawing on my recent social experience in Portugal. But I was looking for something more central, a core understanding of the New World that went far beyond those two areas. The yearning for that special kind of understanding shaped everything that happened that year and focused the options that awaited me back home.

I arrived at Idlewild Airport, soon to be renamed for the young President who then graced the White House. Alone and unmet, I faced what seemed to be enormous confusion. A terrifying Customs Officer required that I unearth my X-ray from the very bottom of my giant suitcase. I dashed to another plane for Cincinnati. No one was waiting so I took a bus to the terminal. Still no one. It was Sunday, everything was closed, nobody was there. I stood on the sidewalk, alone, with two suitcases and one bag—all my belongings for a year.

A taxi managed to find the right address, but it was a long day. I was not afraid, I have always liked adventure, and it all seemed part of discovering a new world, but I was tired. Not too tired however to see things around me. As I look back, I realize that I began my discovery in that taxi, during my ride through an unknown city, trying to find an address. The process went on: the meeting of new people, the finding of new places, discovering a new climate—cold and snow I had never before suffered. The process went in parallel with the news: daily reports of the world as seen and heard from the other side of the great ocean. I was used to seeing Europe as the center, looking East and West. Now America was the center and big things were happening, big things I could not always fully understand. The tensions of the Cuban missile episode and the real dangers of war in October went past me too quickly; I only realized later the frightening dimensions of that crisis.

There were friends, people from all backgrounds and origins. It was clear that America was not a nation in the European sense but rather a complex collection of nations. I learned that Americans called themselves Irish, Italian, Lebanese, often before calling themselves Americans.

And there was creativity: I was surprised at the originality, the sense of independence of American youth, different from what we were used to in Europe. I went from discovery to discovery, through the proces of a progressively deeper understanding of the New World and what it meant for Americans.

The celebration of Thanksgiving a month later gave it all a core meaning. Americans perhaps have forgotten the meaning of that traditional celebration, with its strong national character and its deep human meanings. It is the feast of the nation, with its multiple peoples, and it is the feast of the family, the heart of the nation. Still, the answer to one question eluded me at first: giving thanks for what?

I looked for an answer in the utopian myths of the Promised Land, of the Land of Freedom and Social Democracy of the first Pilgrims, in the myth also of unending search expressed by the movement West, the Moving Frontier of the exlorers and the adventurers. Originating in the earliest days of America, in the very beginnings of the New World, Thanksgiving Day slowly came clear to me as a very old expression of rejoicing, of gratitude for the gift of America, for the finding and possessing of a new land and all it symbolized for the first settlers. If this sounds familiar to an American reader, let me invite reflection on how it looked to a young woman from Salazar's Portugal in the sixties.

My efforts to understand this myth drove me to delve deeply into the history and the writings of those first Americans. The certain passion that pressed me forward stemmed from my own personal history. It is important to understand that I came from a country where political thinking was not encouraged, where the issues of democracy were not discussed. Life at home, for the elites of Portugal in my parents' generation, had been quiet, stable. But in the younger generation, mine, we had the feeling that it was a fragile stability: in the Portugal of the sixties there was no deep creativity, no political discussion. Political power allowed no opposition. Only the outbreak of war in Portugal's former African territories gave rise to unrest and some small contestation, quickly overcome. So my discovery of America was not just an amusement, it was a passionate search for our own future.

Along with the understanding of general democratic political concepts came the discovery of the myths that had to be there to support and enrich them. The myth of adventure, of quest and search for a new land, for a new Frontier, for God's country—all this unfolded before me, not only in the historical records of the pilgrims and settlers but also in tales and stories, in notebooks and diaries, in songs and in jokes. They gave body and texture to the abstractions in my discovery of America, of the America in myself and in my country's future. Understand the myths and the rest is easier: how simple to follow them out in texts like the Declaration of Independence, the Constitution and the Federalist Papers. In Portugal I had studied and read American history. I knew these great texts and the facts that surrounded them. But it took my year on the banks of the Ohio to understand what they all meant.

The idealism of youth, the experience of living through the rapid transformation of a closed society into a much broader and multi-faceted reality—this gave these American myths and the values they contained a special significance and relevance. The dream of freedom, the dream of equality, the dream of democracy as expressed in them remain today the most powerful memories of my American days.

As references to the past, they became tools to understand the present that year; they seemed to me to acquire new meanings in the sixties. There was an atmosphere of questioning and change, a rethinking of concepts and values, a new celebration of the basic principles that had shaped America.

The social realities of the early sixties, for me, flowed from a meaningful past. It was a time of struggle for civil rights, against racism and oppression, the time of the great marches for freedom and equality. The never-ending search for social democracy in America, in those years, reached one of its highest points. With President Kennedy, new hope had filled the nation. He spoke of the old dreams, gave them a new face and used them masterfully to achieve new dreams.

Kennedy's metaphors, his evocation of myth, spoke to the problems of Portugal, as I saw them. We too were poised at a New Frontier, we too had problems but opportunities, we too needed reality in our idealism, we too had to fight poverty and marginalization, to build equal opportunities and genuine freedom for all. His language was something new to me, and I could feel its echoes and impact in my American friends as well. Some of them for example joined the newly-created Peace Corps, and I was witness to their enthusiasm about helping others get their fair deal. As a New York psychologist said at the time, "These kids represent something many of us thought had disappeared in America—the old frontier spirit."

Slow but strong, the revival of old and lost ideals was happening around me. Through the media, I witnessed the climax of the civil rights movement with the March on Washington of August 1963—in three months Kennedy would be gone. Still, in Washington a few days later in early September, I could still feel the emotions the March left behind. Even today I can hear the tones of Martin Luther King's voice—he too would soon be dead—and his speech from the steps of the Lincoln Memorial. Here again were the old myths of freedom and equality, the utopian dream waiting to be fulfilled, the ideas enshrined in the Declaration of Independence, not yet realized but certain some day to be.

Racism was the most visible and dramatic issue, but the turmoil of the sixties went deeper. It amounted to a complete review of American values. My most valuable experience was to watch this challenge, this daring attempt to find new ways of expressing the dreams of the past, in the basic stability of a forward-moving society. Everything was open to question, from politics to morals, from habits and traditions to basic ideals. The American awareness of a past fulfilled, through the achievements of the present, had special meaning for a citizen of Portugal in the sixties. At home, in a closed society, the younger generation questioned these same basic issues, but there could be no political or social consequences until the seventies and our own Revolution in 1974.

Remember that in my Cincinnati college one of the themes beneath all academic endeavor was the issue of equality in the status and role of women. In Lisbon, in my university years, I had worked with women's movements. I had mainly been involved with groups of a social and religious character. I was highly aware that change was needed, was slowly happening, and was on the verge of occurring more vigorously in this area. But in my relatively privileged position as a member of the elite, what was the meaning of all this for me? If we had control over it, what direction should it take? My American year helped me find the meaning of that universal search and translate it into particular terms for myself and my nation.

We all know that the sixties also meant the New Feminism, a whole new kind of women's movement. True, the old tradition of 19th-century feminism and the struggle for suffrage were still alive. Pressure for further legislation against discrimination had continued, even after the vote was granted. But there had been difficult years—the Depression, the World Wars—and the traditional feminine "mystique" was tenacious. The re-birth of feminism came about through many factors—social and demographic changes, changes in the labor market, and so forth. It was also swept along by the tides of the times, by the civil rights movement taken in its broadest sense. Equality for workers, equality for people of color, equality for women—these requirements flowed along the same channels as the quest for social democracy. Democracy was being rebuilt, and the fight for women's rights was part of the rebuilding.

Though it would become more radical in later years, the revival in the sixties in the U.S. of feminist social movements was cautious and general. They were really movements against discrimination and oppression. They were movements as well against a feminine mystique that had long kept women in inferior roles.

The pressures had been building since the forties when the War brought women into new kinds of jobs. In the fifties the number of women lawyers doubled and engineers trebled; the trend was continuing. In the sixties a new element was added: manpower shortages and the consequent rise of demand for womanpower in the labor force.

Discrimination was still the norm. Women got less pay, rose more slowly to managerial positions, and so forth. The daughters of the women of the forties, who had been persuaded to go back home after the War, were unwilling to follow in their mothers' paths. They were becoming aware of their rights: civil rights were for them too. I was undergoing the same process.

The year before I arrived, in 1961, President Kennedy had set up the Commission on the Status of Women. Its report documented areas of discrimination and reinforced the awareness of inequality in the minds of women, especially those already involved in politics and social movements. Legislation for equal pay was put forth, as were recommendations to end certain types of legal discrimination, mainly in the areas of marriage and property. Later, the Civil Rights Act of 1964, intended to combat racism, was enlarged to include gender discrimination. Women were therefore included in the Equal Employment Opportunity Commission which would implement the Act. It would soon begin to have an effect.

This rebuilt legal base strengthened the American women's movement. It was followed by the creation and reinforcement of women's organizations and the development of new ideologies on women, their role and status. Betty Friedan's *Feminine Mystique* (1963) challenged us all. It deflated the old myths of domestic bliss, of the happy homemaker "fluffy and feminine, . . . gaily content in a world of bedroom and kitchen, sex, babies and home." It pointed to the contradictions of hard reality in women's lives.

In 1966 the same feminist leaders created NOW, the first new American feminist organization in half a century. But like black power, radical feminism began to create its own backlash: some women felt comfortable in domesticity, and many others, women and men, were terrified at the implications of the movement's ideas. Still, the world had changed; it would never be the same again. Concern for the rights of women and racial minorities survived even in the more conservative decades which followed, and they would proliferate abroad.

All this was the air I breathed that year in Cincinnati. The opportunity to witness the rebirth of the equal rights tradition, later expanded into human rights, to see it in the historical context of the progress of social democracy and the application of its principles to the situation of women—this was a privilege. It would soon have a transforming impact on my professional life and responsibilities.

*   *   *

I returned to Lisbon in September 1963. I was soon caught up in my former profession. Perhaps I was a better teacher, if only because I knew a lot more literature; but for the rest of it there was little room for political expression in the Portugal of the sixties. I taught, in Portugal and at Cambridge, where I earned another degree in English Studies. I was still in literature and language. In Cambridge I fell in love with the young James Joyce.

Joyce notwithstanding, I also met in Cambridge a future Professor of Chemical Engineering. We returned to Portugal, married, and began raising the three daughters who soon followed. I stepped out of my career and my Fulbright experience drifted into the past. But it was still there, waiting. I began to take on volunteer work with women's projects and issues—as the mother of three future women, I had new reasons for concern.

In 1974, it happend, our Revolution for Democracy. Like all Revolutions, it had its positive and negative aspects. Democracy was the aim however and, notwithstanding difficulties and mistakes, things moved in that direction—democracy takes time.

Women's issues now began to translate from local problems into open political and social issues. What had been unsaid for years began to come into the light of day. Old stereotypes were questioned, and the idealistic views of the early Portuguese feminist movement in the first decades of our century were revived and reinvigorated. The tradition of women's affirmation pervading our history was brought to light. The new Constitution, adopted in 1976, articulated a totally new set of egalitarian principles.

In 1974, my children were old enough for me to re-enter professional life. I was invited to enter the government mechanism entrusted with responsibility for women's issues, our own Commission on the Status of Women. All my past experience flooded back. My Fulbright year came alive.

I have worked in this field ever since, now almost twenty years. We had to make changes in legislation to achieve legal equality. Education and public information programs had to be devised to raise the consciousness of women about their rights. Training programs had to be developed to give women tools for their new responsibilities. New careers opened to women, new strategies for their promotion were set in motion, old myths were discarded.

In those days, I worked passionately in the field. I still do. Over the years I have been involved with research, documentation, and many specific projects. The work requires a versatility I did not know I had—perhaps that too was nurtured in Cincinnati? I have always kept in mind a single principle: real equality is much more than formal equality. Real equality, is the requirement of true democracy, of a true respect for basic human rights.

Today I preside over my government's Commission for Equality and Women's Rights, in the Prime Minister's office: it is the mechanism for designing a global national policy on equality. Since 1983 I have represented Portugal with the Council of Europe's Committee for Equality between Men and Women, in two different years as President. With the European Commission, I represent my country on the Committee for Equality of Opportunity between Men and Women and in 1991 became its President. I chair a working group of experts on Parity Democracy for the Council of Europe. I was a member of Portugal's delegations to the UN Conferences in the International Women's Year (Mexico 1975) and for the Decade of Women (Copenhagen 1980). In the UN I consult on women's issues, especially with regard to the Convention on the Elimination of all Forms of Discrimination Against Women.

In every forum, I have defended the same thing: the concept of equal rights and opportunities as an absolute and basic requirement of democracy. I believe that, without real equality for both women and men, there can be no democracy; equality is both a prerequisite and a consequence of any democratic society. This conviction led me to propose to the Committee of Ministers of the Council of Europe in 1988 that equality be handled in the organization not as a social question but under the heading of Human Rights. This change, not merely structural but philosophical, was made in 1989. It is the achievement of which I feel perhaps most proud.

All this my Fulbright year helped nurture and build; so many things began to take shape in Cincinnati. I wonder what would have happened in Fayetteville.

Willis Wager came early to educational exchanges, having studied in pre-War Germany, but late to the Fulbright Program. Returning to Germany on a teaching Fulbright in 1963 after a substantial career in university teaching, he was successful enough in his assignment to be offered a second teaching assignment to Turkey and a third to Iran. His essay speaks for itself; it reveals much of the spirit of this gentle educator who spent his life, like Montaigne, in search of Man. Willis Wager fell seriously ill in the Fall of 1991. Knowing the end was near, he entrusted the final preparation of this essay to the principal editor, reflecting the quality of a friendship initiated in Tehran. His death came in November 1991.

17

FULBRIGHT, THE HUMANITIES AND HUMANKIND

Willis J. Wager

The Rektor's letter was blunt: "What are the titles of the courses you will teach?" It was 1963 and I was to hold a Fulbright Professorship at the Pädagogische Hochschule in Berlin.

The question was baffling. I had no idea what courses they offered or how they were listed. Thirty years before, in the full spate of the Nazi era, I had studied as a pre-Fulbright Era exchange student at the University of Frankfort-am-Main. But a Pädagogische Hochschule is more like a teachers' college, preparing for secondary teaching. Behind the Rektor's letter lay Germany's pride in its tradition of freedom in learning and teaching: Professors determined what they would teach and no power on earth could interfere.

My own experience in different Boston universities added another dimension. From a base in literature, I had found treasure in teaching "art," defined as material from nature—pigment, stone, words, sounds— that had been subjected to human effort and shaped by the human mind, giving it special value. Some called it The Humanities, but I preferred "art," as the title

215

of my later book betrays (*From the Hand of Man: A History of the Arts*). The idea behind my experiments in Boston: some contact with the arts, not necessarily for professional proficiency or as a lifetime commitment but for first-hand understanding, made the deepest contact with young minds.

For Berlin, the fallback was "Amerikanische Literatur," but that was not enough. "Humanities" was meaningless in German. "Comparative Arts" might have covered it, but not "Vergleichende Kunst." Even "Liberal Arts," or any of the titles we give to general culture courses in the U.S., was foreign to Germany because it was assumed optimistically that such a base had already been built by the Gymnasium or high school. In the end, a Boston colleague wrote to a friend and we agreed to tell the Rektor that I would teach "Der Mensch und die Kunst," Man and Art.

In Berlin, after the usual epic struggle to find housing for my wife and me, I learned that hot controversy was raging between the English and the Fine Arts Departments as to who was stuck with me. I called the bluff by offering to double my load and serving both.

The Hochschule, in contrast to the university, was tightly run. Instructors knew each other, and at the annual Christmas party the Rektor and the head janitor swapped tales of the Russian Front. In German higher education, the Administration is little in evidence. The Rektor carried a full teaching load in contemporary history, including World War II, yet this sizable institution operated smoothly amidst a body of very Prussian regulations. Rektors and Deans were chosen by the teaching faculty; their jobs are little more than committee assignments. *Eppur se muove*—and still, it worked.

The tradition of high academic freedom was tested only once, in my case. The Chairman of Fine Arts, who wanted to make sure I had a sizable class, asked me to teach in German to that end. Only once did he make a request I could not honor. In the fine arts, there was a "party line" favoring a non-representational approach, with stress on available materials and found objects—a rich field, given the junk left behind by the bombs of '45. But it was overdone and became its own kind of regimentation, so in my classes we left the matter open. Some students wanted to work in watercolors, suited to the rapid pace of the classroom, but there were no funds for such materials. I bought some cheap watercolor sets and ordinary paper on my own, for their use.

The Chairman was not happy—the precedent would affect others. "What one of us does," he insisted, "we *all* must do." There was no point in arguing with a determined German Chairman. But I had not come all the way from Boston just to do what the others were doing. Slowing down for a while, we were soon back to watercolors. Nothing further was said, until it came time to leave. As he looked at a collection of my students' work, the Chairman could not hide his delight: "In Germany we talk and talk about the Humanities and the Geisteswissenschaft. *You* have done something about it!"

Discovering difference is a Fulbright commonplace, but difference has its dangers. There was change in the Berlin air; one had the sense that any alternative way looked better, so tightly had the German system been run. Example: when my class visited an "American-type" preparatory school, they were greatly puzzled: "The pupils, on their own, got out their trays and went to work. How is that possible, if no command was given?" Such differences led to the Rektor's agreeing that my successor should give a course on the American School. "*You* ask him," said the Rektor. I doubt it happened.

Back in Boston, the Berlin experience and some of the student work helped bring *From the Hand of Man* to completion and Boston University Press distributed it, as a kind of textbook. Still, Boston after Berlin was less of an adventure than what I remembered. I had developed a taste for the boundless curiosity of students abroad and for the deep satisfactions of working with them. In no time, we were on our way to the University of Istanbul. Having waited fifty-odd years for my first Fulbright, I had few guilts about accepting my second.

For someone interested in the history of humankind, there are few places like Istanbul: it is built on past grandeurs. Coming from the airport, the road passes the sea-walls of the Roman emperors, and the center of the University is a great arch, topping a hill from which the Emperors reviewed the troops as they set forth to bolster the sagging imperial system. No one bothers much with the Greek and Roman columns lying about; little remains to convince us that this was once the focus of the Balkan world. Even the capital has moved to Ankara.

Time disappears during a casual stroll down the main avenue, midst beggars, the underemployed, and several functioning theatres—the legitimate kind. Disappears in fact: no one, literally, can agree on the correct time. The universities operate without a public calendar, meetings happen with no fixed or announced agenda, people depend on their inner timesense more than on their watches. Ask a student to meet you at a fixed time, he answers, "If God wills." Everything—life, human destiny, the future—is in God's hands. Time is one of the wonders of the East.

God's will extended to the flies. They infested the campus and even, outrageously, the faculty dining room. "God's creatures are all free here," explained a straight-faced colleague. Pigeons too are everywhere, as are the delicate traceries they leave behind. The students seem, like the pigeons, to wander about, in a vast roofed-over space near the center of the University, walking and talking and meditating before class. I wondered what my German colleagues would call this version of freedom.

Across the Bosphorus, official Asia began. There was still a ferry then, unless you preferred a rowboat. My wife and I were privileged to spend a summer there at the Uskudar American Girls' School, studying Turkish. Wherever we were, there was the past, a historical continuity which reflects the absence of any sharp catastrophe interrupting the fundamental flow of Turkish life.

Early in the year, one privilege befell me: participating in the election of a new Dean. The faculty had greatly outgrown its traditional procedures: a name was called, the Professor responded, was given a ballot, marked it, walked across the room and deposited it in a big box. Somehow I had become known as Yussuf, a version of my middle name. Yussuf had a full vote. This amazing process went on for four full days. Patience is a strong suit in Turkey.

This time American literature was my field, with a little composition thrown in. The teaching tools I had grown used to in Boston were another matter here. The Department handy-man, a genuine Figaro living largely by his wits, was quick at spotting needs. He made tea, did mimeographing, ran errands, brought chalk, you name it. He had helped me regularize my civil status by standing in endless lines for me, spending days I could not afford. The rumor spread that he was cheating me out of my money. For me, time *was* money, but not for the Turks. I did not automatically assume, as they seemed to, that people's motives until proved otherwise were invariably bad.

I *did* spend a lot of time trying to resuscitate an old mimeograph machine, to little avail. My chairman advised me gently to let such matters be—the faculty does not concern itself with mechanics. Fortunately the U.S. Consulate was there to help.

Turks have a peculiar silence to them. In a tea-shop, they will sit for unbelievable hours, taking apparent notice of nothing. As my Turkish teacher explained it, "A Turk would just as soon be alone."

Affordable excursions by ship showed us Turkey, from within sight of Russia to the southernmost tip, at the frontier with Syria. Classical Greek sites and New Testament geography were endless enrichments, from ancient Antioch to the Dervishes, whirling in their age-old enactment of planetary movement. So were the ritual athletes, going through their amazing actions in rhythm with the chanting of ancient epic poetry; and the Hittite Museum in Ankara displayed Turkey's effort to bring to life its pre-Hellenic glories. Of all the countries where I have lived, I have come least close to exhausting Turkey's fascination, the more so because its claims are advanced with such modesty.

The theatres on the main street turned out to reflect something deep in the character: drama became a major teaching tool.   Students were up on the then-current American playwrights, done in translation on Istanbul's Broadway. We read and rehearsed plays by contemporary Americans leading to a production of Murray Schisgall's *The Typists* at one of the downtown theatres. Rehearsals in our apartment were at first awkward—some of the students had never before been with non-family members of the opposite sex outside the home. Through Turkey's many changes, it remains a deeply Muslim country, especially at the lower social levels.   Segregation of the sexes is especially sharp.

My year in Istanbul was punctuated by an emergency assignment to help out in neighboring Iran. The Muslim holidays were differently placed in the two countries, so I could afford a month in Tehran.   I knew one of the university Deans from Boston days; and the Iran of the late sixties, with the Shah firmly in control, retained all the fascination of ancient Persia as it rose to prominence in the modernizing sector of the Near East.   That busy month precipitated my third Fulbright: I was asked to move from Istanbul to Tehran at the end of the year.

This time we were in Asia and no mistaking it.   Arriving by night, Tehran was a vast jewel in the oriental velvet night.   It was easy to find our way around but harder than ever to cope with the time question. When would the University open?   "When the Shah opens it."   And sure enough, the telephone informed me that tomorrow was the day.

Tehran University was a sizable quadrangle of buildings in stucco, surrounded by a high iron fence, guarded at each gate.   The full assembly of faculty was already in place when the Shah and his Queen arrived by helicopter and took their place, looking out with the faculty at a sea of student faces. After speeches and a student chorus, trained apparently by some survivor of the original Cossacks, the Shah and his Consort distributed gold medallions to the best student from each Faculty or School.   He chatted easily with each of them, recalling common acquaintances I was told. Then the session ended, the royal couple was whisked away, and the faculty moved to an impressive repast laid out on tables in the open courtyard. Classes began the next day, triggered by the Iranian clock.

The students were assiduous, even indefatigable. They had first survived vicious competitive exams, then they were parceled out into the different Schools not by their own desires but by their placement level—the least good went into Theology. Their English was uneven—some had studied at one of the five or six Iran America Societies scattered throughout Iran, some had worked with recordings, some had studied in Europe. But they never gave up.

Early I concluded that this energy was a great strength, so a practice grew up: I would write full revisional instructions on their papers, then they would follow out the suggestions conscientiously, sometimes through several revisions. They also received verbatim mimeographed copies of all lectures. Assignments were flexible: they were asked to read one book, say, by a Puritan author; using my *American Literature: A World View*, they would go to the USIS Library and find a book they could handle. To my delight, few of them chose the easy way.

The University for them, at least for those in the Faculty of Letters, served in their minds neither vocational nor professional objectives but was instead a barrier to be passed, authorizing entry into life as an educated person. Some were already in business: one ran a fabric mill, another had a shop in the bazaar, and so on. Most of them were very poor, beyond our capacity to understand. Yet between us we put together a booklet of serious literary essays, an impressive demonstration of the taste, ability and energy of these children of Hafez and Saadi, Ferdowsi and Khayyam.

Tehran in the late sixties was a bleak kind of city, yet one with many cultural advantages. Intellectual life took place in little circles, called a *dowreh*. A student group meeting at the only student center connected to the University—operated and funded paradoxically by USIS—invited me to talk to them about my former student Joan Baez. Formal and informal groups like this one dotted the city. And the Iran American Society offered its own vigorous and relevant range of programs.

Iranians are polite, almost to a fault. Unlike the Turks, who had no human model to emulate other than the long-dead Ataturk, the Iranians took the Shah as their model. They tended to aspire to his example of correct behavior. On the other hand, when they broke loose, as we would see less than a decade later, they went far beyond ill-behavior.

From my times, a student strike will illustrate the point. One day a student phoned: there was to be a strike the next day and perhaps I might want to stay home? How little he knew his teacher! Next day, our class was proceeding as usual when a crowd of students rushed down the hall, shouting *tatie* (holiday); a leader knocked at our door. *Tatie.* I knew very little Persian, but I informed him that the Dean had informed me of no *tatie*. My excessive politeness melted the student-leader and we began to talk. Meanwhile my class had scooted out the back door; I let the leader go his way.

Soon they all returned, shamefaced. I asked them what they were striking for and we began an elegantly guarded discussion of politics. It seemed that the bus company, under government control, had raised fares. How would poor working women (sic) get to work? Then why demonstrate, I asked, at the *University*? Why not the Ministry of Transportation? Answer: "O-o-oh, they would put us in jail if we did that!" The university in fact enjoyed a certain amount of immunity—the police had to work through the Dean's office. Was this strike a mere flexing of student muscle? The discussion went on.

These students were tightly held and their misbehavior reflected their resentments as well as their lack of political experience. It was certain that the Shah considered the University a dangerous place—an attempt on his life had once taken place there. A decision to decentralize more energetically, creating a number of smaller universities around the country, had been reached in 1968. But a low level of turmoil persisted.

The National University, so-called, was allegedly private. In fact it was neither national (*melli*) nor private. "National" was a name, and the State supported it just like the others. True, the students *did* pay a small tuition fee, and there was more flexibility in hiring faculty, among them a good crop of U.S. returnees. For the rest, there was no difference. Another emergency phone call, this time from the Embassy's cultural office, persuaded me to use my day off to go up there, by bus, to help out.

It was an unruly group, nearly a hundred students. Their expectations were fairly simple: I was to tell them what the assigned reading "meant," so they could give it back to me on their exams, thus saving them the trouble of doing the readings themselves. I refused this deal, so they refused to listen. The impasse lasted several weeks. Then, one day at the USIS Library, the Librarian pointed out several of these students at a table; she said they had told her how pleased they were by my presence, for the simple reason that it permitted them to graduate. The story emerged through discussion. Each student was required to write a bachelor's thesis. They had their topics but they had no idea of what a "thesis" looked like. I promised to do my homework if they would return the following week at the same time. Twice the number returned and the next week twice more than before. Soon most of the class was showing up at the Library. Class behavior fell into place and we returned to the campus.

Another case of unruliness, which I linked even then to the larger political system, was similarly resolved by finding the central cause. One of my students taught English, at a private school, to 40 or 50 children of 12-14 years. During a thesis consultation, she blurted out her troubles with the behavior of her class. She had already lost her temper and screamed at them, something she had never done before. The situation was getting worse.

A visit to her class the next day was enlightening. I had envisioned merely observing from the back of the room. Instead, virtually in a shout, their teacher introduced me as an English-speaker and made herself my translator. The students were in fact being downright unruly.

"You understand, I speak English. What do you want me to tell you? A joke? A story? A proverb?"

"*Shiir*," shouted one of the smaller boys, the Persian word for "poem."

"And you, what do you want?" Again, *shiir*, and so on around the class. "All right, what poet?"

Someone shouted, literally, "Shack-spear." "All right, what poem of Shack-spear?" Again a shout: "Omlette."

"Well all right, what happens in Omlette?" One girl, who had apparently seen a Russian film of Hamlet, stood up and, as though possessed, went through the entire story, at breakneck speed: the Shahinshah did this, Ophélie did that, and so on. It had obviously moved her greatly; she was like a child repeating every detail of a horror movie. Her excitement was clearly reaching her peers.

"Let's put on Omlette. Who wants to be Ophélie?" Hands flew up. "And Omlette?"

We had a herald pretend to blow a big trumpet then begin to read from a scroll. We followed the script as related by the little girl. Everyone had a wonderful time, including the frightened teacher. I then tried a few Elizabethan songs, especially the round "Hi-ho, Nobody home, Meat nor drink nor money have I none, Still I will be merry!" Some of them sang, "I will be married," but all of them sang with great gusto and it didn't matter.

I went back to that class three or four times, once with recordings of famous actors reciting Hamlet's lines. I imagine the children had fun impressing their parents by reporting what they were doing.

The teacher and I analyzed the reasons for their behavior. We came together to two conclusions, though there are certainly more to be drawn. First, the curriculum was an irrelevant bore. That day they had been scheduled to learn the names of the months and the seasons, as they were called in a distant island called England. Tehran was a branch of the Muslim world: months and seasons were differently reckoned; for example the New Year (No Ruz) begins on the first day of spring—a delightful notion, it seemed to me. I doubt these children had ever seen a calendar, as we know it.

Second, they were never involved individually or collectively in the proceedings. They had no control of their destinies, either in that class or probably anywhere else. So they did the only thing they knew how to do, misbehave and rebel.

We learned more from the teacher-student, who became a member of our little family. She was to be married, after graduation, to a doctor from another part of Iran and would not meet him until the day of the wedding. "My father, who is very modern, said I could choose: either marry this man or become a teacher and never marry." We asked her if that felt strange. "No. They know what sort of person I am—better than I do myself. Besides, I have lots of other things to worry about besides finding a husband. Don't they have my best interests at heart?" Another student said the same thing when, sympathizing with Blanche Dubois in *Streetcar Named Desire*, she asked: "What could she do? Her parents would not arrange a marriage for her." The insights of foreign students into our literature and society are often refreshing and sometimes penetrating. They also reveal a lot about their own society and about themselves.

Life has a way of going on, even during Fulbright years. The ordinary things happen to us, some good and some dreadful. Let it simply be said that, during our springtime in Tehran, a long-dormant meningitis virus flared up and swept my wife away in less than a week. The details of coping with ambulances, hospitals and finally with preparations for returning the body to the U.S. are too grim to record here. We had done it all, together, for thirty years and now we would go home together. Everyone tried to help. It was the end of the school year and the end of my Tehran Fulbright.

Helping me pack, through that last night, was one of my students in whose car we careened through Tehran streets to the airport. There another student, a tall soldier wearing the light blue neckerchief of the Shah's Imperial Guard, took charge of getting me through the formalities. As I boarded the plane, I looked back at the crowd and at the friends who had come to see me off. Tehran, by night a jewel on the velvet of night but by day dry, dusty and beige, was left behind. Who knows today where and how those minds I touched are living?

*   *   *

What does it all mean? To get at that question, I confess I often think of these last two decades, after returning to Boston from my three Fulbrights in Berlin, Istanbul and Tehran, as my fourth Fulbright. These years have been a time for looking at my country with the fresh vision I had acquired abroad, a time for tackling some of the problems I saw. The Fulbright experience at its best is not an empty academic honor, it is life itself.

First, books. My *World View*, with its non-national approach to American literature, was published by New York and London University Presses. In Iran it was translated into Persian by my department chairman at the University. Presumably still available there, it provides a coherent picture of our literature from a world-history viewpoint. It contains the essence of many human lives and concludes with the suggestion that we live in an age of martyrs, of whom the third Gandhi to die by an assassin's hand is only one recent example. As for the *Hand of Man*, grown far beyond its beginnings in the Boston of the early sixties, it achieved only local publication at Boston University, all 600 pages of it. It tries, as forthrightly as I could write it, to answer the questions my students everywhere have asked about art and its making. Berlin and Istanbul deepened the sections on pre- and proto-history. For example, the Librarian of the American Indian collection in Berlin, who treated Amerindian literature as "Alt Amerikanische Literatur" on the analogy of Old French Literature, helped me understand ways to enrich the book.

Then, teaching. I had missed much of the violence in the American universities during the Vietnam conflict. Even Boston University called off final examinations as the combined police and fire departments lined up along Commonwealth Avenue—wisely leaving the back exits open for students to leave when their position became untenable. Wise heads talked in all seriousness about the "end of the American era, as we knew it."

To counteract violence, students at BU on their own initiative opened a "Free University"—sounding oddly to my Berlin ears. My early information on this movement was vague: no prerequisites, no tuition, no credits, no salaries for teachers. Student Activities funds, instead of going to the usual ephemera, went into this radically different educational endeavor. The faculty was of course skeptical, but we were all made welcome to join.

A BU student leader, regularly enrolled, carried the incredible administrative load, not unlike the valiant Rektor in Berlin. I got involved by accident: an active and gifted student of mine asked for my help in finding a room with at least two pianos, for a course he was doing on musical improvisation. I ended up volunteering to teach a course I had once tried at a choir school: familiar passages from the New Testament in Greek. No declensions, no conjugations, just familiar passages like the Lord's Prayer, the Beatitudes and the Christmas Story. Was I back in Istanbul? Or was it Tehran?

Two dozen students aged nine to ninety—literally—stayed with me all that year. One physician came all the way from Providence to these sessions in the Chapel basement. The next year the Lighthouse Center of the Salvation Army asked us to do the course again in a rough area of South Boston, with the same success.

Meanwhile life, as it will, was going on. I remarried. I was called upon to serve two years as President of BU's Phi Beta Kappa Chapter. And I retired and moved to Tennessee.

What has the New Testament in Greek to do with the Fulbright Program? To me, it has to do with how education is carried on. I had learned that there is no one correct way to teach anything. As my hardy little group struggled with Greek, I often wondered how many of the traditional formal university courses would have met the scholarly criteria, say, of Erasmus. Yet he would have felt quite at home with us. Unconventional educational procedures abroad fed back in Boston and carried us to the very roots of the Humanities.

As I write the closing pages of this essay, this "attempt" in Montaigne's sense, I receive a letter from a former student, who studied organ performance abroad on a Fulbright. For twenty-five years, she and her Fulbright husband have lived in Idaho and raised five children. She writes: "I have a humanities class of my own to teach this year at Treasure Valley Community College. It includes painting, sculpture, architecture, literature and music. It . . . keeps me hopping." She also notes modestly that she is Idaho's Mother of the Year for 1991. This from one letter, from one who bothered to write. Who says the Humanities are dying?

For me, the Fulbright experience has to do with seeds sown far and wide, each endowed still with life. I doubt that is what the Senator had in mind—or if he did he is an even greater man than we know, as is often the way with sowers of seeds and planters of trees.

It was one of those encounters which only Fulbright can produce: an American school superintendent and an Indian director of a teacher-training college. In the following essay and response, we are privileged to see exactly where that meeting led and what it produced. We are fortunate to have not only the view from India but, in the afterword by Roy Wahle, a sense of how it looked at the American end. It should be noted that the Indian partner in this friendship wrote his essay without suspecting that the American would have his say; in turn the American wrote his piece having seen only an early and very different draft of the Indian contribution.

18

THE MISSION THAT BINDS

D. A. Ghanchi

In the early sixties, beginning my career as a college teacher, the Fulbright Program had an almost mystical appeal for us in India. I was in Ahmadabad, after having been a school teacher and principal for more than a decade. In August 1961 John McCelvie, a Fulbrighter from Illinois visiting Ahmadabad, seeded the idea that the Fulbright path might lie open to me.

The Sardar Patel University, where later I taught at the Secondary Teachers Training college, worked closely with the Indian Fulbright Commission. We had Peace Corps volunteers and American scholars in different disciplines. We worked together in classroom teaching, curriculum planning and community work. We shared various cultural celebrations.

In 1965, two remarkable people came to Patel: Roy Patrick Wahle, then Deputy Superintendent of Curriculum and Instruction for the Bellevue School District in the State of Washington, and his vivacious and charming wife Betty. With three children, this Fulbright family was planted in the midst of a colony of Indian teachers and their families. A process of cultural symbiosis was set in motion, and it caught me in its wake. The Wahles had the will and the art needed to wear down the initial shyness and reluctance of campus families to an experiment in intercultural living. Besides our professional relationships, there were visits to surrounding communities, to homes, to religious festivals. There was much partaking of food and drink, much sharing of joy and sorrow. It was a tiny model of the Fulbright ideal.

The Wahles' message was empathy and cooperation, and they practiced it. They adopted the impoverished village of Rampur on behalf of the people of Bellevue.   The citizens of Bellevue then contributed funds to build an elementary school in Rampur; it stands there today, a symbol of international cooperation.   It also serves as a reminder that self-help can alleviate misery and dispel backwardness.   When the Wahles returned for a visit in 1985, they were received with unprecedented gaiety and effusive thanks by the former students of the "Bellevue" school.

Dr. Wahle helped a number of us on the faculty apply for Fulbright grants, with an energy hard to imagine: he studied our curricula, discussed our candidacies with the Vice-Chancellor, observed our teaching, and spent hours in consultations with each of us in order to refine our goals and expectations. I remember his words in 1965:   "In India you have a tradition of dedication. Here is a chance to carry it forward in new domains." I have tried to live up to that charge.

I have held three Fulbrights, all in the State of Washington: first, as an exchange teacher in 1966-67, then later as a visiting lecturer, and finally as a research scholar.   I have seen more aspects of the Program than most.   For me, it was a means to professional growth and an entry into the process of intercultural understanding and cooperation.   It was not a tourist sojourn, nor a touch-and-go surface affair, nor a transitory socialization, nor a trip to explore commercial pastures, nor a ticket to international conferences.   Its potential is larger than life itself, touching on human destiny, tolerance, harmony and even love.

In August 1966 before leaving India, I was briefed with all the other Indian grantees at Fulbright House in Delhi.   The legendary Dr. Olive Reddick, first director of the Indian Fulbright Commission, inaugurated the sessions.   She spoke of the world as a fractured family, riven by ethnic, political, economic, social and cultural divisions.   This tiny woman, who had long managed a serious infirmity of her own, lifted the hearts of those who heard her.

It was no accident that I was placed at a high school in Bellevue.   At a welcome assembly, the principal said I was not just another teacher of English and social studies but an emissary from the land of Gandhi, one whom he expected to bring a qualitative change in the school's perceptions of the world.

I taught seniors.   They were curious about the world.   Contrary to what we hear about American teenagers and high-schoolers, they were open-minded and inquisitive.   I had some ideas about correlating the teaching of English and social studies, and these classes proved a remarkable laboratory for experimentation.   In India, my teaching was didactic; in Washington it became participatory, a student-centered approach which had various kinds of social fallout. I am still in touch with many of those students, thanks to the mails.

Faculty colleagues were kind and warm-hearted. Encounters in the faculty lounge were invariably enriching for me and the friendships we developed there still feed into our work today, on both the Indian and the American sides of the equation. It was a year of renewal and even rebirth.

I lived with an American family. Henry Tunes was a Spanish teacher: he, his wife Barbara and two children made me part of the family. I was involved in the daily chores, even house-building and gardening; there were celebrations like Halloween and Thanksgiving, to which we added Diwali and India's Republic Day. I remember a rodeo in Ellensburg that even today rattles my spine. The Tunes' home is my second home, as mine is for them in India. Cultural immersion is a product of the Fulbright process.

I early had an experience of culture shock.   Aboard the S.S. Aurelia, chartered to transport 1000 Fulbrighters who had been collected in England to the U.S., the trip took ten days. Western food, scantily-clad young people at the swimming pool, bathrooms without doors, dancing and singing accompanied by hugging and kissing—these were surprising ingredients which embarrassed and dazed me. I fled into my cabin. But a music teacher from Texas dragged me out and my socialization began. By the time I got to Bellevue I was well on the way. Still, the Wahles and the Tunes and indeed everyone took great care to bring me carefully into this new world. There were family visits, dinners, barbecues, churches; and everywhere I was urged to present myself and India to others.

By November Dr. Wahle thought I was ready for the annual conference of the National Council of Teachers of English in Houston. I had never imagined such a mammoth gathering of teachers, all dedicated to a single subject, from kindergarten right through the university.   The exciting days of serious professional deliberation gave me a model, one I have replicated with some success in India, for profession-oriented conferences.

Barbara Tunes' mother lived in Yakima. I wrote my mother that she reminded me of her, and my mother wrote back a letter expressing relief that her role was being filled! When I visited my new mother, she would send me home with cookies or plums from her tree in the backyard. A scarf she gave me hangs before me in my study as I write these words.

Returning to India with a gigantic cultural cargo, I found myself in a new job as Dean of the College of Education. I set about placing parcels of my cargo in the right contexts. Then, after thirteen years, I found myself again headed for Washington, this time to teach Indian history and culture at Matteo Ricci College in the University of Seattle, while handling a doctoral seminar in comparative education at the University's Education School. Teaching India, as it were, to both undergraduates and graduates, I found it a useful opportunity for analysis of my own and American culture. In essence it was a cooperative intellectual exercise in understanding and perhaps even sympathizing with the problems of the Third World.

The freshmen amazed me most—their inquisitiveness was boundless. They were interested in India's past, in her cultural achievements, in her value systems. They examined with great sympathy the suffering of India under alien rulers. I was amazed by their appreciation of Gandhi's theories of non-violence, as practiced by him in the struggle against one of world history's mightiest empires. These young citizens of the American republic gave every hope that they would play out their roles in life with faith in the utility of non-violent means for solving societal problems. In turn I reminded them of the meaning to India's nascent democracy of the American experience over the last two centuries.

I remember one of the students named Roberta, who said this: "India's democracy is a challenge. Look at her problems: over- population, poverty, illiteracy, superstition, insurgency. It is a miracle that democracy survives there!" Does the Fulbright Program build an integrated family? Students like Roberta make me think so.

My doctoral candidates represented a cross-section of students from many walks of life. We spent a lot of time on the crushing problems of Indian education. We talked about how international agencies like UNESCO, UNICEF, WHO and of course the binational Fulbright Commission were helping India and the rest of the Third World with developmental problems. All this, Fulbright included, revolutionized traditional modes of thought by bringing together people of different cultural backgrounds. Taken together, my students' project-papers added up to a suggested course of action for Indian education which my country might have followed to its advantage.

By now the Wahles and I were part of the same extended family, but how different from the extended family system of India—a subject of frequent comparative discussion among us. Threading through it all was the strand of one cardinal principle: tolerance. Without it there can be no harmony, no integration, no continuity. My graduate students were more skeptical: they felt that tolerance was the one quality that modern Western nations were fast losing. Ogilvie, who worked in a prison, said this: "My experience with prison inmates is disheartening. They lose patience, then tolerance goes, and aggressivity arises at the slightest provocation." Did I communicate some hope that the Eastern experience had something to offer? Not only the Indian joint-family system but the Hindu philosophy of divine pluralism? I like to think so.

The Wahles' second India trip in 1985 grew again from Fulbright roots: it was a three-month assignment at my college. We went to Rampur, to be welcomed by tumult. It was now a full-fledged school, and a second generation of students was already in attendance. The first generation had taken up occupations unknown to their parents. There was greater social mobility, and the quality of life in the village had improved markedly. We went to two other districts—Sabarkantha and Panchmahals. I had sent a number of my students to teach in these areas, where there is a sizable tribal population. It is akin to and often worse than the grim things one expects to find in American Indian reservations. Dr. Wahle and I did in-service teaching, Betty worked with women's groups, my wife and daughter interpreted. We visited tribal homes, simple straw huts with no conveniences. Working in these areas was a micro-experiment in social change through cross-cultural cooperation. The project was later taken over by the College of Education because the state government appreciated what had been done and saw its potential as an ongoing movement to enhance the quality of life. The project continues today, though I retired in 1987.

During this trip the Wahles noticed the role of my family in our work: from my home we worked with faculty and students of five colleges and interacted with a cross-section of people from many different levels of society. Before they left, they insisted that if I were to return to the U.S. it must be with my wife. So, in 1986, I was assigned a class in English as a second language at the Central Community College in Seattle, while serving as well as consultant on multi-cultural curriculum in the entire School District of Seattle. My wife, who came along, joined Betty in her work with women.

This time my students, thirty of them, came from twenty different countries. Even language teaching had its social hazards.   One day, working on comparisons, I used the model-sentence: "In a democracy a woman has as many rights as a man." Immediately Fatima, from Turkey, asked whether India did not still practice Suttee, the custom by which a widow throws herself on the funeral pyre of her husband. It led to an animated sociological discussion, with much use of English comparisons.

In the District, I could share ideas with teachers involved in a project on a multi-cultural curriculum. We discussed the concept, developed alternative drafts, tried them out through simulations, visited classes, compared experience in India and the U.S., and in the process we ourselves went through a cultural transformation. In Seattle, ninety languages are spoken—India's fourteen major languages and 2500-odd dialects were a subject of great comparative interest. I told them about the discussions in India of education as a composite orientation, to reduce the chances that India's divisive forces might ever get the upper hand. These forces have by now taken the lives of three people named Gandhi. Such happenings remind us how vital it is to build integration into the national mind.

My wife's presence made everything the richer. She and Betty undertook a socio-cultural mission to the twin cities of Bellevue and Seattle, and in rural Washington. My wife had little English but that did not stop them. She gave presentations, organized exhibits of Indian artifacts, and demonstrated various skills of cooking and dress. To her amazement, she learned that American women shared the important things with her: a desire for a stable, satisfying and safe home life in a world free from war, want and division.

Returning to India in February 1987, I was assigned now to the curriculum-planning project of the Board of Secondary Education in Gujarat state. It was a perfect chance to use everything I had learned and to make it useful to others for years to come. The new curriculum, with a strong component of multi-cultural content, came into force in Gujarat's secondary schools in June of 1991.

One does not stop learning and growing. Three assignments with the Fulbright Program, spanning two decades, have meant a virtually continuous cycle of learning, teaching and sharing, in India and Washington. Is it an accident that Fulbrighters turn almost by instinct in this direction? I think not. Everything in the Program, at least insofar as I know it, points in the same direction. Its goals are clear, its selection procedures are rigorous, objective and beyond reproach of any kind, its orientation procedures are imaginative and effective, its monitoring agencies are personal and sensitive. And there is a periodic renewal of learning and relationships through conferences, travel and visits.

I can only hope the spiritual discourse will be as clear to the generations ahead as it has been to me. May the Program ever set its goals high, extending that great vision of a single human family. As Walt Whitman put it:

> Come, let's make the world indissoluble,
> Let's make the most splendid race
> The sun has ever shone upon.
>
> Let's make divine, magnetic lands,
> With the love of comrades,
> With the life-long love of comrades.

TWO-WAYS TIMES TWO: AN AFTERWORD

Roy P. Wahle

Having read only an early and very different draft of the words of my friend Dr. Ghanchi about his Fulbright experience, I tried independently to get down on paper the essence of what our double-ended Fulbright has meant to me. I thought about how he "looked," about his unique contribution to Indian and American classrooms and about his considerable contribution to India. He is one of the few Muslims in his area who has earned a national reputation for his teaching and writing, and he has held all kinds of responsible positions, even in his so-called "retirement."

India was not our first choice for a Fulbright assignment, but it should have been. Our two assignments, separated by twenty years, were in 1964-65 and 1985. Three of our four children accompanied our first visit. My wife and I returned alone for our second Fulbright visit. In short, Fulbright has been the single most influential experience in our family's growth and in the development of my professional career. Stimulated by our immersion in Indian culture, we have since visited 38 other countries. Our children and their families carry on the tradition.

Both our teaching scholarships were centered at Teachers' Colleges. One was in Vallabh Vidyanagar, the other in Modasa, both in Gujarat state. The late Dr. Haribhai Desai, a Hindu, by his own choice nurtured our first visit. We were the first American family to visit the area.

Our daily inquiries were all met. Education classes were designated and the year's itinerary of village visits was arranged. Our cultural astonishments were quietly explained and discussed. Our family health was maintained. Some years later Desai visited us in Bellevue. We arranged a teaching position in our public schools and cost-free lodging. With his earnings and a scholarship, he remained several years and completed a doctorate in psychology, the first such degree for a member of the faculty of Sardar Patel University. He returned to leadership positions in India. His unfortunate early death left us

232

in sorrow. Two of his sons remain in India but the oldest practices architecture in Saudi Arabia, hoping to return to India for a decent life with his young family. He too is looking forward to an advanced degree in the U.S.

Dr. Dawoodbhai Ghanchi came to America three times under my sponsorship. We met him as a young teacher in India and later he was our sponsor when he and his family were our hosts at his college in Modasa when I taught there in 1985. The Ghanchis continue to be our friends. Our correspondence has never ceased and no subject is taboo.

Our attraction for India was enhanced by many people but our understanding of India's people and problems was significantly centered around these two families. They represented India's middle class, now larger than the population of France, but each from its own unique perspective.

Going to India the first time was a tremendous moment. I was accompanied by an adventurous wife, two sons aged 5 and 9, and a daughter of 13—all blonds! A son of 17, also blond, stayed home to meet a football commitment. Our robust family delighted and entertained their contemporaries endlessly. Every Indian holy day and holiday was observed with Indian friends. The children's acceptance of the adventure was a delight and a fulfillment for us all. We encountered a Salvation Army doctor early in our visit and he tended to our few needs, but there were no health problems. Later our 21-year-old son, who at 17 had remained behind, was so captivated by the family tales about India that he took his bride there via the Peace Corps and had a remarkable experience as one of those who introduced the Green Revolution, in his case focused on aboriginals.

As one might expect, we devoted some time to religion. We came to understand that Hinduism was represented by a group of practices; the Muslims by contrast project an orthodoxy. This was only one of the realities which, according to their varying perspectives, our friends helped us understand and which helped explain the politico-cultural nuances in this fascinating country. The increasing identification in Indian politics of religious perspectives appears to have dubious ramifications for the governance of the world's largest democracy.

Indians we knew intimately, especially some young professionals, seemed ambitious yet resigned. Upward mobility is the hallmark, but beneath it there is the resignation which may be needed to meet adversity. Two of Ghanchi's sons are seeking careers abroad, one a physician in England the other a computer technologist in New Jersey. A third son aspires to practice village medicine in India, and a daughter is a medical technician. One son, when he had recently completed medical studies, put the sense of carefully-limited expectations this way: "We Indians do not expect comfort." The remark of course was intended to point up the contrast with his perception of American behavior.

Americans of course were as fascinating to them as they were to us. Indian educators, especially Ghanchi, were eager to study our educational theory and to experiment with our educational practices. This open stance contrasted with representatives of India's economic endeavors, who sought self-sufficiency in disregard of any dependence on the world economy. Yet I was impressed with the enthusiastic adoption of concepts like quality control and participatory planning within factories—I made a point of visiting industrial plants in Central India.

Both Desai and Ghanchi noted that India's concept of freedom pertains to the group as opposed to the American focus on individual freedom. Ghanchi conjectured that our internal westward expansion contributed to the dominance of this individualist interpretation over the collective.

It is hard to express the deference paid to us as foreigners, perhaps more pronounced among Muslims. It could be confused with politeness, but it went far beyond that. On several occasions we were fêted as befits visiting gods. In Rampur, where we had a school-twinning project that had been instrumental in building a school for 100 children in the sixties, the village patriarch came to us in a gesture of welcome and knelt literally to kiss my feet!

Things do move in eternal India. In 1964, American PL 480 wheat, sent to feed the hungry, helped finance Fulbright scholars in India. In 1985 famine was said to be a thing of the past. Although India has not adequately financed its educational system, especially at elementary levels, we learned that the Green Revolution prospered wherever education was progressive. Educators have reminded the government of this detail but with little discernible effect on educational policy.

Another change: during our first visit, we had enjoyed active evenings. There was much conversation and children were playing merrily. Twenty years later, Indira Gandhi had successfully blanketed the country with television transmitters. Now the village was passive. Even with only one TV set, a village could be very quiet in the evening.

Ghanchi is a remarkable man, an accomplished educator and linguist. He epitomizes energy, dedication and organization. He shatters any stereotype of the indolent Indian. He absorbed with his mind every aspect of the American culture, yet he consistently maintains his Indian and Muslim identity. True, he adapted suitable elements of American family life into his own interrelationships. When I visited him in India in 1985, he had turned the gardening practices he had seen in Bellevue to use in his own landscaping.

He was equally energetic in adapting American classroom techniques to his teaching back in Modasa, where he was principal of the teaching college. In Washington, his services were sought by educators in our schools and colleges. He performed cross-cultural classes and consultation work in secondary schools, school districts, community colleges and at Seattle University. Students fell in love with his authentic and sensitive presentations and his ability to delineate contrasts in the various cultures of India, as distinguished from the conditions of life in the U.S.

With Ghanchi and Desai, their families and ours have gone through the looking-glass of another culture, to such an extent that there are moments when we are not sure whether we are looking at the reality or the mirror image. For them and for us, it was a two-way mission. Two times two is four, and four times four sixteen, and on it goes. I doubt it will ever end, this endless multiplication. Is this the richness of the Fulbright experience, that once initiated it has no ending?

*Beginning with a general esthetic of cultural interchange, Dr. Maini,
Professor Emeritus of English at the Punjab University in Chandigarh,
proceeds to formulate an esthetic specific to the Fulbright Program, in
the history of humankind. The Fulbright "Moment," as he calls it, is a
unique element in a period of human history in which internationalization, the development of an open world culture, has taken place faster
than it can be understood. As a framework for a world-history view of
the Fulbright Program, his seminal yet highly personal essay breaks new
ground. At the same time, his reminiscences of the Harvard experience
bring to life the story of his own growth and his role in the moment to
which he has given a name.*

19

THE FULBRIGHT MOMENT: VOYAGES
THROUGH VALUES

Darshan Singh Maini

Let me define my general esthetic before presenting an impressionistic
melange of memories, insights and concepts. Briefly, I have always sought to
follow even a maverick or marginal experience to its ideational lair; this helps
appease my cognitive imagination. Any writing, to my mind, remains
curiously hollow or insufficient if it fails to connect with the underlying grid
of impulse, energy and dream which animate events and actions. To put it
differently, two elements give form to my discourse: the search for the poetry
of facts, and the need to see structures within a holistic perspective. To reach
the nuclear heart of things, I try to relate all emerging perceptions to a wider
sum of values.

Inclining thus towards a historical context, I do not on the whole accept
the post-modernist esthetic of deconstruction, fragmentariness and complete
subjectivity, despite the partial truths in this metaphysics. For me, there is
always a movement from the mirror to the prism, from reflection to refraction.
Yet even as the elements of personality, fantasy and contingency begin to color

236

the argument, the imagination of fusion is continually at work, keeping things on course.

I say all this as a preamble to these reflections and refractions on my Fulbright days at Harvard in 1969-70. The picture requires a large frame. The Fulbright Moment better than any other phrase sums up for me the unique quality of the experience.

The rationale for cultural exchanges provides the overall context. Cultural, religious and pedagogical visits, exchanges and embassies between communities and races, between countries and nations, have existed since the advent of human civilization. There is no shortage of documentation for such a traffic of thought. All the major classical civilizations, the Indian, the Chinese, the Babylonian, the Egyptian and the Greek, sought in one way or another to establish a hegemony of power and perceptions. There are numerous accounts of scholarly travels undertaken simply to understand the human race in all its richness and diversities; but most such adventures, history affirms, were fostered by ideas of conquest, control and colonization. It is primarily the imperialist ethos which has tended to characterize such efforts in the past.

We may then infer that, before modern modes of travel and levels of consciousness, such enterprises were essentially marginal in character. Only in the second half of the present century did it become possible to institutional-ize such flows of men and minds and then to extend them on a global scale. A radical change in the human situation warranted a movement in that direction. In a world of shrinking geography, closer frontiers and expanding intellectual horizons, competing new cultures and ideologies, as well as the unsettled classical cultures, needed to evolve common grounds for action.

It began to be clear that communities of teachers, scholars and writers interacting with their counterparts abroad could help create a kind of open culture, one which could then empathize with and accommodate all kinds of opposed, adversarial and even sub- cultures. Such interfacing was bound to bring to the surface the truer and nobler aspects of different societies. And to do so, people working in the knowledge industry had to be brought together so that they could experience the common perceptions and varying attitudes that lay hidden beneath the patina of national prejudices and *personae*, of reports and rumors, of cliches and stereotypes.

Of the plans thus conceived and serviced by the world's powers, the Fulbright Program has without a doubt turned out to be the most spectacular and effective enterprise of all, in its dimensions, in its mechanics, in its achievements and in its promise. No doubt its great success is predicated upon the emergence of the U.S. as a supreme post-war power, not only in its military might, material resources, and technological-industrial leadership but also in its new ideas, new challenges and new directions in almost every conceivable aspect of human society.

To project America in this way, in its fullest reach and spread, demanded a corresponding structure, vision and ethic. One wonders today if Senator Fulbright and those who helped him conceive this idea and prepare its blueprints had any firm idea of the form and scale of things. Presumably it developed naturally, as it came to be translated over time and in proportion as it developed an image, an élan and an aura. That dream of a fellowship of scholars from all parts of the world—I think of Poe's vision of the world's poets standing hand in hand across the encircling globe—is happily a living reality now, an affirmation of the magnanimities of the Fulbright Moment. No wonder then, in a period of less than fifty years, that the program has succeeded in establishing large communities of understanding, trust, and honor across the seas. An academic culture has emerged, drawing on the best in American modes of instruction and habits of thought and work; even if in a limited way, it has in turn carried back the freight of experience and insight earned by scholars on both sides of the oceans. An effective Fulbright fraternity is beginning to take shape, with a distinctive *esprit de corps*, a signature and a style.

The Fulbright Moment, as I see it, is an era in American history extending back to Jefferson. If we reach back farther, to the Renaissance and the Elizabethan Age in England, it may even be seen as a link in a longer chain of significant and creative moments in the history of the Western world. To be sure, in its operative agenda and its immediate objectives, it seems at first sight to have been too modest a movement to claim historical importance. But when we ponder its meaning and temper from the heights of its achievement, it is possible to view Fulbright as a significant metaphor for the explosion of knowledge and for the cross-fertilization of scientific and humanistic thought on a scale beyond any initial reckoning.

There is of course a difference between the larger historical moments and the one bearing the Fulbright message. While earlier moments had a voluntary, spontaneous and spiritual character—a kind of breakthrough from within or implosion, the Fulbright Moment was a controlled, directed and sponsored affair, despite its conscious efforts from the beginning to achieve a kind of intellectual autonomy. It is a moment in cultural history when an outward movement of thought became a requirement for the American imagination. Larger historical moments comprehensively subsume the dream, the genius and the character of societies poised for a qualitative leap into the unknown; they carry the mark of identity. The Fulbright Moment instead was an assumption of responsibility flowing from the geo-political status of the American State. And since such dreams begin in responsibilities, as Yeats says, the Fulbright code had to acquire a strong moral dimension in its action.

My own little voyage of discovery involved a Fulbright grant in the senior category, at the end of the explosive sixties. Despite the commonality of the Fulbright experience for grantees, it is certain that the meaning of that experience cannot be the same for any two of them. It will be interesting, over time, to speculate about these different constructions and to collate them when and where possible. My aim here is more modest: to put across my little narrative, a moment within a moment, a dream within a dream. The broader historical concept describes a state of reality that, having its locus in a public event, embodies individual visions. To that extent, it becomes an instrument for the discovery, or rather the rediscovery, of one's self. Such a moment brings into play one's characteristic energies and quiddities, and it authenticates our search for the envisioned *nirvana*. The nature of such a quest constitutes a major theme of my narrative.

The assignment to Harvard brought some of my deepest urges and dreams into the open. The opportunity, the impulse and the readiness of the receiving imagination underwrote the ideas and images that for me had made up the "romance" of America since my youth. America has figured for generations of readers, visitors and settlers as a grand symbol of the felicities and largesse of life. True or not—and there is an entire body of "dark" American classics to challenge the dialectic of the American Dream—the country of Columbus, his providential and fabulous mistake, has come to embody the future of mankind. For all its confusions and contradictions, its ambiguities and ironies, America still speaks to the imagination in a special voice. It brings, if I may say so, collateral styles and responses to bear upon our dreams. From Jay Gatsby's "milk of wonder" to the long dream of riches is one story; but there is as well the story of values and freedoms and enfranchisements along the way. It is this story above all that unfolded for me at Harvard as America began to grow upon my imagination.

The Fulbright experience for me was at once an act of initiation, a ceremony of understanding, and a saturation of sensibility. America had already gotten under my skin, long before I ever set foot on its generous soil in the fiftieth year of my life—it was a kind of homecoming. It remained to be seen how my earlier impressions, gleaned largely from readings, would be vindicated or falsified or confuted. I had to sort out my perceptions and to organize them into a clear statement. It involved the mending of views, here and there, and a realignment of certain lines of thought. In all, my faith in the greatness of America as an idea rich in human possibilities was vindicated over and over again during my ten-month stay. There were distressing sights in America as well, but the dream survived. And during later visits it was to offer me no small comfort amidst moments of doubt and anxiety.

I arrive at Logan Airport on September 15, 1969, after brief stopovers in Kuwait, Beirut, Berlin and London. In transit over a week, musing much over my American prospects and the life at Harvard. First taste of American geniality, relaxed style and academic *bonhommie*, as opposed to Indian formality, German solemnity and British taciturnity: when I check in with Pan Am at Heathrow. Somehow, in the rush and rumble of things—airports can throw even American thoroughness into confusion—the stewardess cannot locate my seat in Economy. Meanwhile the plane is already aloft. She has a bright idea and with a charming smile and a wink beckons me to follow her to First Class. For fifteen minutes, I enjoy the privileges—champagne and other gifts—until my seat is located and I am promptly but graciously conducted back to it. The prettiest part of this mid-air interlude was my discovery that the person seated next to me was a Professor from Harvard. We grew so friendly during the long flight that he and his wife, sensing my need, offered to drive me from Logan to the Harvard Yard. It all started thus on a happy and, as we Indians say, an auspicious note.

Within a couple of days, I had secured accommodations in a 19th-century colonial house—12 Clinton Street. I had arrived. American windows were already opening out onto the landscape of the imagination. My pilgrim soul was pleased. I had a whiff of the perfume of America as I settled down, under a benign Baptist roof, to long hours of labor in the Harvard libraries.

My research project on Henry James, whose papers and manuscripts are preserved in the Houghton Library, was the reason for my stay at Harvard. It took all my energies and exertions. A seven-hour daily work stint, followed by hours of reading and writing until well past midnight, was not enough to cope with the flood of Jamesiana. But 12 Clinton Street had all my love and sentiment. At the touch of a door knob one Sunday morning, it had become my home, an overwhelming presence in my thoughts. In the developing vision of things, home-University-city soon became one integral and comprehensive metaphor for the pursuit of the American essence.

All good things start from home. My imagination first fastens on our dear India House—as it came to be affectionately known because of the number of Indian lodgers over time—and on our gracious landlady Charlessie Humez, whose motherly care and tenderness gave my Harvard labors a family touch, bringing the blessedness of corn, milk and meat to bear upon my long, sustained and difficult dialogue with the ghost of Henry James. In two complementary pieces, I have already recorded a salute to American womanhood, to the American home and its culinary culture, and to American ceremonies, protocols and priorities. Let me dip into those memories.

The scene changes. We are now in the adjoining dining room, with its ornate paneling and its rich mahogany table redolent of family pieties and repasts. The lace and the linen, the plate and the cut glass around bespeak a happier time, and we may not touch these artifacts of the hand and the imagination except on a day of ceremony or celebration. Which reminds me of Mrs. Humez' "high teas"—the sparkling china, the singing kettle, the lace napkins, and a whole generosity of American cakes and cookies and doughnuts and maple syrup, and the Indian "leaf" . . . . Oh, the inebriation of that slow draft and the dialogue and the laughter! I could then understand why Lionel Trilling paraphrasing Mary McCarthy once said that "no people ever had so intense an idea of the relationship of spirit to its material circumstances" as the Americans had . . . . There had been music in her life earlier—her late husband had been a musician. Now the piano in the draped and curtained music room stood silent. Her husband was gone, and her three children—no longer with her—had suffered divorces and broken homes; but Mrs. Humez had not allowed the world to sour her twilight years. And when she would laugh, one heard the sound of a rippling stream cascading over rocks and ravines. Even on the telephone, the voice had a clear, innocent, bell-like quality. I suppose the eternal American girl in her still held sway, still glowed and sparkled. It is thus that I could imagine an Isabel Archer gliding into her old age in slippers of silver and gold! No wonder Henry James made these "frail vessels" carry the full weight of moral life. Mrs. Humez too was a daughter of the stern Puritans, but in her as in the Jamesian heroine the traditional stoicism and sadism of the male Puritan had been purified, as though filtered through a sieve . . . .

I had of course read and taught scores of American novels and plays about the family, some of them extremely distressing—Dreiser, Faulkner, Arthur Miller, Albee, Eugene O'Neill—and it was Mrs. Humez' home that helped dissipate that negative vision and reveal instead those strong moral currents of familial ethics that continue to show despite evidence to the contrary. Without my Fulbright I could not have felt the real truth of the American home, in my pulse as it were.

And there were visits to other homes across the country, as well as brief but beautiful days of hospitality under friendly roofs—in the parlors of Harvard colleagues, in the seaside house of the Simmonses as a sponsored Fulbright guest, and in their Newbury Port neighbors' place, called Egerton House, with its rare first *de luxe* editions of Henry James and Rodin's Eve, in the suburban villa of Dr. and Mrs. James J. Feeney of the Medical School—better than anything I could imagine as a retreat for a congress of minds, in the apartment of Dr. Deeter in New Manchester, in the home of Dr. McLeod of Rider

College, Trenton, New Jersey, in the Circle Way mansion of Helen and Bill Mulder—who still keep their Indian "mark" intact, in Salt Lake City and, finally, in the bungalow of Dr. Allan Wendt of the English Department at Mills College, Oakland, where his delightful family and his huge friendly Alsatian made my California holiday a long ride into the blue. The list is long, and I can at this distance only thank those other friends and strangers who opened their doors, offered drinks and dinners and drives into the country on those smooth silken roads, with their wives and daughters adding their delightful little peck on the cheek at parting.

All those memories take me back again to the American classics from which my fanciful picture of the U.S. had taken form, shape and color. My first encounter with an American book was at the age of 20—Dreiser's *An American Tragedy*. In India, American literature did not become a reality until the Fulbright impact; few before were conscious of its separate identity. But my chance brush with that volume at a holiday resort left me reeling, literally bowled over. It would perhaps be truer to say that the book possessed me for nearly a hundred hours. When fully 38 years later I rose one evening to speak on this book to a graduate class at New York University, the whole memory of Dreiser's harrowing tragedy on the death of the American Dream came rushing back upon me—the fascination, the shock and the horror of it all. Images of fiction and images of reality mesh into an enveloping view of a foreign society, and they stabilize one's responses—something that authenticates the passage of knowledge from book to street and back. Reality does not imitate art, as the inimitable Oscar Wilde quipped, but art does *create* life, creates that life which is lived intensely in one's imagination, as James argued in a famous exchange with H. G. Wells. My exposure to the American reality on the ground eventually prepared the ground for my understanding and assessment of the American classics—a great part of my criticism is directly related to the Fulbright experience. The theory and the concept that year found their correlative in insights that rose, like partridges, before a gathering crack of reality, as I moved from home to home, from campus to campus, from coast to coast.

My Harvard story—I watched *Love Story* being filmed in the Yard on a winter morning—is long and rich enough to lead my eager imagination in a dozen different directions. Let me pick up a few bright strands to bring out a "figure in the carpet." First, Harvard's ways of doing things, its ethos and ambiance, its Ivy League image, culture and style. The university's name, across the Atlantic, conjures up a whole continent of American dreams and historical memories, dreams which no other American university may claim. To be at Harvard in whatever capacity is to become, in effect, a part of the great and glorious tradition going back to the Mayflower. Its aged brick buildings, its old-world charm—mosses and ivy and columns—would not perhaps be enough to delight the modern eye. Nor is Cambridge a pretty place when one sees it in the context of modern American cities, of marble plazas and sparkling fountains. But who expects a vintage wine to come out of a shiny new silver spout? The creepers and the lichen and the elms, the spires and the turrets and the winding stairs still serve the Gothic imagination of poet, pundit, and pedagogue.

One knows that in these precincts some of the noblest American spirits have dwelt, that some of the greatest human minds have cogitated in these rooms and halls. Today's America owes so much to generations of Harvard scholars and scientists that anyone, let alone a visiting Fulbrighter, stands in awe. I soon discovered that Harvard's eminence and aloofness made it no less human nor genial in its day-to-day life. In my case I was thoughtfully left alone to browse among the books in my carrel on the fourth floor of Widener. It worked beautifully, what with a few business trips to the English Department in Warren Hall, and a whole calendar of events to choose from. This was in striking contrast to the fussiness, the red-tape and the clutter of things in our Indian Universities, which sadly continue to be the poor cousins of the British family. The American system is quiet, efficient, non-interfering; it allows the scholar as much freedom and choice as he can take, and it leaves lots of room for improvisation and innovation. Indeed the whole economy of Harvard is well honed to the needs of the scholarly community there. And I could only admire the ethic of work and responsibility that silently touched one's thought. It is this type of academic culture that one seeks to create on returning home. Even if it is mostly frustrating, it is essential because one's work habits have already changed.

Apart from the library hours, with their own solemnity and propriety (what a relief to be spared the book vandalism of my country!), the most fruitful and memorable moments of my stay were those spent in the genial, witty and stimulating company of the English faculty over Tuesday lunch at Eliot House. To invoke the atmosphere of these nostalgic assemblies and wine and victuals is to return to some of the civilities and table talk. As we sipped sherry or claret or burgundy in the anteroom, or collected meals on our trays in a long queue of teachers and students, then drifted into the faculty dining room, the utter ease and informality of the proceedings had a tonic effect. Perhaps twenty faculty showed up, but the faces kept changing. Some, like Trilling, visiting from Columbia that year, Gay Wilson Allen, the Whitman scholar, Chairman Morton Bloomfield, and Harry Levin were all but permanent fixtures, as was I—it was a ceremony not to be missed. What wonderful words flowed down the table, a stream of comments on the world's sad ways, on man's follies, on American quirks and quiddities. I remember best our animated discussion of each major scene in the BBC series *The Forsyte Saga*, the rage that year. No one ever talked about a colleague or his work: it was not done—the Harvard difference. The Brahmins of an earlier era had left their traces in Eliot House.

A place out of some fairy tale? Harvard's greatness does give the imagination of reverence free play. But that particular year included some of the darkest and ugliest in its long history. It was in fact a very wrong time for an outsider to be on any American campus. The youth revolt was still not spent, and like most movements it became particularly shrill before its collapse. It reached Harvard in all its fury towards year-end, and I was in the middle of it, watching scenes of unbelievable violence, abuse and assault in the Yard and in Harvard Square outside. The Vietnam trauma, aggravated by Kent State and My Lai, had at last overtaken Harvard. The hippie culture had all along been in evidence, but now came the sullenness and the rage. We had sit-ins, marches, torchlight processions, police dogs, pickets, stampedes and mélées. All tradition seemed to go up in smoke before one's bewildered eyes. The American Presidency itself was under continual siege—the gags about Nixon and his deputy were nasty ("There's good news, bad news and Ag-news"), but Yankee humor was so clearly an act of therapy.

Even in the midst of all the chaos and confusion, the inner core of Harvard life remained untouched. There were scores of small events, gestures and signs that vouched for the continuing moral strength of the place. The madness would pass, but while it lasted there was no mistaking its authenticity. Is that what prompted Trilling to call his Norton Lectures that year *Sincerity and Authenticity*? It was American youth's hour of truth, a politics of passion and pity and perversity. It was the time when the horror of the racial question in America had begun, only begun, to register with white youth. "Black is beautiful" was posted all over America.

There are so many distressing features of the American scene—street violence, rape, drugs, murder, muggings, prostitution and the destitute homeless—all of which the media magnify enough to frighten any visitor on arrival. Even if you escape these lethal realities, the media heap coals upon the imagination. "Violence," as a TV film called *Violence Sonata* pronounced in its caption, "is as American as cherry pie." It is there in the very composition and being of America, as deep as the urge for absolute freedom and justice. The contraries however do not cancel out the dream of America but instead create a dialectic of accommodation and responsibility. One has to see all that from within to be able to understand.

On the brighter side, my notebooks for that year contain tender and delicate memories, scenes and episodes, some of which enriched my literary consciousness and enhanced my understanding. To begin with, there were three Fulbright conferences: an arrival orientation in Washington, a March meeting also in Washington, and a June wrap-up at USC in Los Angeles. The March conference was a full-blown affair: renowned scholars, Senators and state officials participated, and I saw in action a corporate dialogue of immense importance. The formal dinner at the State Department, in the opulent and elegant Franklin Room, meetings with Secretary of State Rogers and his wife, with Senator Fulbright and other dignitaries—it was a show that underlined the high value of the Fulbright Program in the eyes of the American government and the Nixon Administration. USC had its own stimulating agenda, and visits to Hollywood and Disneyland added to the expanding sum of insights. On my trip home, a stop in Hawaii at the East-West Center brought the wheel of the Fulbright year full circle, even as I circled the globe. My senses had stored a rich harvest, my mind was saturated, and my imagination soared in a new kind of freedom.

I must bring my muses home, to 12 Clinton Street, where all this began. Under Mrs. Humez' vigilant and trained eye, I began to admire the economy, the elegance and the style of that great American daily *The Christian Science Monitor*. She would entertain no other newspaper and I soon saw the virtue of her argument. After a casual first meeting with its book editor Melvin Maddocks, he invited me to review books. Within a few weeks I could admire my name and signature at the head of a column. A beautiful relationship materialized—I recall the warm farewell lunch in downtown Boston, giving body to all the lovely music he and his deputy had been whispering by phone.

The scene shifts to a small Indiana town. I have been invited to deliver the Convocation Address at New Manchester College, plus lectures on Henry James, Shakespeare, Sikhism, an odd assortment. The student revolt had left no campus untouched and my hosts warned me about potential catcalls, eggs and other missiles. I was in awe when I learned that one of the earlier figures to deliver such an address had been Martin Luther King. At the podium, all kinds of thoughts kept my mind in a state of alert, even anxiety. I sailed into my 45-minute address, entitled "East-West Passage." Soon I sensed that it was going well, but the applause and the ovation left me dazed, almost speechless. Here was the Fulbright Moment, mysteriously come to life on an ardent American campus. For at least one Fulbright soul, that piece of Indiana soil had become a "country of the mind." Years later, reading Ross Lockridge's *Raintree County*, that Whitmanesque novel of epic proportions and grandeur, my thoughts kept returning to New Manchester. Let me quote from that address.

> We have, both in the East and the West, tended to give our inevitable but entirely wholesome cultural differences the quality of immutable antinomies, such as we find in life and nature. No wonder, we see the East as feminine, shy, ingrown and reflective, and the West as masculine, vigorous, expansive, and engaged. We associate India and the Orient with dreams, mystery and transcendence, and the Occident with empires, artifacts and machines . . . . What is temporal and relative thus appears spatial and absolute . . . . Basically, the East-West values *cannot* be different, unless of course we posit a schizophrenic God who is playing Dr. Jekyll in the East and Mr. Hyde in the West! . . . We have all, teacher and student, administrator and parent, to learn to discipline our minds. And the mind, we know, is a lawless maverick, insolent and defiant. But as the Founder of Sikhism, Guru Nanak, sang in one of his beautiful and deathless hymns, *Nun jeetey jug jeet*, "The conquest of the mind is the conquest of the world."

Then the farewell to Harvard. On the last day of my stay, the young and charming Sarah Adams, a protegée of Mrs. Humez who had driven me to Cape Cod, the theatre, the Boston Symphony—with complimentary tickets from the Fulbright Office—took me out to the Cambridge cemetery, where the bones of Henry lie in eternal peace near the rest of that great family of minds the Jameses. I saw on his gravestone these thoughtful words: "Interpreter of both sides of the sea." It was a theme which would run through the fruit of my Harvard year, my book *Henry James: The Indirect Vision*.

What does it mean now that an Indian academic, who later would visit the U.S. for many lecturing or teaching assignments and whose involvement with America's literature, life and polity would become a consuming concern, spent a year in Cambridge? In brief, American society, driven by the dream of money, success and power, is at bottom in search of the freedom that the good life affords. Trilling wrote, "Somewhere in our mental constitution is the demand for life as pure spirit." It is not in any fixed form or formula that the American culture of material well-being can be explained. For culture, as he puts it, is "a hum and buzz of implications."

Is the Fulbright Program different from other exchange programs? I have had little chance to experience any others, outside the British Council visits to Great Britain. The Council has an impressive presence in India and Indian scholars, brought up on the British brew until recently, had a few colonial hang-ups. The Old Guard in the English Departments of Indian Universities would not, until the end of the sixties, allow even a single paper or course out of the prescribed three to be on American Literature at the post-graduate level. A good deal has changed since the Fulbright effort. Today almost three-quarters of the Masters' and Doctoral dissertations touch American writers. The most remarkable feature of such developments is the creation of an academic culture which is visibly pluralistic. The American work ethic is not yet significant as a factor, but the American model with regard to university structures—new courses, semester examinations, evaluation methods—these touch higher levels of teaching and research. Compared to the Council, the Fulbright's administration was perhaps a trifle more thoughtful and liberal. Yet my seven weeks at London University in the summer of 1964, Shakespeare's fourth centenary year, was a satisfying experience—I was the only non-white scholar in a group of 140 from all over the world. I learned to live amidst a large community of minds, with ease and facility. Later visits to British universities, to the homes of poets, and to scores of country houses and castles right up to Aberdeen, gave me a wondrous peep into that old and civilized society. The Colonel Blimps still around do not disturb the British picture. British insularity is still there, but the red-brick universities have moved far from conservative mores and moorings.

Yet I must confess, as I lay down my pen, that since my Harvard visit it is America alone that has the power to bewitch my imagination. It ever remains a clear call and a wide call that may not be denied.

PART IV

THE SEVENTIES: SURVIVING CHANGE

In 1970 the Senator was still in place, but he would leave the Senate in 1975; no one would replicate his role as champion of the program. The Vietnam War, in full spate in 1970, was slouching towards its sad end. In the State Department, the stalwart Nixon-appointee John Richardson had taken up the reins of State's cultural programs and had already begun his patient eight-year effort to rebuild the program's image and budgets. But progress was slow, barely faster than inflation. Richardson had the wisdom to recognize the value of a BFS suggestion to foster the birth and early growth of an alumni network, long after the Japanese alumni had organized.

With no new agreements, the death of commissions already in existence became more critical: Iraq, Tunisia, South Africa and Paraguay were gone, Ethiopia, Ghana and Iran would soon follow. A second factor blossomed in the seventies: USIA began operating Fulbright programs with neither country Fulbright agreement nor binational commission. Soon it was done everywhere, most often in small countries where it was argued that administrative costs would be excessive; only in the eighties would USIA Europe hands speak openly of eliminating the great European commissions. In Japan, the remarkable Caroline Yang had begun her tenure at the Commission and had impressive alumni support. Other country commissions, despite rising foreign-government contributions in many countries, slowly pared their ambitions, as U.S. appropriations flattened and inflation took its toll. Instead of full-year grants, the commission in Italy, for example, found itself providing a *mensualità*, a stipend-in-aid measured out in one-month doses, to top off the expenses of scholars who had reimbursed research placements in Italy or the U.S. Commission administrators, reluctant to shrink their program numbers below the point of visibility, found other ingenious ways to stretch funding—on the assumption that U.S. appropriations would soon return.

They did not. Grants continued to become shorter, stipends smaller in real terms. Meanwhile Secretary of State Kissinger, apparently unaware of the potential for building on existing Fulbright agreements, fostered new "joint-commission" arrangements with countries like Egypt and India, diluting further Fulbright's seminal or "flagship" role.

The Stanton Commission Report, in 1975, was the latest and the most powerful of the numerous studies since the early fifties to recommend that cultural relations be separated or insulated in one way or another from "information." The Commission reasoned that "the Spokesman Function" dealt with current policy and had thus to present it in the best possible light, while scholars, educators, and artists on the other hand dealt with a far longer range of concerns and were concerned with seeking truth. Inexperienced Carter staffers seized upon "the USIA question" for their first formal government reorganization. But instead of heeding Stanton, they threw the tiny State Department cultural office, with its 270 staffers, into USIA, with its 5000 employees. USIA, it was said, was together at last.

Four contributors from the seventies appear in this volume, three from the U.S. and one from Spain. One went to Spain to read nineteenth-century literary history and fell victim to the scent of orange-blossoms; another saw the grim realities of post-Prague-Spring Czechoslovakia; a third discovered India during a six-week whirlwind seminar; and a Spaniard studying clinical psychology in California returned to her country to find Franco gone, leaving his country ill-equipped to handle the psychological and moral consequences of democracy and freedom.

This sample cannot claim to speak for the seventies. Yet these four insights, each in its own way, hint at new directions in the Program—shorter programs, greater awareness of the political meaning of the experience, a new critical yet ever-protective sense about Fulbright, and perhaps the merest hint of a need to do something about a world slipping out of control, symbolized by the agony of Vietnam. Even the Fulbright Program, originally designed by bipartisan efforts to soar high above the shifts of earth's weather, seemed to be tossing in turbulent air.

Did the Senator imagine "that his program might some day produce Americans who would gamely step in to probe issues of national identity in the old civilizations of our world?" In his study of Spanish and Portuguese intellectual relations since the nineteenth century, Dr. Utt has focused on the elusive question of national cultural identity, during his more or less continued residence in Spain. In the Fulbright world, foreign and American, national identity is far from an uncommon theme. Like Italy, the Iberian Peninsula has attracted four writers and these essays intersect and interact in unexpected ways. His tribute to the accidental acts of faith that Fulbright represents, and to the usefulness of its generous network of impressive alumni, highlights spires and turrets of the Fulbright structure. No other author in this volume goes so far as to qualify the Fulbright ideal as a religious principle. If Darshan Singh Maini gives us the esthetic of the Fulbright Moment, Roger Utt hints at its metaphysics.

20

HISPANIST AT LARGE

Roger L. Utt

By the summer of 1969, the firestorm in Vietnam had cooled, albeit only by a few degrees. The Selective Service System had given me some slack, just enough so that I could finish my MA in Spanish literature at the University of California at Santa Barbara. Now the inevitable was at hand. Halfway through my induction physical, in the suffocating atmosphere of a windowless building in downtown Los Angeles on a hot, smoggy day in August, I was pulled out of a lineup of naked, sweaty, profoundly unhappy citizens, handed some papers, and told to report to a medical officer down the hall. The doctor examined my ears and solemnly informed me that a significant, and possibly progressive, high-frequency hearing loss of unknown origin in my left ear had rendered me a "combat liability" and that I was consequently disinvited to join the U.S. Army. Heading back toward the locker area to retrieve my clothes, and my life, I noticed something different going on as I passed by the

"Audiometry Station": the sound-proof box, about the size of a small RV, that only a few moments before had scientifically uncovered my flaw was now unattended. Its circuitry had evidently broken down, and the line of future soldiers was now veering toward a sergeant seated at a card table, puffing distractedly on a damp cigar stub. He would briefly hold up a mechanical buzzer to one ear of each passing recruit, ask if he could hear the sound, and then bellow "NEXT!" without removing the cigar, and without waiting too long for a reply.

From that astonishing day to the present, I have held a special reverence and affection for a peculiarly Hispanic notion of fate. Its name is *azar*, which in Spanish means "random chance." Its bluntly iambic pronunciation—in Castilian, a-THAR, with a voiceless, retroflexive tap of the tongue behind the teeth, on the final consonant—is virtually indistinguishable from that of *azahar*, the word for "citrus blossom," because the *h* is silent in modern Spanish. These two words share a common etymological source: they both entered Spanish from the Arabic *zahr*, meaning both "flower" and one of a pair of dice; and the connection between the two terms was the floral symbol placed on one facet of a Moorish gaming die. By the time *azar* entered the English language—via French and eventually English gambling houses, where "Hazard" became a popular game of chance played with dice—the noun *hazard* had lost all its original perfume and most of its innocence, acquiring permanently the connotations of menace and danger we commonly associate with golf courses, run-down tenements, and faulty appliance cords. But in contemporary Spanish, the word *azar* is value-free: not *bad* luck, but rather something more akin to *pure* luck, blind chance, contingency. One may profit by learning to see *azar* as Spaniards see it, not as a malevolent or sinister force, not as *hazard*, but as an aleatory phenomenon, ineffable and mysterious, laced with an indecipherable poetic rhyme and a faint scent of Andalusian orange blossoms. It cannot be invoked, provoked or cajoled; it simply intervenes or intercepts, and moves on. It is the silent engine of all Histories and of all stories—*historias*, indistinguishably for both, in Spanish—and thus of my story too.

"Now what?" I wondered as I left the Army Induction Center, dazed but whole. I had accidentally won two precious years—maybe more—in that bizarre lottery. I decided I would devote them to finding out if I could learn to teach to others what I knew and liked best. So I picked about a hundred schools and sent off my applications, including one to the University of Auckland, in New Zealand, whose exotic catalogue had been misplaced on the library shelf marked "U.S. Four-Year Colleges/Universities." A few months later I became the third member of the Spanish section of the Department of

Romance Languages at Auckland. I reckoned I was in paradise. Outside my classroom window, bellbirds sang their amazing velvet chime in the lush subtropical foliage while I explored Quevedo, Cervantes, and the mysteries of the Spanish subjunctive mood, testing bright, eager, unjaded kids, fresh from the farm many of them, and testing myself, learning how to be a professor, entering Hispanism as a professional. The two years I stayed in that glorious, thriving, clean, uncomplicated place are among the happiest I can remember.

Although my old department at Santa Barbara had expanded noticeably during my absence, I was considering a move elsewhere for doctoral work. "Have you met *him* yet?" former professors inquired pointedly upon my return. "Who?" "You mean you haven't met Jorge de Sena?! Brace yourself," came the reply from more than one. No, I had never even heard of Jorge de Sena, the Portuguese scholar and new chairman who was radically re-energizing the Department. I liked him instantly. I had never seen up close the likes of such a committed teacher, such a ferocious administrator, such a versatile, outspoken scholar and literary critic, such a profound poet, such a gentleman, and such a dreadful hammer to anyone who crossed him unreasonably—all contained in a single powerhouse personality, whose impact on Portuguese letters is without equal in our century. To me, he gave two things: clarity to a professional commitment as a Hispanist and, more precious, friendship.

I was becoming a serious student of the prolific 19th-century Spanish novelist Benito Pérez Galdós (1843-1920), who has only lately begun to acquire abroad the standing he deserves among the major figures in European realism. Neighboring Portuguese writers, I mused, must have taken an interest in Galdós' novels—nearly 80 of them—as well as in those of certain other writers of his generation, so I spent an afternoon in the library poking around, expecting to have my curiosity satisfied in fairly short order. The search proved more far more difficult than I thought it should be, absorbing days rather than hours, without results. "What's going on here?" I complained to Sena. "There should be at least one book on modern Hispano-Portuguese cultural relations, or a few scholarly monographs on mutual influences between the so-called *Generación de 1868* in Spain and the Portuguese *Geração de 1870*, but I haven't been able to find much more than one or two evasive and unsatisfying articles." He winked a knowing wink. "Keep looking. This is a very interesting subject." Stepping up my search to the level of interlibrary loans, I began to sense an odd conspiracy of silence operating somewhere. How could this be? Spaniards and Portuguese have shared the same clearly defined space for centuries, undivided by massive natural barriers; they speak very closely related tongues, and they have a long parallel experience of empire, war, and peace; yet they seem either perfectly oblivious of one another or irrationally hostile in their mutual suspicions and mutually unflattering stereotypes. Granted, Portugal had been absorbed under the Spanish Crown for sixty years, from 1580 to 1640, but that "Captivity," as it is sometimes called in Portuguese history books, could not account for so much silence three centuries later. Had not the Portuguese been instrumental, under Wellington, in driving Napoleon's armies from Spanish soil?

After a while of this, Sena said to me: "You are meddling in one of the best-kept secrets of Hispano-Portuguese historiography and literary history. The subject has been very nearly taboo for decades, and the resources for dealing with it are buried deep. What's more, the issue of political and cultural relations between the two countries became fiendishly complex in the nineteenth century, and, as you have learned, a thorough and objective global study of the phenomenon remains to be written. I'll help you get a grant to work in the National Library in Lisbon this summer."

I returned from Portugal with a fair amount of primary material, which would take months to digest, with doctoral coursework and demanding teaching assignments occupying most of my time, now as a Lecturer. I needed to go to Spain. I had studied at the University of Madrid as an undergraduate participant in the University of California Program and thus felt more linguistically and socially secure about doing complicated research there than in Lisbon or Coimbra. I decided to apply for another grant, a big one this time. But the Fulbright advisor at Santa Barbara quickly shot me down: the deadline for applications had expired only a few days before I came to inquire. "End of subject," I muttered to myself as I stepped in the elevator. The automatic doors were nearly closed when I heard a loud voice from one of the inner offices: ". . . the deadline for. . . ." The advisor was waiting at the elevator when I arrived, on a hunch, back up on the fifth floor of the Administration building. Sheer *azar*. "I've just verified that the Fulbright deadline for candidates applying 'At Large'—that is, without specific institutional affiliation—is still three weeks away. You might qualify, since your doctoral coursework is now nearly finished."

My contact with the Fulbright organization thus begins, literally, on the threshold of an elevator, and figuratively, on the threshold of a career: a sharp administrator took a second look at the possibilities; and a subtle, irrational intrusion of random chance—of blind, indifferent *azar*—once more dropped a splendid opportunity right in my lap.

Of course, *azar* alone achieves nothing. The "achiever" in a person's life, I think, is one's continuity of purpose, without which the unpredictable visitations of *azar* make no lasting sense and may indeed have destructive effects. In fact, I am persuaded that in a rudderless life the neutral actions of *azar* are more apt to resemble the predatory deceptions of its brother Hazard, the notorious crapshooter.   If I had to invent a religion, I would call its supreme deity Azar and its fallen angel Hazard. Continuity of purpose is the conviction that what you are doing is worth doing, that it is right, that it is bigger and more important than you are, and that you ought to keep doing it, in whatever way you can, as well as you can, and for the benefit of as many people as possible. If pressed to restate the case, I would define continuity of purpose both as a fairly effective form of insurance against Hazard's dicey game and as a fertile field for growing sturdy citrus trees whose blossoms, *azahares*, sometimes and for no apparent reason smell especially sweet.

This is where my debt to the Fulbright organization comes in. That it considered my curiosity about Spain and Portugal worth supporting with hard cash, unquestioningly and with no strings attached, was more than an act of conspicuous generosity and of uncommon faith. More transcendentally, it offered the opportunity and the means by which I would locate a fertile field— my continuity of purpose—not merely in narrow terms of scholarly interests, but as a permanent feature of my personal and professional life.

*   *   *

I arrived in Madrid as a Fulbrighter-at-large in October of 1976. The city had been transformed. In 1966 the going joke among the more arrogant American students had been: "You can buy Spain for less than eight million dollars—but then you have to fix it!" It seemed to me, back then, that nothing worked and nobody cared. A decade later, Madrid's population had apparently doubled, and areas of town that I remembered as being on the furthest periphery were now part of the capital's rapidly elongating nucleus. The main avenues bustled with clean, late-model cars, instead of the wheezing, soot-encrusted, 2-hp Citroëns, ugly little Seat 600s, and unmuffled, three-wheeled minivans of yore; and where once there had been total chaos, now the traffic lanes were clearly marked and most drivers were scrupulously observing them. Chains of sleek, new American-style cafeterias with names like California, Nebraska, and Ohio had sprung up in tidy contrast to the thousands of more authentic (and far more appealing) scruffy bars and taverns. The men had abandoned black as the only color in their wardrobe; the women were more stylish, perkier, more articulate, uniformly younger-looking somehow. Everyone was taller. Even the food—*Dios mío*, the spectacularly good foods and wines of Spain!—seemed to taste better. Levi jeans, or convincing imitations of them, were ubiquitous. Kiosks, literally sagging under the weight of a journalistic avalanche, were festooned with layer upon layer of new papers and magazines of every political hue, and long-repressed

Spaniards were developing chronic eye-strain by pretending not to notice the plague of pornography. Everywhere one encountered the slogan, scrawled by confused or hopelessly embittered rightists, "Con Franco se vivía mejor" (With Franco, life was better)—to which more liberal graffitists, schooled in irony, would scribble responses charged with characteristically Spanish dark humor. My favorite was: "¡Con Franco, *llovía* mejor!" (With Franco, the *rain* was better!).

What, indeed, would life be like without the Caudillo? This was the only question that mattered to Spaniards in the fall of 1976. After nearly forty years of authoritarian rule by arbitrary decree, General Franco was not yet a year in his grave, and the entire country was still holding its breath, watching its extraordinary transition from dictatorship to democracy tentatively unfold. Three months earlier, King Juan Carlos had sacked the inept Francoist prime minister Carlos Arias Navarro and then dumbfounded political analysts everywhere by picking an obscure senior bureaucrat of the Falangist party apparatus, Adolfo Suárez, to steer the nation toward the light. Suárez did just that, and brilliantly, but the political cost was devastating: in the municipal and regional elections of May 1991, his reformed centrist party failed to secure even 5% of the vote. The velocity of Spain's transformation in the last fifteen years has thus turned one of the great heroes of the transition into a political non-entity, a common fate of leaders caught between irreconcilable forms of government. Suárez' impossible task of both placating and weakening long-entrenched interests is masterfully detailed by Paul Preston in his *Triumph of Democracy in Spain* (1986).

In a December 1976 referendum, 74% of the eligible voters turned out to declare themselves 94% in favor of a reform package that would legalize all political parties, including the dreaded Communists, and pave the way for the first free elections in 41 years, which were held in June. Installed in a pension directly behind the parliament building, I got used to running a gauntlet of poised machine guns every afternoon on my way home from the National Library. Organized violence, both state-sponsored and clandestine, was never far from the surface: I dodged a few rubber bullets myself and hid out a few times in shadowy stairwells, elbow to elbow with huffing, middle-class shoppers and strollers, as security police swept without warning through this or that downtown district. The aerial percussion of helicopter blades was, invariably, the sound of real trouble on the way.

Sena had corresponded on my behalf with the only scholar in Spain I knew to be working on 19th-century Luso-Hispanic relations—in the Spanish system, access to work like her 1962 dissertation is normally negotiated directly with the author. By the time I got to Madrid my elusive "advisor" had transferred to Salamanca. When I finally tracked her down, she had forgotten her agreement to provide bibliographical orientation: "I have plans for publishing my dissertation," she explained as I caressed the binding of her 600-page tome on my lap in her apartment. "I'm afraid I cannot let you read or photocopy any part of it." She was not the only academic I met who was sensitive about foreign intruders, as if there were room on the turf for only one self-approved scholar at a time. Closed, politicized societies breed suspicions in the most unlikely places. In those days, for example, library clerks—unqualified state functionaries who controlled all access to holdings—would sometimes ask *why* you wanted a certain book. In all important Spanish libraries today, the stacks are still off-limits to researchers; but the service is vastly improved, and Spanish academics, especially the younger ones, are as collegial as their American counterparts.

The phenomenon I was studying is, or was, called "Iberism." Almost clandestinely, like the mounting demands for political and social reform that began seriously to inconvenience Spanish and Portuguese monarchs in the 19th century, the term *iberismo* entered the political vocabulary of the Iberian Peninsula around 1850, as the name for a progressive idea whose time had come. It was a somewhat ingenuously conceived instrument, or pretext, for liberal reform that would eventually entail the formal unification of Spain and Portugal. Proponents of Iberism saw in this idea a healthy alternative to the political, economic, and social stagnation of the prevailing regimes. They were confident that an intimate alliance or fusion of the two countries would lead to numberless improvements in the quality of Peninsular life and would put a welcome end to centuries of absurd and self-defeating estrangement between the two national groups.

In both countries over the next half-century, the *idea iberista* generated a mass of propaganda and counter-propaganda, which became especially shrill during the period between the Spanish Revolution of 1868 and the Restoration of the Bourbon monarchy in 1875. Across a span of fifty years, the banner of Iberism passed successively from liberal monarchists to progressive democrats, to conservative republicans, to socialists, and finally to radical federalists, taking on altered meanings and new political agendas at each stage of the process without ever being clearly defined or put forward as a coherent program of Luso-Hispanic rapprochement. Threatened by the implications of Iberism, the governments of both Spain and Portugal effectively undermined many of the gains that were made by novelists, poets, and journalists in the direction of Hispano-Portuguese cross-cultural communication, so the gains of *cultural* Iberism—the phenomenon that most interested me—were modest and left virtually no traces in subsequent Peninsular historiography. In the end, the very word *iberismo* became anathemized in Portugal as a synonym for antipatriotic socialism; in Spain, it was viewed by the regime as the password for a nefarious plot cooked up by radically subversive, godless federalists. Thus, until the "Revolution of the Carnations" in Portugal in 1974 and the death of Franco the following year, the specter of the long-dead Iberist movement systematically poisoned mutual understanding between the two countries, and *Iberismo* was officially considered a non-topic on both sides of their common border, the bastard child of 19th-century Peninsular liberalism.

In all my writings on this subject, I have insisted on making a distinction between the political manifestations of Iberism and those of a more exclusively cultural orientation. In fact, I may have been the first to use the risky phrase *iberismo cultural*, which lately seems to be gaining currency. For example, in 1990 César Antonio Molina, director of the weekly cultural supplement of *Diario 16*, a well-known Spanish daily, published an interesting volume entitled *Sobre el iberismo*. The book opens with a useful survey on "iberismo cultural," touching on many 19th- and 20th-century Spanish and Portuguese writers, including Sena, who have devoted attention to Peninsular letters from a binational perspective. An early section of this first chapter borrows heavily from a book of mine whose value Molina deems, I blush to say, *extra-ordinario*. No American Hispanist-at-Large could ask for more—but I wonder if the Senator from Arkansas envisioned that his program might some day produce Americans who would gamely step in to probe issues of national identity in the old civilizations of our world . . . ? Side by side, but as perfect strangers to each other, Spain and Portugal entered the European Economic Community on January 1, 1986. Since then, several important binational literary conferences have been held in both countries, and the eighth annual Luso-Hispanic "summit" between the leaders of Spain and Portugal took place in mid-December 1991. It's a beginning. Clearly, the climate of Hispano-Portuguese cooperation is warmer now than it has ever been; but it will be a good long while before any sort of formal program of binational educational and cultural exchange is established to chip away at the foundation of the so-called "Cork Curtain" that still psychologically divides the Peninsula.

By day, then, I was poring over dust-laden newspapers and journals of the mid-1870's, attempting to mediate between two mutually hostile or indifferent cultures that were almost as foreign to me as they still were to each other. By night, I found the noisy, smoke-filled bars and cafés of Madrid alive with debate on the prospect of democracy in Spain exactly a hundred years later. Franco had harped incessantly on the theme that his people were born anarchists and therefore incapable of self-government. He was partly right in the first instance, but he had drawn a grotesquely wrong conclusion in the second because he simply ignored the average Spaniard's deeply rooted sense of justice, antedating the spirit of Montesquieu by about five hundred years: "*¡Dios, qué buen vasallo, si hoviesse buen señor!*"—Lord, he'd be a splendid servant, if there were a worthy master!—says a deathless line in the 12th-century epic poem of the Cid.

All the Fulbrighters that year were especially conspicuous targets of Spanish curiosity about political matters, and we were inevitably drawn, again and again, into the loud and constant exchange of informed opinion, unconcealed prejudice, and outright nonsense on the crucial questions of how, whether, and how soon Spanish society should, or could, embrace democracy and assimilate its consequences. The grilling, often expressed in anti-American terms, could get rough: "So, *amigo americano*, how do you explain the sorry record of race relations in your country? What about your military-industrial complex that is destroying Southeast Asia? What about the two Kennedy assassinations? Why does everyone have guns in the U.S.? This you call democracy? This is what we Spaniards should aspire to now?" The hardest part for an American under such circumstances is knowing when to keep your mouth shut and to let your hosts come around by themselves, if they will, to a point of view you can explore together.

On the other hand, it was disconcerting but wonderfully instructive to find one's self in some hundred-year-old café, engaged in conversation on a lofty topic like Freedom or Democracy, and to be suddenly preempted by a bunch of snarling Blue Shirts who invade the place and angrily demand that everyone present sing "Cara al sol," the triumphant Fascist anthem of 1939. On the occasion I am recalling, the electric silence in the room, until the thugs departed in frustration and disgust, was eloquent. Today, those who want to are still singing that anthem loud and clear—in a society that freely endorses their right to do so—every November 20th, on the anniversary of Franco's death. In 1991 an orderly crowd of about 10,000 assembled for the annual apocalypse in Madrid on the 17th, a Sunday, in front of the Royal Palace, where the Arab-Israeli Peace Conference had concluded two weeks earlier. The mistress of ceremonies was Carmen Franco, daughter of the departed Generalissimo. It was front-page news the next day, as was the report that David Duke had lost the gubernatorial election in Louisiana.

Throughout my Fulbright year, the Spaniards I talked to (and listened to) sharpened my perceptions about what it means to live in a democracy, and they offered me the rare privilege of witnessing first-hand, in indescribably intimate ways, how they would achieve this for themselves by peaceful means, against the grain of their own history. The result, for me, was that I came to admire and love these cocky, stubborn, impetuous, pragmatic people. Oddly enough,

I came to feel that I too was somehow, microscopically, a part of their bold experiment. This was the least visible but most lasting outcome of my Fulbright experience, and it was not unlike the result I have detected, then and since, in other grantees I've met in Spain at Fulbright-sponsored receptions or at the chatty luncheons its alumni frequently hold at the famous International Institute in Madrid.

As I see it, the Fulbright opportunity extends to each of its beneficiaries an unspoken invitation to risk abandoning some part of his or her vision of the way the world works, or ought to work, and to replace it, permanently, with a fragment of a world view shaped by another culture in another place. My guess is that the vast majority of Fulbright scholars and teachers have, with varying degrees of intensity, not only experienced this process but have also sensed that it almost always operates reciprocally. Empathetically, we argue and we learn, we are influenced and in turn influence others, in ways that the average American would probably, if only grudgingly, approve of. Let's not forget that Americans in general are often skeptical of the value of this kind of binational interchange, even though the pittance it costs them to underwrite it (in the U.S.-Spanish arrangement, at any rate) now amounts to a good deal less than their fair share. I am tempted to think that one explanation for this skepticism lies in a peculiar deficiency of the English language, which is so poorly equipped to express the sort of reciprocities and simultaneities I am trying to describe here. Or is it just an accident that our English dictionaries resort to French for *rapprochement*? The word I want, in Spanish, is *compenetración*.

The countless and unpredictable consequences of this intensely personal process amount, collectively and individually, to something we might agree to call the main external feature of the Fulbright difference. The real action, however, takes place at the level of the individual Commissions abroad, where that difference is nurtured in ways that are consistent with local conditions. Spain's Commission, in operation since 1958, has grateful friends everywhere in the country, nearly 4,000 of them, all former Spanish grantees to the U.S. who have achieved high prominence in Spanish universities, or in business, science, government, the arts, and public health. An American operating alone would have trouble getting within fifty feet of any of these busy, influential Spaniards. The genius of the Fulbright system, the real value of the Fulbright credential, is that if I need to talk to any one of them, now or in the future, they are only a phone call away, via the Commission, and they are always ready to listen and to help.

Some of these Spaniards, like the current Minister of Education and his Undersecretary, have had Fulbright awards; others have been supported by a separately funded agency under Fulbright direction, the U.S.-Spanish Joint Committee for Cultural and Educational Cooperation, which was created in 1977 as a logical extension of the Commission to complement and supplement its functions.   As for the Americans, and in the field I know best, the Commission's rosters of pre-doctoral Fulbright grantees from the U.S., together with those of American postdoctoral scholars sponsored by the U.S.-Spanish Joint Committee, amount to something on the order of a Who's Who at senior levels in the field of Spanish Studies in universities all across the U.S., and their work represents a disproportionately large measure of the vigor, breadth, and universally acknowledged high quality of Peninsular Hispanism in the U.S. today.

If I had picked a more conventional topic for my own work, I would surely have made faster progress in my research by tapping into the resources of the Fulbright network in Spain. The Commission staff happily facilitated any contact I requested, but I found only one other scholar that year who knew more about my subject than I did.   So I simply chained myself to my numbered desks in various libraries and archives, slogged across a lot of bibliographical terrain, and brought home a trunkload of photocopies, including reproductions of some choice documents plucked from the vaults of the Galdós Museum-Residence in the Canary Islands.

It was a profoundly sad homecoming for me: Sena was now gravely ill. He died in June of 1978. I was shattered, adrift. And I had not yet written the first sentence of my dissertation. A year later, they graciously gave me a PhD in exchange for an utterly unpublishable lump of a "book" on an early period in the life and work of Galdós (the main text) and on the "Portuguese Connection" with his generation of writers (the footnotes).

A distinguished Midwestern university hired me in 1980 to reorganize, supervise, and teach in its Spanish language program, to cover a need for undergraduate and graduate courses in 19th-century Peninsular literature, and, above all, to publish—to be, in short, a professional Hispanist in its midst. Two years later, my second application to the U.S.-Spanish Joint Committee was approved, and I went "home" to patch up the holes in my previous work and to start writing.

In 1983, "home" looked to be more prosperous and self-assured than ever. Five years earlier, at a moment of excruciating tension in the country, some 70% of those eligible to vote had collectively expressed an 87% approval of the democratic Constitution of 1978.   Spain was now a functioning *monarquía parlamentaria*, with a partially decentralized, proto-federalist structure of 17 autonomous governments. The Basque, Catalan, and Galician languages, whose imprudent use in public had only a few years before been grounds for arrest, were now constitutionally protected tongues, co-official with Castilian in their respective regions. The country had been deeply sobered by the attempted coup d'état in 1981 and would not forget that the crisis had been defused by King Juan Carlos who, while the entire Government was being held hostage in the Parliament building, telephoned the nation's highest military commanders and coolly reminded them of their sworn allegiance to the Constitution and to his sovereign will. The Socialist party, under the leadership of its general secretary, Felipe González, had jettisoned the Marxist underpinnings of its historic charter and had subsequently won an absolute parliamentary majority in the general elections of 1982. Spain had entered NATO, and "Guernica," Picasso's emblematic portrait of the country's savage civil war, had safely returned from its long exile in New York. The helicopters were now just monitoring traffic jams or surveying protest demonstration routes. In a word, the transition was over. Irreversible social and political change was underway, and the country's economic boom was poised for takeoff.

The Cultural Attaché at the Portuguese embassy in Madrid put me in touch with José Antonio Llardent, a Spanish publisher and widely esteemed translator who was then working on a monumental bilingual edition, in verse, of the great 19th-century Portuguese poet Antero de Quental. I had found a kindred soul, the person I had been looking for all along: Llardent opened his black book to me, and I became his occasional "informant," passing on interesting tidbits that kept popping up in my research—and I was now finding exciting new information at every turn. Once more, an invisible thunderbolt of *azar* led me to a remarkable find that spring, one of those scholarly discoveries that take your breath away. It altered the course of my research and determined the shape and subject of my first book.

Back on the Plains, chapters began to spin off at the rate of two a month, and my Spanish—"precise, pristine, somewhat sparse," as one future American reviewer would put it—seemed to be working with me, rather than against me, as is usually the case. Much to my surprise, Llardent asked to publish the book. It appeared in the spring of 1988, dedicated to him, though he never saw it. But a few days before he died he learned that his magnificent annotated sonnets of Antero de Quental—a labor of cross-cultural *compenetración* if ever there was one—had won Spain's National Translation Prize. My contribution to that book was much smaller than his flattering acknowledgements suggest. But my small mark is there; and it does, however slightly, make a difference.

There have been other surprises. Tenure was not to be forthcoming, and my former status as a Hispanist-at-Large was suddenly revived, with a whole new meaning. Then in the fall of 1987, a fresh intervention of *azar* rearranged everything. An American publishing company sent me to Madrid to work with one of Spain's most respected broadcast journalists in implementing a grand idea: a monthly, hour-long taped collection of excerpts from his daily public affairs broadcast for use by private subscribers as well as by high-school and college language students. My task would be to provide a transcription of these taped programs, to annotate them in English, explaining their historical, political, literary, and cultural references and smoothing the student's way through unfamiliar words and tricky grammatical constructions, and finally to produce an accompanying study guide for each issue. The result was a lively, entertaining package that conveyed an authentic image of what contemporary Spain is all about. Alas, the sinking dollar and the recession ended the project; but during the four years it lasted, a million words surged through my computer, giving pleasure and instruction to as many students—including those at good old Auckland University—as most Hispanists see in a lifetime.

Continuity of purpose in one's life entails, as I proposed earlier in this *historia*, a dual consistency. It is both a stable terrain that favors enduring achievement and a lightning rod that bends the random thrusts of *azar* toward useful and constructive purposes. I believe this now as firmly as I ever did. And having studied the clear-cut lessons of perennial conflict and misreckoning between Spain and Portugal, I like to believe that my intuition about continuity of purpose holds true as well for whole societies, which have nothing to lose and everything to gain simply by making a persistent, honest effort to know and understand one another freely, one-on-one, uninhibited by the often clumsy protocols of their respective governments, however well- or ill-intentioned these may be. This is precisely what the Senator intended all along. And now, which of my two religious principles—*azar* or the Fulbright ideal—will guide me through the next steps? I'll know for sure when I catch an unexpected whiff of orange blossoms in the air.

REFERENCES

José Antonio Llardent and Juan Eduardo Zúñiga, trans. *Antero de Quental: Poesias y prosas selectas*, Madrid: Alfaguara, 1986.

César Antonio Molina, *Sobre el iberismo, y otros escritos de literatura portuguesa*, Madrid: Akal, 1990.

Paul Preston, *The Triumph of Democracy in Spain*, London: Methuen, 1986.

Roger L. Utt, *Textos y con-textos de Clarín: Los artículos de Leopoldo Alas en EL PORVENIR*, Madrid, 1882; Madrid: Istmo, 1988.

Carmen Varela is a clinical psychologist at Spain's National Health Institute who teaches at the Complutense University of Madrid. As of this writing, she is president of the Spanish Fulbright Association. Born into a dictatorship, she traces the impact that its social and educational policies had on her and then analyzes the painful delight of encountering democracy in California. Her first Fulbright grant was bestowed upon her in absentia *when she applied from UCLA to the Joint Commission in Madrid, working in parallel with Fulbright and considered in Spain as part of the Fulbright Program. Returning to Spain in 1978 and watching the psychological dilemmas of transition from the Franco regime to a constitutional monarchy, her unusually self-aware intellectual itinerary sheds a dark but hopeful light on the emergence of would-be democracies all over the world. Her article, written in a difficult Spanish reflecting her commitment less to science than to poetry, has been translated with sensitivity and scholarship by Professor Paul Witkowsky, Fulbright alumnus and colleague at Radford University in Virginia, where Dr. Varela was Fulbright scholar in residence in the Spring of 1992.*

21

OF CROSSES AND CROSSINGS

Carmen Varela

The possibilities we ignore are those of which we are ignorant, a Renaissance Italian wrote.

In 1977 I was ignorant. Not illiterate or unable to cope, not lacking in education of a certain kind, simply ignorant. True, in my country I passed for well educated, a bright youngster from the provinces. But I had been educated under a dictatorship, one whose evolution through various stages of authoritarianism did not begin until the sixties and did not reach another kind of plateau until the Constitution of 1978. My understanding of the world, shaped by this regime, was one-dimensional.

Then a Fulbright post-doctoral fellowship in Los Angeles took me many steps further into the endless field of clinical psychology and brought me into contact with other patterns of communication, social organization, community values and group behaviors. I went virtually overnight from a rural to a technologically advanced society, from an oral to a sophisticated information-based culture, from a leveling and censor-ridden community to one in which individual development and expression were everything. My mind learned to approach things critically but positively; I built a progressive and multidimensional understanding of human behavior. It took years.

It began at UCLA though in fact I landed in Oakland. It was early afternoon, in June 1977—it was already early the next morning in my beloved Galicia, the far northwestern corner of the Iberian peninsula.   There the purifying bonfires of St. John's Eve were at that moment giving birth to new life. The same rebirth was happening to me that Midsummer Night's Eve, that June 24. I was twenty-four years old, arriving after a journey that might as well have crossed twenty-four centuries.

When I thought about the U.S. in those days, I steered a jagged course between outright admiration and rejection, provoked by dark fears about power and domination. Education under repression had left my mind paralyzed by dogmatism. Dogma allows only one choice: good or evil, each as easy to understand from the inside as it is to manipulate from the outside. It is surely the most effective psychological strategy ever devised for controlling behavior, as politics and religion long ago discovered. Dogma is clear and simple: the boss says sex is bad or church-going is good. Democracy is harder: it says sex and churchgoing may be good or bad, depending on the circumstances. Dogma shapes minds in a special way: they are innocent, ingenuous, comprehensible only in terms of a single system, comprehending only what that system allows; such minds cannot encompass multidimensional relationships, situational as opposed to eternal values. To me it was incomprehensible that a person could dress like a hippie, act with unthinkable freedom, yet work harder than I had ever seen anyone work.

I went to America on my own, in the first instance. On the plane, while my mind struggled with prejudices about American imperialism, I read a biography of Isadora Duncan, who danced to free America and win back Europe. I saw myself as a heroine from the other side: even educated under a dictatorship, I was ready to leap all barriers, beginning with the Atlantic. I had read Marcuse, whom I linked with Freud; Hemingway, who showed me Italy and my own Spain; I knew Poe and Truman Capote who, like me, admired Isak Dinesen; I knew Allen Ginsberg and through him the Beatles; Ferlinghetti was there in my mind, associated with Rilke, as Dylan Thomas was with García Lorca. Europe and America were the cradle of my culture, but turned another way they twisted around each other like a hangman's noose. I was inexperienced, confused; with a small suitcase under one arm and a few borrowed dollars, I knew I needed to escape to another shore if I were to decipher the codes of my life.

*   *   *

To understand a transformation, the reader must know where it begins. Like Franco, I was born into two cultures, one Galician and one Spanish. In old Galicia, where the name of Cape Finisterre echoes the many Land's Ends of Europe, my mother tongue was *gallego*, closely related to Portuguese. The land, inhospitable and isolated, for millennia has defended itself by means of endless rituals. For example, I was born with a sixth finger, amputated when I was a month old. My parents preserved it in a vial of formaldehyde and it went with me everywhere, my most precious possession, my true identity, my amulet. Where else on earth do children play with reliquaries—let alone with relics of themselves?

My family had its idiosyncracies. In our area it had a reputation for strangeness and I was part of it. Our customs were different: we did not eat certain combinations of foods. We were one of the more prosperous families in the area and we supported the local church, yet it was well known we were fiercely anticlerical. We conformed, but I remember riding through a forest with my father and waiting for hours while he delivered what years later I learned were provisions for refugees from the regime. We were comfortable yet we lived an austere and almost puritan life—we hated alcohol and all drugs, and the wine we drank was sweet and sacramental. We were judged to be stingy and even cowardly, since we tended to shy away from conflict or aggression. We never used our legal name, Varela: our old rural house took its name from the village—Couto—and that was the name by which everyone knew us.

As a child my parents dressed me in both skirts and pants; in school I was excused from sewing because I was smart. My grandmothers and great-grandmothers were all schoolteachers, possibly among the first educated women in Galicia, and by custom they inherited land as men did. For many years I did not know how to tell masculine from feminine behavior. Our house had a lot of books, another oddity in our village; my sister and I devoured them one after another, whatever the subject.

My father's refrain was that knowledge was what mattered. He recounted the lives of important people and warned us to stay away from social conflict. Cultivation of the mind is a source of wealth, he taught us. Great men had been persecuted and martyred but their words remained. "It is ignorance that turns people into slaves." This kind of talk got him elected Justice of the Peace, but his hatred of conflict means he now suffers from insomnia—yet he owns seven alarm clocks. It is that sort of family.

An unusual family in a harsh land produced a strange young girl; at fourteen I was gigantically curious and creative yet always a timid outsider. At sixteen, when I got my first national identity card, I first saw my name written as Carmen Varela; before I had been Carmela, Carmina, Carmen do Couto, and Maica—from Maria del Carmen, which must be my legal name since the non-Catholic name Carmen by itself was not allowed under the regime nor by the church my parents supported.

The identity card, I later understood, was a way of controling people. The "social" or secret police dressed in civilian clothes and passed themselves off as students or workers or whatever. They could take away your card on any pretext and tell you to pick it up at such a police station on such a date. There, various officials interrogated you for hours. Sometimes you were sent to a prison called the "chalet," a euphemism in the secret communication code generated by all repressive regimes.

I went once to the polic station for an "interview". Like other students I had been trained to answer No to all questions. "Do you know X?" No. "Do you know who Franco is?" No. It was a way of avoiding self-contradiction, but it infuriated the police and sometimes led to torture and rape. We are still required to carry our identity card with us, but now it seems legal, even to me. At the very least it protects us against identity crises.

In short, I grew up in an odd family and in an end-of-the-earth culture that still dreams its ancient Celtic legends; among other objects, it worships stone and rocks. When the Christians tried to convert these pagans, they planted the corners of old Europe with great granite crosses. Symbols tell everything, if you ask questions: people all over the world seek the same refuge in their symbols that they knew in their mother's womb. All cultures, even civic cultures, are born in rituals and myths; they are founded at bottom on a religious sense of being.   When I was a child, during the years I found safety in religious rituals, a road passed before my house. At the first crossing on the road leading left was the *cruceiro*, a great white granite cruciform on a stepped pyramidal base. That road led to the city, and to the right lay the mountains; but the *cruceiro* was always there, marking the place where roads began and ended. Roads enchanted my child's mind as much as stones. The pagans worshipped the road itself, or was it the traveler? Perhaps they worshipped the passer-by in all of us. The granite cross offers both the secular security of stone and the light of a new faith. But today the myths have faded.   A psychologist can explain why dictatorships do not tolerate crossroads and why my precious *cruceiro* could not serve them symbolically. Indeed I prefer to think that such a symbol must have seemed an insufferable affront, an intolerable proclamation of free choice.

We bring inherited baggage into the world. Culture functions as the brain does: it selects, shapes and remembers experience. The practice of government, called politics, is a product of culture, like science, art or religion. Democracy is its greatest idea.

Within itself, every culture carries its own baggage of history. Political cultures grow and assimilate experience as infants do: they begin in magic and charismatic authority. Then come more complex forms: a sense of order, a more rational structure associated with wealth, honor and intelligence; but the rules are strict and not to be infringed; everything is simple and clear, so transgressions are punished harshly.   Next, in human growth, comes adolescence: between flattery and attack, we compromise and conciliate, argue and agree, convince each other and band together to convince others. Finally we are adults: we understand, put things together, analyze the options; we are fair and moderate, creative and democratic; we temporize and cope.   But history never leaves us, there is always the memory and the temptation of simpler ways: rigidity, intolerance and repression.

Like many Spaniards raised under the dictatorship, I was born at the edge of a great wound. When history slashes into an old culture, people go blind. They reach out for their remembered treasures; they forget the cruelty, the lack of reason, the filth, the meanness, the squalor that unavoidably go with it. Our revolution, our dictatorship, like so many others, threw overboard the accomplishments of our earlier maturity; it rejected balanced education for rigidity, charisma and mediocrity. It turned every one of us into a miniature dictator, in my case for two-thirds of my life. In our inability to develop harmoniously, we reach for grand theoretical models like Fascism or Marxism; we want change so badly we forget the harshness, the brutish behavior, the injustice.   Dictatorships build dividing walls in our hearts yet provide no shelter for discovery, flexibility or adaptation.

Milan Kundera has explained how dictatorship destroys a society's ideals, abuses its citizens and contaminates a culture with its liturgies of kitsch. There is no morality under dictators, only ideology; no education, only indoctrination; no ideas, only The Idea. The bad news in my country was the beginning of the Civil War in 1936; worse news in 1939 was the outset of nearly forty years of dictatorship—even if it did teach us the virtues of patience and peace. At the beginning: brutal repression, ideology imposed by terror and indoctrination, and economic misery—shortages, hunger and black markets.

Later it eased, with controled liberalization and an economic recovery—but never without the iron grasp of the censor. I grew up in this second phase at about the time the Fulbright Program had its late beginnings in Spain, in the early sixties. What was it all about?

First, recession and economic isolation. Exhausted by the Civil War and snubbed by the Western democracies, Spain's identity survived in our hearts only in the feeble rhetoric of slogans: "Spain is different" aimed at attracting tourists; "Europe's last hope for spiritual salvation" was for internal consumption. As tourists—uncontrolable information-sources—began to flood in, Franco wanted us to believe that our hereditary and moral traditions set us apart from those countries, which of course wallowed in sin. A few slogans endlessly repeated are a supremely efficient means of controling behavior. Dictators, like religious leaders, know what psychological strategies they need to retain power.

Meanwhile, an opposite movement of people brought light into our closed society: in the sixties a wave of emigrants left Spain for menial employment elsewhere in Europe, leaving many of our towns with no one but sad children and sadder old people. The Catholic mind saw them as martyrs bound for glory in the Great Beyond of sinful countries. We said goodby with fear and reverence, as we bid farewell to the dead. And there came back to us the money sent home, the electronic appliances, the idea of indoor plumbing. Inscribed in ideology and enshrined in protective legislation, the family became an economic pillar of society: fathers ruled and everyone obeyed. There was little protection against abuse of women, children, and the aged. An old saying has it that a Spaniard depends on his parents until he is forty and on his children after that.

Second, cultural isolation, visible for example in our curriculum. Languages, geography, mathematics, science, and history were taught at all levels from elementary school through the universities. The universities taught only technical subjects—medicine, law, engineering—that did not threaten accepted social thought. History, for example, began in the endless boredom of antiquity, became mysteriously obscure during the Middle Ages when Christians, Arabs and Jews lived in peace and prosperity and when Spain was the heart of Western civilization, then leapt to the Renaissance. Dismissing the medieval Spaniards as infidels and traitors to the True Spain, the dictatorship stressed the restoration of Ferdinand and Isabella; the Catholic monarchs expelled the Moors who had lived in Spain for eight centuries. Many Moslems and Jews converted; for those who did not, the Inquisition tidied things up. At about this time an Italian adventurer from Genoa showed up, persuaded the monarchy to fund him, and arrived by mistake in an unknown land, a great continent filled with exotic cultures. For us in school, Columbus the Spaniard marked the triumph of Catholicism and the Catholic Monarchs over the pagan world, the extension of our language to these fortunate new peoples.

We also studied National Political Education. It taught a sort of ideological catechism based on the various touchstones of national unity: family, community, and the syndicates—vertically-organized workers' groups, the Fascist version of the union. In all it was a grim guide to the approved way of life and its communitarian values. We were told that Spain had always defended the highest ideals—even the Civil War was a holy war. We learned little about post-Renaissance history, and nothing of course about the Civil War and its aftermath—the school year always seemed to run out before we got there. Not that we were short on time: the girls studied sewing for a couple of hours a day. *Costura* was our *Cultura*—we deserved no more.

Third, isolation in the family and the work-place. The regime prohibited political affiliations, associations or meetings of more than a few people at a time, without prior notice to the Ministry of the Interior. We turned into a nation of individualists who preached at each other—semi-detached monologues in which everyone talked and no one listened. Result: no sense of mutuality, no interdependence, no teamwork, no cooperation. In the family, the largest group permitted, there were pressures and incentives to have more children. With large patriarchal families the true source of authority was never in doubt. In the work-place loyalty to the father translated into loyalty to the boss—the same kind of blind, unquestioning loyalty the military takes for granted. Curiosity or dialogue could easily be taken for mutiny.

Fourth, political and religious training. Freedom of expression being severely restricted, the first three factors were reinforced by rigid one-dimensional training or political indoctrination in the principles of National Syndicalism and by religious training targeted against two dangers: free speech and sexuality. Adultery, abortion were unmentionable; any open conversation about politics, religion or sex was subversive and punishable. As in many dictatorships psychoanalysis was forbidden and thereby acquired the special rebel's fascination that comes with prohibition. Post-dictatorial societies like Spain's often have decades of catching up to do before they can deal deeply with such issues, for example, as psychology, psychiatry, education, or women's rights (tightly limited with regard to property and no rights at all with regard to children). And such societies often revive theories which have gone badly out of date.

*   *   *

In Oakland then, my suitcase was small but my baggage was immense: the analysis above touches only the peaks. The eucalyptus trees lining the highways around San Francisco gave off a pungent perfume I knew from the forests of Galicia. When, a few days later, I was invited to spend a weekend in Columbia, an inland town celebrating a local holiday, I found a small band playing for a parish dance at which attentive parents, seated in a circle of folding chairs, kept benevolent watch as their children danced and flirted. The only thing missing was the sound of the *gaitas*, the Galician bagpipes. Instead there was American folk-music which, together with the men's jeans and denim jackets, gave me the impression of having been dropped onto the set for a Western movie.

In San Francisco the search began for a place to continue studies in clinical psychology. Finally a remarkable medical educator took interest in me. Eccentric and reclusive, extraordinarily alive and intelligent yet languid and with a look of immense sadness in his eyes, he now directs a psychiatric hospital in New Mexico. He pointed me towards the clinical research unit in the Camarillo Neuro-Psychiatric Institute at UCLA as the best site for my needs in California. A month later, in September 1977, I began an internship in that prestigious institution. The shocks and the discovery began.

First there was the director of the unit, a small man slight of build, simple, forceful, with an incisive, sharp and inquiring way of looking at you. Yet the look was familiar, as were his features, his voice, his way of talking. He asked if I was afraid of him; I was so overwhelmed I could barely admit I was. I wrote home that day: "I can't explain it, but his gestures, his features and his way of talking are like ours; he is like a strange kind of Spaniard."

By mere chance I met a Fulbright Fellow at UCLA. He told me about the Program—a subject on which I was woefully underinformed. Without leaving the country, I communicated with the remarkable Ramón Bela, legendary director of the Fulbright Commission in Madrid, and arranged financial support under the Joint Commission program. That is how I became a Fulbright post-doctoral fellow without a doctorate—one of those contradictions in which Spanish surrealists like Dali and Buñuel take special delight.

My worship of knowledge was fierce but private. I went into the clinical investigation unit as though it were a cathedral. There I remained, seated, confused, like a penitent on Jacob's ladder, hearing, seeing, speaking no evil, as if I had entered the novitiate. I felt fortunate and singled out, yet I was the most miserable person on earth. Youth and poverty are related—I was very young. I waited for orders.

Orders never came. What was I supposed to do? The director told me to "take the initiative," which I later learned could mean anything from washing the dishes to carrying out the most sophisticated research programs. My passiveness puzzled everyone. The nurses looked at me curiously and asked me about Spain; they laughed at the severe restrictions on women's behavior. I did not know what to tell them. Why these questions? I wondered if there were social police, even in Los Angeles?

After two weeks the director told me I would have to leave in two weeks if my "attitude" did not change. I could not speak, only listen with a knot in my throat. When the tears began, everyone left the room.

Happiness is a requirement in California. Sins against happiness—like crying or suffering—are punished. Complaints mean cynicism or sadness or depression. Galicians, prone to homesickness and melancholy, with a proud ironic sense of life and death, are lost in such a whirlpool of happiness.

For about thirty hours I was bereft, waiting for some miracle. Trained by our regime to resist adversity, seeing no alternative, I tried to hang on. Psychologists call this "escape conditioning" or "negative reinforcement." It creates strongly persistent behaviors. I learned then I could hold out a long time—as so many of my countrymen have learned to do, putting up with impossible conditions at home and at work.

Yet I was in love, if not yet with America at least with the idea of learning as much as I could. The telephone saved me from drowning in my own despair. A Spaniard, professor of medicine at UCLA, called to ask how I was doing. When I told him I had to leave, he extracted the story and understood immediately: "The only thing you are doing wrong is what you are not doing. No one will manipulate you, no one will make fun of you, no one will think you are weird, no one will punish you. What you've got to do is ask questions."

In the Spanish school system, we were punished for asking questions. In elementary school they made me wear donkey's ears for asking questions. Here questions were a means of learning. Those simple instructions from an experienced Spanish colleague were all I needed. The Monday of my third week at UCLA I woke up ready for anything. My ears have not stopped growing since.

I asked about everything, even what I thought I already knew. With every question I learned something new: facts, subtleties, relationships between things that I had never seen before. I learned that behavior is like a rainbow that appears and disappears according to the circumstances. I learned to live for and in the moment. They called me Maica, spelled Mica and giving way to numerous puns. Life suddenly became a joy.

*   *   *

For a Galician, it was natural that my first contact with democracy should have taken place a few hundred miles away in France, when I was an eighteen-year-old child. But my first real working acquaintance with it came in the U.S., at UCLA, when I was still a child, if a slightly older one. Discovering democracy is an experience I share with many other Spaniards who are struggling today to strengthen and build on the changes that have taken place in my country.

It is impossible for me to find the words to express how painful it was. It does not come easily, learning complex responses like respect, flexibility, willingness to negotiate, taking responsibility for your own behavior, and thinking creatively about how to make things better. My passion for freedom was enormous but my ability to use it and to adapt was slow. This is my country's dilemma with one difference: since it is easier to restore an old pattern of behavior than to learn a new one, those in Spain who were educated before the Civil War learned democracy before many of us who were born under the regime.

As the year progressed, I visited Mexico, which like many Americans had tried to help the Spanish Republic. In the U.S. I learned of the brave idealism of the Lincoln Brigade; in both countries I saw the generosity accorded to political exiles, many of whose families I was able to meet.

Meanwhile the director was teaching me things about myself. He told me about Maimonides, born in Córdoba, about racism in Spain, about the fascination of Toledo—my own history in short. I slowly realized why so much seemed familiar to me, where my family's eccentricities came from, why we were skeptics, noble of spirit, cautious if not cowardly, philanthropic, lovers of books, music and culture. I had known that my family was descended from converted Jews, but I had no idea what it meant—I had never met a Jew in Spain because, as we were instructed, there were none. That explained my family's withdrawal into itself, and our perpetuation of certain family customs.

In short, America was busily burying herself away in my heart, a tiny flame. My two countries became husband and lover—impossible to be with one without missing the other.

There were other places, other countries. After UCLA I spent a semester at the University of Southern Illinois in Carbondale, which will shortly open an extension in Madrid. Later, in 1982 the UCLA connection helped me spend a month with WHO in Venezuela advising the Ministry of Health.

My return to Madrid in 1978 was momentous: I found that even our new Constitution had barely begun to change things. And since then, as in a story by Isak Dinesen, democracy and dictatorship have come to seem to me like two locked boxes, each of which holds the key to the other.

*   *   *

Fifteen years later, in January 1992, I returned to the U.S., this time as Fulbright scholar in residence at Radford University in Southern Virginia. Now Spain is celebrating five hundred years of transatlantic contact in Seville, entertaining the Olympics in Barcelona, and Madrid is Europe's cultural capital for 1992. While the U.S. argues about abortion and its government becomes more rigid, less humane, its personal behavior more conformist, more stereotyped than in the seventies, Spain is moving in the other direction, towards ever-greater flexibility, with bureaucracies ready to bend their rules according to circumstances, with enormous tolerance for variations in human behavior.

A visit to Cuba last year reminded me what we used to have in Spain and I wondered what will happen when *its* Galician leader joins his Spanish forbear. In Venezuela I found a different kind of democracy in transition. In Yugoslavia and East Germany before re-unification I saw other dictatorships, these born in principle out of egalitarian idealism, and I learned that they can be as vicious as dictatorships of the right. There I also learned that, whatever its faults, communism etched into the minds of millions the idea of fundamental individual entitlements to health care, education and employment. Even dictatorships do some things right, while no democracy yet has achieved perfection.

Today Spain is creating nothing less than a distinct new society, on the basis of technology, industrial competitiveness, respect for cultural diversity, and the desire to fit the Spanish piece into the jigsaw puzzle of Europe. The experience of an ever-imminent past is invaluable; nothing brings a community closer than disaster and millions of us have seen that disaster. That we know.

How does human community grow from there? We are emerging from fear into understanding, from authority into individual responsibility; it is a time for dialogue, multidimensional education, encouragement to creativity, cultural sensitivity and, in the Senator's deathless and simple if not always meaningful phrase, "mutual understanding." Psychologists and social scientists improve democracies, at least so they say, by criticizing them. But people also learn by trial and error; they learn if they are allowed to ask questions without fear. As with people, so with nations. Only international cooperation can create open communities based on a common program of mutual respect, constant renewal, personal responsibility and a better quality of life. It has been said that whoever points at the moon may end up staring at his own finger. Spain cannot run that risk. We need to work slowly, looking for the best way, for *our* best way. We need to keep constant contact with other people, systems, cultures, ways of looking at the world.

Galicians are wanderers in the world. More than anyone we ought to be able to learn and relearn how to adapt to our surroundings. Behavior is learned both by imitation and by viral infection—it spreads easily from person to person. Galicia has produced its share of dictators—Fidel Castro as well as Franco. Perhaps now it is time for Galicia to infect everyone with the idea that democracy can be like one of our *cruceiros*, a symbol of security yet a symbol of choice.

When I was little I dreamed I would some day build an immense palace with a great library. Every book would have its place and through them all the authors, living and dead, would speak to me. I awake as an adult and see that the dream has come true: the Fulbright program has built a palace big enough for the whole world, big enough for us all to discover the world's knowledge and the richness of multiple cultures. Dialogue, sharing ideas, working together, peace through the word, understanding each other, looking for other ways—these are mottos carved on the walls of the Senator's palace. To them we might add Pascal's words about "roads in motion that take us where we want to go."

I did not mention earlier that when I left my house as a child there was a third road. It led toward the Atlantic. I chose it in the end, and it led me to that great lady Democracy, so subtle, so sophisticated yet so open to all peoples. It was she who taught me how to be forever in love with the other side of things, the other shore and its many roadways.

The author, Hannah Arendt Professor of Sociology at Rutgers, has held Fulbright lectureships in India, Argentina, and Israel. His Fulbright experience with India contrasts with the other Subcontinental experiences related in this volume: his visit was a whirlwind tour of twenty cities in sixty days, a kind of sociological Chatauqua. For the sociologist, it was a disappointing exercise in superficiality, arrogance and ambivalence. Yet even the sociologist's acerbities soften, with time, and there remain a group of memories and perceptions bordering on poetry. His unusual defense of the Fulbright program as a glorious creature of its weakness illustrates and illuminates its mysterious capacity for holding up to us an unsuspected mirror and bringing to life forgotten facets of our character. To see things as they are and to accept that they must be as they are—is this not one basis for defining the elusive concept of mutual understanding?

22

UGLY AMERICANS, ARROGANT INDIANS, AMAZING INDIVIDUALS

Irving Louis Horowitz

This retrospective has to do with ancient history, or at least events now fifteen years past. That they remain vivid is a testimonial to how memory intersects with history in the affairs of individuals and nations alike. In this case, I am reporting on a two-month Fulbright Senior Fellowship to India many summers ago, in 1977 to be exact. During that time I visited no fewer than twenty cities in every part of the nation, an average of three days per city. Such a trip does not make one expert on a foreign nation, much less on an ancient civilization. Still, it entitles one at least to claim an experiential base that stands above those who think that "theorizing" about the world begins, and worse, ends in Washington, DC. The charge given to participants in the symposium of this volume includes candor and criticism, and avoiding the celebrationist tone which too often misleads those who follow our path "into the field." Of course, one must remember too that the world is not a "field," any more than it is an oyster.

I did not go to India in 1977 as an unknown academic. Because I was an Oxford University Press author, nearly all of my major works on international development and political sociology were well known. Oxford had offices in Bombay, New Delhi, Calcutta, and Madras; though the sun had set on the East India Company and then on direct British rule in India, it had not so much as dimmed with respect to OUP. True, my hosts knew only the 1965 original edition, not the 1972 revision. But a twelve-year time lag in India is not all that bad. Indeed, when my wife, in conversation with a fellow Indian dignitary at one of our meetings, noted that Praeger Publishers had just been sold, he responded with a knowing word. But our Indian host had in mind the sale of Praeger to Encyclopedia Britannica in the mid-1960s, not her reference—the sale of Praeger to CBS in the mid-1970s.

The late seventies were a particularly difficult period in Indian political and economic life. Prime Minister Indira Gandhi's emergency measures had done far more to sustain her in power for the short run than resolve the crisis of governmental legitimacy which her rule ostensibly sought to overcome. It was a time of intense self-doubt as to the efficacy of democracy in India, of breakdown in the shibboleths of the founding fathers. This intense self-questioning went remarkably unexamined by outsiders. But it was the stuff of everyday discourse among Indian scholars and students at the time.

It might well be that what I experienced resulted from the special circumstances of a unique period. Still, I think what I experienced were problems endemic to the uneven distribution of wealth and power in India. And responsibility for this distribution was attributed to embarrassed Americans rather than to tattered Englishmen. With the English largely gone, except for their drinking clubs taken over by the local Indian bourgeoisie, Americans became recipients of animosities and suspicions they did not always deserve. Even when they deserved such calumny, unlike the English they rarely seemed to understand why.

The ugly American of the post-Vietnam epoch turns out to be neither the interventionist ambassador of Burdick and Lederer, nor even the quiet stumbling bureaucrat devised by Graham Green, but the Political Pilgrim described more recently by Paul Hollander in his book by that name. One does not always find upholders of the American empire on Fulbright tours—at least not on the three I took—but those for whom criticism of American culture prevails as an ideological given. At one conference I attended, participants from the U.S. took turns at self-criticism and national self-abasement. The Indian participants must have wondered what was left to say, or for that matter why the U.S. even occupied an exalted global position. They were not the only ones. I had the same curious fascination with wave after wave of "self-criticism" by the nabobs from the West.

It may well be that the short-term traveling social scientists with whom I had the greatest contact in 1977 India suffered most from this malady. It might also be that the impact of Vietnam still weighed heavily on American visitors to South Asia. Perhaps the best explanation is psychological: an attempt at anticipatory socialization, what a colleague has nicely termed the wish to get beyond the boredom of boosterism at one end and a nervous response to attacks of local America-bashers at the other. Whatever the initial motivation, the disturbing fact is that, in place of real analysis, sloganeering prevailed. The analysis of development problems is sufficiently complex as to require some disaggregation; yet time after time one heard diatribes on the evils of capitalism and on the inequities of race in the U.S., all with scarcely a comment on specific Indian conditions or on modes of amelioration.

At one conference center, the major conflict was between the engineers who came from the U.S. to set up a fertilizer plant and the social scientists on Fulbrights. The latter wasted little time in criticizing the engineers and denigrating any effort at amelioration. On the other hand, the engineers were not especially helpful, given their own biases against the "natives" and worse, a sort of linear imagination that disallowed any other "logic" than their own. It reached a point where the engineers sat at one table, the social scientists at another. Just how this helped the Indian community is hard to say. To be sure, the engineers had plenty to say about their Indian technological counterparts, little of it any good. By the same token the sociologists had nothing whatever to say about India. They knew almost nothing about the country to which they had come to lecture.

The most embarrassing moments came during interactions in which criticisms were made of the U.S., with no corresponding awareness of India's problems. The work of Arthur Lall, Philip Mason, or even E.M. Forster seemed unknown.   No real advance preparation or briefing had been undertaken. Diplomacy was reduced to the absence of criticism of one's hosts. As a result, our Indian hosts felt either that Americans were soft in the head, or so lacking in pride that no assault, however coarse, would be challenged. Little wonder that they saw themselves as superior in learning and in wisdom to their American guests; their superiority in the art of dialectical reasoning was obvious.

The words of people like Subrata Kumar Mitra, author of *Power, Protest and Participation*, were simply unutterable during the emergencies of the seventies.   But his themes were well known.   In explaining the state of emergency, he noted the need to move beyond the conventional view of democracy in India as a smooth progression from colonial rule to popular government.   Quite the contrary, he saw the nation as characterized in the emergency by "political insurgency, intolerance of minorities of which communal riots are an extreme manifestation, police violence, 'criminalization' of politics, excessive use of force, and the rise of popular authoritarianism." These are not incidental features of Indian life but germane to the processes that gave support to democracy in the first place. But there we sat across the table in 1977: Americans thoroughly incapable of understanding the society they temporarily inhabited and Indians thoroughly incapacitated by the society into which they were locked.

The anomaly in this microscopic incapacity to understand macroscopic events was played out in lifestyles. Some, with long-term Fulbrights, lived like Pashas. Their salaries, modest in American terms, enabled them to retain full-time servants, maids, and chauffeurs in India—in fairness probably no more than their Indian counterparts. I met one graduate student doing his dissertation who whined that he was only able to have one man-servant and a chauffeur! This same character claimed that Indians were "rupee crazy." In such bizarre circumstances, it is small wonder that it was easier to examine Washington politics in Delhi than Delhi politics in any part of India.

Moreover, some of these long-term junior Fulbrighters, individuals who in the U.S. were politically quiescent or silent on major issues, were not at all averse to speaking out about Indian politics and what Indians should do to make things better. These people, with at best a rudimentary knowledge of basic languages of the country, felt unconstrained in sharing opinions on the Gandhi regime, the Congress Party, the Indian economy, what have you. In short, the ugly American syndrome of the fifties was not alleviated by the behavior of certain Fulbrighters, but rather given new dimensions. The amount of money they received, modest in domestic U.S. terms, was sufficiently large in Indian terms to stimulate discrepancies between ideological venting and personal life-styles, anomalies completely unrecognized by the worst offenders.

I am not suggesting that the funding of long-term Fulbright personnel should be cut back. The contrary. But for those going overseas on federal auspices, taxpayers' money, being temporarily wealthy in a Third World country carries responsibilities for the family as well as the person. Modesty should rule. Otherwise the strange situation in which the largesse of America is denounced by those who are its unique beneficiaries might lead one to believe that hypocrisy rather than principle drives such grand theorizing—true ugliness.

At the other side of the table too often were arrogant Indian intellectuals, legion in their numbers, boundless in their *chutzpah*. Time and again, one heard echoes of the trashiest Marxist dogma, with scarcely any consideration of its appropriateness for Indian conditions. In the many conversations which I held with Indian scholars, I did not hear a single criticism of the Soviet Union. The "orthodox" Indian scholars were simply silent on totalitarianism, while the "Marxists" were positively ecstatic about the glorious "model of development" provided by the Soviet Union.

They seemed to believe that the U.S. was a necessary evil and the USSR the savior from the East. India remained outside the Southeast Asia Treaty Organization; but when border disputes erupted between China and India, and the struggle went badly for India, the U.S., Britain and Canada, the much-reviled English speaking Union of the Second World War, came to the rescue. These uncomfortable facts of recent Indian history remained unspoken, both by Indians and, probably out of ignorance, by those very visiting dignitaries who presumed to know a great deal about what was wrong with America and what India needed to do to solve its problems.

I lunched with one Indian scholar, the head of the Soviet-Indian Friendship Committee. He was unhesitating in his praise of Stalinism. For him, Stalinism was the necessary "model" of development for India. Stalin took a backward, recalcitrant people and brought them, hollering and screaming, into the modern world. True enough, innocent victims, into the millions, were sometimes claimed. But—like Russia—India had people to spare! Development was worth the price. It should be added that this same paragon of socialism, at the luncheon table, snapped his fingers and rang the bell for the attention of the waiter, then dressed him down for poor and delayed service. When I expressed amazement at such a public rebuke, the head of the USSR-India friendship committee said, "Socialism requires its waiters too; they need to be reeducated."

One sensed from these Indian academics, often western-trained, a certainty derived from dogma rather than a careful empirical look at the world. Given the fact that this was the time of Gandhi's "emergency measures," certain lines of criticism may have been easier than others. Those certain that the Soviet path of development would reach to paradise were careful not to speak of domestic events. Indeed, in the entire time I spent there, I heard not a single voice raised against the undemocratic measures of Gandhi's repression, not a single critique of the limits of Indian democracy, not one concern that India might have drawn too close to its Soviet allies at the risk of negating a thinly-based democracy.

The arrogant Indian was more often than not an advocate of more democracy for others, but he had very little to say about democracy at home. Repeatedly, the academics we met represented one or another form of nationalist orthodoxy, with hardly a glance at other ways of doing things. A xenophobic nationalism seemed to prevail widely at the time, a vision that seemed to enthrall the intellectual class precisely at a time when the need for honest and open criticisms was at its highest. It is not that such voices were entirely absent; indeed the journalists of India spoke with extraordinary candor and vigor in the many Indian newspapers. A sense of open dialogue and balanced analysis was readily to be found in the newsweeklies. But when it came to the potentates of Indian scholarship in the social sciences, one saw the dead hand of the ideological past. Ritual replaced reality, and utopia displaced ordinary life. Snapping fingers at the untouchables and wagging tongues at visiting Americans seemed to satisfy them.

What made all of this inevitable was ultimately the Americans' lack of knowledge of the host country. I found myself taking an in-country crash course in the history of India. There is a rich and fair-minded literature, often done by classical scholars, historians and literary people and prepared in a colonial period in which the drive for independence was real enough but tempered by the knowledge that independence was a beginning and not an end. In that literature one learns the roots of the debates in Indian life: the gap between Gandhian pacifism and actual Indian militarism; the continued gap between urban bourgeoisie and rural masses; the corruption of a political party system that boasted hundreds of parties but, at that time at least, was defined in reality by machinations within a single party; a sociability in which religious animosity was far greater than it had been under colonial rule. Whatever their motives, the colonial powers had reduced caste conflict and religious hatred.

It is crucial that the Fulbright Program, as it enters a new and perhaps more uncertain period of its history, reflect a higher level of reality about the character of the U.S., as well as a better sense of the place to which one travels. There can be no real discourse without a common base of knowledge. Precisely this was missing in my Fulbright Indian experience. Even as I prepared to leave India, I remained the only one in our initial group who seemed to feel any urgent need to learn about the subcontinent.

Since books are heavy and hard to lug about, here is a list of bare minimum of titles well worth the ride to Delhi. They are no substitute for experience, and others may have a quite different list, but they do help enrich experience. For a sense of pre-Independence India one can read a turgid tome like William Wilson Hunter's *The Indian Empire: Its Peoples, History and Products* (New York: AMS 1966, originally published in 1893); but a much finer starting place is the great E.M. Forster's *A Passage to India* (New York: Harcourt, Brace, 1924) in which East meets West in uncomprehending dialogue. To read this is to know why independence was not a choice but a necessity. The popular work by Larry Collins and Dominique Lapierre, *Freedom at Midnight* (New York: Simon & Schuster, 1975) remains unsurpassed as a vivid study in the revolutionary moment. It makes clear why India gained its independence, but in the process, lost part of its vaunted "civilization." Ved Mehta's *Portrait of India* (New York: Farrar, Straus & Giroux, 1970) is the other side of Forster—the dialogue by an Indian at home in the West but at peace in the East. A slightly aged work by the incomparable Lady Barbara Jackson (Ward), *India and the West* (New York: Norton, 1961), still makes good sense. Despite all sorts of nonsense written by social scientists and policy-makers from both Indian and American sources, Lady Jackson understood that we are tied by a common belief in democracy, whatever the uncommon nature of Indian traditions may appear. Sarvepalli Gopal's collection, *Jawaharlal Nehru, 1889-1964* (New Delhi: Oxford, 1980) should be read: this man and this family is the dorsal spine of twentieth-century Indian political life. Finally, for those who wish to ponder questions of economic and social development at the higher reaches and who wish to see India in a geo-political regional context, one might turn to Gunnar Myrdal's *Asian Drama: An Inquiry into the Poverty of Nations* (New York: Pantheon, 1971). Myrdal is no Adam Smith, but then again twentieth-century India is no eighteenth-century England. This three-volume effort nearly doubles the weight and pages of all the other books recommended. There are always those who like to travel heavy.

As for me, I wanted to rise above the Emily Post vision of that rich nation, to get beyond the nice-manners style of doing intellectual business. I suspect that until the Indian Fulbright Commission finds ways to ensure that all its American participants move beyond manners into civility, transform ignorance into knowledge, and take observation into criticism, we will continue to have a less than adequate return on our investment in this crucial program.

*   *   *

What my wife and I are finally left with is not memories of the political but feelings of the personal. Apart from the sentiments expressed, the formal lectures are barely a memory, and the conferences that made me so angry at the time raise hardly a hackle now. Is the "secret" of the Fulbright experience the solidarity one forges with other human beings, people whose paths are not to be crossed more than once and even then incidentally? I would like to dwell on these crossings, since in retrospect they are what best defined the events and sustain the memories.

The first episode involved a trip from Coimbatore to Kerala. Because we had changed our booking from Delhi to Kerala, we had to go via Madras; but the plane from Madras to Kerala was totally over-booked. We could fly to Coimbatore and go overland to Kerala, or wait a day, perhaps longer. We chose the overland route, roughly two hundred miles. The roads were essentially impassable, yet the taxi driver drove like a man possessed; the sights and sounds of southern India were spread before us in a way we could never have imagined from the air. To understand population density, I recommend such a trip. We seemed to pass along a string of villages, each a total universe. The world of Indian village life makes one appreciate the organic sense within the Indian peasantry. Things do not so much develop as simply change. The external world of computers, automobiles, and television does not so much change value systems as become one more element in the enduring, continuing rhythms of life.

To move from the abstract to the concrete, on this taxi tour of the south, I managed to tear my trousers. Everything was either back in Delhi or packed to go by plane. So I asked the driver if it were possible to have the pants repaired. He indicated: "No problem. Every village has a tailor." So we stopped at a town roughly 20 miles from Cochin. I got out and went to an open-air tailor. He had erected the rudiments of a shop, but only that. It is not what one expects from a tailor shop in New Delhi much less New York. I explained my problem, showed him the immense tear in the pants. Immediately, matter-of-fact, he told me to remove the pants. "But where do I do this? This is an open air bazaar, we are surrounded by people." He became irritated; it was he who was doing me the favor, not the other way about. So I sheepishly removed my pants inside a sort of booth. My mid-section was protected, but my head protruded and my bare legs showed. Within minutes, a throng of several hundred people formed to gaze at the 6' 2" American. They did more than gaze, they roared with laughter. There I was, without pants, my fellow Fulbrighters sitting impatiently in the taxi, while busloads of natives of Kerala passed by with joyous laughter and the repairman sewed away.

There was nothing much to do but join in the laughter. It was an absurd scene. The tailor was a wise fellow, and we chatted about worldly affairs, but not about politics. I asked how often he went to Cochin. Not often—once about 15 years ago. I exclaimed that Cochin was only a few miles away, virtually within walking distance. He asked me what was the good of such a trip? Could it give him health, could he learn much, could he even enjoy the status as a tailor he has in his village? Being without clothing made it difficult for me to argue against such peasant wisdom. Here we were: the tailor and I discoursing on the meaning of urban life in central Kerala, while hundreds of people made sport of my plight. The tailor refused to take more than the normal payment in rupees for his services, and the caravan started up again on the road from Coimbatore to Cochin.

The experience was all very good-natured. But it made me realize that cultural relativism is not so much a scientific fact as it is a western artifact. For people locked into village life, the norms of the group were absolute, not relative. Foreign tongues like English were foreign, period. People of great height were abnormal, not just different, more to be pitied than reviled. But in this tiny experience, the charade of a universe in which everyone is an intellectual or an academic was cracked. Reality can be less than comfortable in such strange moments. It is easier to talk about "the people" than to be among them.

The second experience involved another taxi ride, this time from New Delhi to Jaipur in Rajastan. We were being taken to the home of a fine intellectual, one who had spent a lifetime studying the Indian peasantry and landed gentry. In fact, his explanation of how the Mogul Empire was defeated, not in battle but in a patient war of attrition that took centuries, has stayed with me all these years. My colleague, then at least a Marxist, painted a clear picture of the architecture and topography of the region to explain how the very notion of a military enclave, impregnable and invincible, finally worked against the Moguls, making them dependent on the poor to grow, harvest and sell the grains by which life is sustained. Finally, in the absence of this system of intimidation on the one hand and payments for foodstuffs on the other, the Moguls were trapped by the very rigor of the division of labor and hierarchical authority that they had built.

More memorable was the ride: in negotiating the winding roads to the top of Jaipur, where the castles are located, the taxi drivers share the road with the elephants. I do not know whether the taxi drivers imitated the honks of the elephants, or vice versa. Perhaps it was a deviant case of art imitating life. I do know that the ride was scary because the elephants had no compunction about putting their trunks right into the car and begging for food. The noises they made were loud. The problem was that the tusks were not removed until food was given. Our taxi driver, however, was a man of principle. He decided against yielding either the road or satisfying the appetites of the elephants.

What happened next best belongs in a Walt Disney film: the elephants honked, the driver honked back. The elephant threatened to remove the car from the road. The driver threatened to run over the elephant. In the end, after at least an hour of this, this Mexican standoff ended: food was given to the elephant, and the elephant in turned yielded the right of way to the road. I am not sure why, but all of this seemed so crazy to me that I laughed in hysterical guffaws. I had no sense of the enormous dangers posed by the elephants (there were more than one). But I began to realize that one reason India is a civilization and not just a nation is that only in India had I ever experienced such a continuity between nature and society. I am not sure I know why, even now. In India, the animal kingdom does not yield to the human species. They simply work out new modes of accommodation in terms of an ever-advancing technology. Somehow they are able to do this without dozens of lobbying efforts for "animal rights" by people speaking for one or another species.

The third event of memory happened the following day, on the mandatory trip to Agra to see the Taj Mahal. I had no idea that the place was overrun by temple monkeys, who must have inhabited the place for hundreds of years. Moreover the Taj had no bathrooms. If you needed to, you squatted and did your duty. Here we were, in the great Taj Mahal, and the bathroom was crowded not with people but with monkeys. I did my thing, monkeys to the right and left of me, sitting as well, eyeing me. I am sure they thought of me as a poor creature, a furless monkey. The furless monkeys leave the Taj every day, the furry monkeys stay on.

The Taj may be a human creation, a veritable wonder of the world (missing stones notwithstanding), but it is owned lock, stock, and barrel by the animal kingdom. It may be a Muslim shrine in a Hindu land, but this place transcends any parochialism of belief. It was a shocking reminder that India was a land of continuities between species. What this means with respect to promulgation of what we call development is hard to say. But it is a world of animals, of which the humans are only one example—perhaps the highest, but still only one. It is not a land stratified into "pets" and "owners." The natural order of things changes, but terribly slowly. At least as long as monkeys own the bathrooms and elephants dominate the highways, the place of the sacred cow is secure in India.

A final point is less an experience than an observation. I was never much impressed by the sari as a mode of clothing. Indeed, it seemed terribly complicated to get into and out of. Then on a side trip to Madras I came to understand it. On the ocean side of Madras, next to a statue of the great poet Tagore, I watched the women of Madras walk along the beach. It was a moving and beautiful sight. The women did not so much walk as undulate, like the ocean waves beside them. It was all so gentle, so perfect. Indeed, the women were far more impressive than the men. At the end of the visit, watching Urdu dancers in a Delhi restaurant, I had this same overwhelming sense of the organic linkage of the women to the land.

When I returned to the airport and saw western women wrapped in saris, I sensed how clumsy, how awkward they were. They could dress in a sari, but they could not imitate that walk, that undulation, that amazing sensuality in which clothing is part of the fabric of life, not simply an artifact of dress. I am not sure to this day why this simple act of walking moved me so. Was it the converse of the animal kingdom's close collusion with the human species? In this instance it was reversed: the humans "dominated" their environment by accommodating to it. The women of Madras were in amazing harmony with the environment. I do not recollect seeing their equal anywhere.

For a brief moment, it is as if I gained entrance into a sense of the eternal India—not the hubbub of its hundreds of political parties, the overcrowding of its villages, the conceit of its intellectuals, the forensic skills of its academics. None of that seemed to matter much. It was the harmony of life, the rhythm of life cycles, the fusion of personal style and world substance that triumphed. It was these things that left an indelible impression on me. For this opportunity to put into personal practice a meeting of East and West, the Fulbright program was responsible.

I realize in this retrospective glance that I have said precious little about the Fulbright program as such or about its office in India. But the beauty of the program no less than its weakness may well have been this absence of intrusiveness. Beyond fulfilling the terms of the agreement, one is left pretty much on his or her own. And this is as it should be. It might have been better had travel schedules been better coordinated. And it might have been better if the local offices of Fulbright had coordinated its efforts with other agencies like the Ford Foundation to give appropriate briefings. But when it comes down to it, the quality of this program resides in its weakness; that is, once a decision to send a person is made, no further interference is undertaken. The Fulbright program never promised a rose garden. But in this instance at least, it made possible a first-hand experience with the jewel that is India, a jewel that needs no crown.

In 1979 Czechoslovakia, like the rest of the world, had no way of dreaming what would happen in the next decade. It remained at that time in the clutches of a totalitarian system which invaded every sector of daily life. Dr. Sugg, Professor of English and Humanities at Florida International University in Miami, has written books on Hart Crane, on Robert Bly, and on Jungian literary criticism. In 1979 he was one of the thousands of tiny windows which the Fulbright Program in the late fifties began opening into the darkness of Eastern Europe during the grim decades of totalitarian control. He recalls his particular experience of totalitarianism in the classrooms of the Purkyne (Masaryk) University. His essay typifies the highly controled experiences of Fulbrighters over the first thirty years of contact with the countries of Eastern Europe, where a single student-informer could end a teaching career or bring about a prison sentence. He reminds us, as do other writers in this volume, not only how far and how quickly totalitarianism has faded since then but also how difficult it will be for the generations indoctrinated in those systems to learn the habits of trust and respect without which democracy cannot live. Meanwhile, as he says, his own approach to American classrooms can never be the same.

23

BEHIND THE CURTAIN: LESSONS IN AND OUT OF SCHOOL

Richard P. Sugg

Living abroad educates by amalgamating many specific lessons about one country and one historical moment with fewer but more valuable insights concerning human nature. Three times before my Fulbright year I had been immersed in a foreign culture, as a Peace Corps Volunteer (West Cameroon 1963-65), as a postdoctoral freelance writer (Ireland and England 1970), and as a part-time professor to the U.S. military (southern Italy 1970-71). But my Fulbright Senior Lectureship as Professor of American Literature at Purkyne (aka Masaryk) University in Czechoslovakia in 1979-80—the year when Russia invaded Afghanistan, America decided to boycott the Moscow Olympics, and Iran despoiled the American Embassy and took the hostages—proved the most enlightening. It was particularly rich on the subject of political and cultural analysis in the classroom, whether abroad or in America. From beginning to end, that Fulbright year taught lessons that have made me see the world differently.

My wife and I began our lesson-learning at the border crossing between West Germany and Czechoslovakia in the autumn of 1979, with a demonstration of what was the effective coin of the realm behind the Iron Curtain. We eased our used VW, newly bought at an automobile flea market in Frankfurt, past the first guard tower, then the tank traps, and up to the Czech station, queuing up in a line of three cars waiting for permission to pass. We handed over our passports and auto registration, the guard disappeared into the station, and we began our wait. After twenty minutes, and the departure of the first two cars in the line, a Mercedes pulled alongside us, honked the horn, and waved a different-colored, diplomatic passport out the window. The guard checked it perfunctorily, and the Mercedes jumped the queue and sped off to the east. More time passed, and then a new vehicle appeared, a chock-full Trailways-class bus from West Germany. The driver left the door open and the motor running as he hurried out, greeted the guard by name, and walked past him into the station; we saw him pull from inside his jacket two cartons of Winston cigarettes, while someone inside approved his passport. Smiling, he returned soon to his bus customers and drove away. After a while, we too were allowed to pass.

Because we had been intimidated by the formidable border, and perhaps because the border bribes were made with a casualness born of routine (or was it because we half-consciously adopted the "when in Rome" attitude and closed our eyes to a scene that would have been shocking at an American border), we did not immediately recoil from either the sleaziness or the political implications of the two crossings we had witnessed. Later, we recounted the experience to our Czech colleague-hosts, whose analysis put the events of the border crossing in a larger moral perspective: they expressed a double bitterness at hearing how the freedom to come and go that was denied to them was sold so cheaply to others, especially by the so-called public servants of their country.

We drove on to Prague, arriving late at night but armed with the address of what turned out to be a posh hotel called the Three Ostriches, where our USIS liaison officer had made reservations for us. Upon entering, we heard loud and occasionally drunken laughter coming from the restaurant, filled with people who might have come over on the bus that passed us at the border.

These uninhibited tourists were among the few groups of people in Czechoslovakia who could stay at the Three Ostriches, because they came with hard currency. Our Czech friends said such hotels catered exclusively to tourists, well-connected Communist Party members, and embassy personnel from countries whose money was worth something. These hotels and the customers they attracted were highly visible symbols of the economic degradation of the general populace by a flawed system. Since 1980 I have told this story many times to American classes, and interestingly enough my Miami lower-middle-class students, with each passing year of the "Greed Decade" of the 1980s, seemed to relate more intensely to the story's imagery of an economically marginalized and déclassé population.

The hotel reservation had been a helpful gesture towards new Fulbright visitors, and the same generosity the USIS personnel displayed in making it was evident generally throughout our stay—they said we got such good attention because we were among the very few non-diplomatic Americans in the country. However, the type of hotel—expensive, touristy, and exclusionary—seemed to suggest the level on which the Embassy people had to live at least their official lives, and this naturally led us to question whether we Fulbrighters should act like "Embassy Americans" or some other kind. The repressive Czech government forced the Embassy people into a bureaucrat-bunker mentality, perforce out of touch with the ordinary people of Czechoslovakia; certainly, our Fulbright year proved that any Czech who befriended Americans, and especially those who worked at the Embassy, might have to explain his or her intentions to the Czech police. But nevertheless it was disconcerting for us to see Embassy people tip waiters in restaurants with cigarettes or bottles of whiskey. Their reasoning, as our USIS friend explained it, was that it didn't matter because everybody knew that Americans were the good guys and would not have played this game if the Communist system and its bad guys were not forcing them into that role. Besides, she pointed out, the Czechs could witness American good will on a daily basis in the classrooms of the Fulbright professors whose year abroad was financially underwritten by the U.S. More to the point, there were problems far greater in Czechoslovakia in 1979 than these petty venalities.

It is never easy to discern a person's or a country's values, but in Czechoslovakia that year it was especially difficult, as the Embassy's Bibles or Calculators Parable illustrates. When we first arrived in Prague, the Embassy liaison told us that the day before a car had been stopped and searched at the border, and the occupants (two known traders) arrested and sentenced to prison. Police harassment was not unusual, but the State Department was internally split on the question of which of two forbidden items had earned them jail time: ten Bibles or twenty-five calculators. As the Fulbright year unfolded, I puzzled over this question myself. In the larger context of cultural analysis, any country can be understood to some extent by examining the difference between what the government names as social enemies (religion was certainly a named enemy in Czechoslovakia—one of my colleagues at Purkyne had been denied his expected and faculty-approved Professorship when "someone" informed the government that his parents had been church-going Protestants), and what it actually works to repress. In the case of Czechoslovakia in 1979-80, an important component of any analysis would be to recognize that the government was removed far from the real and felt needs of the people, so that it had become in fact a pervasive enemy of the people, concentrating on stifling all their impulses toward freedom, whether religious or economic. When I finally knew my Czech colleagues well enough to ask them about the Bibles and Calculator Parable, their answer to what had earned the jail time was swift and sure: "Both."

I was the first-ever Fulbright Professor at Purkyne University. It had been named Masaryk University until the Communists took over the country in 1948 and decided to eradicate all public record of Tomas Masaryk, the professor-politician (married to an American) who had helped found the Czech republic and had become its first President. The Masaryk University Department of English and American Studies had counted among its first professors Roman Jakobsen, and the current faculty and students were of very high quality. But in 1979-80 in the classes of the English Department at Purkyne university there were no common texts. Students learned about American authors by hearing a lecture on the life and work, not by actually reading their writings, and thus not by generating any exchange of ideas debated and honed through reference to words on a page to which all had access. In Czechoslovakia there were no textbooks, no university bookstores, no xerox and no mimeograph machines (these latter were specifically outlawed). What weighty and perhaps unwelcome answers could this leaden Czech reality contribute to questions posed in the current debate in America concerning the canon of texts, or to theories of reader-response criticism, whose inflated, etherial nature was captured nicely by the title *Is There a Text in This Class?* I count as one of the most important accomplishments of that Fulbright year my convincing the Embassy to put thirty texts, copies of the Norton *Anthology*, into the American literature classes of Purkyne University. To be denied a common text is more than just being turned into a tour guide for the blind; it is to understand best how important is an assumption we regularly make in the classroom, of the possibility of a communion of minds—whether in agreement or debate, but always in discussion and development—that underlies the entire project of education. Looking back, I believe the Czech government must have been not just unable to afford common texts, but had decided to be actively against them, at least in the liberal arts, precisely because they recognized the danger. Textbooks are as dangerous as other manifestations of the freedom of speech that the Czech police ubiquitously forbade. The week before we left the country, after classes had finished for the year, I noticed that someone had locked up the 30 Nortons in a cabinet; I wonder now who had the key, and when those books were taken out again. I doubt that any of the Czech professors would have dared to use them while the Communists remained in power.

Because it was said that the government paid approximately one in ten people to report on what others were doing and saying and planted a few of these informers in each classroom, the freedom of expression that we take for granted as crucial to successful education (not to mention democracy) was not possible in classes at Purkyne University. To teach in such a situation, as well as to be a student, was not unlike participating in a psychological experiment, where everyone was forbidden to discuss certain ideas, where the teacher could hear voices changing in mid-thought and even mid-sentence, as the speaker would approach an area too dangerous or too personal to be entered in the presence of informers. In my class there were two students whom the others shunned, for having been admitted to this extremely competitive university through connections to Communist Party members. These two and one other seemed to be informers; whether they actually were, I don't know (I remember one of them refused my suggestion of a subject for a paper-presentation, and instead presented a diatribe that seemed right out of the can on the "politically correct" stance of Dashiell Hammett). Their presence had the effect of censoring any extended discussion.

Censorship takes on new faces in such a pervasively totalitarian context. Everyone in Czechoslovakia had, in a sense, become an agent of censorship by developing this self-censoring habit of mind and mode of expression. I myself experienced increasing self-censorship, first consciously and completely by my own choice, then by insidiously less and less conscious habits; it truly seemed to influence not only what I said but what I thought. I learned from this aspect of the Fulbright year the importance of teaching students in American classrooms to exercise regularly their privilege of free expression, the act which produced literature, after all. A lesson I missed on my way to getting a PhD and that some of my professors seemed to have missed also was that teachers must strive to be aware of the politics of the classroom dynamic, in order to ensure that it will be a place sacred to the exchange of expressions of free and developing selves. American classrooms do not have the informers problem, where one bad evaluation can send a student or even the teacher to jail; but every classroom does have a power dynamic. When one sees the skewed results of a different power configuration, such as Czech informers, it forces one to rethink the classroom transaction in all its aspects; I realize now how deceptively easy it is in an ostensibly liberal context like an American classroom for a red pen, a grade book, and a half-conscious habit of mind to turn the teacher himself into an informer-censor.

What, then, should be the role of the Fulbright professor, or any other teacher, in a situation where the external conditions, both political and socio-economic, impinge so forcefully on the inner world of the classroom? Seeing the difference writ large in Czechoslovakia taught me a lesson regarding an inescapable condition of education, anywhere and anytime: there is a necessary relationship, which the teacher must address, between the world of the student inside the classroom and outside of it. Every time a teacher enters a classroom, he or she should make a conscious decision about how much or little of the reality outside the room shall be brought into it—because a decision perforce *will* be made, consciously or unconsciously. It is not that all teachers must be preachers but that an intellectually honest estimation of how people do in fact receive literature must conclude that it always is, and ought to be, conditioned by the external context in which the reader exists. Thus it is the teacher's duty to show by his or her example that, as the model reader for the students, he acknowledges the interaction of the literature he reads and the life he lives. In this sense, all literature is wisdom literature, whether or not it claims overtly to be a version of truth.

As our Fulbright year went on, the presence of the global political world intensified. From fall through spring the Iranian hostage situation dragged on excruciatingly, only to become horribly worse with the failed rescue mission; and the Winter Olympics, after President Carter's decision to boycott the summer events in Moscow in protest over the Soviet invasion of Afghanistan, became a surrogate battleground. The American and Soviet hockey teams moved toward a climactic showdown—the big game was televised by Austrian TV and picked up somehow (maybe the government did not jam it because the Russians figured to win) by an enterprising Czech restaurant-bar, and when the Americans upset the Russians at least half the crowd applauded and cheered loudly (a potentially incriminating display of anti-Russian sentiment).

Then in late spring the political presence which loomed so large around the globe that year began to assert itself in the microcosm. One day the chairperson of the English department—a plucky and resourceful linguist named Joseph Hladky, who had befriended us from the beginning and who at my urging had applied for and was awarded a six-month Fulbright to America the next year—approached me before class with a frightened look and said I had been summoned to the government bureau that controlled our visas and therefore monitored our in-country actions. This honest man (he is now, in free Czechoslovakia, the Dean of the College), had an uncertain, worried look that was more upsetting than anything else I had seen in the country.

At the office I was met by a friendly bilingual woman who knew me from having issued us several tourist visas to Vienna; she took me into her office, where two new faces waited: a Czech policeman and another man who spoke neither Czech nor English, but who was clearly the boss. He asked all the questions, in a language understood by the Czech policeman, who then repeated them in Czech to the visa woman, who said them in English to me. The first question was why America had insulted the world by boycotting the summer Olympics; he then moved on to other general political topics, asking my opinion of the Russian invasion of Afghanistan, the coming Presidential election campaign (could Ronald Reagan win?—in April 1980 I declared, "No Way!"), and the treatment of blacks in my country. But then came the questions whose answers had real consequences: have you made many friends during your stay in Czechoslovakia? My answer was no, since our friends would likely become his enemies. Did I like the students? Yes, of course. Did any of them ask you to do anything special for them, like mail things out of the country? No, they only asked me to teach them about American literature. Do you believe in God and go to church? Sometimes. After about twenty minutes the questioners turned from serious to jovial—for approximately three minutes—and then concluded the interrogation by asking if I would like to have a drink with them sometime. I said I was busy and it would be difficult. When I left the big building, passing the usual lines of Czechs waiting to apply for exit visas, I went straight home, took my wife out of our bugged apartment, and told her the story. We decided to go straight to the American Embassy and tell them what happened, to avoid any confusion. We drove to Prague that day and told our USIS colleague the story. She was mildly upset but not surprised; she said the Embassy would speak to somebody. That was the last I saw of the man who knew no Czech.

The interrogation had its effect on the classroom. When final exam time came round three weeks later, none of my students showed up. It was not because I was a lame-duck Visiting Professor on his way out of town, because the chairperson had clearly stated that there must be a final. But the students must have been told by somebody to disappear. We had been fêted at an end-of-semester party the week before, and had spoken with many of the students and all of our colleagues, but no one had mentioned then that the exam had been canceled; I do not think they knew at the time. But on exam day, when I reported the empty room to the chairperson, he said that the Dean of the College had changed the rooms and in effect canceled my exam; he could not do anything about it. My question at the time, unspoken: Did the Dean speak Czech?

We left two weeks later, but not without a final demonstration of the power that had been behind the politicization of my Czech classroom. At the border a guard decided to look into the glove compartment of the VW, where he found a map to the American Embassy in Budapest, given to us two months before when we had been invited to a party as participants in that year's convention of the American Studies Association of Europe. The guard, who spoke as little English as I did Czech, took my wife and me into the border station, where a plainclothes person who knew some English asked us about the map. Then he told us that we must be searched, in another room, and told another guard to lead me away. The guard made me take off my clothes, down to my briefs, and he looked through all the pockets (my wife said they searched her pocketbook); when he found ten dollars worth of Czech money, he set it aside. Finally, he motioned for me to put the clothes back on. We went back to the plainclothesman, and he told me that I could not take money out of the country: I could either deposit it on the spot in the Czech Central Bank or else "give it to a friend," nodding toward the border guard. I chose the Bank, and they in fact gave me a receipt, which I kept for a souvenir until the next year, when my old Czech chairperson Joe Hladky visited us in Miami during his Fulbright to America. Over a beer (aka *pivo*) we decided he should carry it back to the Department's library fund, though he was not sure that the bank would cash it. They did not, and now we both consider the receipt a relic of the Cold War that was.

Life's most important lessons always have to do with people, and I would like to conclude with a catalogue of the remarkable souls I met during my Fulbright year. Thirteen years have passed, and the revolution has brought the Czechs a playwright for a President. My old chairperson Joe Hladky, whose career had been blocked by his refusal to join the Communist Party, has been promoted to Dean of the College. Last year I spotted, in the Program of the annual MLA Convention, a paper to be presented by someone with an American-sounding name who cited his affiliation with Masaryk University. And then a recent Christmas card from my old colleague Lidmilla Pantuckova (whose daughter in the 1970s was denied entrance to college and forced to become an apprentice sausage-maker instead, because of her father's political satires) informed me that Masaryk/Purkyne now has annual appointments both from the Fulbright program and from a British exchange program. Don Sparling, the Canadian expatriate who married a Czech and started a family in the 1970s, has now become chairperson. Several years ago the Department's senior member, Jan Firbas, was made the Professor for the department, after having been denied his rightful place for many years for being Christian. My former colleague Jessie died, a poetess from Scotland who married a Czech freedom fighter during the War and returned with him to live in Czechoslovakia and preach the virtues of Communism long after most Czechs had given up on it. And two colleagues in their thirties, Madame Chernov and Alex Tichy, died of cancer, perhaps victims of the unregulated environment that was a dispiriting aspect of every Czech's life. The most striking statement of our entire Fulbright year, made by a man in his sixties whom we met just before we left, still sticks in my mind as the epitaph to so many of the life-stories we heard in 1980 from the Czechs: "I have lost everything I had—four times."

The turbulent experiences of that year behind the Iron Curtain have been smoothed by time and memory, but their core lessons endure and are not forgotten. My Fulbright experiences, and surely those of other Fulbright professors, have taught lessons that we cannot help but translate anew for American students every time we enter our classrooms.

PART V

THE EIGHTIES: SEEKING THE NEW

Early in a new and radically different administration, USIA threatened to focus the heavy cuts it faced on Fulbright, some say as a wily tactic to turn them aside. The Congress, even without the Senator's leadership, was stung to counter-action by widespread protest on the part of Fulbright's American constituents and foreign friends; it mandated that exchanges be doubled over a five-year period. Defining "exchanges" to serve its purposes, USIA followed orders. Fulbright budgets drifted upwards; but inflation nibbled at the increase and much of the new money was set aside for "innovative" programs and costly orientation and enrichment seminars. The five-year doubling produced no appreciable rise in participant numbers and failed to arrest the trend to shorter grant-periods. Congress then kept the budget flat for the next five years.

Only two commissions were opened in the eighties: Morocco in 1982 and Ireland in late 1988. Commissions continued to shave stipends to keep participant numbers high. Laments about lowered quality began to be heard on both sides of the oceans. Among Washington innovations were new opportunities for teachers in secondary schools and the smaller universities and colleges in the form of six-week summer traveling "seminars" abroad. These contributed to a decline in the person-months going into traditional academic exchanges for study and research—the same numbers went for shorter periods. By now American universities were relying increasingly on Department of Education funding to maintain their language and area studies programs, and USIA's Congressional mandate to play a role in coordinating U.S. government educational diplomatic efforts was fading from memory. A major task-force study touching Fulbright concerns, the Council on Area and Foreign Language Studies (1988), neglected to include USIA in its deliberations.

Overseas, the staffing of USIS cultural positions for Americans continued to shift from cultural specialists to informational generalists: in two of the major cultural capitols of Europe in the late eighties, gifted USIA officers with no previous cultural experience became Cultural Attachés. The committed cultural-educational professionals drifted away.

Of thirteen contributors to this section, only one is foreign, a further reminder that there are no statistical conclusions to be drawn from what has

297

fallen into this volume. The reason for fewer foreign participants can only be hypothesized: the Fulbright Newsletter reaches more alumni in the U.S. from the period since 1978—mailing lists still suffer from the inexplicable loss of Fulbright records in the 1977 reorganization; by definition it reaches younger ones who have had less time to think about their experience. These returnees from the eighties have fresher memories; they have had correspondingly less time to grow in their careers and reflect on their experience.

Of the twelve Americans, most are academics (it is estimated that 80% of American alumni are in education, of which only 8% in primary or secondary). Among these, a city-planner tells of the impact of his Fulbright tours and consultancies; an American Studies belles-lettrist relates her discovery of the meaning of American culture in Europe in the cruel Aprils of her two Fulbrights; a spouse with her own career tells of her husband's assignment to Europe's northernmost university and its impact on their family; an artist-educator learns in the UK to extend the concept of design to all teaching; a political scientist relates his experience of French social science to the history of the dialog between French and American liberal thought; a Fulbright couple analyze their efforts to come to terms with a resurgent Germany; a professor of business administration reports rebirth in the new Portugal; an American Studies lecturer in Poland discovers that the onions of irony in a "Bloc" country have many layers; and two African hands, a nursing educator and a comparative historian, describe the rigors of maintaining morale and intellectual dignity in countries where the annual per capita income is less than $300. On the shorter-term side, a secondary teacher remade by an Indian "seminar" becomes international studies coordinator for a university; and a "professional" one-semester grant to teach journalism in Pakistan turns a newspaperman into a professor by act of Fulbright and leads into the politics of the Afghan War. The single foreign contributor, a British neuropsychologist, discovers light in the cornfields of Ohio.

From the viewpoint of the Program's history and its health, it is a decade of decline and erosion, gentle and invisible but persistent. Yet neither custom nor dearth seems to have staled Fulbright's variety.

Professor Allor, director of the School of Planning at the University of Cincinnati, has a background in architecture and planning at the University of Michigan and holds a doctorate in social science from Syracuse. In this essay he displays rather than describes the kind of mind-change and insights produced by three separate Fulbright experiences and then by consultancies all over the world. His calm assertion that it is the mind itself that is reshaped by international immersion, recounted in what one reader has called a post-modernist style, makes an unusual statement about the ultimate Fulbright effect. At the same time, he draws attention to the potential disconnections between these new minds and everyday American life, focusing on the ironies of American professors of planning who are everywhere in demand except in their own country.

24

HABITS OF THE MIND

David J. Allor

My three Fulbright experiences have changed my life, not so much in the character of behavior, but in the character of thought. A Fulbright experience is itself one of intensified perception, broadened comprehension, and sober alteration of the mind and its habits. Fulbright experiences are carried forward and enter on-going experience. In ways that I cannot fully explain to myself, I find that recollections of my Fulbright experiences penetrate my everyday life. My everyday life is of course quite different from those of others. The great majority of my time is devoted to professional instruction in urban planning, organization theory and mediation skills, and in academic administration. Yet like most people, I buy my own groceries, cut the lawn when necessary, take out my own garbage, and pay my bills with acceptable tardiness. The reality I create about me is different but not wholly separate from that of others.

As each Fulbright experience required me to see more in a different culture, I am now disposed to see more in my own culture. As each Fulbright experience required that I understand more of another culture, I am now disposed to understand more of my own culture. As each Fulbright experience required me to evaluate my conduct in a foreign culture, I am now disposed more fully to evaluate my conduct in my home culture. It is not that I have become "enlightened," "sophisticated," or "cosmopolitan." There is no grand synthesis of experience. There is a heightened sensitivity to other perceptions, other interpretations, and other justifications. Perception is no longer a casual recording of appearances; it requires mental discrimination. Understanding is no longer common; it requires a mental tolerance for diversity. Justification is no longer universal; it requires a mental humility in the reconciliation of personal and societal values. The Fulbright experience induces the mind to look always for something else, to interpret it as something other, and to reflect upon it in the search for something better. Ongoing experience is changed because habits of the mind are changed. While experience is continuous, at times I find myself startled by the vividness of certain mental associations. Fulbright experiences of the past are suddenly brought forward and embed themselves in present thought.

The chronology of my experiences has little significance, except to provide for the reader a grounding for what might otherwise appear to be a set of random memories. My first international experience was during the summer of 1974—I went to Iran as a tourist and to Saudi Arabia as an invited guest of the Arabian-American Oil Company. For a Midwestern American, superficially educated in democratic doctrine but thoroughly educated in Catholic dogma, immersion in a Moslem culture was disorienting. I sensed the growing tension between the Pahlavi secular autocracy and the underlying Shi'ite theocracy. While I experienced no overt hostility to Americans, my left-handedness might rub Moslem religious sensitivities, said the briefers. There were some contradictions as well. Saudi Arabia, with the seat of the Moslem faith at Mecca, nevertheless had made a lucrative accommodation of Middle Eastern theocracy to western capitalism. The isolation of foreigners in such company towns as Ras Tanura engendered an aberrant American culture within Saudi Arabia. Frenetic effort was directed toward both recreating the American "home" and demonstrating the breadth of international experiences through acquisition of selected artifacts. Conversely, the segregation of foreigners had failed to prevent the penetration of that American culture into Saudi Arabia through conspicuous consumption of Western goods. From that experience, I became more sensitive to the dynamics of religious commitment, political power, and economic order.

My first Fulbright appointment was in 1980 as a Senior Scholar at the Economics Research Institute of the University of the Andes, Mérida,

Venezuela. I performed evaluations of urban-industrial development projects in the Andean region, which had been authorized under the Fifth National Plan (1976-80). I was invited to return as a Visiting Professor in 1984 to replicate my evaluations during the penultimate year of the Sixth National Plan (1981-85); both were published there (Allor 1981, 1985). In Venezuela I first became aware of social, political, and institutional positioning. I was a Fulbright appointee, with an earned doctorate, and certain social courtesies were extended to me; conversely certain forms of social behavior were expected of me. While initially embarrassed, I grew accustomed to being addressed as *Asesor* or *Consejero*. I was bound to a higher social class. My Venezuelan colleagues were perplexed to discover that my father, a carpenter, had not completed high school because of the exigencies of the Great Depression. The ability to "jump social class" within a generation is a popular fiction in the U.S. While much desired, it is a near impossibility in Venezuela. My colleagues were more comfortable with my being a Democrat rather than a Republican, even though as an American I was expected to be a defender of capitalism. Americans see capitalism as a state of affairs but not as one of several ideologies. For Venezuelans, economic systems have correlative political ideologies.

Immediately thereafter, early in 1985, I served as Advisor in Urban Planning to the Institute of Urban Research and Planning, Curitiba, Brazil, under sponsorship of the Ohio-Paraná Program of the Partners of the Americas. By great good fortune, I was living in Brazil at the time of restoration of civilian governance. Despite severe and continuing economic crisis, it was inspiring to witness the depth of commitment to democracy by Brazilians so long deprived of the right of national franchise. Yet their joy in the present and their hope for the future were tempered by the sorrow felt at the death of president-elect Tancredo Neves.

In the summer of 1986, Cincinnati colleagues and I had the privilege of participating in a Fulbright multi-university travelling seminar in India, under a university-affiliation program sponsored by USIA, organized by USEFI in Delhi, and headed by then-Fulbright Association President David Johnson. Touring thirteen cities in a period of six weeks left intense impressions: masses of individuals struggling to overcome economic and social disparity and religious division to sustain and promote an intendedly democratic nation-state. Images of the communalism of the ashram in Ahmadabad, of the mercantilism of Bombay and Madras, of the socialism of Kerala revealed a diversity of both social and economic orders. At times the images were all too vivid, distorting perception, confusing comprehension, and summoning conflicting justifications.   Air-conditioned hotels became places of mental refuge as well as physical comfort.

My third Fulbright experience was in 1987 as a Senior Research Scholar at the Graduate Faculty of Human Settlements Planning, the Autonomous University of Nuevo León, Monterrey, Mexico. The idea was to broaden activities between my university and Nuevo León, as coordinated by my colleague in economics Haynes Goddard; it was supported by a Fulbright-USIA university affiliations grant. I participated cooperatively in the preparation of a research project for the evaluation of industrial park developments surrounding the Monterrey metropolitan area. In attempting to construct a research strategy to explain the urban development consequences of metropolitan industrialization, I became increasing aware of the dynamics of rural-urban migrations, the transformation of social structures, and the dependency of the population upon corporate economic development and international trade. During the celebrations of the seventieth anniversary of the Mexican Federal Constitution of 1917, newer variations of older problems emerged. The earlier focus upon agrarian land reform had turned toward urban-industrial enfranchisement. The political order established by the Institutional Revolutionary Party (PRI) for nearly fifty years experienced severe stress. International debt refinancing required that those already in poverty bear additional economic hardships.

This above record of experience may have some cumulative effect upon the character of my thoughts; but, in the everyday activities of my life, specific recollections emerge in unanticipated association to readdress perception, understanding and justification. The discussions which follow are reconstructions of recollections, brief summaries of on-going experiences, seeking to demonstrate certain habits of the mind.

I recall a small dinner meeting of Fulbrighters at a hillside restaurant overlooking the Ohio River at Cincinnati—a visiting Fulbright Association officer was being entertained by various Fulbrighter colleagues—Sam and Lynn Noe (Turkey, Pakistan, India) and Barbara Ramusack (India). A slow, cold mid-January rain partially obscured the lights of the city before a darkening sky. There was conviviality around the table. Discussions turned to past experiences in the Middle East and in South America and then to new opportunities in Eastern Europe. There was expression of concern for the future of the Fulbright program, given domestic political climate and economic recession. There was also discussion of expanding the participation of the Fulbright Association through local chapter creation.   Over appetizers, comments centered on solicitation of essay proposals for the present anthology. Then, while presenting the entrees, the waiter announced, in a timbre struggling to retain a matter-of-factness, "We have begun to bomb Iraq." Despite the warmth of good company, I sensed a chill in each of us, especially in those whose Fulbright experiences and academic careers related to Middle Eastern history, culture, and architecture. For all of our hopes and efforts to promote "international peace and understanding," I sensed a failure of the human spirit. While driving home in a heavier and colder rain, I struggled to maintain a matter-of-factness in the situation about me. But my mind summoned other events to view and words to hear. As in Iran more than ten years earlier, should we not have seen the bitter fruits of a militarily-supported autocracy? Given the prosecution of the carnage of the Iran-Iraq War, how could we have so misperceived the tenaciousness of Saddam Hussein in his occupation of Kuwait? Given the long history of slaughter among Arab brothers, it seemed an irony to me for Saddam Hussein to now call for a "Holy War" uniting Arabs against the U.S. Such a call would surely plunge the entire world into expanding military aggression and random terrorism. Later, that same evening, I heard the words of President Bush characterizing the bombing as a "just war," subconsciously alluding to the German invasion of the Czechoslovakian Sudetenland as historical precedent. But the precedent seemed shallow. Had not the U.S. supported Iran militarily through the reign of the last Pahlavi Shah? Had not the U.S. tacitly supported Iraq throughout the Iran-Iraq War? In that neither Iran, nor Iraq, nor Kuwait, nor Saudi Arabia were or were soon likely to become democracies, what objectives were being pursued by the "liberation" of Kuwait? With perceptions so obscured by the patriotic images of the national media and with misunderstandings so confounded by deception and complicity, it seemed impossible to justify the "War in the Gulf" on either the merits of its intentions or the value of its consequences. If the U.S. sought to secure oil and engender democracy in the Middle East, it achieved only the former but at great human and economic cost.

At the end of that Winter academic quarter, I was in a hurry to complete grading final examinations, so that I could participate in the Annual National Planning Conference of the American Planning Association. A second-year graduate student from Ecuador entered my office to discuss the progress of his thesis on squatter-settlement upgrading and environmental protection in Quito. As discussion concluded, he commented that he thought it odd that there would be such a thing as a national planning conference in a nation where there was no national planning. I found myself amused and embarrassed as I returned to grading; my mind drifted. The U.S. had once initiated a national planning effort. In 1933 the National Planning Board was created inside the Public Works Administration, converted into the National Resources Board in 1934, twice reorganized and abolished in 1943, all this in response to the economic crisis of the Great Depression. It ended when the Congress refused funding for fear of the "socialist" connotations of a national planning agency. This brief experiment passed into history, given little attention except by planning historians. The U.S. has never perceived itself as needing national planning, despite continuing and severe regional imbalances of human and material resources, deteriorating urban and industrial infrastructure, and increasing infant mortality, poverty, homelessness, illiteracy, and structural unemployment, all compounded by increasing racial and ethnic heterogeneity. The theories and processes which American planning consultants had been so eager to apply to other nations had never been applied to the American context. I felt the value of my own consultation diminished.

Even as these thoughts rushed painfully through the mind, they inverted themselves, to ask what I had learned from these foreign nations. I recalled my afternoon visits to the bookstores of Monterrey and Mexico City. I saw myself sitting cross-legged on the display floor of Fondo de Cultura Económica, reviewing the works of Gonzalo Robles, Arturo Guillén, and Jaime Ruiz Dueñas. I recalled my joy in discovering the works of Allan-Randolph Brewer-Carias, Carlos Rangel, and Julio Corredor in the bookstores of Mérida. My visits to the Higginbottom's Bookstores in India were secular pilgrimages, rewarded by the discovery of the works of M. Visvesvarya, M.L. Seth, and M.L. Jhingan. Of all these nations, Brazil offered the greatest treasures. In addition to the works of Celso Furtado, E. Roberto Grau, and Celson Ferari, there were works from Spain, England, France and Germany, translated into Brazilian Portuguese. I took a superficial solace in that many of these works were now safely contained within my home library. Yet I felt a sudden disappointment, for they had not been widely used in my teaching of American students. I had collected knowledge and assimilated some of it; but my Fulbright experiences had not been brought home to America. In forcing myself to complete the grading, I was confronted by the narrowness of American planning education. Late one evening, while editing the draft of a conference paper comparing the national planning processes of Brazil, Mexico and India (Allor 1991), I listened to the television replay of the national evening news. While paying only scant attention, I heard the words of President Bush suggesting that Iraqis should consider removing Saddam Hussein from political and military power and more obliquely encouraging the Kurdish minority to revolt. It was not difficult to condemn Saddam Hussein as evil, given his rise to power, his sponsorship of terrorism, and his apparent delight in naked aggression. But the less-than-veiled exhortation to "remove" him might come to haunt the President. No doubt the opponents of Bolivar felt politically justified in their assassination of Antonio José de Sucre (1830) to prevent the political integration of Gran Colombia.   No doubt Victoriano Huerta felt politically justified initiating the "removal" of Mexican President Francisco Madero (1913) to usurp the presidency for himself.   No doubt her Sikh bodyguards felt politically and religiously justified in their assassination of Indira Nehru Gandhi (1984) in response to the suppression of ethnic independence and the desecration of the Golden Temple at Amritsar. Exhortations to remove an apparent evil may themselves lack merit.   The removal of an apparent evil is not a guarantee of the triumph of goodness.

During an administrator-skills training session the following Spring, conducted by the American Council on Education for school directors and department chairs at the University of Cincinnati, the facilitator commented that academic administrators at times alienate their colleagues and staff members through the use of "trite phrases," "tired metaphors," and "veiled references," which can offend accidental listeners when addressing others.   I recalled another work session, in Venezuela, in 1984.   While the director of the research institute was discussing the accelerated marginalization of rural population peripheral to industrial development projects, a number of the staff members seemed distracted, annoyed at some comment they had heard.   While wishing to remain attentive to the "business" before us, I was increasingly interested in overhearing the other conversation.   The comments were critical of then-President Reagan.   Perhaps these staff members, like many other Venezuelans, were being discreet, not wishing to offend this American visiting professor and former Fulbright scholar.   It took some time for me to discern what had offended them, my comprehension of spoken Spanish often lacking accuracy.   Then, quite suddenly, the comment that had offended them was repeated and understood, "Communism would not be permitted to enter through the back-door of the Western Hemisphere."   Spoken then with reference to Nicaragua, I felt that I had heard it before; but, I did not yet understand the depth of its offensiveness.   After recessing the meeting for a long Andean lunch, I took the local Volkswagen *porpuesto* to my *pensión* in Los Chorros de Milla.   As I crossed the street to enter the courtyard, I looked down the alley and saw the day-servants carrying the garbage out the back door of the *pensión*.   Was that the worth of Central and South America to the North American mind, a source of servants and a site for garbage?   Were Central and South Americans so weak as to have to be protected from Communism even at the loss of self-worth?   Would our hemispheric "good neighbors" ever be permitted to enter the front door of North American consciousness and be accorded respect?

I returned to the Institute later that afternoon. Overtly passive, I was nevertheless deeply angry. How was it possible that a nation with such intellectual resources as the U.S. could articulate "foreign policy" in so offensive a manner? I also felt embarrassment at my political naiveté. Certainly, the words of the President were directed towards both frustrating the Sandinistas and marshalling anti-communist sentiments of Americans. But the President ought to have understood that news media are global. A warning to our enemies had offended our friends.

Early one morning in late Spring, I took the bus to the University of Cincinnati. I recalled another, longer bus ride, across the breadth of Monterrey. From my middle-class apartment in Residencias Anahuac, the bus carried me south, past the very large public Autonomous University of Nuevo León, along the railroad lines and steel mills of San Nicolás de los Garza, past the bullfighting arena and the Cuahautemoc brewery, through the 1910 Arch of Reforma, then crossed the major streets of the commercial center, over the River Santa Catarina, along the southern edge of the low-income Colonía Independencia, and ended at the well-kept campus of the Technological Institute of Monterrey. The buses of Monterrey were not air-conditioned so that I felt more directly the harsh diversity of the urban-industrial environment. Yet, for all the immediacy of that experience, I was the observer of the culture. The Fulbright appointment as research scholar was clearly so specialized a function as to isolate me from the everyday reality of Monterrey. I had been *in* Monterrey but not part of Monterrey. As I exited the bus, my consciousness returned to Cincinnati. I wondered whether I was a part of this reality. Was I an observer rather than a contributor to my home culture? What purpose did my strained perceptions and imperfect understandings serve? Passing my office, I went directly to my classroom to give a lecture on problem-solving processes.

In this narrow and peculiar setting, I felt that I was competent and I belonged. In a foreign context, seeking to belong requires conscious effort to behave as expected. As a North American, and especially as a Midwesterner, I carry within me a self-comforting but imperfect egalitarianism. I tend to be rather irreverent of class distinctions. Nevertheless, I would dress up for a concert by the Cincinnati Symphony Orchestra and I would dress down for shopping at the Findlay (farmers) Market. I deceived myself that I could slip across social classes with such apparent ease and success. While living in Mérida, during my first Fulbright appointment, I found it particularly enjoyable to hike along the mountain slopes above La Hechicera. Early on Saturday mornings, I would dress in worn blue-jean pants and jacket, filling the pockets with roles of camera film, light filters, and lens paper. Outfitted with heavy boots, camera, Swiss Army knife, and small backpack, I took the *porpuesto* down to the public market to buy bottled fruit juice, dry white cheese, and small breakfast rolls. I recall that an older woman always served me at the *panadería*. I always ordered one dozen rolls; they lasted through mid-afternoon. At first, she addressed me with the level of courtesy accorded *turistas*, pleasant but not engaging. But as one Saturday followed another, she became more distant, more formal. Anxious that I had offended her, but unassured of my command of Spanish, I asked one of my friends to inquire if there were a problem. The response was direct. The woman in the *panadería* thought it odd that a university professor would not send his servant to buy the breakfast rolls. Whatever my perception of social reality and fluidity, I had been put in my place. University professors did not dress down and do their own grocery shopping.

My research has often required a narrow focus upon macro-economic changes. I tend to overlook more immediate changes in everyday life. It was a rare experience to be able to return to Venezuela to assess changes in the economic development of the Andean region between 1980 and 1984. The once massive oil export revenues had diminished. Massive programs of heavy industrialization were paralyzed. Trapped between stagnant industrial employment but continually inflating prices for consumer goods, the slowly urbanizing populations made mounting demands upon public social services. Despite massive oil reserves, Venezuela could not continue to fuel the economic development. After leaving the research institute early in the evening, I would run the inclined ring road of the campus of the University of the Andes at La Hechicera. This served as much to clear my mind, as well as get much-needed exercise. When I had done this in 1980, I was alone. My Venezuelan colleagues conceived of exercise only in service to athletic competition. As I did not play soccer, my exercise served no constructive purpose. It was my silent observation that these Venezuelans spent far more time watching soccer than playing it.

When I resumed this practice in 1984, much had changed. The ring road had been discovered not only by waves of young soccer players, but also by female students, young couples and middle-aged businessmen. All of us had our own objectives, routines, and paces. As we passed each other, there was a short glance, a thin smile, or a silent nod, all gestures of encouragement. We were all achieving our goals, quite independently of public policy, development incentives, and governmental coordination. It became apparent to me that I had looked for change in all the wrong places. Change is initiated and supported at the micro-level, in those everyday routines of our lives. The macro-level measures of balance of import/export payments and the net regional product lost preeminence in my assessment of change.

                    *   *   *

Even though my thoughts often turn inward, they may have significance for others.   Promoting international peace and understanding requires an extraordinary continuity of effort. In a world so distracted by episodic conflict and random violence, peace is often experienced as the absence of war and understanding is often limited to diplomatic protocol.   While formally-sponsored programs of international exchange are functionally necessary, the U.S. has not capitalized upon the experiences of former Fulbrighters in promoting international peace and understanding in our everyday lives. The Fulbright experience is neither an escapist adventure nor a permanent credential. Its value is derived by its extension to other domains of continuing experience.   Whatever the contributions to other nations, the Fulbright difference has not yet been created within the U.S.

Former Fulbright appointees often fail to continue to promote peace and understanding once having returned to their homes.   Ironically, Fulbright alumni are accomplished at bringing home the memorabilia of their experiences.   Their professional offices, studios, dining rooms, and dens are adorned with artifacts, selected to demonstrate cultural diversity tempered by the good taste of the former appointee.   Yet it is clear that much of the breadth of experience and depth of understanding has not been brought home to the U.S. The U.S. persists in its self-deception that it has more to teach others than it might learn from others. The Fulbright experience has yet to penetrate and in turn be absorbed by American thought, pedagogy and conduct. The wealth of knowledge held in the minds or within the private libraries of former Fulbrighters is disseminated poorly, most frequently to other learned colleagues, professional societies, and special interest groups, but rarely to the society at large.   For those of us in teaching professions, conventional pedagogues resist balanced accounts of cultural diversity and global perspective. While many former appointees are recognized experts in the disciplines and professions, their conduct with the larger society does not reveal an extension of international understanding.

For some former appointees, the Fulbright experience itself may be confusing.   Perhaps the multiplicity of perceptions, the compounding of alternative interpretations, and the apparent fragility of justifications frustrate cognitive management.   The Fulbright experience may produce a higher sensitivity to the depth of ignorance rather than to the breadth of knowledge. Where former appointees have been so humbled, they may lapse into passivity and silence. The potential of a continuing contribution is lost. Both American culture and policy are left interculturally-impoverished.

Yet of all of those who could comprehend the variations of human personality, the subtleties of expression, and the conventions of culture, the former Fulbright appointee must be among the foremost. The Fulbright experience irrevocably alters the mind's habits, empowering it to relate concept to context, cause to effect, intention to consequence. To give voice to knowledge is to risk its test as wisdom.

REFERENCES

David J. Allor, *Desarrollo industrial sub-regional y desarollo urbano: el caso de La Fría, Desarrollo urbano sub-regional en el Estado Tachira*, University of the Andes: Mérida, 1981 and 1985.

_____, "The Institutionalization of Planning and the Tradition of Grand National Plans in Brazil, India and Mexico," paper presented at the Joint International Conference of Associations of European Schools of Planning and the Association of Collegiate Schools of Planning, Oxford, July 1991.

After the pre-Fulbright culture shock of moving from Los Angeles to Indiana, Dr. Mossberg came late to the real thing. She was twice a Fulbright in Finland, the second time in the prestigious Bicentennial Chair of American Studies, and served as resident specialist in American Studies for USIA, traveling to dozens of foreign assignments. She reports total self-transformation. With a traditional view of literature and culture in the belles-lettres tradition, she discovered that the U.S. is seen abroad primarily through its popular culture and set out to understand the European fascination for cultural products like "Dallas" and McDonald's. This led to a pedagogical revolution on one campus and, ultimately, to leave the university career for a life, as she says, of cultural entrepreneurship. Her Fulbright set off a consuming search for the links between popular culture and traditional high culture, and for the relevance of academic study to individual life. A fish must leave water to understand it, but water seen from above becomes the mirror in which self-awareness begins. This essay has been reworked from earlier publications, lectures and seminars.

25

AND WHERE YOU ARE IS WHERE YOU ARE NOT

Barbara Clarke Mossberg

> *Traveling is a fool's paradise.*
> —Ralph Waldo Emerson

> *I went to the woods because I wished to live deliberately.*
> —Henry David Thoreau

I thought I was so smart. My Fulbright like a novel would end and real life resume. I knew what journeys were and the purpose and destination of my travel. This is a travel essay, not about my literal journey, but about where temporary travel takes us; how it leads to a more permanent, perpetually transforming process of mental leaps and departures. This essay, in other words, is about how Fulbright turned me into a traveling fool. I am in the woods. There is no turning back.

"There is nothing people hate so much," mused D.H. Lawrence as he read American "classics," "as a new experience." This seems unfairly insulting to the national pride about our well-known stomach for adventure, played to brilliantly by a popular and commercial culture where newness is progress and difference a prestigious commodity. Unlike Toyota and Volvo, Lawrence just didn't know! We crave new experience. He just liked to tweak and pique.

I was leaping, only because gravity necessitated touching down at all, across Jogjakarta's Temple, in my high heels and lecture suit. My host had just said, "If you are very quiet (I became very, very quiet), and very still (his voice was now a whisper and I became very, very still), you will see the black snakes of Borabadur. . . ." He may have said more but I was already in the air, ululating and trying to transcend physical laws to get back to the jeep. New experience? Who are we kidding? The world had been heaping doses of new experience upon me this day—first escaping Bangkok's floods and snakes in trees only to discover myself in malaria country (malaria?), then being robbed; then being taken on diversionary routes "to avoid terrorists" (terrorists?); eating unrecognizable fruit then reading instructions to soak such fruit first in decontaminants. I had read Paul Bowles, I knew what happened to people who leave Kansas.

That I was in Bowles' eerie world was confirmed when I arrived in Jogjakarta, still trembling from a ride in a rusted and minimalist airline, chest wounds oozing from being rubbed raw jogging in Thailand's 100% humidity, to see a hand-lettered sign bobbing towards me. I'M NOBODY! WHO ARE YOU? ARE YOU NOBODY TOO? A voice behind it spoke: "Barbara Mossberg, the Dickinson scholar?" Was this Bowles or Lewis Carroll? A Dutch consultant to Indonesia, hearing of my lecture, brought his jeep to intercept a fellow poetry-lover. I had to see the Temple. A penultimate experience, worthy of Emily Dickinson; and I would make my 5 PM lecture. Dazed, glazed with repellent and cod-liver rash ointment, I went, Alice in Wonderland dubiously following the White Rabbit. I knew better, yet I was already in the Hole.

Now, as I ungratefully leapt to avoid new experience with amazing alacrity given my flummoxed state, my flimsy heels smashing on rocks in vain efforts to fly, I marvelled at Lawrence's wisdom. My family was right: I led a foolhardy life, perilous and bizarre; and for what, I asked myself? I had plenty of time to ponder, for in spite of traveling all day through storms and robbers and terrorists and mosquitoes and now risking my life on a road with rickshaws, elephants and trucks to be on time for this lecture, no one came— for three hours. Rubber time, and the slide-projector for which I had carried two hundred slide twenty thousand miles didn't work anyway. I was on the road for American culture, the granddaughter of immigrants who didn't speak English now representing the U.S. People from villages three hours away came to learn about the U.S. with me. This was all in a day's work for a Fulbrighter—it was 1987 and I had been one for five years. If I lived, would I trade my life? Now was the moment to ask.

How did I get into it all? Perhaps my motto, from Henry James: "Try to be one of those on whom nothing is lost." The disaster, boredom—whatever challenges the spirit that James implies is opportunity for conversion into Something—is a sense of travail, tribulation, ignorance. James was not telling us to seek it; he only told us what to do when it came.

Fulbright, conversely, sets us up for it. The first Fulbright I blithely accepted in 1982 led straight to this present predicament. I was in Fulbright terrain, an arduous, disconcerting, humbling, dazzling and infinitely renewing state of mind. Lawrence was on the mark—we hate new experience—yet isn't this what Fulbright is all about?

The purpose of academic exchange may be to uncover bases of understanding which generate a sense of logic and urgency about living peaceably together on this planet. But the process of going abroad as an American Fulbright to teach or to study is essentially and necessarily one of giving us new experience. Not a by-product—toxic or benign—but the point, for a people for whom flight from new experience is in the grain, common as corn.

Americans can go straight for 3,000 miles over swamps, saltbeds, headlands, prairies, snow-covered peaks, redwoods, rain forests, and diverse communities, yet never have a new experience. Cajun land or Cree, blizzard or sizzling, we can eat the same hamburger with the same secret sauce, sleep under the same orange roof, or tune into the same TV or radio show. Franchises along the strips into every city, and shopping malls at every major highway crossing, make Iowa and Texas interchangeable. This is how we diffuse, transform and tame the reality of one of the most ethnically and geographically diverse nations on earth.

In fact, evidence of our ambivalence to new experience is everywhere. American commercial and popular culture capitalizes on it. Holiday Inn reassures the national psyche: "No Surprises." The beloved "E.T." features a homesick alien in a new land, an only slightly disguised version of every newcomer to a community—by definition 25% of America's population at any one time. Baseball, our national pastime, is a drama whose plot involves getting "home"; its action is circular—get "home" or die. Store cookies are Almost-Home-Made. For every product labeled "New! Improved!" another one boasts "Original Recipe," "Made the Same Way Since 1836," "Old World Flavor."

Anne Tyler's parable *The Accidental Tourist* concerns a man who writes travel guides for those traumatized by anything "foreign." Seeking the familiar, a home-away-from-home, a home *manqué*, the "accidental" tourist is a wary and closed mind resisting the notion and reality of difference. This mind wants meatloaf in Paris, dreads *croissant*. The possibility of alternative ways of doing, thinking and valuing is erased as we try to recreate a known world, Tyler argues, from a threatened sense of too much out there that is different and new.

History documents hostility to discovery, be it the round world or the lightning rod. It may seem ironic that fear of the new flourishes in a country whose self-image pivots on the concept of a "new world" and whose Dream depends upon the possibility of a "fresh start" for a "new life." Perhaps it is precisely an emerging culture's cult of the new, a pluralistic culture's cult of difference, and a definition of success as a function of change—of freedom as the ability to "make a difference"—which accelerate the need for sameness and continuity. No wonder New Coke failed. Hating new experience may be as American as apple pie—or as tofu burrito.

This is Fulbright's challenge. Our very training creates an attitude which can keep new experience at bay. Like T.S. Eliot's hopeless J. Alfred Prufrock, who insists that he has known it all, we block any chance for new experience, and thus for the hope which can sustain us during crises of self-worth. Unable to imagine anything new and different, like mermaids who might sing to him, Prufrock's emotional paralysis comes from tragic arrogance. His depression is a function of a limited, limiting intelligence, a consequence not of seeing reality but of not being able to imagine enough. Eliot, who gave himself a Fulbright of sorts as an antidote to the Prufrock mentality, describes the process he literally transacted in his moves from Missouri to Boston and London. England, his metaphoric as well as literal destination, is only possible upon giving up one's known world; hope and redemption pivot on an open mind willing to risk getting lost, as in "East Coker":

> . . . In order to arrive there,
> To arrive where you are, to get from where you are not,
>   You must go by a way wherein there is no ecstasy.
> In order to arrive at what you do not know
>   You must go by a way which is the way of ignorance.
> In order to arrive at what you are not
>   You must go through the way in which you are not.
> And what you do not know is the only thing you know
> And what you own is what you do not own
> And where you are is where you are not.

Fulbright provides the necessary existential crisis Eliot calls for. We surrender our sense of knowing and certainty in moving to a different culture with different foods, places and ways to shop and go to work, language inside and around us, climate, clothes, pots and pans and spices and laundry methods. More is gained than the flexibility we acquire when our lecture notes are lost, our books are ruined in a flood, the slides for the lecture three hundred people wait to hear do not fit in the projector, or our disks are incompatible with our new computer: I mean the humbling and liberating experience of oneself as different and foreign.

Until the point of cross-cultural encounters, our complacency goes unchallenged. We are parochial in peace. I first learned this when I left Los Angeles for graduate school in Indiana—prompted by the exasperated reaction to my naiveté of a visiting East Coast professor. As we read the "Waste Land," he asked why April is the cruelest month. I knew. "Because," I said, "in the Spring the world is so fertile that it is intolerable to look within, to see our own sterility in contrast, our own lack of growth . . . ." He cut me off: "Miss Clarke, that could only be said by someone who was raised in California. If you want to understand American literature and culture, you must go East, where April is muddy, icy—and cruel." Humbly setting out for a cruel April, I ended in Indiana.

I had thought my undergraduate years in the late sixties at UCLA were normal—library, beach parties, pep rallies and televised marches; we wore jeans and workshirts, shoes optional. Arriving for an orientation picnic in Indiana, dress "casual," I was dangerous. They were further alarmed when I later emerged during a thunderstorm in my brand-new first-time-ever storm gear—boots, wool sweater, and insulated raincoat. I was not just sinister, I was crazy too. My six-year sojourn among the Hoosiers transformed my identity from run-of-the-mill to oddball. Suddenly I was a Westerner. As my permanent tan faded, as leaves turned color not in books but on trees, I began to realize how my upbringing differed from the rest of the world. Coming from LA, I considered lilies of the field in Indiana as undeveloped land yet to be paved, rain as romantic, stores not open 24 hours a day as un-American, things as all wrong: no bagels, pasta, tortillas; people swimming in quarries, not backyard pools; adults riding bicycles; women sweating. I was critical of the differences I saw between "right" and "normal" LA life and this new culture, and I was demoralized by them. With my double vision, through the lens of green pastures, I could *see* for the first time—the golden tumbleweeds blowing across freeways and cement river beds. But I knew being away had truly changed me when my mother called from Pasadena one April day.

Mentioning it was snowing, I was bewildered when she said, "OH, MY GOD!"

Like Eliot's London, Indiana was a kind of self-conferred Fulbright brought on by chagrin at my parochial knowledge of April. So that, offered a Chair in Finland during my 1982 sabbatical, I agreed in the name of intellectual growth to extend my pursuit of authentically cruel Aprils. By now "seasoned," I knew who I was and what I was getting into—a year in an exotic place, then back to normal. By then I was tenured in an English Department in Oregon, and my book on Emily Dickinson was out. I could not imagine a different way of being.

But even Dickinson knew the consequences of departures: "Can the Lark—resume the Shell?" Leaving the U.S. only gave me a *new* new understanding of myself and my culture which made the "real life" I assumed I would resume no longer possible. They say, "If you want to know about water, don't ask a fish." Why or how should the fish know it—water is "natural," "how things are." But take the fish out of water by hook or crook or Fulbright and the shocked fish comprehends water, waterhood, air and airness, fish and fishity. The changes in me as a scholar and teacher in Finland were a function of cross-cultural internal-external re-vision, and the intimacy with my own complacency and ignorance it brought. In the culture shock of air, fish are as homesick as E.T. and the accidental tourist. But they begin to know water and themselves. Discovering I did not know "it all" was liberating, for what we think we know when we are in water can make for Prufrockian doldrums and even intellectual dead-ends. Air instructs the fish.

The air, that foreign angle of vision, is the advantage which enables insights into our culture that may by definition be invisible from within. Whether Lawrence's provoking potshots or Tocqueville's or Crèvecoeur's beloved or respected generalizing, theory on American comes from outside. Perhaps it has to. Fulbright gives us a chance, or forces us, to be our own Lawrence or Tocqueville—refreshingly disrespectful or wise.

We Americans tend to assume we do not have a culture. We identify with a region, class, profession, race or ethnic group. We are too diverse regionally and ethnically, we say, to have a culture. Even though my doctorate was done in American literature and I professed to teach it, the Americanness of our literature was difficult to assess; in any case it was an optional issue. I did not think of myself as "American." There was no need to. Nor would I have felt entitled to. Academically, I was an outsider, born in Hollywood, female, immigrant family, public schools, feminist critic, poet: I took it for granted I did not belong to a culture that I did not believe really existed.

In Helsinki later, I held the Bicentennial Chair in American Studies, responsible for officially representing "America"—idea and political construct —as well as the field of American Studies. When I confessed before taking the Chair that I was in English, not American Studies, I was told, "That's fine: whatever you do is American Studies." The casual approach to the field aside, the to-me preposterous view of me as a generic American who represented an entire national culture at first bemused me. Was I an archetypal American because the Finns did not know better, or was it because from the perspective of so many countries and time zones away, they more clearly could see the "American" in me? But I immediately began to see what identified an "American." At a corner, I would join people waiting for the light to change. Suddenly I would notice the street was empty. Unembarrassed, I would cross. Disconcerted at my own obliviousness, I was even more so to see people still waiting for the light to change when no cars were visible. And staring at me. What was going on? Crossing the street at will was so automatic that it took time to work through the meaning of the stares: why is this woman breaking the law, risking her life, and . . . being different? Reflecting on an indifference to time and tolerance of rules obeyed even when illogical prompted questions: not only why do *they*, but why do *we* live and dream and see as we do? What in our history and geography creates such values? What would I accomplish in the seconds I saved—invent electricity, write a Constitution or a poem? A supposed specialist on American culture without a sense of the need or even the possibility of defining such a culture, I now began to experience myself as an "American," always in a hurry, frustrated at the two hours my washing machine took for four pounds of laundry, the two weeks for film developing or dry-cleaning.

The sense of difference and self-consciousness led to the recognition that such responses are in my culturally-implanted computer, part of my default drive. Swimming in our own water, we do not connect our own behavior with the history, experience and psychology of a people or see in ourselves the deep values of our culture. Leave the water, look back, and it becomes a mirror. Where do behaviors and values originate? Forced to challenge our own assumptions about the right and natural ways to go about a subject, we see that we come from one culture and environment. These ideas come from somewhere: a red light is a suggestion, an authority to question, a challenge to our independence and autonomy. One is responsible for one's fate. Time is to save.

U.S. literature and history remind us of the economic motivations for being the first to cross the land—160 free acres to the first to arrive. There were political imperatives for moving—and moving fast. There is folk wisdom on success—"the early bird gets the worm," and an ethic of independence which scorns government regulation of private behavior, raises thinking for oneself to heroic proportions, and praises nonconformist—even rebellious—actions towards community and coercive authoritarian structures, from fishing regulations to parking meters.

The knowledge I had absorbed in my training was being mined anew, a vein of revelation. In this history I found myself. Studying the world from LA in the fifties, history and culture were things that happened "back East" helped by men wearing overcoats and hats. In school, one never got the impression that LA was *the* or even *a* real world. It was a-cultural, a-historic terrain. The reality we knew was not Reality, not Educated Reality. U.S. history was not quite exotica but what Emerson calls the "not me." It had never occurred to me to consider myself part of U.S. history nor to believe that study of it could illuminate a world I knew. Neither did I expect my own experience to provide insights into what I studied. I did not expect education, in this sense, to be relevant to identity or to a sense of possibility.

In my first visit to Finland, 7000 miles of separation connected me to my culture; my own life was a microcosm of U.S. history. Hollywood origins were no longer to be obscured for academic respectability but examined for what they revealed. I was part of American history. Indeed, my family history—immigration from beleaguered island nations in rickety boats, arriving poor and scorned, enduring ethnic strife, leaving New York in the largest internal migration in U.S. history, continual transplantation as outsiders in a succession of "new lives," and a complex gene pool—all this placed me in a historical mainstream that included myth and cultural ethos. The Finns were right: I was an archetypal American, a veritable Case Study.

What a discovery! What I knew beyond my formal training in criticism was relevant to an understanding of my own culture! My mother's indignant "I-am-an-American" when I proudly introduced her as Italian was of a piece with the generational conflicts in Italian-American and other ethnic writers. My map of American cultural studies included the West Coast as well as my Sicilian grandmother from Queens hoarsely shouting "More whiskey!" The personal is historical. The Brooklyn Bridge is part of my past—and LA is part of America's. It is amazing to think back and recognize that neither idea was being taught at the time. Having to come to terms with "water" gave me the freedom and impetus both to discover and recover my cultural identity and more, my mandate as a scholar of American culture.

The consequences for my intellectual life amounted to a paradigm shift. As a teacher of literature, I had asked why an author wrote as he or she did and what that said about the culture. But it was another matter to regard oneself as a product of this culture. Not only had I not been trained to see myself as an authentic American, I was also distanced from the way in which America was known in Helsinki. I arrived in Finland to find a 7-foot Mickey Mouse decal in my apartment. At the Arctic Circle, leading a seminar for business chiefs on the U.S. with my maps and charts and books, reindeer outside, I began with a question of perceptions of the U.S. "Duh-less" said one after another. "Duh-less?" "JR?" "Oh, DALLAS!" Unfortunately, I had not seen it—not untypical of Americans abroad who are frequently appalled, embarrassed and dismayed when they discover the U.S. image abroad— Marlboro Man, Coke, McDonald's, violent movies and so on.

Teaching Melville and Dickinson in the context of the so-called "popular" culture my students and colleagues associated with us produced a tension. A first reaction to being confronted with imported "popular" culture is to dismiss it: this is not American Studies, American culture, or me. I don't watch "Dallas," I don't even own a TV. Doubting I was a representative American in my lack of participation in popular culture, or that any one person could responsibly speak for the nation, the Chair made me accountable, if not for the U.S. at least for explaining it. It made no sense to side-step how the U.S. is manifest abroad. If it is known for Mickey Mouse, could I leave it at that? If I was going to explain the U.S. in any way that was both responsible and credible for people trying and needing to understand us, could I say this and this are American culture—and all the rest you don't have to worry about? Neglecting perceptions as jumping-off points or windows into the culture, refusing to deal with the reality of the ways the U.S. is known abroad not only is wasteful, it creates a credibility gap and a conviction of scholarly irrelevance.

From a scholarly perspective, I began to feel it unnecessary and finally inaccurate to try to separate out the ways the U.S. is known—the real, the *faux*, the *manqué*, the beside-the-point. Faced with the necessity to connect artifacts of American culture present in Helsinki with the political, intellectual and cultural history of the U.S., I soon saw it was not an either/or situation. Each was a product of the American experience. It was not Moby Dick or Mickey Mouse, Dickinson or "Dallas." The same culture, my culture, produced it all, and in my sense of responsibility for making the connections explicit and comprehensible lay an opportunity for thinking about my culture, one in which the concepts of high or low, popular or academic, dismaying or praiseworthy are irrelevant. For myself as well as my students, I had to answer "Why McDonald's?"—how it got there, what it meant. In other words, I had to apply the same methodology to cultural images, icons and institutions that I had been applying to literary texts. Thomas Jefferson's seeing the Constitution as "an expression of the American mind" suggests a rationale for integrating into our study of culture all of its ingredients as valid "expressions" of a pluralistic mind which was diverse and conflicted even in Jefferson's time.

My mandate to represent the U.S. "whole" in all its diversity with the hodge-podge of seemingly unrelated ways in which the culture expresses itself—this brought changes in my own attitudes and identity, deepening my teaching and scholarship. Accounting for a diverse, pluralistic country that would make sense in an international context led to transcending affiliations of discipline, department, college, institution and region. My teaching broadened to an interdisciplinary treatment of topics—environment, ethnicity, and technology—rather than a focus on syntax and theme. The role of landscape is an issue in literature; but different attitudes about nature in Finland threw into relief the variety of American attitudes towards the land (as ally, resource, source of survival and wealth, antagonist to be subdued, conquered, tamed, transformed, exploited or developed, as place of mystery, apprehension, salvation, recreation). People seeing land without a sense of the threat, fear, awe, or guilt, as exploring and settling Europeans portrayed it, or the spirits which America's indigenous peoples saw in it—this informed my effort to explain the history and interconnections of these attitudes and their results in literature, art, economics, politics, public policy and law. The focus shifted from the writer's craft to values and their origins. I found myself using the Western film, musical comedy, Senator Wayne Morse's advocacy for the Wilderness Act, Cole Porter's "Give Me Land," Indian litigation with the U.S. government, Teddy Roosevelt, *New Yorker* cartoons, Remington sculptures, Bierstadt paintings, the Watts Towers, Ansel Adams photography, Ralph Lauren designer jeans, and ads for liquor, cigarettes, and cars, along with Jefferson, Poe, Thoreau, Muir, Alice Walker, Shepard, Stein, and Zane Grey. My "texts": Letters to the Editor, Congressional bills, film, theme parks, public parks.

Not only was my sense of the "text" enlarged but my students were asked to connect, instead of dismiss as irrelevant, surface manifestations of the U.S. with the history, psychology, and experience of the American people. What the Finns brought to the study was a valuable and necessary part of the learning process: the perspective of fish swimming a different stream on the meaning of a culture that seemed incomprehensibly trivial, reckless, chaotic. At an international conference in Finland, a journalist asked, "How does it feel to come from a country with no culture?" After a year in a culture defined by consistency and hegemony, by what is predictable and rests on reliable sameness and shared knowledge and values, I could understand the question.

From her perspective the U.S. did lack visible, unambiguous roots and traditions. How can we be a culture if we are black and white and polylingual and so newly arrived, practicing so many religions—if we can't tell by looking or even talking to them whether people are from Egypt, France, Thailand, Jamaica or merely the U.S.? By all the traditional ways in which culture is understood, how can the U.S. have a culture? Or as one student said, "In Finland, whatever is different makes us less Finnish, but in the U.S., whatever is different makes you more American." My students and I together began to examine the concept of culture itself as we tackled "Mickey Mouse." I bought a TV so that I could relate the U.S. in programs abroad to the cultural history I was teaching.

My scholarship incorporated such changes. The idea that American culture is an oxymoron is held with great conviction, even within the U.S., by specialists on culture as well as by the public at large. On my way to conduct an American Studies seminar in Spain, explaining my work to a flight attendant, she said, "But you can't! If you talk about American culture you are saying Santa Fe is the same as Phoenix or Miami and they aren't." The reasoning: we are too different to be construed or understood as a nation. But such logic can be a defining characteristic, arguing for a national ethos, for putting a unique value on difference and diversity. In fact the flight attendant herself made my case. Describing matter-of-factly her family's seven moves in six states for her father's career, and her own efforts to "get a change" and "see the world" and "find out who I am," she joined the Army ("I wanted a different experience"), got a "fresh start" in the airline industry ("I needed a change and wanted to travel"), and now planned to return to school to learn to be a Washington lobbyist "because I want to make a difference." Her sense of the possibility of moving to change her life for the better, her expectations that she could change her life and location at will, her desire to "make a difference," her assumption that she can always begin again, her own family history—all this bespeaks a mindset formulated in the American historical experience. In the water, she could take her values and assumptions for granted—they were normal, not "cultural."

Any of our stories could make the case for our culture. However unconscious, marginal or alienated in our own world, leaving the water we learn that our identity, behavior, assumptions and ideas come from the larger culture we express—the message in Fulbright's ingenious deep structure.

Thus in Finland I began to be a talking fish. I gave lectures, seminars and institutes on "American" attitudes and values, using the images, icons and institutions by which Americans are known and know themselves. I went from Dickinson to Mickey Mouse and the Marlboro Man and integrated them. Like a symbolic anthropologist or a cultural geographer, I was studying phenomena of the everyday, the ways we live and dream and create and imagine, curious and fascinated by our culture. I was going beyond what I had been trained to know and to value. I was literally an "amateur." Workshops and institutes for scholars, teachers, students, journalists, and others, led to a manuscript in progress: "America As Text: Reading A Culture." Its thesis: if we want to understand a culture "whole," we confront a hodgepodge of seemingly unrelated elements. Just as seeing earth from space reveals its essential wholeness, shape and patterns, looking at the U.S. in a cross-cultural context reveals its inter-connectedness.

Thus as a textual and contextual cultural critic, a "cultural chaoticist," I "read" traditional and non-traditional texts—drama, poetry, fiction, essays, but also graffiti, the language on parking signs, the Vietnam Memorial, 2000 Pennsylvania Avenue, Portland, New Coke, Pizza Hut's policy of free meals to those served too slowly, the Immigration Reform Act, the statistic that we move every four years and go 58 feet further west every day—all as "expressions of the American mind." I show how they interrelate in terms of the experience of the people, how the surface culture reveals the deep structure of values and the experience which shapes them, how the Constitution embodies ideas of an immigrant, diverse, insecure and fragmented culture, as a resolution to the on-going value-drama of New Coke, baseball, Emerson, Stevie Wonder, supermarkets and campaign rhetoric. There is a pattern of "value clusters," simultaneously interactive, paradoxically opposed strains that constitute our culture and characterize "the expressions of the American mind": the tension between new and old, change and tradition, diversity and conformity, the individual and the community—all these tensions fuel the culture and keep it dynamic.

Returning home after my initial thirteen months abroad in 1983, I could not give up the challenges and stimulation of interdisciplinary interaction or the comparative approach to cultural studies. I wanted to make the U.S., *my* U.S., continually whole and new and fresh, raising new questions and keeping complacency at bay. I sought a way for students to bring to their studies the advantages of overseas students, the same relevance of their own experience. Former Fulbrighters helped create an interdisciplinary American cultural studies degree program for the University of Oregon, involving thirteen departments and seven professional schools. Both degree requirements and curriculum for the one-year team-taught core course came out of my Fulbright teaching. I used my Fulbright experience to fight for the logic of this program ("Why do we need to study America," a student asked me, "when we live here?"). Once begun, the program seemed irresistible to a wide constituency:

traditional undergraduates, re-entry students, continuing education students, international students in law, education, business, liberal arts, journalism, and health sciences, and subsequently, foreign educators and community members for continuing education and in-service programs. Faculty went into dormitories to lecture on favorite research topics that did not fit into their departments (the Apple Pie Seminars), and into the community to seniors, high schools, service organizations. Learning about the U.S. was so strange that it was media news. The program was good for the university and state. But my motivation was also selfish—creating faculty development and outreach programs to support the program was a way to foster a challenging interdisciplinary, international, comparative and cross-cultural environment I now could not live without.

I became the first director of this program in 1984. At home and abroad I worked on American Studies, interdisciplinary programs and international education. Lessons from the Arctic became keynote speeches and seminars for before-breakfast business groups, high schools, library groups, educators, service organizations, journalists, patrons, civic leaders, and professionals on U.S. culture in colleges and universities. I became an entrepreneur, designing programs for international educators as well as participating in State Department projects overseas. In 1986 I became the "American Studies Scholar in Residence" for the U.S. Information Agency, "Telling America's Story to the World." This unique position was a new kind of Fulbright, at-large style. I became a tour guide for diplomats and educational leaders of "the U.S. as a living text"—its monuments, architecture, alleys, porches, and everything in between. I wrote, lectured and consulted on American Studies as conceived and practiced here and worldwide. Daily, I tackled "Who we are and why." I went to North Africa, East and West Europe, Southeast Asia, as well as throughout the U.S. I met representatives of virtually every nation on the globe to discuss education and culture.

Fulbright transformed me first into an American and then into an advocate for American Studies, interdisciplinary studies, international education, the Fulbright Program, and higher education on a national and international level—from a respectable scholar of distinguished writers to a professor of Mickey Mouse. It transformed my family. I enrolled my 6-year-old son in Washington's International School; at the end of the school day he would put on a tie for embassy events. My husband became an international lawyer and joined me in Washington. Every day we passed the Capitol, the Smithsonian, the Jefferson and Lincoln Memorials, Watergate. I spoke at the Library of Congress. By now my leave from Oregon was going on three years and I faced a crisis. I gave up tenure and put my university life on hold to become a full-time Washington expert on "water." By now I have spoken to over nine thousand people interested in the fish's perspective.

When I consider my work now with institutions and governments in the U.S. and worldwide, often officially representing the U.S., I think of my Sicilian grandmother not knowing English, baffled at "the Americans." My parents blame Fulbright, as they should. And I, lecturing during a monsoon in Bangkok where more people were dying from snake bites than drowning, or giving a slide lecture with no slides at 11 PM in Jogjakarta, or being put in plaster in a hospital in Budapest so that I can resume my seminar on "Ethnicity and American Culture" the next morning, wondering how I got into these sitations—in these times I think of Fulbright, too.

Fulbright gave me gills. I could no longer live only in water. I left the water again and again. And then back for a recharge of the original Fulbright, to immerse myself again in difference, shake out my theories and the complacencies developed in the previous decade, to become new again and see who I was. In 1991 I returned to the University of Helsinki to take what was now the Fulbright Senior Distinguished Lectureship, the Bicentennial Chair in American Studies. My topic: "Educating for the 21st Century: The American Challenge," the logic and mandate for international, cross-cultural, and multicultural education in an increasingly diverse society—and the dire consequences of educating a people to believe that education does not serve reality.

Now I was a deliberate tourist, literally and intellectually. A tourist among disciplines and fields, no "native" or even "naturalized" cultural geographer, anthropologist, political scientist, nor historian, sociologist nor linguist, I had been freed to wander among political theory, anthropology, philosophy, sociology, history, linguistics, landscape architecture, chaos theory, cultural geography, and everything in between. One reward of such wandering is the exposure to truly original thinking in works which stretch and defy categories and engage in irresistible disciplinary trespassing. Not taking the disciplinary water for granted, not knowing "what everyone knows" in each discipline, region or institution, I am free to ask questions. I can behave as a tourist— curious, critical, comparative, enthusiastic; and my sojourns among and between fields and cultures alter and constantly correct my vision.

In other words, I have tried to remain a full-time Fulbrighter and to act on what that means. Fulbright institutionalizes disruption, the decision to have a new experience, to leave the water, to go to the woods to live deliberately. By definition, one has to keep moving. Thoreau left his woods after two years: "I have other lives to live." I suppose my answer is that I continue to try to destabilize what I know, to not know things, to be the "fool." We go Fulbrighting to be as wise as Emily Dickinson's cosmic, divine Clown:

> A little madness in the Spring
> Is wholesome even for the King,
> But God be with the Clown—
> Who ponders this tremendous scene—
> This whole Experiment of Green—
> As if it were his own!

Once out of water, with each new pair of eyes experiencing them for the first time, ancient worlds seem new, an experiment. They are worlds we continually make new with attitudes of openness, worlds of possibility Emerson called "paradise" for the "fool" who travels. So I thank Senator Fulbright for his vision of the new, newer, renewed and constantly renewing life that exchange and change make in our lives, a continuing birth-day. As e.e. cummings said, "This is the birthday of life, and love/And the gay great happening illimitly earth." Cummings, who had lived abroad, was being literal. The earth does "happen." Our attitude towards the new and unknown gives us access to a sense of extraordinary reality. We tend to forget that the earth moves, and we with it. The trick is to be aware of such travel and what it brings—stars and miracles like morning sun.

Fulbright begins with travel, but it is a journey we soon learn has no destination other than departures. D.H. Lawrence was probably right, when he said we hate new experience: it is arduous to live in a constant state of unsettling. But we need an outside perspective and an open, humble mind if we are to retain a sense of hope. If Prufrock had gone on a Fulbright, I suspect he would not have been depressed, he would not have assumed he already knew it all. He would not have been so foolish as to think he was not traveling and could not hear the mermaids singing.

Dr. Johnson, who has taught at Kansas, Illinois State, Cleveland State, Howard, and Georgetown universities and has published extensively both scholarship and more general writing, is director of publications for Science Applications International in Virginia. She is unique in this volume in writing not as a Fulbrighter but as an accompanying spouse and mother of three sons. Her attention to the total experience of the family's year in the world's northernmost university ranges from the effects of darkness through the schooling of her sons to the search for her forbears and the problems of five people returning to their native soil transformed by an experience of otherness. Yet in this poetic telling of a year in the life of a family, the same themes recur—anti-American attitudes, the distortions of a selective media, disorientation, and self-discovery.

26

CIRCLE OF LIGHT: A YEAR IN ARCTIC NORWAY

Abby Arthur Johnson

"Where?" people still ask when we say that we spent the 1983-84 academic year in Tromsø, Norway, 215 miles above the Arctic Circle. "Why?" they continue, when we explain that the location is so far north that the sun remains hidden below the horizon for two months in the winter. One of Ron's colleagues in the History Department at Georgetown University even remarked, "Why did you ever choose such a desolate site for a Fulbright experience?"

"Well," we invariably reply, "Tromsø is a wonderful place." The University of Tromsø, where Ron was a Fulbright lecturer in American history, is distinguished not simply because it is the northernmost university in the world. The school, which has a student body of about 2,400, has an international reputation in such areas as Lappish studies and Arctic biology. Tromsø, an island city of approximately 45,000 people, is rich in human history, replete with evidence of Stone Age communities and relics from the years when Vikings dominated the region and early Lapp groups moved across the territory. More recent history features Roald Amundsen, who launched his polar expeditions from this "Gateway to the Arctic."

With our three sons (then thirteen, nine, and six years), we believe our experience in Tromsø was unique in large part because it was sponsored by the Fulbright Program. We were expected to live on the economy and in the community, not in some separate American compound. The Tromsø community encompassed Ron's colleagues, who had invited us to the university and, as their many kindnesses showed, felt a responsibility for our professional and personal well-being. The community also extended to our neighborhood in the newer part of town, where we lived with several Norwegian families in a four-story apartment building. Eager to extend hospitality, our neighbors took us blueberry picking, helped us identify bargains in the local *matsenter* (grocery store), and listened to our Norwegian, providing we would listen to their English. We felt free in our dealings with both neighbors and colleagues. As the information provided by the Fulbright program made clear, Ron was not expected to be a spokesperson for the U.S., although we certainly understood that our conduct in this new environment reflected on our home institutions, as well as on America in general. In sum, we remember our Fulbright year as an extraordinary opportunity for exploring Arctic culture and for rethinking our definitions of life.

It was an old land to which we went. After a summer of increasingly frantic preparations, we flew from the Baltimore-Washington International Airport in July 1983. Our first destination was Göteborg, Sweden, where we had a rendezvous with an old friend—our 1974 Volkswagen station wagon, which we had shipped out of Baltimore a month earlier. The car had its drawbacks: it had already logged 128,000 miles, leaked in the rain, and sometimes stalled unexpectedly. We had opted against the purchase of a new car for persuasive considerations—the value of our stipend, about 40 percent of our joint income in the States; the economy in Tromsø, which Arthur Frommer described as "a real boomtown . . . with prices comparable to those of Alaska in the gold rush days"; and the uncertainty of driving conditions in Arctic Norway, where tire studs were required from October to May.

Retrieving our car, we headed toward Telemark in southern Norway, where we wanted to scratch after family roots. The serendipitous discovery there of a family line reaching back into the fourteenth century and perhaps earlier underscored our sense of a cultural stability in Norway that was not possible in the U.S. This discovery provided a framework for our entire year—a perspective for drawing ongoing cultural comparisons. Like most Americans, I had known little about my Old World origins, other than that my ancestors were Norwegian or Swedish. Sometime in the second half of the nineteenth century, my maternal great-grandmother Gunhilda Karine Larson had left Norway for the States with her Swedish husband, Carl Johan Anderson. They eventually homesteaded on 160 acres in Brule County, South Dakota, where they lived out their lives, raising seven children.

On the eve of our departure for Norway, I received a letter from my aunt Erma Anderson that spoke, with some memorable phrasing, to Gunhilda's Norwegian past: "There is a city named Drangedal in the township of Drangedal, in Telemark." The letter, the result of dogged genealogical research on her part, gave us some of the old family and place names we needed to trace Gunhilda's past.

On August 9, we drove into Drangedal. We could do nothing to announce our arrival, for we did not have the names of any living relations and we had no command of Norwegian, only some scraps of grammar. Using a 1935 map purchased in a local bookstore, we proceeded to track down families with the old names Moen and Vraalstad. The initial results were discouraging. At the first farmhouse, an elderly woman shut her door on my opening salvos constructed from terms looked up in our Berlitz English-Norwegian dictionary. With dogs baying at several windows, she kept muttering, "Jeg forstår ikke" (I do not understand). At the next house, we enjoyed a pot of coffee in silence with a smiling couple who had replied to my "Jeg ikke snakker norsk" (I do not speak Norwegian) with "Vi ikke snakker engelsk" (We do not speak English).

In the early afternoon, we struck gold. With the help of a young translator, found at yet another farmhouse down the road, we met fourth cousins. One of them was a local genealogist who had a family tree reaching back to the seventeenth century and a valley history—*Drangedal med Tørdal* (728 pages)—that later made it possible to trace the clan into the fourteenth century. From a section of this history entitled "Dei som er reist til Amerika føre 1885" (Those who emigrated to America before 1885), we learned that Gunhilda, her brother Halvor, and her husband Carl had been among twenty-three emigrants from Drangedal in 1867.

These newly-discovered cousins told us old stories about the family; showed us fading photographs and other artifacts, including a rifle my great-great grandfather Lars had used in an 1812 skirmish against the Swedes; took us on a tour of the valley, pointing out farms that had been in the family for generations; and led us to the site of the home where Gunhilda had been born. The day came to a resounding conclusion as Steinar Vraalstad, a charismatic farmer in his eighties, drew his arms about us and exclaimed, "Samme blod! Samme blod!" (Same blood).

The excursion to Drangedal had large meaning for us. The first members of the family to return to the valley, we had the privilege of breaking the silence of more than a century. We discovered a continuity there that exceeded all expectations, accustomed as we were to urban mobility and change. The experience primed me, in particular, to look for cultural continuity elsewhere in this old land. Upon reaching Tromsø in mid-August and then in the following months, I measured my evolving perceptions of life back home against the cultural coherence I saw from our first days in Norway.

We were already moving into the dark. After a seven-day drive north, which included several difficult ascents of rugged mountain ranges, we arrived in Tromsø on August 16. We had already got our feet wet in this old land, our car having leaked rain throughout the trip. It took much longer to feel at ease in our new environs, which initially seemed all mountains and water. By early spring, we would have a fuller picture of the larger environment and had found some metaphors. Watching the sun climb over the mountains, I saw the Arctic cycle of darkness and light as a parallel to our own experiences. Autumn, the period of the setting sun, was a time of transition for us, a search for redefinitions and new interpretations of several subjects, including day/night and life back home.

We were intrigued all fall with the widely divergent interpretations of the two-month *mørketida* (dark time), which began in Tromsø on November 24. Some people, particularly native north Norwegians, claimed that the long night inspired their creativity. Others, especially those from southern Norway, said that the season made them both psychologically and physically sick. In similar manner, some were prone to see light and others dark during the approximately two-hour period at midday, when reflections from the distant sun could color the sky over Tromsø and create a type of twilight.

Musing over differing understandings of daylight and dark, we had questions about another topic we had thought solid—direction. Having grown up in Minneapolis, I had long considered myself a northerner. This label was challenged as we crossed the moonlike landscape in Norway at 60° 32´ north (the parallel demarcating the Arctic Circle), as we stood one fine late summer afternoon on the shores of the beautiful Lyngen Fjord and looked past snowy mountains toward the Arctic Sea, and as we compared Tromsø temperatures with the weather back home. On August 24, for example, our sons walked off to their first day at the local public schools dressed in winter jackets, woolen hats, and rain boots. The temperature topped 37° F. According to the *International Herald Tribune*, the recorded highs for American cities on the same day included 73° F for Anchorage, 102° F for Chicago, 86° F. for

Minneapolis, and 97° F for Washington, DC. Suddenly, North America seemed a rather southern place.

Language was an additional subject for speculation. Early on, we had thought of our new context as a vast stage where we could observe and record our sons' progress in language acquisition at an accelerated rate. As we quickly discovered in Tromsø, the actual learning process differed considerably from what we had expected. Our language enterprise began on an uncertain note. "Tromsø Information for Fulbrighters," a document provided by the U.S. Educational Foundation in Norway, informed us that there were no English or American schools in the Tromsø area and that the children of Fulbrighters had all attended the local public schools. "Children who speak no Norwegian should expect," the document added, "to have some problems the first few months. After that, experience indicates that on the whole, things work out quite well." The relaxed tone of the statement was reassuring. We did wonder over the casual allusion to "some problems" and "on the whole."

Our sons, who had learned no Norwegian before leaving the States, did indeed have some linguistic misadventures. Their initial problems were perhaps best conveyed by our oldest son Adam (thirteen years). Coming straight home from the first day of classes, he declared: "I didn't understand anything, and I have no friends there."

Nevertheless, "things [did] work out quite well," in part because of a few hours of language instruction each week at school and especially because of long periods spent with other children on various playgrounds, where they picked up the Tromsø dialect. Contrary to our previous thinking, Adam gained facility in the language more quickly than Alex (nine years) and Karl (six years). While his brothers reached a reasonable proficiency by the turn of the year, Adam was speaking Norwegian all day at school by mid-November. His teachers announced then that he would have to participate in the regular curriculum and take examinations in Norwegian with the other students.

Adam, we felt, had no greater language capabilities than his brothers. One reason for his rapid progress had to be his classmates, who had studied English in school for three years and could meet him halfway. Another was his age. As a young teenager, he was more susceptible than his brothers to social pressures and wanted to conform to the ways of his peers, which meant that he had to learn their language.

The parents were on a different language track from the sons and even from each other. We were both enrolled in the two-semester, four-hour per week Norwegian course offered by the University of Tromsø free of charge to associated faculty and researchers. Ron, however, taught in English and spent most of his days speaking English.

Assigned to the University's Institute of Language and Linguistics, he gave the standard course in American civilization, as well as offerings in American history since 1945 and African-American history and culture, the latter of which drew the most student interest. The students wanted to hear him talk in American English and to challenge his interpretations of U.S. race relations, politics, and international policies. They would gather around him after class for further conversation. After the topic had been aired, however, they usually shifted unconsciously to Norwegian, where Ron could not follow.

On a number of occasions, I also fell silent before Norwegian, although I prepared diligently for our language class, worked my way patiently through the local newspaper *Nordlys* (Northern Lights), and tried out my new words regularly on shopkeepers and neighbors. Enthusiastic over my progress, which far surpassed my learning rate during years of German and French language study back home, I eagerly went at first to school meetings, political rallies, even occasional plays, all staged in Norwegian. On September 15, for instance, I sat through a 1.5-hour lecture in Norwegian on reading problems associated with the vowels, ø, and å. I grasped not a word and determined to stay clear of such sessions until I had progressed further in the language.

For all of us, the experience of language that autumn was novel without question. Our immersion in Norwegian was stimulating and exciting but also at times daunting, especially for Ron and me. Back in the States, a person would never have been expected to know much about another language after a few months of study. In Norway, our language sensibilities and expectations were heightened. In addition, we were humbled by the language proficiencies of our new friends, several of whom spoke not only English, but French, German, and perhaps Italian. To them, languages were a hobby, something to be picked up during the summer holidays. In terms of language, and despite the considerable progress we were making, we felt monolingual and very American.

At the same time, we were struggling with definitions of "American." We found ourselves preoccupied with social comparisons. During our early months in Tromsø, the culture we saw locally and glimpsed on a broader level appeared remarkably cohesive on a range of measures, from religious and cultural traditions to social programs. While many of the churches were nearly empty on Sunday mornings, ninety-five percent of Norwegians belonged to the Evangelical Lutheran state church, supporting it with their taxes and returning to local parishes for major passages: baptisms, confirmations, marriages, and funerals. While novelists Bjørnstjerne Bjørnson, Knut Hamsun, and Sigrid

Undset explored a variety of differing subjects and themes, their work seemed unified on several scores, including a common preoccupation with light and dark. Norwegians were also unified by a health and social services network that cost a sizable price in taxes but that provided them with generous protection from cradle to grave.

The more stable and orderly Norway looked, the less coherent the U.S. appeared. The diversity that seemed the strength of America when we were in the States appeared fragmentary, even confusing, from overseas. I began to have trouble identifying American culture, a term that had not seemed so difficult back in the States. It was obvious that we in the States share economic, political, and judicial systems. It was just as clear that we share the work of notable authors, artists, and musicians. The problem was in identifying a common culture that could incorporate, for example, the different experiences of F. Scott Fitzgerald, Zora Neale Hurston, and Chaim Potok. Was there anything, I thought, more culturally powerful in the States than popular culture, exemplified by fast-food restaurants, hit movies and songs, and big television events like the Superbowl?

I also became critical of the American work ethic, which was so much a part of my own nature. New friends, whose work day ended in mid-afternoon, seemed surprised over my office hours as a writer-editor in metropolitan Washington. By the time I would leave my office in the States, at 6:30 or 7 PM, most Norwegians had not only consumed but digested their dinners and were well into the delights of the evening.

Two events in autumn 1983 particularly tested our cultural comparisons and search for new definitions. The first was a visit the U.S. Ambassador to Norway made to Tromsø during late September. We met the Ambassador briefly at a reception held in his honor by the U.S. Information Office in Tromsø. The meeting was not remarkable in any way. We certainly, then, did not expect the ensuing uproar.

The Ambassador had been invited to the high school in neighboring Tromsdalen on September 21 with the expectation that he would discuss U.S. relations with Central America, especially Nicaragua. Instead he used the occasion to praise the U.S. and Norway as bulwarks of freedom. He also asked his audience, which consisted not only of students and teachers but also a sizable number of area residents, to try to understand the U.S. The September 22 issue of *Nordlys* introduced its coverage of the event with the following quotation from the Ambassador's remarks: "All you here with your beautiful white skin, you are one community. Try to understand the U.S.A., which is such a mixture of peoples." The headline ran: "You have beautiful and white skin, try to understand the U.S.A." Another headline in the same issue went: "Pleased that the students had fine, white skin." Before these and other comments appeared in the press, we heard them repeated by angry neighbors who had attended the presentation.

The speech fueled a controversy over race relations in the States and U.S. foreign policy in Central America that continued for weeks. We were not comfortable with the reverberations, although no one appeared to connect us with any statements made on September 21. A teacher at the local elementary school spoke to the heart of the larger problem, however, when she said that the incident reinforced stereotypes some Norwegians had of Americans as condescending, bigoted, insensitive.

Another challenging event for us that autumn was a televised program on the Ku Klux Klan aired by the *Norsk rikskringkasting* (NRK), the Norwegian Broadcasting System. The focus was on the 1979 rally of the Communist Workers Party in Greensboro, North Carolina, broken up as Klan onlookers shot and killed five Party members. The program highlighted the subsequent court proceedings and the finding that the indicted Klan members were innocent.

Because NRK provided only one television channel, anyone watching TV that evening saw the program. The audience included a sizable percentage of Ron's students, who came to class the next day with many questions. A number of the most vocal students criticized the U.S. for gross inequities they saw in its judicial and social systems. They did not understand how the Ku Klux Klan had managed to survive for so long. They did not, moreover, understand race relations in the States. They wanted quick and simple answers which, of course, were difficult to formulate. Ron drew upon resources and analyses he had gained over the years. The explanations, which involved reexamination of his customary approaches to American history, were more difficult in this new context than they had been in the States. The Norwegian students of American history often expected more from the U.S. than did American students, who had grown accustomed to the nation's vulnerabilities. Lecturing in this different environment, Ron could understand and share the disappointment many of his students felt.

As the long polar night closed over Tromsø, we found ourselves pondering the basics—light and dark, the North, language, and culture, both American and Norwegian. Needing more time to think, we welcomed the start of *mørketida*.

By now our life was lived under the moon. *Nordlys* announced the beginning of *mørketida* on November 23 with a photograph of two people standing under a streetlight, lifting an umbrella against the dark and snow. Translated from Norwegian, like the other passages in this article quoted from

Nordlys, the caption read: "On the Way Into the Dark Time." Replete with diverse literal and metaphorical meanings, the two-month winter night is surely the most challenging season of the Arctic calendar.

On the positive side, *mørketida* is a time for cooperation and creativity. Erling Nilsen, director of the Tromsø city museum Skansen, told me about the social significance of the winter night. He sensed community most then, saying that people have historically crossed class lines and other barriers to help each other through this difficult period. In addition, he described the cultural significance of the period. During winter, "we developed our culture," wrote poems, gave concerts, and staged plays. Among the novelists who wrote about the polar night was Cora Sandel (1880-1974), who spent eight years of her youth in Tromsø. In *Alberta and Jacob* (1926), she described the unique blend of colors possible from reflected light in the southern skies: "to see the miracle accomplished; to see the glow turn blood-red and then fade, the mountains darken against a green sky, the moon be lit."

Sandel concentrated, however, on the pain and suffering more frequently associated with *mørketida*. The extended dark forces people indoors, where they must confront their friends, their families, and themselves. Too often, the darkness of the season deepens physical and psychological disorders. The most common complaints involve sleeping problems, usually an insomnia probably attributable to hormonal imbalances brought on by the absence of sunlight. Other difficulties include depression and various physical ailments, such as arthritis. "You believe perhaps that this is an exaggeration, but each year I fear that the dark time shall take my life," seventy-two-year-old Magnus Larsen said in a comment repeated in *Nordlys*. Small wonder that Henrik Ibsen associated the winter darkness with "the old tragedy" in *The Lady from the Sea* (1888).

The people of Tromsø use various approaches to work their way through the dark time. Some fly the direct route to the Canary Islands, or they frequent the local sun tanning centers, which totaled at least twelve in 1983-84. "Don't be pale!" the tanning parlors admonished in their advertisements. Graphic images of their success were sightings of deeply tanned individuals standing under streetlights against mounds of snow—a record-breaking fifty-two inches by Christmas. Mostly, however, the citizenry depend on the old celebrations, the traditional festivities of Advent, Christmas, and the New Year. The Christmas Gospel, John 1:1-14, was particularly meaningful against the backdrop of *mørketida*: "The Light shines in the darkness and the darkness did not overcome it."

As for our family, we were too new to the area to share in any of the old *mørketida* complaints. We were fascinated, instead, by the drama of life lived without any sunlight and by the special beauty of the dark time—the aurora borealis shifting across the sky in a blend of rich colors, a full moon circling above Tromsø twenty-four hours a day at Christmas, and much more. We were moved as well by occasional comments that reverberated far beyond the actual words. Erling Nilsen, for example, remarked that people thought the sun would return, they surely hoped it would, but they could never be certain. Nils Knutsen, instructor in Norwegian literature at the University of Tromsø, liked to say that *mørketida*, not the period of the midnight sun, is "the exotic time."

Mostly, we were grateful for the opportunity to concentrate on the larger resonances associated with the long night. We did not gain any sharper definitions of American culture, probably because we were so overwhelmed by the season. We did, however, realize as never before the importance of community, including family, during the dark times of life.

Then the sun returned. With a four-minute showing on January 21, known as soldag (sun day), the sun reappears over Tromsø, shattering the power of the winter darkness. The citizenry herald the new day with traditional foods, including *berlinerboller* (special donuts filled with jelly) and hot chocolate, and with festive gatherings and songs. The first grade class at the local elementary school kept singing a simple refrain at their 1984 celebrations: "Sun out/ Sun in/ Sun in the heart/ Sun in the mind/ Sun, only sun." The crowd that assembled at the city museum remembered the old Tromsø songs, which described an awakening "in the sun from Skansen to Sommerlyst," or from the lowest to the highest elevations in town. Meanwhile, a number of organizations chose sun queens, staged *soldag* bazaars, and gave concerts of seasonal music.

People rejoiced, for their former uncertainties, their *mørketida* complaints, evaporated in the new day. *Soldag* signaled a return of confidence, singularly expressed by the resounding conclusion to Halvdan Sivertsen's song "North of the Polar Circle": "We are strong and can take whatever comes when it comes/ We have the sun and soon it is summer."

The "soon" was appropriate, for the sun quickly gained ascendancy over Tromsø. The two-month period of the midnight sun, the flip side of the long winter night, began on May 17.

Susceptible to the rhythms and moods of the prevailing culture, our family felt renewed strength and confidence with the return of the sun. Like so many others in the far North, we embarked upon a more active period. We traveled, for example, to the storied places we had heard about during *mørketida*: the frozen desert of Svalbard (Spitsbergen Islands), last stop before the North Pole; the tundra surrounding Kautokeino, where the Laplanders graze their reindeer;

the fishing villages of the Lofoten Islands, famed since the Middle Ages for their rich catches of codfish each spring. We also spent long hours skiing the limitless cross-country trails in the area's mountains.

In addition, of course, we continued with our regular school and work schedules. As one of only two Fulbrighters in north Norway, Ron was asked to speak at a number of schools in the region, one of which was historic Kongsbakken high school in Tromsø. During early March, he met fourteen one-hour classes, addressing topics selected by the students and teachers. Nine of the topics centered on the contemporary experience of minorities, especially African Americans, in the U.S. Representative titles, as provided by the classes, included "Racism and Ku Klux Klan Activities" and "Blacks after Martin Luther King, Jr." From the titles, and from in-class discussions at the university in the autumn, Ron knew the questions that would be asked and was ready with answers.

He began each class with a fifteen-minute statement on the unique diversity of American culture, focusing on the experiences of African Americans and the history of the Civil Rights movement. In the ensuing discussion, students invariably recalled the televised program on the Greensboro killings aired in the fall and suggested that black-white relations had not really improved in the States since Martin Luther King's 1963 march on Washington. Acknowledging the tragedy at Greensboro and the ongoing challenges concerning race and poverty in the States, Ron emphasized the progress made, including the end of legal segregation in the South and the growing number of black students in higher education. As evidence of a more equal distribution of income and opportunity, he cited the increasing expansion of the black middle class. Ron left Kongsbakken thinking that one of his larger responsibilities as a Fulbrighter was to respond to the ongoing questions triggered by the televised images of Klansmen shooting demonstrators.

Focusing on their immediate surroundings, our sons did not wrestle with such questions. As the months rolled on, they became increasingly Norwegian. They spoke in the Tromsø dialect, making jokes with their peers concerning the "sissy" Norwegian spoken in Oslo. They could hear the foreign accent in our Norwegian, which had progressed substantially since the preceding fall. Occasionally, they urged Ron and me not to speak in Norwegian, or even in English, when we were with them in public places. I had sudden insight into the linguistic experiences of immigrants to the U.S., of great-grandparents Gunhilda and Carl speaking a broken English, surrounded by their glib children.

Watching our sons standing in clusters of blonde boys on the playground or in the grocery store, we thought they looked and sounded much like their friends. They had the same haircuts, wore the same style of tennis shoes, listened to the same music, watched the same television programs. We could see them shifting their expectations to this new context and thought that in another year, were we to stay on in Tromsø, they would have a distinctly Norwegian identity.

Well before the end of our year in Tromsø, we recognized that Norwegian society has its own cracks and strains, exemplified by the sometimes difficult relations between the predominant culture and differing groups, including foreign workers and the country's 30,000 Laplanders. Nevertheless, it has a continuity from the local to the national level that cannot be found and is probably not possible in the States, given our diverse cultural groupings. We saw a clear example of this cultural cohesion in Norwegian television, which had been one of our social yardsticks throughout the year.

Compared to commercial networks in the States, the Norwegian Broadcasting System had a larger purpose and scope. As explained in a *Nordlys* editorial during the spring, the major goal was "to secure our own culture and identity against a supposedly much stronger foreign influence from TV transmission by satellite." Focusing on this end, NRK showed a substantial number of programs made at home and focusing on Norway: interviews with fishermen, poets, and politicians; documentaries on reindeer herding in Norwegian Lapland; portraits of life in particular Norwegian *fylker*, or counties. Yet the programming was not provincial. A small country in a large world, Norway cannot afford to be isolated. NRK accordingly aired films from around the globe, including North Korea, China, and the former Eastern bloc countries.

NRK also broadcast "Dynasty," one of the big hits of the 1983-84 season. During the fifteen minutes preceding the show, the playground outside our apartment building emptied as people called out the hour from their balconies. During the autumn, "Dynasty" ran at prime time: around 10 PM on Saturday. In the spring, it was relocated to start between 9 PM and 10 PM on Wednesday, seemingly as NRK officials searched for Saturday programming more consistent with their objectives. The rescheduling, however, brought protests from clergy, who had trouble attracting parishioners to meetings on Wednesday nights, and with the owners of movie theaters, who reported a thirty-percent drop in attendance during "Dynasty." In late spring, NRK officials, despite the popularity of the series, canceled the show altogether.

NRK programming could anger the general public, as with the decisions concerning "Dynasty," and it could fan controversy, as with the film on the shootings in Greensboro. In addition, the shows were sometimes monotonous, particularly the extended discussions over local political issues. On the whole, however, the one Norwegian channel was informative, entertaining, and cosmopolitan—decidedly superior in quality to the standard fare of the many commercial stations in the States. Moreover, Norwegian television was a unifying force in the larger culture, a statement that could not be made about TV in the U.S.

Our opinions of Norwegian and American television paralleled several conclusions we had come to concerning Norway and the States. Life in Norway seemed coherent, stable, safe compared to life back home. During late spring, as the sun circled over the city day and night, we all declared that we could have spent much more time in Tromsø, that one year, after all, was much too short. We could well understand our nine-year-old son Alex, who announced in the spring that he wanted to be a Norwegian citizen.

At the same time, we began to devour news from the U.S. We snatched up *Time* magazine as soon as it became available at the university. We bought the *International Herald Tribune*, at a pricey $1.50 per issue, nearly every other day. We could not wait for results from the 1984 presidential primaries. Astounded over Gary Hart's early victories, we speculated, along with our friends and neighbors, over the chances of "native son" Walter Mondale. In the process, we were surprised to find ourselves missing the excitement, the chaos, the brawl that often comes with life in the U.S.

It was time to go home. We returned to the U.S. on July 31, exactly one year after our departure for Norway. Since that time, we have had ample opportunity to reflect on the enormous difference a well-placed year makes.

At home in northern Virginia, we began fielding telephone calls and could not, at first, recognize the deep, manly voices of Adam's friends, then fourteen years. We read mail collected for us by our renters, who had left about three hours before our return, and were shocked by news of a good friend's death, on the very day we had left Tromsø. We went to our neighborhood swimming pool and saw babies who had not been conceived when we left for Norway. We learned of marriages, divorces, promotions, disappointments, serious illnesses. I went to my office in an area of northern Virginia experiencing explosive commercial development and lost my way among the new buildings, roads, and stop signs.

Feeling almost disoriented by the change we saw everywhere, we recognized that we too had changed. The most vivid example was Karl, who was placed at the start of the 1984-85 school year in a second-grade class with a significant number of good readers. In the opening days of the term, the teacher was surprised to hear him reading English as if it were Norwegian, saying "ēs" for "is" and "hōōs" for "house," for example. At her recommendation, he was transferred for the year to a class of students working with

English as a second language. The new class, consisting largely of children from immigrant families, was reading well below grade level and was not expected to manage even the easiest second-grade readers by the end of the school year. Karl caught up in reading with his peers in other classes by late winter, but only because we got permission from the instructor to tutor him at home.

In terms of the standard American school curriculum, our sons had fallen behind the other students in certain subjects, Karl in English and Alex and Adam in mathematics. But the gains far surpassed the setbacks, which were only temporary anyway. Our sons' eyes had been opened to the world beyond our borders and they could never, we felt certain, be the same again.

Ron and I also experienced shifts in perception, beginning with very basic matters like sunlight and darkness. Thinking about the light imagery common to much Scandinavian literature, I recalled a characterization in Knut Hamsun's *Pan* (1894) of a 70-year-old Lapp blind since the age of twelve. With an optimism shaped by life in the North, this man lives with the expectation that one day he will see the sight he misses most: "He sat . . . in front of the fire, full of hope that in a few years he would be able to see the sun." We had gone to the Arctic, lived through a two-month winter night, and returned with an unexpected benefit—a capacity to appreciate the sun.

In addition, Ron and I experienced a type of cultural reawakening. Arriving in Tromsø, wet feet and all, we had a relatively secure sense of American culture and of ourselves as Americans. As the autumn sun set over the city and then during the dark time, we went through a period of cultural introspection and critique, prompted by the unity we saw in Norwegian culture and by questions concerning American culture that emerged during the year. As the daylight increased, we felt a renewed sense of our own identity as Americans and could better understand, appreciate, and explain the diversity basic to American culture.

Back in the States, we were poised for the types of discussion, particularly the debates over definitions of American culture, that have been prominent in academic circles throughout the 1980s and into the 1990s. Having been sensitized once again to America's multicultural historical development, we readily joined the critique of the traditional Anglo-centric canon—that the old literary, historical, and socio-cultural standards cannot represent the larger whole. To colleagues wondering about the value of his Arctic experience, Ron explained in part that the year in Norway caused him "to look more objectively at U.S. culture and to rethink the essential dimensions of American society." He came away from this experience emphasizing the need for a "much more relevant, multicultural perspective of ourselves as a people." In the following years, as Director of American Studies at Georgetown University, he has initiated curriculum changes that substantially modify the old canon. One such change was the establishment in 1985 of a required American Studies course that explores the lives of Native Americans, African Americans, and women in the context of an increasingly diverse cultural framework.

As for me, I too saw the changes wrought by our year and the need for a refined, much more inclusive approach to American culture. We had traveled to the top of the world to learn about another way of life. In the process, we developed a better understanding of the U.S., as well as of ourselves. Given this gain and all the rest, our Fulbright year was an unqualified success. "Tromsø," we will continue to say, "is a wonderful place."

The author is a neuropsychologist at the Great Ormond Street Hospital for Sick Children in London. She tells a tale of a young British maverick who ends up in a new American medical school lost in the cornfields of Ohio, in a place appropriately—or symbolically—called Rootstown. What she learned there, as she tells us, is still being sorted out; but it will be clear to readers who entertain stereotypes of the British character that Deborah Christie is not one's everyday Brit. Among themes that emerge from her essay, she articulates the notion of a binational Fulbright personality, an idea that can easily be illustrated elsewhere in this volume. And she tells of the identity search that began in Ohio. As of the present writing, Dr. Christie is Chair of the British Fulbright Scholars Association.

27

NOTES FROM ROOTSTOWN

Deborah Christie

Like the blind men who touched the elephant, each of us can only describe part of the whole. But without polling some 130,000 foreign Fulbrighters I suspect we all felt one identical thing: the great beating heart of that marvelous and terrifying beast America. Eight years later I can still feel that heartbeat, and it is always there to remind me that the person who came home to Britain was not the one who went.

Experience is our conscious interpretation of events, thoughts and actions—all emergent properties of our brain-states. Do the multiple events and relationships of the Fulbright years cause physiological change? Do encounters with people, places and ideas make a real and tangible difference? Practically, at least in the UK, the status of Fulbright speaks loud. True or not, we are seen as special, even gifted. I learned I was capable and that brought me confidence. To use language I learned in the U.S., "I was empowered," bringing to reality what my parents tried to teach me—that I could do anything I wanted if I tried hard enough. That has helped over these years to shake off self-doubt, the kind that plagues us all. But it is only now, as I relive that year for these notes, that I realize this discovery of self was engendered and nurtured during my time as a Fulbrighter.

Back home in Britain, the experience has left an indelible mark upon me. Afterwards I no longer wanted to play the game, do as I was told. I no longer wanted to read the text of a chapter from the reading list and call it a lecture. I no longer wanted to be treated like a second-class citizen because I was not on the faculty. I also discovered that behaving like an American is fine if you talk like an American. Otherwise it is hard to find your place.

As I review these notes, I see that they imply another dimension: the search for the soul of a nation, perhaps two nations. The idea behind stereotypes assumes there is such a thing as "an American" and by extension "an America." Is there? Would all foreigners describe the same thing? No, differences flow from the writers themselves. There is the point. Most of the obvious discoveries I made in the U.S. reduce to this: that there is no such thing as "an American," even in Rootstown.

And what of the effect we have on our hosts? I seem to have spent much of my life upsetting stereotypes about how a white-British-female-academic (choose one) should look, sound and behave. My father called me "Britain's Revenge"! Foreign perceptions result not only from the nature of our encounters but from who we were. Who then do we become?

I had always had a clear idea of what I wanted to be. Psychology caught my attention at the age of 12. I traveled to my professional commitment not by a calm voyage but rather more like a trip over Niagara in a barrel—you get there but it is not easy. I discovered in myself a habit of clashing with my elders and betters—I must have seemed a bit of a Bolshevik. And although my exam results were underwhelming I found myself with a first degree, lots of ambitions, and nowhere to go.

Working part-time as a sales-girl in a shoe shop had brought me through college; they wanted me to work full-time while I sorted out career questions so I joined the real world and its targets. Getting in at 8:30 with no proper breaks, dealing with the extremely bad-tempered general public, putting up with the worse-tempered area manager, that sort of thing. It wasn't college life.

Twelve months and a trail of interviews later, one of my professors offered to take me on as PhD candidate. No money, just a room and a chance to do what he said I should be doing. No money meant more shoes, but in the American movies the heroes and heroines always worked their way through college and if they could do it so could I! So I began my apprenticeship to Academia.

Intellectual training? I'm not sure I had any. I cannot honestly say that I ever sat down to discuss how best to frame a theoretical question. Life in the Unit—Department, in American terms—was empirical. There were questions to ask and paradigms to use. Administration took up much of my supervisor's time, so I tended to get on with things my own way and present him with things after the fact. This suited him in the main; if I waited around for him to discuss the future it would have meant things never got done at all. To be honest this did not really worry me much. I pick up things quickly enough and I like being responsible for my own destiny, even when it means the ride is not of the smoothest.

In Orwell's fateful year 1984, at age 25, I was finishing my PhD in London when over the horizon rode—well actually he walked—Ted Voneida. A devout American anglophile on sabbatical, he expressed friendly concern at the haphazard approach to science I had acquired over the past few years. We discovered a mutual empathy, having much to do with humor and with a love for malt whiskey, and we worked on a project together for a few months. Before he left for the U.S. he asked if I would be interested in coming to work with him—in Rootstown, Ohio. Something about that name . . . .

Put in more formal terms, I was asked if I would like to work at the North Eastern Ohio College of Medicine by the Chair of the Department of Neurobiology, Professor Theodore J. Voneida. He would soon become one of the greatest influences in my life, one of the most gifted teachers I have ever known, and one of the nicest men I have ever met.

The image of America and its people portrayed in the popular media was appealing to me, if less so to others. The thought of someday going there had always been interwoven with my ambition, but it had never occurred to me as I drew near the end of my doctorate that I would get there so soon. Saying Yes to his invitation was easy and instantaneous, but it took longer to follow through with the Fulbright Commission in London. Memory psychologists worry about why we retain some memories and bury others. I still remember what I wore to the interview at the Fulbright Commission. I remember looking at the photo of Senator Fulbright, trying desperately to memorize the list of Commission members who—without knowing it, or did they?—were about to make such a difference in my life. The first question was not too difficult: "Where exactly is Rootstown?" I told them all I knew: a small town near Kent, Ohio—at least everyone had heard of Kent. Only two nail-biting weeks later when I discovered I had been chosen did I go out to the nearest bookshop and buy a map of the U.S.A.

My next memories come into focus at the Cleveland airport where Ted—or should I say Professor Voneida—was waiting. The drive from

Cleveland to Kent was exciting, though I doubt many Ohioans ever felt that way. The houses, so different from Southeast English red brick and inner-city grey, were made of wood, painted blues and creams, browns and greens; they had screen doors and porches and people sat out on them. The yards had no fences or hedges and everyone seemed to be out at the same time cutting the grass. Only as time moved on and I traveled around the country did I begin to see that the houses were all slightly different. To me at first they were a single continuous painting by Norman Rockwell. Sitting in Ted's car, driving on the wrong (!) side of the road, I was scared and excited and brave and different. I had been there only a few hours.

The Department of Neurobiology at the College of Medicine, part of a consortium composed of Youngstown, Akron and Kent Universities called NEOUCOM for short, was special in the mid-eighties. We sat in the middle of what had been an enormous cornfield in the Midwest, heartland of America, with hardly an all-American to be seen. Alex and Pascal of Ukrainian and Italian heritage respectively, Gad the Israeli, Teresa the daughter of a Taiwan diplomat and Durriyya, a Malaysian graduate student, wandered the corridors. Faculty members claimed second-generation heritages with Norway and Serbia. Larry wore his long hair in a pony tail with a great beard framing his philosophical musings on various subjects. This contrasted with A.T. Perkins III, our token All-American Boy, but no one held it against him.

It is tough, they say, when you don't speak the language. Anglophones assume this is no problem in the U.S. But I soon learned that the scope for misunderstanding was widened by this very assumption. It is not what you say, it is how and where you say it. I was initially disconcerted as I walked through the Medical School corridors, greeted by people I had never met who enquired about my health and general well-being. It took a while to realize I was not expected to stop and answer, only repeat the enquiry with equal cheeriness and concern and continue along my way. This involved training on my part—the process requires careful timing. Too early an enquiry results in forcing the greetee into a conversation, but waiting too long results in a verbal collision or in missing your target. I soon got marvelously adept at this form of communication and could sing out "Hi, how ya doin'" with the best. In fact I found it dreadfully hard to break the habit back in Britain and have since made it a mission in life to introduce this custom to every Department I visit, with appropriate colloquial adjustments of course.

My problems with the American language were soon set aside and I began, neo-colonialists that we all are, trying to establish a bit of British tradition in Ohio. The people in the shops "jus' loved" the way I talked; they would delight in telling me about their English ancestry and how their cousins planned to come and visit. In the Department, there was a small debate over whether or not I was a true "Brit." Those who had been to the UK were quick to point out that nobody in Britain had such a loud laugh—in which they were not entirely wrong. Ultimately my daily yearning for a "nice cup of tea" firmly established my claim to the other side of the pond. I began giving evening classes in Cockney rhyming slang, and among my colleagues a certain amount of linguistic pollution could be detected: soon "yoo-hoo" and "sooopah" and "bloody hell" began to echo down the halls, along with "Hi, how ya doin'."

A matter I forgot to mention, *pace* the memory psych people, was Alexander, my Fulbright baby boy. When I began my Fulbright grant in August, I was five months pregnant. I popped home in November, had Alexander in December, spent Christmas with the family, and arrived back in Ohio in the midst of a January blizzard. It had taken 24 hours from Heathrow, it was 4 AM, and I had husband Andrew—who took six months of leave from his work—and a 6-week-old baby in tow. Clearly, part of the Fulbright experience is learning that anything is possible.

From the first day, one of the differences I noticed was in the atmosphere. It would be cheating to say there was no politics, but the Department managed nonetheless to be cohesive both at a personal and a professional level. Not that everyone agreed with each other all the time. But they met, they discussed, they argued, and ultimately they decided on policies and actions. What's more, everyone was involved. Not just faculty but graduate students and technicians. Everyone had a voice and a contribution to make, and these were all heard and acted upon.

At NEOUCOM I was surrounded by colleagues who were first of all friends. What I learned from my time with these people was devastating: research and teaching can really be fun! These students and faculty colleagues were more like family than anything else. We ate donuts, drank beer, made popcorn, had birthday parties with soda and ice cream and cake. In case my interview panel is reading this, we worked too, extremely hard in fact. The faculty meanwhile was giving the best lectures and courses I have ever heard or participated in, to this day. They inspired the students—it is a big word, inspire, but they did it—they inspired *me*.

The teaching in general was a revelation. At NEOUCOM I was assigned part of the course in Functional Neuro-Anatomy for medical students. We worked in pairs and, as part of the course, we were expected to go to each other's lectures. Interaction, class participation and thorough preparation were central parts of the teaching style for most of the faculty. Teaching became part of my learning. Handouts defining key words and complicated diagrams for labelling presented well in advance meant students were prepared to learn and even to enjoy the lectures. At 8 AM when they began, the halls were packed—few lectures in Britain begin so early. Another element of organization: the course organizer held weekly meetings with all course contributors and discussed lecture content and level of difficulty, also shedding light on the learning process by reporting on previous years' results. Cohesiveness and continuity were the norm, even when several different lecturers were involved.

At NEOUCOM they stressed teaching in every way they could, for example providing a special seminar on professional lecturing skills; all faculty attended, at the College's expense. It was hoped—no, it was expected—that I would put in the effort and time to do things right. I learned simple lessons: e.g., the advantages of showing enthusiasm, both for your subject and your audience. At the end of each year, all course directors received grades on individual lecturers and overall course quality from the students and other course teachers, which meant accurate and at times painful feedback on performance.

Then there are the famous seminars, so characteristic of American university education. In the U.S. I was given responsibility and I was expected to accept it and take it on my own. In the Department I organized a graduate seminar series, corralling speakers, advertising the talks, chairing the sessions.

And what difference did America make to my abilities as a researcher? Ted tried hard to get me to focus on precise research questions. He taught me to pay attention to detail. He tried to make me methodical, and for a while I actually was—though I think the reader of these notes may be skeptical. And he taught me to be brave enough to write for myself. He edited my texts, not by rewriting them, but by showing me where I had to rewrite them myself. He made me think about what I had written and he taught me self-criticism, helping me recognize my weaknesses and build on my strengths.

At the same time Ted taught me the opposite: that there were things in life more important than a research project—things like being a decent human being, generating a sense of community around one, and making a difference to others. He taught me that if I dropped dead tomorrow my experiment would not matter so much as the effect I had on others.

Everything was moving forward far too fast: Alexander was soon crying with an American accent sitting under my desk while I worked at the computer—the click of the keys seemed to put him to sleep. He never complained. Beyond Kent, there were conferences in Dallas and Louisville, friends in Washington, DC and Toronto; we toured Philadelphia, Baltimore, and New York with my sister. And we spent many weekends with Ted and

Swanny in their beautiful cottage on a lake near the Southern Ohio-West Virginia border.

Fulbright means the development of special relationships with a country and its people through deep immersion over time and shoulder-to-shoulder work on important problems. Fulbright means a spirit and a vision, the spirit embodied by the Senator himself. It means confidence, it means touching people, it means changing other people's lives and one's own. Being a Fulbrighter for me meant travel, new people, new languages, and friendships which persist over thousands of miles.

Getting there is half the fun but getting home is rugged. Things are cut and dried in England; people know their place. Where was mine? When I left I was not sure. When I returned I was even less sure. Today I still wonder. Did I feel special, that lifetime ago when I set out? No, just scared. Was there ever a point where I could say I noticed a difference? Not really. I'm still scared, but I don't let on.

My return to the chillier climes of British academia has been difficult at times. Here the pursuit of intellectual excellence supersedes everything, including family and humanity. Strict hierarchies prevail, research is the key to rank. The classic British lecture consists of a list of facts delivered to bent heads scribbling furiously, or so it seems to me. Before Fulbright, expatriate Americans who hated the system had sensitized me to it; and my father—who directed marketing for an American multinational—implied the same when he tried to teach me that you had to sell ideas just as you sold a car. In Britain, if anyone in your learning career ever formally takes you aside and says, "This is how to do it," you have hit a lucky day. A guest lecturer in the UK is told to talk about what he or she wants and is seldom given any information about the other lectures in the course. Things had not changed while I was away. And although teaching accountability is slowly creeping into British universities, I was so hooked on the idea when I first came home that I asked students to complete a questionnaire on anything I did. Oddly enough this kind of effort was appreciated by few students and seen as bizarre by many colleagues. British students are used to the list-of-facts method and confused by interaction. They want precise instructions, not just guidelines showing them how to find out for themselves. Changing customs can disorient even the best. Yet when I began organizing a seminar series back home I tried things the Rootstown way and it worked out very well, although my senior colleagues complained about the excessive amount of time and commitment I expended.

The biggest but the most difficult difference to define is attitude. Just as in the sixth form, where my fundamental Bolshevism first emerged, my return home has meant clashes. As I analyze the reasons, they flow from good habits contracted in Rootstown: a commitment to teaching, an independence of mind and initiative. Yet I know that a commitment to teaching short-changes research and that independent initiatives require consultation if they are to succeed. So I pay the price. But in the final analysis if I had not left the UK the system would have worn down my Bolshie side and knocked me out. If I had not gone away, I'd be better behaved, no doubt. And I'd probably have lower expectations of people, which would save me a lot of daily disappointment. But then would I be better? Would I even be me? Professionally, am I a better researcher after my time in Rootstown? Painful as it is to admit, I think the answer is No. I don't have the single-minded determination to concentrate on a single question. I do too many things, try to please too many people. I need to learn to say No, I need to learn to play the game. Do I really want to? The Fulbright experience does not make you into something you were not already; instead it lets you find the person you are, and it gives you the courage—and a certain amount of intellectual and experiential equipment—to stick with that person. So much for roots.

My passport says I am still a Brit, not an American. The problem is that when I go back to the U.S. and step off the plane, there is part of me that feels it has come home. How can I explain this? The question I ask myself: do my American counterparts have this same feeling when they return to the country where they spent their Fulbright year or years? I would bet the answer is Yes. The location doesn't matter. There are almost 200,000 people just like me all around the world. We no longer have just one nationality, we are Fulbrighters, once and for ever.

Patricia Hutchinson went to England as a mature adult, for highly implemental purposes. Curious about a development in British education called CDT, or Craft, Design and Technology, she wanted to study its applicability to American schools. What she learned there turned a hypothesis into a commitment to introduce CDT techniques to the U.S. She does this from a base at Drexel University in Philadelphia, where she edits a magazine dedicated to this educational approach. Around the serious focus of her essay, there emerge more discreet references to the kind of personal journey her British saga meant in her life as a teacher, an artist, a woman and an American, as well as a thoughtful consideration of educational reform that sheds additional light on the other essay about the UK in this volume.

28

TRANSFORMATION BY DESIGN

Patricia A. Hutchinson

At our first official Fulbright occasion, a welcoming reception at the Embassy, my husband Hutch and I found ourselves in conversation with a British Aerospace executive who showed considerable interest in my project. I planned to investigate Britain's development of an innovative teaching approach called Craft, Design and Technology, CDT for short. I already knew that the cream of UK academia was oblivious to this initiative. Yet here was a prominent industrialist grilling me about it. "CDT," he said, "is probably the only reason my son got into university. His grades and test scores were only average, but once he got out his design portfolio, there was no stopping him. One minute he was just the sum total of his A-levels, and the next moment he had the entire department and all the admissions officers in the palm of his hand. His design work was the evidence of his ability to perform—and that was all they needed!"

This testimonial was not typical of the awareness level or attitudes I normally discovered outside of the public education community. But I knew I was on to something after that enthusiastic encounter, and it set the tone for the following year's work. The structural changes in British education promised by CDT had already begun, but the evidence was subtle, and I would clearly have to seek it out.

In the broadest terms of politics, education has two possible objectives: to maintain the status quo or to transform society. British education has long been a good example of the power of education to institutionalize an idea. Through the system of public schools and state schools, the latter with grammar schools for "gifted" students and a vocational track for all the rest, traditional class structure was maintained for many decades. In today's fast-paced world, that situation is changing. A more telling example is Soviet education where until recently school was the vehicle for maintaining a highly consistent, if contrived, view of reality for all pupils. Education as a change agent is typified by post-World War II Japan. The American educational system transplanted to Japan after the War helped bring that society from an essentially feudal nation with a reputation for shoddy products to the modern technological power it is today, even if the speed of that change probably owes much to traditional Japanese class values, inherent in that society, and certainly built into educational policy as well.

As an educational program, Fulbright is transformational by design. Its goal is the kind of intercultural understanding that will make future wars untenable, and it operates on an underlying assumption that this goal is best achieved on a person-to-person basis. Since the Second World War, when Senator Fulbright proposed the exchange, students from many countries have experienced their own personal transformations. Many of us have felt the magic of a shared insight over a cup of coffee or the sense of having, just for a moment, broken through the language barrier. These moments can happen on a very short visit, but given a chance to develop they are only the first steps in breaking down stereotypes and gaining cultural sensitivity. Fulbright provides those chances, and for each of us, the awakening is unique.

My own passion for international living was sparked by a trip to Amsterdam some years before my Fulbright exchange, and I will always give much of the credit to Billy Joel. My friend Jane and I, on vacation without our spouses, were visiting Holland for the first time. To our surprise, we were greeted at the airport by two flight attendants, daughters of a friend of Jane's boss. They had promised their parents to drive us two "matrons" (fully eight or ten years older than they were) into Amsterdam to find a hotel, and were determined to honor this obligation. Conversation was tough—their English was limited to the beverage choices on KLM, and our Dutch ranged from "Vermeer" and "Van Gogh" to "Ginever" and "Gouda." We were squirming in frustration as the Fiat crossed the city limits, when suddenly

"Piano Man" blared from the radio. On the downbeat, we all burst into song and then into laughter. We sang and laughed our way through several suburbs and ended by spending the holiday at their apartment. Typical natives, they had never been to the Rijksmuseum, so we treated them to the Arthur Frommer tour of the city. And every time we found ourselves at a verbal impasse, we'd laugh and sing a few bars of "Bottle of Red. . ." or "Come out, Virginia."

Since then there have been lots of similar moments, glimpses through a cultural barrier of something deeply familiar. But I think it was my musical Dutch holiday, and the experience of fellow-feeling it inspired, that strengthened my resolve someday to live and work abroad. And the kind of "cultural immersion" I envisioned presented itself several years later in the form of a Fulbright exchange to the UK in 1985-86.

I was 36—a "mature" student, as the Brits sympathetically put it—at the time of my study in England. Determined to find out first-hand about British education for my doctoral project, I was also eager to build on the feeling I had had in Holland. I wanted to know just what I had in common with people raised in a different country, with a history and traditions all their own. I hoped that this experience might allow me to see my own culture and assumptions in a new light. Over the course of a year, I got both closer to and farther from my goal. Of one thing, though, I am certain—it must have been a Fulbrighter who said, "I can tell you everything about a country I've visited for two weeks, but after six months or a year, I know a lot less."

My search for clues about British schooling began with an immersion in the literature. Some thirty years ago, a diverse group of British writers from education, industry and government began to publish articles and essays about the challenges facing the UK in the coming decades. Divested of its empire, Britain no longer had access to cheap raw materials. The factories and mills that had made it an industrial empire were outdated, and a thoroughly unionized work force meant high labor costs. In these three domains of former strength, Britain was finding it hard to compete. None of these writers expected or advocated a return to the mixed blessings of colonialism or the industrial revolution. And the labor movement had greatly improved the quality of life for British workers. Yet the cost of progress had been high for the UK, as unemployment lines, social unrest and the loss of international prestige indicated. To reverse this downward spiral, the writers proposed changes in technology, in economics—in society itself—through education. New strategies for schooling had to be found, they suggested, which would seek not to preserve the status quo but would redirect students' attitudes toward themselves, others, work, class and competition. The goal of schooling, they felt, must be to prepare every Briton to live—to succeed in a technological world. Only through a dramatic educational transformation could Britain regain its competitive edge. Critical to this transformation, said the writers, was the design process, applied throughout the curriculum, and especially in relation to technology.

American educators had looked with interest on experimental programs in British schools for decades. But the growing parallels between the UK's economic problems and our own dictated that the U.S. take a closer look at Britain's response to the challenges of national competition for the twenty-first century. Criticism of American education by parents, employers and government commissions suggested that we needed to consider some transformations of our own.

Transmission, transaction and transformation are three views of how learning takes place. Some see teaching and learning as a transmission of knowledge, from those who have it to those who don't. The facts are written on the clean slate of the student's mind and remain there or in some mental filing cabinet for future reference. Facts, skills and attitudes can be passed on in this way from generation to generation, but no attempt is made to foster the kind of thinking that results in creative leaps. In fact, transmissionist teaching preserves the status quo and tends to discourage potentially disruptive innovations.

A second school of thought looks at education as a transaction between curious learners and sensitive teachers. In this case, the transactions between each pupil and teacher are unique, since the learner brings different experiences to a transaction and therefore asks different kinds of questions. Although this "transactional" learning is an appealingly personal vision, it easily fits into the model of K-12 schooling where, for a given learner, knowledge can eventually be complete.

Transformationists are a third group. They view learners as people in a constant state of change, continually picking up clues from the whole environment and revising their world views with every new input. Teachers who work from this perspective facilitate learning, provide stimulating settings, and pose probing questions. For transformationists, learning is forever.

To many educators today, perpetual learning is the only kind that makes sense for a fast-changing technological world. New jobs and career skills, relocation and its accompanying culture shock, even changes in the artifacts of everyday life can be disturbing. Technology and its by-products challenge us to expect change as the norm and require a major adjustment of attitude. As early as the 1960s, British curriculum designers set out to challenge the nature of traditional schooling by developing educational strategies around the transformationist perspective. By organizing learning around the process of thinking rather than the content of a variety of changing disciplines, they intended to help students gain really valuable skills and flexible attitudes toward their world. They hoped that their graduates would know how to find out what they needed as each new challenge or opportunity arose, and would recognize lifelong education as a fact of life.

My research at NYU into British technology education had revealed the discipline as an interesting mix. As a student of both art and technology, I found the idea of combining the thinking processes used in design work with the practical goals of technology highly attractive. During twelve years of painting, graphic design and teaching, I had come to think of the design process—whether technological or aesthetic in outcome—as a metaphor for a way of living, of taking charge of one's life. I had seen my students initiate and carry out design work, and come away from the process with a feeling of real satisfaction. Planning and making—whether for functional or purely expressive reasons—allowed them to assume responsibility for and feel capable of effecting change. They had to take risks, and sometimes they failed; but in design-oriented classes, failures are part of the learning process, and success is achievable by anyone through resourcefulness and perseverance. They found they had to draw upon a personal reservoir of learning and life experience, but this was a very natural kind of activity. Designing solutions to problems, after all, is the fundamental adaptive strategy of the species. Also fundamental to the species, however, is the need to pass on knowledge through education. Being a successful designer, and learning to approach the world from that perspective, must be learned. These qualities are not instinctive, and they are certainly not fostered by simply memorizing facts or performing programmed activities.

British educators' suggestion that, while facts and formulas have their value, it takes design activity to put them into context, echoed my own feelings. But what I really wanted was a chance to study their rationale and their methods, and to start building a case for a similar approach at home, where design education in public schools was non-existent.

My proposal to the Fulbright committee at NYU outlined a plan to examine design-oriented technology education programs in the UK, for possible adaptation to an American setting. Most of the committee were from the traditional liberal arts disciplines, and I could tell that both technology education and the mission—a chance to have an immediate effect on a new educational direction—clearly seemed "offbeat." They recognized a true zealot when they saw one. Notwithstanding, I received notice of my award in April. I left in September 1985 for Oxford.

The decision to pursue a Fulbright in England in order to develop an argument for design-based technology education in this country posed nearly as many problems for me as it presented opportunities. My husband, known by everyone but his parents as Hutch, is a teacher-educator in a New Jersey State College. We are both in technology education, but our backgrounds in fact are very different, which flavors our approaches to the subject and probably keeps us from trying too hard to compete. Uprooting Hutch for a year from his teaching and other professional activities was not easy. In fact, from both a personal and financial standpoint, it turned out to be impossible. We compromised: he took a half-year sabbatical in Oxford, after which he returned to New Jersey, and we spent the second semester as "pen pals." Although living and working abroad was definitely not his idea of an adventure, he will be the first to admit that the Fulbright experience, unsolicited in his case, has provided continuing benefits. Professionally, it has changed his career. He has spearheaded curriculum development efforts at Trenton State that have resulted in an entirely new kind of teacher-training program. This program emphasizes thinking skills and technical problem-solving, a considerable leap beyond the technical skill-building that has always been the hallmark of industrial education. In addition, several courses within the new program are being offered to all liberal arts students as part of fundamental preparation for living in a technological world. Trenton State's technology education program is recognized nationally as a model of educational innovation and has been similarly cited in reports by visiting researchers from Australia, Egypt, Holland, and Canada. The guiding vision for this unique hybrid of American and British approaches has put Hutch in considerable demand for lectures and articles, largely thanks to his "Fulbright" experience. From a personal standpoint, his stay in Oxford was equally significant. It provided him with many friends and a wealth of cherished memories, as well as the prestige at home of having visited nearly every pub between Lands' End and John O'Groats.

Another impact of the decision to apply for a Fulbright became fully evident only after my return to the U.S. In essence, Fulbright had called my bluff in a game of careers I had been playing for several years. I found myself forced to make a choice: would I be a painter with some strong views on education, or would I be a design educator who tried to work art into her life during off-hours? The ramifications of my choice were not as clear as they now seem and were obscured by the anticipation of the year's adventures. But I felt that accepting the offer of a scholarship carried an obligation to do the most with the opportunity provided; when I applied, I agreed to accept that obligation. Perhaps because of my own inability to juggle, painting has taken a back seat to education for the past six years, and this is a constant source of frustration. Apparently, there is no such thing as an unmixed blessing.

At any rate, it is a premise of this essay that a single Fulbright award affects not one but many lives, in many ways. It upsets the equilibrium of daily life, that is part of the experience. Fortunately for me, there is a certain artist's instinct to keep gathering material for future projects, and it has never suspended operations. I have always kept sketch-notes of my surroundings, particularly on vacations and visits. During my stay I sketched our cottage and village, as well as many of the people I met. The cottage held particular charm for me—its scale and textures, the extremely organic nature of its materials struck a deep cord and allowed me to indulge myself in some romantic time-travel.

Six years later, I have finally begun work on a series of oil paintings, reflections on my British stay, full of images of stone, thatch and hedge, the faces and forms of folk musicians, the Celtic book illuminations I pored over at Lindisfarne and York, surfacing and enriching the mix. I have found that such images collect for only so long, then they have a way of asserting themselves.

Our first few weeks in England were spent finding our niche. Since I would be doing a lot of traveling and would have a car, we decided to look for a house or apartment to rent in one of Oxford's outlying villages. Oxfordshire is a delightful mix of farmland, modern housing estates and medieval villages. Renting a thatched cottage had been beyond my wildest dream, but one nevertheless threw itself in our path. The advertisement read: "Fifteenth-century thatched cottage. Wanted: couple (preferably foreign), non-smokers, no children, keen gardeners." To this point in my life I had shown no sign of a green thumb, but I determined to develop one on the spot. A few days later we moved in.

Renting in England is an education in itself. Problems with squatters and an ancient law that makes them almost impossible to evict makes owners of income property very cautious. We spent most of our first day at Merrick Cottage walking through the five tiny rooms listening to an estate agent tape-recording a description of every feature, down to the chips in the well-worn teacups. (This procedure was repeated on the last day of our stay and the transcripts were assiduously compared for signs of property damage.)

Hutch's sacrifice in agreeing to these living arrangements only became clear after he had nearly knocked himself out several times on the 6-foot-high living room ceiling beams and the considerably lower doorway to the kitchen. My fairy tale was his recurring nightmare—the high price of romance! Despite this considerable hazard, the village of Forest Hill managed to charm us both.

All through September we were assailed by the sweet smell of burning fields as the farmers replenished the ash in the soil that had supported many of their families for centuries. (Environmentalists have now all but stopped this tradition, a necessary move—what a loss!)

Our village, according to a history left by our landlord, had been chronicled in the Domesday Book of 1086. Its residents had suffered repeatedly from the ravages of the plague. John Milton had met and married his bride there, and Merrick Cottage, a relatively recent fixture of the main street, dated from the reign of Henry VIII. Although a trendy guidebook described Forest Hill as "unremarkable," we noted and doted on every detail. What if there were no shops—there was a postbox, a bus stop, and two pubs!

The city of Oxford too was a constant source of awe—and frustration. Sharing streets laid out for pedestrians and horsemen with double-decker buses and maniac bicyclists was a real challenge. Part of the magic of Oxford, however, is the fact that, just by turning a corner or ducking through a low gateway, a pedestrian can be transported to another time and place, somehow leaving behind even the noise and exhaust fumes.

My own corner of Oxford was on the second floor of the Clarendon laboratory, an edifice haunted by the ghosts of countless brilliant scientists and regularly besieged by animal rights activists. Because Oxford is not one institution but forty separate entities, purely academic affiliations through the school of education or the science labs provide no direct connection to the colleges, where the real tradition of Oxford resides. Thanks to our acquaintances through Fulbright, we visited many of the colleges, even dining in the Hall at Christ Church, taking tea at New College and sherry at Nuffield. Like all college towns, Oxford itself had much to offer—from the Ashmolean and city museums, to musical evenings with the "Oyster Band" at the Jericho Tavern. May morning on Magdalen bridge was magical, with the sun rising over the tower to the strains of madrigal singers, followed by a medieval market atmosphere featuring Morris dancers on the steps of the Sheldonian Theatre and mulled wine at the Turf, Oxford's most ancient pub. For romance and atmosphere, we never tired of the sense of history or the aura of poetry pervading the town.

Connection with Oxford opened many needed doors for my study of design education; it also provided a library, a telephone and a parking space. In my dealings with the university, I was repeatedly impressed with the unhurried pace and the rule of tradition in all things. For example, in order to get a library card for the Bodleian, I had to appear before the chief librarian and solemnly swear to refrain from setting fires. Curbing my pyromania, I nevertheless made a serious faux pas by outrageously presuming that morning coffee at the Department of Education was optional—I was nearly ejected bodily from the library, which they locked daily for the ritual from 11 to 11:30.

Public education is not a specialty of Oxford, but the library provided a wealth of excellent resources for my study. It was clear that many disciplines had contributed their insights to the design model evolving in Britain, and that the result was an integrative and potentially more relevant vision of education. According to my readings, new theories and practices stressing hands-on design and problem-solving were in place in Britain in a number of secondary schools, through a course called CDT (Craft, Design and Technology). Evidence of the success of this approach was promising, but mostly anecdotal. Testimony which appeared in print at that time came largely from sources such as technical training boards and institutions of "further" (vocational) education, where recruits who had experience of design and technology seemed to be better trainees—self-starters, good communicators and team members, adaptable to a variety of situations. These qualities seemed to be just the ones that the politicians were hoping for in their new generation of "school-leavers," and they were clearly the kinds of skills needed at the policy-making level as well.

Design-based learning had found a proving ground in CDT classes, the equivalent to American industrial arts; but in neither country did this discipline command much prestige. Engineering commands greater respect in the U.S. than in Britain, but even here, the supposed route to industrial excellence through engineering is assumed to be science. Yet in neither country do science classes emphasize practical problem-solving, the essence of engineering innovation. Therefore, despite its potential for broad impact, I expected relatively few people at Oxford to be familiar with design and technology education—even in their own country. I was right about academia, but, as suggested by the encounter with our British Aerospace friend, the ears of industry were firmly fixed to the ground.

My plan for exploring the nature of design and technology education in Britain had three tracks. First, I wanted to search British texts for the origin of their design model, to make sure we were all talking about the same activity. Second, I wanted to develop a network of experts, from the founders of the initiative to the administrators and the classroom practitioners. This latter group then supplied the third component: a chance to observe the design process in classrooms. The network of teacher-trainers, county advisors and inspectors were the logical sources to direct me to examples of good practice.

I started my search by attending a design and technology conference at Wembley stadium, convinced that there I'd get a capsule history and overview of developments to date. By the seventh or eighth jargon-laden presentation, Hutch and I had begun to suspect a conspiracy. The speaker had just finished a sentence containing about a dozen acronyms, some of whose letters stood for other acronyms, we later discovered. We started to laugh and could not stop. When we apologized and explained our bewilderment, the presenter smiled sheepishly and with typical British understatement, admitted to having got somewhat carried away. (Having "got" rather than "gotten" turns out to be the current form of a verb in evolution, according to the Brits: "gotten," they tell me, is Elizabethan, a throwback typical of remote colonial outposts. Two things I had not anticipated were a language barrier—and insults!)

A later presentation confirmed the language problem. At that session, a leading figure in technology education described the project he directed. When asked how he'd accomplished so much, so quickly, and with so few resources, he solemnly replied: "Hard work and graft." Clearly, "graft" in Britain had another meaning than the common American application of the word. Later we told him that in our country graft could certainly be used to supplement your resources, unless you were caught and jailed.

Britain—on the map—is a small island, so I made some ambitious travel plans. I determined, just for starters, to see the author of every book I had read. An acquaintance from King Alfred's College in Winchester put me in touch with the first of these, and from that moment the connections proliferated. Hearing about my project, everyone from ministry officials to classroom teachers was more than willing to share. I had bought a used car and a road atlas, determined to drive to my meetings and see some of the countryside on each outing. I soon discovered that, aside from motorways, British roads go through, and not around, each hamlet. It also became clear that the no-speed-limit highways can only be reached by mile after mile of 15 mph B-road. Since every destination took twice as long to reach as I had planned, I had to revise my itinerary. Nor had I factored the latitude into my schedule, and by November I was running out of daylight hours by mid-afternoon. Imagine my frustration—to plan a route past Stonehenge on my way to or from a meeting in Bath, only to find (or not find) the stones completely obscured by darkness!

My network-building activities led me to the Royal College of Art, the government's Department of Trade and Industry, the Design Council, the University of London, and the headquarters of Her Majesty's Inspectors of Schools. Each contact had a network of his own, and I left most meetings with several new interviews to schedule. In Nottingham I joined teachers in learning about electronics, pneumatics and structures. I followed some of these teachers back to their classrooms, where the same content was explored through an endless variety of design activities.

In Hampshire I visited students aged 12 to 14, where one young designer explained a hovercraft innovation he had developed. I asked if his teacher was a specialist in hovercrafts, and he replied that, after the first couple of weeks, he had become the class expert on that subject. Without a moment's hesitation, the teacher agreed: "If they can't each teach me something new by the end of term, the program just hasn't worked." As noted by my British Aerospace acquaintance, the students' design portfolios were remarkable, documenting a thinking process that could never have been reflected by grades and test scores alone.

In Buckinghamshire, I joined primary teachers in workshops with David Jinks, the developer of a new technique for building structures. His materials included square-section wood—square dowels, I called them—and triangular cardboard gussets, which could be easily manipulated by small hands. Components were joined with glue using gluing templates and yielded amazingly strong, light and elegant structures of almost unlimited proportions. The technique required no nailing, and for young children, wood lengths were precut with simple jigs. Second-level work allowed for the construction of mechanisms for use with the structures. Back in the classroom of one participant, I saw students building dynamic models with the technique—drawbridges and boats and catapults that were used to make lessons in literature come alive while youngsters worked out technical problems.

Other visits revealed some drawbacks of the program I had come to study, including the logistical problems posed by 25 students working on independent projects: storage, scheduling, safety, limited resources; the problems of assessing interpretive work; and the ever-present examination system. But they also revealed a wealth of creative energy on the part of both teachers and students. Best of all, they hinted at a feeling of real purpose on both sides. I was grateful to realize that I could contribute something back to the teachers I visited. Most of them worked in isolation, with little chance for feedback or sharing ideas. Many asked me how their programs compared to others I had visited and seemed truly amazed and touched to find they had been recommended as experts by the advisors and inspectors I had contacted. This little bit of recognition, I later reflected, was one of the subtle impacts of a project like mine—a benefit not to be undervalued.

By June I had visited over thirty schools in England, Scotland and Wales. I had discovered a growing interest in the expansion of design and technology into the primary school, and I had met several outstanding talents in that area. I may even have given the primary technology movement in England a boost by nominating one dynamic Wiltshire advisor to speak at a U.S. conference in the fall of 1986. Outside of his usual context, he managed to capture the attention—and imagination—of a visiting British official from the Department of Trade and Industry, and went home to head up a national educational research project. The results of that project will produce benefits to both countries for years to come.

Throughout my ten-month stay in Britain, I was able to balance my research with exploration of the countryside. I visited museums, saw plays, and stormed castles and cathedrals in England, Wales and Scotland. Many of the acquaintances I made have since ripened into solid friendships and have been renewed by visits in both directions. From that September to June, I spent hours in conversation with other American Fulbrighters, reflecting on new perspectives of home. Thanks to the efforts of an energetic staff at the Fulbright Commission at 6 Porter Street, I joined other Fulbrighters behind the scenes at parliament and traced the path of Stanley and Livingston at the Royal Geographic Society. I lived the fantasy of spending most of a year in a 15th-century cottage and ran out of fuel oil in mid-January, just to add to the authenticity. I shared Christmas plum pudding with an English family, played skittles at the local pub with my classmates after a long day of teacher workshops, and tried my feet at Morris dancing. I did not waste a day.

A Fulbright scholarship is an investment, but the dividends are rarely tallied. Most of us finish our projects, aware of our personal gains, and move on without reflecting on the impact we've had. But those impacts are not incidental. I have been particularly fortunate—I have seen those dividends gather interest. During the past five years, the support that sent me to England in 1985 has generated and fostered a much more intimate dialogue between educators in the UK and the U.S. This dialogue has had significant impact on decisions being made in both countries. From my desk at Oxford, I had the chance to talk to the architects of Britain's evolving design and technology effort, now a central component of their new National Curriculum; to arrange visits to schools where enthusiastic teachers collaborated with motivated students; and sometimes even to introduce an isolated Yorkshire teaching whiz to a kindred spirit in the south. (While we might expect a straightforward international exchange of benefits from such a project, there is something quite magical about helping a Briton effect change at home.) Since returning, I've seen my experiences in the UK influence curriculum planning in a number of American states. The growing network of American colleagues has facilitated student and teacher exchanges in both directions; this has resulted in dozens of individualized study tours, often with the personal touch of home stays.

In a very real sense, the project underwritten by Fulbright helped set in motion a great many initiatives in support of educational change. Of perhaps greatest impact is TIES Magazine (Technology, Innovation, and Entrepreneurship for Students), a new international journal for teachers created by Ronald Todd, a former professor at NYU, and myself. TIES addresses a common concern of most countries today: how to prepare children for life in a changing technological world through a strong grounding in the design process. The publication is only one manifestation of an expanding network of design and technology educators, working to infuse new values into public schooling.

Many of these developments are dividends of a project that Fulbright helped make possible. Fulbright support gave me a means of articulating an alternate way of seeing the world, of enlarging upon and spreading a powerful new idea in which I firmly believe—what we call nowadays empowerment. Should we call it Fulbright empowerment?

The author, Associate Professor of Political Science at the George Washington University, practices comparative government with a strong base in political theory. Not untypical of his generation, he did his junior year abroad—at Sciences Po' in Paris—as a spin-off from first-generation Fulbrighters. Thus his Fulbright year was less an introduction to France than a rite of passage: he re-entered Sciences Po' as a senior researcher, becoming a colleague of his former teachers. His essay, while a personal memoir, focuses more broadly on the interaction between French and American social thought beginning with the Founders' borrowings from Montesquieu. Tracing the growth of intellectual relations over time, he documents the era in which, through Fulbright energies, the borrowing process became a genuine exchange of ideas, with little concern for imbalances of trade.

29

EXCHANGES AND EXCURSIONS IN FRANCE

Harvey B. Feigenbaum

The Fulbright Program may not always have been conceived as an exchange, that is a two-way transmission of ideas, cultures, conceptions. Some of its advocates were seduced, though certainly never the Senator even in his off-moments, by the notion that the principal reason for Americans to voyage abroad was simply to disseminate the scholarly, cultural and scientific achievements of the U.S. to those less fortunate than ourselves. The beneficiary scholars coming to the U.S. from abroad would similarly drink from the American font and bring back the good news to their respective home countries. Viewed in this sense, the Fulbright Program was not unlike the imperial concept of Cecil Rhodes, whose scholarship fund permitted more than one future U.S. Senator to cross the Atlantic and attend Oxford.

Yet scholarship, and ideas generally, are necessarily the products of interaction. Interacting with their research, scholars are necessarily both the transmitters and receivers of ideas. The carriers of these abstractions were and are people, with individual experiences inherent in their humanity. The impact of the exchange has always been collective as well as individual. Early administrators, academic advisors and policy-makers in the Fulbright Program were supremely aware of this necessary two-way flow, despite strong propagandist pressures to "tell America's story to the world." Not only were the individual lives of legions of scholars changed by their Fulbright experiences, so too were the disciplines in which these scholars were actively engaged. It would be too much, and too disparaging of the nearly 200,000 participants in the program, to suggest that parochials were invariably transformed into cosmopolites as a result of their respective experiences. However it is not an exaggeration to remark that intellectual worlds changed, thanks to the Fulbright process. Worlds of ideas became richer, more varied—indeed, more sophisticated—as scholars navigated the globe.

My own area of expertise is political science. The country I have inhabited most, other than my native America, has been France. And at least part of my French experience I owe to the Fulbright program. Thanks to it I have had an opportunity to examine the reciprocal intellectual influences between the two countries close at hand. The social sciences in the two countries have clearly benefitted from a long period of mutual contact, beginning (officially) with Benjamin Franklin and Thomas Jefferson. But the earlier contacts burgeoned as a result of the Fulbright Act of 1947. In the years since the establishment of the Fulbright program, upwards of 7000 Americans have lived, worked, and otherwise been immersed in France because of it. Many of these Fulbrighters were social scientists. Even if the reciprocating flows of French scholars did not numerically balance the torrents of Americans gushing into France, the effect on both sides of the equation has been prodigious.

My own amalgam of French and American culture was acquired in large part at the Institut d'Etudes Politiques de Paris, known affectionately to all as Sciences Po'. Initially I attended Sciences Po' not as a Fulbrighter but as one of the many American undergraduates who take their third year of university study abroad in programs often launched by returnees from a Fulbright experience. In my case, I arrived the year after the turmoil of 1968. I had the luxury to be able to study. I could do so without the punctuation of mass chanting, unpeaceful demonstrations, or the pungent odor of tear gas. Indeed it was a time which allowed me to acquire a taste for studying in cafés. To be fair, it was not only cafés for which I had acquired a taste—coming from the staid, then all-male University of Virginia, the co-educational charms of Paris did not escape my notice. Sitting in those cafés, more than automobiles crossed my field of vision.

Paris was a collection of sounds, smells, and above all, sights. It was a very long way from Charlottesville. I champed at the bit when I returned to Mr. Jefferson's University. My goal was to get back to Paris as soon as possible. I initially tried to do this via a student Fulbright proposal immediately after graduation, but my project was too transparent. Fulbright grants facilitate travel, but fortunately the contrary does not apply: failure to obtain them does not necessarily keep you home. After my BA, I returned to a two-year stint at Sciences Po'. The modesty of the tuition costs allowed me to pay most of my expenses from summer earnings. My Fulbright experience would come later, as a scholar in the West European Research program, when I could greet my former teachers as, or almost as, an equal.

The Institut d'Etudes Politiques was and is the *sine qua non* for those of the French who wish a career in the political establishment of France. The original purpose for which the Institute was founded was to imbue the soon-to-be elite of France with a degree of political sophistication, as well as with the rudiments of public law, history and economics. As is common in France, it is an institution where form and style weigh as heavily as substance, and where, at the undergraduate level, acquiring the Master's ideas are preferred to any apprentice's attempts at originality. To the few American students trying for the two-year *diplôme* (many junior-year abroaders did the one-year *certificat*), the emphasis on form seemed enigmatic and the low premium on our personal ideas and originality proved a persistent source of frustration. As one professor said, "When one of my students tells me he has an idea, I tremble." Nevertheless, we persevered and as it turned out we actually learned a great deal. As I look back, I see that the French and American educational systems are remarkably complementary. Americans put a premium on originality, but undergraduate students frequently know so little that they end up reinventing the wheel. Even innovative thought needs rigor, an attention to intellectual order and facts. Here, the French system excels.

The emphasis on form should not surprise anyone familiar with a people who revere Descartes. Curiously, however, Sciences Po', despite its Establishment pedigree (almost every important French politician and administrator has spent time in its halls on the Rue St. Guillaume) teaches the virtue of the dialectic: all arguments are defended by way of a two-part exposition in which clashing ideas culminate in a conclusion supporting the thesis. Connoisseurs will of course note that the preferred dialectic is Hegelian, based on ideas, rather than Marxist, derived from material conditions. The members of the French establishment are no fools.

Like any good alumnus of Sciences Po', I learned quickly to have a thesis ready for any occasion. I have one here. My thesis: the dominant idea of

American social science is that of liberalism. If that is so, then contact with French social science both supported and dialectically undermined that liberal tradition. Note that I use "liberalism" here in its 19th-century sense, a view which advocated both freedom of markets and freedom of individuals.

Let me first consider French social science as a source of American liberalism. In the early fifties, Louis Hartz wrote an extremely influential book: *The Liberal Tradition in America.* Crowned by the American Political Science Association, it was perhaps the most influential study of its time. Hartz had conceived his work as an attempt to reinvigorate Tocqueville, a figure in no need of reinvigoration in the U.S. but who had been less influential in informing the French, many of whom were more inclined to the musings of Marx. The ideas of Tocqueville dominated Hartz' book, as they generally have much of American political science and social thought since they first came to these shores. One hundred sixteen years ahead of his time, Tocqueville was, spiritually at least, the first French Fulbrighter to the U.S. when he arrived in the New World in 1831. The notion that not only does America have something to offer the world but also that America's most important invention is modern democracy surely traces its roots to the liberal aristocrat from France.

Hartz argued that America was basically a fragment of British 17th-century liberal culture, minus a conception of feudal class relations. Without a concept of class, or consequently of class struggle, Americans viewed themselves as a collection of individuals; ideas which accommodated this view then were easy to accept. The whole was nothing more than the sum of the parts. Methodologies which made the same assumption found a ready audience in the U.S., and French social science had such methodologies to offer.

Philosophical conceptions which maintained that truth was not only knowable but observable, that all one needed to do was catalog facts for the laws of human behavior to become apparent—these ideas attracted Americans. One such philosophy was Positivism, deriving essentially from the intellectual excursions of such nineteenth-century French social "scientists" as Henri de Saint-Simon or Auguste Comte (Anglophiles and Anglophones tend to trace all this to David Hume). Positivism insinuated itself easily into America's adaptation of 17th-century British culture. Positivists maintain that those who study society can and should use the same techniques that physical scientists use to study the world around them. Those who disagree with the positivists argue that knowledge of the social world cannot be acquired in the same way as knowledge of the physical world because all observation is tainted by the social context of the observer. Broadly, these debates about what is knowable and how knowledge is acquired fit into the branch of philosophy known as epistemology.

Amazingly enough, most Americans do not read French. The epistemology of Saint-Simon and Comte influenced America only indirectly through their positivist disciple John Stuart Mill. Based on Saint-Simon, Comte and Mill, the foundations were laid in the U.S. for a social science of generalized "laws" derived from patterns of observable facts and suitable to statistical manipulations. This latter characteristic was also an import: the statistics-oriented methods of Emile Durkheim influenced not only American sociology but the entire range of the social sciences as practiced in America. After World War II, Talcott Parsons, the most influential sociologist of the period, constructed an "American" approach to sociology wherein the Alsatian Durkheim and his trans-Rhenic neighbor Max Weber were elevated to icons.

The influence of French social science however went beyond sociology. The attraction of statistical methods could only be felt if one understood the world to be the sum of individual parts, where actions and objects could be divided into incremental bits. These notions reached their apogee, of course, in neoclassical economics. We normally trace American economic thought directly to the Scot Adam Smith, whose *Wealth of Nations* was first printed in the banner year 1776; we also attribute importance to the English Marginalist School associated with Alfred Marshall in the nineteenth century. Yet French economists are very much part of the neoclassical heritage. Jean-Baptiste Say (1767-1832) and Léon Walras (1834-1910) weigh in on equal terms with Marshall or the Italian Vilfredo Pareto (I apologize for adding another nationality, especially as the latter's late and reluctant conversion from fascism to democracy does not signal one of the economics profession's finer moments—Pareto could never have held a Fulbright).

Indeed, if we weigh the practical impact of early economists, Say may have beaten them all. The latter's claim to fame is, not coincidentally, "Say's Law," which stated that "supply creates its own demand." It does not take an economic genius to recognize the origins of the "supply-side economics" touted so recently, and with not inconsiderable impact, in the U.S. In fact, the Republican Party may owe more to French economists than they acknowledge. No less a stalwart than Pierre Rinfret, erstwhile Republican candidate for Governor of New York, has been heard to say that the only economics of value he ever learned was picked up in Dijon on a two-year Fulbright.

Still on the French contribution, in political science one cannot underestimate the early French contributors, notably Montesquieu and Tocqueville. Montesquieu is usually considered to have laid the base for the drafters of the American constitution by his emphasis on the value of separating institutional powers (in *De L'Esprit des lois*); his musings on political culture virtually created my own field of comparative politics and other elements of contemporary social science. It was Montesquieu who was, if not the first, then one of the earliest to demonstrate that there was something to be gained from comparing political systems. While he theorized quaintly that different "climates" produced different behavior (to be fair, Montesquieu's notion of climate included the "moral climate"), the sources of culture for him became less important than the fact that different countries had different cultures. Had Woodrow Wilson thought more about comparative politics rather than writing his influential book on *Congressional Government*, the Virginia lawyer and Princeton political scientist might have fared better in the negotiations at Versailles. He surely would have realized that different political leaders negotiated from different cultural perspectives. He might also have taken a less interventionist and more understanding approach to our neighbors to the South, rather than insisting on "teaching [Mexicans] to elect good men" by intervening militarily.

No less a conscious but latter-day Wilsonian than J. William Fulbright wanted to correct for the insulated character that inhibited the achievement of Wilson's goals for peaceful relations among nations. His idea, as he has put it in his folksy way, was to educate "these goddam ignorant Americans." Montesquieu had alerted comparative politics to differences in culture, and the Fulbright program helped alert, or in some cases remind Americans of Montesquieu.

If the impact of Montesquieu on American social thought tended to accent differences, the generalizations of Tocqueville highlighted the similarities in human responses to political incentives. For Tocqueville especially, institutions could correct human failings; competing centers of power could ward off authoritarian tendencies at the top, while power given to local government could strengthen the democratic experience of most citizens. Tocqueville learned this by comparing the centralized and authoritarian France he knew to the riotous and libertarian politics of the U.S. he visited. Thus, all political scientists interested in the impact of culture on institutions and in the impact of institutions on culture owe a debt to Tocqueville and France.

Twentieth-century icons from France are by like token not rare. In the field of international relations, Raymond Aron, along with the German-American Hans Morganthau, is one of the founding fathers of "political realism," an academic approach to issues of war and peace that has dominated the views of diplomats and statesmen since World War II. If Wilson and his successors drank too little from the cup of Montesquieu, later generations—certainly those who did Sciences Po'—may have been too strongly influenced by the so-called realism of Aron.   Despite his Jewish roots and Gallic education, Aron's world was Anglo-Saxon.   It was the world of Hobbes, because of whom Aron's *La Guerre et la paix entre les nations* was more *Guerre* than *Paix*.

By way of a parenthesis, Aron's book was a bible at Sciences-Po'.   I used to see him rummaging around in the card catalog room of the library and I would secretly curse him.   My reasons, however, were not intellectual: the tome was soporific.   I preferred Aron's rival from the same class at the Ecole Normale Supérieure Jean-Paul Sartre: his books, excepting the opaque and ponderous *L'Etre et le Néant*, were at least entertaining.

Closer to the point of the present volume, much of the post-war transatlantic influence discussed above was facilitated by the Fulbright program.   Young French scholars reanimated the thought of Tocqueville and Durkheim back in their native land, where more rigid ideological categories had intervened.   Michel Crozier, Henri Mendras, and Alain Touraine, perhaps the three best-known French sociologists, who brought back American thinking to France, worked at the University of Chicago and Harvard in the early years of the exchange in 1950-52, two of them financed by Fulbright.   It was a happy *échéance* as well that the best-known French diplomatic historian, Jean-Baptiste Duroselle, directed the Fulbright program in France for many years, assuring a Franco-American exchange of ideas which reverberates as vibrantly today as it did at the dawn of the postwar era.   To be a student in Duroselle's large lecture course was pure delight.   He presented diplomatic history without reference to notes and with a rollicking sense of humor that made the weekly lecture more like a visit with a stand-up comic.   His *L'Histoire des relations internationales de 1919 à nos jours* was a standard reference at Sciences Po'.   Less of his work has been translated, but my own students are familiar with him thanks to his chapter on French foreign policy in the influential volume *In Search of France*, of which Duroselle was a co-author, along with Stanley Hoffmann, Charles Kindleberger, Jesse Pitts, and Laurence Wylie.

Under the stewardship of Duroselle and the Fulbright Program, French scholars relearned their own traditions, as well as new ones, in the U.S.   Meanwhile Americans went to France.   Thanks to Fulbright, American liberalism came full circle.   In the vocabulary of travel, the idea of liberalism completed a round trip.

If French social thought supplied support for liberalism in the U.S., French thinkers have also challenged and even undermined the liberal hegemony, both in France and the U.S.   Liberalism has always had its critics on both sides of the Atlantic.   America obviously owes its current discourse to the multiple facets of liberalism: Republicans focus on keeping the state from intruding on the freedoms of businessmen, while Democrats focus on protecting individuals' (including alleged criminals') civil liberties. By the same token, both parties pervert classical liberalism. Democrats do so by advocating government intervention in the market, while Republicans advocate, in essence, state-prescribed moral and religious conduct under the guise of promoting "traditional" values. This, of course, does not exhaust the range of American political debate, but setting the distortions aside, most divisions in the U.S. are, in a sense, family quarrels within the broader context of liberalism.

Certainly, any mode of thought and action, positivism and liberalism included, will generate dissent. The critique of liberalism gained force as U.S. policy-makers decided to promote, or perhaps fell into the trap of promoting without complete awareness of what they were doing, the philosophy worldwide. The Vietnam War rent the American social fabric. Some critics of the war saw American foreign policy as essentially motivated by the machinations of capitalists to secure more markets (the economic side of liberalism), while others in the opposition saw it as the product of a messianic zeal to impose American ideology on others. Positivism, which denied a role for values in social science, lost favor. Liberalism seemed to lead to its opposite, the American state's intrusion on others, be they Vietnamese nationalists or American dissenters. Here too, Senator Fulbright and his program played two roles: Fulbright's personal reaction to the Vietnam war, where the Senate Foreign Relations Committee he chaired gave voice to the war's opponents, and the Fulbright Program's promotion of intellectual exchange, which facilitated the transmission of critical thought between the world's academies—both these factors contributed to the debate. Conservative critics of the Fulbright program were well aware of the danger of this allegedly left-wing contaminant from abroad; yet they tended not to notice that American-trained foreign scholars, who studied in the U.S. thanks to Fulbright, often challenged the frequently deep-seated Marxism of their home academies when they returned to Europe.

The Vietnam War discouraged many social scientists in the U.S. It also encouraged them to look for, if not ulterior motives, then the sets of incentives which guided politicians. This led, I think, to an attraction for structuralism in the U.S. True, the groundwork had been laid long before American troops set foot in Indochina. The work of Claude Lévi-Strauss, especially the notion of irreducible underlying structures which he saw guiding human behavior, greatly influenced American anthropology in the 1950s. Lévi-Strauss' ideas may, of course, have been influenced by his long sojourn in New York during World War II—in this sense, he like Tocqueville was a kind of "pre-Fulbrighter." Certainly, there was an element in his notion of social structure that had a twist of America: his structuralism focused on the unchanging dimensions of culture. It was, in a word, a-historical. Lévi-Strauss' ideas in turn led farther than he anticipated, to a spread of the more simplistic "structural-functionalism" in sociology and political science, despite the French anthropologist's personal aversion to the approach. These ideas aimed to uncover invisible, underlying motivations of human comportment and provided a tradition upon which the critics of the Vietnam War could draw.

In the 1960s and 1970s, writers began to look for some kind of capitalist logic to the behavior of the American government, which seemed to some to do whatever it wanted, despite broadly-based and growing popular protest. French structural Marxists, especially Louis Althusser and Greek expatriot Nicos Poulantzas, offered an explanation: the capitalist state was autonomous, that is, insulated from the influences of society. It had to be independent of different factions so as to provide optimum conditions for capital accumulation.

This notion of the autonomous state appealed not only to leftist scholars but to more conservative critics of liberalism, like Stephen Krasner or Theda Skocpol. These thinkers rejected the view that states merely reflected society and asserted instead that a state could incarnate the national—or at least its own—interest. Here they also received support from France: Jean Bodin's *Six Books of the Commonwealth*, like Tocqueville less influential in France than in the U.S., had made the same claims in the sixteenth century.

Beyond political science and sociology, French social thought extended to history in the post-Vietnam world. Traditional American historical scholarship, which emphasized (and critics said, glorified) the actions of governments, gave way to the New History, influenced by Marc Bloch and the Annales School in France and its foremost practitioner Fernand Braudel. The State University of New York at Binghamton opened a Braudel Center, under the direction of Immanuel Wallerstein, to study long-term structural trends in world history. Wallerstein's approach, grafting Marxist vocabulary onto a view of the world that could only be termed structural-functionalist (Wallerstein's earlier intellectual loyalty), offered attractions to a wide range of scholars: professions of Marxism appealed to the left, while the inherent functionalism, presenting world society as an organic whole, appealed to the right. The most prestigious university presses added a multitude of new titles in social history to their already impressive lists.

The thesis of structuralism has, in a sense, led to its antithesis. The search for hidden structures of power led to seeing power in unusual places, by previous standards. The writings of Michel Foucault suggested that power was everywhere. He looked for signs of politics in everything from prisons to sexual relations. Since power is a relational concept—you only have power over someone who does not—power everywhere meant power nowhere. The structuralist critique of liberalism, carried to its ultimate conclusion, self-destructed.

This did not end the influence of the new wave of French social thought in the U.S. One form of structure is law, the quintessential expression of the Establishment. As structuralism provided fuel for critiques of the American policy, deconstructionism (as represented by philosopher Jacques Derrida's literary criticism) gave ammunition to many, including left-of-center critics of legal theory.

Legal scholarship in the U.S. has traditionally been a closed system. Legal reasoning has its own standards, where laws and judicial opinions are taken at face value. Dissent from this view has traditionally taken the form of attributing legal ideas to ethereal notions of "Natural Law," which claims values are "objective"; but it is murky as to the source of those values or as to the actual meaning of "Nature." Long somnolent, issues of Natural Law recently arose again in American consciousness (after, some might say, a two-century hiatus) as Clarence Thomas weakly defended the approach in his confirmation hearings for appointment to the Supreme Court. French ideas gave critics of traditional legal scholarship a different intellectual basis upon which to criticize the Establishment. Ephemeral allusions to "nature" were not necessary. The Critical Legal Studies movement based at the Harvard Law School borrowed deconstructionist ideas. If, as followers of Derrida contend, the authority of those who write words is less important than the context within which the words appear, the authority of legal decisions is less important than the political context of the law. If the original liberalism of Locke and Tocqueville delegitimized arbitrary authority, the ultimate critique of liberalism delegitimized all authority.

Yet authority survived. The assault on authority generated a conservative reaction. The 1980s saw a full scale counter-attack against intellect. The verdict of populist irrationality as articulated in Gustave Le Bon's *Psychology of Crowds* (1895), seemed to be an up-to-date assessment of Republican presidential campaigns. The late Lee Atwater, a PhD candidate in Political Science at the University of South Carolina, concocted his Willy Horton ads; they may not perhaps have been directly inspired by Count Gobineau, but they played to the same emotions. Nevertheless, intellect survives. The base, xenophobic instincts of *la foule* seem only to be short-term. In the end cooler heads seem to be prevailing. When the dust settles, I suggest we may wish to give some measure of credit to the Fulbright Program.

*   *   *

Things have a way of turning into their opposites. The liberalism of America ultimately led to a kind of global interventionism. This then generated dissent at home and ill-will abroad. Ultimately, the excesses of both phenomena were self-correcting, although not without a great deal of pain.

In my view, the American story has nonetheless been one of liberalism triumphant. The country may indeed have been a fragment of British political culture, but in the four centuries since the founding of Jamestown American culture has taken on a cast of its own. An important ingredient of the American amalgam has been the contribution from France. Thinkers like Tocqueville learned from America and in return spurred us to new heights. Other French social thought reinforced our virtues. And messianic liberalism, which governed our foreign policy in the world's limitrophes, not only failed to accomplish its objectives but ricocheted back on us. Deeply-held beliefs came into question. Ultimately, the experience was healthy. The schisms caused by liberal misadventure in foreign affairs led in the end to greater tolerance, both at home and abroad. The route was tortuous, but the destination grand. I am an optimist. I like to think that we are stronger for having taken that road.

The vital mechanism which assists a society to self-correct is the free flow of ideas. Observation and critique are the functions of intellectuals. These functions are all the more critical when they involve or affect those who exercise political power. Emperors need to know when they are wearing no clothes. Thus, the intellectual interchange facilitated by the Fulbright Program has served more than the principle of knowledge for its own sake. The freshness of outlook afforded by the visitor serves the interest of the host. At both ends of the exchange, we learn from travel, and we learn from inviting travelers to our homes—the effects of travel are a tonic to mind and soul. Since 1949 generations of Fulbrighters have tried to create better worlds. This experience has illuminated the route, as we all have pursued our collective journey, shaping history as we progress.

Alan and Jacqueline Paskow, who profess philosophy and romance languages respectively at St. Mary's College in Southern Maryland, went to Germany in 1987, to the University of Konstanz, where Alan taught American Civilization. In a joint article written after that experience for an annual publication in Konstanz focusing on the city, they reflected on aspects of life in Germany. Three years later, for this volume, they restated this article and appended some later thoughts. Given its focus on town rather than gown and its intended audience of citizens of then-West Germany, there is little that explicitly touches the Fulbright Program or the intellectual challenges of teaching in a foreign university or relating to foreign colleagues. Instead we find an analysis of U.S.-German relations, of difference, of the effort to come to terms with the meaning of Germany today by Americans sensitive to history and to the values of America and Europe. This facet of the Fulbright experience, an encounter with another nation's identity bringing Americans face to face with the complexities of their own cultural synthesis, reflects the search of other writers in this volume.

30

GERMANY REMEMBERED AND RECONSIDERED

Alan and Jacqueline Paskow

Three or more years ago, in the summer of 1988, a German friend of ours in Konstanz invited us to set down some of our impressions of that city and of Germany. He made his request as an editor of the *Konstanz Jahrbuch*, where the essays were to be published, in German, the following year. Then two years later the principal editor of this volume read our essays and suggested that, with modifications for the new readership, they might be appropriate for this volume of Fulbrighters' recollections and reflections. What follows are revised versions of the original essays, plus a jointly-produced afterword that expresses our current sentiments about our stay in Germany. Here first is what Alan wrote in 1988:

"I came to Germany excited and apprehensive. My wife, also a college professor, and I were beginning our sabbatical year. I was being paid by a senior research Fulbright grant to undertake the kind of reading, conversing, and writing (on current issues in literary theory) that I had longed to do, but which I had necessarily deferred for years. Our eleven-year-old daughter was with us too. She would, we hoped, make good friends, learn a new language, and be stimulated by the different 'world' of Germans.

"However, I felt a sense of uneasiness in many of the towns and cities that we visited on our way to the Lake of Constance. For this was the country of 'the Germans,' a people who at one time had enthusiastically supported a government that had sought to annihilate people virtually indistinguishable from some of my friends and all of my relatives, i.e., fellow Jews.

"Since I had known very few Germans before coming to Germany, initially the 'meaning' of Konstanz, of the country itself, was defined almost exclusively by its architecture. The buildings of the oldest section, especially the cathedral, bespoke a city that had predated and would postdate me by 'eons.' I felt comforted by this, sensing that something human and magnificent would not soon be leveled in favor of something 'new' and technologically 'necessary.' North of the old quarter was a different cast of buildings, in the manner of Jugendstil, which imitated, in the framing of windows and doors, the arabesque patterns of nature. I often contemplated this architecture. It had grace, imaginativeness, and (except for one massive, helmet-like cupola) proportion; it strengthened my belief that while new styles like Jugendstil cannot totally supplant the old, we need them nevertheless—for a proper sense of our own *current* identity, distinct from that felt by people in earlier periods, and at the same time for a proper sense of our own *historical* identity, since the opposing quality of the recent and contemporary necessarily refers us to 'another' time, whose values are able to wait for our re-exploration and re-appreciation.

"Other visual impressions: shiny and clean, red busses endlessly repeating by the clock their city-wide circulations; a litterless environment, achieved in part by citizens who actually use the large metal waste bins to deposit, in the appropriate holes, their green, brown, and clear glass bottles and jars; boats on the Lake of Constance, and especially the slow, silent, effortless movements of pale, white sails, heading not to destinations, but simply and fully participating in the moment of wind and current.

"At the same time, from the beginning of our stay there were for me inexplicable contrasts to this eminently habitable world of Konstanz. A watch tower soared above the railroad tracks at the center of town. No sinister purpose here, obviously. And yet something about that tower—was it the uncompromising geometry of its weathered facade or the fact that a watchman within it would be quite isolated from the people below?—compelled me to think of the Nazi period (in particular, of the watchtowers at the four corners of concentration camps). And then there was the bank and office building now occupying the site of Konstanz's principal synagogue, destroyed a half-century earlier. The bank was . . . well . . . a bank. And yet for me, having met some of the old Jewish Konstanzers who, in a specially set-aside room within, participate in Sabbath services, the bank refused to even look like just a bank. When I would look at it carefully, it simply stood there in a kind of defiant, ugly functionality. And I recall as well the immense stone (or cement?) building near the people's high school, standing by itself, alone, abandoned, connected to nothing in the here and now: its long, vertical windows boarded up, the unattractive yellow-beige face thoroughly pockmarked (from old wounds of bullets?), the bushes and trees surrounding it appearing diseased and stunted by that which they were intended to grace. No thing, not even a simple sign, acknowledged—much less gave testimony to—this place.

"These impressions were necessarily qualified as we became acquainted with many Konstanzers—parents of our daughter's friends, colleagues from the university, and of course the city's merchants, auto mechanics, doctors, dentists, public officials, et al. I cannot say that I was ever able completely to integrate and reconcile my initial contrasting impressions. But I can say that I grew very fond of a few Konstanzers and very grateful to many, many more.

"I suppose that what affected me earliest and most strongly was the earnestness, thoroughness, and sense of responsibility that Konstanzers showed to the stranger. Some illustrations come immediately to mind. I wanted, within days of our arrival in the city, to buy for my wife a pair of earrings for her birthday. I asked advice from a goldsmith in the city center. She listened to my halting German, asked many questions, understood the intricateness of my request, sensed as well that she had on her hands a fastidious and perhaps unsatisfiable customer. Yet she was able, even after several return visits on my part, to respond to me with useful information, warmth, and even humor. We eventually collaborated on the design of the earrings which she fabricated. But I'm certain that she would have responded in precisely the same way had I finally left the store with no purchase. Another time, one morning, the printer of my computer wouldn't work and, needing to send in a conference paper immediately, I hoped for its instantaneous repair. 'I'm sorry,' apologized the store repairman; 'I won't be able even to look at it for several days.' 'Whatever you can do,' I said somewhat desperately. That afternoon the technician, an extremely friendly and polite person, told me over the telephone that my computer printer was fixed. I could hardly believe it.

"As with all virtues, there is in this trait of public conscientiousness an obverse side—the excess which becomes a vice. Consider my first experience at the local indoor tennis club. During my first visit, I enjoyed playing at a temperature of 16 degrees Celsius (about 61 degrees Fahrenheit) on beautifully cared-for courts. But then, at exactly six minutes before the hour, flashing lights started blinking at my partner and me. What's that? I asked. 'We must stop now,' he said. Let's hit these two balls and then stop, I suggested. 'No,' he said, 'we must stop now. Watch what I do.' He found a huge net-like object and started dragging it across the court. Its wake was a perfectly even surface. I fetched a similar 'net' and copied my partner. Around and around he went, like a donkey at a grist mill. I became a donkey too. Then he found a device for cleaning the lines of the court. Up and down and back and forth he went with his click-click machine—quickly. I was a little slow. The next players, ready for at least three minutes, walked onto the court and started hitting the ball to each other while I anxiously finished cleaning the lines. 'Next time try to clean up more quickly,' he told me in a friendly way. 'You know how it is in Germany.' (I noticed on the wall clock that it was two minutes past the hour.) On the way back to the locker we stopped before a small electric machine. I watched my partner insert first one foot, then the other. The whirring motor was removing bits of fine surface composition that had stuck to each of his tennis shoes. I imitated him, fascinated by, and eager to understand, this utterly rationalized world of rules and instruments designed to help people play a game with maximum efficiency. In the locker room we undressed and I followed my partner into the shower room. I turned on the shower, which blasted me with hot water for about ninety seconds. Then nothing. I called to my partner for an explanation. 'You need to push the button again.' Why again? I asked. 'Well,' he said, 'the hot water output is timed so as not to waste any water.' With five or six button pressings, I managed to finish my shower. The wall hair dryer was waiting for me when I stepped out.

"There was one domain where I frequently saw—I was mystified by this—the very opposite of public conscientiousness, although, to be sure, rules were being carefully observed: this occurred in Autobahn driving. The images of cars in my rear-view mirror would appear *ex nihilo*. And suddenly their drivers would be applying their horns and blinking lights with rage. I always seemed to move too slowly from the left lane of the Autobahn to the middle lane. Why couldn't these drivers wait a bit for me to pull over? And why was it necessary for them to travel at 160, 180, or 200 kilometers per hour in the first place? A friend from Schwelm assured me that it had to be so. Why? I insisted. 'Commerce,' he said. 'In Germany we need to move our products very quickly and efficiently.' They can't wait a little longer for delivery? 'Certainly not,' he stated categorically. Once on a narrow street in the downtown area of Konstanz I was driving a bit too much to the left, thus making it difficult for a woman driver in the opposite lane to get easily by me. There was such anger in her eyes and distorted mouth (words I could not hear), such frustration and even (it seemed) hatred, that I felt for a moment . . . condemned.

"The experience of that woman, as well as a few other similar experiences, assert themselves as strange, even eerie, in that place in my life called Konstanz, Germany. I cannot help feeling that they are significant. Still this supposed significance is contradicted by so much else—especially by the warmth, affection, and attention to detail shown to us by Konstanzers who became our friends. Illustrations: the careful preparation and presentation of seemingly every course of each meal that various friends treated us to. The way in which one couple whom we became close to planned each phase of a day celebrating my forty-ninth birthday—from a hike to a lake in the Swiss Alps to our eating together at a superb local restaurant. The effortless care and imaginativeness that the wife of our friend from Schwelm showed in organizing our (collective) children and arranging daily bicycle trips around the Lake of Constance when she and her three young daughters stayed with us in our modest Konstanz apartment for an entire week. The attentiveness with which my sponsor at the University of Konstanz, Professor Hans Robert Jauss, read my own philosophical writings and his insistence, obviously for my sake alone, that we discuss them, and his writings as well, in German for two hours each week.

"I could continue these recollections of experiences that define my sense of who Konstanzers and Germans are. But it is also useful to compress and summarize what that complex year *meant* to me. Overall, I enjoyed being in Germany enormously; I have strong affection for the people and find myself wanting to know them in a deeper way. I read newspaper articles and essays in magazines and journals that pertain to Germany whenever I can. I know that part of my fascination with the country has to do with its past culture, which has given the world so much in the realms of science, art, and philosophy, but which also brought about the Second World War and all of its attendant horrors. Just as I am unable to reconcile some of the particular events with others that I was witness to in Germany, so too I am unable to reconcile various historical events with its cultural achievements. But I am grateful for the way in which Germans do not hide, but conscientiously try to come to terms with, their past—in frequently appearing magazine stories, television programs and books, as well as in private conversation. The

Germans, it seems to me, have, on the whole, done much better in this regard than the Austrians, the Hungarians, the French, and the Poles. And they have done much better than we Americans have done with our own past in Vietnam. "

*   *   *

Here is what Jacqueline wrote: "I found many aspects of life in Konstanz, Germany very provoking in their differentness. It is probably only in their differentness, perceived from the point of view of 'elsewhere,' that certain ways of being even become visible in the first place. And it is in turn this experience of estrangement, with its wonder, frustration, even indignation, and after it the achievement of an uncanny familiarity, that can make living in another culture, as opposed to touring through it, so quickening and productively unsettling to the spirit.

"Overall, I was most struck by how much of a distinct culture has survived both a cataclysmic past and the 'Americanization' of Western Europe. What seemed to me most distinguishing of German culture compared to American culture is the important role that boundaries and distinctions themselves play in daily life.   There are surely more differentiations in everyday life in Germany that do not exist in America than there are different kinds of bread in an ordinary German bakery.   But I will mention only the very most mundane ones, those that are, I am assuming, the commonest currency for a German.

"When I go to the bakery and have done my best at choosing and naming my daily bread, I mustn't forget to mark my departure with a 'good-bye' to the shopkeeper before I leave the premises. And I must learn that there is a time for everything and that not everything can be done at any time, depending on my fancy. The time, for example, between twelve o'clock and two o'clock is staked out as pausing time. School is over for the day, most stores close, and families eat their midday meal together and rest without outside disturbances. I must never telephone people at home during this private time. A second daily island of time, which is likewise not to be invaded by noise or telephone calls, runs from nine o'clock in the evening until seven in the morning. Shops, of course, close earlier; that is, when 'Feierabend' begins. The term has no tidy English translation, but you know when it strikes, because the shopkeepers will brusquely terminate their relationship with you and show you the door. Similarly, there is no mistaking a weekend for a week day. If

"The seasons too have their German boundaries. They are often defined by popular celebrations—festivities which are subsidized by city hall, and by citizens divided up into guilds, fraternities, or neighborhood associations. In November, for example, I watched as winter was let loose in the center of town. She was allowed to roam about and misbehave until February, when she was imprisoned again to prepare for the resurrection of spring. The seasons of a person's life too, or even of the life of a firm or organization, are delineated not only by birthday celebrations and retirement receptions, but by anniversary festivities commemorating the sheer fact of their continued existence (of their 'Bestehen'). Even death is given a time limit, after which your grave is removed from the cemetery to make way for the next generation of the dead.

"If weekends are markedly different from week days because work stops and friends and families go walking or bicycling together in nature, the remarkable fact that there still exists some nearby nature to go walking in at all is due to the persisting boundaries between town and countryside. When you leave Konstanz and walk in a northerly direction, for example, buildings along the highway actually stop at a certain point and do not reappear until you come to the village of Litzelstetten, or again until Dingelsdorf. Likewise, the villages of Allensbach or Dettingen are still separated from Konstanz by woods, albeit the tidiest, most manicured woods I have ever seen, with hardly a trace left of underbrush or fallen timber.

"And if towns and villages keep their distance and distinctness from one another, so do people, especially in town. It is as though the closer the space, the greater the formality. I never felt more lonely, for example, than in the elevator of my seven-story apartment building, travelling with fellow residents to whom I had never been introduced. There was such a silence and an avoidance of eye contact that I didn't dare say anything, much less introduce myself. The message seemed to be that we should pretend that the other person wasn't really there. I was so unsettled at first by this elevator custom, and by the positing of my nonexistence, that I took to using the staircase instead.

"Outside of the elevator, however, on sidewalks and steps, passing conversation—even though it occurred less frequently than I was used to in America—was often more significant and interesting. The rhetorical question, 'How are you?', which in America is used merely as a greeting and an assurance of undiscriminating friendliness, but rarely as a sincere question, in Germany, much to my delight, usually provoked—instead of the equally rhetorical, American 'Fine'—a considered reply. In the end, I appreciated more than anything else a German's ability to be fully present to your question and to take the actual content of conversation seriously, showing me that the subject matter at hand could be distinct from, and not just an alibi for, the performance of an easy ritual. This generosity of attention and readiness to discern has, since my return home, made me obsessively aware of a distractedness, a kind of spiritual dispersion or avoidance on the part of my compatriots (and myself) in our daily greetings.

"However, the most difficult line of demarcation for me as an American to live with at first was that which lies between 'Du' and 'Sie' and that between first-name address and titled last-name address. In America, the social world is merely divided up between people whom you know and people whom you don't know. The former are more or less indistinguishably called 'friends' (unless you actually despise them), while the others aren't called anything. They are simply the people whom you don't know; in other words, a vast reserve of potential friends, were you to meet them. Within the broad American category of 'friends,' Germans, on the other hand, distinguish between 'Freunde' and 'Bekannte' which, translated into American notions, mean very good friends versus casual friends. Of the first category, that is, those to whom you say 'Du,' you don't want to have too many, I've been told, because there is a big responsibility that goes with having a Du-relationship. In general, Germans probably take longer and better care of their 'Freunde' than Americans take of their 'friends,' which may explain why an American can usually accommodate many more friends than a German —the more, in fact, the merrier—whereas a German will be more cautious and selective about whom to admit to this denomination.

"Is it because Germany is smaller and more crowded that doors to rooms are kept closed, that so many fences are constructed, lines drawn, and distinctions made, as though to make space? And conversely, is it the legendary wide-open spaces that have brought Americans together so uninhibitedly? Quite likely. But now that space is no longer so abundant in many parts of America, now that an almost continuous city runs down the northern third of the eastern seaboard, for example, why then do Americans continue to minimize differences, even at the price of esthetic sloppiness, educational and political superficiality, and psychological dispersion? Or how, on the other hand, do Germans dare insist on differences without their social fabric being torn apart? Perhaps, given the plurality of ethnic cultures in the U.S. and the all-too-real differences among people, it would be truly dangerous for democracy and sociability to leave the thin layer of commonality and go looking for distinctions. Whereas, given that Germany has, relatively speaking, a remarkably homogeneous ethnic majority, distinctions may be needed to create diversity.

"Whatever the reasons for these differences between German and American manners, my stay in Germany taught me that from distinguishing and discerning comes, paradoxically, the possibility for more exciting contact. And when I say Germany, I primarily mean certain people in Konstanz and its surrounding, but separate, villages, in which I learned how to cross the boundary from 'Sie' to 'Du.'"

*   *   *

It is time now for an afterword, written in late 1991. All of what we wrote in 1988 is still valid today as a record of our feelings about our stay in Germany.   But three intervening years have provoked re-thinkings and clarifications of our experience. The following brief reflections take up what we wrote above, rendering some of our previous thought explicit, other parts of it reshaped or further developed.

It may seem a little odd to say that the first respect in which we felt a loss in returning to America concerned the architectural environment with which we were confronted—odd because Germany's architecture is not that extraordinary (compared with that of, say, France or Italy) and because a country's architecture would not seem to be a definitive cultural feature. Still, we did find ourselves depressed by the general level of architectural unimaginativeness of the area in which we live (Southern Maryland).   Much of it seemed so crassly functional, exhibiting little care for overall proportionality, environmental and other-dwelling integration, or esthetic attention to details (e.g., manner of disrupting the flatness of a façade, recessing of window frames, design of porch railings). Our fondness for certain features of German architecture is probably more of a comment on our particular esthetic interests than it is on German culture. Yet these features reminded us of what seemed to be the greater overall concern, the conscientiousness, on the part of Germans. We do not know whether it is really true that Germans manifest a kind of care in attending to details that is superior to Americans' care.

Perhaps our status as obvious foreigners already disposed many people to be more helpful to us. Perhaps we as foreigners, at the mercy of a culture in many ways strange to us, were always ready to acknowledge whatever thoughtfulness Germans showed toward us. And perhaps, finally, there is something about communicating with people in a language you do not yet know so well that is very stimulating—fun, even, in a way, erotic—and this sense of our own enjoyment may have provoked our friends and acquaintances to respond to us in a similar manner. Our delight was due to our achievement of sharing feelings and incipient ideas with people of extraordinarily different backgrounds.

It is analogous to reading with gratitude a superior piece of fiction about another land in another time, but the satisfaction is greater, for in the face-to-face encounter you not only understand another, you communicate back to him or her, and then your own initial understanding as well as previously unexpressed sentiments are taken up, confirmed, sometimes developed further. In this kind of encounter in Germany, we felt closer not simply to the person or persons with whom we were conversing; we sensed we were getting nearer to the heart of a whole people. The fundamental consequence of this sort of experience was the feeling of becoming "cosmopolitan"—not urbane or sophisticated, but at home in, kindred with, another "world." Now we are more eager to understand Germans and Germany's problems. And we think we can say with sincerity that we are more eager to understand other peoples and other nations' problems as well.

Sometimes, however, our deepening sense of kinship took peculiar turns. In the spring of 1988, we decided, against the advice of colleagues at the University of Konstanz, to visit Frau Heidegger, wife of Martin Heidegger, arguably the greatest philosopher of this century, yet someone sympathetic to, and supportive of, many of the grandiose ideals of Nazism. Elfride Heidegger was in a nursing home in Freiburg (in Breisgau). When we arrived at the care facility, we were told that Frau Heidegger was blind and frail and could only talk with us for about five minutes. Despite this warning, she was sufficiently strong and so eager to talk that we spent over an hour with her.

It was fascinating being with Frau Heidegger. After a three-hour drive to Freiburg, we were all at once transported from a very academic world of scholarship whose occasional subject was the larger-than-life genius-philosopher, Martin Heidegger, to the very mundane bedroom of this particular woman who had spent approximately sixty years of life with her husband. We asked Frau Heidegger all sorts of questions: How did she become acquainted with Martin? Did he have much to do with the upbringing of their children? Was she interested in philosophy? Did she understand and appreciate her husband's work? What did she and her husband think of Hitler? In answer to this last question she said:

> From 1933-36 Hitler did much good for Germany. He built the Autobahn from Freiburg to Hamburg, and from Freiburg to Basel, and by those projects many unemployed people were able to find work. [But] from 1936-39 Hitler became bad. My husband always said that it was not right that people destroyed the synagogues of the Jews, when we too wouldn't have liked it if the Jews had burned down Christian churches. But from 1939-45 the overall situation became terrible, and we Germans wrote him off . . . He was a good-for-nothing (*Taugenichts*).

Alan asked: Because of her disillusionment with Hitler, did she consider emigrating? "But why should we?" she replied. "We *weren't* Jews."

In these simple replies it is easy to detect Frau Heidegger's anti-semitism. For us questioners, this prejudice was no longer tied to images of Hitler and Himmler and Gestapo agents; it was here, right before us, in its distressing ugliness. Yet it was virtually impossible for us to despise this earnest, ninety-year-old woman, lying in her bed, her blind eyes vaguely directed upward, eager to oblige her American visitors in any way that she could. It would be wrong to say that the contradictions within past German culture were at that moment in an important sense reconciled; but we *can* say that the cultural issues that we had read about, discussed, and pondered for years assumed a greater intensity and complexity, and that despite what we had just heard we felt sympathy, even warmth, towards this woman before us.

Because of this kind of experience, when later we were back in our college classrooms in America, it became psychologically unacceptable for us to repeat with the same self-assurance many of our previously enunciated generalizations about Germans who were alive during the period of the Third Reich.

In this regard, but speaking more broadly, Germany will always have a peculiar fascination for us, as something more than another foreign country that we know well. As Alan indicated, Germany has given us incredible gifts in its scientists, artists, and philosophers; but it also gave us Dachau, Birkenau, and Auschwitz. It would be easy to assert that the latter "gift" was aberrational. One could then put the primary responsibility for World War II in Europe on Hitler and the Nazis. On the other hand, some historians take the opposite position and see something sinister in the German people themselves, since they, after all, democratically elected Hitler to power and since many Germans supported Hitler throughout his reign. But we believe that both positions—either that the Nazis were the culprits or that the Germans as a whole were the culprits—are perhaps wide of the mark. For Germany prior to World War I was apparently no more, perhaps less, anti-semitic than other European countries. And Germany was as Western in its cultural outlook as any other European country. These two important facts suggest the hypothesis that there may be something inherently wrong with some aspect of *our* Western outlook itself, that German behavior in the third and fourth decade of this century, while extreme, was manifesting the realization of a possibility that was an ingredient in our modern Western orientation. To say this is not fundamentally to exculpate Germany (as several prominent German historians have tried to do over the past ten or fifteen years), for it cannot be ignored that the French, British, or Belgians did not do what the Germans did. But it is to raise a question about our own American culture—to see it as Western, as profoundly kindred in its values to those of Germany since at least the time of Bismarck, and therefore as perhaps in an important way containing, if only implicitly, a danger. We mention this last point in order to explain our intense continuing interest in Germany. For it is for us now something more than a country of intriguing cultural paradoxes. It does still have these paradoxes—some of them even embodied in individuals whom we remember—and our affection for so many of its people will always goad us to want to understand and appreciate more about them. But we strongly suspect that the proper untangling of modern German history may be the key to comprehending some important truths about modern Western peoples.

Thus the Fulbright experience has led us first to what might be called the otherness and strangeness of the other; but this experience in turn has led us to wonder more about the onlookers themselves, which is to say that we now have a more intense wonder about, a sense of strangeness concerning, ourselves, Americans, as a people.

Four essays in this volume treat Spain and Portugal. In this one the writer, Professor of Management at Pepperdine University in California, tells a tale of self-discovery and renewal. On the recommendation of a perceptive Dean, he went as a Fulbright to Portugal at the precise moment in history when Portugal was beginning to awaken to the need for alternate structures to those torn down after the years of Salazar's dictatorship, and specifically in his case to the need for modern managerial methods. At the time of writing, he had found ingenious ways of returning for three further tours of service to Portugal's universities and has no intention of stopping now. This new connection with a country where he sees his potential contribution as vital and which rewards him in a hundred subtle and surprising ways has become a permanent part of his life. To be useful, to be appreciated, to be able to live with simple pleasures—these three factors make petty inconveniences like faulty wiring disappear. In a letter of gratitude to his thoughtful Dean, he conveys the poetry of a life renewed and turned to purposeful activism.

31

LETTER FROM LISBON

R. Grandford Wright

How did he know the time was ripe for another person? What did he sense occurring to or within me to give such advice? It was at a midpoint in my academic career—not too soon, not too late—that then-Dean Kenton L. Anderson forthrightly instructed me that it was time to get involved in a growth experience beyond the emotional comfort of my own site. Some five years later he confided that he knew a Fulbright would provide honors and experiences beyond those our University could provide. Hence, I sought and won the award that reinfused passion into my teaching and made continuing service psychologically palatable.

At the end of my Fulbright adventure in small measure of thanks, I penned the reflections that follow to the mentor who inspired me to apply for the award.

UNIVERSIDADE NOVA DE LISBOA
Faculdade de Economia
Gestão/M.B.A.

Rua Marquês da Fronteira, 20
1000 LISBOA

14 December 1987

Dear Ken,

It is raining at long last in sunny Portugal, cozy in the living room of the flat and cold elsewhere.   Winter is bearing in.   Tables and chairs are corralled in the cobble-stone corner of what once was our favored sidewalk café. After three sets of company, between term papers and finals, I treated myself to a deep cold requiring abundant self-indulgence with deference from others.   And in that state of insulation, I take the further selfish opportunity to share with you a bit of what has been.   The remarkable events here are nearly over, and this is a nostalgic chronicle impervious to dates.

To me, things here are always fascinating—often emotionally draining —but always commanding.   They all started for Suze and me on the flight deck of a Trans Air Portugal Tri-star locked in on Lisbon with a Portuguese pilot who had studied air safety at my alma mater—USC.   A neighboring school yard's continuing chorus of excited children's voices. The trill of the fife of a passing umbrella repairman.   A world-class European city with a rooster harkening each morn in its center.   A busload of Mongoloids passes, a truly gentle people.   The misfunctional stuff: the old telephone with the confoundingly sticky dial, the drunken streetlight across the street that nearly passes into dimness when it's most needed.   Bobé, the scrappy little honey-colored dog next door, whom we visit with a yummy Bonio— "The biscuit that thinks it's a bone."   Then we visit the Communist co-op "CCD do CNP," where politics and aesthetics bow to some good buys.   Lisbon is getting itself dressed up for Christmas, a simple traditional frock that she has been wearing for years.   Over a million cobblestones we walk.

Then on to the central shopping district with its elegant past, then the powerful statuary of Rossio. A moment of distraction to view the blackened remains of the Chiado district, following the fire that razed the shops and stores and now dampens the spirit.

That evening, it is a joy to be with the Dennis Shaws, the Cultural Attaché, and his wife Dana (pronounced DĂNA), watching a tape of the Dodgers vs. Mets final playoff game (sent to me by a former student from back home). But this evening it is a reception and sit-down dinner with an international assortment of intellectuals and artists. Introduced to squash at Jaime Reis' club (he is the Dean). Quick! His boy Kanga let me win one. Next, Jacques Delors, head of the EEC, is awarded his first honorary doctorate by our department of economics (must be a good man—was once an associate prof of Management!) Finished a white paper for the University here. Like to lunch with students in the charming informal breakfast room at the palace.

Interviewed by Martha De la Cal, *Time/Life* and *WSJ International* correspondent here, on how our Program would make a difference in Portugal, especially with EEC deregulations coming in 1992. Hope she doesn't misquote—will find out when piece is published. Went to a reception at U.S. Ambassador's home to honor 18 years (can you believe?) of contributors to the Salzburg Seminars, held annually at the dramatic Schloss Leopoldskron, a unique intercultural, interdisciplinary dialogue among horizontal thinkers and mid-career professional leaders. Ambassador Edward M. Rowell's home is a showplace highlighted by hand-drawn American quilts hung as tapestries. (A Beatles' tape is beating out a popular piece from the flat across the street.) And we plan to play tennis, weather supporting, at the Embassy court and to attend the annual Marine Corps birthday celebration on the weekend.

A later day . . . the Marine Corps Ball *was* one! The 213th year of pomp, circumstance and service. It is a tradition for the Ambassador to cut the first pieces of cake for the youngest and oldest Marine present. Dennis Shaw told the Detachment Commander that I was a former Marine of Korean War vintage. So there we stood at attention, black-tie up front, with the Hymn and all—me, the "oldest," and the youngest (looking like a baby, he was the same age as I was when the War began for me and when I acquired the illusion of a mantel of manhood).

Tennis is superb on the excellent Embassy hard courts. Rare to find hard courts here. Suze and I played against a couple of fun characters—Al Griffin, a rock musician dependant of the only Vietnamese-born Embassy attaché anywhere, and Dick Burns who as Naval Attaché claims he's a physician—he is one of several alternately rumored to do intelligence. Both solid players.

Gorgeous, palatial setting for the court, overlooking an aqueduct and valley, a point where George Bernard Shaw mused and wrote.

Back "home" we find comfort in the sounds of the train with its bi-tonal shrill whistle. We like the Embassy folk—especially Dennis and Dana. Sort of characters from America's heartland in the best meaning of that heritage—generous and gracious hosts. Senior USIA/State servants—Iran, Brazil, Tunisia . . . then here. Suze saw a fine poster that she wanted on the wall of the local telephone exchange. After a lovely Embassy dinner meeting held at the hunting lodge of a great old palace, Dennis and his wife brought us home. Stopping to see Suze's favorite poster, she decides to carefully remove and quickly abscond with it while we three and a number of our "host" citizens look on. Only two problems: since the Revolution, removing such an announcement is "forbido" as a violation of freedom of speech; and the other: the poster is clearly marked CONFERENCIA DO PCP with vivid red star, hammer, and sickle. I can see the headlines now: U.S. Embassy attaché and Fulbright accomplice offend Soviet bloc . . . .

We took a group of people aboard the battleship USS Missouri on Thanksgiving. What a display of power! I hadn't seen her since she was softening up matters for our assault on Inchon, September 15, 1950. She may have acquired the nickname of "Big Mo" honestly, but to me she's the "Mighty Mo." Now she is a bulwark of a peace-keeping armada serving on the southern perimeter of NATO. Ominous, angry, dark profile, angularly chiseled as only a warship—especially a battleship—can be. No civilian craft has so menacing a presence. Yet with responsible government behind the force, she is welcomed at anchor in the river Tejo as a friend by most Portuguese, a foe only to our mutual enemies.

Can you picture strolling through the gentle rolling hills of a 770-acre cork tree forest in central Portugal? It has been owned since the 1800's by the family of a special lady at the University—Maria dos Anjos de Serpa. After the Revolution of April 25, 1976, the Communists lifted 348 acres—the issue is in the courts. We call Maria dos Anjos, "Angel." She springs from an old family of landed gentry with two marvelous farms, a flat in the city, and membership in the most discerning of social clubs in Lisbon. Angel and her family find themselves impaled on the barbs of a socio-political class conflict. The Communists, so prevalent in the rural communities, are convinced that the De Serpa's land was a political spoil from the dictator Salazar that should be returned to "the people." The family counters by pointing out that the family's ownership of the land precedes the dictator's reign. Whatever the outcome, the locals know the family's eminence. Hence, Angel responds to the peasants in nearby villages as a person of the landed gentry. The villagers respond by acting as respectful and compliant peasants. This farm has cork, corn, rice, cane, vegetables and sheep. On the second visit, we saw the birth of a lamb—the eighth this season. An active little creature who will add a new generation to a cross-sectional flock with old, crippled, middle-aged, young. Angel's parents, who have a second farm and city house, are remarkably proper old-generation elites. All members of a gorgeous social club in Lisbon.

The weather is now crisply clear, brisk and invigorating. We journey to the mouth of the Tejo River where three ancient castles (now *pousadas*) staunchly stood guard against attacks by Moors, where now in a national forest the forces of NATO stand. Then we set off for points north to Oporto, the industrial city where Eiffel practiced up for the main event with impressive bridges. At least one is suspect: people leave the train to take a cab home by another route. We travel south to Sintra, Fatima, Nazaré, and Obidos where alone we climb the wall (1148) surrounding the city. I suppose castles heralded city expansion just as freeways today are bellwethers of suburban growth. Then to Cascais (pronounced COSH-CYSH), and Estoril, where a 13th-century "Westminster Abbey" emerged. Hard to explain why, until we learned that the dull king had a bright English queen.

Home to warm, replete dinner parties, a thrilling European circus (*circo*) with three rings in your lap. An evening at the "Cow Palace" to see a bull fight. Dramatic! One's enough. Excellent lunches in the confines of the walls of St. Jorge's castle that towers over Lisbon on one of its seven hills, as with Rome and San Francisco, to Alfama, the "Latin Quarter" that alone survived the earthquake in the mid-1700's. This is where the *fado* music is played, tugging at one's heart strings tautly. All about love—just as New Orleans has its blues to give vent to the sad side of the affections of man and woman—so the Portuguese have *fado*.

Back to the well-appointed apartment, where our friendly, well-intentioned maid has been dutifully moving things and leaving them in new places (a tactic of day-help, whatever their national origin or allegiance). This marvelous *casa*, with day-help furnished, and all for only 60,000 escudos monthly, only a bit over $400 U.S. Warm and dry for Portugal. We are experiencing inundation by torrential rains. Much needed rain. Then a break. And that new moon, shockingly immense, ostentatiously bright, rises. And Suze quietly sews her rich Arraiolos rug, while I try vainly to tell a simple children's story about a mythical character I could only have created here. The fairy-tale was inspired by the daughter or son (who knows which?) of the *portaria* who helped its mother sweep the marble back stairs that lead down to the courtyard, in the swish-tick rhythm of the broom striking stone. The child sings a happy and innocent song. His or her self-amusing lyric was a sweet gift to listeners given unknowingly, but altering their lives forever. The book is called *Frumpé* after the little singer. Having carved out my career locked on linear logic, how refreshing and difficult this blithe fantasy is to write.

The dining room becomes the focal point of activity—sewing, writing, corresponding, reading, TV, and—oh yes, dining. And it became more rivetingly so as a gathering place when the weather grew cold. A little room with windows to the street, a happily vocal school yard across the street, a funny old mahogany table, open-leafed with piano-like legs, two marble stands of early Roman inspiration, a China hutch for a book case and all other office stuff, a study lamp Suze thoughtfully bought, and a small Siemens heater. The things produced here in comfort: *Frumpé*, working paper #104 for the University, the article on mentoring with friend Bo Werther, the consulting paper to *Business Forum*, a symposium design, the Wilson Center research proposal, all that it takes for two graduate classes, and now, the galleys for the strategy text. What fun!   Truly, it was . . . .

Our flat is plain but adequate (the Communist poster enlivens the place). It backs up to a glen of cedars and beyond, to a playground so that a lilting banter of kids' voices makes its presence known daily: it fronts on a reflection pool. A couple of weeks ago, the water had to be shut off for over a day. The local people had been prepared (same thing occurred earlier with power), but two uninformed visitors were not. You guessed it!   When I returned from the University, the water level of the otherwise tranquil pool had dropped discernably, as Suze had hauled enough of the stuff up to our place to open an ice rink had the weather changed dramatically. The dearth of good books and TV surely helps to get something done during those long, cold evenings and weekends. Typically Sunday finds TV beaming Catholic Masses and European soccer on its two-channel system, meeting a viewer's diverse needs for peace and violence respectively.

I wrote a white paper on the Program and two papers for U.S. journals, then contributed the first paper from a Fulbright business professor to the Department's series of Working Papers.

From the first moment of contact the University people have been wonderful. Director Carlos Barral met us warmly when we arrived at 4:30 AM. Our economics division chap, Jaime Reis, is quite a man. Cambridge-trained, and 20 years there made a mark of class.

Unlike most American universities perched centrally in cultural islands, here the new university is scattered around Lisbon with a school or division here and there. One of many such sites houses the School of Economics. A restored monastery used for a time as army barracks after the religious orders were expelled from Portugal in the nineteenth century. We teach in a five-star eighteenth-century palace. A beautiful, ornate edifice set in spacious rolling grounds overlooking the Gulbenkian Museum within walking distance of downtown Lisbon (of course, most everything is within walking distance for me).

Picture the stereotypical American academic hall, then come with me to the MBA Program site. Driving up Rua Marquês da Frontiera turn right through the great iron gates to the guard tower, where a friendly aging couple and two wary young dogs live and welcome wanted guests. Motor up the bowed drive to the carriage entrance. Then enter and inhale the grandeur. Warm Philippine mahogany, marble steps, joint gas/electric lamps for contingencies set in massive chandeliers, frescos everywhere, a million-dollar dining room, Della Robbia ceramic, gilded sculpture on door handles, a fully furnished sitting room, the added elevator that fails to work, a charming informal kitchen café. In sum, four stories of the elegant baroque milieu demanded by the princely few of the 1750's. The requirements for students carved out carefully to preserve the ambiance. A library tucked away here, a computer lab there, and the major seminar room. Imagine further this classroom, a long rather narrow hall with high ceilings and heavily draped cathedral windows designed for dining. In typical style, students' one-armed chairs face the teacher's raised lecture platform. Untypically, the walls are adorned with a priceless collection of ceramic tiles, called *azulejos* for the blue of the Portuguese sky. These blue and white tiles portray dramatic hunting scenes serially from prehistoric cave man, to the use of slings, to spears, to the use of early firearms. And midst these remarkable cultural carryovers from the 1700s we discuss socio-technical configurations of business enterprises for the 2000s.

What poignant teaching experiences. A student population that *needs* help—and knows it. To be listened to actively. To have students inquire "May I?" before entering one's office or classroom, if late. What a joy it is to have João Especial as a student, a budding brain trust in artificial intelligence (to Stanford) and Rita e Cunha, a PhD candidate, whose dissertation I will have the joy of guiding with three Portuguese colleagues and Fred Herzberg who was here last year. Tremendous intellectual and professional experience. Powerful!

The oral defense of our first PhD candidate. Dramatic, worth the price of a ticket! Remarkable rites and rituals that mark the degree-holder for life. In the U.S. it is customary for a dissertation defense to be attended by the candidate's committee members, several faculty members interested in the research conducted, and several interested in becoming graduate faculty members.   The examination can be conducted thus in a small class or conference room.

Not so in Portugal. Picture the stage: an amphitheater, with raised platform for examiners with massive table, and a lower desk for candidate, stage left. High walls with shining windows at the top. Imagine the drama: the audience assembles unevenly, senior faculty take the orchestra seats, the PhD student's considerable family gather colorfully, students of the candidate mingle noisily, and of course PhD students who will later endure the process—*if* all goes well. Now, representing eight years of study, the young candidate seats himself nervously at his modest desk, pawing through the dissertation to find the response to a belated obscure query that he has imagined will be asked. A hush befalls the crowd as the academic tribunal enters, bedecked in somber black robes, tightly fitted, with glistening black high hats topped with pom-poms (the red and green colors of Portugal). Preliminary statements introduce the research, then the fusillade of probes and measured returns, occasionally spiced with humor, but back to the main mood of solemnity. After each inquisitor has had his questions fielded, after some two hours, the candidate and audience are admonished to leave the assembly so that the committee can make its decision. We now huddle in nearby halls, for a time that seems interminable, awaiting the decision.

Unlike the mere pass-fail consequence in the U.S. way, in this process there are varying levels of pass from marginal to "highest distinction." If the candidate scores a pass with less than the highest mark, he is not acceptable as a teacher at the University. It is tantamount to telling the graduate to leave Academia. So the decision marks the person beyond the degree requirements —for life.

The double doors open. The crowd expectantly returns, silently. The chairman's vibrant pronouncement brings applause, cheers and tears of relief, then champagne to mark the spot—on the faculty. A pass with "highest distinction!" Somehow their way makes ours seem trivial and, if one has studied eight years, anticlimactic.

Now it's back to temporal necessities—and it's also cultural whiplash time. A fleeting air-conditioned train rocks me to Vila Nova de Gaia to teach something called "Leadership: Entrepreneurship and Productivity" (such a lot of words) to people in the new MBA Program at the Instituto Superior de Estudos Empresariais da Universidade do Porto and to return me to Lisbon that afternoon to teach later at the Universidade Nova de Lisboa's MBA/ Management School. From a kibbutz-like, squat building at Oporto back to the grand palace at Lisbon.

It is the beginning of the end of the adventure in Portugal. The time races by, so charged is it with events. And they continue—the people, papers, proposals. Seems that Pepperdine and the New University of Lisbon will link in an educational alliance. I hope it is fruitful. Sat in a "faculty jury," as the outside (I guess, *outside!*) member to review the preparation of a candidate for *associato* level. PhD-trained statistician at Germany's Bergischen Universität-Wuppertal, smitten with Japanese management ways. Deming revisited. (The poor Portuguese worker will never know what hit him.) The mix of colleagues at the "trial" is hysterical. All sizes, all shapes, and *all* academics. Could be a gaggle from the groves of academe *anywhere*. Especially when trying to find another date and time to meet. Calendars out, serious search ensues, no date good for all, Chair decision, junior prof out of next meeting. Ah, sweet justice and harmony prevail.

As we prepare to leave, it's a bittersweet experience. To return to the people, places, puppies, and things that we've left at home is sweet: to leave this most charming, less efficient culture and its warm people is bitter. Especially when one cares about them and their destiny—1992 and beyond. And the Portuguese riding in on waves of two recent revolutions, one political the other cultural. Live now, pay later. And the capitalists come from afar, and a baby boom from here, and a mighty European economic machine needy of unskilled hands. A people who desperately need the lessons of economic productivity that I exported, yet who—if they take that all too seriously—will lose a way of life far more precious. So one wonders . . . as do the MBA students. Representative of such concern were the responses of Isabel Marques, a graduate student, to my questions:

How will the MBA Program impact on Portugal?

The MBA Program . . . will have a very positive impact on our country, because we do not belong to the developing countries' category anymore, and the progress we are making in every area is enormous. I think that Portugal has lots of potential . . . but the problem is that it doesn't know yet how to take advantage of what it has. People are not well-educated (not enough), amateurism is everywhere, and ignorance is a major barrier to successful development.

We are starting now a period where many opportunities are arising, in every area, and we have a strong will towards getting close to our developed international partners. That is why I believe that, with better prepared managers who could allocate more of our limited resources, who could innovate, organize, prepare people, etc., our products would be more competitive, our society would be going forward, our people would be more productive, our economy would be more prosperous.

The MBA Program gives us the chance to get acquainted, not only with techniques which are fundamental to managerial functions, but also the overall idea that a manager should be, nowadays, an open-minded person with the needed flexibility to make the best decisions in a permanently changing and defying environment.

How will you be better able to contribute to Portugal?

My basic motivation . . . is that I want to be a happy person, and this implies professional happiness. Management is the complement I needed in order to be able to work efficiently in the business area. I know I can be a good professional, and I will feel fulfilled if I can feel that what I have achieved has a purpose, a meaning, and is useful to the society . . . .

If I can make one enterprise prosperous—not only profitable, although this is a main objective—but also an organization where people, which is for me the most important element, can be productive and motivated . . . and feeling happy for belonging to the organization, I believe I will be doing something for Portugal.

What conditions currently prevail that may impede your ability to so contribute, e.g., values, law, religion, family, social structures, or whatever?

I think this is a good opportunity to say something about what are some of Portugal's weaknesses. Portugal is, first of all, a country with old traditions, where people are conservative and reactive to changes. Most people accommodate themselves to their situation, rather than to make something change it. It doesn't mean that they are lazy; maybe they are not ambitious enough. In my working experience I have noticed some major barriers to what could change the organization for the better.

First of all, the businesses are small, and usually the older member of the family is the leader. He tends to centralize all decisions, which can be inefficient. The companies are *traditional*, the employees work there for 10, 15, 20 years. One problem is that, because it is a paternalistic corporation, if there is an employee who is not productive enough to contribute to the firm's development, we act rather like a charity home, maintaining him/her there just for humanitarian reasons. What I am saying is that *sentimentalism* still plays a major role in these traditional businesses (which are still the biggest share of all businesses), in detriment to efficiency.

. . . Our *labor laws* are still very rigid, which means that sometimes you cannot fire someone even if you have a good reason. The flexibility of these laws (which are not yet possible due to our Constitution, which is going to be revised) are very important to attract foreign investment and therefore promote our development, as well as to encourage internal investment also.

. . . *Ignorance* can still be a major barrier to development. That is why in the next years the great emphasis will be made in education . . . . A problem which I could face would be that older people and usually not well educated would not accept easily management authority from someone new in age with less experience although highly qualified. I referred to Portuguese people being conservative and, in a way, traditional. A traditional belief would be that you know nothing unless you have lived many years, and mainly, if you have suffered a lot . . . .

A remarkable genetic riptide between Europeans and Moors brought forth these appealing people—these Portuguese—not without strife, conflict and buffeting. Now a cultural riptide is at work—between parochial, simpler ways and ways required by the need for advancement, which shall not be reconciled without considerable social upheaval and personal pain. So, certain of the mores, values and customs that have served well in the past mean the people of Portugal may now have to bend in the path of economic progress. Not break, for the people, products of ancient genetic happenstance, are up to the stress demanded by today's cultural wrenching.

The De la Cal article in the International Edition of the *Wall Street Journal* reflected my views accurately:

> Visiting American Professor . . . of Pepperdine University, who is teaching (here) for the second time, believes the MBA graduates will change Portugal. He believes they will break down the values. He says they are making an impression in management, consulting and teaching. "These people are like our own business people. They are political moderates who want to see free enterprise work. They see the old rule where the government was like Big Brother—a patriarch—as a web to be pierced." He likens their training to a "conspiracy" to change things. "We already have 300 'conspirators' out there getting into responsible positions across economic sectors . . . . Their influence is being felt.

And the jury is still out, not on the issue of the Program's societal impact, but only on the ultimate magnitude of the cultural collision.

Then, turning from the macro-scene, there is a painfully injured drunken Gypsy, many cripples, a proud cab-driving historian, a colleague—Anibal Cavaco Silva—who is Prime Minister. And again, a deep appreciation for the remarkable genetic riptide between Europeans and Moors that brought forth such a handsome cultural happening.

Then back to the reality of Portugal today. Eighty-five percent of its heavy industry nationalized, and the disillusionment of the achievers with post-revolutionary lethargy, egalitarian, pseudo-democracy, disestablishment and the anti-disestablishment. One major economic setback in this small democracy and the people could look back with longing to images of other governments that seemed to work better. The people deserve better. But I don't know if they can compete with the pervasive economic powers of the EEC. Yet pride and perseverance has kept them free from others for centuries.

The day has melted away pleasantly as these words to you have flowed. And the Atlantic storm has passed, leaving the pastel houses across the courtyard water-stained and brightly cleansed. It is time to wind down the stay, to position myself to leave grudgingly, to consult with the future Universidade do Madeira, to say adieu to Oporto with a last visit, to tenderly revamp the dining room for mere dining. It is tranquil here. Now the little person, the child of the *portaria*, sweeps the marble stairs and sings that infectiously innocent song; and the dial on the telephone doesn't seem to stick so badly, and the drunken street light across the way seems to recover just as one needs light. And the walks over miles and miles of cobblestones, walks, and walks, and walks. There is no doubt about my returning. If Hemingway had his Spain, I have my Portugal. The wise man cautioned:

Don't go *to live* as an expatriate in Lisbon or London or Paris or wherever just because it sounds like fun. This is one of the most important moves ever you will make. Things and people that you didn't like before may be more appealing to you, while those that had held attraction for you may become unattractive. You will grow in differing ways than others here from living abroad. So . . . take a good look in the mirror before you go because you'll *never* see that person again.

So it is, one moves on from the man in the mirror. And without your inspiration, Ken, none of it would have happened. No one can repay a mentor, except through one's own protégés. I hope nonetheless that through this epistolary form of sharing you can sense the depth of my appreciation.

From the beginning of the Fulbright Program, secondary and primary teachers have participated, if usually in a university context. Even after extensive overseas visiting, student tours to Greece and Italy, and a Fulbright traveling seminar in China, a six-week summer seminar in India for secondary-school teachers brought to Anne Thomas a new vision of the world and her role in it as a teacher, as a woman, as an American, perhaps even as a human being. One of two American secondary educators represented in this volume, both India veterans, she tells a story of discovery and revitalized professional commitment, of a mission to carry her new insights to others. Now foreign student and scholar advisor at Lehigh University, a career-change directly prompted by her brief but immersive tour in India, the author by her own admission has touched the Fulbright spirit and will never be the same.

32

HANG RIGHT AT THE COW: TEACHER IN INDIA

Anne Horsfall Thomas

India—vast, variegated, diverse, a nation of contradictions. Elegant wealth, miserable poverty; drought, monsoon; fragrant flowers, stinking sewage; parrots flashing green and flying free, starving dogs; bullock carts, BMW's; beggars, Brahmins; temples to the glory of God incarnated in an ele- phant-headed god; marble temples more sophisticated than the Parthenon; bride burnings, Indira Gandhi.

Eleven American high school teachers with our Fulbright director went to study and absorb, to learn as much as we could about this complicated culture. We tried to understand and reconcile these stark contradictions—so often we saw one thing but it meant another. We reached out our hands and our minds to these hospitable and fascinating people, and in return they captured our hearts.

We were only a passing-through, a brief dot in the landscape of their lives. But as we faced each other and talked, we were changed forever. What do they see when they look at me in my Rockports, with my camera, my watch, my cotton T-shirts, and my sweaty face, my white skin and blue eyes, colorless and drab? I can only guess. They are too polite to tell.

What do I see looking at my counterpart, the Indian woman? Her deep black eyes and her beautiful long black hair, carefully tended. She is smaller, more self-contained, more dignified and reserved. She is a survivor, she seems to know more than I do. She teaches me what I knew in my head but now I know in my soul—I belong to a minority of Caucasians.

The Fulbright experience changed me forever. Never again can I look at my life, my profession, my country, my sex, in the same way. And what I thought I knew about India, from careful reading and study, has turned upside down—India does that to visitors. She is sophisticated, gracious, complicated, and ancient, more full of color and of decay than expected.

The essence of the Fulbright program is to live it by being there. The intensity of being submerged in another's culture molds values and thoughts into permanently new forms. These forms say the human being everywhere is a creature to be marveled at, struggling to maintain existence, adaptable and prolific, anxious to reach and touch those who also inhabit the earth, and like all humanity, looking for the meaning of reality.

Our thoughtful hosts outdid themselves in teaching us. We saw change and contrast with the recent past. There is rapid growth in industry and per capita income. India is the seventh largest industrial nation in the world. The land of famine has become a food exporter. Keeping pace with the new wealth is the ever-increasing population, well over 750 million, more than double the number of people since Gandhi's time. India adds the equivalent of a new Australia every year and is rapidly closing the gap with the 1.1 billion of China. Unable to make it on the land, millions move to the cities, creating more and more slums. The slum story is universal: lack of sanitation, filth, disease and hopelessness. This is a dramatic contrast to the new cars, luxurious homes, and children educated abroad.

Americans like tidy answers, but there is no tidiness in India. The only way to make sense of it all is to accept this fact, and to seek out patterns that give some meaning to this great paradox of a land. In the search, a glimmer of reality can emerge. My students worry about reality; they need to understand that reality and truth are not simple but infinitely complicated concepts, that the American way is not the only way, and that there are no easy answers to the vast dilemmas of the human condition. For this, India is the ultimate teacher.

Take the superstition about the sacred cow. The foreigner has the idea that cows wander the streets, eating food that is desperately needed for people, leaving manure behind, and causing a general nuisance. Although this is true, the reality has another side to it. The cow does wander freely, but each one belongs to someone. Except for an occasional bull, all the cattle are female. The males have conveniently been eaten somewhere along the line, probably by Muslims or untouchables—orthodox Hindus do not eat beef. The cows eat the garbage dumped on the streets thus relieve the landfills (I never knew cows ate banana peels). The manure is scooped up by the poor to use for fuel, thus saving trees. The cow gives daily milk to the owner's children. And, surprisingly, the cows wisely tend to stay inside the traffic islands. The pragmatists claim that by keeping the cow sacred it has been preserved through times of famine. In any case, when Indira Gandhi ordered the sacred cows penned up there were riots and she quickly abandoned the policy.

We became fond of our local cows. "Cow Corner" became a favorite landmark. We found ourselves giving directions by "turn right at the cow" or "go two blocks past Cow Corner."

The teacher summer seminar was planned meticulously by the U.S. Educational Foundation in India, the Fulbright arm. We were plunged into the culture and the people in a way no other type of visitor can be, thanks to USEFI. Why did all this happen? Teachers shape our nation's future leaders, through us the Fulbright program reaches the young people of the U.S. and the teaching profession is enhanced. By studying and experiencing India herself, we could take first-hand lessons to our students. We spent many of our days in lectures by faculty from Pune University, other days visiting sites of religious, historical, or contemporary significance. India is one of the oldest civilizations in the world, tracing her 4,500-year-old roots to the banks of the Indus River and the city states of Mohenjo Daro and Harrappa. Our Indian hosts were eager to teach us, and we tried to absorb it all.

Some evenings featured dinners on the open-air rooftop of our hotel lit by a sliver Moghul moon with a temple to the goddess Parvati in the background, illuminated on a distant hill. On other evenings we were thoughtfully entertained in Indian homes. The hospitality of India is legendary, a fact we discovered time and again. All twelve of us would troop in and our hosts and hostesses would try to make us comfortable, serve us food we could eat and beverages that were safe for sterile American stomachs. On our side we tried valiantly to eat the spicy food and prayed that Mother Kali would not haunt us in the night. As the days added up, so did the impressions, sometimes so many that it was difficult to sort them all out. Our own vision of reality was constantly challenged. Understanding India is like peeling an onion—beneath one thin layer there are dozens more. Our eyes were like that onion—layers kept coming off.

We happened on a lavish Hindu wedding in our hotel, and the family insisted we stay and join in. Claridge's Hotel in Delhi has a winding marble staircase in the front hall and a Sikh doorman elegant in a white suit and red turban, Mr. Babasingh by name. Wedding customs tell a great deal about people and their values, especially those reflecting the place women have in the society, from the bride to the mother and the in-laws.

I was prepared for much of what I saw, but the important place of the groom was an eye-opener. The women, among the most beautiful in the world, were gowned in sparkling sarees hand embroidered with gold and silver thread and jewels, bangles up their arms, henna designs on their palms, their oiled black hair down their backs, with jewels in their noses, in their hair, adorning their necks, wrists, ankles, fingers, and slippers. Then the groom arrived on a decorated white horse, to the accompaniment of a band and firecrackers. He was dark mustached, gorgeous in a white suit and red turban dripping with flowers, escorted into the banquet room and seated on one of two red velvet thrones.

The bride appeared through a back door, preceded by little girls throwing flowers, supported by women attendants and carrying a gold garland. Her red wedding saree, heavy with gold, weighed her down. She was covered with gold and jewels and had gold dust in her hair. She was properly downcast. In the Hindu tradition a bride leaves her family and becomes part of the household of her new husband and his family. She returns to the home of her birth only for visits.

At the exact auspicious moment, determined by the astrologer, the couple moved to the makeshift temple set up on the grounds of the hotel where two Hindu priests presided at the ceremony. The mothers were much in evidence. The couple took vows and walked around the sacred fire. With us, the guests were welcoming, speaking English and several other languages. They were interested in the U.S., and many had been there. One young man, dressed in a Miami Vice tee-shirt, stood with his friend, a young Sikh in full beard and red turban.

They told us that this was an arranged marriage, and that the bride and groom, although they had met, did not know each other. The young people we spoke with, although modern in their education and careers, emphasized that they planned to have their parents arrange their marriages. They agreed that the families knew best who would serve them well as a spouse. In the usual course of affairs, the young couple does meet and can decide at that point for themselves. Divorce is rare in India. The first reaction to this of my American class of freedom-loving students was shock and disgust. Later, after talking about it further, the other side of the arranged marriage began to emerge. Although no one was ready to accept it, the students were aware of their own misconceptions about the idea. Our children of split families do not think divorce is such a great idea.

Life in the villages is another matter. The Fulbright program showed us many sides of Indian life. We had to see villages—70% of India's population is rural. Sonori made a dark contrast with the elegant urban wedding. A large and fairly affluent walled village about 15 miles from Pune in the state of Maharashtra, it has emerged recently from its feudal state. The town is still surrounded by thick walls dating from the 14th century, its heavy gates studded with spikes to repel elephants. Once inside, thick stone walls twist and turn to keep invaders at bay. The walls are in ruins now. The land of the wealthy ruling family has been broken up, redistributed by the government in the land reform movement that came with independence in 1947. The landlord family, maintaining a heavy stake in this dry soil, has had wells dug and irrigation projects built. This family is the only one with the capital to invest in such projects.

The countryside was on the edge of severe drought and the monsoons were late. The well-being, indeed the very life, of the village depends on the fluctuations of nature. With rain, prosperity; without rain, poverty and possible famine. Most of India's population lives with this reality.

The village school, grades 1-8, has a total enrollment of 357 out of an eligible 500. Bright-eyed children stand on command and chirp "Good morning madam." There are 50 or more to a class, seated on the floor in perfect order, reading, writing and doing sums. The number of students falls off in the upper grades—the older children are needed on the farm. By grade eight the class size is down to 30, the majority boys. The girls are kept home to help with chores and tend younger siblings. The problem of the inequality of education for boys and girls is serious; it reflects on many aspects of Indian life, including the population explosion and female life expectancy. The teachers are anxious that their pupils perform well for us. Their salaries are less than those of railway porters so they live in the same poverty as their students. On the walls are the usual portraits of Gandhi, Nehru, and Indira.

We had tea in a farmer's house, a relative of the original landlord family. There were no BMW's or televisions here. The tea was prepared by the wife of the day-laborer while her three-month-old baby girl was tended by her older brother. He pushed the baby in a swing until she fell asleep. The love between Indian brothers and sisters is important in the social structure; when an Indian girl is in need, she often turns to her brother. There is a special brother-sister day every year when gifts are exchanged. In addition to careful non-exploitive arranged marriages provided by many families, this is a safe-guard for women in Indian society—another lesson for the feminists among us.

Our group sat, shoes off, on a matted floor. Two bullocks were tied nearby. The hostess, her saree scarf carefully pulled over her hair, showed off her kitchen, with a wood-fueled oven where she squatted to bake the unleavened bread. In fuel-short countries, flat bread is common, and much of the fuel is dried cow-dung patties. The village houses have one or two rooms, with animals sharing the space. One of the wealthy houses had a new baby, a son, showed off with pride. A newborn goat was also in the room, staggering around on shaky legs. Goats and sheep often are allowed to wander freely, eating the roots of the sparse vegetation and contributing to a severe erosion problem.

Government programs encourage reforestation and we saw many dry areas planted with new trees. Preserving trees is not easy in a land where fuel is scarce. The only tree not cut is the sacred bodhi, or peepul tree, frequently painted orange at the base. It is considered sacred because Buddha sat beneath a bodhi tree about 500 BC in Varanasi when he achieved Enlightenment. As with the sacred cow, religion has preserved an important resource.

In another much poorer small village in Maharashtra state we stopped for a rest from a long bus ride while our driver had tea. A woman was standing in her dirt yard, goats and a water buffalo tied nearby. Beside her were three brass pots used by the village women to carry both water from the well and milk to be delivered. Kept shiny with a sand scrubbing, they are family heirlooms, probably handed down as dowry for a new bride or from the mother-in-law to her son's wife. They are heavy and even three empty ones are a burden. Full, they would have been nearly impossible for us to carry. The village women carry such heavy loads on their heads as a matter of course, which may explain their elegant posture and swaying walk.

The village woman displayed her pots, and her family gathered around. She was the mother-in-law and matriarch of this family, with her daughter-in-law and granddaughter standing submissively nearby. Although she spoke no English and we could not speak Marathi, we were able to communicate as women. This happened many times. The women would speak with us and show us things, where they would be shy and retiring around the men, quickly pulling their saree scarf over their heads.

During the visit there were many onlookers, most of them male. It was never certain which ones, if any, were part of the family. In India the separation of the sexes is understood, so as women we were left to set this scene ourselves. We managed, with much laughter and sign language.

The contrast between the primitive rural life of the majority of the Indian population and the urban rich was disturbing. In the villages we felt as if we had stepped back in time to an almost feudal existence. Despite the efforts of the government to redistribute the land, most Indians live in poverty. This is caused in part by the population explosion, in part by bureaucratic regulations which actually limit free enterprise, in part by the stratified Indian social system. And yet, despite the wildly rising number of bellies to feed, the Indian farmer has not only kept pace but has excelled. India really does export food.

The life of village women in India, heavily governed by tradition, is not easy. Girls are considered a burden and an expense; they are often neglected as children in favor of their brothers. In a poor family, during illness, the medical care is often reserved for the sons. The sons tend to get the better food, including the limited protein from eggs or meat. A girl baby often is breast-fed for a shorter period of time because the mother is anxious to become pregnant with a son. Sometimes girl infants are smothered at birth.

It can be dangerous to be born a girl in India, as in many countries of the world. The ratio of women to men is 960 to 1,000. The usual ratio is the reverse. The higher death rate for women is caused directly by their low status which leads to neglect, starvation, female infanticide, and later, childbirth death and suicide. We visited a Mother Teresa orphanage and child-care center in Agra and were shown babies which had been abandoned on the doorstep. Almost all were girls. When a family is too poor to raise its children, it is often the girls they give up.

This is well-known information, but in India the reality of the statistics hit home. As often seems to happen there is another side to these bare facts. The population explosion is the death knell for India and all of Asia. The fewer girl babies who live to grow up, the fewer women of child-bearing age. Cruel and tragic, female infanticide is a form of population control. When one actually experiences the horrors of over-population, the complexity of solutions becomes more obvious. India cannot afford the luxury of debating the morality of abortion, for example. Only wealthy societies can do that. India is in a struggle for survival for all her people. The effects of over- population can be seen everywhere—the contaminated water supply leading to disease and death, erosion of the land, poverty on the streets and in the villages, malnutrition, crowded schools.

The reasons behind the treatment of girls go back to the roots of the marriage and family patterns of the traditional society. Before reaching puberty a girl is "married out," which means that as a virgin she left her village and her home for the home of her husband and his family. This trend is still true in the rural areas and among the urban poor, despite the new law setting the marriage age for girls at eighteen. Her family has to raise a dowry for her and also has to provide an expensive wedding. It is not unusual for a family to go into lifelong debt to pay for the marriage of a daughter.

Perhaps the most startling paradox in the whole of India is that Indira Gandhi could be a powerful Prime Minister in a country where the status of women is one of the lowest in the world. The literacy rate for women is 25 % in the urban areas and 18 % in the rural. Mrs. Gandhi is still criticized by feminists in India for failing to enact legislation to protect and help women.

Low status for women actually contributes to the high birth-rates. Studies done in India and elsewhere show that once women are educated and their status improved they demand and choose family planning. In the state of Kerala, where the literacy rate of women is high, the birth-rate is low. Where the women tend to be illiterate, such as in Uttar Pradesh, the birth-rate is very high. Literate women are more willing and able to practice family planning. They long for smaller families. Usually this is true, however, only if they can produce a son and have a reasonable assurance that he will survive.

Despite the odds against them Indian women are dynamic and capable; they work the fields, carry bundles of bricks on their heads at construction sites, teach school, run day-care centers, organize entrepreneurships, administer factories, serve in Parliament, run the Fulbright program in India, and zip around on their motor scooters, scarves flying.

In 1989, the government declared runaway population growth the number one priority. So far however the government has done little to implement its declaration, and the burden of birth control continues to fall to the women with little help from the system. Through the Fulbright office, we were able to arrange visits to two types of family planning centers, headquartered in New Delhi, both organized and financed privately with local overseas funding. One program, the Parivar Seva Sanstha, established family planning clinics throughout the country side of India. These clinics offer family planning advice, birth control devices, and abortions in safe and sanitary conditions. The other program, the Family Planning Foundation, was organized to provide information and long term studies about the birth rate and family planning.

And then there were the schools. We visited the prestigious Ahilyade Vidyaloya Girls' School in Pune. The school has grades 5-10 and is attended by 2,200 girls. They pay partial tuition, and the rest is tax-funded. The faculty were proud that 90 % of the girls pass examinations and attend 11th and 12th standard (grade), junior college in the Indian system. The other 10 % go into the work force or into vocational training. The school, like many others, is on double session and the classes have up to 60 students. There is a serious shortage of teachers and facilities while the Indian educational system struggles to keep up with the population explosion.

This school is located in Pune, an intellectual and cultural center with several colleges and universities, including the well-known University of Pune. According to law, the girls living in the neighborhood attend this school, as in our system of tax-supported education. However, because good schools are at a premium the parents seek a relative or friend living in the area to claim their daughters so they will be eligible to attend here. The school is named for a wealthy Hindu noble widow who was left with a large inheritance. She refused to submit to suttee (widow burning) and used her inherited wealth to establish facilities for women in the Pune area.

The girls wear green jumpers and white blouses. The younger girls have short hair, but as they reach high school age they let their hair grow, usually wearing it in braids. All the girls have pierced ears and wear the red dot on the forehead. The school follows the state curriculum, like all Indian schools. Lessons are taught in Marathi, the local language, or in English and Hindi, the national languages. In the eighth standard the girls may choose to study Sanskrit, the language of the ancient sages. In practice, English skills are lacking, despite the efforts of the enthusiastic English teacher assigned to us as translator. Since English is the one language spoken throughout India among the educated, the lack of English puts these girls at an immediate disadvantage when they graduate. If a student is to get ahead in the working world she must be fluent in English. Some of our colleagues visited a boys' school in Pune where the language of the lessons was English. These young men were fluent, a great advantage for the future.

The curriculum of the educational system is rigorous, and in the upper standards several hours of homework are required every night. The parents, especially the mothers, have to become involved in their children's lessons if they are to succeed in school. The Indian woman, ambitious for her children, is pressured to stay at home until they are grown and graduated from "junior college" or the 12th standard.

India lacks enough institutions of higher education, and competition to be accepted into the universities and colleges is fierce. There is also a certain amount of corruption in admissions standards with the purchasing of grades and test scores. In addition, political unrest closes down many of these institutions, leading to the famous "brain drain." Thousands of Indian students study in the U.S., and close to half of them still remain to enter our professions and businesses.

Indian teachers are proud that there are no serious discipline problems in their schools, unlike what they have read about in American schools. Drugs, alcohol, teen-age pregnancy are almost non-existent. The students are serious about their school work, and the social life of the typical American teenager lies beyond their wildest dreams. This lends a certain delightfully ingenuous quality in the Indian high school student. By comparison, many of my own students seemed spoiled and demanding, rude and self-centered, and not especially happy with all their freedoms and choices.

There is an increasing demand by the Indian families for the education of women, and the government and the educational system are striving to meet it. Opportunities for women have expanded in all fields. Not only does it create upward mobility, it also contributes to their marriageability. Families of potential husbands are looking for brides with an education, and they advertise that fact in the newspaper marriage ads. Where once caste and good family were the primary requisites, now it is education. "Caste no bar," say the ads. The more education a woman has, the higher salary she can command in the job market. For example, gynecologists—whose salaries are high and who are almost all women—can often name their own husbands. The effect of the increased education for women leads to status-quo-shaking results. As the women become more upwardly mobile, the under-girding of the society comes into question. What will happen to the extended family, the arranged marriage, the dominance of men? It is already known that educated women are refusing to have large families. The changes taking place for women are bound to destabilize the already unstable culture. For every move in a culture, there are counter moves, and many elements of a society cannot handle the changes. Any change in the age-old status of women in the society has such profound implications that the very foundations of that society tremble.

For example, one development, horrifying to Indians and outsiders alike, is the rise in "dowry deaths." In these cases, if a husband or his family does not consider the dowry of the bride to be sufficient, or the bride's family does not pay up, the bride is set afire. Although considered murder in the legal system, these cases are difficult to prove. Most Indian women wear the long scarves of the saree, and cook over open flames, so accidental death by burning is not uncommon. Out of shame, the bride's family often does not press charges.

We were told that this development is not frequent, is relatively new, and is a direct result of dislocations of the family. In a more stable time the husband and his family would not dare such a thing out of fear of reprisals from the bride's family and her home community. The husband would never be able to find another wife—the dead bride's family would see to that. But today the extended family is no longer as strong and reprisals are less likely. The repercussions of change cannot always be anticipated.

What does this mean to our students at home? Even in the current national mood of teacher- and school-bashing, Americans consider education the answer for all society's ills. Yet these experiences in India demonstrate that education can bring about results that are not always good. Education can effect societal change, but only over time can it also soften attitudes and bring about solutions. The quick fix does no good. True, the immersion of the Fulbright program has an immediate impact on us, reflected quickly in the thought-processes of our students. Teachers use what they have experienced because they have been changed themselves. The effect ripples out.

Religion arches over it all. Sacred traditions, sacred cows, sacred trees, sacred monkeys, sacred temples, sacred mosques, India is a land where religion is a way of life, a daily experience, not a sometime Sabbath phenomenon. Hindus, who make up 80% of the population, believe that there are many ways or paths leading to God. Hinduism absorbs many religious teachings and still maintains a common thread. This leads to a kind of tolerance which gives power to her pluralistic democracy, even if religious fundamentalism continues to demand its right to the one true way, making tolerance its victim.

We visited temples—Sikh, Jain, and Hindu—and Muslim mosques. We sat at the feet of gurus expounding on the meaning of life and we listened to a variety of Indian attempts to bring order to human existence and to find "Truth." They preached non-violence and love for all God's creatures; they extolled the life of sacrifice and serving others. We visited Hindu homes— each with a puja corner where daily devotions are performed, including ritual baths of the small statues of the gods and saints, placing of fresh flowers, and burning of incense.

Hindus claim that there are as many deities as there are Hindus, but there is also only one god. They refer to a single god, the great power, and over and over we heard, "thanks be to God" or "if God wills" or "God is good."

We saw countless shrines to Ganesh, the elephant-headed, pot-bellied, beloved deity who is the son of the Lord Shiva and his wife Parvati. One path to the truth is through the ever popular Ganesh. He sits with one crossed leg, and with one leg dangling, missing a tusk, and his trunk usually swinging to the viewer's right. He is accompanied by his vehicle, the rat, and one of his two right hands is raised in a blessing. It is difficult for the Westerner to reconcile the worship of the particular deity with an advanced civilization. And yet, there it is.

Stories from the legends of Hinduism are retold in comic book form in the Amar Chitra Katha, published in Bombay by the India Book House. These books, popular and readily available, encourage both literacy and the spread of knowledge about the great epics of Hinduism. We brought these books home into our classrooms where they make fascinating reading, as complicated and mystical stories become comprehensible. A favorite describes how Ganesh got his elephant head. As an adolescent boy, he was asked by his mother Parvati to guard her bedroom against the unannounced visits of Shiva. Shiva arrived, was stopped by Ganesh, and became so enraged that he cut off the boy's head. Realizing what a terrible deed he had committed, he called on the great god Brahman to help. He was told to go into the woods, remove the head of the first animal that came along, and return with it to the dead body of his son and attach the head; the boy would then come back to life. Shiva did as he was told, saw the elephant first, and followed directions.

There are shrines everywhere, dedicated to the whole pantheon, especially to the Lord Shiva who dances through the universe destroying evil. He rides on his vehicle, the bull Nandi, and is often represented by a lingam, a phallic symbol representing the life force, bathed in yogurt and curd and strewn with fresh flowers. He has four arms, and his head is wreathed in a halo of fire.

The female aspect of Hinduism is symbolized in the powerful and elusive Parvati. She has a changing personality, now wise, now bloodthirsty, and is a contradiction in herself. She is gentle and compassionate, female and motherly, but she has another side. Manifesting herself as the death-dealing Kali, she represents the destructive side of life. From time to time we would happen upon roadside shrines dedicated to her. The shrines had garlanded pictures showing Kali as black-skinned, usually as an old woman with sagging breasts, and a necklace of human skulls. Her many arms hold the severed heads of mustached men, never of women, and a sword dripping with blood. She has a huge red tongue hanging from her mouth, long black hair streaming down her back, and most frightening of all, she stands triumphant on the dead body of Shiva himself.

We witnessed a whispered-about but rarely-seen Kali incident. In a busy shopping area in Hyderabad, a filthy couple banging on drums approached us shrieking. They carried a flat basket with the mutilated body of a probably drugged, not dead, infant exposed for all to see. They were shouting that they had performed a blood sacrifice to Kali on our behalf, and we needed to pay them for this in order not to be cursed by the goddess. Several passersby furtively put money in the basket. Eventually they were chased away by our Fulbright guide, who threatened them with the sole of his shoe.

Kali is also a positive force. She is referred to as "Ma," Mother, and she holds the promise that out of death comes reincarnation and a renewal of life. In dying, one can be reborn, physically or mystically. Feminists everywhere are fascinated by the symbolism of the Kali-Parvati legends which explore the depths of the often-contradictory feelings about women. The love-hate, worship-fear relationship with this many-sided goddess represents basic, atavistic human emotions. Her story intrigues our students, as they slowly became aware of the conflicts that exist within the human condition and culture. And she fascinates India. The teeming city of Calcutta gets its name from Kalighat, the bathing place of Kali on the banks of the Holy Mother River Ganges. A relatively new feminist magazine is named Kali.

With 76 million Muslims, India is also one of the largest Islamic countries in the world. We visited mosques, simple and stark in contrast with the wildly decorated Hindu temples. Women are not allowed into the inner sanctum, which is usually a small room with a cloth-draped marble tomb of some long-dead holy man. Despite our willingness to cover our hair and arms (in the 90-degree heat), the women were forced to wait outside while the men went in. We waited with the Muslim women and girls, draped in black, squatting outside in the courtyard.

Indian religion is surely the biggest puzzle of all for the Westerner. The legends and color, the deep faith and devotion—all this can make Western spiritual life seem sterile. But it has frightening power to unleash emotions among the Indian people. The siren song of mysticism has drawn many Westerners to Indian religions; the negative side of fanaticism and the Hindu caste system has served as a brake.

We lived surrounded by deep religious faith and we were led to a greater understanding of the power of religion and spirituality. It is impossible fully to understand the actions and goals of the Indian people unless you take this power into account. As an example, the contradictory attitudes towards women are symbolized in the variety of manifestations of female goddesses, or the many sides of the same goddess: sexy temptress, bloodthirsty judge and punisher, creator of life, all rolled into one. Religion says much about the place of women in Indian society, as it does about everything else.

*   *   *

Looking back, there is no way to resolve India's essential paradox what is reality, what is truth? Just when you think you have part of it sorted out, she hands you another question. This makes her a source of fascination, enticing you ever to return.

One fact should be fairly obvious: India is a linchpin of Asian politics. Of all the world's people living in a viable democracy, 50% are Indian. It is an open society with a vigorous free press which constantly challenges the status quo. Indian scholars, engineers, teachers, doctors, skilled workers, merchants, live across the world and have become an integral part of global society. The U.S. needs India as much as India needs the U.S.

The Fulbright impact comes from cultural immersion and participation—we were forced to experience things first-hand. The message in its most basic terms was this: there is no single way, we are all part of a seamless web. We cannot afford to analyze and judge quickly the actions of others based only on a Western framework and context. That path leads to ignorant and dangerous decisions for a nation.

Our responsibility now, as teachers and as citizens, is to share this message with our students and with other Americans. As the U.S. struggles to mature, we must begin to see the cultural depth in our fellow-denizens of this planet, as they need to see ours—and as we need to see our own. This does not mean we must tolerate injustice and poverty, but it means we need to look ever more closely at their causes. If I can spread that idea through teaching, writing, and personal discussion, then I will fulfill my obligation to the Fulbright program.

The Fulbright program for secondary teachers adds a new professional dimension to the careers of dozens of teachers each year. The results are life-changing, for students as well. If students can learn that there are no simple solutions, that there is value in the human being wherever it is found, the Fulbright goal of "waging peace through understanding" comes a step nearer. Our students, who will take this nation into the 21st century, must be armed with deeper ways of looking at the world than their predecessors.

After return, I found I needed more direct contact with international students, a larger role in the establishment of an international educational community. Our survival as a nation, indeed our survival as a species, depends on establishing a global environment: an international climate in our institutions of learning is the road that leads there. Why not, for example, by integrating foreign nationals into our campuses, letting them too be teachers? The world has long beaten a path to the doors of our nation's outstanding colleges and universities. To retain that excellence, we must move beyond complacency into an international way of thinking and acting. At all levels of development—as individuals, as institutions, as nations—maturity comes as we begin learning to cope, however tentatively, with irrevocable and irreducible complexities and contradictions. For this kind of maturation, India is the master teacher.

As her dutiful student, I changed careers. Today I am helping internationalize a university. In my broader career I still teach seminars and workshops, but now as a foreign student and scholar advisor in a university. Who I am, who we all are—this has been changed forever. Sharing this with others will help them touch the Fulbright spirit. It touched me and I will never be the same.

*The author is professor of history at Florida Atlantic University. Like
many of the American Fulbrighters who spend time in Africa, he found
that more time was consumed by mere coping with problems than by
paradigm shifts. As the old joke asks, who's got time to change? With
the other Fulbrighters at his university in Lesotho, he and his wife found
their time heavily absorbed by matters of basic everyday survival. In
that, they were brought to live at the edge of subsistence in ways that
most Americans have forgotten. At the same time they found themselves
drawing together into a close mutual-support network of fellow Americans. With few students of his own, the author got deeply involved in
primary and secondary education and through this involvement was
brought to the challenges of comparative history. His essay is descrip-
tive of the resilience of Americans and the flexibility of the Fulbright
experience—there is always something useful to be done. Persistence
in giving generously of themselves where others might give up yielded
only to his wife's illness. With all this, Dr. Kersey manages as well to
give a vivid portrayal of a strange world on the roof of the unknown
continent.*

33

FULBRIGHTING ON AFRICA'S ROOF

Harry A. Kersey, Jr.

Will I ever forget the look on my wife's face that day in 1988 when I
opened the envelope and proudly announced, "We're going to Lesotho!"
"Where's that again?" she asked, her face betraying more of a "My God,
what's that?" look. It was a question that I would often get over the next few
months, and to a degree ever since.

Fortunately, experience as a Fulbrighter at the University of Zimbabwe
four years earlier had left me with an insatiable curiosity concerning life in
Southern Africa, which correspondence and reading had helped to fill. So it
was possible to give a quick briefing to those who inquired. My first point
was always to emphasize that the country's name is pronounced *le-SOO-to*; my

410

second was to note that "Lumela" means "hello" in the Sesotho language. From there it was all downhill.

I will be forgiven, I hope, for offering some basic information about the country. The Kingdom of Lesotho, a minute country about the size of Maryland, comprised almost entirely of rugged mountain ranges or arid upland valleys, lies totally land-locked within the Republic of South Africa. Because of its altitude the country is often referred to as the "Roof of Africa." The population of around 1.6 million is overwhelmingly Basotho, a Bantu-speaking people whose ancestors migrated into the region several centuries ago. Although it is often erroneously identified as one of the "homelands" set up by the Pretoria government to isolate large segments of the black South African population, Lesotho has historically remained a politically independent enclave owing to a remarkable set of circumstances.

Unlike most of the indigenous peoples in the region, the Basotho never totally succumbed to the economic and military pressures exerted by the Dutch Boers during their Great Trek to settle the interior during the 1800s. Instead, under the leadership of their venerated founder King Moshoeshoe, from their strongholds in barren moonscape mountains, they appealed to Queen Victoria for protection. The English monarch took a humanitarian interest in the people; her government was also seeking ways to thwart Boer expansion, so the British Basutoland Protectorate was established in 1868. A colonial goverment would oversee affairs until Lesotho became independent in 1966.

The overweening reality in Lesotho today is the economic and military dominance of the Republic of South Africa. The capital city, Maseru, sits on the border; consequently every aspect of both the public and private sector economies is dependent on keeping that border open. In recent years South Africa brought pressure to bear by simply constricting the flow of goods across the Maseru bridge and instigated a military *coup d'état* against a Lesotho government considered "un-cooperative" by Pretoria. The present governmental structure vests legislative and executive power in King Letsie III, who ostensibly rules in conjunction with a Military Council that is necessarily committed to co-existence with its powerful neighbor. The major source of government revenue is derived from its share of tariffs collected by the Southern African Customs Union, which includes Lesotho, Botswana, Swaziland, and the Republic of South Africa. At the same time, Lesotho joins with other black African nations in condemning the apartheid system and calling for majority rule in Tanzania. It is at best a precarious and sensitive relationship between disparate partners.

Overall, the largest portion of Lesotho's national wealth comes from the remitted pay of migrant laborers employed in the mines of South Africa. At least one-half of the adult male work force is occupied in this manner, and any cut-back in mine employment creates serious economic problems among the Basotho. This system has also led to severe dislocations in family and community life, with women and children left responsible for subsistence farming in a land that is far from self-sufficient in feeding its own population. Outside the few towns most of the Basotho still live in small villages on land allocated by the headmen or chiefs, who are appointed by the King. Some villages in the lowlands—that third of the nation which lies at about 5,000 feet—have electricity, sanitation, and a good water supply, but most do not. Throughout the countryside families still reside in the colorful *rondavel*, a traditional round hut made of stone with a conical thatched roof. Livestock is still considered a standard of wealth, and the bride price is normally paid in cattle. So much for general background.

*   *   *

It was a clear, cold August day—still late winter in the southern hemisphere—when we arrived in Lesotho. The drive from the airport to the National University at Roma took only thirty minutes on what passed for a paved road, but it was like journeying back through time on a strange planet. On either side of the road were clustered the *rondavels* of small villages, thin curls of dark smoke arising from coal fires that had already been kindled against the late afternoon chill. It was Saturday, a shopping day, so great numbers of Basotho were out and about along with their children. Everyone seemed to be walking somewhere, mostly to local market centers. All were muffled in their colorful wool blankets decorated with striking designs, worn as outer garments against the biting wind. Occasionally we passed men riding horses and young boys astride donkeys which carried sacks of mealy-meal; other youngsters drove herds of goats or cattle before them, often crossing the unfenced right-of-way. Many of the men and women balanced enormous parcels, water containers, or loads of firewood on their heads as they walked. All in all, it was a new cultural kaleidoscope which bombarded the eye.

One never forgets that first view of the Roma Valley, seen from the top of a pass after ascending a steep grade. Stretching away as far as the eye could see were treeless mesas, with the snow-fringed front range of the Maluti Mountains as a magnificent backdrop. The villages blending with a dark reddish earth, the huge Aloe plants growing to form natural kraals, the great sky filled with whispy winter clouds, all reminded me more of New Mexico rather than Africa as it was thought to be by most Americans. Descending into the valley floor we passed through more villages and skirted deep erosion ravines called *dongas*. Because the road was under repair—a constant state of being in Lesotho—streams were crossed on single-lane temporary bridges which drivers approached from both directions with a kamikaze zeal. Finally we arrived at the university, a fenced enclave in the middle of the valley surrounded only by fields and villages. A tiny shopping center across from the main gate was the only semblence of a town. We soon learned that one of these buildings was our local branch of the Queen's Egg Circle—a concession of the royal family and the only source for eggs in the country. Our new address was a recently constructed faculty-staff housing area known as Soweto—believe it or not, that is its official university designation—where the other Fulbright families were located. This would become a very close-knit, highly supportive group—Jim and Barbara Mathieu, Mary Holly, Dick and Nancy Miller and their son Bradley; we shared incredible experiences and formed lasting friendships.

We all learned our first smattering of the Sesotho language from our domestic helpers who became friends as well as employees and who took a proprietary interest in our welfare. Our flat was spartan but adequate and clean; moreover, thanks to the USIS director and his wife, it was stocked with a starter supply of bottled gas, food, boiled water, and even a bottle of wine to celebrate the safe arrival!

The National University of Lesotho (NUL) evolved out of a Catholic mission and seminary begun in 1946, and the original stone structure is still part of the administrative complex. Everything was in short supply. We were each given a box of chalk and an eraser to last the year; I dutifully took both to class daily and guarded them zealously. Many of the buildings and much equipment on the campus have been donated by western nations, although they suffer from lack of maintenance. As is generally the case throughout Africa, most labor is unskilled; there is no lack of gardeners and grounds-keepers, but few electricians and plumbers. My office, for example, was maintained spotlessly, but we never managed to get the telephone connected during my stay. A lecture hall door fell from its hinges the first day of class and remained that way for most of a term. Interestingly, the Basotho are horse people, and NUL is perhaps one of the few campuses in the world where many workers ride their horses to work and leave them tethered to graze on the grounds during the day. We stepped carefully when crossing the lawn.

My Fulbright assignment was to teach courses in American history and twentieth-century world history—neither of which was required for history majors. Moreover, American history had been offered as an elective for the preceeding five years, so virtually all our majors had already taken it. Consequently, I had only one small class for the twentieth century and no enrollees for American history.

The Basotho students were polite and receptive and were generally well prepared. Initially they had some difficulty adjusting to my rather informal method of instruction, having come through a British-oriented system which featured lectures rather than discussion. The smattering of South African students on the campus were more politically attuned to the world and perhaps a bit more socially aggressive than the native student population. This became quite apparent during demonstrations when Bishop Desmond Tutu paid a visit and addressed the student body. Tutu had been a faculty member at NUL in the 1970s and was close to many of my colleagues.

With an abundance of free time I was able to give guest lectures, participate in departmental activities such as reading MA theses, and work on a variety of interesting projects. One week was spent as a visiting professor at the University of Zimbabwe, where I lectured on my academic specialty, the ethnohistory of the North American Indians. Also, that particular year the NUL history department had planned a series of field trips to the famous historical sites in Lesotho, including the sacred mountain Thaba Bosiu where the Boers were defeated by King Moshoeshoe I, and the burial site of many subsequent kings. We also visited Mount Moorosi in the Orange River basin, site of the opening encounter in the Gun War of 1880-81. These entailed difficult trips to remote regions and rugged climbs, but they cemented close relations between the faculty and students as we shared in their country's national historical experience. This was a rare opportunity for a visiting academic to see the interior and talk with local elders. It also led to a departmental decision to plan a future national oral history project which will be a cooperative affair between my home institution and NUL, perhaps with funding from USIA. This will initially focus on oral traditions in those villages which are soon to be displaced by the massive Highlands Water Project diverting water resources to the Transvaal region in South Africa.

Several of the Fulbright wives became involved with the NUL International Primary School, which we affectionately called NULIPS. This school is a study in contrasts. It occupies a very marginal physical facility in a setting of great scenic beauty. From every direction the mountains overlook the cramped buildings and a very sparsely equipped play yard. The only water fountain for several hundred students is a single standing pipe and spigot in the play yard. Although the school is located on the university campus it has no relationship with the academic program per se.

In Lesotho as throughout much of the world elementary teachers do not receive their education in a university, but at special teacher-training institutions. Neither does the school have a research or curriculum development function, although it is acknowledged to be one of the exemplary primary schools of the country by the Ministry of Education. The Head Teacher, a dynamic Kenyan of Indian descent, had promoted it as an International Primary School—and indeed it had a sprinkling of expatriate children—but it was certainly not independent either from the university budget or from national curriculum guidelines. The students come almost exclusively from university-related homes, and the very high tuition by Lesotho standards is subsidized for children of staff members.   Thus the primary school, like the provision of staff housing, has become an institutional perk. This excludes all but the most affluent non-university Basotho families from sending their children to the school and lends it an air of exclusivity which is incongruous for such an impoverished country.   There is a stark contrast between the well groomed youngsters in their red-and-gray uniforms at the campus school and the sparsely clad, barefoot, poorly fed children in the nearby village schools.

My wife, a school media coordinator, and her partner—whose husband was a Fulbrighter in mathematics, undertook a reorganization of the primary school "library." This turned out to be a small room with several large shelves filled with uncatalogued books, which shared space with an assortment of old tires, bags of cement, wheelbarrows, gardening tools, and various other junk. Each day everything had to be removed before the cataloguing could begin and returned at day's end; in Lesotho nothing is summarily thrown away because someone might be able to use it in the future. It took most of a year to sort things out in the "library"—the wheelbarrow is still stored there! After returning home both wives organized local drives to send learning materials to both NULIPS and other schools in our valley, and they still stay in touch with the faculties.

The Head Teacher soon learned of my involvement with American Indians, which in the past had included directing a number of state and federally funded education programs and the development of textbooks and instructional units for the State of Florida. She approached me with the idea that if a model American History unit could be developed during my stay in Lesotho, it could possibly be passed on to teachers around the country through the Basic and Non-Formal Education System (BANFES)—a rural teacher-training project funded by the U.S. Agency for International Development.

The efforts of many western nations—primarily Canada, Germany, the Netherlands, the U.S., and Ireland—are being poured into agricultural, economic, and educational development projects.   There is also a very large contingent of Peace Corps volunteers in the country, many serving in the rural schools.   For all its impoverishment Lesotho has a surprisingly extensive, if marginally effective, primary school system, most of which is operated by religious groups in cooperation with the government. Approximately 98% of the school structures have been built by either the Catholic Church or the Lesotho Evangelical Church, with minuscule teacher salaries paid by the Ministry of Education. The adult literacy rate is perhaps the highest in Africa, approaching 59%, even though school attendance is not compulsory. Moreover, many young boys attend school only irregularly as they have to tend the herds in place of adults who are away in the mines. Traveling with the BANFES team, my wife and I were able to visit numerous schools in the mountain villages and had nothing but admiration for teachers who labored under truly primitive conditions with as many as 100 children in unheated, unlighted, often dirt-floored classrooms. Yet, we were always greeted with great courtesy and friendliness—a hallmark of the Basotho.

In a country which has so little in the way of school facilities, materials, and trained teachers it would be reasonable to expect a limited curriculum in the area of Social Studies. At the very least one would not expect to see an emphasis on non-African history in the primary grades; but such is not the case. The national curriculum guide for Standard (Grade) Seven issued by the Ministry of Education calls for extensive study of world history.

Quite obviously the degree to which history is taught varies from school to school and teacher to teacher. The training of most elementary teachers in Lesotho prepares them to deal with only the most elemental concepts of world history and geography, and that is a major stumbling block to realizing these curriculum goals. So when the opportunity was presented to help develop a model instructional unit on American History, I eagerly accepted.

The Social Studies unit that we planned with the teachers was introduced in the school with great initial success. NULIPS is an English medium primary school and the students have a good command of the language, as well as a grasp of African history, especially that of their particular region. Unlike their peers in other Lesotho primary schools, these students have been encouraged to raise questions and engage in western-style dialogue with teachers; they generally had active, inquiring minds—plus teachers who were interested in encouraging discovery skills. In the Basotho culture it is usually considered impolite to ask too many questions, especially of adults; this carries over into the elementary classrooms throughout the country where most learning is by rote memorization due to extreme overcrowding and a lack of adequate materials, as well as marginally skilled teachers. However, the university school students were very responsive to the concept of comparing elements of South African history with similar occurences in North America during the 18th and 19th centuries, when Europeans confronted native cultures.

For example, the experimental unit which we introduced dealt with some causes of the American Revolution in 1776, comparing it with the Great Trek of the 1830s and the subsequent Boer Wars. The regular teachers introduced this unit with map work and a glossary of terms that would be used. My role was to provide the basic content using a lecture-discussion technique which had proven successful with the eighth graders in our university laboratory school at home, where I had taught a course on American Indians for several years.

The Basotho students were quick to grasp some fundamental similarities between the Boer penetration of the South African interior and the inexorable westward push of European settlers from the American seaboard colonies. They understood that both the Boers and American Colonists were resisting the imperial policies of their European metropoles, while seeking economic and political freedom for themselves; in both instances the native populations which had long inhabited the land were militarily and politically overwhelmed. The students were surprised to learn that in the case of Amerindian tribes the populations were decimated by diseases which Europeans brought, but the same fate did not befall the African peoples as an aftermath of contact. In fact just the opposite was true in South Africa where the native peoples became a subjugated majority. Student questions also indicated they were aware that racism was an important element underlying expansion on both continents. In a short examination at the conclusion of the unit, the students evidenced a mastery of the major objectives, and in informal questioning expressed positive feelings about their experience.

Unfortunately, unanticipated medical problems forced my wife and me to return to the U.S. before the end of the academic year, so the project was placed on hold until my next extended visit. Nevertheless, certain observations can be made about the prospects for utilizing the comparative history approach to introduce American History in village schools throughout Lesotho. At the present time, under prevailing economic and political conditions, the prospects are not promising for two reasons.

First, the quality of the teaching staff in the vast majority of rural schools is marginal. Most have not completed a teacher training course, and would have to be brought up to speed in social studies content and methodo-logy before comparative history techniques could be introduced. The NULIPS teachers were exceptionally well trained and highly motivated, while the Head Teacher was supportive of curriculum innovation. In addition, it was possible for me to share with them the basic concepts of such works as Howard Lamar and Leonard Thompson's *The Frontier in History: North America and South Africa Compared*, and George M. Fredrickson's seminal work *White Supremacy: A Comparative Study in American & South African History*. In fact some of the NULIPS staff knew Professor Thompson, a former South African resident who has been at the university frequently and has written extensively about the history of Lesotho. This would not be the case with teachers in the remote mountain schools where they are hard pressed to deliver even the most rudimentary instructional program.

Second, the students in the rural schools have a very limited experiential backround. Unlike the NULIPs children, many of whom have traveled extensively in Africa and Europe, the average Lesotho school child has rarely been any distance from his or her home district. Thus most lack the background necessary to conceptualize issues in comparative history. Certainly this could be overcome, but it would take a great deal of effort by already overworked and undertrained staffs. Even so, a goal of the BANFES project and the Ministry of Education should be to focus on innovative techniques which will enable these teachers to broaden the horizons of their charges. Hopefully we can return to assist in that process.

In the two years since the Fulbright assignment we have stayed in close touch with our Basotho friends. In fact, my NUL department chairman who is finishing his doctoral work in the U.S. visited us for a week and lectured to our university students on contemporary issues in South Africa. In addition, I was able to return to Lesotho in June of 1990 to attend a planning conference for the oral history project mentioned earlier. This, plus continuous correspondence, has enabled us to maintain an intimate first-hand knowledge of conditions in the country.

In reflecting on our time in Lesotho, there was such a variety of experiences that it is difficult to isolate those which were truly transforming. Perhaps the most striking thing to both of us is that we became keenly attuned to survival in Lesotho; and, where a few months earlier we had no inkling about this remote corner of the earth, we were soon resonating to the tempo of life in a culture of scarcity. Little things became magnified: would there be too much rain that would keep us slogging in mud, or not enough so the university reservoir might go dry?   Would the road to Maseru be passable if anyone got sick?   Could the power lines survive the high mountain spring storms, could the electricity remain on through dinner?   Would we be able to find enough dry kindling to start a coal fire this evening?   Who had the gardening tools that we shared?   Will the telephones ever operate again? How much colder could it get at this altitude? All of the Fulbright families have been indelibly marked by these months shared with a truly unique people; not surprisingly, we often recall them fondly, if still with a little dismay.

And none of us will ever again be able to watch the television news reports on the violent upheavals in South Africa without wondering what is going on in that little postage stamp-sized country in the middle of the African map.

The author teaches in the Religion Department at the University of South Carolina. In 1988-89 he taught American literature at the Jagiellonian University in Kracow, where a line of Fulbrighters had preceded him. In January 1989 he was invited to write a piece for a clandestine publication and did so, concealing his hand to a certain extent by adopting an ironic and self-mocking tone. Invited for this volume to review his original statement, he did so in 1990 and then in 1991 added a few more thoughts. At three different levels of time then the reader can watch the deepening understanding of this unusual experience, at a time when Poland was poised on the brink of a new era.

34

POLAND: DURING, AFTER AND LATER

Kevin Lewis

During my stay in Poland, in January 1989, I published an article. It was translated into Polish by Piotr Pienkowski for, and published by, the Polish free press quarterly *Arka* (No. 25, March 1989, pp. 13-16) under the title, "Wizyta Na Koszt Wlasny," "A Visit at One's Own Expense." This is what I wrote:

"A small number of my colleagues at the public, state-supported University of South Carolina envy my coming to Poland for a year as a Fulbright lecturer. But most of my acquaintances and some of my family think it strange—at best, a puzzling decision. What is this man, they probably think, a masochist? I claim no Polish blood and have never previously visited Poland. The only Polish-American I can remember in my distant past was an inspiring university professor, a linguist who told us he had fled Poland on skis during the War. No scholarly research and no journalistic project brings me to Poland. So what gives? Why did I come? I continue to ask this question myself.

"Reader of this journal, you whom the truths of this country's situation elude far less than they elude me, you who will smile when I confide my latest insight into the Polish reality, you who have seen American tourists and

American writers come and go, perhaps you can help me understand why I sojourn among you, speaking no Polish, interrupting my small career in mid-life to learn what I can learn and to enjoy what I can enjoy in this curious region of the mind, this baffling text of Poland. Read on. Observe the academic at his introspective investigation. Treat kindly his reckless, provisionary bill of explanation.

"1.1. In the country in the Soviet orbit in which I have been led to believe the human spirit enjoys its fullest play, I wanted to discover whether a better answer can be given than in America at present to the question: How then shall we live? As my wife, a native of the American South (an inheritor of its distrust of work for work's sake), constantly reminds me, I am a Puritan. Mine is the New England tradition. My forbears were Scotch-Irish Calvinists-—Protestant forefathers whose transmitted teachings prepared my personal embrace of the slogan that appears, albeit in a terribly dislocated ironic context, over the gate at Auschwitz, "Arbeit macht frei" (My phrase was: Work will bring forth the Kingdom of God). These same teachings prepared the character of my American attraction to Freud. I make jokes about the old New England ideal of plain living and high thinking, but my family tradition places me in spiritual opposition to the conspicuous consumerism of my society. It propels me into the field in search of socio-political contexts elsewhere where a Puritan might find better support for a better life.

"1.2. Though I wanted to test in a socialist state the possibilities for the realization of a more authentic way of living, I am thwarted by my visitor's privileges, my dollars, my unrestricted travel, my access to the best hotels and restaurants, and by the support system that follows me everywhere. I live in a cocoon, protected by an unremovable screen on all sides separating me from the images of reality I observe from a distance. My discoveries, such as they are, remain theoretical, never ontological. And I am comfortable with my frustration! So how in the space of a such a year can I ever learn to understand what is being said here in public and written here in "official" publications?

"1.3. I came in order to determine whether it is possible for a man of average intelligence, curiosity, and imagination coming from the west with no previous local experience to begin successfully to read between the lines of publications approved by the state. Apparently it is not, at least not after five months.

"1.4. I am not such a Puritan. I came to Poland with dollars in hopes of finding Cuban cigars at a price an academic can afford. I have been cruelly disappointed, not in the prices, but in the unavailability of these ambrosial materials. And Poland has brought out in me the follower of the Eastern Bloc Cargo Cult of consumption in hard currency stores.

"**2.1.** I wanted to understand the historical-social-cultural context which produced a work as strange to me as *Ferdydurke*. I have felt as though I can begin to grasp Dostoevsky's underground man. Not Gombrowicz. That work could have been written on the far side of the moon, for all the light it sheds on my previous experience of the human reality. For this very reason I have been drawn to it, vexed by its mystery. Is Gombrowicz the only Polish Modernist? Is this what a Polish Modernism, or perhaps Post-Modernism would look and feel like? I know something of Faulkner, and of white-black social tension, but Faulkner is no guide through the darkness of deformed personal relations I enter in Gombrowicz. I can neither see nor, still less, see through that face, or those faces. And I am still drawn.

"**2.2.** He makes a loud noise in the West, but we listen to Kundera in spite of it. We are suckers for prophets—they titillate us, we consume them—and Kundera's know-it-all pose is seductive to those, like myself, who tend to remain thoroughly and shamelessly uninformed about *Mitteleuropa*. I came to Poland because Kundera commanded me. 'Central Europe represents the destiny of the West in concentrated form,' he has warned, implying that there is still time to reverse our neglect of this region and, in the process, to learn something about *ourselves*. But does our destiny lie fifty years in the past? in economic ruin, corruption of conscience, and the complete works of Lenin? What does he mean? Does he find his material in the apocalyptic *Planet of the Apes*? I came here in order to work this one through.

"**2.3.** I came to Poland because here, in the last Christian country in Europe, men kiss the hands of women. I wanted to discover the connection. The flowers are not only a means of relieving the drabness of the socialist workers' paradise, they are surely also a romantic gesture, of a piece with other Romantic, occasionally self-martyring gestures of defiance. Romantic Christianity within Opposition Christianity (see 6.2). Question: when is Romanticism unreconstructed by Modernism *not* kitsch? Answer: when what remains uncorrupted in a tragically embattled nationalism seeks political expression in tribal Romanticism. But this is difficult for me, believing with Auden that Romanticism ran its course from Goethe to Hitler.

"**2.4.** I came here curious about the evolving role of the writer in Central Europe. American writers have envied what seems from afar the spiritual security of the vocation of writer as intransigent national hero. But my Puritan conscience suggests that a constellation of dishonesties equivalent to, but mysteriously different from, that with which I am familiar must haunt the writer here. Surely keepers of the word in different traditions suffer differing forms of this common complaint. I want to understand the present sense of "calling," the religious term, in the Polish writer together with its inherent dangers to the self. I want better to grasp the dimensions of this problem as suggested in self-torturing, nearly impenetrable translated prose by my new acquaintance, Jan Prokop, several years ago in a piece he wrote for the American journal *TriQuarterly*.

"2.5. If the Western modernisms, "high" and "low," have not crossed the borders into Central Europe (Kundera), or if they have snuck across and remain incognito, what is the Western visitor to make of the literary modes and vehicular forms adapted or devised by Polish writers today? To be modernized or to modernize oneself must carry different meaning in the different traditions. An intriguing issue which for me must remain academic, lacking Polish. But I did hope to develop my own sense of just how Polish writers negotiate an authentic means of engaging the forces at play in their lives, from both the personal and literary points of view.

"3.1. I came in hopes of understanding two or three Poles well enough to be welcomed finally as an intimate friend into the privacy of your notoriously guarded personal life. The English journalist who spent several years in Moscow as a young man, Malcolm Muggeridge, once defined love as 'the discerning affection for the private side of others.' I accept this. I attempt to universalize it. But the guarded Polish private reality throws up obstacles to the realization of such love for me, and I am haunted by the prophetic warning of Gombrowicz's 'faces.'

"4.1. I came because I have been challenged by the expression on the face of Milosz when he visited my university several years ago, and by what he has written about the vacuity and untroubled innocence of his California students in their tight jeans and cultivated sun-tans. The look said to me, 'You will never know the suffering depths of the human reality I have seen and assimilated in Central Europe—you are forever prevented from adding this essential revelation about the human heart to your personal store of knowledge of the world and of yourself.' I have read the poem 'Child of Europe' several times in hopes that it might yield at last these secrets. I have devoured his autobiographical *Native Realm*. Yourcenar's *Coup de Grâce*, as well as Wiesel's *Night*, Borowski, and the Hungarian doctor Miklos Nyiszli on Auschwitz, suggest that Milosz is correct. But intellectual pride and curiosity thrust me vocationally into this personal project of attempted discovery.

"4.2. Like many visitors to Poland, born luckily too late
and too far away to have experienced the years of war, I have come to reflect at first hand upon the Nazi death camps, to make the obligatory on-site visits, and to find my own way into the labyrinthine tangle of the discussion of

historical Polish-Jewish relations. I came here tantalized by Lanzman's comment at the end of 'Shoa' that the sites of the Nazi killing factories struck him by their great natural beauty. I can become a familiar of Auschwitz, I find after several visits. But the apparent local truths upon which I stumble in Poland—historian Norman Davies helps descry them—defy integration, let alone accumulation, into a larger truth. But do my readers adequately understand why Auschwitz, the flagship of the line and the focus of what remains our unbelieving astonishment at what occurred in Poland caught between Stalin and Hitler, has become a tourist mecca and not only for Jews? Auschwitz as a celebrated but remote geographical location is *information* denied in western societies surfeited by information and accustomed to getting it when we want it. Until our voracious media discover or invent a still more unbelievable image of nightmare atrocity, Auschwitz will remain the ultimate shock, a marketable holy ground. Hence its cachet.

"**5.1.** I came to experience and to understand a little of what life is like, conditioned by the prolonged death throes of the kind of socialist state imposed here by the Soviet Union after Yalta. The humiliations and corruption accompanying this brutal joke may linger long under various succeeding displays of self-reform. But so impractical a system in which so few are rewarded with so little save the scorn of their countrymen cannot last forever, not even in a society where traditional values, in spite of Western influence, seem weighted against the disciplined individualism (and pluralism) which energizes the western democracies. Yes, I came to see what the lines in the shops are like by standing in them, to learn the daily frustrations by living a few of them myself, to get angry over the sheer nonsense of making travel arrangements. Only after arrival, did I find I had come in order to find Poles who have not watched television and not read a state newspaper since the imposition of martial law.

"**5.2.** What I have discovered is not ineptness in specific high places—from its recognizable effects all around me I am partially shielded by my cocoon—but thieves in low places. I am a natural target of the pick-pocket gangs who operate with apparent impunity in Warsaw Central Station, and of the would-be magicians among the koniki ('little horses,' the money changers), working the bait-and-switch trick under the benign surveillance of the milicja (police). I came to discover where personal enterprise may find expression in Poland, and I have found it. Is bribe-taking the principal free enterprise in a socialist state?

"**5.3.** I came not with political theory, not with a journalist's list of questions, but rather to an academic appointment with specific tasks to accomplish. But the satisfactory accomplishment of my assigned tasks seems virtually impossible, owing to the damaging effects of a dismal socio-political system upon the academic life. No institution in a society can function independently of the larger system of which it is a part. If the whole is diseased, so must the parts be. One symptom of disease is the mistrust of the beneficial service universities render to a society by demonstrating and inculcating the free exercise of the disciplined critical faculties.

"**5.4.** I wanted to get a clearer grasp of those elements in a socialist system which may indeed need to be integrated into the faltering systems deployed by the western democracies. I have not yet found these elements. Nor have I found clues for possible solutions to the numerous imperfections of which analysts of the various western diseases complain.

"**5.5.** I came here with a view to taking Conrad's troubling river upstream into the heart of darkness to its source, that is, in ambitious hope of penetrating the related mysteries of Socialist Central Europe: the tribal feuds, the killing grounds, the palpable absence of the Jews, the economic chaos, the discredited elitist puppet power structure, the depthless chasm separating theory and practice, the refusal to imagine the burdens of freedom, the festering resentment, the will to leave (the will to remain), the stony public face, the fouled air, the sick children, the trumpeter of Krakow every hour on the hour from the Mariacki tower pleading for the End. I came in order tentatively to name these mysteries for myself, suspecting that some permutation of an alien master-slave system of human relations may partially account for the distortions I seek to understand. Finding myself in the thick of unexplained contingencies, a player in a drama broken off and begun again as often as the story in Diderot's *Jacques the Fatalist*, I wonder whether, were it possible to penetrate further into the mysteries, I might ultimately descry the revealed inner face of an Ivan Karamazov and, at the heart of it, hear the soothing assurance, 'All is permitted.'

"**6.1.** I am a Protestant Christian humanist for whom personal prayer remains valid while most dogmatisms and evangelisms effectively remain shallow idolatries serving an admixture of worldly gods. I came to Poland to ascertain how seriously the secularized and embattled Christian communities further west should regard the appearance in Poland of so great a display of religious practice. I am not especially encouraged by what I have found so far. Can any one human institution perform so many important human functions as the Polish Church appears to be performing? A bright student reports of her reaction to reading Thomas Merton, 'The richness of his inner experience made me dizzy!' Does the harried Polish reality currently leave any room for the inner life?

"**6.2.** I have come to discover whether the last remaining Christian nation in Europe will be required, under the laws of heaven, to die for our sins (again). I hope to gauge whether the population at large can yet be made ready for such a recapitulative messianic assignment.

"**6.3.** As a trained theologian-analyst of folk Christianities—for theological purposes *all* Christianities can be approached usefully with a view to identifying their 'folk' dimensions—I want to appraise so that I might better appreciate the role in salvation ascribed to the Virgin in the romantic Christianity of this place and tradition. Exploration of the terrain of Polish Mariology: my contribution to the ecumenical dialogue with American Protestants begun by Pope John Paul II at my university (of South Carolina) in September 1987.

"But this is enough. I am made to feel uneasy in Poland when I press too hard dialectically for truths about the Polish reality. I am made to feel (by my translator, for one, whose services I greatly appreciate while I cannot assess them critically), and hardly ever intentionally, that I am participating in a colossal joke, in part a joke on me, and that I will be unable to get the point, now and perhaps never."

*   *   *

After my return, in December 1990, I reconsidered all this. The reflections entitled "Wizyta Na Koszt Wlasny" were occasioned by an invitation to contribute something on a topic of my own choosing to the then-underground literary and political Polish quarterly *Arka*, published in Krakow. The invitation came from a younger colleague in the Institute of English Philology at the venerable Jagiellonian University in that city, the cultural center and seat of kings until the capital was moved to Warsaw in the seventeenth century. It came midway during my year as the Fulbright Lecturer in American Literature in that institute (1989-90), one of the original Fulbright positions in Poland. The article was published three months before my wife and I returned home to South Carolina.

This scatter-shot "bill of explanation" may provide an instructive kind of response to the vexed "Polish reality" of that time by a Fulbrighter with no previous connection to Poland and no familiarity with the language. I went to Poland with nothing more at stake than curiosity about the place and about life generally in the Eastern Bloc under the control of imposed Communist regimes.

In January, when I submitted the piece to *Arka*, not even our tuned-in Polish academic friends were able to envision the rapid political changes which ensued. Far from it. Socially, economically, and politically, the Polish reality of that moment was indeed volatile. But this was nothing new. The inept, discredited Communist-controlled government was hanging on, and our Polish friends remained sunk in their impatient, pervasive pessimism about the immediate future. That January, any achievement of what Poles endearingly refer to as a "normal" (Western) life appeared to lie as far in the precarious future as ever.

If the West was normal, the situation in Poland was one of prolonged "crisis" following upon precedent crises extending back into the eighteenth century—long enough to have forged a most "abnormal" cultural identity. If in my response to the *Arka* invitation I could open myself "recklessly" to the serendipitous experience of immersion in the surrounding "otherness" of the Polish personality, perhaps insight into its mind and spirit might flow and genuine contact follow. So I attacked it with my own spirit, with theater, and I winged it. Although the course of events then swiftly altered the political scene, perhaps something of value in the piece remains, some contact with the enduring Poland, even if only in one impressionable American's mimicry of Polish irony.

Innocently, I had expected to encounter in Poland at least some allegiance to Marxist ideology. My students laughed at me when I told them this and when I asked their advice on behaving so as not to attract the unwanted attention of the security arm of the state. They told me I had seen too many movies. Neither my wife nor I ever did meet even a party card-carrier of the opportunist, preferment-seeking kind. By the fall of 1988, Poland had become a society in which anyone could say and do practically anything without fear of trouble from the authorities. Even policemen were changing money on the black market! The occasional street demonstration staged in Krakow that year by groups on the radical (radically conservative) fringe of the political spectrum served merely as outlets for undergraduate street theater parody and for rock-throwing high-schoolers eager for a piece of any action. Materials produced by the underground desk-top publishers were available openly around the university.

And yet, when my young colleague, Piotr, in January identified himself as a member of the editorial committee for *Arka* and invited a contribution from me, his wary pessimism made this form of still-illegal expression of political dissent seem at least a moderately risky business. Recall that in no other Eastern Bloc country during the 1980's, and especially following the martial law crackdown of December 1981, did underground publishing flourish as it did in Poland. Hundreds of books and dozens of regularly appearing newspapers and journals served to keep every Pole who wished it in touch with dissident viewpoints of every description.

I slowly discovered the meaning of this phenomenon. That year in Poland shocked me into a fuller grasp of the social function of language. Those who have never known the absolute corruption of language imposed by a Stalinist type of regime can only begin to imagine the importance of such un-"controlled" publications to a society threatened by apathy, moral deteriorization, and paralysis through otherwise unrelieved suspicion of the "lie." *Arka*, founded in 1983 by a group of Krakow intellectuals including several former internees under martial law, quickly became a highly regarded vehicle of truth-telling throughout Poland and in the expatriate Polonia communities abroad. Saul Bellow, Melvin Lasky, and Norman Podhoretz had lent their names to its international council of patrons, doubtless in virtue of their sympathy with the traditional, anti-leftist values which undergirded the politics of the Polish opposition.

Although *Arka* has republished in translation or summarized articles originally appearing in periodicals such as *Encounter*, *Partisan Review*, *Commentary*, and *The New Republic*, Piotr informed me that mine would be the first contribution from an American resident in Poland at the time of publication. It is one indicator of the Polish reality of the time that this fairly prudent appointee of the USIA guessed correctly that his appearance in *Arka* would do harm neither to the Fulbright program nor to himself as a foreign employee of a university answerable to the state-controlled Ministry of Education. The invitation appealed to my sense of adventure. I put other work, including course preparation, temporarily aside. I did not bother to consult our helpful contacts either in the Krakow consulate or the Warsaw embassy.

But why the tone I used? To have fun with the assignment was in order, so it seemed. I had come to believe that, in that cultural context, the appearance of making fun had more currency than the appearance of taking one's task with solemn seriousness. I was learning the local use of irony. One student whose candor I trusted upon reading it expressed appreciation of my unusually "confessional" voice. Another, caught up in opposition political activities, advised me that I was paranoid!

Poland is a difficult, elusive read. Poles like it this way. Under long, imposed gangster rule, first, by the three partners in the Partition (1795-1918), and then by the Communist puppet state following World War II, Poles have apparently grown ever more feisty, cunning, obstinate, and ironic. The Polish way of coping with the various uninvited occupying powers for two hundred years has been stubbornly to subvert the illegal "authorities" in any and every way short of sacrificing life, though even here the cherished myth of patriotic martyrdom is intrinsic to the tradition of the Polish intelligentsia. The "otherness" of the evolved Polish mind, shaped for generations by geographical and political conditions totally unlike those affecting any other people to the West, throws Americans especially off balance, that is when we stay long enough really to engage it. Words spoken and written in public in Poland, like behavior generally, as in other such hostage countries, have not meant what they mean elsewhere in free societies.

Further to confuse, the politics of dissent have taken their bearings from the very principles which provoke liberal dissent in the western democracies. Paul Goodman's title *Growing Up Absurd*, would be, if anything, far more appropriate for an autobiographical account of growing to maturity in the Poland of the last forty years—and yet such a story would be unrecognizable to us, so difficult is it to imagine that experience well enough to *feel* it and to identify with the local pattern of learned responses to events. In Poland it has become natural to disbelieve even the truth when spoken by official representatives of the "lie." It has become second nature to believe the most outrageous rumors if transmitted privately by friends. And learned habits of mind carry over. Even sympathetic truths eventually become suspect. It is to the infinite credit of Polish perversity and persistence that the nation managed its heroic triumph over the sceptical apathy and paralysis the lie induces, at least to the initial extent of winning back self-government. How the ingrained traits of the evolved Polish mind will serve the nation as it pursues reconstruction and stabilization in the image of the "normal" is indeed another and troubled issue. But I was only beginning in 1989 to break out of my own differently conditioned mind to engage the depths and the potential of despair in that irony of the Poles.

Piotr was one of my teachers of this attitude to life, and he was elusive. I owe to his informal tutorials the theme of the visitor from the West destined to misunderstand the motivations, paradoxes, and the improbable throwback romanticism of the local intellectual life. Piotr unknowingly supplied me the stagey, wiseacre, role-playing voice of the piece I wrote. For, if of nothing else, I could be certain of my numerous uncertainties about Poland. By playing the open-hearted, well-intentioned fool, perhaps I could prevent being made an unwitting fool. (I remember well sitting in embarrassment at a long lunch table with Krakow intellectuals courteously hearing out a visiting American academic in his native arrogance and ignorance presuming to offer advice on Eastern European affairs.) One of my favorite Polish paintings is the great history painter Jan Matejko's image of the court jester in red from head to foot, seated deep in melancholy reflection—a cultural icon. Its universal theme provides an emotional bridge to the particular historical experience of those embattled people on that tragic land.

The feeling of being lost but strangely at home in a world beyond my grasp remains as true now when I think back on our experience as it was then when we were immersed. That lostness was wonderfully exciting, providing as it did a life-expanding intellectual challenge of integrating ourselves into that otherness as we could. Doubtless like other returnees, I am prodded by the temptation to add the character, expressions, and legacy of the Eastern European "captive mind" to my ongoing research concerns. Tantalized, I learned something but not enough. I seemed to learn that most Western journalists and political scientists had no better grasp of the evolving Polish reality than do I on the basis of elementary new acquaintance with its fabulous literary tradition and our ten-months' immersion in the text itself. Surely no American policy guiding relations with the emerging Poland can achieve success by any measure unless informed by serious, catch-up, historical cultural studies, and specifically by a thorough, well-coached reading of Polish literature from Adam Mickiewicz forward. In the *Arka* piece, dated as it is, I still wish to signal this conviction.

*   *   *

Later still, in December 1991, I reread the above. By then I had drifted still further away from immersion in the Polish experience. I see one omission: I have not done justice to our American colleagues, our well-meaning handlers among the diplomats. A concluding word then about that relationship against the play of Polish-American encounters and politics.

During summer orientation in 1988, for Fulbrighters headed for appointments in Poland and other Eastern Bloc countries, Washington USIA officials pointedly insisted that we were *not* to be or to be regarded as employees of USIA. If ever given cause by locals wary of the Fulbright program's possible connection with foreign policy goals, we were to claim the status of independent academics on cultural exchange. The understanding with which I subsequently operated was that, while "selected" by a committee of academic peers, and while "appointed" by USIA, I was technically "employed" by my Polish university. The dollars deposited into my bank account in South Carolina by USIA were some sort of enabling stipend, whereas the all-but-worthless zloties doled out to me from a cash box in the Dean's office at the Jagiellonian once a month were my salary.

This theoretical distinction, however tricky, seemed useful at the time and I was grateful for it. I was to hold myself responsible solely to my profession and to my new students and colleagues. I was not to be burdened or tainted by politics. At the same time, I was urged to avoid any political behavior my presumed good judgment might deem foolhardy, such as participation in street demonstrations.

In fact, I never needed to invoke the appointed/employed distinction—we never once knowingly met *that* kind of suspicious Pole. Equally notable, or so I was to learn, we encountered not even a trace of suspicion that my Fulbright appointment had been secured by any process other than fair competition on a reasonably level playing field. At the time, Polish Fulbright academics were perceived to be "selected" with a heavy input from Party politicians rewarding loyalty, despite the efforts of USIS to frustrate this practice. In that system, Fulbrights were rarely dispensed to Jagiellonian scholars, hard scientists excepted: Krakow remained a seat of cultural and political resistance to the Communists. But my immediate colleagues, as English language and literature teachers, had enjoyed a certain access to short-term exchanges in England and had observed a relatively un-politicized academic world.

The USIA position as presented seemed fair and conducive to the carrying out of my duties, both assigned and self-initiated. And USIS kept the bargain: I never once felt any kind of interference or attempt to influence us by the Warsaw Embassy or the Krakow Consulate. At the Embassy, the Fulbright program was serviced by two fine USIS women. Handling the Fulbrighter motley was not easy, and opinion that year divided over how well they accomplished it. (A USC colleague had taken his family to Greece earlier in the eighties; dismayed by the total lack of assistance given him by Fulbright Commission or Embassy in Athens, he nonetheless stayed two years.) My wife and I were nothing but grateful for aid rendered, given working conditions in Poland and the limits of USIS job descriptions. Even more helpful, and not only because we saw him more often at the Krakow Consulate where we enjoyed mail privileges, was a remarkable USIS officer, a Princeton PhD in Russian History. He read my article in Polish in his copy of *Arka* and complimented it with genuine interest—the more impressive in that I had neglected to mention it to him previously.

There was a small flap in Krakow in the spring of 1989. Without consulting the Jagiellonian, USIS Warsaw decided it had to remove the longstanding Fulbright position in Linguistics from Krakow and divert it to another university perceived to be in greater need. The news shocked the English Institute, where I taught with my Linguistics Fulbrighter colleague. Our Polish colleagues were dismayed; they had come to rely on this appointment, and the following year was especially crucial. We were told Fulbright budget constraints were to blame, USIS wanted to distribute the benefits of the program more widely. Joining our protest with those of our Polish colleagues, we managed to delay the decision for a year. I have not heard what has happened since.

With the return of Polish independence, the administration of the Fulbright program has now been removed from the Warsaw Embassy, to be vested in a new binational commission. Fulbrighters will now have less immediate on-site contact with USIS. Gone too are the commissary and pouch privileges which made life for Fulbrighters a little easier in the eighties. Poland was an often frustrating challenge for us, and the diplomats, for whom we developed a reciprocated affectionate regard, made it easier. Having them was better than not having them. In our best moments we seemed to be working in concert for mutually agreed ends. They had more perks but we had the better job—occasionally we felt sorry for them in their insulated world. And the isolation imposed upon diplomats seems to attract or to shape borderline eccentrics similar to those attracted to academic life. All said, we are something of a poetic match for each other.

Whether one was an academic or a diplomat in Poland ultimately made little difference. The Poles I met loved the idea of America and coveted what Americans have. But they had grown sceptical about an individual American's ability ever to understand the Polish reality or ever to evince critical curiosity about it. They were more apt to see Americans as friendly, fatuous, and lucky than as civilized, "intellectual," and ironic. Experience of Americans seemed to have taught them to expect neither depth, nor acuity, nor survival cunning. Western political liberalism as a source of ideas seemed irrelevant. And so both Fulbrighters and American diplomats in Poland were treated with a combination of material respect and intellectual condescension, and both for fairly good reasons, or so it seemed to me then.

Our association with representatives of U.S. foreign policy in Poland simply did not matter where gaining or losing the confidence of Polish acquaintances might have been concerned. I connect this with a related social phenomenon. I cannot remember even once being asked by a Pole about my politics or about anything else personal, for that matter. The Poles I met ("exhausted," lacking time for the amenities) were truly not interested. If, well-tutored in survival and subversion, they had come to believe perversely that whatever the Communist state might say would be a lie, they were not prepared conversely to believe that whatever a Fulbright lecturer from a world-powerful democracy might say would be true or even intellectually useful. The Polish reality is not framed by such logical symmetries.

Whether I was associated with U.S. foreign policy or even held political views of my own made little apparent difference to the Poles I met. My battle that year was to be heard at all, to be taken seriously. My battle, more basically, was with real cultural naiveté (my own, first and foremost) and with the local assumption that, as an American, I could not be expected to hold interesting or relevant views on Polish history and politics. The good reasons Poles seemed then to have for dismissing American ideas as such—they did rather like Reagan's description of the USSR as an "evil empire"—now in retrospect seem colored by the traditional cultural arrogance and related intellectual isolation which shapes the Polish mind.

The "crisis," as our print and broadcast media dutifully report, continues albeit in a different form, deepening the impatience and resignation of an embattled people. Three years of freedom from the noxious interference of the "gangsters" on hire to the former USSR have brought surface change. But whatever the structure evolved for any tradition-based Polish "democracy" (in which every man would be a king), Poles will still be dreaming of an elusive "normal" state of affairs. A Fulbrighter's notes on his one-time privileged immersion in that culture, dusted off, may contribute to understanding why.

Frank Jossi, now with the World Press Institute at Macalester College in St. Paul, Minnesota, tells one of the strangest stories in this volume. Recruited from a newspaper job in the South, with no graduate training or teaching experience, he was catapulted through Fulbright into a program referred to as a "Professional" Grant into a one-semester position as the first Fulbright Professor of Journalism at the Punjab University, then found himself in Peshawar, at work with the Afghan resistance movement as a public information officer, or in his word a "flak," a full-fledged propagandist in a mad-hatter war-support operation. No essay in this volume more clearly illustrates the issues involved in pushing the Fulbright program towards short-term policy-relevant purposes. Yet to the author's credit, he analyzes the experience clearly in positive terms; he raises a variety of serious questions about the integrity of the press, about journalistic education and implicitly about the Fulbright Program in its more recent manifestations. But, like others in the volume, after these two kinds of front-line experience he will never be the same.

35

FRONT-LINE JOURNALIST

Frank Jossi

Not so long ago I found myself in Pakistan teaching journalism in two different front-line situations. The first, a three-month teaching assignment with the Fulbright program, placed me in a university in Lahore, where I was the first Fulbright journalism-educator in Pakistan. The second took me to Peshawar during the Soviet withdrawal from Afghanistan. The first situation transformed me, for the occasion, from a journalist to a college journalism instructor and a test case for Fulbright's so-called Professional Program. The second turned me from a journalist and educator into a flak—that is the only word—for an alliance of Afghan guerrilla groups, holy warriors or freedom fighters, depending on your nomenclature, all this during a set of events which changed history. My story begins in Lahore.

*   *   *

This was her day of reckoning. Behind her veil she stood just behind a cement pillar on the third floor of the humanities building of Punjab University, hiding from some unknown. She looked shaken and uneasy, not at all like the articulate and happy young woman that I had come to know as a good student and a class leader.

Just a few weeks before, she and a group of female students had collected a few hundred dollars from students and faculty and bought blankets for flood victims whose homes had been destroyed after the Indus River spilled over after torrential downpours. Confident and cheerful, she arranged a visit with the other female students to a town an hour from Lahore where electricity was still a concept and the closest thing to a house was a 10-foot-high reinforced mud hut. On that trip I saw her and the others practice a highly selective process of choosing blanket recipients, one which made getting into Harvard Medical School look unremarkable. They conducted interviews and told anyone having a bed or even a rag remotely as large as a blanket that they had to give way to the truly needy, those who had nothing at all to sleep on but the clothes on their backs. At the end of the day we gave the last blanket to a pregnant woman who, making her way through a crowd that had grown aggressive and unruly, nearly fell into a ditch. Moments later our van sped back to Lahore, leaving behind an angry and disappointed mob.

Back at school, things had changed. She rarely wore the veil over her face and she had never displayed the edgy nervousness so apparent to any passerby on this sunny and desert-dry day. I asked why. "I'm meeting my husband for the first time and I have never met him before. My parents arranged the marriage."

Even Benazir Bhutto had succumbed to an arranged marriage, revealing openly that it represented more of a career move than anything to do with love. She knew she had no chance at office without practicing Islamic customs.

A few weeks before, the tall, lanky and handsome class poet had come into my office for a private conference in which he shyly and tearfully told me how much he wanted what he labeled a "love marriage." My meager and poor advice—where is Ann Landers when you need her?—pointed out that even love marriages end in separation and that my country led the world in divorces. Love may have little to do with successful marriages and love can grow from nothing at all; going through life's travails with someone can eventually lead to love, I suggested. I had been alerted to this question: at a party a woman radio personality had told me, perceptively: "You in the West, I admire your technology, your ability to quantify everything in numbers, your great science and your freedom. But sometimes I think you've given up love for freedom."

Love was about the last thing I thought I would learn about in Pakistan. Pakistan is not France. Pakistan, I had envisioned, would be all social upheaval and guns and dictators and fanatical fundamentalism and tribal factionalism. You do not assume you will encounter much discussion of love and the polarity of its practices in the East and West, nor do you figure to discover in the pleading look of a young man in love with the idea of love, how much freedom we have in the West or that we may have given up love for freedom.

I was a Fulbright instructor in the Department of Mass Communication of the University of Punjab for the last three months of 1988. Overnight I went from writing in the U.S. about rock and jazz and the inscrutable lyrics of groups like R.E.M. to advising international journalists covering the Afghan War on what guerrilla parties would be the best company inside Afghanistan. I went from having politicians and public relations agents avoiding my phone calls to being called "Professor," without a master's degree. I went from a Southern seaport town graced by 100-year-old magnolias to a densely populated city where trees were a luxury, where the air forever held a thin film of soot. I went from nights of concerts and movies to nights of book-reading and watching, once a week, a video or "The Cosby Show," the one American television show deemed harmless enough to air each week on the government-operated television station.

If the changes were dramatic, I was ready for them. I longed for adventure and the Fulbright offered it. It took the form of teaching Third World students about how journalists work in a free-press system. I had a great deal of experience in reporting, from the investigative kind to general assignment news and arts writing. Now I was confronted with the challenge professionals face when they have an opportunity to teach and they have to figure out how to condense what they have learned all those years into a course. In my case, and in that of many a Fulbright, the additional task is how to make it all relevant to students living 10,000 miles away in a country with no history of democracy or a free press.

I was frightened by teaching. A friend suggested I write out my lecture notes. I sent off almost 100 pages via diplomatic pouch to Pakistan a few weeks before I left.

This was my first taste of the developing world and the first time the Fulbright Program had ever sponsored a Fulbright "Professional" award in Pakistan for journalism. I had no idea what a "professional" grant was, only that I practiced a profession and was given a grant. I had no way of knowing what it was like to face a class, much less a class for whom English was a second language. I had no clue it would take three hours to open a bank account and that almost anything I ate could haunt me for days. I had only a vague idea of what the Fulbright people expected or what my Pakistanis colleagues wanted. Armed with textbooks and notes, I hoped I was prepared for anything. In fact, I was prepared for almost nothing.

I survived, and well. The Department gave me an embarrassingly large office, bigger than anyone else's, and offered me anything I required. The Chairman, Dr. Miskeen Ali Hijazi, was committed to improving the Department despite his politicized staff and the politics of Pakistan. Soft-spoken and sage-like, Dr. Hijazi juggled the sensitive politics of the Department and University with the aplomb of an acrobat. The staff leaned right except for the journalism historian, a tall and thin man whose company I sought on occasion to hear an alternate viewpoint. As with any academic staff, there were petty jealousies and ideological splits, idle gossip and party rivalries, favoritism toward certain students and rejection of others.

Laid out like an American campus, sprawling in every direction, Punjab had 10,000 students and several hundred staff. Originally a British college, it still had afternoon tea, cricket and soccer fields and English library books. Constructed of cheap cement and bricks that crumbled with the scratch of a pen, the school, the largest college in the country, had the decaying look and feel so persistent in the developing world, where things made out of fabric appear more durable than most buildings. Chalk more than two inches long broke in my hand.

The students alleged great problems in understanding my flat, Midwestern accent of the kind commonly heard on the nightly American news. British English they seemed to understand. Since I could find no one to translate my American into British English, I employed one of the department's many staffers—whose main job was to provide tea and cookies in the morning for the professors—to copy my voluminous notes. I could see his shoulders sag when I came into the office with yet another sheaf.

Every classroom and every office had to be locked the minute it emptied. "Someone could leave a bomb in the office if we leave the doors open," Dr. Hijazi explained to me my first day, adding: "A few people are upset that an American is here and they don't like America." There's nothing like a death threat to start you thinking how important you must be. American students are frequently criticized for not taking school seriously enough, but at this juncture I figured Pakistani students were taking it a little too seriously.

I taught two classes: an upper-level course for those in the master's program had eight students; the other, for first-year students, had 35 or 40, depending on the day. By the end of the quarter, the first class dwindled to one or two students while the other grew by four or five. The Punjab master's degree in journalism requires only a final paper and tests; course work did not matter. No one graded anything because grades were irrelevant. Take the final test and write the final paper and you pass. Class attendance was not required during the second year. The system encouraged sloth. The first-year course, since at least attendance was required, was popular even though students did not receive grades.

Motivation and discipline, forever the lamentations of American educators worried about the coming generations of TV-watching dumbbells, were absent as well from classes at Punjab. The women sat to the right of me in two rows and the men sat to the left or in back of the women, with a row separating the sexes. The women were an island of good manners, while the men, hormonally unbent, disrupted class with rude remarks in Urdu. They made jokes among themselves about women in the class and angered serious students with their antics.

"Some of these students are unqualified, but they have to be admitted because they come from a certain province and we must accept a certain number from every province," a professor told me. Another colleague had a different take: "I think because they do not get to date that they are always thinking of women. They may keep their attention just a few minutes on the class but then they think of women and try to impress them by doing stupid things." While I was in Pakistan, a British theater troupe's performance was so badly disrupted by young men during the first act that an older Pakistani woman stood up at intermission and chastised them for their behavior.

Other professors told me I was not alone in my frustration with the generally disruptive classes. But bad behavior was the least of my troubles. I often had to walk a political tightrope. Pakistan is an overwhelmingly political country, a place where a simple conversation invariably turns to ideology and power. I sat in on meetings of the Lahore Press Club, held at a local hotel; they consisted mainly of the country's right-wing editors sitting around a circular table and jawing over politics for hours while chewing sweet cookies and drinking strong, hot tea. After Benazir's election in November 1988, the press club members were distraught. At a December meeting they spoke at length, in Urdu, about what measures they could take that would lead to the fall of Ms. Bhutto. Suddenly the club members turned their stares on me. A Punjab colleague whispered in my ear: "Mr. Jossi, they want to know what you would do to de-stabilize Benazir's government." It was not my expertise, I replied, noting that I quite liked her programs and ideas.

Obviously it was difficult to teach students how the press functions in a free society. The ideal of even vaguely objective reporting was even more difficult to transmit. The Pakistani press mostly reflects a political party except at the most extraordinary media outlets; rarely are both sides of any issue discussed. The British English employed in news copy is antiquated and incomprehensible, reading like a VCR instruction manual. Obfuscation is more common than elucidation in news stories, as they might put it. Journalists compete at sounding intellectual rather than cogent, leaving some Pakistani analyses looking like academic decontructionism. True, the press is being slowly freed from government constraint but the kind of freedom enjoyed in the West is a long way away.

What could I contribute at this frontier of journalism education? My presence at least allowed students to learn the importance of clarity and the concept of impartiality in news reporting, at least to the level of giving both sides of a story a chance to speak. The function of the press does not only involve reflecting political beliefs or quoting government press releases but in transmitting thoughtful and balanced information on events and ideas of significance. And even if the nascent free press in Pakistan could not accomplish these sometimes impossible tasks—American journalism does not always achieve this, either—I advised my students on a basic but forgotten lesson of journalism: be accurate.

Accuracy was such a problem with the Pakistani press that the office of then-Ambassador Robert Oakley would provide journalists with same-day transcripts of press conferences and interviews. That way the journalists could check their quotes and interpretations with what the ambassador actually said and have no excuse for misquoting him. I had a similar experience. One night I gave a speech to a small group of businessmen that for some strange reason received coverage by the Associated Press, which sent a reporter who quoted me as saying the FBI and American publishers controlled the American press (he got one part right). What I had said was that publishers impose their own form of control on editorial content in response to advertisers and special interest groups, while at the same time denying, after a question, FBI influence on the American media. This was much too complex an explanation for that particular reporter to handle and I was left to look stupid in the following day's newspaper.

Rather than the mouthpiece of the government, Americans believe the press should be its watchdog. From investigative reporting to simple general assignment reporting, the American press serves not just to reflect what the American government does but to probe why it is doing it, at what cost and with what likelihood of success. Some Pakistani newspapers—especially the

Western-oriented *Nation*—do remarkably well at this but on the whole the media is the lapdog of the government. Government-imposed shackles, ranging from intimidation to controlling newsprint, obviously hurts the cause of the press, but so does the lack of aggressiveness and professionalism on the part of Pakistani journalists. And so does a highly politicized readership which sometimes collects into a mob at the behest of a political party to storm newspaper offices for the crime of reporting issues or presenting opinions it does not enjoy—such a mob nearly destroyed a paper in Karachi during my stay in Pakistan.

Journalistic education in Pakistani is abysmal, requiring almost nothing of students; few campuses have a student newspaper. During my tenure classes were canceled whenever the slightest opportunity for amusement came up. No one showed for classes one day because a national cricket championship was being shown on television; a week later the classroom was empty again because the department's student cricket team had a match.

While many students may not have taken the educational aspect of college seriously, they did actively and violently participate in political activities. Campus violence was endemic—more than 70 students had been killed in the 1980s on Pakistani college campuses—because students have no outlet except protest. National political parties routinely use student parties to stir discontent in the collegiate community and student government had become so dangerous it had to be banned. One of my brighter students, involved in a liberal student political movement, was kidnapped by a competing student faction and held hostage for a day.

One American journalist-educator cannot save this system from its own corruption. What we can offer is a vision of a more responsible and aggressive press, ideas for writing with greater clarity, a sense of professionalism and enthusiasm, and faith in what we are doing. On a personal level, we can begin to destroy myths about our country and to confront genuine curiosity on intense questions of culture, such as divorce, marriage, drugs and love. As a real-life information booth for the U.S., I fielded hundreds of inquiries and guessed at what I did not know.

At the end of the semester, I wondered if I had achieved anything at all. During the final class I asked students to raise their hands if they planned to become journalists; a scant three or four confessed to that career goal. Had this first-time teacher persuaded most of them to stay out of the media? While that may have been a noble achievement in the U.S.—where too many journalists chase too few jobs—what Pakistan needed was more bright minds in the media. When I asked what their career goals were, nearly everyone told me they sought a safe job in government public relations or government-owned television, which in Pakistan meant secure employment and decent wages for life, regardless of talent, competence or effort.

To make matters worse, I received a meager 13 papers out of 39 in the first-year reporting class. Yet the Department chair was astonished, as was the rest of the staff. No faculty member in years was ever able to drag that many papers out of a first-year class, especially one in which the students had to write in English. I thought this comment was invented to make me feel good but I checked around with other professors, who reported the motivational level of most students hovered somewhere around brain-dead. Students will respond if you show you care by preparing for lectures, attempting to engage them in discussion, offering office hours and staying the course when a few disruptive elements get out of hand. Teaching, like writing, is harder than it looks, but the rewards can be richer than those in other professions. As a journalist you rarely meet your audience, as a teacher they show up everyday.

Should people like me, with little or no teaching experience, be allowed to teach as university faculty abroad in the Fulbright program? In highly sensitive programs involving international understanding, should first-timers be allowed to test their teaching skills on unsuspecting foreigners? After all, I would not want untrained journalists joining newspapers or appearing on network news shows, even in a time when many a pretty face qualifies as a "television journalist."

My conclusion surprises even me: modesty aside, the right kind of person, one with ambition and appropriate experience, can have an impact as great as a trained teacher; the burnout phase has not been reached and the freshness of coming from the real world remains potent. Especially in the liberal arts, in law and in journalism, the Fulbright grantors are wise to look beyond academia to the professional community for a select few future Fulbrights. The basic Fulbright paradigm, university-to-university transfers, must continue as the main context of the program. Within this context, professionals can play an important role if placements are done with sensitivity and intelligence—and with more training than I received (I had none).

Considering the reports of two colleagues who followed me—one who thought the Fulbright a waste of time, the other who enjoyed it—I believe "Professional" Fulbrights might achieve several purposes. International journalists and students tell me their developing countries sorely need expertise in business, computers, journalism and law. While the academy can certainly provide people in some of these areas, the professional world offers just as many uniquely qualified individuals who want to work abroad but are unable to find opportunities. The Peace Corps, for many, requires too large a time commitment; other programs I have researched nearly always cater to academics. With the rapid changes going on around the world, more than a few Americans I meet want to participate in front-line, epoch-making transformations. These same individuals would increase the Fulbright's recognition and broaden support for the program at home—it needs new friends.

Then came Peshawar. My final month in Lahore, December 1988, I was rewriting my notes into a textbook for publication in Pakistan. A one-month extension of my Fulbright helped me finish the book. I had left my previous job in the U.S. and I had not lined up another. I wondered how I could get to Peshawar, the hotspot of Asia even before the final Soviet withdrawal from Afghanistan in February 1989. Suddenly an opening came: Peshawar's USIS American Center inquired if I might like to work at something called "The Afghan Media Resource Center." The salary was generous enough—about the same as a Fulbright grant—and the chance to work in Peshawar was incredibly appealing, whatever the AMRC was. After lying on a beach in Indian Goa for a week, I headed for Peshawar.

In honesty, I was a rube. I had no real knowledge of either what the AMRC was or what the war was about. It was a distant, confusing and brutal conflict that held a cherished place on the front pages of every Pakistani newspaper. It made former Pakistani President Zia-al-Huq a power in central Asia and a major American ally (and killed him in a mysterious plane explosion), it left a million Afghans dead, it created an alternative Afghan leadership in Peshawar composed of cruel, conservative Islamicists, and it produced a flourishing heroin trade between Pakistan and the West, as well as a huge internal drug problem for Pakistan. The war was the last great *jihad* between East and West, between the Soviet Union and America, but it was fought on one side by a surrogate army, poorly trained and badly armed.

Peshawar is a complex place. The intrigues that come with any border town are always intense, but it seems especially true in Peshawar, home to the famed Pathan warriors. They have not changed all that much since Kipling's days. It is a city where with a little luck you can find any drug you want, where men openly carry guns and use them with great frequency to end disputes or to start them, where caravans of camels can be seen late at night on their way toward the Khyber Pass. Darra, a nearby town, boasts a gun market where you can rent an AK-47 and wander back into the hills for a shooting session, or you can simply shoot those rounds into the air in the middle of the street—and attract no attention at all—or you can buy hashish playfully disguised as animal statues placed in display cabinets next to health accoutrements such as British breast-developing creme.

The AMRC was located in a large white Miami-style house on a dusty street in the University Town section of Peshawar, an area full of relief agencies dealing with Afghan refugees. Armed guards checked for bombs under every car that entered through the walled gates, using a contraption that looked like an oversized dentist's mirror. Everyone in Peshawar had enemies.

More than three million Afghans had moved to Pakistan to live in mud-hut villages with barely drinkable water, where summer temperatures hit 120 degrees. The staff of the AMRC had fled Afghanistan, some with families, others entirely on their own. One staffer literally walked to Peshawar from Kabul after seeing 17 family members killed and spending two years— often under torture—in Pul-e-Charki, a perennial on Amnesty International's list of hellish prisons.

The AMRC was the brainchild of the USIA. The Afghan War had been under-covered by the media, in part because going "inside" with the mujahideen could be so dangerous. The USIA figured it was the Afghan mujahideen's war, why not let them cover it? The job went to Joachim Maitre, former dean of Boston University's School of Journalism and noted ideolog, who lost his position in 1991 after charges of plagiarism. Maitre's great vision was to let Afghans cover the war and transmit their stories to the West via the Hearst Corporation's King Features Syndicate. When several unflattering articles surfaced concerning the project, King quickly dropped out. But BU remained to train the initial crew that would run the operation. *Newsweek* reported the initial cost for the AMRC at $500,000.

It did not take me long to realize the primary duty of the Center was propaganda clothed as "journalism." The operation had a staff of 40, including cameramen, photographers, writers, secretaries, two cooks, video editors and print editors. Older staff members had come from Kabul University, where they had taught a form of journalism akin to public relations. The center helped coordinate trips inside Afghanistan with the seven different factions of the mujahideen; it sent its own reporters, photographers and video crews inside Afghanistan and gathered reports from the mujahideen parties. Stories and videos collected from all sources were transmitted daily to the wires, and videos were sent sporadically to London and points beyond.

My job consisted of editing copy sent daily to the international and national wire services, a process of taking out phrases like "praise Allah" that appeared after sentences describing the destruction of Russian tanks; writing news items and scripts for the video department; encouraging better and fairer coverage of the war, and teaching classes to refugees on the craft of journalism. My boss at the USIS American Center, though supportive, gave me little guidance on what I should be doing as American "advisor," so I improvised. The video department asked me to write scripts that eventually appeared on Cable News Network. The friendly director of the AMRC, a quiet and dignified Afghan named Haji Daud, sought advice on how to make the operation run more smoothly. I pushed the young reporters, translators and editors to write more thorough and engaging stories. I spoke to international correspondents trying to get a handle on the war and I met countless visitors in the relief community. I taught classes of turban-headed men with rugged faces who not only paid attention but constantly asked questions. And I enjoyed helping a dozen Afghans fill out U.S. immigration forms and inventing for each a birthday, since they only knew their year of birth. The taste of power!

After six months at the Center, I concluded it had achieved an important if not necessarily journalistically correct niche in Afghanistan's history. In its first year of operation, the AMRC collected 20,000 photographs, produced 400 stories (often only a few paragraphs) and recorded 300 hours of tape. The quality left much to be desired but these documents are a valuable repository for future historians. Dozens of journalists, photographers and video cameramen and editors were also trained; they may someday form the basis of a journalistic community in Kabul, if peace ever comes. Without the pressure of wars, I am convinced many of the younger staffers will someday be competent journalists.

Yet the AMRC had myriad problems of the kind that were bound to arise when the U.S. hands over an institution to barely-trained Afghans with a thinly disguised hatred of the Soviet Union. No country that had been decimated as Afghanistan had could expect its journalists to be anything but patriots, not truth-seekers eager to tell the real story of war and the inevitable power struggles that go with it. I thought my function was to instil a measure of journalistic criteria into the copy and into the thinking of the reporters, but by the end of my stay the newsprint editor informed me AMRC staffers were Afghans first, mujahideen second, and journalists last.

Could the American media hold to the criteria of fairness in a war in which the U.S. was invaded, lost one million men and saw another five million people displaced? If the coverage of the Gulf War is any indicator, the American media is embarrassingly easy to manipulate, to cajole into a cheerleader's posture. Did anyone other than I expect Afghans to "cover" the war, offering critical comment and analysis?

Each member of the Center carried a mujahideen party-affiliation that the Pakistani government required of all refugees. The affiliation had an important effect: it prevented staffers from ever saying anything publicly critical about the party to which they belonged. I cannot recall the AMRC ever critically studying the frayed mujahideen leadership, forever bickering among themselves at the expense of the movement.

However hard I tried, stories always came out reading like laundry lists of tanks destroyed, soldiers killed, garrisons captured. While the AMRC had a few reporters in the field, Afghanistan had an acute shortage of field telephones or any other modern form of communication that could have given us daily reports. The Center had to rely on reports from the mujahideen parties, who sent word of victories to their Peshawar offices, then called the AMRC with the news.

Despite the opportunity to minimize losses, the parties always noted wounded and dead mujahideen accurately, which came as a surprise. The first instinct of the American military, at least in Vietnam, was to cover up casualties. To the Afghan way of thinking, each soldier who died in this *jihad*, or Holy War, was a martyr and therefore on the quick path to Allah's after-life.

No story I ever edited made elaborate claims of great victories. I never quite ascertained the truth of AMRC stories, but I did see dozens of foreign correspondents come in to talk to the staff about traveling with the mujahideen and to find out battle plans. The Western media paid attention to AMRC stories that went out on the AP wire, but never relied on them for the whole story. Neither I nor the staff were under any illusion about that fact; we knew that good reporters would dismiss most of the information offered.

The overall picture of the war AMRC stories painted in 1989 after the Soviet withdrawal was deeply flawed. The Center reported the mujahideen were moving effortlessly toward the capture of the nearby city Jalalabad, just inside the Afghan border. Meanwhile, the Western press corps found the mujahideen's attacks on Afghan-government-held Jalalabad badly coordinated and poorly executed and marred, remarkably, by fighting between factions. I suggested the Center report problems between parties. I figured, naively, that if the mujahideen's leading news agency discussed these issues the commanders and party leaders would have to discuss their differences and eventually work together. A few of these parties liked each other as much as the Serb leadership likes its Croatian counterpart.

All the rushing weirdness of Peshawar, all those nights of drinking beer at the American Club and listening to foreign correspondents tell tales, all the fascinating folks in the relief community, all those earnest young Afghans waiting for a new dawn in their country—all this made Peshawar a difficult place to leave. In the summer, with dry heat and temperatures above 110 degrees, I decided it was time to travel on—first to China from Islamabad on the Karakoram Highway, then to Europe.

Anything more would have to come from the Afghans themselves. I knew that the editor of the AMRC print section, the man I had to deal with on a daily basis, would never encourage his reporters to dig deeper or to investigate fighting in the fractured mujahideen alliance. He was a member of the party of Hikmatyar, a tyrannical Islamicist who thought of the media solely as a propaganda tool for his party. To him I was naive. I expected his reporters to be like those in the Western media. I judged that his young men were much smarter and wiser than he figured. I did not expect the AMRC to produce a Woodward or a Bernstein—that kind of reporting could only result in death for the journalists who practiced it in covering the war.

Yet with encouragement and training the operation could have been so much better. The AMRC itself was not a good idea. If USIA really wanted to train a new generation of Afghan journalists, it should have gone through a journalistic foundation or exchange program or funded a media center. An Afghan information center run by an intelligent and political moderate had been serving the needs of many visiting reporters before the AMRC was established. It continued operation while I was in Peshawar, always scoring high marks from correspondents. Improving something that already exists and is independent of political power-brokers makes more sense than creating a new center that would have a shaky legitimacy owing to its USIA connections.

When I arrived home in the U.S. I received a call from the AMRC director, Haji Daud. He had moved with his family to suburban Washington, DC so he could do a master's. He told me that after I left the AMRC print department was transferred to the mujahideen's interim government. It would serve as a public relations section for a shadow government to be put in place once Kabul fell to the mujahideen, an event that seems as unlikely now as in 1989. The heinous Hikmatyar and his Hezb-e-Islami faction—the recipient of a lion's share of U.S. military aid during the mujahideen's war with the Soviets—had long wanted to merge the AMRC with their propaganda outfit. Now, the center no longer even bothers trying to practice "journalism"; it now offers honest-to-goodness press releases, not news stories, a sad ending to a bad idea.

*   *   *

My year in Pakistan changed me more than I changed any of my students or colleagues. The abstraction of the Third World, seen through television documentaries and commercial appeals, dissolved when I saw the reality. Yet what I saw, however unappealing, was oddly compelling and wonderful. The awesome poverty of Pakistan—the endless slums and countless disease-ridden children—does not stop the people from enjoying a strong family structure, a calm dignity and a great sense of hospitality.

I found open doors and smiles when I walked through the poorest neighborhoods, a willingness to ask a stranger in for tea and sit through strained conversation with hands and gestures. I know I am an American, and I know this is why the invitations were extended. But I also know few Americans would do the same for foreigners. Friendship and conversation are important in the Pakistani culture. No office or home visit could ever last only ten minutes; tea and sweet baked goods lengthened every stay. At first this irritated me. Then I realized the importance of a simple visit and the need for communication beyond the usual banalities. A slower society with a bad phone system and one horrible television network leaves people more time for each other, more time to investigate personal and political issues on a human basis.

I no longer believe that American society offers the only viable path to happiness. Perhaps a mixture of our strengths and those of other cultures might be a more appropriate goal. I have come to understand the cultural dimensions of their problems and how U.S. policies, good and bad, have an enormous effect—whatever their intent—on these countries. Most Americans have no idea how central their country is to the rest of the world, nor do we have a clue how others live. The smugness of American culture was hard to accept upon my return; often I have been tempted to send some self-centered snob or whining teenager to an Afghan refugee camp for a few weeks.

I read more about other cultures than ever before; I take more classes, I seek out international visitors when I can. I try to understand the intense role religion plays in local, regional and international politics, especially the clash of Islam and Christianity. The cultural differences of East and West, highlighted for me during the riots in Islamabad over *The Satanic Verses*, intrigue, baffle and infuriate me. I grope for understanding and for common ground on issues like this, and it is elusive. Can we ever reconcile differences between the freedom of inquiry and religious faith? Understanding comes hard.

My Fulbright experience tested skills I did not know I had. Like many journalists, I used to prefer the role of an outsider looking in, a critical observer unwilling or unable to enter the debate. Now I find myself joining community boards, doing volunteer activities and taking small leadership roles in the Saint Paul and Minneapolis area. My job also forces me to make decisions for a fairly large group of not always malleable malcontents. Suddenly, I am a leader—did Fulbright teach me that?

My heart has changed. Once a cynical critic of society who would sit back and watch it all go to hell, I may still be a cynic but now I prefer to try to bring about social change in small ways. In reporting, you learn more about tearing things and people apart then about building them up. I find I can contribute an occasional article somewhere. I can teach, I can learn, I can share knowledge with those I think can benefit. When I returned, I vowed to contribute something to the community where I relocated: now I find myself serving on the board of directors of a theater and of my apartment complex, volunteering to work with troubled juveniles and starting conversation groups dealing with social issues. Did Fulbright give me that?

There is a darker side. I grew callous, stepping over bodies sleeping in the streets, ignoring beggars throwing babies in my face in Lahore and the sight of limbless Afghan children in Peshawar. The world is an unfair and unkind place and to feel for everyone is to be forever depressed. I also grew hardened to American foreign policy in action in Afghanistan and Pakistan, and I came away concerned that the more ill-conceived and lame-brained a policy, the more likely its adoption and implementation. Did Fulbright teach me that?

There is also the painful discovery of anti-Americanism. Yet even in the tensest of times I found an unbelievably friendly attitude toward Americans in Pakistan. There is some goodness even in the most violent places. I know Fulbright taught me that.

I discovered non-verbal communication, struggling to describe myself and my feelings to Pakistanis, Indians and Chinese, while they suffered the same problem with me. We had great conversations consisting of inane gesticulations and rough Urdu and English. I remember the sheer exultation of teaching classes of Afghan refugees at the moment when their faces told me they finally understood. I remember endless conversations with intellectuals over Christianity and Islam, over supposedly heartless Western lifestyles and the family-centered Central Asian ideal, over technology and whether it destroys or enlightens human lives. I remember the banter of bored correspondents, over too many beers, about an obscure war in an obscure part of the world. Conversation can be a cerebral pursuit but it also breeds friendship and love. Another lesson, perhaps attributable to Fulbright.

Pakistan was the most difficult place I ever worked. But there were endearing rewards—the smile of understanding from a student struggling to learn, my reception of a lovely book and engraved plate from my Punjab students during a last celebratory lunch together. No politician or editor ever did that for me. People ask how I ever lived in such an under-developed country. Why not? Europe is a dull and easy ride compared to the front lines of Central Asia, where daily life is unpredictable, occasionally dangerous and ultimately fascinating. Even in an Islamic country you learn that the rest of humanity is not so different from you and that they share many of the same aspirations for happiness, economic well-being and love. The dramatic transformation of Eastern Europe is there to remind us what it is all about. We can and must learn to live together. I know Fulbright taught me that.

At the beginning of this volume, we were reminded that the first foreign Fulbrighters ever sent to the U.S., in 1949 from Burma, were two nurses. Since that time, in most Fulbright Programs throughout the world, there have been few participants in the applied sciences and especially in the medical professions. Professor of Nursing at the University of Miami, Dr. Keen's experience in Malawi, by her own admission no different from the work she would have done as a WHO or a Rockefeller Foundation grantee or a Peace Corps volunteer, resembles the other African experience in this volume: there was enough to do so that policy and program differences mattered little. With a dozen foreign programs working in Malawian medicine, with little or no cooperation from the government, with no advance briefing and with no more than the instinctive coordination of consummate professionals facing overwhelming need, an American nursing educator worked daily in a hospital jammed full of sick and dying patients. She rolled up her sleeves and did what had to be done. Yet two years later she has already begun to articulate the kind of question that should be pondered by those who shape the policies of exchange programs between the U.S. and the desperately poor nations of our planet. The questions raised in Burma more than forty years ago still obtain: are policy distinctions between technical assistance and exchange programs like Fulbright, shaped and codified by well-fed bureaucrats in Washington, valid in a country like Malawi? Does the Fulbright difference perhaps lie in its overarching diversity, its ability to meet the most critical needs in any place, at any time? Or should Dr. Keen have gone to Malawi under other auspices?

36

THE DIFFERENCE IN MALAWI

M. Frances Keen

This essay began and then evolved from an apparently simple question: the difference my Fulbright experience in 1989-90 has made in my life and in the lives of those with whom I worked in Malawi. As I reflected on my experiences over time, I realized that the question, in fact, was not so simple.

Let me begin with the second point—the lives of those with whom I worked in Malawi. Years of colonialism, followed by 28 years of a tight authoritarian political system, have shaped the character and the nature of the people of this dreadfully poor country. Part of this pattern of inheritance is a reticence and hesitancy to express opinions and feelings. Thus, reliable measures of impact or effectiveness becomes difficult. I quickly learned to look for impact in terms of small changes and hopes for the future. True, Malawian faculty colleagues came to the U.S. to study. However, their U.S. education in no way resulted from my efforts; the process for making these opportunities available was already in place when I arrived. I could provide encouragement and information about the U.S. education system, and perhaps set an example. Beyond that, little more.

Thinking about the impact of the Fulbright experience on my own life is simpler. One insight: in contrast to my earlier teaching experiences in the Caribbean, the readjustment to the U.S. upon my return was much more difficult. The root of this difference was the even greater gap between this poor country and our own, not the Fulbright Program. What I describe below will hopefully illustrate what I mean.

In Malawi, I was rarely aware of the fact that I was a Fulbright— there was simply too much to do for me to reflect much on my status. I am proud of having received a Fulbright award, but it is not in my nature to view myself as privileged for that reason, any more than it is my nature to flaunt advanced degrees. In international work, the first job is to prove one's credibility; and that depends upon knowledge, skills, ability to adapt to the culture, sincerity of purpose. Credentials or titles may open doors, but from then on it is up to you.

The Fulbright Program in Malawi is one of dozens of agencies at work. U.S. government agencies include the Peace Corps, USAID, and USIA; private and international organizations include the World Health Organization, Project HOPE, the Rockefeller Foundation, the UN Development Programs, the UN High Commission on Refugees, Habitat for Humanity, and a variety of church missions, among others. Even though I received no information about these various organizations before I left for Malawi, the roles and functions of each were quickly sorted out after I arrived. I was living in the capital city where most of the agencies were located, and the expatriate community was small enough so that we knew one another and were aware of one another's responsibilities. I can honestly say that the roles and programs did not overlap or conflict with one another. There was more than enough for everyone to do.

In one sense the "influence" and prestige of having a Fulbright matters most in the U.S. I have tried to use this element after return by writing, by speaking, and by attempting to share my experience with others. That is why I have undertaken to write this essay—in the hope that portraying life in a lesser-developed country, an experience that few Americans have, may itself make a difference.

*   *   *

I arrived in Lilongwe, Malawi, Central Africa, in September 1989, to teach nursing at Kamuzu College of Nursing, University of Malawi. In some ways I was better prepared than many would have been for teaching in Malawi; I had spent summers teaching in developing countries in the Caribbean and was accustomed to a scarcity of chalk, erasers, and overhead transparencies, periodic power failures and water shortages and the like. But I had never lived so far removed, both literally and figuratively, from the U.S.; nor had I ever lived in a country so poor as Malawi.

Moreover, I never anticipated the questions of intellect and the dilemmas of spirit that my experiences would present. I did not fully anticipate the continuing difference that the experience would make in my life. What do I mean?

Malawi is the sixth poorest country in the world, with 90% of the population employed in subsistence farming. The major exports are all agricultural, and the primary food production crop is maize. The Gross National Product (GNP) per capita per annum is $160. This compares with a GNP of $340 for Haiti, the poorest nation in the Western Hemisphere. The life expectancy is 46; the number of infants who die before their first birthday is 151 for every 1000 live births (compared with 10 in the U.S.); 30% of all children die before their fifth birthday. The leading causes of both mortality and morbidity are infectious diseases and malnutrition. The situation is now considerably worsened by the AIDS epidemic, with an HIV-positive rate of approximately 20% in urban heterosexual populations.

The day-to-day reality of these abstract statistics was a hospital filled to capacity, with many units having two to three times more patients than they were originally designed and equipped to handle. Extra mattresses were placed on the floor underneath beds, between beds, along hallways, and on the porches. In the children's ward, two or three children occupied each bed. Items that are disposable in the U.S. were used over and over again; and the sheer number of patients and lack of adequate numbers of health personnel left no option but to provide care in true assembly-line fashion as patients lined up to receive their pills or have their dressings changed. At other times nursing care was a disjointed pattern of rushing from one emergency to another, as changes in the patients' conditions were brought to the attention of the nurse by family members. The sickest patient *at the moment* received the care; prevention of complications was often impossible simply because no one was available to monitor the patient.

How could I teach nursing students under such conditions where I questioned whether *I* would be a nurse? More importantly, I began to wonder how I would be able to share my impressions with members of the nursing profession back in the U.S. How could I discuss the condition of the country without offending my Malawian counterparts? Could I be objective, presenting the deep and complex underlying reasons, when Americans frequently demand a quick look and capsule summary?

Children with kwashiorkor or marasmus, both severe forms of malnutrition, were common sights in the hospital; and malnutrition was a frequent primary or secondary cause of death in children. Children who were fortunate enough to have survived the critical first five years were often thin, stunted in growth, and walked on legs deformed by vitamin deficiencies. Adult deaths as a result of motor vehicle accidents, malaria, and AIDS were all too frequent. Death became a familiar part of everyday life, many times greater than the situation in the U.S.

As a nurse, I was certainly accustomed to trying to help patients and their families cope with the emotions of death. I had watched people die; I had taken dead bodies to the morgue; I had asked families to consider organ donation at the most difficult of times; I had cried with families; and I had ached as I watched my students lose their first patient. I certainly had not been one who had been able to "compartmentalize" or deny the existence of death in my life.

Yet somehow in Malawi death was different. As I sat in my office, I could hear the wailing of a funeral service at the hospital morgue through my open windows; and when the spouse of a staff member died, school closed immediately so everyone could attend the funeral. Why was death so much more a part of life in Malawi? Was it that the country was densely populated and everybody knew everybody, as in a small town? Was it the sheer number of deaths? Was it the short life-expectancy and the fact that causes of death were most often accidents and infectious diseases, as opposed to diseases of old age and environmental stress—did this bring death closer to one's reality? Or was it a culture that accepted death as an inevitability—a culture that could not fight that inevitability with high-tech equipment and numerous medications?

The health care situation in Malawi, as in other countries, was further complicated by the political situation. The nation's health was adversely affected by the President-For-Life's reluctance to acknowledge publicly the seriousness of malnutrition and starvation in his country. Without acknowl-edgement, international assistance could not readily be provided. The million Mozambican refugees living within Malawi's borders were able to receive food and health care; these people, recognized as a major world refugee population, were officially welcomed by the Malawian government and international aid was made available. The result: often Mozambican refugees had greater access to food, education, and health care services than Malawians.

If direct aid in the form of food supplements could not readily be provided to Malawians, what about aid to the hospital itself? I soon learned that most international aid programs were no longer willing to fund daily operating expenses, providing the rationale that an expense this basic in nature should be met by the government. The rationale has merit and is certainly within the framework of First World philosophies and ideologies; but that ideal was of little comfort when I looked around the children's ward and saw children dying simply because they had not had enough to eat or because the hospital was lacking necessary supplies. I understood long-term objectives, but I wanted short-term solutions too.

International aid was more readily available in the form of bricks and mortar and sophisticated, technical equipment. But one has to examine the appropriateness of the donation in light of the country's needs. What happens to a hospital or school building when personnel is not adequately trained in the maintenance of a facility or when the materials to maintain the facility are not available or affordable? One could easily suggest that a government institution should be able to meet these day-to-day expenses. But limited natural resources and shortages of man-made materials meant most products were imported from South Africa, via an armored convoy, through war-torn Mozambique. The end result was a cost three to four times the South African or U.S. price. The sixth poorest nation in the world could not afford such expenditures.

For example, was an intensive care unit, complete with infusion pumps, cardiac monitors, and mechanical ventilators, appropriate given the over-whelming number of basic health needs that could be corrected with clean water, vaccines, and simple medications? On the other hand, can a country turn down such a gift when it is offered? Is it reasonable to expect a country not to want such capabilities? What about the members of the middle and upper class, albeit small, aware of the facilities elsewhere, who want to live after trauma or a heart attack? And what of the appropriateness of such a donation when personnel are unfamiliar with the operation and maintenance of such equipment and when replacement parts are not available?

I was confronted with an example of problematic international assistance at the school of nursing. When I arrived, I was informed that the school had a computer for faculty use. Naturally I was pleased: I was worried about writing out everything by hand again! But the computer at Kamuzu College of Nursing soon became a saga. As the days passed, using the computer became more and more complicated. I had to: (1) locate the room where the computer was stored; (2) find the key to the room; (3) enter the computer room to find that the computer had a password; (4) learn who knew the password and get it; and (5) enter the computer room again. When I did all this, I found that the donor had given only a computer and printer and almost nothing else.

The hard drive was loaded with programs, but the donor had copied not only the programs but the donor university's data files as well. The donation did not include paper, extra ribbons for the printer, diskettes, or program and instruction manuals. Most importantly, the computer was not protected with a voltage regulator—a necessity in Malawi because of frequent changes in power.

The computer soon became the bane of my existence as I finagled deals for supplies via contacts in South Africa, England, and the U.S.; every time I knew of someone entering or leaving Malawi I would badger them to bring back supplies. By the end of my year, I had begged donated supplies, enlisted the assistance of a Peace Corps Volunteer in computer science to clean up the hard drive and substitute word-processing and data-base programs that were compatible with those being used throughout the country in various government ministries; I had developed a manual with basic operating and word processing instructions, offered individual instruction to interested faculty members and staff, and written a grant proposal with a Peace Corps Volunteer to obtain Corps funding for a voltage regulator and more plentiful supplies. The reader can imagine how much time and effort went into this secondary project. On the surface the results were successful. Yet I knew the computer would continue to be a problem in terms of maintenance, repairs, parts, and supplies—and this for years to come.

Was a computer without continuing support an appropriate use of foreign assistance funds? If the U.S. Embassy and foreign firms with additional resources and support systems outside Malawi had difficulty maintaining their computers, what hope was there for an under-funded government school? In any case, once the computer was presented, was it not reasonable to make it operational, especially in a university which expected its faculty to conduct research?

How does one resolve the disparities between the so-called First World and the Third? I am not convinced that there are any answers or that the disparities can be resolved. Perhaps the incongruities exist to encourage us to question our own values and ideologies. I came away from Malawi with more questions than answers and I drew only a few conclusions—partial conclusions that continue to be modified by my experiences back in the U.S. Let me try to articulate some of these tentative hypotheses.

Conclusion I: *Life and its relationships are precious and fragile.* Death is compartmentalized for most of us in the U.S. Without the observed frequency of death and with an extended life expectancy, we are easily able to get away with denying our mortality if we wish. With our sense of reality so shielded from death, we can fail to recognize that the relationships in our lives, as we know them today, could also be inalterably changed this same day.

Conclusion II: *Look for little changes, assuming change is even desirable.* One of the courses I taught was Nursing Management and Leadership. How does one discuss leadership roles and functions and encourage critical thinking when elements in a society block concepts of individuality and freedom of expression? In Malawi, I had to accept the fact that something I said—or was perceived to say—or the role model I presented—or was perceived to present—might one day influence another's thinking or questioning. For example, I hoped that my enthusiasm for nursing would encourage students to continue with a career in nursing. While the working conditions, opportunities, and salaries were by no means commensurate with those in the U.S., nursing in Malawi did present some advantages. Nursing offered a career with day-to-day relevance to the problems of the country; nursing also offered a career ladder, although limited, and provided opportunities for advancement in nursing education or administration; and nurses were assured of employment. Malawian nurses also shared professional status and identity with one another and with nurses from throughout Africa and the world, as a result of their professional organization and its international affiliations. The Nurses' Association of Malawi, established in 1979, became the first organized group of health care professionals in the country. The organization may prove to be instrumental in the promotion of health and also in the advancement of women in Malawi. In addition the organization may provide opportunities for my students to develop their future leadership potential.

Conclusion III: *Assess the appropriateness of our national and personal philosophies, ideologies, and actions within the context of the culture.* Is our aid or assistance of real benefit by the country's assessment, or is it simply a matter of what *we* believe to be of benefit, leading the country likewise to believe it would be of benefit? The position of an American outside the U.S. is often privileged—Americans are esteemed and our opinions are valued.

With the privilege comes responsibility—a responsibility to evaluate the relevance of our assistance.

I learned in Malawi that I myself frequently needed assistance with life outside the context of my culture and experience. One day in the middle of my stay, an administrator at the College informed me that he had a gift for me and that the gift was in front of the building. Out front, I saw a basket with several live chickens. The administrator proudly told me that the largest chicken was mine. I knew that in Malawian culture the gift of a live chicken or goat was a great honor. I was grateful and humbled simultaneously, knowing how much a chicken cost to raise. At the same time I was wondering what to do with a live chicken. My relationship with the administrator was such that I could freely admit, with only mild embarrassment, that I had no idea how to kill a chicken. He assured me that my helper at home would be able to kill it. At this point I was forced to admit, with greater embarrassment, that I did not even know how to carry a live chicken. We both laughed, and the tale of the professor who did not know how to kill or carry a chicken spread through the College. Meanwhile, I made arrangements with one of the cooks to kill the chicken at the College so I could carry it home in the manner to which I was accustomed.

My chicken story does not end in Malawi. In December 1991 I gathered with four of my former Malawian faculty colleagues for a holiday celebration in Philadelphia. My counterparts had all since arrived in the U.S. to study for advanced nursing degrees with the help of scholarships from the UN or the Rockefeller Foundation. A local church had given them a seventeen-pound frozen turkey, with all the fixings, so that they could share in the U.S. Christmas tradition. But my colleagues had never prepared or stuffed a turkey before, let alone a seventeen-pound frozen bird—a task that daunts many American cooks. As I provided instructions on stuffing and roasting a turkey, I reminded my friends of my chicken. Amidst tremendous laughter, we realized again that our so-called expertise was only defined within the context of our culture and experience.

This leads to Conclusion IV: *Perhaps an even greater responsibility of such an experience is to encourage and enable Americans to broaden their view of the world.* Before I left Malawi, one of my colleagues at the university said, "Be sure to take some pictures of our modern buildings and development, not just our villages." He had studied in England and found that a persistent image of Africa was one of big-game safaris, mud huts, and the days of Isak Dinesen's "Out of Africa." On return I encountered those same perceptions, and I was glad he had suggested photos of downtown office buildings and suburban homes so that I could show both sides of today's Africa.

My teaching and lecturing has changed. I now make a point of integrating global perspectives and comparisons into my classroom teaching. I have also attempted to influence the development of curricula to include global issues. Owing to recent interest and the increasing necessity to "internationalize" curricula and professional organizations, I have found that a variety of opportunities to present and incorporate global perspectives are available if one is motivated and persistent.

I have also encountered unique opportunities to inform educators and the public about the Fulbright Program. For whatever reasons, post-doctoral awards tend to be associated with the humanities and social sciences as opposed to the applied sciences and professional disciplines. Fulbright awards are rare in nursing, medicine, dentistry, health care management, epidemiology, and other health care disciplines. In many countries, these health care professionals receive their education in professional schools outside the mainstream of the university system and thus are frequently not eligible for Fulbright programs. Even when professional schools lie within the mainstream of university education, the schools often do not share equal recognition and status with their colleagues in the arts and sciences. Professional colleagues in the U.S. likewise are often unaware of the opportunities in their disciplines and may not pursue a Fulbright for this reason.

In the year of my Fulbright experience, there were only three requests worldwide for Fulbrights in nursing education. In the 1992-93 bulletin announcing research and lecturing awards, seven countries requested Fulbrights in nursing education, including Botswana, Greece, Iceland, Jordan, Malta, Norway, and Pakistan. The awards varied from a request to "teach community and psychiatric nursing and conduct clinical research in psychiatric nursing" to a request to "assist in curriculum development at the doctoral level."

Malawi convinced me that there is or ought to be a place for Fulbright awards in the health sciences and other professional practice disciplines. The developing countries need resident teachers of professional fields. Professionals may be viewed and utilized in more of a consultative and service-oriented role than other disciplines, while impact or effectiveness may be more difficult to measure because of the sheer enormity of the task. But if the program and the individual can be responsive to these needs and attack the task at hand, the ultimate outcome of the experience remains the same—a difference in the lives of all those involved.

PART VI

1990-92: LOOKING AHEAD

By the beginning of the decade, the world had turned over. How "the end of history" will affect the Fulbright Program remains to be seen.

One trend is already clear: agreements and commissions have already begun to crop up in previously unlikely places. In Canada and Mexico, good neighbors overlooked for forty years as potential Fulbright countries, commissions now exist. Both, however, have been designed in a totally new way, in Canada reflecting uncertainties about future Congressional funding and the assumption that without predominantly private-sector support there can be no survival, and in Mexico showing the same partial reliance on the private sector. The other new commissions are in Hungary (1990), the best-prepared of the former "Bloc" countries, and in Prague (1991). As of this writing, binational agreements are being discussed or negotiated in Indonesia, Jordan, Poland, Rumania, and some republics of the former Soviet Union. Sadly, on September 1, 1992, events in Yugoslavia resulted in the closing of that commission after twenty-eight remarkable years.

After five years of flat budgets, a rise of about 10% was appropriated in 1991, less than 2% per annum for those five years—eight such appropriations would still not build one Stealth bomber. Suggestions from USIA to the overseas commissions to raise private and foreign government funding for their programs have produced results in some areas of the world, notably in East Asia and especially in Japan, where the alumni raise half a million dollars a year to expand the commission's scholarship program. But elsewhere there is little to show for the effort, beyond the confusion of the commission directors at being asked to learn and practice the fine-tuned profession of fund-raising in countries where the philanthropic practices of the U.S. are not shared.

In 1992, American voters opted for a new President. Bill Clinton is a Rhodes scholar from the northwest corner of Arkansas who once worked in the Senator's office. The implications of this close personal and intellectual relationship and of the political changes in America remain to be seen, but observers were quick to point to the internationalist orientation of the President-elect. In the Los Angeles Times of November 8, Guardian correspondent Martin Walker related a 1967 event when Clinton, then president of the Georgetown University student body, met German Fulbright

Scholar Rudi Loewe: "Since you're a Fulbright, how would you like to meet Senator Fulbright?" The next day they took breakfast with the Senator in his office. The Washington Post also on November 8, speculating on the foreign policy of the new team, quoted a German official: "Clinton and Gore belong to the successor generation . . . they are the exchange generation—the people who did the Rhodes and the Fulbright scholarships. They are internationalists." It is tempting to believe the future for Fulbright may look brighter.

Only one essay marks the nineties, a self-aware study by an American Studies practitioner—meaning study of the U.S., not the interdisciplinary "American Studies"—of the ambiguities involved in teaching foreign university students about the U.S. The contribution was largely composed at the Catholic University in Nijmegen in the Netherlands, where the author held the chair of American Studies in 1990-91, but it draws on his pre-Fulbright work surveying American Studies teaching in the Far East. It is difficult to imagine that the writer's concerns would have meant much to the Fulbrights of the fifties. The ironies and tensions he notes speak for more than one Fulbrighter of the seventies and eighties. But the nineties remain to unfold, as the different demands of a multipolar world begin to make themselves known.

Yet, tensions and all, it seems ever more likely that the Fulbright ideal and the Program that defines it will go on, that it will keep on trying to deal with the new challenges of history in its old but never-ending search for understanding. Perhaps today it may sound less naive to articulate the hope, indeed the implicit assumption of every author in this volume, that Fulbright will go on forever.

The author teaches American Studies at the University of Iowa. After frustrating experiences with two Fulbright nominations, he spent a year in Taiwan on a research program funded by the Taiwan government. Focussing on experts on American culture in the Far East, many of whom were Fulbrighters, he found in their envy of his own "freedom" certain questions about the irreducible cultural imperialistic dimension built into exchanges between a super-power and smaller states, especially in a field like his the job of which—like that of USIS—is to some extent to "tell America's story abroad." By the time he received his own Fulbright, in the John Adams Chair of American Civilization in Nijmegen, he was sensitized to the ambivalence of his position as a scholar in the service of a political mission, the more difficult in that the mission evoked his broad sympathies. His struggle with this dilemma lies at the center of this essay.

COMING TO TERMS WITH INTERNATIONAL AMERICAN STUDIES

Richard P. Horwitz

I grew up remarkably ill-equipped for cross-cultural communication. Until very recently, I did not even realize how serious a handicap that was. I may still have it, but thanks in part to opportunities for academic work overseas, it seems less debilitating. Although a professor of American Studies and thus vocationally fixated on the country of my birth, I have found ways to function cross-culturally, maybe even to spare others my mistakes. This essay is an autobiographical account of the experiences that taught me about my place as a cultural critic in the wider world.

My most severe limitations could be blamed on circumstances surrounding my birth in Connecticut just after World War II. There was the comforting embrace of an allegedly homogeneous New England town. Anything other than English was a "foreign language." In an age when even hoods dressed up for the prom, youth culture was considered threatening, not to mention the cultures of Puerto Rican- and African-Americans in the next town. The rest of the world was associated with the insanity and terror of Europe that my ancestors recently fled, the Pacific theater, or The Bomb. In school I learned about countries outside the U.S.—Korea, the Philippines, Cuba, "Banana Republics," Vietnam—only as they became troublesome to the Department of State. They were "problems." Learning about the U.S. was called "civics," meaning the glorious privileges of democracy, but learning world geography meant guessing who would be on "our" side in World War III. We spent more time rehearsing for nuclear attack—"duck and cover"—than developing our minds or strategies to avoid it.

Of course, there were contrary influences. Great-grandparents and grandparents had come from Eastern Europe. Those who survived in the U.S. were people for whom global conflict and cultural divides were visceral experiences. Shouting matches about Israel, trade unionism, U.S. policy in the Middle East, and the global history of "my" people were not unusual. For them, the U.S., my home, was still the land of "goyim" (i.e., non-Jews, akin to "honkies") even if a particularly nice bunch. Such *Yiddishkeit* signaled the mix of envy, fear and loathing for an American culture that would never be theirs. Even after seven or eight decades in this country, most of my ancestors died "greenhorns." My parents were bilingual, using Yiddish in parental pidgin over dinner for developing a united front about my bedtime. Since I had a stake in learning the code (and not letting them know I knew), I received early training both in quasi-anthropological participant observation and in a language that gave me a jump-start in Dutch. I was usually the rare Jew in my school, but this was hardly something to advertise at the time, at least without protected flanks. Like so many children of the Baby Boom, I thought it my responsibility to get with the program of the American melting pot. Whether as a good student of civics, a Jew or an adolescent, when faced with difference, duck and cover.

Some of this fearsome conformity withered with maturity. But most of it was more ruthlessly hacked apart in the sixties, when I was a student at the University of Pennsylvania. There the smart people among whom I counted myself were non-conformists, at least in the sense that we began to see bright spots wherever the State Department saw gloomy ones and vice versa. Although active in the anti-war movement (a "community organizer" for SDS), I found the field of American Studies an hospitable academic niche in my search for relevance in a Talmudic vein.

From an international point of view, that proved an unfortunate choice. American Studies was at the time still dominated by tweedy WASPs who clung to intellectual dispositions that, though radical for the 1950s and early 1960s, seemed hopelessly accommodative to the status quo a few years later. In hindsight I should have recognized that many of the deficiencies in American Studies were attributable to its almost exclusive focus on the U.S. and, to a lesser extent, its European connections. But like rebel academic peers I concentrated on easier targets: the mushy methodology, the privileging of Euro-American belles-lettres, the neglect of working people and popular culture. The preoccupation with American "exceptionalism" was a target too, but only because of the way it invited xenophobic jeremiads, harkening back to Jeffersonian ideals rather than real cultural diversity within the U.S. Diversity outside the U.S. or connections between the U.S. and other nations were low on the reform agenda. By drawing attention to cultural divides within the U.S., we rebels may have made it even easier to ignore much greater ones beyond it. (Davis 1990, Winkler 1985, Wise 1979)

Whatever the latent urges, the first overt push overseas came to me from a different source. I had long been interested in cultural anthropology and gained some fame in American Studies for applying fieldwork routines to the U.S. But I had trouble gaining much legitimacy in anthropology itself because I had no experience with anyone radically "other," a standard initiation rite in that field. A mentor in anthropology and American Studies at Penn and then at the University of Maryland, John Caughey, kept urging me to head for other lands to strengthen what he saw as a decent but undeveloped sense of culture outside my own experience.

When I applied for a Fulbright to Rumania for 1982-83, I came close to doing so for the first time. As best I can recall I picked that location for four reasons: 1) I thought a communist country would be sufficiently "other" to educate me, or at least to please anthropological skeptics; 2) my family hailed from that region; 3) Fulbrights in Eastern Europe were supposed to be relatively easy to win; and 4) I had seen Herzog's "Nosferatu," which made the Transylvanian Mountains look gorgeous. I readied my application, received a nomination, took an unpaid leave from my job (as did my wife Noni), rented our house, and waited for the phone to ring with my assignment in September. At the end of August, CIES was still trying to get the right person to answer the phone in Bucharest. When I showed signs of panic, they offered me an alternative in Yugoslavia, but they would have to begin again to arrange visas and what not. Since we had no income and no place to live, I opted for a colleague's cabin on an island off the Maine coast and a job in the plumbing supply department of a local hardware store. CIES never bothered to let me know how the transatlantic cables turned out. This experience piqued my interest in internationalism only insofar as I had one good reason never to trust my future to Fulbright again. But while working in Maine I finished a book that helped secure my promotion and another leave in 1984-85. This time I would better prepare, take the half-salary to which I was entitled, and keep a wary eye on alien bureaucrats in Washington. John Caughey was fresh back from a Fulbright in Pakistan and advised that India was the place for me—quite "other" but less Byzantine than Byzantium, and English would do. Again I applied and received a nomination from Fulbright. We arranged leaves, rented the house, and waited for the phone to ring. This time, I would begin reading everything I could about India well in advance, call Washington weekly, and prepare alternatives if there were a repeat performance. In fact, there was. This time I bailed out before the money ran out to head for the Republic of China where we had some indirect contacts and Noni had a good paying job (supposedly!).

While we were packing for Taiwan at the end of August, CIES called to say that they had "just about" succeeded in arranging my passage to India. With barely repressed glee, I declined. We flew to Taipei, joyously independent of Washington whims. After a series of tumultuous disasters and good fortunes, I was awarded a research grant from the National Science Council of the Republic of China to work at Academia Sinica, the national center for advanced research. I would deliver a series of lectures on American Studies in the U.S. and conduct research on American Studies in Taiwan. I remain monumentally indebted to the NSC and colleagues in Taiwan for their staggering generosity. My research entailed a history of institutionalized American Studies in China and analysis of interviews and questionnaires that I administered to Taiwan Americanists on their backgrounds, beliefs and practices. Since I have published my findings elsewhere (Horwitz 1989), I will not repeat them here. But that experience dramatically affected the broader orientation I have toward American Studies overseas and the cross-cultural business in general.

Since I was surely mistaken about the particular mix of estrangement and kinship I felt toward the Taiwanese at the time, I would not claim to have "understood" their culture, but even in failing to do so I much better understood my own. As everyday life confounded my common sense, it increased my sensitivity to the potential variety, scale and significance of cultural divides. I could no longer assume that common sense was quite so "common" or "sensible." Even working in the plush environs of Academia Sinica, I gained a much deeper appreciation for the dedication that studying the U.S. from abroad may require. The English language, the relative poverty of research and teaching facilities, the fractional academic politics, and the geopolitical valence of American Studies for a quasi-client state—these represent hurdles that internationally-oriented Americanists could better take into account. As my attention was drawn to such hurdles, I developed lasting doubts about the potential effectiveness of academic exchanges for producing mutual understanding. In fact, I still wonder how fortunate or unfortunate that limited potential may be. In evaluating it and trying to imagine improvements, I developed a new awareness of the limits of my own "liberal relativism."

I realized that being open to a foreign culture was insufficient. In challenging circumstances, even as limited as a debate with a Chinese colleague about "the lesson" of U.S. experience in Asia, it is hard to tell how much of our disagreement is attributable to cultural difference in the first place. Since that colleague, as likely as not, was trained in the U.S. and we get our facts from the same sources, it is worth considering that we are working from within a single academic culture, and for that reason our "foreignness" has nothing to do with it. We just disagree. Moreover, even if the source of our differences is properly considered cultural, I may remain convinced that this foreign culture errs no less than my own. Finally, whatever my private analysis of the situation, the simple fact of my presence abroad has contradictory, institutional repercussions that a commitment to open-mindedness may help in assessing but does not resolve. In Asia I had to confront this troublesome reality, one that cultural diplomats take for granted but that intellectuals can too gleefully ignore. At the very least, cultural communication had better be arranged with due attention to the potential for conflicting circumstances and interests of both parties and their sponsors.

Although my identity as an American opened a lot of doors, I felt that working for an agency formally disconnected from the U.S. government greatly helped me reach these conclusions. For example, Fulbrighters and cultural diplomats whom I interviewed in Asia spoke to me as if I presented a rare opportunity for them to let their hair down. They were startlingly critical of the official exchange industry and spoke as if its disappointments had been a guarded secret: "Gosh, you're lucky to be able to look into this without any connection to the U.S. government; I bet you're getting some great stuff, and you can say whatever you want."

Since at the time I saw only the vaguest of connections between the government and what Fulbrighters actually did (certainly most of them were not Reagan's sort of folks), I was puzzled by this response. I was also struck by the large amount of time and energy foreign scholars put into courting U.S. cultural diplomats to fund their travel, research, conferences, and publications. Since they knew I interviewed in the embassy, Asian colleagues even pumped me for advice in shaping proposals that U.S. diplomats would support. Naturally, I felt exceedingly awkward when the same diplomats asked me which of the competing factions of foreign academics should get limited U.S. resources.

My analysis of these puzzles progressed little beyond a naive wish for greater candor about the exchange industry and concern for the clumsy way that my tax dollars were being used, like it or not, to shape the intellectual life of foreigners. I had thought that this was supposed to be a cross-cultural business, an equitable trade of gifts rather than the reflagging of American ships.

Nevertheless, I was glad to have USIA grants of my own to compare situations on short lecture trips in Japan and the Republic of Korea and on a longer stint, alas, courtesy of Fulbright in India. The change in funding source certainly did not incline me to alter my lectures. They fit the slightly left-of-center fare typical of U.S. Americanists. I noted only modest changes in other realms. For example, it was clear that being welcomed at the airport or depot by a bilingual host, supplied with advice on day-to-day living and ready-to-wear respectability, greatly eased my way into foreign countries. It was also clear that this ease exacted a price in the depth and breadth of my exposure to those countries when compared with Taiwan. As much as I appreciated the creature comforts, they made it easier to remain ignorant of the culture of the hosts, a deficiency I recognized in myself and that I thereafter better understood in the American turbo-profs whom I met.

With the intense experience in Asia behind me, I returned to the U.S. to discover that my professional association, the American Studies Association, was in the midst of a frenzy to "internationalize." With USIA support, a cadre of largely self-appointed ASA representatives were jetting around the globe to network and negotiate terms of cooperation with (and thereby canonization of) Americanists overseas. The U.S. government had primed the pump, and colleagues rushed to help with little more than a glance at the potability of the supply or integrity of the pipes. I was deeply troubled to find not only little discussion of the concerns that confronted me but also resistance to their public discussion. I felt like a heretic for daring to challenge the culture of our own professional impulses in the critical manner that I took to be the distinctive feature of the field.

As far as I know, I was the first person outside of USIA ever to study what these particular exchanges actually do in a foreign environment. Proposals to present my work at the national meeting of the ASA were repeatedly rejected by the ASA international committee. Instead, they featured cliché-ridden testimonies of turbo-profs (often jetted in with USIA funds) on the wonders of exchange. Sessions were co-chaired by cultural diplomats from

Washington who steered discussion toward effective recruiting for the existing system.

Easily finding contradictions if not hypocrisy rampant, I became determined to make international American Studies itself a legitimate subject in the field. Despite (or maybe because of) significant obstacles, I set out to edit an anthology on the subject, one that would sweep away the platitudes to address the academic, personal, and political challenges that I feel cultural exchange has always entailed. I would do my part for candor. As best I could, I tried to finesse the star system to allow dissident voices to emerge (Horwitz, forthcoming). Since Europe has the oldest and most distinguished tradition of American Studies outside the U.S., I was determined to learn about it first-hand. This time, in part because I was more secure in my own professional status, I dared to trust Fulbright a little more and was not disappointed. In fact, I was showered in good fortune and remain grateful.

For 1990-91 I received a distinguished senior lectureship, the John Adams Chair, established in 1984 by the Netherlands America (Fulbright) Commission for Educational Exchange to rotate in Dutch universities. I was assigned to Catholic University (Katholieke Universiteit) in Nijmegen, a very pleasant place. I have only begun to reflect on this recent experience, but I can already see some advantages and disadvantages relative to those in Taiwan.

Teaching full-time (as opposed to research) helped me better understand the practical—organizational and financial—limits of doing American Studies overseas in the manner to which I am accustomed. It also put me in slightly closer contact with students. But the sheer effort involved put me less in communication with faculty and sorely compromised my research. The perks of the position—the pay, the prestige, the opportunity for funded travel, help in finding food and shelter—were wonderful. But I again suspect that they also made it easier for me to learn little about the necessities of everyday life in the Netherlands. I would not relish retaking the crash-course in survival that my position in Taiwan required, but I know that I learned more because of it. Similarly, while the Fulbright helped me gain serious responses from European "heavyweights" in my field, it also made it harder to see their world from the outside. As a Fulbrighter, I was presumed to be enough of an insider to have a stake in the existing system of cultural exchange and thereby to be an inappropriate person for sharing gripes. Through such rarefied experiences I gained important lessons in cross-cultural ideology. In the simple, largely unspoken niceties of becoming or being treated as a Fulbrighter, boosterism is normalized, unspoken secrets established, and heresy defined—all without any visible agent.

I gained much the same sense on sundry lecture tours, courtesy of foreign universities, embassies and Fulbright commissions. After a lecture, members of the audience would routinely ask me to explain some U.S. government policy (as likely as not on a totally unrelated subject) that had made the local news. It was usually plain that they asked because the policy seemed to them transparently wrong. The justifications that made the press were entirely unpersuasive, and they wanted me to come up with a better one to test their initial judgment. Since I aim to please my hosts and normally welcome such conceptual challenges, I would do my best to improvise a new, improved rationale, imaginatively placing myself in Washington shoes.

But I was also struck by the fact that I, too, usually found the policy wrong and the justifications wanting. Since I am hardly a policy analyst, much less an ambassador, why should I be trying to persuade the audience that their and my instincts were wrong, that lurking behind official pronouncements was some higher wisdom we were obliged to concoct and respect? I began to learn first-hand how simple decorum and intellectual integrity can turn a Fulbrighter into a spin-controller for the powers that be.

These challenges reached their breaking point during the Gulf War. A classmate in my intensive Dutch class, a Kurdish refugee from Iraq, often confided in me about the horrific circumstances of his escape and of his an-guish over family members whom he had not been able to contact in months. He could easily imagine the worst. He knew about terror in the desert in ways that I could not easily project onto the homefront flag-wavers broadcast on CNN. "I am grateful for the Americans," he said, "but why does President Bush have to sound like Saddam Hussein? How can he talk about 'heroes'?" This time I just shrugged, "I don't know. He probably doesn't have to and shouldn't."

Of course, there have been times when I am sufficiently ambivalent about or supportive of the dominant American line to relish the opportunity to do some image management on its behalf. The first generation of Americanists, after all, touted the U.S. overseas to solidify the Alliance against the Axis powers, hardly an ignoble calling. I felt just as self-righteous in "correcting" Dutch students' understanding of U.S. history, when, for example, they blamed the U.S. entirely for the Cold War, as if only certified paranoids could worry about Stalin.

Similarly, I could not help but temper their view of U.S. race relations. Self-styled progressives often spoke as if the only races worth acknowledging were in one of two exclusive, essentially uniform categories, white and "other," oppressor and victim. They needed help to understand why "others" often do no get along, why many are not pleased to be considered victims, and why, quite apart from bigotry, separate facilities such as black university dormitories might be considered attractive by the "victims" themselves. Often their impressions of the U.S. bespoke images from the mass media which featured poverty and violence unknown in most of northwestern Europe. When contrasted with the predominantly white, well-groomed talking heads who packaged the news, you could understand how their bifurcated images were warranted but over-generalized. In such ways, I have found myself alternating between moments of feeling soiled or at least compromised and self-righteous by virtue of my position.

There have also been moments where the tensions were present at once but refused to blend into some manageable mix. The most memorable ones occurred in the classroom when I was trying to help Dutch students bear in mind the importance of Christianity for many Americans. On average, when compared to other peoples around the world, Americans are especially church-going people, and it is impossible to make much sense of everyday life in this country without a sense of the weight of Christian traditions.

As a Jew, constantly embarrassed by references to "goyim" but knowing full well what they mean, I may be oddly sensitive to this issue. Furthermore, at the time I was living in Nijmegen, an easy bike-ride from the German border (an object of irrational fear), teaching at a Catholic, albeit libertarian university. The house where my family lived was literally in the shadow of the church that was the main landmark for the town. But just around the corner were the remains of a humble synagogue, now converted to an art gallery named for a saint. It was rarely open, and news that I had been sighted peering through a window occupied neighborhood gossip for a couple of weeks. Everyone who could have been a relative worth reckoning had been efficiently removed or more likely annihilated within a few years of my birth. My son went to a Catholic school at the end of the street, also in the shadow of the church. Furthermore, nearly everyone around me had the blue eyes and fair hair of the Protestant elite in the U.S., people who if they are liberal still boast of having someone like me among "some of my best friends," like a cocker spaniel. I may have had a Distinguished Fulbright, but I was not feeling terribly secure or proudly American.

Students, though, tended to treat talk of organized religion, especially heart-felt religious devotion, as a sign of ignorance. To be proudly Christian was analogous to being a member of the Klan. Church-goers are a kind of rabble, spouting mumbo-jumbo that could turn at any moment to terrorism. Given European history, it is an understandable worry, but it is also a serious obstacle to understanding life in modern America (and, I must say, much of it in the Netherlands). Their proud insistence on tolerance and dispassion limited them to viewing American Christians as mental or moral defectives. I could use my Fulbright to help them get past such presumptions, at least provisionally to grant American Christians enough integrity to consider how their faith could be reasonably related to other facets of everyday life.

So, this Jewish American—a descendant of the Holocaust, living in the shadow of the church, alternately fearful of mainstream America and determined to represent it well—spent many hours trying to evoke a sense of the beauty of Christian devotion that my compatriots know, distancing it from the version that helped justify the slaughter of my (and a goodly share of the students') ancestors. I cannot imagine a moment better capturing the way Fulbright has helped me confront the dilemma of my position in the world.

These competing dispositions—on the one hand to worry about academic exchange as U.S. cultural imperialism and on the other to relish it as an opportunity to do the right thing—are still at the heart of my understanding of the difference a Fulbright makes. I cannot consider "just doing my work," apart from weighty personal and global, ethical and geopolitical considerations. Working overseas in brief but diverse encounters has led me to doubt the value of sorting ourselves into categories of "self" and "other," least of all according to geopolitical borders. Of course, those borders reinforce lines of inequality. They remain important especially as long as the agencies that coordinate and fund our exchanges are themselves instruments of the state. However unwittingly, those agencies have helped teach me to beware and encouraged me to help others more critically participate in addressing the cultures that unite and divide the world.

REFERENCES

Allen F. Davis, "The Politics of American Studies," *American Quarterly*, 42(3) 1990, pp. 353-74.

Richard P. Horwitz, "'Foreign' Expertise: American Studies in Taiwan," *American Studies International*, 27(1) 1989, pp. 38-62.

Richard P. Horwitz, ed., (forthcoming) *Exporting America: Essays on American Studies Abroad*, New York: Garland.

Karen J. Winkler, "Scholars Chide American Studies for Ignoring the Rest of the World," *Chronicle of Higher Education*, November 13, 1985.

Gene Wise, "'Paradigm Dramas' in American Studies: A Cultural and Institutional History of the Movement," *American Quarterly*, 31(3) 1979, pp. 293-337.

Professor of History at Yale, Robin Winks writes of three Fulbright incarnations yet passes over others. One of the prestigious academic figures pressed into service on occasion by USIA to serve as Cultural Attaché in various capitals of world culture, in his case London 1969-71, he is unique in having sustained continuous dedication to the health of the Program, maintaining detailed information through close observation, producing special reports, lecturing to USIA training groups and alumni, shaping the American studies component of the bicentennial celebration in 1976, helping USIS abroad during his travels, serving on the board of the Fulbright Association, and producing a generous flow of correspondance with those who care about Fulbright destinies.

AFTERWORD

Robin W. Winks

The Fulbright Experience, surely by now qualified for capital letters, is bound together by common features of change, most of which are attested to, consciously and unconsciously, in these essays. As the principal editor notes, there can hardly be any former Fulbrighters who do not believe that the experience changed their lives; the present essayists would not have agreed and tried to write about that experience were it otherwise.

What do they have in common? Americans who went abroad, perhaps for the first time, learned about their own country, often more than they learned about their hosts. Those who came to study in the U.S. from elsewhere, from Italy and France and India and from all of those countries whence nearly a hundred and thirty thousand foreign Fulbright scholars were drawn, had their eyes opened to the diversity and energy that mark American society. If "anti-American" when they arrived, they appear to have returned home as warm friends of the U.S., even when still concerned or even angry about aspects of American life, especially its unusual and appalling history of preoccupation with matters of race. But after return and with time, their concern and anger take their place in a context and no longer consume them.

This kind of change works largely at the surface level, of course. Only over a lifetime do we become aware of just how deeply change has penetrated. As perhaps the broadest example, there surely can be no doubt that the

Fulbright Experience has contributed in a significant manner to an improved understanding of, and in most cases a sympathy for, the U.S. both at home and abroad. At the same time, it has opened the eyes of Americans—who have often arrived at positions of influence, especially in the educational world—to better ways of understanding, relating to, learning from other societies. To this transformation in understanding, and thus in international relations, brought about by this shared experience, these essays offer abundant evidence.

An historian can only be surprised that as yet there has been no substantial written history of the Fulbright Program, at least since the early efforts of Walter Johnson and Francis Colligan thirty years ago. Senator Fulbright's idea was truly unique and, in its application, revolutionary. Educators had traveled to other cultures before—indeed the medieval university was based on such a presumption—and on occasion had worked out one-on-one exchanges through institutional ties of church, college or discipline. But had a government ever committed itself to the idea that educators might be valuable as ambassadors, that the exchange of educational ideas might have a significant impact on international relations? To be sure, there are still bean-counters among those who examine the Fulbright premise, those who think that its major significance is that this or that cabinet officer in this or that nation was once a Fulbrighter and (as an unproved assumption) has been a friend of the U.S. while in office. And there are those who, detecting an imperialist plot in everything the U.S. does, believe that the Fulbright Program was not genuinely binational, that it was an attempt to promote American educational ideas and organizations abroad, to supplant traditional values, and so to create a mutual community of the educated elite which would, in less "advanced" nations, be dependent on American technology, American books and American scholarship.

Many of us believe that the experience was far more than this, even when it was this. Yet, to the extent that there has been any history of the program, it has been left to the instrumentalists to write. Where is the life of the Senator that focuses on his unique contribution to world peace through education, rather than on his role as an opponent of the war in Vietnam? Where is the history of the Fulbright Difference as an aspect of intellectual and social history, rather than as yet another exercise in bureaucratic and diplomatic history? Rich primary sources, including the essays in this volume and many more that surely could be invoked, await the scholar who knows how to ask the right questions. There is, as yet, simply no Fulbright historiography, though essays like these lay the crucial groundwork for dispassionate inquiry.

For a brief two years, well after my own two Fulbright experiences, I served as Cultural Attaché in the American Embassy in London. In those days, an annual task descended upon the Cultural Office from Washington, the preparation of a report called "Evidence of Effectiveness" (I remember it as "Proof," but friends assure me that memory exaggerates). I was and am an educator and I argued then, as I do now, that in the life of the mind one cannot provide proof, nor even evidence that is conclusive, that any given action produced any given direct result. Education, we know, is diffuse, slow and intangible; it is a process. Perhaps one could count the number of young people who, in Iran for example, learned English as a result of an American's visit, and this might reasonably be thought to prove *accomplishment* of some kind. But *effectiveness*? Surely not.

In London, as we prepared these reports, we knew we were engaging in a fantasy. We knew that we had been effective as a group, and highly so; we knew that the office had helped X number of individuals to find places in American education programs, that Y musicians from the U.S. had performed before audiences of Z proportions. We could show that more and more British universities were introducing formal instruction in American Studies, or in the study of America—not at all the same thing, as some of these essays suggest. And thus we knew that *information* about America, and one hoped knowledge as well, was more readily available than before. But could we prove that the study of America made N number of people in the UK feel more friendly toward current American foreign policy? Of course not. Indeed, in the short run, formal study may on occasion have provided more structured information to support anti-American sentiments. The Fulbright Experience is based, as all education must be based, on the non-quantifiable belief that knowing about other societies increases understanding and that understanding at the very least lessens the likelihood of preemptive judgments.

Yet these essays attest to far deeper changes. Scholars substantially altered their courses as a result. Individuals changed career paths. Some wrote books they had not previously thought to write. Many learned languages. Some married while in the host country, so that the Fulbright Experience remained a fundamental part of their social environment. Many, from Europe and elsewhere, learned to work truly hard for the first time in an American university. Many Americans learned for the first time to work more reflectively. Even those who are not represented in this volume learned. And this includes the few who discovered within themselves a loathing for being out of their accustomed settings and who returned home with the formal tasks of learning unfinished—even these, we may presume, learned about themselves.

These essays demonstrate all these responses, and they demonstrate more, for the careful reader, in what they say and do not say. I am struck for example by the desire of virtually everyone in this volume to "do the right thing" when abroad. I am struck with the value of a new educational environment, *any* new environment. I note again the discovery by some of these writers that meeting one's countrymen abroad is a different proposition from encountering them in one's own halls of ivy. Reading these essays reminds me that when one writes about another country one writes in fact about one's own.

My own tripartite Fulbright Experience bears witness to all these conventional observations. As a Fulbright student I attended Victoria University in New Zealand, pursuing that nation's history as a facet of the larger imperial history of which it was part. At the same time I did research among the Maori, in order to understand the syncretic movements by which, to use a Western concept, their religious beliefs sought to accommodate to the teachings of the missionaries. The exemplary Eric Budge, the Commission's director, opened my eyes to New Zealand; and the gentle historian Winston Monk, who taught American history despite a single four-day visit to the U.S., made me see my own country very differently. So I wrote a book, fell deeply in love with Avril, proposed on the third day and was married in a matter of weeks. This was 1952 and I encountered almost no anti-Americanism.

Just ten years later I was Fulbright Lecturer at the University of Malaya, as it then was. Here the tiny Fulbright Program was run from the American Embassy in Kuala Lumpur. All went smoothly, after a brief run-in with a USIS officer who wanted to have a look at my lecture notes—a request politely declined and never raised again, perhaps because of the supportive intervention of the Ambassador. We had arrived only a few days after my daughter's first birthday, and in Malaya we had the exquisite pleasure of living through her second year while discovering a new and very complex society. We ate everything, saw everything, grasping the whole of Southeast Asia to us—even its nagging anti-American elements. Again I wrote a book, taught several classes, learned enough Malay to get along in the villages, and formed friendships that have lasted a lifetime. My wife developed her interest in Asian dance, theatre and music. In today's terms, we had a ball.

The third experience in 1969-71 took us to London, where I was an academic on loan serving as Cultural Attaché. The Chairmanship of the U.S.-UK Binational Commission went with the territory. Kept on course by its able director, John Herrington, working with Vice-Chancellors of universities and eminent members of the American business community, I learned Fulbright from the other side: about what Washington hoped for, about the desperately depleted funding, about the relative values attached by different societies and bureaucracies to different academic disciplines. Whether the quality of the program was following its budgets into decline, or whether Washington was interfering, I was too obtuse to determine. I know we sent excellent people back and forth across the Atlantic. Oh yes, now and then a missive would arrive from Washington that struck us as wrong, we would say so, and Washington would fall silent. I knew enough about the lifestyle of bureaucracies to know that such attempts would be made and I did not resent them but merely sought, usually with success, to reshape them to more appropriate goals. It is naive to expect bureaucracy *not* to try to interfere, provide "guidance," give direction. No one in London at the time was naive, least of all my boss, the remarkable William Weld, who had earned his PhD in literature at Columbia and had served as a Cultural Attaché more than once. And so we responded in kind, with our own evidence or proof of effectiveness. A Republican was in the White House but no one, in those ancient times, asked me about my political affiliation—as they have taken to doing in more recent times. Perhaps they already knew. But all that was thirty years ago.

Pondering these three experiences, as I read through this collection of fine essays, I could not help but be struck by Ms. Geyer's perception that the Fulbright Experience has taken place virtually in its entirety within the framework of the Cold War. Notions and definitions of effectiveness, decisions about the shape of programs, a Fulbrighter's self-consciousness about personal purpose and mission, all this and so much more—I am inclined to say *of course*—were deeply influenced by this inescapable reality. The program was obviously of a time, in a place, to a purpose. Yet it had throughout a rich specificity that transcended any simple collection of people, programs, policies or nations.

What then will the Program become now, with the Cold War at an end? Is there less need for it? Emphatically No. The capacity for human beings to misunderstand one another has in no measure diminished—some worry that it may have increased. Americans must still go abroad to learn about themselves and their country, and in larger numbers than ever. Scholars from "abroad"— an odd term now that Canada and Mexico have joined the Program—need access to American institutions, far more than ever before. Even if it cannot be quantified, the unquestioned success of the Fulbright Program in the past reminds us that it will be needed fully as much in the future.

These essays then are a kind of stock-taking, a look inward. Yet they also provide abundant evidence of effect, a persuasive and appealing look outward from the vantage point of forty-odd individual authors from fifteen countries. All are reflections on a time and a process. They are about education, to be sure, but they are also autobiographies, some of them meeting the highest demand of that difficult form of literature in that we can virtually see the author changing in the very act of writing about past events which, through the effort to recapture them, become present events. All these essays, as Dr. Mossberg notes, are a form of travel literature, as we share in visits to Delhi and Dijon, St. George, Utah and Cincinnati, Ohio, seeing places and people through the eyes of another. Indeed this is travel literature at its best, not descriptions of monuments and mountains but revelations of the life of the mind. Of course, the careful reader will find inadvertent revelations in these essays—subtle prejudices unveiled, human and written texts explicated in a manner at once unexpected and revealing. These essays are more than interesting and significant; surely they are true as well.

This Afterword, these reflections after many words, might as easily be called an Afterward. If pundits now deem the Cold War to have come to some kind of end, if Mikhail Gorbachev can stand where Churchill stood in Fulton, Missouri, in the heartland of America, to declare the end of the war Churchill symbolically framed, then we need to look ahead and ask, what is to be afterward?

It seems to me there should be many afterwards: new programs, new intellectual endeavors, the restoration of what has been demonstrably good, the prolongation of the Fulbright Difference into the future. Perhaps too there should be more volumes like this one, books which capture the rich particularity of human experience, and this before the opportunity passes. Might there not be volumes organized by themes, asking, for example, what was the Fulbright Difference in discipline X or Y, for pre-doctoral students, for post-doctoral researchers, for women, for minorities? Might there not be volumes dedicated to the Difference vis-à-vis specific countries: what difference did it make, to cite my parochial experience, in Britain, Malaysia and New Zealand? If this book does its job, many more books will use it as their point of departure.

Whatever comes next, it should be blindingly obvious that the Fulbright Experience has been too valuable to lose. It was, as Anna Maria Martellone remarks, a time of Good Encounters. I fear the world will need an abundance of Good Encounters in the years ahead.

Carmen Varela's vision of the Fulbright Program as a vast living library of humankind inspires our indexing, which begins the process of cataloguing. Though this volume contains the work of but forty authors, the places, organizations and names mentioned in their texts reach far in space and time. We have chosen the inclusive mode, in the belief that the range of these references allows in itself an insight into the rich humanism of the Fulbright process. To facilitate its use, we have provided three separate listings: the first for countries and political entities, another for institutions and organizations, and finally one for people, from Socrates and Maimonides to Frank Jossi's Afghan friends and the hostess of Dr. Maini's rooming-house.

—The Editors

INDEX I

COUNTRIES, REGIONS AND POLITICAL ENTITIES

INDEX II

ORGANIZATIONS AND INSTITUTIONS

INDEX III

PARTICIPANTS AND PEOPLE